Ṣaḥīḥ Muslim

صحيح مسلم

Ṣaḥīḥ Muslim

With the Full Commentary by

Imam al-Nawawī

Translated and Edited by

Adil Salahi

VOLUME
·THREE·

THE ISLAMIC FOUNDATION &
ICMG AUSTRALIA

Ṣaḥīḥ Muslim: With Full Commentary by Imam al-Nawawī, volume 3

First published in England by

THE ISLAMIC FOUNDATION,

Markfield Conference Centre,
Ratby Lane, Markfield,
Leicestershire, LE67 9SY,
United Kingdom
Website: www.Islamic-foundation.com
Email: Publications@islamic-foundation.com

Quran House, PO Box 30611, Nairobi, Kenya

P.M.B 3193, Kano, Nigeria

Distributed by
Kube Publishing Ltd
Tel: +44 (0) 1530 249230
Fax: +44 (0) 1530 249656
Website: www.kubepublishing.com

2nd impression 2022

With special thank you for the immense contribution of ICMG Youth Australia.

Cataloguing-in-Publication Data is available from the British Library

ISBN: 978-0-86037-733-7 *casebound*
ISBN: 978-0-86037-728-3 *paperback*
ISBN: 978-0-86037-738-2 *ebook*

Cover Design by: Jannah Haque
Typesetting by: Naiem Qaddoura
Printed by: Elma Basim, Turkey.

بسم الله الرحمن الرحيم

CONTENTS

BOOK OF MENSTRUATION

BOOK OF PRAYER

TRANSLITERATION TABLE

Arabic Consonants

Initial, unexpressed medial and final: ء ’

ا	a	د	d	ض	ḍ	ك	k
ب	b	ذ	dh	ط	ṭ	ل	l
ت	t	ر	r	ظ	ẓ	م	m
ث	th	ز	z	ع	‘	ن	n
ج	j	س	s	غ	gh	هـ	h
ح	ḥ	ش	sh	ف	f	و	w
خ	kh	ص	ṣ	ق	q	ي	y

With a *shaddah,* both medial and final consonants are doubled.

Vowels, diphthongs, etc.

Short:	ـَـ	a	ـِـ	i	ـُـ	u
Long:	ـَـا	ā	ـِـي	ī	ـُـو	ū
Diphthongs:			ـَـوْ	aw		
			ـَـيْ	ay		

In the name of God, the Most Compassionate, the Ever Merciful

PREFACE

We live in a time when people can spread their views around the globe at the touch of a button. Yet such views may come from people of little knowledge who can confuse and even misguide others. This is a concern that has become particularly acute with the widespread misrepresentation of Islam, both by those hostile towards it, and, unfortunately, even those who claim to profess it. Through their evil but eloquent schemes, such people can misrepresent the sacred teachings of this religion, and direct the ignorant and the ill-fated to perpetrate heinous crimes against both an innocent public and an innocent religion. Such deception and misinterpretation has sadly become all too common in our day, and among its causes is, undoubtedly, the relative inaccessibility of sound Islamic scholarship and literature in the English language. An additional cause is the suggestion that there is no difference between experts and non-experts. It is as though God never declared in His Book: '*How can those who know be equal to those who do not know?*' (39: 9)

A plethora of problems can arise when non-experts begin to consider themselves experts on a subject matter. One can vividly illustrate with the example of a person who requires medical attention. A sensible individual would choose to be treated by a medical professional—an expert in the field—rather than risk their health by consenting to a medical procedure from someone who fancies themselves a doctor simply because they have read a medical textbook in their spare time. Indeed, there are serious legal consequences for those who claim to practice medicine without a recognized licence—one which is granted because they have been through rigorous training and examination. Such legal repercussions are entirely appropriate of course, for such frauds place people's worldly lives at risk. Yet why is it that when it comes to our health we seek an expert opinion, but when it comes to our everlasting Hereafter so many of us prefer to follow someone who considers himself an expert after reading just a couple of books? Simply put: why do we risk our eternity by following those who are not qualified? Why do we not seek out recognized experts? As God the

Almighty says: *'ask the people of knowledge if you do not know.'* (16: 43) It is precisely to address this gap between scholarly works and non-scholarly opinions that we have endeavoured to produce this invaluable resource.

After reading the entirety of *al-Minhāj* in Turkish, the Director of Organisational Management at Islamic Community Milli Gorus (ICMG) Youth Australia, Adem Temel, conducted a meeting with our small team in which we studied the book and recognized how blessed we were to have access to such a stupendous work. It was evident that the renowned scholar and author of *al-Minhāj*, Imam al-Nawawī, may God have mercy on him, had wisdom and knowledge many today are in desperate need of. Indeed, *al-Minhāj* is one of the greatest and most respected commentaries on *Ṣaḥīḥ* Muslim. While an English translation of a hadith can struggle to convey its apparent meaning, let alone the appropriate context and other subtleties, commentaries by experts like Imam al-Nawawī can shed light on hadiths more comprehensively and thus give us greater access to the intended meaning while guarding us against misunderstanding. During a subsequent meeting, our team compared the Turkish translation of *Fī Ẓilāl al-Qur'an* with the English translation by Dr Adil Salahi and were impressed by the remarkable consistency between the two translations. Immediately thereafter, the team made the decision to contact Dr Salahi with a view to proposing that he translate Imam al-Nawawī's *al-Minhāj* into English. We were overjoyed to hear his positive response.

A number of people and organizations have contributed to this project. Firstly, this work would not have been possible without Adil Salahi's mastery of both the Arabic and English languages. His love of Prophet Muhammad, peace and blessings be upon him, and his dedication to making knowledge accessible has led to the translation of significant works from the Islamic literary heritage. Second, the ICMG Youth Australia and Kube Publishing (UK) teams worked closely to meet all project timelines. Third, many individuals and groups volunteered to support this project both physically and financially. Lastly, and most importantly, God, the Almighty, guided us, brought ease, and opened closed doors to make everything possible.

'... and my success can only come from God. In Him I put my trust, and to Him I will return.' (11: 88)

Halim Erbasi
ICMG Youth Australia
Director of Education

BEFORE YOU READ

There are some important points that the reader, particularly a student of Hadith, needs to bear in mind when using this book. Although these have been explained in the Introduction to the first volume, it is considered worthwhile to remind readers of the editorial method followed in this work.

1. Numbering and references

It is surprising, but there has never been a full and serial numbering of hadiths in *Ṣaḥīḥ* Muslim, and hence references to hadiths vary. A hadith is often referenced by book and chapter: 'Related by Muslim, Book of Faith, Chapter so-and-so', and so forth. This is a difficult method of referencing, particularly because the headings of some chapters run into two or three lines, or even longer. The fullest numbering of the hadiths in *Ṣaḥīḥ* Muslim is that given in *al-Muʿjam al-Mufahras li-Alfāẓ al-Ḥadīth*, but many hadiths are left without numbers. These are versions of the previous hadith, differing only in their chains of transmission, and it was probably felt that they should count with the earlier and often more complete version.

Al-Muʿjam al-Mufahras is a concordance of the words of the Prophet's hadiths listed in the most important nine anthologies: al-Bukhārī, Muslim, Abū Dāwūd, al-Tirmidhī, al-Nasā'ī, Ibn Mājah, as well as Mālik's *al-Muwaṭṭa'*, Ahmad's *al-Musnad* and al-Dārimī's *Sunan*. It was prepared by a group of forty Western researchers of Islamic studies under the supervision of Arent Jan Wensinck (1882–1939) and edited by the Egyptian scholar Muhammad Fu'ād ʿAbd al-Bāqī (1882–1967).[i]

---

i. Shaykh Muhammad Rashīd Riḍā gave an English copy of *A Manual of the Early Muhammadan Traditions* by Arent Jan Wensinck, Professor of Arabic and Islam at the University of Leiden in Holland, to one of his regular students, Muhammad

However, *al-Muʿjam al-Mufahras* gives a serial number to each 'book' in Muslim's *Ṣaḥīḥ*. Thus, it lists the numbers of the hadiths in the Book of Faith from 1 to 380, and then begins the numbering in the Book of Cleansing from 1. As such, it does not give a complete serial numbering to the entire anthology. I have therefore decided to provide serial numbering, giving every hadith its own numbered identification. In doing so, I follow the method adopted by the late hadith scholar Mūsā Shāhīn Lāshīn (1920–2009) in his 10-volume commentary, *Fatḥ al-Munʿim fī Sharḥ Ṣaḥīḥ Muslim*. This method does not assign a number for a hadith that differs from the one before it only in its chain of transmission, but that has exactly the same text.

Muslim's *Ṣaḥīḥ* has been translated into English by Abd al-Hamid Siddiqui. The translation is well circulated and its better known edition, published by Dār al-Salām, is available online. After looking carefully at this translation, I have decided to provide my own. However, the translation gives a full serial numbering of the hadiths listed by Muslim, bringing the total to 7,190 hadiths. This is different from Lāshīn's method of numbering, which brings the total to 6,571 hadiths. To make it easier for readers who wish to refer to Dār al-Salām's translation, I give the number in that translation in brackets before the chain of transmission.

Fu'ād ʿAbd al-Bāqī, and asked him to translate it into Arabic. ʿAbd al-Bāqī, who was working as a translator at the Agricultural Bank in Cairo at the time, complied and translated the book, but first he wrote to Wensinck for his permission. Wensinck expressed delight at the idea and also sent ʿAbd al-Bāqī a copy of the first part of a concordance of the Prophet's hadiths that he and other researchers were working on. ʿAbd al-Bāqī reviewed the work and found many mistakes. He made a list of these and sent it to Wensinck, who was delighted with the input and recruited ʿAbd al-Bāqī as editor of the entire *al-Muʿjam al-Mufahras* concordance.

Al-Muʿjam al-Mufahras is published in Arabic in eight volumes and is indispensable for any researcher in Islamic Studies. Words are listed alphabetically, and a short sentence or phrase in which the word occurs is given. Then the hadith which includes the sentence or phrase is referenced to any of the nine anthologies. ʿAbd al-Bāqī's role is acknowledged by Wensinck in the Introduction, and working on this concordance enabled Muhammad Fu'ād ʿAbd al-Bāqī to subsequently undertake his own highly acclaimed concordance of the Qur'an.

Thus, three sets of numbers are included before the chain of transmission of each hadith. The first is a complete serial number following Lāshīn's method. The second is that of *al-Muʿjam al-Mufahras* and the third is that of Dār al-Salām's translation given in brackets. Where Lāshīn or *al-Muʿjam al-Mufahras* does not give a hadith a number, because it is the same as the hadith before it, I follow the convention of giving it the mark '000'. Thus, either of the first two numbers may be replaced by 000. Where Dār al-Salām's translation omits a hadith or does not give it a number, I give it the mark '0'. The pattern of numbering is simplified, as follows:

Lāshīn – *Al-Muʿjam* – (Dār al-Salām)

This applies to all the hadiths that are entered in the anthology itself, beginning with the Book of Faith. Imam Muslim wrote a long introduction to his work, explaining his method. In it, he includes ninety-two hadiths and statements by the early scholars of Hadith. These are given separate numbers, from 1 to 92. Only a few of these are entered in *al-Muʿjam al-Mufahras*, because the majority are attributed to scholars of Hadith. Whichever is entered in *al-Muʿjam al-Mufahras* its number is stated. Dār al-Salām's translation does not include this introduction.

When a hadith is entered in any of the other five anthologies considered to be the most authentic, I mention these in a footnote. Where no such information is given, it means that the hadith is entered only in Muslim's anthology. The Arabic original of each hadith is given immediately after the English translation, but this applies to the main body of the anthology, not to Muslim's introduction.

Imam Muslim divided his anthology into books, each covering an important area of the Islamic faith, such as the Book of Faith, the Book of Prayer, etc. He did not make further classification. It was left to Imam al-Nawawī to divide each book into chapters, and give headings to these. These chapters were later given numbers in *al-Muʿjam al-Mufahras*. The headings and their numbers are given in this translation. However, as many headings tend to be long, I have tried to reduce them while retaining the elements highlighted in the headings. It should be pointed out, however, that some of these chapters are not given numbers. Where no number is given to a chapter in *al-Muʿjam al-Mufahras*, it appears without a number in this translation.

There are a few instances where the same number is given to two consecutive hadiths. In order to indicate that this is not an error, but merely following the Arabic original, the repetition is indicated by the symbol [R].

2. The chain of transmission

Hadith scholars were very specific in their terminology. Therefore, when they used synonymous words, they imparted clear distinction to them. Thus, the words *ḥaddathanā, akhbaranā, anba'anā,* and *ʿan,* have different meanings, although linguistically speaking they are very similar and denote receiving information from a named person. However, *ḥaddathanā* is used to refer to a process whereby the teacher reads out the hadith to his students, whether he is narrating from memory or reading out loud directly. *Akhbaranā* and *anba'anā* are practically identical in meaning. However, the first refers to a process whereby a student is reading aloud from his teacher's books in the presence of the teacher. *Anba'anā* does not specify this process, but means that the information was passed on by the teacher or in his presence. *ʿAn,* on the other hand, does not specify any process, nor does it specify that the reporter actually heard the teacher's narration or his student's reading out in his presence. Indeed, it could, thus, mean that the reporter heard the hadith from a colleague who was in the teacher's circle at the time.

In order to reflect these differences, 'narrated' is the term used here for *ḥaddathanā*, 'reported' for *akhbaranā*, 'mentioned' for *anba'anā*, and 'from' for *ʿan*. However, any of the first three ways could involve a one-to-one situation in which the reporter is the only one present with his teacher. In Arabic, this is marked by changing the last letter in the three Arabic words, using 'ī' instead of 'ā'. Thus the words become *ḥaddathanī, akhbaranī,* and *anba'anī.* To reflect the difference in the English translation the words 'to me' have been used after 'narrated', 'reported' and 'mentioned' to indicate the one-to-one situation, while the three words on their own indicate the presence of others when the narration took place.

Readers will also note that in some hadiths the chain of transmission includes the mark [H]. This is indicated in Arabic by the use of the letter [Ḥ], and it may occur once, twice, or even more in the chain of transmission of the same hadith. What this signifies is that the hadith is narrated by two or more chains of transmission, but these join up at some stage. Rather than give them separately, repeating the names of reporters from where they join up to the Prophet's companion, Hadith scholars use this way to indicate that the different chains are joined at this point.

Another symbol used in the chain of transmission is [R], but this is much less frequent. It simply indicates that the number given to a particular hadith is repeated, which means that the number has been given to more than one hadith instead of giving each of them a separate number.

Sometimes Muslim narrates a hadith from three of his teachers and uses the word 'narrated', but their methods of learning from their teacher whom they quote differ. Muslim is too careful and meticulous to overlook this fact. He makes this clear by immediately adding something like: 'The first said "narrated" and the other two said "reported".'

3. Word usage

The usage of some Arabic words need to be explained. The word 'imam' is often used in reference to some scholars quoted in this work. It is also used in reference to both Muslim and al-Nawawī. There is, however, a very clear difference in the use of this word by Sunni Muslims and the Shia.

Linguistically speaking, *imām* means 'leader' and is often used, particularly in books of Islamic Jurisprudence, or *fiqh*, to refer to the ruler or the head of state, whether he has the title of caliph or some other title. It is also commonly used to refer to the person who leads congregational prayer. In this second usage, there is no difference between the one who leads the prayer and anyone in the congregation, except that the imam leads and the congregation follow.

A far more common usage of the word is as a title of respect added before the name of a scholar who is recognized for his high achievement and scholarship. This is how it is mostly used in this work. It may, however, also be used here in the sense of the 'leader of congregational prayer' when this topic is discussed, but as such will be clearly identified at that juncture. A scholar who is considered an imam has no special distinction, apart from what his scholarship gives him; he does not enjoy any special status. It will be noted in this work that the views of some such scholars are outlined, and discussed or rejected. This is clearly a matter of scholarly difference that does not detract from the high standing of the scholar or the one who differs with him.

The Shia have a totally different concept of 'imam'. They give this status to twelve people starting with 'Alī ibn Abī Ṭālib, the Prophet's cousin, followed by eleven of his descendants through Fāṭimah, his wife and the Prophet's daughter. To the Shia, those imams were infallible and enjoy a rank that is almost equal to that of the Prophet. Indeed, the way some Shia speak of the third Imam, al-Ḥusayn, the Prophet's grandson, gives at times the impression that they rank him above the Prophet himself. Moreover, the Shia believe that the twelfth Imam was taken away and did not die: he will return at some point when he will bring justice to the world. This Shia concept is absolutely unacceptable to Sunni Muslims who do not recognize any such status as belonging to anyone.

We speak of a hadith having a chain of transmission and we mention 'transmitters'. We also use the words 'reporter' and 'narrator'. These three words are used interchangeably and they refer to the people named in the chain of transmission. These have the same status with regard to how the Prophet's statement or action is taught and learnt. When we use the verb 'narrate' we are referring to the action of stating the hadith, whether by reading it out loud or otherwise. However, the word 'narrate' is often used in Islamic literature in reference to the works of the leading scholars of Hadith and what they include in their anthologies. Thus, we often see phrases like 'al-Tirmidhī narrated ...', 'al-Bukhārī narrated ...'. It is felt that it is better to distinguish the mere quoting of a hadith and its entry in an anthology. Therefore we use the word 'narrate' to indicate quoting a hadith and the word 'relate' to mean the 'entry in a Hadith anthology'. Thus, we say: 'al-Bukhārī relates in his *Ṣaḥīḥ*', or 'al-Bayhaqī relates in *Shuʿab al-Īmān*', or 'al-Nasāʾī relates in *al-Sunan al-Kubrā*'.

The words Abū and Abī are often used in the names of hadith reporters and scholars. These two are the same word, but the endings are case markers according to their position in the sentence. Invariably, Abū is used at the beginning of the sentence and when not preceded by a name, while Abī is used when preceded by the word 'ibn'. There are other situations that indicate which of the two should be used. Both words mean 'father of' and their use indicates an appellation of respect.

The word *mawlā* is used to describe some reporters and other persons mentioned in the commentary. This word is one of the few Arabic words that denote opposite meanings. Linguistically, it means both 'master' and 'slave', and it is used in the Qur'an to refer to God as the *mawlā* of the believers. When someone is referred to as the *mawlā* of another or of a tribe, it most frequently refers to a slave who was set free. He then allied himself with his former master or with his tribe, as this was a recognized practice in Arabia both under Islam and prior to it.

It will be noted that the phrase 'but God knows best' is used very frequently in al-Nawawī's commentary and by the scholars he quotes: this is a mark of humility. They express their views but shy away from presenting these as the true and correct view, to the exclusion of anything different. It is akin to saying that 'this is what I know, but ultimate knowledge rests with God'.

The word hadith is used with a capital or small 'h' and this usage indicates a difference. When it is used with the lower case first letter it refers to a single statement by the Prophet. Hence, the reference to one or more statements by the Prophet is always with the lower case. When it is used with a capital first letter, it refers to the Hadith discipline, which is a specialized branch of study, concerned with the Prophet's statements, actions and approvals.

4. Arrangement

Imam al-Nawawī discusses three areas in relation to every hadith included in Muslim's anthology: 1) The general meaning of the hadith and its message. He also outlines the important points it includes and highlights any rulings that it stipulates or may be based on it. 2) The chain of transmission: he identifies the different reporters, giving some information about them and their full names if they are mentioned by first name or by appellation. He also highlights any useful point that the chain provides, and explains any subtle point that reflects Muslim's careful and meticulous scholarship. 3) He explains the language of the hadith, stating the meanings of individual words, particularly those that may be unfamiliar to readers or became rarely used. Where a word, phrase or sentence may have more than one meaning, he discusses these and shows which, if any, is unacceptable. However, he does not follow a single pattern in the arrangement of his commentary. Sometimes, he begins by discussing the chain of transmission, but often he discusses the general meaning first. He may also start by explaining the language and the meaning of individual words.

In this English version, liberty has been taken to follow a consistent pattern. The meaning of the hadith is given first and then its explanation, under the subheading 'text explanation', is provided. This is followed with any discussion al-Nawawī gives concerning the chain of transmission, using the subheading 'transmission'. The information al-Nawawī provides about the meaning of individual words and the pronunciation of unfamiliar words and names has been ignored, because these are already reflected in the translation. However, when he discusses alternative meanings, what is considered useful to English readers is included. If it is a matter of pronunciation or a grammatical aspect that does not affect the meaning or the message of the hadith, this has been disregarded.

5. Quotations and references

In his monumental work, al-Nawawī cites numerous quotations from various scholars. At times, he mentions the work from which the quotation is made, but in most cases this is not done. Although his work has been checked and verified several times, and published many times in different countries, none of these undertook the task of checking the original works in order to provide detailed references. There are several reasons for this omission. Many of the original works have not been published, but remain in manuscript form held in different libraries in various countries. Moreover, many of these works are voluminous. For example, al-Nawawī often quotes from Imam al-Ḥaramayn, who wrote a large number of books. As mentioned in the biographical note on Imam al-Ḥaramayn, one of his books is published in twenty-one volumes. Although a discerning scholar may have a good guess as to the book from which a particular quote is taken, finding it may require several hours, if not days of hard work. Imam al-Nawawī died 750 years ago and we cannot blame him for not citing his references according to modern methods of citation. It should be remembered that all the books he read were written in long hand and manuscripts of the same book differed in size, number of pages and style of writing. Readers and students must simply trust to his scholarship and piety with all that he quotes from other scholars. May God bless them all for their meticulous and faithful scholarship.

6. Notes and editorial liberty

In certain cases, it is felt that a note should be added within the text to explain certain points or add a particular perspective. This is not surprising considering that the book was written nearly eight centuries ago. In order to make the addition very clear, it is preceded by the word 'Note' and given an independent paragraph.

In a few cases, a sentence is started by mentioning the author's name before mentioning what he says, such as 'al-Nawawī considers these hadiths self-explanatory, adding only …', and in a very few cases, a short comment by the author is not included in the translation, because time has made it irrelevant and including it would be either confusing or require a long explanatory footnote. Since it is unlikely to concern the reader, it is felt that omission is better. Such liberty is taken only in cases where it is felt that had the author lived in our time, he would have approved of such omission.

Adil Salahi
London
February 2019

THE BOOK OF CLEANSING

CHAPTER 1

THE IMPORTANCE OF MINOR RITUAL ABLUTION (*WUḌŪ'*)

[397–1]. (Dār al-Salām 0432) Isḥāq ibn Manṣūr narrated:[i] Ḥabbān ibn Hilāl narrated; Abān narrated; Yaḥyā narrated; that Zayd narrated to him; that Abū Sallām narrated to him; from Abū Mālik al-Ashʿarī; that God's Messenger (peace be upon him) said: '**Cleansing is half the faith. "Praise be to God" [i.e. *Alḥamd lillāh*] will fill the scales. "Limitless is God in His glory" [i.e. *Subḥān Allāh*] and "Praise be to God", will fill all that is in between the skies and the earth. Prayer is light; charity is a proof; patience in adversity spreads light; and the Qur'an is a clear argument for or against you. Everyone goes out in the morning, and everyone sells themselves: one either frees oneself or sends oneself to ruin**'.

حَدَّثَنَا إِسْحَاقُ بْنُ مَنْصُورٍ، حَدَّثَنَا حَبَّانُ بْنُ هِلَالٍ، حَدَّثَنَا أَبَانُ، حَدَّثَنَا يَحْيَى، أَنَّ زَيْدًا، حَدَّثَهُ أَنَّ أَبَا سَلَّامٍ، حَدَّثَهُ عَنْ أَبِي مَالِكٍ الْأَشْعَرِيِّ قَالَ: قَالَ رَسُولُ اللهِ صَلَّى اللهُ عَلَيْهِ وَسَلَّمَ: «الطُّهُورُ شَطْرُ الْإِيمَانِ وَالْحَمْدُ لِلهِ تَمْلَأُ الْمِيزَانَ، وَسُبْحَانَ اللهِ وَالْحَمْدُ لِلهِ تَمْلَآنِ - أَوْ تَمْلَأُ - مَا بَيْنَ السَّمَاوَاتِ وَالْأَرْضِ، وَالصَّلَاةُ نُورٌ، وَالصَّدَقَةُ بُرْهَانٌ وَالصَّبْرُ ضِيَاءٌ، وَالْقُرْآنُ حُجَّةٌ لَكَ أَوْ عَلَيْكَ، كُلُّ النَّاسِ يَغْدُو فَبَايِعٌ نَفْسَهُ فَمُعْتِقُهَا أَوْ مُوبِقُهَا»

Text Explanation

This is an especially important hadith as it speaks of a fundamental aspect of Islam and a number of important rules. The Prophet says

i. Related by al-Tirmidhī, 3517.

that 'cleansing is half the faith'. The term the Prophet uses here for cleansing is *ṭuhūr*, which literally means 'cleansing', and in Islamic terminology refers to minor ritual ablution for prayer, i.e. *wuḍū'*, or to the major ritual ablution, i.e. *ghusl*. Scholars explain the statement 'Cleansing is half the faith' in different ways. It is said that multiplying its reward may go up so as to be equal to half the reward for belief. It is also said that when one accepts the faith, one's acceptance wipes away all previous sins. The same applies to ablution, because ablution is not valid except when performed by a believer. As it is dependent on faith, it acquires the meaning of being its half. Another view mentions that 'faith' in this instance means prayer, as this usage occurs in the verse that says: '*God would never have let your faith be in vain*'. (2: 143) Prayer's validity is conditional on cleansing oneself, and as such it becomes like one half of it. In addition, the term 'half' is often used figuratively, so as not to mean an exact half. This is perhaps the best view. It may also be interpreted in the following way: since faith means mental conviction and apparent action of obedience indicating commitment, then conviction and action are the two halves of faith. Cleansing incorporates prayer and as such it falls under the action of obedience, but God knows best.

The Prophet (peace be upon him) says in this hadith 'Praise be to God will fill the scales'. This means that the reward for praising God is so great that it will fill the scales. There are numerous texts in the Qur'an and the Sunnah which confirm that actions will be weighed and that some will be heavy while others will have little weight.

The Prophet then said that '*Subḥān Allāh*' and '*Alḥamd lillāh*', which respectively mean 'limitless is God in His glory' and 'praise be to God', will fill all that is between the skies and the earth. This may be explained in the following way: if their reward is to take physical form, then it will be so great as to fill all the space between the earth and the sky. That they are so richly rewarded is because *Subḥān Allāh* stresses God's uniqueness and that nothing bears any comparability to Him, while *Alḥamd lillāh* emphasizes our need of God's help and our dependence on Him, but God knows best.

The Prophet then says: 'Prayer is light'. This means that prayer prevents a person from committing sin and stops people from doing what is wrong and sinful, while always guiding them to what is right. As such, it is like light which allows us to see our way clearly as well as what is around us. It is also said that its reward on the Day of Judgement may be in the form of light. Another suggestion is that because prayer involves concentration on addressing God and turning to Him with all our senses and mental faculties, it gives us insight into things and enables us to learn about the nature of things. God says: '*Believers, seek strength in patience and prayer*'. (2: 153) Furthermore, scholars say that this statement means that prayer will impart to the worshipper a light that is reflected on his or her face on the Day of Judgement, and that it imparts brightness that is seen on their faces in this life. This is unlike those who are unbelievers, but God knows best.

The hadith then describes charity as a proof. Imam Ismāʿīl ibn Muhammad al-Taymī, the author of *Al-Taḥrīr*, said: 'This means that it is resorted to as a proof. In the case of someone questioned about how he spent his money during his lifetime, he would resort to whatever he gave in charity as a proof supporting his claim: "I have given part of it as charity". Alternatively, a person who frequently donates to charity will be given a mark identifying him. This mark will be a proof and he will not then be asked how he spent his money'. Other scholars said: 'This means that charity is a proof that the one who pays it is a believer. A hypocrite does not give charitable donations, because he does not believe in its reward. Therefore, what one donates to charity has the proof that confirms one as a believer', but God knows best.

The next sentence in the hadith says: 'Patience in adversity spreads light'. This refers to patience that Islam approves of. This includes patience when doing what pleases God and patience in tolerating the inconvenience that may attend refraining from doing what is forbidden. It also includes patience in adversity, whatever life may bring of adverse situations. What is meant in the hadith is that such patience is a virtue and that a patient person will continue to receive guidance that enlightens his way. Ibrāhīm al-Khawwāṣ said: 'Patience refers to holding on to the Qur'an and the Sunnah'. Ibn 'Aṭā' said: 'Patience means remaining steadfast and well behaved in situations of adversity'. Abū 'Alī al-Daqqāq said: 'True patience is not to entertain any objections to one's lot. To show one's adversity, without complaint, is not inconsistent with patience. In reference to Prophet

Job, God says: *'We found him patient in adversity. How excellent a servant of Ours; he would always turn to Us'*. (38: 44) Yet addressing his Lord, Job said: *'Affliction has befallen me'*. (21: 83) But God knows best.

The hadith then mentions that the Qur'an is an argument that counts for or against any person. The meaning is clear. If one recites the Qur'an and acts on its commandments, it becomes an argument defending one; otherwise it is an argument against one.

The last part of the hadith says: 'Everyone goes out in the morning, and everyone sells themselves: one either frees oneself or sends oneself to ruin'. This means that everyone will follow the path they choose. The one who sells himself to God, obeying His orders and doing what He has laid down frees himself from punishment in Hell. The one who sells himself to Satan and follows his own desires sends himself to ruin, but God knows best.

Transmission

The chain of transmission of this hadith has been discussed by al-Dāraquṭnī and others. They said that one reporter is dropped between Abū Sallām and Abū Mālik, and the name of this missing reporter is ʿAbd al-Raḥmān ibn Ghunm. They explain that Muʿāwiyah ibn Sallām reported it from his brother, Zayd ibn Sallām, from his grandfather, Abū Sallām, who reported it from ʿAbd al-Raḥmān ibn Ghunm from Abū Mālik al-Ashʿarī. This is how the hadith is related by al-Nasā'ī and Ibn Mājah. This argument may be countered in Muslim's defence by saying that it appears that Muslim was aware that Abū Sallām heard this hadith directly from Abū Mālik. As such, Abū Sallām would have heard the hadith twice, once directly from Abū Mālik, and on the other occasion he heard it from ʿAbd al-Raḥmān ibn Ghunm reporting it from Abū Mālik. Whichever way it was, the text is authentic and may not be questioned, but God knows best.

Abū Sallām's name is Mamṭūr and he is known as al-Aʿraj al-Ḥabashī al-Dimashqī. Al-Ḥabashī means the Abyssinian, but his ancestry goes back to a clan from Ḥimyar in Yemen, not to Abyssinia. Abū Mālik's name is subject to controversy, and it is variably reported as ʿUbayd or Kaʿb ibn ʿĀṣim or ʿAmr. He is counted among the Hadith reporters from Syria.

CHAPTER 2

CLEANSING REQUIRED BEFORE PRAYER

[398–000]. (Dār al-Salām 0433) Saʿīd ibn Manṣūr, Qutaybah ibn Saʿīd and Abū Kāmil al-Jaḥdarī narrated (and this is Saʿīd's text):[i] Abū ʿAwānah narrated; from Simāk ibn Ḥarb; from Muṣʿab ibn Saʿd: '**ʿAbdullāh ibn ʿUmar visited Ibn ʿĀmir when he was ill. [Ibn ʿĀmir] said: "Would you not pray for me, Ibn ʿUmar?" [Ibn ʿUmar] said: "I heard God's Messenger (peace be upon him) say: 'No prayer is accepted without ablution, and no charity from an unlawful source is accepted'. You were a governor of Basrah".**'

حَدَّثَنَا سَعِيدُ بْنُ مَنْصُورٍ، وَقُتَيْبَةُ بْنُ سَعِيدٍ، وَأَبُو كَامِلٍ الْجَحْدَرِيُّ، - وَاللَّفْظُ لِسَعِيدٍ -، قَالُوا: حَدَّثَنَا أَبُو عَوَانَةَ، عَنْ سِمَاكِ بْنِ حَرْبٍ، عَنْ مُصْعَبِ بْنِ سَعْدٍ، قَالَ: دَخَلَ عَبْدُ اللهِ بْنُ عُمَرَ عَلَى ابْنِ عَامِرٍ يَعُودُهُ وَهُوَ مَرِيضٌ فَقَالَ: أَلَا تَدْعُو اللهَ لِي يَا ابْنَ عُمَرَ؟ قَالَ: إِنِّي سَمِعْتُ رَسُولَ اللهِ صَلَّى اللهُ عَلَيْهِ وَسَلَّمَ يَقُولُ: «لَا تُقْبَلُ صَلَاةٌ بِغَيْرِ طُهُورٍ وَلَا صَدَقَةٌ مِنْ غُلُولٍ، وَكُنْتَ عَلَى الْبَصْرَةِ»

[000–000]. (Dār al-Salām 0434) Muhammad ibn al-Muthannā and Ibn Bashshār narrated: Muhammad ibn Jaʿfar narrated; Shuʿbah narrated [H] Abū Bakr ibn Abī Shaybah narrated: Ḥusayn ibn ʿAlī narrated from Zāʾidah. Abū Bakr said: And

i. Related by al-Tirmidhī, 273.

Wakīʿ narrated from Isrāʾīl: all of them from Simāk ibn Ḥarb, with this chain of transmission, from the Prophet: **the same text**.

حَدَّثَنَا مُحَمَّدُ بْنُ الْمُثَنَّى، وَابْنُ بَشَّارٍ، قَالَا: حَدَّثَنَا مُحَمَّدُ بْنُ جَعْفَرٍ، حَدَّثَنَا شُعْبَةُ ح، وَحَدَّثَنَا أَبُو بَكْرِ بْنُ أَبِي شَيْبَةَ، حَدَّثَنَا حُسَيْنُ بْنُ عَلِيٍّ، عَنْ زَائِدَةَ - قَالَ: أَبُو بَكْرٍ - وَوَكِيعٌ، عَنْ إِسْرَائِيلَ كُلُّهُمْ عَنْ سِمَاكِ بْنِ حَرْبٍ بِهَذَا الْإِسْنَادِ عَنِ النَّبِيِّ صَلَّى اللهُ عَلَيْهِ وَسَلَّمَ بِمِثْلِهِ.

[399–2]. (Dār al-Salām 0435) Muhammad ibn Rāfiʿ narrated:[i] ʿAbd al-Razzāq ibn Hammām narrated; Maʿmar ibn Rāshid narrated; from Hammām ibn Munabbih, Wahb ibn Munabbih's brother, who said: This is what Abū Hurayrah narrated to us from Muhammad, God's Messenger (peace be upon him). He mentioned several hadiths which included: **'And God's Messenger (peace be upon him) said: "The prayer of any one of you who has invalidated his ablution shall not be acceptable unless he performs [a new] ablution"**.'

حَدَّثَنَا مُحَمَّدُ بْنُ رَافِعٍ، حَدَّثَنَا عَبْدُ الرَّزَّاقِ بْنُ هَمَّامٍ، حَدَّثَنَا مَعْمَرُ بْنُ رَاشِدٍ، عَنْ هَمَّامِ بْنِ مُنَبِّهٍ أَخِي وَهْبِ بْنِ مُنَبِّهٍ، قَالَ: هَذَا مَا حَدَّثَنَا أَبُو هُرَيْرَةَ، عَنْ مُحَمَّدٍ رَسُولِ اللهِ صَلَّى اللهُ عَلَيْهِ وَسَلَّمَ فَذَكَرَ أَحَادِيثَ مِنْهَا، وَقَالَ رَسُولُ اللهِ صَلَّى اللهُ عَلَيْهِ وَسَلَّمَ: «لَا تُقْبَلُ صَلَاةُ أَحَدِكُمْ إِذَا أَحْدَثَ حَتَّى يَتَوَضَّأَ»

Text Explanation

The first hadith states that 'No prayer is accepted without ritual ablution', which is a clear statement that cleansing is a condition for the validity of prayer. *Qāḍī* ʿIyāḍ said: 'Scholars differ as to when ablution was made obligatory for prayer. Ibn al-Jahm said that in the early

i. Related by al-Bukhārī, 135; Abū Dāwūd, 60; al-Tirmidhī, 76.

days of Islam minor vitual ablution, i.e. *wuḍū'*, was recommended as a Sunnah, then it became obligatory when the Qur'anic verse permitting *tayammum*, i.e. dry ablution, was revealed. The majority of scholars, however, maintain that it was made obligatory before that. Scholars differ as to whether performing the ablution is obligatory to everyone who wishes to pray or only to those who do not have a valid ablution. A number of scholars of the early generations expressed the view that ablution is obligatory before every prayer. They cite in support that the verse stating the details of ablution starts with the sentence: '*Believers, when you are about to pray, wash your faces…*'. (5: 5) Some suggest that this was true in the early days but that it was later abrogated. It is also suggested that the order to perform the ablution before every prayer is only an order of recommendation, rather than obligation. A different view is that the ablution was not made obligatory except for one who has no valid ablution, but to renew it before every prayer is recommended. All scholars have subsequently adopted this view and there is no longer any difference between them. They explain the order in the above-quoted verse as applicable to everyone who is without valid ablution'.

Scholars of our Shāfiʿī School of *fiqh* express three different views on what makes performing the ablution obligatory. The first is that it becomes generally required when one has gone to the toilet, thus invalidating one's earlier ablution. The second is that ablution is obligatory only when one wants to pray, and the third view is that the two things together make ablution obligatory. This is the one upheld by our scholars.

The Muslim community is unanimously agreed that to pray without a valid ablution or dry ablution is forbidden. There is no distinction in this respect between obligatory or voluntary prayer, or a prostration of gratitude to God or one recommended at reciting or listening to one of fifteen particular verses of the Qur'an, or for *Janāzah* Prayer, i.e. the funeral prayer. The only exception is what is attributed to al-Shaʿbī and Muhammad ibn Jarīr al-Ṭabarī that the *Janāzah* Prayer is valid without ablution. Such a view is definitely incorrect. Scholars are unanimous that the opposite is the correct view. If a person deliberately prays without ablution and has no excuse, he commits a sin. He is not, in our view and that of the majority of scholars, an unbeliever. It is reported, however, that Abū Ḥanīfah considers him an unbeliever because he is frivolous in essential religious matters. However, disbelief is a matter of belief and conviction. Such a person appears to be a believer.

All this applies if the one who prays without ablution has no excuse or justification for so doing. What is the ruling, then, concerning the case of one who has a valid excuse, such as a person who cannot find water to perform ablution or dust for dry ablution? Four views have been expressed by al-Shāfiʿī and these became the views of different scholars. The most correct of these four, according to our Shāfiʿī scholars, is that such a person must offer his prayer in the condition he is in, and it is obligatory for him to repeat his prayer when he can find the means to perform ablution. The second view is that it is forbidden for him to pray, but he must later offer his missed prayers when he can perform the ablution. The third is that it is recommended that he offers the prayer during its time but must pray again later. The fourth view is that he must pray on time and no repeat is required of him. This last view is the one preferred by al-Muzanī, and it is based on the strongest evidence. He must pray because the Prophet says: 'If I give you a specific order, then fulfil it as best you can'. That he need not repeat his prayer is based on the fact that repeating any deed becomes obligatory only on the basis of a fresh order, and the normal situation is that no such order is made. Al-Muzanī says in this respect: 'Every prayer that is required to be done on time, despite some defect, need not be offered again', but God knows best.

In the second hadith, No. 399, the Prophet says: 'The prayer of any one of you who has invalidated his ablution shall not be acceptable unless he performs [a new] ablution'. This means that the prayer is only acceptable when one has cleansed oneself by performing an ablution with water or dust. The hadith mentions water ablution only because it is the normal way to cleanse oneself and it is by far the most common, but God knows best.

In the first hadith, No. 398, Ibn ʿUmar quotes the Prophet as saying: 'No charity from an unlawful source is accepted'. The Prophet uses here the word *ghulūl*, which is translated here as 'unlawful source'. The general meaning of this word is 'treachery', and its original meaning is 'to steal from war gains before they are divided among the beneficiaries'.

In the same hadith, Ibn 'Āmir[i] requested Ibn 'Umar to pray for his recovery, but Ibn 'Umar said to him: 'I heard God's Messenger (peace be upon him) say: "No prayer is accepted without ablution, and no charity from an unlawful source is accepted. You were a governor of Basrah".' Ibn 'Umar meant that in his post, he had numerous duties towards people, in addition to his responsibilities towards God and people. He could not have discharged all these fairly, and as such he was accountable for them. Prayer for such a person is not acceptable, in the same way as the prayers and charity by one who does not refrain from sinful deeds is unacceptable. It appears, but God knows best, that Ibn 'Umar meant his words by way of admonition, to urge Ibn 'Āmir to repent and stop all violations and suspect actions. He did not mean that prayer for transgressors is unacceptable. The Prophet and all Muslim generations prayed for unbelievers and transgressors to mend their ways and follow God's guidance.

Transmission

The chain of transmission of the first hadith includes Abū Kāmil al-Jaḥdarī, who is al-Fuḍayl ibn Ḥusayn, and he is known as al-Jaḥdarī after one of his ancestors called Jaḥdar. Abū 'Awānah's name is al-Waḍḍāḥ ibn 'Abdullāh.

The chain of transmission of the second narration of the first hadith, No. 398, goes as follows: 'Muhammad ibn al-Muthannā and Ibn Bashshār narrated: Muhammad ibn Ja'far narrated; Shu'bah narrated [H] Abū Bakr ibn Abī Shaybah narrated: Ḥusayn ibn

---

i. 'Abdullāh ibn 'Āmir was a cousin of 'Uthmān ibn 'Affān, the third of the Rightly-guided Caliphs. He was appointed by 'Uthmān as Governor of Basrah, and he was the commander who extended the Muslim state into Khurāsān. He remained Governor of Basrah until the end of 'Uthmān's reign, then was reappointed Governor of Basrah for some time during Mu'āwiyah's reign.

ʿAlī narrated from Zā'idah. Abū Bakr said: And Wakīʿ narrated from Isrā'īl: all of them from Simāk ibn Ḥarb'. Muslim says: 'all of them from Simāk'. This refers to Shuʿbah, Zā'idah and Isrā'īl as all of them reported from Simāk. Muslim also says: 'Muhammad ibn al-Muthannā and Ibn Bashshār narrated: Muhammad ibn Jaʿfar narrated; Shuʿbah narrated [H] Abū Bakr ibn Abī Shaybah narrated: Ḥusayn ibn ʿAlī narrated from Zā'idah. Abū Bakr said: And Wakīʿ narrated from Isrā'īl: all of them from Simāk ibn Ḥarb'. This means that Abū Bakr ibn Abī Shaybah narrated this hadith from Ḥusayn ibn ʿAlī who narrated it from Zā'idah, and Abū Bakr also narrated it from Wakīʿ from Isrā'īl. The way this is reported has the same meaning as 'Wakīʿ narrated to us', but in some original manuscripts the word 'narrated' is missing after Wakīʿ, leaving the words: 'Abū Bakr and Wakīʿ from Isrā'īl'. This is also correct as it implies that what follows is joined to what Abū Bakr said in the first instance: 'Ḥusayn narrated'. Thus, the meaning in this case would be: 'And Wakīʿ narrated from Isrā'īl'. In some original manuscripts it appears: 'Abū Bakr said: and Wakīʿ narrated'. All these versions are correct, but God knows best.

CHAPTER 3

THE DESCRIPTION OF PERFECT RITUAL ABLUTION

[400–3]. (Dār al-Salām 0436) Abū al-Ṭāhir Ahmd ibn ʿAmr ibn ʿAbdullāh ibn ʿAmr ibn Sarḥ and Ḥarmalah ibn Yaḥyā al-Tujībī narrated to me:[i] Ibn Wahb narrated; from Yūnus; from Ibn Shihāb; that ʿAṭāʾ ibn Yazīd al-Laythī reported to him; that Ḥumrān, ʿUthmān's *mawlā* reported to him: '**ʿUthmān ibn ʿAffān called for water and he performed the ablution: he washed his hands three times, then rinsed his mouth and blew his nose. He then washed his face three times, then washed his right hand up to the elbow three times, then washed his left hand in the same way. He then wiped his head, then washed his right foot up to the ankles three times, then his left foot in the same way. He then said: "I saw God's Messenger (peace be upon him) performing the ablution in a way similar to what I have done then God's Messenger (peace be upon him) said: 'Whoever performs the ablution in a similar way to what I have done now, then stands up and offers two *rakʿahs* during which he thinks of nothing [other than his prayer] is forgiven whatever sin he did'".**'

Ibn Shihāb said: '**Our scholars used to say: "This is the most perfect ablution anyone can perform for prayer".**'

i. Related by al-Bukhārī, 159, 164 and 1934; Abū Dāwūd, 106; al-Nasāʾī, 84, 85 and 116.

حَدَّثَنِي أَبُو الطَّاهِرِ أَحْمَدُ بْنُ عَمْرِو بْنِ عَبْدِ اللهِ بْنِ عَمْرِو بْنِ سَرْحٍ، وَحَرْمَلَةُ بْنُ يَحْيَى التُّجِيبِيُّ، قَالَا: أَخْبَرَنَا ابْنُ وَهْبٍ، عَنْ يُونُسَ، عَنِ ابْنِ شِهَابٍ أَنَّ عَطَاءَ بْنَ يَزِيدَ اللَّيْثِيَّ، أَخْبَرَهُ أَنَّ حُمْرَانَ، مَوْلَى عُثْمَانَ، أَخْبَرَهُ أَنَّ عُثْمَانَ بْنَ عَفَّانَ رَضِيَ اللهُ عَنْهُ: «دَعَا بِوَضُوءٍ فَتَوَضَّأَ فَغَسَلَ كَفَّيْهِ ثَلَاثَ مَرَّاتٍ، ثُمَّ مَضْمَضَ وَاسْتَنْثَرَ، ثُمَّ غَسَلَ وَجْهَهُ ثَلَاثَ مَرَّاتٍ، ثُمَّ غَسَلَ يَدَهُ الْيُمْنَى إِلَى الْمِرْفَقِ ثَلَاثَ مَرَّاتٍ، ثُمَّ غَسَلَ يَدَهُ الْيُسْرَى مِثْلَ ذَلِكَ، ثُمَّ مَسَحَ رَأْسَهُ، ثُمَّ غَسَلَ رِجْلَهُ الْيُمْنَى إِلَى الْكَعْبَيْنِ ثَلَاثَ مَرَّاتٍ، ثُمَّ غَسَلَ الْيُسْرَى مِثْلَ ذَلِكَ». ثُمَّ قَالَ: «رَأَيْتُ رَسُولَ اللهِ صَلَّى اللهُ عَلَيْهِ وَسَلَّمَ تَوَضَّأَ نَحْوَ وُضُوئِي هَذَا» ثُمَّ قَالَ رَسُولُ اللهِ صَلَّى اللهُ عَلَيْهِ وَسَلَّمَ: «مَنْ تَوَضَّأَ نَحْوَ وُضُوئِي هَذَا ثُمَّ قَامَ فَرَكَعَ رَكْعَتَيْنِ لَا يُحَدِّثُ فِيهِمَا نَفْسَهُ غُفِرَ لَهُ مَا تَقَدَّمَ مِنْ ذَنْبِهِ»

قَالَ ابْنُ شِهَابٍ: وَكَانَ عُلَمَاؤُنَا يَقُولُونَ: هَذَا الْوُضُوءُ أَسْبَغُ مَا يَتَوَضَّأُ بِهِ أَحَدٌ لِلصَّلَاةِ.

[401–4]. (Dār al-Salām 0437) Zuhayr ibn Ḥarb narrated to me: Yaʿqūb ibn Ibrāhīm narrated; my father narrated; from Ibn Shihāb; from ʿAṭāʾ ibn Yazīd al-Laythī; from Ḥumrān, ʿUthmān's *mawlā*, that **he saw ʿUthmān when he called for a jug. He poured water over his hands three times and he washed them. He then put his right hand into the jug [taking out some water] and he rinsed his mouth and blew his nose. He then washed his face three times and his arms up to the elbows three times. He then wiped his head, and washed his feet three times. He then said: "God's Messenger said: 'Whoever performs the ablution in a way similar to mine, then prays two *rakʿahs* during which he thinks of nothing [other than his prayer], will be forgiven whatever sin he did'".**'

وحَدَّثَنِي زُهَيْرُ بْنُ حَرْبٍ، حَدَّثَنَا يَعْقُوبُ بْنُ إِبْرَاهِيمَ، حَدَّثَنَا أَبِي، عَنِ ابْنِ شِهَابٍ، عَنْ عَطَاءِ بْنِ يَزِيدَ اللَّيْثِيِّ، عَنْ حُمْرَانَ، مَوْلَى عُثْمَانَ أَنَّهُ رَأَى عُثْمَانَ دَعَا بِإِنَاءٍ فَأَفْرَغَ عَلَى كَفَّيْهِ ثَلَاثَ مِرَارٍ فَغَسَلَهُمَا، ثُمَّ أَدْخَلَ يَمِينَهُ فِي الْإِنَاءِ فَمَضْمَضَ وَاسْتَنْثَرَ، ثُمَّ غَسَلَ وَجْهَهُ

ثَلَاثَ مَرَّاتٍ وَيَدَيْهِ إِلَى الْمِرْفَقَيْنِ ثَلَاثَ مَرَّاتٍ، ثُمَّ مَسَحَ بِرَأْسِهِ، ثُمَّ غَسَلَ رِجْلَيْهِ ثَلَاثَ مَرَّاتٍ»، ثُمَّ قَالَ: قَالَ رَسُولُ اللهِ صَلَّى اللهُ عَلَيْهِ وَسَلَّمَ: «مَنْ تَوَضَّأَ نَحْوَ وُضُوئِي هَذَا، ثُمَّ صَلَّى رَكْعَتَيْنِ لَا يُحَدِّثُ فِيهِمَا نَفْسَهُ غُفِرَ لَهُ مَا تَقَدَّمَ مِنْ ذَنْبِهِ»

Text Explanation

The hadith No. 400 mentions that 'Uthmān washed his hands three times, which indicates that washing one's hands before the ablution is a recommended Sunnah. This is agreed by all scholars.

He 'then rinsed his mouth and blew his nose'. What is meant by 'blowing his nose' is to extract the water from one's nose after having inhaled it. Ibn al-A'rābī and Ibn Qutaybah mention that what is meant is inhaling the water, but the first is the right meaning. This is confirmed by another version which mentions both actions of inhaling water and blowing one's nose. Rinsing one's mouth means taking some water into one's mouth and turning it around before spitting it out. The minimum required in this regard is to take some water into one's mouth and then spit it out. To turn it around is not essential according to the majority of scholars. However, some of our scholars say that it is essential. This difference of opinion is like that of wiping one's head. The question in this case is whether it is enough for a person to place his wet hand on his head, without moving it around. The more correct view is that it is sufficient, just like it is sufficient to wet one's other body parts without rubbing. Inhaling water means to put it in one's nose and to pull it up with one's breath. It is recommended to do mouth rinsing and inhaling water to the full, unless one is fasting when such exaggeration is discouraged. This is based on the hadith narrated by Laqīṭ quoting the Prophet: 'Inhale fully unless you are fasting'. This is an authentic hadith related by Abū Dāwūd and al-Tirmidhī with sound chains of transmission.

Scholars of our school of *fiqh* maintain that in whichever way water reaches the mouth and the nose, the acts of rinsing and inhaling are considered complete. As for the preferable method, there are five views: (1) to do the rinsing of one's mouth and inhaling the water, taking three handfuls of water and using some for rinsing and the rest for inhalation each time; (2) to take one handful of water and rinse one's mouth with this water three times and then inhaling water three times; (3) to take one handful of water and rinse one's mouth and inhale water, then repeat the complete process two more times; (4) to take two handfuls of water and rinse one's mouth three times with the first one and inhale three times with the other; and, (5) to do it with six handfuls of water, rinsing one's mouth with three and inhaling with the other three. The correct procedure is the first, and it is specifically mentioned in authentic hadiths related by al-Bukhārī, Muslim and others. The hadith that mentions the fifth procedure is poor in authenticity. Therefore, the one mentioning three handfuls is the appropriate one, confirmed by the hadith narrated by ʿAbdullāh ibn Zayd and mentioned in Muslim's anthology. Scholars agree that rinsing one's mouth is done before inhaling water, whichever method is chosen. The question here is whether this is obligatory or recommended. There are two views on this point, and the weightier one is that it is obligatory because these actions involve two separate organs. The other view is that it is only recommended to do the rinsing of one's mouth first, just as washing one's right arm first is recommended, but God knows best.

The hadith then says: 'He then washed his face three times, then washed his right hand up to the elbow three times, then washed his left hand in the same way. He then wiped his head, then washed his right foot up to the ankles three times, then his left foot in the same way'. This hadith is a particularly important one in explaining the proper way of ablution. Muslims are unanimous that washing all organs that should be washed in the performance of ablution is obligatory once only. To wash them three times is a Sunnah or recommended practice. Authentic hadiths speak of washing every organ once only or three times, as well as washing some organs three times, and others twice or once only. Scholars say that these differences show that all these methods are acceptable and sufficient. This means that three times brings the matter to perfection, while once only is sufficient for validity. This is how the difference in what the relevant hadiths state is explained. However, narrators quoting the same companion of the Prophet relating the same hadith may differ. This is explained as a case of forgetfulness by some and remembrance by others. What a reliable reporter adds is upheld as this is agreed by scholars.

Scholars have different views on wiping one's head. Al-Shāfiʿī and others are of the view that it is recommended to do it three times, like the rest of the organs washed in ablution. Abū Ḥanīfah, Mālik, Ahmad and the majority of scholars are of the view that the recommended practice is once only. Authentic hadiths mention wiping one's head once only, while some just say, 'he wiped his head'. Al-Shāfiʿī cites in support of his view the hadith that we shall see in Muslim's *Ṣaḥīḥ* mentioning that 'the Prophet performed the ablution, doing each action three times', and the hadith related by Abū Dāwūd that the Prophet 'wiped his head three times'. He also draws an analogy with the other organs. In reply to those quoting the hadiths that mention the wiping once, al-Shāfiʿī says that these tell us that this is permissible, but the Prophet continued to do what is preferable, but God knows best.

Scholars are unanimously agreed that it is obligatory to wash one's face, arms and feet fully. The Shiah are the only ones who take a different attitude, saying that the obligation is only to wipe one's feet. This is definitely wrong, as there are numerous texts confirming the obligation to wash one's feet when performing the ablution. Moreover, all those who report how the Prophet performed the ablution confirm that he washed his feet.

Scholars are also unanimous that wiping one's head is obligatory, but they differ as to the extent of what is obligatory. Al-Shāfiʿī and other scholars say that the obligation applies to what the term applies, even as little as one hair. Mālik, Ahmad and several others maintain that the obligation applies to all the head. Abū Ḥanīfah says that what is obligatory is to wipe one-quarter of one's head. Scholars also differ as to whether rinsing one's mouth and blowing one's nose are obligatory, giving four different views: (1) Both are recommended [i.e. Sunnah] in both the normal ablution, *wuḍū'*, and the major ritual ablution, *ghusl*: this is the view of Mālik and al-Shāfiʿī and their schools of *fiqh*. It is also the view of al-Ḥasan al-Baṣrī, al-Zuhrī, al-Ḥakam, Qatādah, Rabīʿah, Yaḥyā ibn Saʿīd al-Anṣārī, al-Awzāʿī and al-Layth ibn Saʿd. It is also reported as one view expressed by ʿAṭā' and Ahmad; (2) both are obligatory in both types of ablution, *wuḍū'* and *ghusl*, and neither ablution is valid without them. This is the best-known view of Ahmad ibn Ḥanbal. It is shared by Ibn Abī Laylā, Ḥammād, Isḥāq ibn Rāhawayh and reported as a second view of ʿAṭā'; (3) both are obligatory in the major ritual ablution, *ghusl*, but not in *wuḍū'*. This is the view of Abū Ḥanīfah and his school of *fiqh* as well as Sufyān al-Thawrī; (4) inhaling water through one's nose is obligatory in both types of ablution, but rinsing one's mouth is recommended in both. This is the view of Abū Thawr, Abū ʿUbayd, Dāwūd al-Ẓāhirī, Abū Bakr ibn al-Mundhir and it is also reported to be expressed by Ahmad, but God knows best.

The majority of scholars agree that in washing body organs, it is sufficient in both types of ablution that water runs over the organs and that to rub them is not a requirement. However, only Mālik and al-Muzanī consider it essential that they should be rubbed. Likewise, the great majority of scholars agree that it is obligatory to wash one's elbows and ankles, but Zufar and Dāwūd al-Ẓāhirī say this is not obligatory. Scholars also agree that the ankles mean the two protruding bones above one's feet and at the bottom of one's legs. There are two ankles in each leg, but the Shiah take a different view saying that there is only one ankle in each leg, which is the bone on the outside of the leg. This is also reported to be expressed by Muhammad ibn al-Ḥasan, but this report is incorrect. In support of their view, scholars cite the linguistic usage and this hadith we are discussing. It says that the Prophet washed his right foot up to the ankles, using the dual form in Arabic, and then washed the left foot in the same manner. The hadith thus confirms that there are two ankles in each leg. Evidence concerning this point is plentiful. I have explained all of it and their origins in *Al-Majmūʿ fī Sharḥ al-Muhadhdhab*, where I speak in detail of the evidence concerning such matters, the differences between schools of *fiqh* concerning them, and the arguments offered by all and how they are responded to. Furthermore, I have spoken there about reconciling evidence and discussed all such matters in full detail. Here, I am only concerned with what is relevant to the hadith I am discussing, but God knows best.

Scholars of our Shāfiʿī School of *fiqh* say that if a person is created with two faces, both must be washed for ablution. If a person is created with three arms or three legs, and they are equal in length, all three must be washed. If the third hand is incomplete and it begins within the area that is obligatory to wash, it must be washed together with the original hand. If it appears above the elbow and is not parallel with the part that is required to be washed in ablution, it need not be washed. If it stretches to be parallel with the obligatory part, it should be washed up to the line that is parallel with the elbows. This is the correct view, although some of our scholars say it need not be washed. If a person's hand is amputated above the elbow, he need not wash the remaining part, but it is recommended that he wash a part of it so that his hand is involved in the ablution. If the amputation is below the elbow, washing the remaining part up to the elbow remains obligatory, but God knows best.

The Prophet says: 'Whoever performs the ablution in a similar way to what I have done now, then stands up and offers two *rakʿahs* during which he thinks of nothing [other than his prayer] is forgiven whatever sin he did'. It should be noted that the Prophet said 'in a similar way to what I have done'. He did not say, 'in the same way', because doing exactly the same as the Prophet is unattainable by anyone. The forgiveness of sins mentioned in the hadith relates to minor, but not major, sins. The hadith recommends offering two *rakʿahs* or more after every ablution. Such a prayer is a confirmed Sunnah. A number of our scholars say that offering such a Sunnah prayer is recommended even in those periods when voluntary prayers are discouraged,[i] because there is a special cause recommending it.

i. These periods are: (1) after one has offered Fajr Prayer until the sun has risen well into the sky (about 20 minutes after sunrise); (2) at midday when the sun is at its highest point until it has started on its decline; (3) after one has offered ʿAṣr Prayer until the sun has set; and, (4) after one has offered Witr Prayer until dawqn.

They cite in evidence the hadith narrated by Bilāl and related by al-Bukhārī in his *Ṣaḥīḥ*, stating that when the Prophet performed the ablution, he offered a prayer. He said that this was the action for which he hoped to receive a great reward. If a person prays an obligatory or recommended prayer after ablution, he achieves this merit, in the same way as greeting the mosque is fulfilled with any such prayer, but God knows best.

The Prophet mentions offering a prayer of two *rakʿahs* 'during which he thinks of nothing'. What is meant is that he does not think of ordinary affairs that have nothing to do with prayer. If something occurs to him but he dismisses it when it occurs, then this is overlooked. The reward will be his, God willing, because such occurrence is not of his own action. God overlooks thoughts that occur to us but do not stay with us. We explained this fully in the Book of Faith, but God knows best.

Imam al-Māzarī expressed the same meaning as I have mentioned and this was echoed by *Qāḍī* ʿIyāḍ who said: 'The reference made here is to thoughts that one recalls or raises within one's mind. Thoughts that come across one's mind by themselves are not meant here'. The Prophet said: 'during which he thinks of nothing', and this refers to something done deliberately because it is attributed to the person himself who does the thinking. *Qāḍī* ʿIyāḍ adds: 'Some say that it is hoped that the prayer of one who accidentally experiences some thoughts is acceptable. It will remain of a lesser grade than the prayer of one who entertains no thoughts other than what relates to his prayer. The Prophet guarantees forgiveness to the one who takes care to do so, because prayer is hardly ever free of some thoughts that are not related to it. This high grade is given to the one who strives to free himself of thoughts prompted by Satan, keeping himself focused on his prayer all the time. He thus ensures by hard effort that his prayer is kept free of such thoughts'. This is what *Qāḍī* ʿIyāḍ said, but what I mentioned earlier is the correct view, but God knows best.

Ibn Shihāb said: 'Our scholars used to say: "This is the most perfect ablution anyone can perform for prayer".' This comment means that this is the perfect ablution. Scholars are unanimous in discouraging adding to washing any part more than three times. This refers to three washes that cover the full organ. If it is not covered by less than two handfuls of water, then the two count as one wash. If one doubts whether one has washed, say, one's face two or three times, one considers them as two times and adds a third. This is the correct view, but Shaykh Abū Muhammad al-Juwaynī of our Shāfiʿī School said that in such a case the person concerned should treat them as three times, as a safeguard against deviation by adding a fourth. The first view is the one that is consistent with the proper rules. A fourth wash becomes a deviation if it is purposely done to add to the three, but God knows best.

What Ibn Shihāb has said may be cited in support of the view that discourages washing what is above the elbows or the ankles. This is not discouraged in our view; on the contrary, it is a desirable Sunnah. We will discuss this at the proper place, God willing. Moreover, what Ibn Shihāb said does not give any suggestion of discouraging this. He is only referring to the number of times washing is done in ablution. However, had Ibn Shihāb or anyone else stated that it is discouraged, the Prophet's practice takes precedence, but God knows best.

The second hadith that describes ʿUthmān's ablution shows that the proper practice to be followed with regard to rinsing one's mouth and blowing one's nose is that one should take water with one's right hand for this purpose. It may also be taken as evidence that one handful of water should be used for both rinsing one's mouth and blowing one's nose. This is one of the five methods I mentioned earlier. The evidence is based on the fact that the hadith mentions the repetition of washing one's hands and face, but leaves the reference to the rinsing and blowing general, but God knows best.

The hadith is evidence supporting the desirability of washing one's hands before putting them into the water container, even though one has not just woken up. This is particularly the case if one has any doubt that one's hand has touched an impurity. This is the view of our school of *fiqh*, and the meaning here is clear. We shall presently discuss this point more fully at its proper place, God willing.

Transmission

The chain of transmission features Ibn Shihāb reporting from 'Aṭā' ibn Yazīd al-Laythī from Ḥumrān. These three belonged to the Tābi'īn generation and they reported from each other.

CHAPTER 4

THE IMPORTANCE OF RITUAL ABLUTION AND FOLLOWING IT WITH A PRAYER

[402–5]. (Dār al-Salām 0438) Qutaybah ibn Sa'īd, 'Uthmān ibn Muhammad ibn Abī Shaybah and Isḥāq ibn Ibrāhīm al-Ḥanẓalī narrated (this is Qutaybah's text):[i] Isḥāq said: Jarīr reported and the others said: Jarīr narrated; from Hishām ibn 'Urwah; from his father; from Ḥumrān, 'Uthmān's *mawlā*: **'I heard 'Uthmān ibn 'Affān as he was in the yard of the mosque. The *mu'adhdhin* [caller to prayer] came to him at 'Aṣr time. He asked for water and performed the ablution. He then said: "By God, I shall narrate to you something I would not have narrated to you except for a verse in God's Book. I heard God's Messenger (peace be upon him) say: 'Whenever a Muslim person performs the ablution well, and then offers a prayer, God will forgive him whatever he does until the next prayer'".'**

حَدَّثَنَا قُتَيْبَةُ بْنُ سَعِيدٍ، وَعُثْمَانُ بْنُ مُحَمَّدِ بْنِ أَبِي شَيْبَةَ، وَإِسْحَاقُ بْنُ إِبْرَاهِيمَ الْحَنْظَلِيُّ، - وَاللَّفْظُ لِقُتَيْبَةَ، قَالَ إِسْحَاقُ: أَخْبَرَنَا، وَقَالَ الآخَرَانِ - حَدَّثَنَا جَرِيرٌ، عَنْ هِشَامِ بْنِ عُرْوَةَ، عَنْ أَبِيهِ، عَنْ حُمْرَانَ، مَوْلَى عُثْمَانَ، قَالَ: سَمِعْتُ عُثْمَانَ بْنَ عَفَّانَ، وَهُوَ بِفِنَاءِ الْمَسْجِدِ فَجَاءَهُ الْمُؤَذِّنُ عِنْدَ الْعَصْرِ فَدَعَا بِوَضُوءٍ فَتَوَضَّأَ، ثُمَّ قَالَ: وَاللهِ لأُحَدِّثَنَّكُمْ حَدِيثًا لَوْلاَ آيَةٌ فِي كِتَابِ اللهِ مَا حَدَّثْتُكُمْ، إِنِّي سَمِعْتُ رَسُولَ اللهِ صَلَّى اللهُ عَلَيْهِ وَسَلَّمَ

i. Related by al-Bukhārī, 160 (in a longer version); al-Nasā'ī, 146.

يَقُولُ: «لَا يَتَوَضَّأُ رَجُلٌ مُسْلِمٌ فَيُحْسِنُ الْوُضُوءَ فَيُصَلِّي صَلَاةً إِلَّا غَفَرَ اللهُ لَهُ مَا بَيْنَهُ وَبَيْنَ الصَّلَاةِ الَّتِي تَلِيهَا»

[000–000]. (Dār al-Salām 0439) Abū Kurayb narrated: Abū Usāmah narrated [H]. Zuhayr ibn Ḥarb and Abū Kurayb narrated: Wakīʿ narrated [H]. Ibn Abī ʿUmar narrated: Sufyān narrated; all of them from Hishām, with this chain of transmission: **the same text. In Abū Usāmah's narration: 'When a Muslim person performs his ablution well and then offers an obligatory prayer'**.

حَدَّثَنَا أَبُو كُرَيْبٍ، حَدَّثَنَا أَبُو أُسَامَةَ ح، وَحَدَّثَنَا زُهَيْرُ بْنُ حَرْبٍ، وَأَبُو كُرَيْبٍ، قَالَا: حَدَّثَنَا وَكِيعٌ ح، حَدَّثَنَا ابْنُ أَبِي عُمَرَ، حَدَّثَنَا سُفْيَانُ، جَمِيعًا عَنْ هِشَامٍ بِهَذَا الْإِسْنَادِ وَفِي حَدِيثِ أَبِي أُسَامَةَ فَيُحْسِنُ وُضُوءَهُ ثُمَّ يُصَلِّي الْمَكْتُوبَةَ.

[403–6]. (Dār al-Salām 0440) Zuhayr ibn Ḥarb narrated: Yaʿqūb ibn Ibrāhīm narrated; my father narrated; from Sāliḥ. Ibn Shihāb said: But ʿUrwah narrates from Ḥumrān that he said: **'When ʿUthmān completed his ablution, he said: "By God, I shall narrate to you something. By God, I would not have narrated it to you, except for a verse in God's Book. I heard God's Messenger (peace be upon him) say: 'When any person performs the ablution well then offers the prayer, he shall be forgiven whatever he commits between that prayer and the one that follows'."' ʿUrwah said: 'The Qur'anic verse referred to is: *"Those who conceal the clear proofs and guidance We bestowed from on high ... who curse"*.'**[i] (2: 159)

i. The full text of the verse is: *'Those who conceal the clear proofs and guidance We bestowed from on high, after We have expounded it clearly for mankind in the Book, shall be cursed by God and by others who curse".'* (2: 159)

وَحدَّثَنَا زُهَيْرُ بْنُ حَرْبٍ، حَدَّثَنَا يَعْقُوبُ بْنُ إِبْرَاهِيمَ، حَدَّثَنَا أَبِي، عَنْ صَالِحٍ، قَالَ: ابْنُ شِهَابٍ، وَلَكِنْ عُرْوَةُ، يُحَدِّثُ عَنْ حُمْرَانَ أَنَّهُ قَالَ: فَلَمَّا تَوَضَّأَ عُثْمَانُ قَالَ: وَاللهِ لَأُحَدِّثَنَّكُمْ حَدِيثًا وَاللهِ لَوْلَا آيَةٌ فِي كِتَابِ اللهِ مَا حَدَّثْتُكُمُوهُ إِنِّي سَمِعْتُ رَسُولَ اللهِ صَلَّى اللهُ عَلَيْهِ وَسَلَّمَ يَقُولُ: «لَا يَتَوَضَّأُ رَجُلٌ فَيُحْسِنُ وُضُوءَهُ ثُمَّ يُصَلِّي الصَّلَاةَ إِلَّا غُفِرَ لَهُ مَا بَيْنَهُ وَبَيْنَ الصَّلَاةِ الَّتِي تَلِيهَا» قَالَ عُرْوَةُ الْآيَةُ: «إِنَّ الَّذِينَ يَكْتُمُونَ مَا أَنْزَلْنَا مِنَ الْبَيِّنَاتِ وَالْهُدَى» [البقرة: ١٥٩]- إِلَى قَوْلِهِ - «اللَّاعِنُونَ» [البقرة: ١٥٩]

[404–7]. (Dār al-Salām 0441) ʿAbd ibn Ḥumayd and Ḥajjāj ibn al-Shāʿir narrated: both from Abū al-Walīd. ʿAbd said: Abū al-Walīd narrated to me; Isḥāq ibn Saʿīd ibn ʿAmr ibn Saʿīd ibn al-ʿĀṣ narrated; my father narrated to me; from his father. He said: **'I was at ʿUthmān's and he called for water [for ablution] and said: "I heard God's Messenger (peace be upon him) say: 'Whenever a Muslim finds himself at a time of an obligatory prayer and he performs its ablution well, and attends to it with serenity and performs its bowing [and duties] well, then it will be a forgiveness to what preceded it of sin, unless a major sin has been committed. This applies for all time'".'**

حَدَّثَنَا عَبْدُ بْنُ حُمَيْدٍ، وَحَجَّاجُ بْنُ الشَّاعِرِ، كِلَاهُمَا عَنْ أَبِي الْوَلِيدِ، قَالَ: عَبْدٌ، حَدَّثَنِي أَبُو الْوَلِيدِ، حَدَّثَنَا إِسْحَاقُ بْنُ سَعِيدِ بْنِ عَمْرِو بْنِ سَعِيدِ بْنِ الْعَاصِ، حَدَّثَنِي أَبِي، عَنْ أَبِيهِ، قَالَ: كُنْتُ عِنْدَ عُثْمَانَ فَدَعَا بِطَهُورٍ فَقَالَ سَمِعْتُ رَسُولَ اللهِ صَلَّى اللهُ عَلَيْهِ وَسَلَّمَ: «يَقُولُ مَا مِنَ امْرِئٍ مُسْلِمٍ تَحْضُرُهُ صَلَاةٌ مَكْتُوبَةٌ فَيُحْسِنُ وُضُوءَهَا وَخُشُوعَهَا وَرُكُوعَهَا، إِلَّا كَانَتْ كَفَّارَةً لِمَا قَبْلَهَا مِنَ الذُّنُوبِ مَا لَمْ يُؤْتِ كَبِيرَةً وَذَلِكَ الدَّهْرَ كُلَّهُ»

[405–8]. (Dār al-Salām 0442) Qutaybah ibn Saʿīd and Aḥmad ibn ʿAbdah al-Ḍabb narrated: ʿAbd al-ʿAzīz, who is al-Darāward, narrated; from Zayd ibn Aslam; from Ḥumrān, ʿUthmān's *mawlā*: **'I brought water for ablution to ʿUthmān ibn ʿAffān**

and he performed the ablution, then said: "Some people narrate things and attribute them to God's Messenger (peace be upon him), but I do not know what these are. However, I saw God's Messenger (peace be upon him) perform the ablution like I did then he said: 'Whoever performs the ablution thus shall have his past sins forgiven, and his prayer and walk to the mosque will be a gain'".'

Ibn ʿAbdah's narration says: '**I came to ʿUthmān and he performed the ablution**'.

حَدَّثَنَا قُتَيْبَةُ بْنُ سَعِيدٍ، وَأَحْمَدُ بْنُ عَبْدَةَ الضَّبِّيُّ، قَالَا: حَدَّثَنَا عَبْدُ الْعَزِيزِ وَهُوَ الدَّرَاوَرْدِيُّ، عَنْ زَيْدِ بْنِ أَسْلَمَ، عَنْ حُمْرَانَ، مَوْلَى عُثْمَانَ، قَالَ: أَتَيْتُ عُثْمَانَ بْنَ عَفَّانَ بِوَضُوءٍ فَتَوَضَّأَ، ثُمَّ قَالَ: إِنَّ نَاسًا يَتَحَدَّثُونَ عَنْ رَسُولِ اللهِ صَلَّى اللهُ عَلَيْهِ وَسَلَّمَ أَحَادِيثَ لَا أَدْرِي مَا هِيَ؟ إِلَّا أَنِّي رَأَيْتُ رَسُولَ اللهِ صَلَّى اللهُ عَلَيْهِ وَسَلَّمَ تَوَضَّأَ مِثْلَ وُضُوئِي هَذَا، ثُمَّ قَالَ: «مَنْ تَوَضَّأَ هَكَذَا غُفِرَ لَهُ مَا تَقَدَّمَ مِنْ ذَنْبِهِ، وَكَانَتْ صَلَاتُهُ وَمَشْيُهُ إِلَى الْمَسْجِدِ نَافِلَةً»

وَفِي رِوَايَةِ ابْنِ عَبْدَةَ أَتَيْتُ عُثْمَانَ فَتَوَضَّأَ

[406–9]. (Dār al-Salām 0443) Qutaybh ibn Saʿīd, Abū Bakr ibn Abī Shaybah and Zuhayr ibn Ḥarb narrated (this is Qutaybah's and Abū Bakr's text): Wakīʿ narrated; from Sufyān; from Abū al-Naḍr; from Abū Anas: '**ʿUthmān performed the ablution at al-Maqāʿid. He said: "Shall I show you how God's Messenger (peace be upon him) performed the ablution?" He then performed the ablution doing each part three times**'.

Qutaybah added in his narration: '**Sufyān said: Abū al-Naḍr said from Abū Anas: "With a number of the Prophet's companions present"**.'

حَدَّثَنَا قُتَيْبَةُ بْنُ سَعِيدٍ، وَأَبُو بَكْرِ بْنُ أَبِي شَيْبَةَ، وَزُهَيْرُ بْنُ حَرْبٍ، - وَاللَّفْظُ لِقُتَيْبَةَ، وَأَبِي بَكْرٍ، قَالُوا - حَدَّثَنَا وَكِيعٌ، عَنْ سُفْيَانَ، عَنْ أَبِي النَّضْرِ، عَنْ أَبِي أَنَسٍ، أَنَّ عُثْمَانَ تَوَضَّأَ بِالْمَقَاعِدِ فَقَالَ: «أَلَا أُرِيكُمْ وُضُوءَ رَسُولِ اللهِ صَلَّى اللهُ عَلَيْهِ وَسَلَّمَ؟ ثُمَّ تَوَضَّأَ ثَلَاثًا ثَلَاثًا»

وَزَادَ قُتَيْبَةُ فِي رِوَايَتِهِ قَالَ: سُفْيَانُ: قَالَ أَبُو النَّضْرِ: عَنْ أَبِي أَنَسٍ قَالَ: «وَعِنْدَهُ رِجَالٌ مِنْ أَصْحَابِ رَسُولِ اللهِ صَلَّى اللهُ عَلَيْهِ وَسَلَّمَ»

[407–10]. (Dār al-Salām 0444) Abū Kurayb Muhammad ibn al-ʿAlā' and Isḥāq ibn Ibrāhīm narrated:[i] both from Wakīʿ. Abū Kurayb said: Wakīʿ narrated; from Misʿar; from Jāmiʿ ibn Shaddād Abū Ṣakhrah: **'I heard Ḥumrān ibn Abān say: "I used to place the ablution water for ʿUthmān. Every day he poured a little over himself. And ʿUthmān said: 'God's Messenger (peace be upon him) told us when we finished this prayer of ours (Misʿar said: I believe it is ʿAṣr Prayer): "I am not sure whether I should tell you something or remain silent". We said: "Messenger of God, if it is good then tell us; and if it is something different, then God and His Messenger know best". He said: "When a Muslim cleanses himself and performs well the ablution which God made a duty for him, then prays these five prayers, they will count as atonement for anything done between them""".'**

حَدَّثَنَا أَبُو كُرَيْبٍ مُحَمَّدُ بْنُ الْعَلَاءِ، وَإِسْحَاقُ بْنُ إِبْرَاهِيمَ جَمِيعًا عَنْ وَكِيعٍ قَالَ أَبُو كُرَيْبٍ: حَدَّثَنَا وَكِيعٌ، عَنْ مِسْعَرٍ، عَنْ جَامِعِ بْنِ شَدَّادٍ أَبِي صَخْرَةَ، قَالَ: سَمِعْتُ حُمْرَانَ بْنَ أَبَانَ، قَالَ: كُنْتُ أَضَعُ لِعُثْمَانَ طَهُورَهُ فَمَا أَتَى عَلَيْهِ يَوْمٌ إِلَّا وَهُوَ يُفِيضُ عَلَيْهِ نُطْفَةً وَقَالَ عُثْمَانُ: حَدَّثَنَا رَسُولُ اللهِ صَلَّى اللهُ عَلَيْهِ وَسَلَّمَ عِنْدَ انْصِرَافِنَا مِنْ صَلَاتِنَا

i. Related by al-Nasā'ī, 145; Ibn Mājah, 459.

هَذِهِ - قَالَ مِسْعَرٌ: أُرَاهَا الْعَصْرَ - فَقَالَ: «مَا أَدْرِي أُحَدِّثُكُمْ بِشَيْءٍ أَوْ أَسْكُتُ؟» فَقُلْنَا يَا رَسُولَ اللهِ إِنْ كَانَ خَيْرًا فَحَدِّثْنَا، وَإِنْ كَانَ غَيْرَ ذَلِكَ فَاللهُ ورسوله أَعْلَمُ، قَالَ: «مَا مِنْ مُسْلِمٍ يَتَطَهَّرُ، فَيُتِمُّ الطُّهُورَ الَّذِي كَتَبَ اللهُ عَلَيْهِ، فَيُصَلِّي هَذِهِ الصَّلَوَاتِ الْخَمْسَ، إِلَّا كَانَتْ كَفَّارَاتٍ لِـمَا بَيْنَهَا»

[408–11]. (Dār al-Salām 0445) ʿUbaydillāh ibn Muʿādh narrated: my father narrated [H]. Also, Muhammad ibn al-Muthannā and Ibn Bashshār narrated: Muhammad ibn Jaʿfar narrated: both said: Shuʿbah narrated from Jāmiʿ ibn Shaddād who said: I heard Ḥumrān ibn Abān narrating to Abū Burdah in this mosque, during Bishr's governorship that ʿUthmān ibn ʿAffān said: **'God's Messenger (peace be upon him) said: "Whoever performs the ablution well, as God has commanded, then [prays] the obligatory prayers ensures forgiveness of what is committed between them".'**

This is Ibn Muʿādh's narration. Ghundar's narration does not include 'during Bishr's governorship' nor does it mention 'the obligatory'.

حَدَّثَنَا عُبَيْدُ اللهِ بْنُ مُعَاذٍ، حَدَّثَنَا أَبِي ح، وَحَدَّثَنَا مُحَمَّدُ بْنُ الْـمُثَنَّى، وَابْنُ بَشَّارٍ، قَالَا: حَدَّثَنَا مُحَمَّدُ بْنُ جَعْفَرٍ قَالَا جَمِيعًا: حَدَّثَنَا شُعْبَةُ، عَنْ جَامِعِ بْنِ شَدَّادٍ، قَالَ: سَمِعْتُ حُمْرَانَ بْنَ أَبَانَ، يُحَدِّثُ أَبَا بُرْدَةَ فِي هَذَا الْـمَسْجِدِ فِي إِمَارَةِ بِشْرٍ أَنَّ عُثْمَانَ بْنَ عَفَّانَ، قَالَ: قَالَ رَسُولُ اللهِ صَلَّى اللهُ عَلَيْهِ وَسَلَّمَ: «مَنْ أَتَمَّ الْوُضُوءَ كَمَا أَمَرَهُ اللهُ تَعَالَى، فَالصَّلَوَاتُ الْـمَكْتُوبَاتُ كَفَّارَاتٌ لِمَا بَيْنَهُنَّ»

هَذَا حَدِيثُ ابْنِ مُعَاذٍ وَلَيْسَ فِي حَدِيثِ غُنْدَرٍ: «فِي إِمَارَةِ بِشْرٍ، وَلَا ذِكْرُ الْـمَكْتُوبَاتِ».

[409–12]. (Dār al-Salām 0446) Hārūn ibn Saʿīd al-Aylī narrated: Ibn Wahb narrated saying: and Makhramah ibn Bukayr reported to me; from his father, from Ḥumrān, 'Uthmān's *mawlā*: '**'Uthmān ibn 'Affān performed the ablution well one day then said: "I saw God's Messenger (peace be upon him) performing the ablution well and then said: 'Whoever performs the ablution like this then goes out to the mosque, having no reason for going out other than the prayer, will have all his past sins forgiven'".**'

حَدَّثَنَا هَارُونُ بْنُ سَعِيدٍ الْأَيْلِيُّ، حَدَّثَنَا ابْنُ وَهْبٍ، قَالَ: وَأَخْبَرَنِي مَخْرَمَةُ بْنُ بُكَيْرٍ، عَنْ أَبِيهِ، عَنْ حُمْرَانَ مَوْلَى عُثْمَانَ، قَالَ: تَوَضَّأَ عُثْمَانُ بْنُ عَفَّانَ، يَوْمًا وُضُوءًا حَسَنًا ثُمَّ قَالَ: رَأَيْتُ رَسُولَ اللهِ صَلَّى اللهُ عَلَيْهِ وَسَلَّمَ تَوَضَّأَ فَأَحْسَنَ الْوُضُوءَ ثُمَّ قَالَ: «مَنْ تَوَضَّأَ هَكَذَا، ثُمَّ خَرَجَ إِلَى الْمَسْجِدِ لَا يَنْهَزُهُ إِلَّا الصَّلَاةُ، غُفِرَ لَهُ مَا خَلَا مِنْ ذَنْبِهِ»

[410–13]. (Dār al-Salām 0447) Abū al-Ṭāhir and Yūnus ibn 'Abd al-A'lā narrated:[i] 'Abdullāh ibn Wahb reported; from 'Amr ibn al-Ḥārith; that al-Ḥukaym ibn 'Abdullāh al-Qurashī narrated to him; that Nāfi' ibn Jubayr and 'Abdullāh ibn Abi Salamah narrated to him; that Mu'ādh ibn 'Abd al-Raḥmān narrated; from Ḥumrān, 'Uthmān ibn 'Affān's *mawlā*; from 'Uthmān ibn 'Affān: '**I heard God's Messenger (peace be upon him) say: "Whoever performs the ablution for prayer and he performs it well, then walks to [join] the obligatory prayer and he offers it with the people, or with the congregation, or in the mosque, shall be forgiven his sins by God".**'

وَحَدَّثَنِي أَبُو الطَّاهِرِ، وَيُونُسُ بْنُ عَبْدِ الْأَعْلَى، قَالَا: أَخْبَرَنَا عَبْدُ اللهِ بْنُ وَهْبٍ، عَنْ عَمْرِو بْنِ الْحَارِثِ، أَنَّ الْحُكَيْمَ بْنَ عَبْدِ اللهِ الْقُرَشِيَّ، حَدَّثَهُ أَنَّ نَافِعَ بْنَ جُبَيْرٍ، وَعَبْدَ اللهِ بْنَ أَبِي سَلَمَةَ، حَدَّثَاهُ أَنَّ مُعَاذَ بْنَ عَبْدِ الرَّحْمَنِ، حَدَّثَهُمَا عَنْ حُمْرَانَ، مَوْلَى عُثْمَانَ بْنِ

i. Related by al-Bukhārī, 6433; al-Nasā'ī, 855.

عفَّانَ، عَنْ عُثْمَانَ بْنِ عَفَّانَ، قَالَ: سَمِعْتُ رَسُولَ اللهِ صَلَّى اللهُ عَلَيْهِ وَسَلَّمَ يَقُولُ: «مَنْ تَوَضَّأَ لِلصَّلَاةِ فَأَسْبَغَ الْوُضُوءَ، ثُمَّ مَشَى إِلَى الصَّلَاةِ الْمَكْتُوبَةِ، فَصَلَّاهَا مَعَ النَّاسِ أَوْ مَعَ الْجَمَاعَةِ أَوْ فِي الْمَسْجِدِ غَفَرَ اللهُ لَهُ ذُنُوبَهُ»

Text Explanation

In the first hadith, No. 402, ʿUthmān is said to have been 'in the yard of the mosque', which means close to it, but God knows best. ʿUthmān says to the people 'By God, I shall narrate to you'. This shows that it is permissible to swear by God even though one does not need to do so. In the hadith, ʿUthmān says to the people that he was only narrating the hadith to them because of a verse in the Qur'an. ʿUrwah then said that the verse he meant was the one that said: *'Those who conceal the clear proofs and guidance We bestowed from on high, after We have expounded it clearly for mankind in the Book, shall be cursed by God and by others who curse'*. (2: 159) This means that had it not been for the fact that God has made it a duty for everyone who learns something to communicate it to others, he would not have been keen to tell them of it.

In most original manuscripts, the wording of the hadith means 'except for a verse in the Qur'an'. However, al-Bājī narrates it as meaning: 'except for the fact that it is in the Qur'an'. The difference is in the way Arabic was written before its similar letters were dotted to indicate their differences. These two ways of reporting the hadith differ in one three-letter word that without dotting may be pronounced as *āyah*, meaning 'a verse', or *annahu*, meaning 'the fact that'. *Qāḍī* ʿIyāḍ said:

> Scholars differ in their explanations. In Muslim's *Ṣaḥīḥ*, ʿUrwah is quoted as stating that the verse referred to is *'Those who conceal the clear proofs and guidance We bestowed …'*. This does not allow the second reading of the word in question. In *al-Muwaṭṭa'*, Mālik said: 'I think he meant the verse that says:

> *"Attend to your prayers at both ends of the day and in the early watches of the night"*'. (11: 114) This admits both readings. If we take this second reading, ʿUthmān meant that the meaning of what he was about to tell the people is already stated in the Qur'an. Had it not been so, he would not have reported it to them so that they would continue to be diligent in attending to their Islamic duties and would not slacken.
>
> Although the verse mentioned by ʿUrwah speaks about the people of earlier revelations, it implies a warning to everyone who follows in their footsteps. Indeed the Prophet gives a general warning in the well-known hadith: 'Whoever suppresses knowledge God will rein him with a rein of fire'.

This is what *Qāḍī* ʿIyāḍ said, but the correct meaning is that mentioned by ʿUrwah.

The Prophet refers to doing the ablution well. This means that it is done in full, and with the proper approach. The hadith encourages us to look carefully at ablution and learn how it should be done, and to make sure that we perform it in the way that combines all that scholars identify as necessary for its validity. We should not be so relaxed as to rely on the differences in their views. This means that one should make sure to start by mentioning the name of God, have the proper intention, rinse one's mouth, inhale water and blow one's nose, wipe all one's head, wipe one's ears, rub one's face, hands and feet as one washes them, do the ablution in the right order and without interruption and other matters on which scholars differ, in addition to ensuring that one's water is pure; but God knows best.

The Prophet says that when a person does this, 'he shall be forgiven whatever he commits between that prayer and the one that follows'. This means the prayer that comes next. The version in *Al-Muwaṭṭa'* says: 'and the one that follows until he offers it'.

In hadith No. 404, the Prophet says that when one performs the ablution well and offers a prayer after it, 'this will be a forgiveness to what preceded it of sin, unless a major sin has been committed. This applies for all time'. This confirms that all minor sins will be forgiven, but not the major ones. *Qāḍī* ʿIyāḍ said: 'What is mentioned in this hadith of the forgiveness of sins, except for major ones, is the view upheld by all Sunni scholars. Major sins are forgiven either through repentance or by God's grace and mercy', but God knows best.

In this same hadith, No. 404, the Prophet says: 'Whenever a Muslim finds himself at a time of an obligatory prayer and he performs its ablution well, and attends to it with serenity and performs its bowing [and duties] well, then it will be a forgiveness to what preceded it of sin, unless a major sin has been committed'. In the earlier version, the Prophet mentions forgiveness for the one who performs the ablution well and offers two *rakʿahs* in which he focuses fully on his prayer, and in the other version he will be forgiven whatever he commits between that prayer and the next. In another hadith, the Prophet says: 'Whoever performs the ablution in this way, he is forgiven his past sins and then his prayer and walk to the mosque will be a gain for him'. In another hadith: 'The five daily prayers ensure the forgiveness of what is committed in between them'. And in yet another hadith, the Prophet says: 'The five daily prayers, and the Friday Prayer to the next, and Ramadan to Ramadan ensure the forgiveness of what is committed between them provided that major sins are refrained from'. All these statements are mentioned by Muslim in this chapter. It may be said that if ablution ensures the forgiveness of sins, what will prayer forgive? And if prayer ensures forgiveness, what will Friday Prayer and Ramadan forgive? The same question holds in respect of fasting on the Day of Arafat, which ensures the forgiveness of two years, and fasting on the 10 al-Muharram, which ensures the forgiveness of one year. Likewise, if when we say 'Amen' this coincides with the angels saying it, our past sins are forgiven. The answer is that given by scholars: each one of the actions the Prophet mentions serves for the forgiveness of sins. If such an action encounters minor sins, it will ensure their forgiveness. If it meets no minor or major sin, it will give credits of good deeds and enhance the status of the person concerned. If it encounters one or more major sins, but no minor ones, we hope that it will serve to reduce these, but God knows best.

The hadith No. 406 mentions that 'Uthmān performed the ablution at al-Maqā'id. These were shops close to 'Uthmān ibn 'Affān's home. It is also said that it was a staircase. Another explanation mentions that it was a place close to the mosque, where 'Uthmān used to sit and look into people's affairs, perform the ablution and do other things. 'Uthmān performed the ablution washing every part three times. This is an important hadith making clear that the recommended, i.e. Sunnah, practice in ablution is to wash every part three times, but the obligatory practice is to wash once only. This hadith serves as evidence in support of al-Shāfi'ī's view, and that of scholars who agree with him, that it is recommended to wipe one's head three times, like the rest of the body organs involved in ablution. There are several hadiths in support of this and I have listed them together and explained them in *Sharḥ al-Muhadhdhab*, pointing out which of them is authentic and which is not. The hadith mentions that there were a number of the Prophet's companions present. This means that none of them objected to what 'Uthmān did. In a version related by al-Bayhaqī and others, 'Uthmān performed the ablution doing every part three times, then said to the Prophet's companions: 'Did you see God's Messenger doing this? They said: Yes'.

In hadith No. 407, the narrator says that 'Uthmān ibn 'Affān used to pour a little water over himself every day. He meant that he took a quick shower every day, because he was keen to cleanse himself and earn the great reward he mentioned in the hadith he narrated from the Prophet, but God knows best.

In this hadith, the Prophet says to his companions: 'I am not sure whether I should tell you something or remain silent'. They said: 'Messenger of God, if it is good then tell us; and if it is something different, then God and His Messenger know best'. He probably meant that he was unsure whether telling them this hadith at that particular point was good for them. He then immediately realized that it was good for them, and he stated it to encourage them to always cleanse themselves with ablution and to do other reward-earning actions. His initial reluctance was because he feared that they might slacken and rely on small matters. Then he decided that it was to their benefit that they should learn what he told them.

They said: 'If it is good, then tell us'. This probably means that if it brings us good prospects and encourages us to do what is a good deed and to refrain from evil and disobedience of God, then tell us so that we will be eager to fulfil our duties. If it is something that does not relate to good actions and avoidance of sin, then God and His Messenger know whether it is better that you tell us or not. They thus left the matter to him.

When they said this, the Prophet told them: 'When a Muslim cleanses himself and performs well the ablution God made a duty for him, then prays these five prayers, they will count as atonement for anything done between them'. This version of the hadith states something very useful. It tells us that when a person performs the ablution, confining himself to cleansing the parts that are required as a duty, and omitting what is recommended or desirable, this great reward will accrue to him or her. However, to add what is recommended is better and ensures greater reward, but God knows best.

Hadith No. 409 mentions that when a person performs the ablution well and goes out to the mosque, having no reason for going out other than to offer his prayers, will have his past sins forgiven. The hadith stresses the importance of doing one's duty with sincere intention and total devotion.

Transmission

The chain of transmission of hadith No. 403 features: 'Ṣāliḥ, Ibn Shihāb said: But ʿUrwah narrates from Ḥumrān'. These four belonged to the Tābiʿīn generation and they report from each other. It has another interesting point which is the narration of an elder person from a younger one. Ṣāliḥ ibn Kaysān was older than Ibn Shihāb al-Zuhrī, and he reports from him.

The chain of transmission of hadith No. 406 mentions Abū al-Naḍr from Abū Anas. Abū al-Naḍr's name is Sālim ibn Umayyah. He was the *mawlā* and scribe of ʿUmar ibn ʿAbdullāh of the Taym branch of the Quraysh. Abū Anas's name is Mālik ibn Abū ʿĀmir al-

Aṣbaḥī of Madinah, who was Anas ibn Mālik's grandfather and the father of Abū Suhayl, Mālik's uncle.

In the same chain we have: 'Wakīʿ narrated from Sufyān from Abū al-Naḍr from Abū Anas'. This is one of the chains of transmission questioned by al-Dāraquṭnī and others. Abū ʿAlī al-Ghassānī al-Jayyanī observed: 'It is mentioned that Wakīʿ ibn al-Jarrāḥ erred in the transmission of this hadith as he said that Abū al-Naḍr reported it from Abū Anas. In fact, Abū al-Naḍr reported it from Busr ibn Saʿīd from 'Uthmān ibn ʿAffān. We have reported this from Ahmad ibn Ḥanbal and others ... . Similarly al-Dāraquṭnī said that this is one of Wakīʿ's errors from Sufyān al-Thawrī. Other good memorizers of al-Thawrī's associates differ with Wakīʿ on this point. They include ʿAbdullāh al-Ashjaʿī, ʿAbdullāh ibn al-Walīd, Yazīd ibn Abī Ḥakīm, al-Firyābi, Muʿāwiyah ibn Hishām and Abū Ḥudhayfah. They report it from al-Thawrī from Abū al-Naḍr from Busr ibn Saʿīd that 'Uthmān ... . This is the correct chain'.

The chain of transmission of hadith No. 409 includes al-Ḥukaym ibn ʿAbdullāh, Nāfiʿ ibn Jubayr, Muʿādh and Ḥumrān. Al-Nawawī mentions this fact, adding nothing, but most probably he meant to add that these four all belonged to the Tābiʿīn generation.

CHAPTER 5

THE FIVE PRAYERS, FRIDAY PRAYER AND RAMADAN WIPE OFF SINS

[411–14]. (Dār al-Salām 0448) Yaḥyā ibn Ayyūb, Qutaybah ibn Saʿīd and ʿAlī ibn Ḥujr narrated:[i] all from Ismāʿīl; Ibn Ayyūb said: Ismāʿīl ibn Jaʿfar narrated; al-ʿAlā' ibn ʿAbd al-Raḥmān ibn Yaʿqūb, al-Ḥuraqah's *mawlā*; from his father; from Abū Hurayrah: God's Messenger (peace be upon him) said: **'The five [obligatory] prayers, and Friday Prayer to Friday Prayer will wipe off what is committed between them unless major sins are committed'**.

حَدَّثَنَا يَحْيَى بْنُ أَيُّوبَ، وَقُتَيْبَةُ بْنُ سَعِيدٍ، وَعَلِيُّ بْنُ حُجْرٍ، كُلُّهُمْ عَنْ إِسْمَاعِيلَ، قَالَ ابْنُ أَيُّوبَ: حَدَّثَنَا إِسْمَاعِيلُ بْنُ جَعْفَرٍ، أَخْبَرَنِي الْعَلَاءُ بْنُ عَبْدِ الرَّحْمَنِ بْنِ يَعْقُوبَ مَوْلَى الْحُرَقَةِ، عَنْ أَبِيهِ، عَنْ أَبِي هُرَيْرَةَ، أَنَّ رَسُولَ اللهِ صَلَّى اللهُ عَلَيْهِ وَسَلَّمَ قَالَ: «الصَّلَاةُ الْخَمْسُ، وَالْجُمْعَةُ إِلَى الْجُمْعَةِ، كَفَّارَةٌ لِمَا بَيْنَهُنَّ، مَا لَمْ تُغْشَ الْكَبَائِرُ»

[412–15]. (Dār al-Salām 0449) Naṣr ibn ʿAlī al-Jahḍamī narrated to me: ʿAbd al-Aʿlā reported; Hishām narrated; from Muhammad; from Abū Hurayrah; from the Prophet (peace be upon him) who said: **'The five [obligatory] prayers and Friday prayer to Friday Prayer will wipe off what is committed between them'**.

---

i. Related by al-Tirmidhī, 214.

حَدَّثَنِي نَصْرُ بْنُ عَلِيٍّ الْجَهْضَمِيُّ، أَخْبَرَنَا عَبْدُ الْأَعْلَى، حَدَّثَنَا هِشَامٌ، عَنْ مُحَمَّدٍ، عَنْ أَبِي هُرَيْرَةَ، عَنِ النَّبِيِّ صَلَّى اللهُ عَلَيْهِ وَسَلَّمَ قَالَ: «الصَّلَوَاتُ الْخَمْسُ، وَالْجُمْعَةُ إِلَى الْجُمْعَةِ، كَفَّارَاتٌ لِمَا بَيْنَهُنَّ»

[413–16]. (Dār al-Salām 0450) Abū al-Ṭāhir and Hārūn ibn Saʿīd al-Aylī narrated to me: Ibn Wahb reported; from Abū Ṣakhr; that ʿUmar ibn Isḥāq, Zā'idah's *mawlā*, narrated to him; from his father; from Abū Hurayrah; that God's Messenger (peace be upon him) used to say: '**The five [obligatory] prayers, Friday Prayer to Friday Prayer and Ramadan to Ramadan wipe off what is committed between them if major sins are refrained from**'.

حَدَّثَنِي أَبُو الطَّاهِرِ، وَهَارُونُ بْنُ سَعِيدٍ الْأَيْلِيُّ، قَالَا: أَخْبَرَنَا ابْنُ وَهْبٍ، عَنْ أَبِي صَخْرٍ، أَنَّ عُمَرَ بْنَ إِسْحَاقَ مَوْلَى زَائِدَةَ، حَدَّثَهُ عَنْ أَبِيهِ، عَنْ أَبِي هُرَيْرَةَ، أَنَّ رَسُولَ اللهِ صَلَّى اللهُ عَلَيْهِ وَسَلَّمَ كَانَ يَقُولُ: «الصَّلَوَاتُ الْخَمْسُ، وَالْجُمْعَةُ إِلَى الْجُمْعَةِ، وَرَمَضَانُ إِلَى رَمَضَانَ، مُكَفِّرَاتٌ مَا بَيْنَهُنَّ إِذَا اجْتَنَبَ الْكَبَائِرَ»

Text Explanation

These hadiths are self explanatory, and al-Nawawī's only comment on them is that it is perfectly acceptable to refer to the month of Ramadan by its name, without preceding it by the word 'month'. This will be discussed in more detail in the Book of Fasting.

Transmission

Hadith No. 413 includes in its chain of transmission Abū Ṣakhr, who is Ḥumayd ibn Ziyād, but his father's name is also said to be Ṣakhr. He is also mentioned as Ḥammād ibn Ziyād, and referred to as Abū al-Ṣakhr al-Kharrāṭ. He was from Madinah and lived in Egypt.

CHAPTER 6

RECOMMENDED GLORIFICATION AFTER ABLUTION

[414–17]. (Dār al-Salām 0451) Muhammad ibn Ḥātim ibn Maymūn narrated to me:[i] ʿAbd al-Raḥmān ibn Mahdī narrated; Muʿāwiyah ibn Ṣāliḥ narrated; from Rabīʿah, meaning Ibn Yazīd; from Abū Idrīs al-Khawlānī; from ʿUqbah ibn ʿĀmir [H]. Also, Abū ʿUthmān narrated to me; from Jubayr ibn Nufayr; from ʿUqbah ibn ʿĀmir: '**We were assigned the duty of tending the camels. When it was my shift, I [finished and] drove them home in the evening. I caught up with God's Messenger standing up and speaking to the people. I heard him say: "Any Muslim person who performs the ablution and does it well, then stands up and offers two *rakʿahs*, attending to them face and heart, is certain to be in heaven". I said: This is splendid indeed. A man close to me said: "The one before it was even more so". I looked up and he was ʿUmar. He said: "I saw you coming a short while ago. He said: 'Any one of you who performs the ablution and does it well, following it by saying: I bear witness that there is no deity other than God and that Muhammad is God's servant and messenger will have all eight gates of heaven open to him to enter from any one he chooses'"**.'

i. Related by Abū Dāwūd, 169 (in a longer version) and 906; al-Nasāʾī, 148 and 151; Ibn Mājah, 470.

حَدَّثَنِي مُحَمَّدُ بْنُ حَاتِمِ بْنِ مَيْمُونٍ، حَدَّثَنَا عَبْدُ الرَّحْمَنِ بْنُ مَهْدِيٍّ، حَدَّثَنَا مُعَاوِيَةُ بْنُ صَالِحٍ، عَنْ رَبِيعَةَ يَعْنِي ابْنَ يَزِيدَ، عَنْ أَبِي إِدْرِيسَ الْخَوْلَانِيِّ، عَنْ عُقْبَةَ بْنِ عَامِرٍ. ح، وَحَدَّثَنِي أَبُو عُثْمَانَ، عَنْ جُبَيْرِ بْنِ نُفَيْرٍ، عَنْ عُقْبَةَ بْنِ عَامِرٍ، قَالَ: كَانَتْ عَلَيْنَا رِعَايَةُ الْإِبِلِ فَجَاءَتْ نَوْبَتِي فَرَوَّحْتُهَا بِعَشِيٍّ فَأَدْرَكْتُ رَسُولَ اللهِ صَلَّى اللهُ عَلَيْهِ وَسَلَّمَ قَائِمًا يُحَدِّثُ النَّاسَ فَأَدْرَكْتُ مِنْ قَوْلِهِ: «مَا مِنْ مُسْلِمٍ يَتَوَضَّأُ فَيُحْسِنُ وُضُوءَهُ، ثُمَّ يَقُومُ فَيُصَلِّي رَكْعَتَيْنِ، مُقْبِلٌ عَلَيْهِمَا بِقَلْبِهِ وَوَجْهِهِ، إِلَّا وَجَبَتْ لَهُ الْجَنَّةُ» قَالَ فَقُلْتُ: مَا أَجْوَدَ هَذِهِ فَإِذَا قَائِلٌ بَيْنَ يَدَيَّ يَقُولُ: الَّتِي قَبْلَهَا أَجْوَدُ فَنَظَرْتُ فَإِذَا عُمَرُ قَالَ: إِنِّي قَدْ رَأَيْتُكَ جِئْتَ آنِفًا، قَالَ: «مَا مِنْكُمْ مِنْ أَحَدٍ يَتَوَضَّأُ فَيُبْلِغُ - أَوْ فَيُسْبِغُ - الْوَضُوءَ ثُمَّ يَقُولُ: أَشْهَدُ أَنْ لَا إِلَهَ إِلَّا اللهُ وَأَنَّ مُحَمَّدًا عَبْدُ اللهِ وَرَسُولُهُ إِلَّا فُتِحَتْ لَهُ أَبْوَابُ الْجَنَّةِ الثَّمَانِيَةُ يَدْخُلُ مِنْ أَيِّهَا شَاءَ».

[415–000]. (Dār al-Salām 0452) Abū Bakr ibn Abī Shaybah narrated: Zayd ibn al-Ḥubāb narrated; Muʿāwiyah ibn Ṣāliḥ narrated; from Rabīʿah ibn Yazīd; from Abū Idrīs al-Khawlānī and Abū ʿUthmān; from Jubayr ibn Nufayr ibn Mālik al-Ḥaḍramī; from ʿUqbah ibn ʿĀmir al-Juhanī who said that God's Messenger (peace be upon him) said: **He mentioned the same hadith except that it differed in that he said: 'Whoever performs the ablution then says: "I bear witness that there is no deity other than God, the One who has no partners, and I bear witness that Muhammad is God's servant and messenger".'**

وَحَدَّثَنَاهُ أَبُو بَكْرِ بْنُ أَبِي شَيْبَةَ، حَدَّثَنَا زَيْدُ بْنُ الْحُبَابِ، حَدَّثَنَا مُعَاوِيَةُ بْنُ صَالِحٍ، عَنْ رَبِيعَةَ بْنِ يَزِيدَ، عَنْ أَبِي إِدْرِيسَ الْخَوْلَانِيِّ، وَأَبِي عُثْمَانَ، عَنْ جُبَيْرِ بْنِ نُفَيْرِ بْنِ مَالِكٍ الْحَضْرَمِيِّ، عَنْ عُقْبَةَ بْنِ عَامِرٍ الْجُهَنِيِّ، أَنَّ رَسُولَ اللهِ صَلَّى اللهُ عَلَيْهِ وَسَلَّمَ قَالَ: فَذَكَرَ مِثْلَهُ غَيْرَ أَنَّهُ قَالَ: «مَنْ تَوَضَّأَ فَقَالَ أَشْهَدُ أَنْ لَا إِلَهَ إِلَّا اللهُ وَحْدَهُ لَا شَرِيكَ لَهُ وَأَشْهَدُ أَنَّ مُحَمَّدًا عَبْدُهُ وَرَسُولُهُ»

Text Explanation

The Prophet's Companion, ʿUqbah ibn ʿĀmir, says that they were assigned to tending the camels. This means that a group of them would gather up all their camels and they would take turns in tending them so that the others would have a chance to look after their other interests. The narrator said that he drove the camels to their different places at the end of the day before joining the Prophet as he was speaking to some of his companions.

The Prophet speaks about how the prayer should be performed, stating that after doing the ablution a person 'offers two *rakʿahs*, attending to them face and heart'. Thus, the Prophet includes in these two words, 'face and heart', all types of submission and serenity because, according to many scholars, submission is physical while serenity is mental.

On hearing what the Prophet said, ʿUqbah said: 'This is splendid indeed'. This means that the Prophet's statement, or the benefit it describes, or the good news it gives, or the worship involved is splendid. It is certainly so on more than one count, including that it is easy for everyone who wishes to do it, and that its reward is great, but God knows best. The Prophet speaks of a person who performs the ablution well. This means that one should do it correctly, washing every part fully, ensuring that the water reaches the whole of each part, as the Prophet showed us.

It is recommended when having performed the ablution that one should say: 'I bear witness that there is no deity other than God, the One who has no partners; and I bear witness that Muhammad is God's servant and messenger'. This is agreed upon by scholars, but it is better to add what is stated in the version related by al-Tirmidhī in his narration of this hadith: 'My Lord, make me one of those who often turn to you in repentance [of my sins] and make me one of those who always cleanse themselves'. This reads in Arabic: *'Allāhumma ijʿalnī min al-tawwābīn wajʿalnī min al-mutaṭahhirīn'*. It is better still to add what al-Nasāʾī mentions in his book, *ʿAmal al-Yawm wal-Laylah*: 'Limitless You are, my Lord, in Your glory, and all praise be to You. I bear witness that there is no deity other than You, the only God. You have no partners. I seek Your forgiveness and I turn to You in repentance'. In Arabic, this goes as follows: *'Subḥānak Allāhumma wa biḥamdik. Ashhad an la ilāha illā ant, waḥdak lā sharīka lak. Astaghfiruka wa atūbu ilayk'*. Our scholars say that these glorifications are also recommended after performing the major ritual ablution, but God knows best.

Transmission

In the first version, Muslim says: 'Muhammad ibn Ḥātim ibn Maymūn narrated to me: ʿAbd al-Raḥmān ibn Mahdī narrated; Muʿāwiyah ibn Ṣāliḥ narrated; from Rabīʿah, meaning Ibn Yazīd; from Abū Idrīs al-Khawlānī; from ʿUqbah ibn ʿĀmir [H]. Also, Abū ʿUthmān narrated to me; from Jubayr ibn Nufayr; from ʿUqbah ibn ʿĀmir'. And in the second version, Muslim says: 'Abū Bakr ibn Abī Shaybah narrated: Zayd ibn al-Ḥubāb narrated; Muʿāwiyah ibn Sāliḥ narrated; from Rabīʿah ibn Yazīd; from Abū Idrīs al-Khawlānī and Abū ʿUthmān; from Jubayr ibn Nufayr ibn Mālik al-Ḥaḍramī; from ʿUqbah ibn ʿĀmir'.

Scholars differ as to the identity of the reporter mentioned in the first version by his appellation, Abū ʿUthmān. Some said that he is Muʿāwiyah ibn Sāliḥ while others said that he is Rabīʿah ibn Yazīd. In his book *Taqyīd al-Muhmal*, Abū ʿAli al-Ḥusayn ibn Muhammad al-Ghassānī al-Jayyānī said:

> The correct view is that he is Muʿāwiyah ibn Sāliḥ. Abū ʿAbdullāh Muhammad ibn Yaḥyā ibn al-Hadhdhā' wrote in his copy: 'Rabīʿah ibn Yazīd said: Abū ʿUthmān narrated to me from Jubayr from ʿUqbah'.
>
> What is recorded in the copies reported from Muslim is what we have mentioned first—meaning what I have stated at the beginning. This is the correct view. What Ibn al-Hadhdhā' says is mistaken, and this is clear in the narration of the highly reliable narrators. This hadith is narrated by Muʿāwiyah ibn Ṣāliḥ in two chains of transmission, one of which is from

> Rabīʿah ibn Yazīd from Abū Idrīs from ʿUqbah, and the other from Abū ʿUthmān from Jubayr ibn Nufayr from ʿUqbah. Abū Masʿūd al-Dimashqī relates it in the correct way we have mentioned, stating it clearly as he says: Muʿāwiyah ibn Ṣāliḥ said: 'Abū ʿUthmān narrated to me from Jubayr from ʿUqbah'.

Abū ʿAlī then mentions numerous chains of transmission which mention the reporter clearly as Muʿāwiyah ibn Ṣāliḥ. Indeed, Abū ʿAlī goes into great detail to illustrate what he considers as the correct view.

Likewise, the correct view is mentioned in Abū Dāwūd's *Sunan*, as Abū Dāwūd said: 'Ahmad ibn Saʿīd narrated; from Ibn Wahb, from Muʿāwiyah ibn Ṣāliḥ from Abū ʿUthmān—and I think he is Saʿīd ibn Hāni' from Jubayr ibn Nufayr from ʿUqbah. Muʿāwiyah said: 'And Rabīʿah ibn Yazīd narrated to me from Abū Idrīs from ʿUqbah'. This is what Abū Dāwūd said and it clearly confirms what we have already said. His statement in the second narration given by Abū Bakr ibn Abī Shaybah: 'Muʿāwiyah ibn Ṣāliḥ narrated from Rabīʿah ibn Yazīd from Abū Idrīs and Abū ʿUthmān from Jubayr' is understood according to what we have already said. Thus, the words 'and Abū ʿUthmān' means 'Muʿāwiyah narrated from Rabīʿah from Abū Idrīs from Jubayr; and Muʿāwiyah narrated from Abū ʿUthmān from Jubayr'. The proof of this interpretation and understanding is in what Abū ʿAli al-Ghassānī narrates with his chain of transmission from ʿAbdullāh ibn Muhammad al-Baghawī: 'Abū Bakr ibn Abī Shaybah narrated: Zayd ibn al-Ḥubāb narrated; Muʿāwiyah ibn Ṣāliḥ narrated; from Rabīʿah ibn Yazīd; from Abū Idrīs al-Khawlānī from ʿUqbah. Muʿāwiyah said: 'And Abū ʿUthmān; from Jubayr from ʿUqbah'. Abū ʿAlī said:

> This chain of transmission explains the problem concerning Muslim's narration from Abū Bakr ibn Abī Shaybah. ʿAbdullāh ibn Wahb also narrates this hadith from Muʿāwiyah ibn Ṣāliḥ, stating both chains of transmission and how they differ. He states what we have already mentioned of Abū Dāwūd's narration from Ahmad ibn Saʿīd from Ibn Wahb … .

Abū ʿĪsā al-Tirmidhī relates this hadith with a chain featuring Zayd ibn al-Ḥubāb from a teacher of his whom he does not specify. Al-Tirmidhī strongly criticises Zayd ibn al-Ḥubāb for this, but Zayd is innocent in this point. The confusion is either from al-Tirmidhī or from his teacher who narrated the hadith to him. We have already mentioned some reports by leading Hadith scholars, which contradict al-Tirmidhī's report. Al-Tirmidhī also mentions this in his book *al-ʿIlal*, and the questions he put to Muhammad ibn Ismāʿīl al-Bukhārī who did not rate it. He quotes him saying something different from what we have reported of leading Hadith scholars. Perhaps he did not record accurately what al-Bukhārī said. Its best chains of transmission are those mentioned by Muslim ibn al-Ḥajjāj quoting ʿAbd al-Raḥmān ibn Mahdī and Zayd ibn al-Ḥubāb from Muʿāwiyah ibn Ṣāliḥ.

ʿUthmān ibn Abī Shaybah, Abū Bakr's brother, narrated this hadith from Zayd ibn al-Ḥubāb adding one reporter, Jubayr ibn Nufayr, in its chain of transmission. Abū Dāwūd relates it in his *Sunan* in the chapter on doubts occurring to a person during prayer, stating: 'ʿUthmān ibn Abī Shaybah narrated, Zayd ibn al-Ḥubāb narrated, Muʿāwiyah ibn Ṣāliḥ narrated, from Rabīʿah ibn Yazīd, from Abū Idrīs al-Khawlānī, from Jubayr ibn Nufayr, from ʿUqbah ibn ʿĀmir' and he then mentions the hadith.

This is what Abū ʿAlī al-Ḥusayn ibn Muhammad al-Ghassānī had to say about the transmission of this hadith, and it is absolutely perfect and to the point, but God knows best. Abū Idrīs's name is ʿĀ'idhullāh ibn ʿAbdullāh.

CHAPTER 7

HOW THE PROPHET PERFORMED HIS RITUAL ABLUTION

[416–18]. (Dār al-Salām 0453) Muhammad ibn al-Ṣabbāḥ narrated to me:[i] Khālid ibn ʿAbdullāh; from ʿAmr ibn Yaḥyā ibn ʿUmārah; from his father; from ʿAbdullāh ibn Zayd ibn ʿĀṣim al-Anṣārī (who was a companion of the Prophet): **'It was said to him: "Show us how God's Messenger (peace be upon him) performed his ablution". He called for a jug [of water] and he poured out of it onto his hands, washing them three times. He then put his hand in the jug and brought it out. He rinsed his mouth and inhaled water using one handful. He did this three times. He then put his hand in the jug and brought it out, and he washed his face three times. He again put his hand in the jug and brought it out, and he washed his hands, up to the elbows, doing each hand twice. He then put his hand in the jug and brought it out, wiping his head with it, moving his hands forward and backward. He then washed his feet up to the ankles. He then said: "Such was the Prophet's ablution".'**

حَدَّثَنِي مُحَمَّدُ بْنُ الصَّبَّاحِ، حَدَّثَنَا خَالِدُ بْنُ عَبْدِ اللهِ، عَنْ عَمْرِو بْنِ يَحْيَى بْنِ عُمَارَةَ، عَنْ أَبِيهِ، عَنْ عَبْدِ اللهِ بْنِ زَيْدِ بْنِ عَاصِمٍ الأَنْصَارِيِّ، - وَكَانَتْ لَهُ صُحْبَةٌ - قَالَ:

i. Related by al-Bukhārī, 185, 186, and in 191, 192 and 199 in shorter versions; Abū Dāwūd, 100 (in a shorter version), 118 and 119; al-Tirmidhī, 28, 32 and 47 in shorter versions; al-Nasāʾī, 97, 98 and in 99 in a shorter version; Ibn Mājah, 405, 434 and 471.

قِيلَ لَهُ: « تَوَضَّأْ لَنَا وُضُوءَ رَسُولِ اللهِ صَلَّى اللهُ عَلَيْهِ وَسَلَّمَ: فَدَعَا بِإِنَاءٍ فَأَكْفَأَ مِنْهَا عَلَى يَدَيْهِ فَغَسَلَهُمَا ثَلَاثًا، ثُمَّ أَدْخَلَ يَدَهُ فَاسْتَخْرَجَهَا فَمَضْمَضَ، وَاسْتَنْشَقَ مِنْ كَفٍّ وَاحِدَةٍ فَفَعَلَ ذَلِكَ ثَلَاثًا، ثُمَّ أَدْخَلَ يَدَهُ فَاسْتَخْرَجَهَا فَغَسَلَ وَجْهَهُ ثَلَاثًا، ثُمَّ أَدْخَلَ يَدَهُ فَاسْتَخْرَجَهَا فَغَسَلَ يَدَيْهِ إِلَى الْمِرْفَقَيْنِ مَرَّتَيْنِ مَرَّتَيْنِ، ثُمَّ أَدْخَلَ يَدَهُ فَاسْتَخْرَجَهَا فَمَسَحَ بِرَأْسِهِ فَأَقْبَلَ بِيَدَيْهِ وَأَدْبَرَ، ثُمَّ غَسَلَ رِجْلَيْهِ إِلَى الْكَعْبَيْنِ، ثُمَّ قَالَ هَكَذَا كَانَ وُضُوءُ رَسُولِ اللهِ صَلَّى اللهُ عَلَيْهِ وَسَلَّمَ»

[000–000]. (Dār al-Salām 0454) Al-Qāsim ibn Zakariyyā' narrated to me: Khālid ibn Makhlad narrated; from Sulaymān (who is Ibn Bilāl); from ʻAmr ibn Yaḥyā; with this chain of transmission: **a similar hadith, but he did not mention the ankles**.

وَحَدَّثَنِي الْقَاسِمُ بْنُ زَكَرِيَّا، حَدَّثَنَا خَالِدُ بْنُ مَخْلَدٍ، عَنْ سُلَيْمَانَ هُوَ ابْنُ بِلَالٍ، عَنْ عَمْرِو بْنِ يَحْيَى، بِهَذَا الْإِسْنَادِ نَحْوَهُ وَلَمْ يَذْكُرِ الْكَعْبَيْنِ.

[417–000]. (Dār al-Salām 0455) Isḥāq ibn Mūsā al-Anṣārī narrated to me: Maʻn narrated; from Mālik ibn Anas, from ʻAmr ibn Yaḥyā; with this chain of transmission. He said: **'He rinsed his mouth and blew his nose three times, but did not say, "using one handful". After "moving his hands forward and backward", he added: "starting with the front of his head moving them back to his rear, then brought them back until he reached the point where he started. Then he washed his feet".'**

وَحَدَّثَنِي إِسْحَاقُ بْنُ مُوسَى الْأَنْصَارِيُّ، حَدَّثَنَا مَعْنٌ، حَدَّثَنَا مَالِكُ بْنُ أَنَسٍ، عَنْ عَمْرِو بْنِ يَحْيَى، بِهَذَا الْإِسْنَادِ وَقَالَ: مَضْمَضَ وَاسْتَنْثَرَ ثَلَاثًا وَلَمْ يَقُلْ: مِنْ كَفٍّ وَاحِدَةٍ،

وَزَادَ بَعْدَ قَوْلِهِ، فَأَقْبَلَ بِهِمَا وَأَدْبَرَ بَدَأَ بِمُقَدَّمِ رَأْسِهِ، ثُمَّ ذَهَبَ بِهِمَا إِلَى قَفَاهُ ثُمَّ رَدَّهُمَا حَتَّى رَجَعَ إِلَى الْمَكَانِ الَّذِي بَدَأَ مِنْهُ وَغَسَلَ رِجْلَيْهِ .

[418–000]. (Dār al-Salām 0456) ʿAbd al-Raḥmān ibn Bishr al-ʿAbdī narrated: Bahz narrated; Wuhayb narrated; ʿAmr ibn Yaḥyā narrated, with the same chain of transmission: **He stated the hadith, but said in his statement: 'He rinsed his mouth, inhaled water and blew his nose using three handfuls [of water]'. He also said: 'He wiped his head, moving his hand forward and backward once'.**

Bahz said: **'Wuhayb dictated this hadith to me, and Wuhayb said: "ʿAmr ibn Yaḥyā dictated this hadith to me twice".'**

حَدَّثَنَا عَبْدُ الرَّحْمَنِ بْنُ بِشْرٍ الْعَبْدِيُّ، حَدَّثَنَا بَهْزٌ، حَدَّثَنَا وُهَيْبٌ، حَدَّثَنَا عَمْرُو بْنُ يَحْيَى، بِمِثْلِ إِسْنَادِهِمْ وَاقْتَصَّ الْحَدِيثَ وَقَالَ فِيهِ: فَمَضْمَضَ وَاسْتَنْشَقَ وَاسْتَنْثَرَ مِنْ ثَلَاثِ غَرَفَاتٍ وَقَالَ: أَيْضًا فَمَسَحَ بِرَأْسِهِ فَأَقْبَلَ بِهِ وَأَدْبَرَ مَرَّةً وَاحِدَةً

قَالَ بَهْزٌ: أَمْلَى عَلَيَّ وُهَيْبٌ هَذَا الْحَدِيثَ، وقَالَ وُهَيْبٌ: «أَمْلَى عَلَيَّ عَمْرُو بْنُ يَحْيَى هَذَا الْحَدِيثَ مَرَّتَيْنِ»

[419–19]. (Dār al-Salām 0457) Hārūn ibn Maʿrūf narrated [H].[i] Also, Hārūn ibn Saʿīd al-Aylī and Abū al-Ṭāhir narrated to me. They all said: Ibn Wahb narrated; ʿAmr ibn al-Ḥārith reported to me; Ḥabbān ibn Wāsiʿ narrated to him that his father narrated to him, that he heard ʿAbdullāh ibn Zayd ibn ʿĀṣim al-Māzinī mention that he saw God's Messenger (peace be upon him) perform the ablution: **'He rinsed his mouth then blew his nose, then he washed his face three times, his right arm three times and the other three times. He wiped his head**

i. Related by Abū Dāwūd, 120; al-Tirmidhī, 35.

with water other than that on his wet hand, and he washed his feet until he cleansed them'.

Abū al-Ṭāhir said: 'Ibn Wahb narrated from ʿAmr ibn al-Ḥārith'.

حَدَّثَنَا هَارُونُ بْنُ مَعْرُوفٍ، ح وَحَدَّثَنِي هَارُونُ بْنُ سَعِيدٍ الْأَيْلِيُّ، وَأَبُو الطَّاهِرِ، قَالُوا: حَدَّثَنَا ابْنُ وَهْبٍ، أَخْبَرَنِي عَمْرُو بْنُ الْحَارِثِ، أَنَّ حَبَّانَ بْنَ وَاسِعٍ، حَدَّثَهُ أَنَّ أَبَاهُ، حَدَّثَهُ أَنَّهُ سَمِعَ عَبْدَ اللهِ بْنَ زَيْدِ بْنِ عَاصِمٍ الْمَازِنِيَّ، يَذْكُرُ أَنَّهُ: «رَأَى رَسُولَ اللهِ صَلَّى اللهُ عَلَيْهِ وَسَلَّمَ تَوَضَّأَ فَمَضْمَضَ ثُمَّ اسْتَنْثَرَ ثُمَّ غَسَلَ وَجْهَهُ ثَلَاثًا، وَيَدَهُ الْيُمْنَى ثَلَاثًا وَالْأُخْرَى ثَلَاثًا، وَمَسَحَ بِرَأْسِهِ بِمَاءٍ غَيْرِ فَضْلِ يَدِهِ، وَغَسَلَ رِجْلَيْهِ حَتَّى أَنْقَاهُمَا»

قَالَ أَبُو الطَّاهِرِ: حَدَّثَنَا ابْنُ وَهْبٍ، عَنْ عَمْرِو بْنِ الْحَارِثِ.

Text Explanation

The first hadith mentions that the Prophet poured water out of the jug to wash his hands. The Arabic word used here, *akfa'*, means 'to hold the jug at an angle so that he could pour the water'. This sentence makes clear that it is desirable to wash one's hands before putting them into the jug to take out some water.[i]

The narrator said that the Prophet rinsed his mouth and inhaled water to blow his nose using the same handful and that he did this three times. In the later version, 'he rinsed his mouth, inhaled water and blew his nose with three handfuls'. This hadith gives us clear evidence in support of the correct view which suggests that the recommended practice is to do this with three handfuls of water, using each one for both rinsing one's mouth and blowing one's nose. We have already spoken about this point in detail in the first chapter in this book, stating the different views concerning it, but God knows best. In the second narration, the hadith states that the Prophet 'rinsed his mouth, inhaled water and blew his nose'. This

i. We have to remember that during the Prophet's lifetime, there was no water supplied into houses as we have today. Moreover, water was scarce in Arabia and there was always need to economize in its use.

supports the view of the great majority of Arabic scholars and others who maintain that inhaling water is different from blowing one's nose. This is contrary to what Ibn al-Aʿrābī and Ibn Qutaybah said, suggesting that they mean the same thing. This is made clear in the first chapter, but God knows best.

The hadith mentions that the Prophet 'put his hand in the jug and then brought it out'. This is how it is stated here in Muslim's *Ṣaḥīḥ*, mentioning one hand. The same occurs in most of al-Bukhārī's related versions. However, in one narration of this hadith by ʿAbdullāh ibn Zayd related in al-Bukhārī's *Ṣaḥīḥ*: 'He put his two hands and took a cupped handful with them washing his face three times'. In al-Bukhārī's *Ṣaḥīḥ* there is also a hadith narrated by Ibn ʿAbbās that states: 'He then took a handful of water like this and joined it with his other hand and washed his face with it'. He then said: 'This is how I saw God's Messenger (peace be upon him) perform his ablution'. In the *Sunan* by Abū Dāwūd and in al-Bayhaqī a hadith narrated by ʿAlī, describing the Prophet's ablution, says: 'He then put both his two hands in the jug, taking out a handful of water and washed his face'. We note that some of these hadiths mention his one hand while others mention his two hands and a third version mentions one hand being joined by the other. They make clear that all three ways are acceptable and are Sunnah. We reconcile these hadiths by saying that the Prophet used these three methods at different times. They show three ways approved by our scholars. However, the correct and best-known of them approved by the majority and stated by al-Shāfiʿī and confirmed by his two main disciples, Yūsuf ibn Yaḥyā al-Buwayṭī and Ismāʿīl ibn Yaḥyā ibn Ismāʿīl al-Muzanī, makes clear that the preferable way is to take the water to wash one's face with one's two hands, because it is easier and more suited to ensuring the washing of all one's face, but God knows best. Our scholars say that it is preferable to start washing one's face from the top because it is easier to wash it all, but God knows best.

The first narration also mentions that the Prophet washed his face three times and his two hands twice up to the elbows. This makes clear that it is permissible to wash different parts differently, washing some three times, some twice and others once only. To perform the ablution in such a way is certainly acceptable, but it is more desirable to wash every part three times, as we explained earlier. That at times the Prophet did them differently was simply to show that this is permissible and acceptable. Indeed, on some occasions he washed every part once only to show that this is permissible. At those times, this method was the best for him because explaining what is permissible is a duty incumbent on him. It may be suggested that this could have been done by verbal explanation. This may be true, but showing it in practice is more effective and does not admit different interpretations, but God knows best.

The Prophet then 'wiped his head, moving his hand forward and backward'. All scholars agree that this is desirable, because it is the easy way to cover all one's head and allow the water to reach all one's hair. Our scholars say that moving one's hands backward after having covered one's head moving forward is only desirable for a person with plenty of unplaited hair. For a bald person or one with plaited hair it is not recommended that he bring his hands backward when wiping his head, because it is unnecessary. If he brings his hands back, this does not count as a second wipe, because the water on his hands is now considered used water, but God knows best.

This hadith does not indicate that it is obligatory to wipe one's whole head, because this hadith describes the perfect ablution, not what is essential.

Hadith No. 419 mentions that the Prophet 'wiped his head with water other than that on his wet hand'. This means that he used new water, and did not merely wipe his head with his already wet hand. However, this does not mean that used water may not be used in ablution. This statement merely indicates that the Prophet used new water, but this does not necessarily mean that it is obligatory to do the same, but God knows best.

Transmission

The first hadith in this chapter is narrated by ʿAbdullāh ibn Zayd ibn ʿĀṣim, who is different from ʿAbdullāh ibn Zayd ibn ʿAbd Rabbih, the narrator of the hadith concerning the call to prayer, i.e. the *adhān*.

This is stated by reliable hadith scholars of the early and later days. They say that Sufyān ibn ʿUyaynah was wrong when he said that the two are the same person. Among those who said that Sufyān was wrong is al-Bukhārī, who makes this clear in the Book of Prayer for Rain in his *Ṣaḥīḥ* anthology of authentic hadiths. It is said that the one who narrated the hadith concerning the call to prayer is not known to have narrated any other hadith, but God knows best.

In hadith No. 419, the chain of transmission begins as follows: 'Hārūn ibn Maʿrūf narrated [H]. Also, Hārūn ibn Saʿīd al-Aylī and Abū al-Ṭāhir narrated to me. They all said: Ibn Wahb narrated; ʿAmr ibn al-Ḥārith reported to me; Ḥabbān ibn Wāsiʿ narrated to him ...'. At the end of the hadith, Muslim adds: 'Abū al-Ṭāhir said: Ibn Wahb narrated from ʿAmr ibn al-Ḥārith'. Here is a mark of the precaution Muslim used to take and it tells of his rich knowledge and meticulous reporting. He distinguished between the way each of his two teachers named Hārūn narrated, saying of the first 'narrated' and of the second 'narrated to me'. In the first case, he learnt the hadith as it was narrated by his teacher to a group of his students, when Muslim was present. In the second case, he was the only one with each of his two teachers as they narrated the hadith to him. I have already stated that it is desirable, though not obligatory, to distinguish between the two, using 'narrated' in the first case and 'narrated to me' in the second. Muslim was very careful in such cases, as we have seen in previous examples, but many more will be mentioned, God willing.

His final statement, 'Abū al-Ṭāhir said: Ibn Wahb narrated from ʿAmr ibn al-Ḥārith', is also a mark of Muslim's meticulous reporting. He reports the hadith first from his three teachers, the two named Hārūn and Abū al-Ṭāhir, as they all reported from Ibn Wahb who said: 'ʿAmr ibn al-Ḥārith reported to me'. However, Abū al-Ṭāhir's version differed in the fact that he did not say, 'reported to me', but said, 'from'. This way of reporting, using 'from', is interpreted differently by scholars, with most of them saying that it confirms direct reporting, but all scholars agree that it is a lesser form than 'reported'. Therefore, Muslim takes the precaution of clarifying the exact method of reporting. His book is full of such gems of meticulousness. May God shower His mercy on him and may He bring us together with him in Heaven.

CHAPTER 8

THE PREFERABILITY OF ODD NUMBERS

[420–20]. (Dār al-Salām 0458) Qutaybah ibn Saʿīd, ʿAmr al-Nāqid and Muhammad ibn ʿAbdullāh ibn Numayr narrated:[i] all from Ibn ʿUyaynah. Qutaybah said: Sufyān narrated from Abū al-Zinād; from al-Aʿraj; from Abū Hurayrah; from the Prophet (peace be upon him) who said: **'When any of you cleanses himself with small stones, let him use an odd number. When any of you performs the ablution, let him inhale some water then blow his nose'**.

حَدَّثَنَا قُتَيْبَةُ بْنُ سَعِيدٍ، وَعَمْرٌو النَّاقِدُ، وَمُحَمَّدُ بْنُ عَبْدِ اللهِ بْنِ نُمَيْرٍ، جَمِيعًا عَنِ ابْنِ عُيَيْنَةَ، قَالَ قُتَيْبَةُ: حَدَّثَنَا سُفْيَانُ، عَنْ أَبِي الزِّنَادِ، عَنِ الْأَعْرَجِ، عَنْ أَبِي هُرَيْرَةَ، يَبْلُغُ بِهِ النَّبِيَّ صَلَّى اللهُ عَلَيْهِ وَسَلَّمَ قَالَ: «إِذَا اسْتَجْمَرَ أَحَدُكُمْ فَلْيَسْتَجْمِرْ وِتْرًا، وَإِذَا تَوَضَّأَ أَحَدُكُمْ فَلْيَجْعَلْ فِي أَنْفِهِ مَاءً ثُمَّ لِيَنْتَثِرْ»

[421–21]. (Dār al-Salām 0459) Muhammad ibn Rāfiʿ narrated to me: ʿAbd al-Razzāq ibn Hammām narrated; Maʿmar reported; from Hammām ibn Munabbih. He said: This is what Abū Hurayrah narrated from Muhammad, God's Messenger (peace be upon him): he mentioned a number of hadiths and said: **'And God's Messenger (peace be upon him) said: "When any of you performs the ablution, let him inhale through his two nostrils some water then blow his nose".'**

i. Related by al-Nasāʾī, 86.

حَدَّثَنِي مُحَمَّدُ بْنُ رَافِعٍ، حَدَّثَنَا عَبْدُ الرَّزَّاقِ بْنُ هَمَّامٍ، أَخْبَرَنَا مَعْمَرٌ، عَنْ هَمَّامِ بْنِ مُنَبِّهٍ، قَالَ: هَذَا مَا حَدَّثَنَا أَبُو هُرَيْرَةَ، عَنْ مُحَمَّدٍ رَسُولِ اللهِ صَلَّى اللهُ عَلَيْهِ وَسَلَّمَ - فَذَكَرَ أَحَادِيثَ مِنْهَا - وَقَالَ رَسُولُ اللهِ صَلَّى اللهُ عَلَيْهِ وَسَلَّمَ: «إِذَا تَوَضَّأَ أَحَدُكُمْ فَلْيَسْتَنْشِقْ بِمَنْخِرَيْهِ مِنَ الْمَاءِ ثُمَّ لِيَنْتَثِرْ»

[422–22]. (Dār al-Salām 0460) Yaḥyā ibn Yaḥyā narrated:[i] 'I read out to Mālik; from Ibn Shihāb; from Abū Idrīs al-Khawlānī; from Abū Hurayrah; that God's Messenger (peace be upon him) said: **'Whoever performs the ablution let him blow his nose, and when using stones to cleanse oneself, one should use an odd number'**.

حَدَّثَنَا يَحْيَى بْنُ يَحْيَى، قَالَ: قَرَأْتُ عَلَى مَالِكٍ، عَنِ ابْنِ شِهَابٍ، عَنْ أَبِي إِدْرِيسَ الْخَوْلَانِيِّ، عَنْ أَبِي هُرَيْرَةَ، أَنَّ رَسُولَ اللهِ صَلَّى اللهُ عَلَيْهِ وَسَلَّمَ قَالَ: «مَنْ تَوَضَّأَ فَلْيَسْتَنْثِرْ وَمَنِ اسْتَجْمَرَ، فَلْيُوتِرْ»

[000–000]. (Dār al-Salām 0461) Saʿīd ibn Manṣūr narrated: Ḥassān ibn Ibrāhīm narrated; Yūnus ibn Yazīd narrated [H]. Also Ḥarmalah ibn Yaḥyā narrated to me; Ibn Wahb reported; Yūnus reported to me; from Ibn Shihāb; Abū Idrīs al-Khawlānī reported to me; that he heard Abū Hurayrah and Abū Saʿīd al-Khudrī say: God's Messenger (peace be upon him) said: **the same text**.

حَدَّثَنَا سَعِيدُ بْنُ مَنْصُورٍ، حَدَّثَنَا حَسَّانُ بْنُ إِبْرَاهِيمَ، حَدَّثَنَا يُونُسُ بْنُ يَزِيدَ، ح وَحَدَّثَنِي حَرْمَلَةُ بْنُ يَحْيَى، أَخْبَرَنَا ابْنُ وَهْبٍ، أَخْبَرَنِي يُونُسُ، عَنِ ابْنِ شِهَابٍ، أَخْبَرَنِي أَبُو إِدْرِيسَ الْخَوْلَانِيُّ، أَنَّهُ سَمِعَ أَبَا هُرَيْرَةَ، وَأَبَا سَعِيدٍ الْخُدْرِيَّ يَقُولَانِ: قَالَ رَسُولُ اللهِ صَلَّى اللهُ عَلَيْهِ وَسَلَّمَ بِمِثْلِهِ.

---

i. Related by al-Bukhārī, 161; al-Nasā'ī, 88; Ibn Mājah, 409.

[423–23]. (Dār al-Salām 0462) Bishr ibn al-Ḥakam al-ʿAbdī narrated to me:[i] ʿAbd al-ʿAzīz (meaning al-Darāwardī) narrated; from Ibn al-Hād; from Muhammad ibn Ibrāhīm; from ʿĪsā ibn Ṭalḥah; from Abū Hurayrah; that the Prophet (peace be upon him) said: **'When any of you wakes up from sleep, let him blow his nose three times because Satan stays the night over his nose'**.

حَدَّثَنِي بِشْرُ بْنُ الْحَكَمِ الْعَبْدِيُّ، حَدَّثَنَا عَبْدُ الْعَزِيزِ يَعْنِي الدَّرَاوَرْدِيَّ، عَنِ ابْنِ الْهَادِ، عَنْ مُحَمَّدِ بْنِ إِبْرَاهِيمَ، عَنْ عِيسَى بْنِ طَلْحَةَ، عَنْ أَبِي هُرَيْرَةَ، أَنَّ النَّبِيَّ صَلَّى اللهُ عَلَيْهِ وَسَلَّمَ قَالَ: «إِذَا اسْتَيْقَظَ أَحَدُكُمْ مِنْ مَنَامِهِ فَلْيَسْتَنْثِرْ ثَلَاثَ مَرَّاتٍ، فَإِنَّ الشَّيْطَانَ يَبِيتُ عَلَى خَيَاشِيمِهِ»

[424–24]. (Dār al-Salām 0463) Isḥāq ibn Ibrāhīm and Muhammad ibn Rāfiʿ narrated: Ibn Rāfiʿ said: ʿAbd al-Razzāq narrated; Ibn Jurayj reported; Abū al-Zubayr reported to me; that he heard Jābir ibn ʿAbdullāh say: God's Messenger (peace be upon him) said: **'When any of you cleanses himself with small stones, let him use an odd number'**.

حَدَّثَنَا إِسْحَاقُ بْنُ إِبْرَاهِيمَ، وَمُحَمَّدُ بْنُ رَافِعٍ، قَالَ ابْنُ رَافِعٍ: حَدَّثَنَا عَبْدُ الرَّزَّاقِ، أَخْبَرَنَا ابْنُ جُرَيْجٍ، أَخْبَرَنِي أَبُو الزُّبَيْرِ، أَنَّهُ سَمِعَ جَابِرَ بْنَ عَبْدِ اللهِ، يَقُولُ: قَالَ رَسُولُ اللهِ صَلَّى اللهُ عَلَيْهِ وَسَلَّمَ: «إِذَا اسْتَجْمَرَ أَحَدُكُمْ فَلْيُوتِرْ»

Text Explanation

Before we pick up Imam al-Nawawī's explanation of this chapter, we may include an explanatory note. People sometimes use stones to cleanse themselves after defecation, particularly when they are away from their homes or travelling, because water is scarce and

i. Related by al-Bukhārī, 3295; al-Nasāʾī, 90.

is needed for drinking. At the time when Prophet Muhammad advocated his message, there was nothing of the modern means of comfortable living, like water supplied into houses or toilet paper. Indeed, paper was not known in Arabia until the eighth century. Therefore, in the absence of water, cleansing oneself had to rely on some solid material, and stones are available everywhere.

Stones may be used to wipe off the traces of urine and stools. The word *istijmār* mentioned in these hadiths means the use of small stones for this purpose. This is the meaning agreed by the majority of language, Hadith and *fiqh* scholars. *Qāḍī* ʿIyāḍ said: 'Mālik and other scholars express different meanings of *istijmār*. The meaning stated earlier is mentioned, but some say that it refers to incense, taking three pieces of it or using it three times in succession. However, the first explanation is more likely, but God knows best'. The explanation we mentioned first is indeed the correct and better-known one.

The Prophet speaks of using an odd number, three or five or more. The view of our school is that what is more than three is desirable. However, the sum of the Shāfiʿī School's view is that complete cleansing, leaving no trace, is a duty and wiping three times is a duty. If the complete cleansing occurs with three wipes, there is no need for more, but if it does not, then more is required as a duty. Moreover, if the cleansing is complete with an even number of wipes, such as four or six, then adding an extra one is desirable to make it an odd number. However, some of our scholars say that it is obligatory to make it an odd number, as the apparent meaning of this hadith suggests. The majority of scholars say that the odd number is not a duty, citing in support of their view the authentic hadith mentioned in *Sunan* anthologies, which quotes the Prophet: 'Whoever uses *istijmār* should use an odd number: the one who does so does well, and the one who does not is faultless'. They understand the hadith in this chapter as meaning three times, while whatever is above that is desirable, not obligatory, but God knows best.

The Prophet says that when a person performs the ablution, he should inhale some water and blow his nose. This makes clear that the inhalation of water is different from blowing one's nose, because the latter means bringing the water and whatever is mixed with it out of one's nose. We have already mentioned this. This statement supports the view of those who maintain that inhaling water during ablution is obligatory because it is expressed in the hadith in the imperative form. Scholars who do not make it obligatory say that the imperative is meant as recommendation, not obligation, because what is really ordered is blowing one's nose, and this is agreed to be recommended, not obligatory. If it is argued that the other narration says that one should 'inhale through one's two nostrils some water and blow his nose', this provides clear evidence in support of making it obligatory, but to understand it as recommendation is acceptable, so that it can be reconciled with other statements that indicate desirability rather than stating an obligation, but God knows best.

In hadith No. 423, we have the statement that 'Satan stays the night over one's nose'. *Qāḍī* 'Iyāḍ said: 'It is probable that this statement is meant literally. The nose is a body opening that may be a way to the mind. All body openings have shutters except for the nose and the ears. A hadith mentions that Satan does not open what is shut. Moreover, an order is given to suppress yawns in order to prevent Satan going through the mouth. Having said this, we should say that the statement may be meant figuratively, because dirt accumulates as a result of dust and the wetness of the nostrils. Such dirt suits Satan, but God knows best'.

CHAPTER 9

COMPLETELY WASHING BOTH FEET

[425–25]. (Dār al-Salām 0464) Hārūn ibn Sa'īd al-Aylī, Abū al-Ṭāhir and Ahmad ibn 'Īsā narrated: They said: 'Abdullāh ibn Wahb reported; from Makhramah ibn Bukayr; from his father; from Sālim, Shaddād's *mawlā*, who said: **'I went into the home of 'Ā'ishah, the Prophet's wife, on the day when Sa'd ibn Abi Waqqāṣ died. 'Abd al-Raḥmān ibn Abī Bakr came in and he performed the ablution at her place. She said: "'Abd al-Raḥmān, do your ablution fully. I heard God's Messenger (peace be upon him) say: 'Woe to heels from the Fire'".'**

حَدَّثَنَا هَارُونُ بْنُ سَعِيدٍ الأَيْلِيُّ، وَأَبُو الطَّاهِرِ، وَأَحْمَدُ بْنُ عِيسَى، قَالُوا: أَخْبَرَنَا عَبْدُ اللهِ بْنُ وَهْبٍ، عَنْ مَخْرَمَةَ بْنِ بُكَيْرٍ، عَنْ أَبِيهِ، عَنْ سَالِمٍ، مَوْلَى شَدَّادٍ، قَالَ: دَخَلْتُ عَلَى عَائِشَةَ زَوْجِ النَّبِيِّ صَلَّى اللهُ عَلَيْهِ وَسَلَّمَ يَوْمَ تُوُفِّيَ سَعْدُ بْنُ أَبِي وَقَّاصٍ فَدَخَلَ عَبْدُ الرَّحْمَنِ بْنُ أَبِي بَكْرٍ فَتَوَضَّأَ عِنْدَهَا فَقَالَتْ: يَا عَبْدَ الرَّحْمَنِ أَسْبِغِ الْوُضُوءَ فَإِنِّي سَمِعْتُ رَسُولَ اللهِ صَلَّى اللهُ عَلَيْهِ وَسَلَّمَ يَقُولُ: «وَيْلٌ لِلأَعْقَابِ مِنَ النَّارِ»

[000–000]. (Dār al-Salām 0465) Ḥarmalah ibn Yaḥyā narrated to me: Ibn Wahb narrated; Ḥaywah reported to me; Muhammad ibn 'Abd al-Raḥmān reported to me; Abū 'Abdullāh, Shaddād's *mawlā*, narrated to him that: **'He entered 'Ā'ishah's home and he reported from her, from the Prophet, the same text'**.

وَحَدَّثَنِي حَرْمَلَةُ بْنُ يَحْيَى، حَدَّثَنَا ابْنُ وَهْبٍ، أَخْبَرَنِي حَيْوَةُ، أَخْبَرَنِي مُحَمَّدُ بْنُ عَبْدِ الرَّحْمَنِ، أَنَّ أَبَا عَبْدِ اللهِ مَوْلَى شَدَّادِ بْنِ الْهَادِ، حَدَّثَهُ أَنَّهُ دَخَلَ عَلَى عَائِشَةَ، فَذَكَرَ عَنْهَا عَنِ النَّبِيِّ صَلَّى اللهُ عَلَيْهِ وَسَلَّمَ بِمِثْلِهِ

[426–000]. (Dār al-Salām 0466) Muhammad ibn Ḥātim and Abū Ma'n al-Riqāshī narrated to me: 'Umar ibn Yūnus narrated; 'Ikrimah ibn 'Ammār narrated; Yaḥyā ibn Abī Kathīr narrated to me; Abū Salamah ibn 'Abd al-Raḥmān narrated to me, or narrated; Sālim, al-Mahrī's *mawlā*, narrated to me: '**'Abd al-Raḥmān ibn Abī Bakr and I followed the funeral of Sa'd ibn Abī Waqqāṣ, and we passed by 'Ā'ishah's compartment. He reported from her, from the Prophet, the same text'**.

وَحَدَّثَنِي مُحَمَّدُ بْنُ حَاتِمٍ، وَأَبُو مَعْنٍ الرَّقَاشِيُّ، قَالَا: حَدَّثَنَا عُمَرُ بْنُ يُونُسَ، حَدَّثَنَا عِكْرِمَةُ بْنُ عَمَّارٍ، حَدَّثَنِي يَحْيَى بْنُ أَبِي كَثِيرٍ، قَالَ: حَدَّثَنِي أَوْ حَدَّثَنَا أَبُو سَلَمَةَ بْنُ عَبْدِ الرَّحْمَنِ، حَدَّثَنِي سَالِمٌ، مَوْلَى الْمَهْرِيِّ، قَالَ: خَرَجْتُ أَنَا وَعَبْدُ الرَّحْمَنِ بْنُ أَبِي بَكْرٍ فِي جَنَازَةِ سَعْدِ بْنِ أَبِي وَقَّاصٍ فَمَرَرْنَا عَلَى بَابِ حُجْرَةِ عَائِشَةَ فَذَكَرَ عَنْهَا عَنِ النَّبِيِّ صَلَّى اللهُ عَلَيْهِ وَسَلَّمَ مِثْلَهُ.

[000–000]. (Dār al-Salām 0467) Salamah ibn Shabīb narrated to me: al-Ḥasan ibn A'yan narrated; Fulayḥ narrated; Nu'aym ibn 'Abdullāh narrated to me; from Sālim, Shaddād ibn al-Hād's *mawlā*, **'I was with 'Ā'ishah (may God be pleased with her). He reported from her, from the Prophet, the same text'**.

حَدَّثَنِي سَلَمَةُ بْنُ شَبِيبٍ، حَدَّثَنَا الْحَسَنُ بْنُ أَعْيَنَ، حَدَّثَنَا فُلَيْحٌ، حَدَّثَنِي نُعَيْمُ بْنُ عَبْدِ اللهِ، عَنْ سَالِمٍ، مَوْلَى شَدَّادِ بْنِ الْهَادِ، قَالَ: كُنْتُ أَنَا مَعَ عَائِشَةَ رَضِيَ اللهُ عَنْهَا فَذَكَرَ عَنْهَا عَنِ النَّبِيِّ صَلَّى اللهُ عَلَيْهِ وَسَلَّمَ بِمِثْلِهِ.

[427–26]. (Dār al-Salām 0468) Zuhayr ibn Ḥarb narrated to me:[i] Jarīr narrated [H]. Also, Isḥāq narrated; Jarīr reported; from Manṣūr; from Hilāl ibn Yasāf; from Abū Yaḥyā; from ʿAbdullāh ibn ʿAmr: **'We came back with God's Messenger (peace be upon him) from Makkah to Madinah. When we were at a water spring on the way, some of us went ahead at the time of ʿAṣr Prayer and they performed the ablution in haste. We reached them and their heels showed clearly that they were untouched by water. God's Messenger (peace be upon him) said: "Woe to the heels from the Fire. Perform the ablution well".'**

وَحَدَّثَنِي زُهَيْرُ بْنُ حَرْبٍ، حَدَّثَنَا جَرِيرٌ، ح، وَحَدَّثَنَا إِسْحَاقُ، أَخْبَرَنَا جَرِيرٌ، عَنْ مَنْصُورٍ، عَنْ هِلَالِ بْنِ يِسَافٍ، عَنْ أَبِي يَحْيَى، عَنْ عَبْدِ اللهِ بْنِ عَمْرٍو، قَالَ: رَجَعْنَا مَعَ رَسُولِ اللهِ صَلَّى اللهُ عَلَيْهِ وَسَلَّمَ مِنْ مَكَّةَ إِلَى الْـمَدِينَةِ حَتَّى إِذَا كُنَّا بِمَاءٍ بِالطَّرِيقِ تَعَجَّلَ قَوْمٌ عِنْدَ الْعَصْرِ، فَتَوَضَّئُوا وَهُمْ عِجَالٌ فَانْتَهَيْنَا إِلَيْهِمْ وَأَعْقَابُهُمْ تَلُوحُ لَمْ يَمَسَّهَا الْـمَاءُ فَقَالَ رَسُولُ اللهِ صَلَّى اللهُ عَلَيْهِ وَسَلَّمَ: «وَيْلٌ لِلْأَعْقَابِ مِنَ النَّارِ، أَسْبِغُوا الْوُضُوءَ»

[000–000]. (Dār al-Salām 0469) Abū Bakr ibn Abī Shaybah narrated: Wakīʿ narrated; from Sufyān [H]. Also Ibn al-Muthannā and Ibn Bashshār narrated: Muhammad ibn Jaʿfar narrated; Shuʿbah narrated: both from Manṣūr, with this chain of transmission. Shuʿbah's narration does not include 'Perform the ablution well', but his narration includes: 'from Abū Yaḥyā al-Aʿraj'.

حَدَّثَنَاهُ أَبُو بَكْرِ بْنُ أَبِي شَيْبَةَ، حَدَّثَنَا وَكِيعٌ، عَنْ سُفْيَانَ، وَحَدَّثَنَا ابْنُ الْـمُثَنَّى، وَابْنُ بَشَّارٍ، قَالَا: حَدَّثَنَا مُحَمَّدُ بْنُ جَعْفَرٍ، قَالَ: حَدَّثَنَا شُعْبَةُ، كِلَاهُمَا عَنْ مَنْصُورٍ، بِهَذَا الْإِسْنَادِ وَلَيْسَ فِي حَدِيثِ شُعْبَةَ أَسْبِغُوا الْوُضُوءَ وَفِي حَدِيثِهِ عَنْ أَبِى يَحْيَى الْأَعْرَجِ.

i. Related by Abū Dāwūd, 97; al-Nasāʾī, 111 and 142; Ibn Mājah, 450.

[428–27]. (Dār al-Salām 0470) Shaybān ibn Farrūkh and Abū Kāmil al-Jaḥdarī narrated:[i] both from Abū ʿAwānah. Abū Kāmil said: Abū ʿAwānah narrated; from Abū Bishr; from Yūsuf ibn Māhak; from ʿAbdullāh ibn ʿAmr: '**The Prophet (peace be upon him) was behind us when we were on a journey. He caught up with us at the time of ʿAṣr Prayer. We were wiping our feet. He loudly said: "Woe to heels from the Fire".**'

حَدَّثَنَا شَيْبَانُ بْنُ فَرُّوخَ، وَأَبُو كَامِلٍ الْجَحْدَرِيُّ، جَمِيعًا عَنْ أَبِي عَوَانَةَ، قَالَ أَبُو كَامِلٍ: حَدَّثَنَا أَبُو عَوَانَةَ، عَنْ أَبِي بِشْرٍ، عَنْ يُوسُفَ بْنِ مَاهَكَ، عَنْ عَبْدِ اللهِ بْنِ عَمْرٍو، قَالَ: تَخَلَّفَ عَنَّا النَّبِيُّ صَلَّى اللهُ عَلَيْهِ وَسَلَّمَ فِي سَفَرٍ سَافَرْنَاهُ فَأَدْرَكَنَا وَقَدْ حَضَرَتْ صَلَاةُ الْعَصْرِ فَجَعَلْنَا نَمْسَحُ عَلَى أَرْجُلِنَا فَنَادَى: «وَيْلٌ لِلْأَعْقَابِ مِنَ النَّارِ»

[429–28]. (Dār al-Salām 0471) ʿAbd al-Raḥmān ibn Sallām al-Jumaḥī narrated: al-Rabīʿ (meaning Ibn Muslim) narrated; from Muhammad (Ibn Ziyād); from Abū Hurayrah: '**The Prophet saw someone who did not wash his heels, and he said: "Woe to heels from the Fire".**'

حَدَّثَنَا عَبْدُ الرَّحْمَنِ بْنُ سَلَّامٍ الْجُمَحِيُّ، حَدَّثَنَا الرَّبِيعُ يَعْنِي ابْنَ مُسْلِمٍ، عَنْ مُحَمَّدٍ وَهُوَ ابْنُ زِيَادٍ، عَنْ أَبِي هُرَيْرَةَ، أَنَّ النَّبِيَّ صَلَّى اللهُ عَلَيْهِ وَسَلَّمَ رَأَى رَجُلًا لَمْ يَغْسِلْ عَقِبَيْهِ فَقَالَ: «وَيْلٌ لِلْأَعْقَابِ مِنَ النَّارِ»

[430–29]. (Dār al-Salām 0472) Qutaybah, Abū Bakr ibn Abī Shaybah and Abū Kurayb narrated: Wakīʿ narrated; from Shuʿbah; from Muhammad ibn Ziyād; from Abū Hurayrah **who one day saw some people performing the ablution [with water] from a container. He said to them: "Perform the**

i. Related by al-Bukhārī, 60, 96 and 163.

ablution well, because I heard Abū al-Qāsim say: 'Woe to heels from the Fire'".'

حَدَّثَنَا قُتَيْبَةُ، وَأَبُو بَكْرِ بْنُ أَبِي شَيْبَةَ، وَأَبُو كُرَيْبٍ، قَالُوا: حَدَّثَنَا وَكِيعٌ، عَنْ شُعْبَةَ، عَنْ مُحَمَّدِ بْنِ زِيَادٍ، عَنْ أَبِي هُرَيْرَةَ، أَنَّهُ رَأَى قَوْمًا يَتَوَضَّئُونَ مِنَ الْمَطْهَرَةِ فَقَالَ: أَسْبِغُوا الْوُضُوءَ فَإِنِّي سَمِعْتُ أَبَا الْقَاسِمِ صَلَّى اللهُ عَلَيْهِ وَسَلَّمَ يَقُولُ: «وَيْلٌ لِلْعَرَاقِيبِ مِنَ النَّارِ»

[431–30]. (Dār al-Salām 0473) Zuhayr ibn Ḥarb narrated to me: Jarīr narrated; from Suhayl; from his father; from Abū Hurayrah: **'God's Messenger (peace be upon him) said: "Woe to heels from the Fire".'**

حَدَّثَنِي زُهَيْرُ بْنُ حَرْبٍ، حَدَّثَنَا جَرِيرٌ، عَنْ سُهَيْلٍ، عَنْ أَبِيهِ، عَنْ أَبِي هُرَيْرَةَ، قَالَ: قَالَ رَسُولُ اللهِ صَلَّى اللهُ عَلَيْهِ وَسَلَّمَ: «وَيْلٌ لِلْأَعْقَابِ مِنَ النَّارِ»

Text Explanation

In this chapter, the Prophet is repeatedly quoted as warning that heels may suffer burning and he continually urges that the ablution should be done fully and well. Muslim's aim of including these hadiths is to provide evidence in support of considering washing the feet obligatory as part of the ablution, and to make clear that merely wiping them is not sufficient. There are different views on this point. A large number of scholars of high standing in different countries and generations are of the view that washing the feet, including one's heels, is obligatory and that wiping them is not enough. Moreover, when they are washed, wiping them is not necessary. No counter argument is given by any scholar whose view should be considered when we speak of unanimity. The Shia say that the obligation is to wipe them, while Muhammad ibn Jarīr and al-Jubbā'ī, the head of the Mu'tazilah, say that one may choose between wiping one's feet and washing them. Some of the followers of the Ẓāhirī School say that it is obligatory to combine wiping one's feet with washing them.

These groups holding views that differ with the great majority of scholars make their argument on the basis of what does not support it. I have explained the relevant evidence in the Qur'an and the Sunnah, as well as the refutation of the counter arguments in clear and simple language in *Sharḥ al-Muhadhdhab*, so as to leave no doubt in the mind of anyone holding a different view. My purpose here is to explain the text of the hadiths and the language used in them. It is not my aim to present detailed evidence or discuss arguments. Perhaps the shortest point we can make is that all those who describe the Prophet's ablution on different occasions and in different ways agree that he washed his feet.

The Prophet says: 'Woe to the heels from the Fire'. He warns that heels may be burnt in the Fire because they are not cleansed. Had wiping them been sufficient, he would not have warned those who do not wash their heels. ʿAmr ibn Shuʿayb narrates from his father from his grandfather that a man said: 'Messenger of God, how is ablution performed?' The Prophet called for water and then washed his hands three times … describing the ablution and adding that the Prophet finished by washing his feet three times. He then said: 'Such is the ablution. Anyone who adds or omits does badly and unfairly'. This is an authentic hadith related by Abū Dāwūd and others with perfect chains of transmission, but God knows best.

Transmission

In one version, a narrator called Sālim, Shaddād's *mawlā* is quoted; in another, it is Abū ʿAbdullāh, Shaddād's *mawlā*, and in a third. Sālim, al-Mahrī's *mawlā*. All three refer to the same person. He is known by several descriptions: Sālim, Shaddād ibn al-Hād's *mawlā*, Sālim, al-Mahrī's *mawlā*, Sālim Bādūs, Sālim the *mawlā* of Mālik ibn Aws ibn al-Ḥadathān al-Naṣrī, Sālim Sabanān, Sālim al-Barrād, Sālim the *mawlā* of al-Baṣriyyīn, Sālim Abū ʿAbdullāh al-Madīnī, Sālim ibn ʿAbdullāh, Abū ʿUbaydillāh Shaddād ibn al-Hād's *mawlā*. All these refer to the same person. Abū Ḥātim said: 'Sālim was one of the best Muslims. ʿAṭā' ibn al-Sā'ib said: 'Sālim narrated to me and in my view, he was more reliable than I am'.

In the fourth hadith, Sālim is mentioned as 'Ibn Sahddād's *mawlā*'. This is how he is mentioned in original manuscripts, and it is said that this is wrong. The correct thing is to delete the word 'ibn'; it is correct because Shaddād's *mawlā* is the *mawlā* of his son. If we can interpret an authentic report in an acceptable way, we should not discard it, particularly in this case which refers to a man who has been given all the aforementioned descriptions, but God knows best.

The chain of transmission of hadith No. 426 features: ''Ikrimah ibn 'Ammār narrated; Yaḥyā ibn Abī Kathīr narrated to me; Abū Salamah ibn 'Abd al-Raḥmān narrated to me, or narrated; Sālim, al-Mahrī's *mawlā*, narrated to me'. Here we have four people from the Tābi'īn generation reporting from each other. Sālim, Abū Salamah and Yaḥyā are well known as belonging to the Tābi'īn and 'Ikrimah ibn 'Ammār is also a Tābi'ī, as he heard from the Prophet's companion, al-Hirmās ibn Ziyād al-Bāhilī. This is clearly stated in Abū Dāwūd's *Sunan*, but God knows best. We also note in this chain that Muslim says 'Abū Salamah ibn 'Abd al-Raḥmān narrated to me, or narrated'. This is a fine point of accurate reporting and we have spoken about it earlier. The same chain of transmission begins with 'Muhammad ibn Ḥātim and Abū Ma'n al-Riqāshī'. Abū Ma'n's name is Zayd ibn Yazīd, and we spoke about him in the early part of the Book of Faith.

The chain of transmission of hadith No. 427 includes Hilāl ibn Yasāf from Abū Yaḥyā. Yasāf is pronounced in two other ways, Yisāf and Isāf. Ibn Qaraqūl, the author of *Maṭāli' al-Anwār*, said: 'Most Hadith scholars mention him as Yisāf, but some call him Yasāf, because there is no Arabic word that starts with Y followed by "i" except Yisār'. The better known pronunciation among linguists is Isāf, which is mentioned by Ibn al-Sukayt, Ibn Qutaybah and others, but people change it and give it a wrong pronunciation. He is Hilāl ibn Isāf'. According to the majority of scholars, Abū Yaḥyā's name is Miṣda', but Yaḥyā ibn Ma'īn said that his name is Ziyād al-A'raj al-Mu'arqib al-Anṣārī, but God knows best.

Also mentioned in the chains of transmission are Abū 'Awānah and Abū Bishr. Abū 'Awānah's name is al-Waḍḍāḥ ibn 'Abdullāh, and Abū Bishr's name is Ja'far ibn Abī Waḥshiyyah.

CHAPTER 10

COVERING ALL PARTS INCLUDED IN THE ABLUTION

[432–31]. (Dār al-Salām 0474) Salamah ibn Shabīb narrated to me:[i] al-Ḥasan ibn Muhammad ibn Aʿyan narrated; Maʿqil narrated; from Abū al-Zubayr; from Jābir; ʿUmar ibn al-Khaṭṭāb reported to me: '**A man performed the ablution, omitting a spot as small as a nail on his foot. The Prophet (peace be upon him) saw him and said [to him]: "Go back and perform your ablution well". The man went back and then offered his prayer**'.

حَدَّثَنِي سَلَمَةُ بْنُ شَبِيبٍ، حَدَّثَنَا الْحَسَنُ بْنُ مُحَمَّدِ بْنِ أَعْيَنَ، حَدَّثَنَا مَعْقِلٌ، عَنْ أَبِي الزُّبَيْرِ، عَنْ جَابِرٍ، أَخْبَرَنِي عُمَرُ بْنُ الْخَطَّابِ، أَنَّ رَجُلًا تَوَضَّأَ فَتَرَكَ مَوْضِعَ ظُفُرٍ عَلَى قَدَمِهِ فَأَبْصَرَهُ النَّبِيُّ صَلَّى اللهُ عَلَيْهِ وَسَلَّمَ فَقَالَ: «ارْجِعْ فَأَحْسِنْ وُضُوءَكَ» فَرَجَعَ، ثُمَّ صَلَّى.

Text Explanation

This hadith makes clear that the ablution of a person who leaves out a small part of what needs to be included is invalid. This is universally agreed. However, scholars differ about the case of one who performs dry ablution, i.e. *tayammum*, and leaves out a part of his face. The view of our school and the majority of scholars is that his cleansing is invalid, just like his ablution is invalid if he omits any part of what should be washed. Three different verdicts are attributed to Abū Ḥanīfah. The first is that if what he leaves out is less than one half

i. Related by Ibn Mājah, 666.

of his face, his dry ablution is valid. The second is it is valid if what he leaves out is less than the size of one dirham, while the third suggests that for the dry ablution to be valid the omitted part should be one quarter of his face or less. The majority may cite analogy in support of their view, but God knows best.

Some scholars take this hadith as evidence that what is required in cleansing one's feet during ablution is to wash, not wipe, them. *Qāḍī* 'Iyāḍ and others also suggest that the hadith indicates that doing the whole ablution consecutively, without interruption, is a duty, citing in support the Prophet's words: 'Go back and perform your ablution well'. He did not tell the man to wash the part he left out. This argument is weak, or rather incorrect. The Prophet's words may equally be taken as requiring the man to complete his ablution or to start it anew. To make either meaning more valid is not right, but God knows best.

CHAPTER 11

SINS GOING OUT WITH THE WATER OF ABLUTION

[433–32]. (Dār al-Salām 0475) Suwayd ibn Saʿīd narrated:[i] from Mālik ibn Anas [H]. Also, Abū al-Ṭāhir narrated, and this is his text: ʿAbdullāh ibn Wahb reported; from Mālik ibn Anas; from Suhayl ibn Abī Ṣāliḥ; from his father; from Abū Hurayrah that God's Messenger (peace be upon him) said: '**When a Muslim (or a believer) servant of God performs the ablution, then as he washes his face, every sin he looked at with his eyes goes out of his face with the water (or with the last drop of water). When he washes his arms, every sin he committed with his arms goes out of his arms with the water (or with the last drop of water). When he washes his feet, every sin to which he walked goes out with the water (or with the last drop of water) so that he will be cleansed of all sin**'.

حَدَّثَنَا سُوَيْدُ بْنُ سَعِيدٍ، عَنْ مَالِكِ بْنِ أَنَسٍ، ح، وَحَدَّثَنَا أَبُو الطَّاهِرِ، وَاللَّفْظُ لَهُ أَخْبَرَنَا عَبْدُ اللهِ بْنُ وَهْبٍ، عَنْ مَالِكِ بْنِ أَنَسٍ، عَنْ سُهَيْلِ بْنِ أَبِي صَالِحٍ، عَنْ أَبِيهِ، عَنْ أَبِي هُرَيْرَةَ، أَنَّ رَسُولَ اللهِ صَلَّى اللهُ عَلَيْهِ وَسَلَّمَ قَالَ: «إِذَا تَوَضَّأَ الْعَبْدُ الْمُسْلِمُ - أَوِ الْمُؤْمِنُ - فَغَسَلَ وَجْهَهُ خَرَجَ مِنْ وَجْهِهِ كُلُّ خَطِيئَةٍ نَظَرَ إِلَيْهَا بِعَيْنَيْهِ مَعَ الْمَاءِ - أَوْ مَعَ آخِرِ قَطْرِ الْمَاءِ -، فَإِذَا غَسَلَ يَدَيْهِ خَرَجَ مِنْ يَدَيْهِ كُلُّ خَطِيئَةٍ كَانَ بَطَشَتْهَا يَدَاهُ مَعَ الْمَاءِ أَوْ مَعَ آخِرِ قَطْرِ الْمَاءِ -، فَإِذَا غَسَلَ رِجْلَيْهِ خَرَجَتْ كُلُّ خَطِيئَةٍ مَشَتْهَا رِجْلَاهُ مَعَ الْمَاءِ - أَوْ مَعَ آخِرِ قَطْرِ الْمَاءِ - حَتَّى يَخْرُجَ نَقِيًّا مِنَ الذُّنُوبِ»

i. Related by al-Tirmidhī, 2.

[434–33]. (Dār al-Salām 0476) Muhammad ibn Maʿmar ibn Ribʿī al-Qaysī narrated: Abū Hishām al-Makhzūmī narrated; from ʿAbd al-Wāḥid (who is Ibn Ziyād); ʿUthmān ibn Ḥakīm narrated; Muhammad ibn al-Munkadir narrated; from Ḥumrān; from ʿUthmān ibn ʿAffān: **'God's Messenger (peace be upon him) said: "Whoever performs the ablution and does it well, his sins go out of his body, to the extent that they go out from beneath his nails".'**

حَدَّثَنَا مُحَمَّدُ بْنُ مَعْمَرِ بْنِ رِبْعِيٍّ الْقَيْسِيُّ، حَدَّثَنَا أَبُو هِشَامٍ الْمَخْزُومِيُّ، عَنْ عَبْدِ الْوَاحِدِ وَهُوَ ابْنُ زِيَادٍ، حَدَّثَنَا عُثْمَانُ بْنُ حَكِيمٍ، حَدَّثَنَا مُحَمَّدُ بْنُ الْمُنْكَدِرِ، عَنْ حُمْرَانَ، عَنْ عُثْمَانَ بْنِ عَفَّانَ، قَالَ: قَالَ رَسُولُ اللهِ صَلَّى اللهُ عَلَيْهِ وَسَلَّمَ: «مَنْ تَوَضَّأَ فَأَحْسَنَ الْوُضُوءَ خَرَجَتْ خَطَايَاهُ مِنْ جَسَدِهِ، حَتَّى تَخْرُجَ مِنْ تَحْتِ أَظْفَارِهِ»

Text Explanation

In the text of the first hadith we have the description of 'a Muslim' or 'a believer' servant of God, and we have 'with the water' or 'with the last drop of water'. In all these cases, the reason is the narrator's doubt. The sins referred to in the hadith are minor ones, not major sins, as we have explained earlier. In another hadith, it is stated 'unless major sins have been committed'. *Qāḍī* ʿIyāḍ said: 'The statement that sins go out with the water is a figurative one, meaning that they are forgiven. Sins do not have bodies so that they go out physically', but God knows best.

This hadith refutes the argument of the Shia and stresses that it is a duty to wash one's feet when performing the ablution.

Transmission

The chain of transmission of the second hadith mentions Abū Hishām al-Makhzūmī. This is how he is mentioned in all original manuscripts in our areas, and it is the correct version. This is also how *Qāḍī* ʿIyāḍ attributes it to some reporters, but adds: 'Most reporters give his name as Abū Hāshim, but the other spelling is the correct one'. His name is al-Mughīrah ibn Salamah. He was known for his goodness, devotion and humility. May God be pleased with him.

CHAPTER 12

THE DESIRABILITY OF EXCEEDING THE MARK

[435–34]. (Dār al-Salām 0477) Abū Kurayb Muhammad ibn al-ʿAlā', al-Qāsim ibn Zakariyyā' ibn Dīnār and ʿAbd ibn Ḥumayd narrated to me:[i] Khālid ibn Makhlad narrated; from Sulaymān ibn Bilāl; ʿUmārah ibn Ghaziyyah al-Anṣāri narrated to me; from Nuʿaym ibn ʿAbdullāh al-Mujmir: **'I saw Abū Hurayrah performing the ablution. He washed his face and did it fully. He then washed his right arm going right into the upper arm, then washed his left arm going right into the upper arm. He then wiped his head and washed his right foot going up the shin, then washed his left foot going up the shin. He said: God's Messenger (peace be upon him) said: "You are the ones who will have the distinctive marks on your foreheads and limbs on the Day of Judgement because you fulfil your ablution. Whoever is able to should elongate his distinctive marks".'**

حَدَّثَنِي أَبُو كُرَيْبٍ مُحَمَّدُ بْنُ الْعَلَاءِ، وَالْقَاسِمُ بْنُ زَكَرِيَّا بْنِ دِينَارٍ، وَعَبْدُ بْنُ حُمَيْدٍ، قَالُوا: حَدَّثَنَا خَالِدُ بْنُ مَخْلَدٍ، عَنْ سُلَيْمَانَ بْنِ بِلَالٍ، حَدَّثَنِي عُمَارَةُ بْنُ غَزِيَّةَ الْأَنْصَارِيُّ، عَنْ نُعَيْمِ بْنِ عَبْدِ اللهِ الْمُجْمِرِ، قَالَ: رَأَيْتُ أَبَا هُرَيْرَةَ يَتَوَضَّأُ فَغَسَلَ وَجْهَهُ فَأَسْبَغَ الْوُضُوءَ، ثُمَّ غَسَلَ يَدَهُ الْيُمْنَى حَتَّى أَشْرَعَ فِي الْعَضُدِ، ثُمَّ يَدَهُ الْيُسْرَى حَتَّى أَشْرَعَ فِي الْعَضُدِ، ثُمَّ مَسَحَ رَأْسَهُ، ثُمَّ غَسَلَ رِجْلَهُ الْيُمْنَى حَتَّى أَشْرَعَ فِي السَّاقِ، ثُمَّ غَسَلَ رِجْلَهُ الْيُسْرَى حَتَّى أَشْرَعَ

i. Related by al-Bukhārī, 3 (in a shorter version).

فِي السَّاقِ، ثُمَّ قَالَ: « هَكَذَا رَأَيْتُ رَسُولَ اللهِ صَلَّى اللهُ عَلَيْهِ وَسَلَّمَ يَتَوَضَّأُ. وَقَالَ: قَالَ رَسُولُ اللهِ صَلَّى اللهُ عَلَيْهِ وَسَلَّمَ: «أَنْتُمُ الْغُرُّ الْمُحَجَّلُونَ يَوْمَ الْقِيَامَةِ مِنْ إِسْبَاغِ الْوُضُوءِ، فَمَنِ اسْتَطَاعَ مِنْكُمْ فَلْيُطِلْ غُرَّتَهُ وَتَحْجِيلَهُ»

[436–35]. (Dār al-Salām 0478) Hārūn ibn Saʿīd al-Aylī narrated to me: Ibn Wahb narrated to me; ʿAmr ibn al-Ḥārith reported to me; from Saʿīd ibn Abī Hilāl; from Nuʿaym ibn ʿAbdullāh that **'he saw Abū Hurayrah performing the ablution. He washed his face and his arms, almost reaching his shoulders, and he washed his feet going up his legs. He then said: "I heard God's Messenger (peace be upon him) say: 'My community will come on the Day of Judgement with distinctive marks on their foreheads and limbs left by ablution. Whoever is able to elongate the mark on his forehead should do so'".'**

وَحَدَّثَنِي هَارُونُ بْنُ سَعِيدٍ الْأَيْلِيُّ، حَدَّثَنِي ابْنُ وَهْبٍ، أَخْبَرَنِي عَمْرُو بْنُ الْحَارِثِ، عَنْ سَعِيدِ بْنِ أَبِي هِلَالٍ، عَنْ نُعَيْمِ بْنِ عَبْدِ اللهِ، أَنَّهُ رَأَى أَبَا هُرَيْرَةَ يَتَوَضَّأُ فَغَسَلَ وَجْهَهُ وَيَدَيْهِ حَتَّى كَادَ يَبْلُغُ الْمَنْكِبَيْنِ ثُمَّ غَسَلَ رِجْلَيْهِ حَتَّى رَفَعَ إِلَى السَّاقَيْنِ، ثُمَّ قَالَ سَمِعْتُ رَسُولَ اللهِ صَلَّى اللهُ عَلَيْهِ وَسَلَّمَ يَقُولُ: «إِنَّ أُمَّتِي يَأْتُونَ يَوْمَ الْقِيَامَةِ غُرًّا مُحَجَّلِينَ مِنْ أَثَرِ الْوُضُوءِ، فَمَنِ اسْتَطَاعَ مِنْكُمْ أَنْ يُطِيلَ غُرَّتَهُ فَلْيَفْعَلْ»

[437–36]. (Dār al-Salām 0479) Suwyad ibn Saʿīd and Ibn Abī ʿUmar narrated:[i] both from Marwān al-Fazārī. Ibn Abī ʿUmar said: Marwān narrated; from Abū Mālik al-Ashjaʿī Saʿd ibn Ṭāriq; from Abū Ḥāzim; from Abū Hurayrah that God's Messenger (peace be upon him) said: **'My pool will be longer than the distance from Aylah[ii] to Aden, and it will be whiter**

i. Related by Ibn Mājah, 4282.
ii. Aylah is the town in Palestine at the head of the Gulf of Aqabah, and which is known today as Eilat.

than snow and sweeter than milk and honey. Its cups are more than the stars. I shall be turning people away from it like a man turns away other people's camels from his water pond'. People asked: 'Messenger of God, will you recognize us then?' He said: 'Yes, because you have a feature that belongs to no other community. You shall come to me with distinctive marks on your foreheads and limbs left by the ablution'.

حَدَّثَنَا سُوَيْدُ بْنُ سَعِيدٍ، وَابْنُ أَبِي عُمَرَ، جَمِيعًا عَنْ مَرْوَانَ الْفَزَارِيِّ، قَالَ ابْنُ أَبِي عُمَرَ: حَدَّثَنَا مَرْوَانُ، عَنْ أَبِي مَالِكٍ الْأَشْجَعِيِّ سَعْدِ بْنِ طَارِقٍ، عَنْ أَبِي حَازِمٍ، عَنْ أَبِي هُرَيْرَةَ أَنَّ رَسُولَ اللهِ صَلَّى اللهُ عَلَيْهِ وَسَلَّمَ قَالَ: «إِنَّ حَوْضِي أَبْعَدُ مِنْ أَيْلَةَ مِنْ عَدَنٍ لَهُوَ أَشَدُّ بَيَاضًا مِنَ الثَّلْجِ، وَأَحْلَى مِنَ الْعَسَلِ بِاللَّبَنِ، وَلَآنِيَتُهُ أَكْثَرُ مِنْ عَدَدِ النُّجُومِ وَإِنِّي لَأَصُدُّ النَّاسَ عَنْهُ، كَمَا يَصُدُّ الرَّجُلُ إِبِلَ النَّاسِ عَنْ حَوْضِهِ» قَالُوا: يَا رَسُولَ اللهِ أَتَعْرِفُنَا يَوْمَئِذٍ؟ قَالَ: «نَعَمْ لَكُمْ سِيمَا لَيْسَتْ لِأَحَدٍ مِنَ الْأُمَمِ تَرِدُونَ عَلَيَّ غُرًّا، مُحَجَّلِينَ مِنْ أَثَرِ الْوُضُوءِ»

[438–37]. (Dār al-Salām 0480) Abū Kurayb and Wāṣil ibn ʿAbd al-Aʿlā narrated (and this is Wāṣil's text). Both said: Abū Fuḍayl narrated; from Abū Mālik al-Ashjaʿī; from Abū Ḥāzim; from Abū Hurayrah: God's Messenger (peace be upon him) said: **'My community will come to me at the pool, and I will turn people away from it like a man turns someone's camels away from his own camels'. People said: 'Prophet, will you recognize us?' He said: 'Yes, you will have a feature that belongs to none other. You shall come to me with distinctive marks on your foreheads and limbs left by the ablution. Some of you will be blocked from me and they will not reach me. I will say: "My Lord, these are also my companions". An angel will reply to me and say: "Do you know what they have invented after you?".'**

وَحَدَّثَنَا أَبُو كُرَيْبٍ، وَوَاصِلُ بْنُ عَبْدِ الْأَعْلَى، - وَاللَّفْظُ لِوَاصِلٍ -، قَالَا: حَدَّثَنَا ابْنُ فُضَيْلٍ، عَنْ أَبِي مَالِكٍ الْأَشْجَعِيِّ، عَنْ أَبِي حَازِمٍ، عَنْ أَبِي هُرَيْرَةَ، قَالَ: قَالَ رَسُولُ اللهِ صَلَّى اللهُ عَلَيْهِ وَسَلَّمَ: «تَرِدُ عَلَيَّ أُمَّتِي الْحَوْضَ، وَأَنَا أَذُودُ النَّاسَ عَنْهُ، كَمَا يَذُودُ الرَّجُلُ إِبِلَ الرَّجُلِ عَنْ إِبِلِهِ» قَالُوا يَا نَبِيَّ اللهِ أَتَعْرِفُنَا؟ قَالَ: «نَعَمْ لَكُمْ سِيمَا لَيْسَتْ لِأَحَدٍ غَيْرِكُمْ تَرِدُونَ عَلَيَّ غُرًّا مُحَجَّلِينَ مِنْ آثَارِ الْوُضُوءِ، وَلَيُصَدَّنَّ عَنِّي طَائِفَةٌ مِنْكُمْ فَلَا يَصِلُونَ، فَأَقُولُ: يَا رَبِّ هَؤُلَاءِ مِنْ أَصْحَابِي. فَيُجِيبُنِي مَلَكٌ، فَيَقُولُ: وَهَلْ تَدْرِي مَا أَحْدَثُوا بَعْدَكَ؟»

[439–38]. (Dār al-Salām 0481) ʿUthmān ibn Abī Shaybah narrated:[i] ʿAlī ibn Mushir narrated; from Saʿd ibn Ṭāriq; from Ribʿī ibn Ḥirāsh; from Ḥudhayfah: God's Messenger (peace be upon him) said: **'My pool is longer than the distance from Aylah to Aden. By Him who holds my soul in His hand, I shall be turning people away from it like a man turns stranger camels away from his water'. People asked: 'Messenger of God, will you recognize us?' He said: 'Yes, you shall come to me with distinctive marks on your foreheads and limbs left by the ablution. These do not belong to anyone else'**.

وَحَدَّثَنَا عُثْمَانُ بْنُ أَبِي شَيْبَةَ، حَدَّثَنَا عَلِيُّ بْنُ مُسْهِرٍ، عَنْ سَعْدِ بْنِ طَارِقٍ، عَنْ رِبْعِيِّ بْنِ حِرَاشٍ، عَنْ حُذَيْفَةَ، قَالَ: قَالَ رَسُولُ اللهِ صَلَّى اللهُ عَلَيْهِ وَسَلَّمَ: «إِنَّ حَوْضِي لَأَبْعَدُ مِنْ أَيْلَةَ مِنْ عَدَنٍ وَالَّذِي نَفْسِي بِيَدِهِ، إِنِّي لَأَذُودُ عَنْهُ الرِّجَالَ كَمَا يَذُودُ الرَّجُلُ الْإِبِلَ الْغَرِيبَةَ عَنْ حَوْضِهِ» قَالُوا: يَا رَسُولَ اللهِ وَتَعْرِفُنَا؟ قَالَ: «نَعَمْ تَرِدُونَ عَلَيَّ غُرًّا مُحَجَّلِينَ مِنْ آثَارِ الْوُضُوءِ لَيْسَتْ لِأَحَدٍ غَيْرِكُمْ»

[440–39]. (Dār al-Salām 0482) Yaḥyā ibn Ayyūb, Surayj ibn Yūnus, Qutaybah ibn Saʿīd and ʿAlī ibn Ḥujr narrated: all from

i. Related by Ibn Mājah, 4302.

Ismāʿīl ibn Jaʿfar: Ibn Ayyūb said: Ismāʿīl narrated; al-ʿAlāʾ reported to me; from his father; from Abū Hurayrah: **'God's Messenger (peace be upon him) went to the graveyard [in Madinah]. He said: "Peace be to you. This is the place of people who are believers. We shall be joining you, if God so wills. It would have given me pleasure to see our brethren". People said: "Are we not your brethren, Messenger of God?" He said: "You are my companions, but our brethren are not born yet". They asked: "How will you know those of your community who are not born yet, Messenger of God?" He said: "Suppose a man has horses with white marks on their foreheads and on their limbs but they are in the midst of completely dark horses. Does he not know the horses that belong to him?" They said: "Indeed, he does, Messenger of God". He said: "They will come with distinctive marks on their foreheads and limbs left by the ablution. I shall lead them at the pool. Some people will be turned away from my pool like stray camels. I shall call out to them: 'Come along'. It will be said: 'They have altered things after you were gone'. I will say: 'Far removed they are. Far removed'".'**

حَدَّثَنَا يَحْيَى بْنُ أَيُّوبَ، وَسُرَيْجُ بْنُ يُونُسَ، وَقُتَيْبَةُ بْنُ سَعِيدٍ، وَعَلِيُّ بْنُ حُجْرٍ، جَمِيعًا عَنْ إِسْمَاعِيلَ بْنِ جَعْفَرٍ - قَالَ ابْنُ أَيُّوبَ حَدَّثَنَا إِسْمَاعِيلُ - أَخْبَرَنِي الْعَلَاءُ، عَنْ أَبِيهِ، عَنْ أَبِي هُرَيْرَةَ، أَنَّ رَسُولَ اللهِ صَلَّى اللهُ عَلَيْهِ وَسَلَّمَ أَتَى الْمَقْبُرَةَ، فَقَالَ: «السَّلَامُ عَلَيْكُمْ دَارَ قَوْمٍ مُؤْمِنِينَ، وَإِنَّا إِنْ شَاءَ اللهُ بِكُمْ لَاحِقُونَ، وَدِدْتُ أَنَّا قَدْ رَأَيْنَا إِخْوَانَنَا» قَالُوا: أَوَلَسْنَا إِخْوَانَكَ؟ يَا رَسُولَ اللهِ قَالَ: «أَنْتُمْ أَصْحَابِي وَإِخْوَانُنَا الَّذِينَ لَمْ يَأْتُوا بَعْدُ» فَقَالُوا: كَيْفَ تَعْرِفُ مَنْ لَمْ يَأْتِ بَعْدُ مِنْ أُمَّتِكَ؟ يَا رَسُولَ اللهِ فَقَالَ: «أَرَأَيْتَ لَوْ أَنَّ رَجُلًا لَهُ خَيْلٌ غُرٌّ مُحَجَّلَةٌ بَيْنَ ظَهْرَيْ خَيْلٍ دُهْمٍ بُهْمٍ أَلَا يَعْرِفُ خَيْلَهُ؟» قَالُوا: بَلَى يَا رَسُولَ اللهِ قَالَ: «فَإِنَّهُمْ يَأْتُونَ غُرًّا مُحَجَّلِينَ مِنَ الْوُضُوءِ، وَأَنَا فَرَطُهُمْ عَلَى الْحَوْضِ أَلَا لَيُذَادَنَّ رِجَالٌ عَنْ حَوْضِي كَمَا يُذَادُ الْبَعِيرُ الضَّالُّ أُنَادِيهِمْ أَلَا هَلُمَّ فَيُقَالُ: إِنَّهُمْ قَدْ بَدَّلُوا بَعْدَكَ فَأَقُولُ سُحْقًا سُحْقًا».

[441–000]. (Dār al-Salām 0483) Qutaybah ibn Saʿīd narrated:[i] ʿAbd al-ʿAzīz, meaning al-Darāwardī [H]. Also, Isḥāq ibn Mūsā al-Anṣārī narrated to me; Maʿn narrated; Mālik narrated; all from al-ʿAlā' ibn ʿAbd al-Raḥmān; from his father; from Abū Hurayrah: **'God's Messenger (peace be upon him) went out to the graveyard. He said: "Peace be to you. This is the place of people who were believers. We shall be joining you, if God so wills".' He added the same as the hadith narrated by Ismāʿīl ibn Jaʿfar, except that Mālik's version says: 'Some people shall be turned away from my pool'**.

حَدَّثَنَا قُتَيْبَةُ بْنُ سَعِيدٍ، حَدَّثَنَا عَبْدُ الْعَزِيزِ يَعْنِي الدَّرَاوَرْدِيَّ ح، وَحَدَّثَنِي إِسْحَاقُ بْنُ مُوسَى الْأَنْصَارِيُّ، حَدَّثَنَا مَعْنٌ، حَدَّثَنَا مَالِكٌ، جَمِيعًا عَنِ الْعَلَاءِ بْنِ عَبْدِ الرَّحْمَنِ، عَنْ أَبِيهِ، عَنْ أَبِي هُرَيْرَةَ، أَنَّ رَسُولَ اللهِ صَلَّى اللهُ عَلَيْهِ وَسَلَّمَ خَرَجَ إِلَى الْمَقْبُرَةِ فَقَالَ: «السَّلَامُ عَلَيْكُمْ دَارَ قَوْمٍ مُؤْمِنِينَ وَإِنَّا إِنْ شَاءَ اللهُ بِكُمْ لَاحِقُونَ» بِمِثْلِ حَدِيثِ إِسْمَاعِيلَ بْنِ جَعْفَرٍ، غَيْرَ أَنَّ حَدِيثَ مَالِكٍ فَلَيُذَادَنَّ رِجَالٌ عَنْ حَوْضِي.

Text Explanation

These hadiths make clear that it is desirable to go further than is required when doing the ablution. This is expressed in Arabic as elongating the *ghurrah* and the *taḥjīl*. The first means to wash a bit of the first part of one's head that is next to one's face, so as to go beyond what is obligatory to wash, making sure that the whole of one's face is washed. To elongate the *taḥjīl* means to wash above the elbows and the ankles. There is no disagreement among our scholars that this is desirable, but they differ as to how much it is desirable. They advance different views, with some saying that it is desirable to go above the elbows and the ankles, without specifying a limit. Others say that it is desirable to go up to the middle of one's upper arm and the middle of one's shin. A third view makes it desirable

i. Related by Abū Dāwūd, 3237; al-Nasā'ī, 150.

to go up to the shoulders and the knees. The hadiths in this chapter apply to all these. The claims of Imam Ibn Baṭṭāl al-Mālikī and *Qāḍī* ʿIyāḍ that scholars are agreed that ablution should go beyond the elbows and ankles are wrong. How could they be right when we have clear and reliable evidence that the Prophet and Abū Hurayrah did just that. The increase is indeed the view of our Shāfiʿī School of *fiqh*, and there is no disagreement among our scholars about it. Anyone who takes a different view will come against these clear and authentic hadiths. They cite in support of their claims the hadith that says: 'Anyone who adds or omits does badly and unfairly'. This, however, is no evidence confirming their claim, because it applies to how many times each part is washed during the ablution, but God knows best.

These hadiths describe the Muslim community as having distinctive marks on the Day of Judgement. As mentioned earlier, the Arabic words *ghurrah* and *taḥjīl* and their derivatives are used here. *Ghurrah* is a whiteness in a horse's forehead, while *taḥjīl* is a whiteness on a horse's front and back legs. Scholars say that the brightness that shows on the parts washed during ablution is called *ghurrah* and *taḥjīl* by way of comparison, but God knows best.

In hadith No. 437, the Prophet says: 'You have a feature that belongs to no other community. You shall come to me with distinctive marks on your foreheads and limbs left by the ablution'. Some scholars say that the ablution applies to none other than the Muslim community (may God increase its honour). Other scholars say that it is not the ablution that is especially required of the Muslim community but the *ghurrah* and *taḥjīl*. They cite in support another hadith which says: 'This is my way of ablution and the way of prophets before me'. The first group reply that this hadith is well known to be poor in authenticity. Moreover, even if it is authentic, it is probable that only prophets were required to perform the ablution, but not their followers, and that the only community required to perform the ablution for prayer is the Muslim community, but God knows best.

In hadith No. 438, the Prophet says: 'Some of you will be blocked from me and will not reach me'. This is explained differently by scholars. One view suggests that this refers to hypocrites and apostates. They may be resurrected with the marks of ablution on their faces and limbs, and the Prophet will then call them to join him, because of these marks. Another view is that this applies to some people who lived at the time of the Prophet and then reverted to disbelief after him. Although these may not have the marks of ablution, the Prophet will call on them because he knew them to be believers in his life time. A third view is that it applies to sinners who commit major sins, but died believing in God's oneness, and to those who followed some deviant creeds but their creeds did not take them out of the fold of Islam. According to this view, such people who are blocked from the Prophet's pool are not definitely going to Hell. That they are blocked may be a punishment meted out to them, but subsequently God's mercy will be granted to them and God may admit them into Heaven, without any suffering in Hell. Scholars who share this view say that such people may have the distinctive marks of *ghurrah* and *taḥjīl* and they might belong to the Prophet's own time or to later generations and that he would know them by this distinctive mark. Imam ibn ʿAbd al-Barr said: 'All those who introduced some alien ideas into religion, such as the Khawārij, the Shiah and the followers of other deviant creeds, as well as those who are unjust and go hard in denying people their rights, and also those who publicly commit major sins will be blocked from reaching the Prophet's pool .... All such people are feared to be meant by this hadith, but God knows best'.

In hadith No. 439, the Prophet says: 'By Him who holds my soul in His hand ...'. This indicates that it is permissible to state an oath, even though one is not asked to swear and there is no need for it. There is plenty of evidence confirming this.

In the last two hadiths, the Prophet goes to the graveyard and describes it as the place of believers. He then says: 'We shall be joining you, if God so wills'. He thus attaches the question of death to God's will, although death is a certainty and will come to all creatures. So, why does he make it dependant on God's will? Scholars have discussed this point and given more than one interpretation. Perhaps the best is that it does not mean doubt about death, but is rather meant for blessing and implementation of God's order as He says: *'Never say about anything, "I shall do this tomorrow", without adding, "if God so wills".'* (18: 23–24) A second interpretation is stated by al-Khaṭṭābī and others who said that it is a good habit that one should have in one's speech. A third view is that the conditional applies to the place, thus meaning that the Prophet and his companions will be joining them in that place of burial, if God so wills. It is also said that it means: since God has so willed. Other interpretations are given but these are flimsy and I would rather not go into them, such as the one that says that with the Prophet on that occasion were some believers and some hypocrites, and the exception applies only to the latter, but this is clearly wrong, and God knows best.

The Prophet says to his companions that he dearly wished to see his brethren. To their question whether they are not his brothers, he tells them that they are his companions but his brethren are those who are not yet born. Scholars say that this hadith shows that it is permissible to wish for something, particularly when it is definitely good, such as meeting good and pious people. The Prophet's wish was to see them in this present life. *Qāḍī* 'Iyāḍ said: 'It has been suggested that the wish was to see them after death'. Imam al-Bājī said: 'The fact that the Prophet said to those who asked him whether they were not his brothers: 'You are my companions', does not mean a negation of their brotherhood with him. He only mentioned their higher grade imparted to them by their companionship with him, in addition to being his brothers. Those who were not born yet would be his brothers but not his companions. God says: *'Believers are but brothers'*. (49: 9)

Qāḍī 'Iyāḍ said:

> Abū 'Umar ibn 'Abd al-Barr interprets this hadith and others that speak of the merits of people who will be in future generations as meaning that some people who live after the generation of the Prophet's companions may be better than some individuals among the Prophet's companions. They take the Prophet's statement, 'the best of you are my generation',

as referring to the earliest of the Prophet's companions among the Muhājirīn and the Anṣār and those who followed their example. These were the best of the Muslim community, and they were the ones referred to in this hadith. A companion of the Prophet who mixed good actions with bad ones, or who was not among the earliest ones, or had no particular influence may be lesser than some who live in later generations, according to the meaning of some hadiths. Other scholars who speak about language and meanings share this view, although the majority of scholars do not. They say that anyone who saw the Prophet even once and benefited by his company is of a superior grade to anyone who came later, because the Prophet's companionship imparts a merit that is higher than everything else. They add that this is an aspect of God's grace which He granted to whomever He chose. In support of this argument, they cite the hadith: 'Should any of you spend [for God's cause] the like of [Mount] Uḥud in gold, he would not attain what is equal to the fill of the cupped hands of anyone of them, or even half that'.

Transmission

The first hadith is narrated by Nuʿaym ibn ʿAbdullāh al-Mujmir. He is given this nickname, al-Mujmir, because he used to bring incense and light it in the Prophet's mosque to give it a pleasant smell. Al-Mujmir was the description of ʿAbdullah but it applied to his son, Nuʿaym, by extension.

CHAPTER 13

EXTENDED ADORNMENT

[442–40]. (Dār al-Salām 0484) Qutaybah ibn Saʿīd narrated:[i] Khalaf (meaning Ibn Khalīfah) narrated; from Abū Mālik al-Ashjaʿī; from Abū Ḥāzim: '**I was behind Abū Hurayrah when he was performing the ablution to offer a prayer. He stretched his arm so as to wash up to his armpits. I said to him: "Abū Hurayrah, what sort of ablution is this?" He said: "Banī Farrūkh; are you here? Had I known that you were here, I would not have performed the ablution in this way, but I heard my friend (peace be upon him) say: 'The believer's adornment reaches as far as his ablution reaches'".**'

حَدَّثَنَا قُتَيْبَةُ بْنُ سَعِيدٍ، حَدَّثَنَا خَلَفٌ يَعْنِي ابْنَ خَلِيفَةَ، عَنْ أَبِي مَالِكٍ الْأَشْجَعِيِّ، عَنْ أَبِي حَازِمٍ، قَالَ: كُنْتُ خَلْفَ أَبِي هُرَيْرَةَ، وَهُوَ يَتَوَضَّأُ لِلصَّلَاةِ فَكَانَ يَمُدُّ يَدَهُ حَتَّى تَبْلُغَ إِبْطَهُ فَقُلْتُ لَهُ: يَا أَبَا هُرَيْرَةَ مَا هَذَا الْوُضُوءُ؟ فَقَالَ: يَا بَنِي فَرُّوخَ أَنْتُمْ هَاهُنَا؟ لَوْ عَلِمْتُ أَنَّكُمْ هَاهُنَا مَا تَوَضَّأْتُ هَذَا الْوُضُوءَ، سَمِعْتُ خَلِيلِي صَلَّى اللهُ عَلَيْهِ وَسَلَّمَ يَقُولُ: «تَبْلُغُ الْحِلْيَةُ مِنَ الْـمُؤْمِنِ، حَيْثُ يَبْلُغُ الْوَضُوءُ»

Text Explanation

Abū Hurayrah addresses his interlocutor as 'Banī Farrūkh', which means Farrūkh's descendants. Al-Khalīl ibn Ahmad al-Farāhīdī, the author of *al-ʿAyn*, said: 'We have learnt that Farrūkh was one of

i. Related by al-Nasāʾī, 149.

Abraham's sons, born after Ishmael and Isaac. His offspring were numerous, and the people of central Persia were his descendants.

Qāḍī 'Iyāḍ said: 'Abū Hurayrah was referring here to the non-Arabs, and he was addressing Abū Ḥāzim … . Abū Hurayrah meant that a person who is taken as an example to be followed should not do in front of uneducated people something that he may take as a concession in a difficult situation or what is more difficult than normal, because of his particular understanding or excessive care. Otherwise, they may follow his concession when they do not need it, or may think that the excess that he does is obligatory, but God knows best.'

CHAPTER 14

DOING THE FULL ABLUTION DESPITE DIFFICULTY

[443–41]. (Dār al-Salām 0485) Yaḥyā ibn Ayyūb, Qutyabah and Ibn Ḥujr narrated:[i] all from Ismāʿīl ibn Jaʿfar. Ibn Ayyūb said: Ismāʿīl narrated; al-ʿAlāʾ reported to me; from his father; from Abū Hurayrah; that God's Messenger (peace be upon him) said: **'Shall I tell what ensures that God will wipe off [people's] sins and raise their grades?' People said: 'Yes, please, Messenger of God'. He said: 'Doing the ablution full well despite difficulty, walking longer to mosques and waiting for one prayer after another. That is [equal to] standing guard'**.

حَدَّثَنَا يَحْيَى بْنُ أَيُّوبَ، وَقُتَيْبَةُ، وَابْنُ حُجْرٍ جَمِيعًا عَنْ إِسْمَاعِيلَ بْنِ جَعْفَرٍ - قَالَ ابْنُ أَيُّوبَ: حَدَّثَنَا إِسْمَاعِيلُ - أَخْبَرَنِي الْعَلَاءُ، عَنْ أَبِيهِ، عَنْ أَبِي هُرَيْرَةَ، أَنَّ رَسُولَ اللهِ صَلَّى اللهُ عَلَيْهِ وَسَلَّمَ قَالَ: «أَلَا أَدُلُّكُمْ عَلَى مَا يَمْحُو اللهُ بِهِ الْخَطَايَا، وَيَرْفَعُ بِهِ الدَّرَجَاتِ؟» قَالُوا بَلَى يَا رَسُولَ اللهِ قَالَ: «إِسْبَاغُ الْوُضُوءِ عَلَى الْمَكَارِهِ، وَكَثْرَةُ الْخُطَا إِلَى الْمَسَاجِدِ، وَانْتِظَارُ الصَّلَاةِ بَعْدَ الصَّلَاةِ، فَذَلِكُمُ الرِّبَاطُ»

[444–000]. (Dār al-Salām 0486) Isḥāq ibn Mūsā al-Anṣārī narrated to me:[ii] Maʿn narrated; Mālik narrated [H]. Also, Muhammad ibn al-Muthannā narrated; Muhammad ibn Jaʿfar

i. Related by al-Tirmidhī, 51.

ii. Related by al-Nasāʾī, 143.

narrated; Shu'bah narrated; both from al-'Alā' ibn 'Abd al-Raḥmān, with this chain of transmission. **Shu'bah's narration does not mention standing guard, but Mālik's narration mentions it twice: 'That is [equal to] standing guard. That is [equal to] standing guard'.**

حَدَّثَنِي إِسْحَاقُ بْنُ مُوسَى الْأَنْصَارِيُّ، حَدَّثَنَا مَعْنٌ، حَدَّثَنَا مَالِكٌ ح، وَحَدَّثَنَا مُحَمَّدُ بْنُ الْمُثَنَّى، حَدَّثَنَا مُحَمَّدُ بْنُ جَعْفَرٍ، حَدَّثَنَا شُعْبَةُ جَمِيعًا عَنِ الْعَلَاءِ بْنِ عَبْدِ الرَّحْمَنِ، بِهَذَا الْإِسْنَادِ. وَلَيْسَ فِي حَدِيثِ شُعْبَةَ ذِكْرُ الرِّبَاطِ وَفِي حَدِيثِ مَالِكٍ ثِنْتَيْنِ «فَذَلِكُمُ الرِّبَاطُ، فَذَلِكُمُ الرِّبَاطُ»

Text Explanation

Qāḍī 'Iyāḍ said: 'Wiping off sins means forgiving people their sins. Or it may mean that they are wiped off the records of the angels charged with recording people's deeds. This serves as evidence that they have been forgiven. Raising the grades means giving people higher and better positions in Heaven. Doing the ablution "full well" means perfecting it, and the difficulty may be because of the weather or the water is too cold or when one is in pain. Walking longer to mosques is due to one's home being far, or due to repeated walks to the mosque. *Qāḍī* Abū al-Walīd al-Bājī said that waiting for one prayer after another refers to two prayers that are close to each other in their due time. As for other prayers, waiting was not the normal action. The Prophet said "That is equal to standing guard". This refers to what is encouraged as standing guard. The Arabic word used here is *ribāṭ*, which linguistically means dedicating oneself to a particular thing. Thus, it is comparable to standing guard as one is waiting for the next prayer. It may also refer to whatever is available or feasible of waiting, meaning that it is a kind of standing guard'.

All this is fine except what al-Bājī said about waiting for prayer, which is questionable, but God knows best.

In the second hadith 'That is equal to standing guard' occurs twice, and in Mālik's *al-Muwaṭṭa'* it is repeated three times. The reason for the repetition is to highlight its importance. It is also said that the Prophet repeated it so that it would be better understood. It was his habit to repeat what he said, but the first view is more likely, and God knows best.

CHAPTER 15

CLEANING TEETH

[445–42]. (Dār al-Salām 0487) Qutaybah ibn Saʿīd, ʿAmr al-Nāqid and Zuhayr ibn Ḥarb narrated:[i] Sufyān narrated; from Abū al-Zinād; from al-Aʿraj; from Abū Hurayrah; from the Prophet (peace be upon him). He said: **'Were it not that I may be setting the believers—in Zuhayr's narration "setting my community"—a task that is too hard, I would have commanded them to brush their teeth at the time of every prayer'**.

حَدَّثَنَا قُتَيْبَةُ بْنُ سَعِيدٍ، وَعَمْرٌو النَّاقِدُ، وَزُهَيْرُ بْنُ حَرْبٍ، قَالُوا: حَدَّثَنَا سُفْيَانُ، عَنْ أَبِي الزِّنَادِ، عَنِ الْأَعْرَجِ، عَنْ أَبِي هُرَيْرَةَ، عَنِ النَّبِيِّ صَلَّى اللهُ عَلَيْهِ وَسَلَّمَ قَالَ: «لَوْلَا أَنْ أَشُقَّ عَلَى الْمُؤْمِنِينَ - وَفِي حَدِيثِ زُهَيْرٍ عَلَى أُمَّتِي - لَأَمَرْتُهُمْ بِالسِّوَاكِ عِنْدَ كُلِّ صَلَاةٍ»

[446–43]. (Dār al-Salām 0488) Abū Kurayb Muhammad ibn al-ʿAlāʾ narrated:[ii] Ibn Bishr narrated; from Misʿar; from al-Miqdām ibn Shurayḥ; from his father: **'I asked ʿĀʾishah: "What was the first thing the Prophet did when he entered his home?" She said: "Brush his teeth"**.'

حَدَّثَنَا أَبُو كُرَيْبٍ مُحَمَّدُ بْنُ الْعَلَاءِ، حَدَّثَنَا ابْنُ بِشْرٍ، عَنْ مِسْعَرٍ، عَنِ الْمِقْدَامِ بْنِ شُرَيْحٍ، عَنْ أَبِيهِ، قَالَ: سَأَلْتُ عَائِشَةَ، قُلْتُ: بِأَيِّ شَيْءٍ كَانَ يَبْدَأُ النَّبِيُّ صَلَّى اللهُ عَلَيْهِ وَسَلَّمَ إِذَا دَخَلَ بَيْتَهُ؟ قَالَتْ: «بِالسِّوَاكِ»

---

i. Related by Abū Dāwūd, 46; al-Nasāʾī, 533; Ibn Mājah, 690.

ii. Related by Abū Dāwūd, 51; al-Nasāʾī, 8; Ibn Mājah, 290.

[447–44]. (Dār al-Salām 0489) Abū Bakr ibn Nāfiʿ al-ʿAbdī narrated to me: ʿAbd al-Raḥmān narrated; from Sufyān; from al-Miqdām ibn Shurayḥ; from his father; from ʿĀʾishah: **'When the Prophet entered his home, the first thing he did was to brush his teeth'**.

وَحَدَّثَنِي أَبُو بَكْرِ بْنُ نَافِعٍ الْعَبْدِيُّ، حَدَّثَنَا عَبْدُ الرَّحْمَنِ، عَنْ سُفْيَانَ، عَنِ الْمِقْدَامِ بْنِ شُرَيْحٍ، عَنْ أَبِيهِ، عَنْ عَائِشَةَ أَنَّ النَّبِيَّ صَلَّى اللهُ عَلَيْهِ وَسَلَّمَ: «كَانَ إِذَا دَخَلَ بَيْتَهُ بَدَأَ بِالسِّوَاكِ»

[448–45]. (Dār al-Salām 0490) Yaḥyā ibn Ḥabīb al-Ḥārithī narrated: Ḥammād ibn Zayd narrated; from Ghaylān (who is Ibn Jarīr al-Maʿwalī); from Abū Burdah; from Abū Mūsā: **'I entered the Prophet's home and [I saw] the end of his tooth stick [i.e. *miswāk*] on his tongue'**.

حَدَّثَنَا يَحْيَى بْنُ حَبِيبٍ الْحَارِثِيُّ، حَدَّثَنَا حَمَّادُ بْنُ زَيْدٍ، عَنْ غَيْلَانَ وَهُوَ ابْنُ جَرِيرٍ الْمَعْوَلِيُّ، عَنْ أَبِي بُرْدَةَ، عَنْ أَبِي مُوسَى، قَالَ: «دَخَلْتُ عَلَى النَّبِيِّ صَلَّى اللهُ عَلَيْهِ وَسَلَّمَ وَطَرَفُ السِّوَاكِ عَلَى لِسَانِهِ»

[449–46]. (Dār al-Salām 0491) Abū Bakr ibn Abī Shaybah narrated:[i] Hushaym narrated; from Ḥuṣayn; from Abū Wāʾil; from Ḥudhayfah: **'When God's Messenger (peace be upon him) woke up for his night worship, he would have a quick brush of his teeth'**.

حَدَّثَنَا أَبُو بَكْرِ بْنُ أَبِي شَيْبَةَ، حَدَّثَنَا هُشَيْمٌ، عَنْ حُصَيْنٍ، عَنْ أَبِي وَائِلٍ، عَنْ حُذَيْفَةَ، قَالَ: «كَانَ رَسُولُ اللهِ صَلَّى اللهُ عَلَيْهِ وَسَلَّمَ إِذَا قَامَ لِيَتَهَجَّدَ يَشُوصُ فَاهُ بِالسِّوَاكِ»

---

i. Related by al-Bukhārī, 245, 889 and 1136; Abū Dāwūd, 55; al-Nasāʾī, 2, 1620, 1621, 1622 and 1623; Ibn Mājah, 286.

[450–000]. (Dār al-Salām 0492) Isḥāq ibn Ibrāhīm narrated: Jarīr reported; from Manṣūr [H]. Also, Ibn Numayr narrated; my father and Abū Muʿāwiyah narrated; from al-Aʿmash; both from Abū Wā'il; from Ḥudhayfah: **'When God's Messenger woke up at night ... the same text, but they did not say "for worship".'**

حَدَّثَنَا إِسْحَاقُ بْنُ إِبْرَاهِيمَ، أَخْبَرَنَا جَرِيرٌ، عَنْ مَنْصُورٍ ح، وَحَدَّثَنَا ابْنُ نُمَيْرٍ، حَدَّثَنَا أَبِي، وَأَبُو مُعَاوِيَةَ، عَنِ الْأَعْمَشِ، كِلَاهُمَا عَنْ أَبِي وَائِلٍ، عَنْ حُذَيْفَةَ قَالَ: كَانَ رَسُولُ اللهِ صَلَّى اللهُ عَلَيْهِ وَسَلَّمَ «إِذَا قَامَ مِنَ اللَّيْلِ» بِمِثْلِهِ وَلَمْ يَقُولُوا لِيَتَهَجَّدَ.

[451–47]. (Dār al-Salām 0493) Muhammad ibn al-Muthannā and Ibn Bashshār narrated: ʿAbd al-Raḥmān narrated; Sufyān narrated; from Manṣūr; and Ḥuṣayn and al-Aʿmash from Abū Wā'il; from Ḥudhayfah: **'When God's Messenger (peace be upon him) woke up at night, he would have a quick brush of his mouth with his tooth stick'**.

حَدَّثَنَا مُحَمَّدُ بْنُ الْمُثَنَّى، وَابْنُ بَشَّارٍ، قَالَا: حَدَّثَنَا عَبْدُ الرَّحْمَنِ، حَدَّثَنَا سُفْيَانُ، عَنْ مَنْصُورٍ، وَحُصَيْنٌ، وَالْأَعْمَشُ، عَنْ أَبِي وَائِلٍ، عَنْ حُذَيْفَةَ: «أَنَّ رَسُولَ اللهِ صَلَّى اللهُ عَلَيْهِ وَسَلَّمَ كَانَ إِذَا قَامَ مِنَ اللَّيْلِ يَشُوصُ فَاهُ بِالسِّوَاكِ»

[452–48]. (Dār al-Salām 0494) ʿAbd ibn Ḥumayd narrated: Abū Nuʿaym narrated; Ismāʿīl ibn Muslim narrated; Abū al-Mutawakkil narrated; that Ibn ʿAbbās narrated to him that: **'One night I stayed in the Prophet's home. The Prophet woke up towards the end of the night. He went out, looking at the sky, and then recited these verses from Surah 3: "*In the creation of the heavens and the earth, and in the succession of night and day, there are indeed signs for men endowed with insight, who remember God when they stand, sit and lie down, and reflect on the creation of the heavens and the earth: Our Lord, You have not created all this in vain. Limitless are You***

***in Your glory. Guard us, then, against the torment of the Fire".* (3: 190–191) He came back to the house, brushed his teeth and performed the ablution, then stood up and prayed. He then lay down, woke up, went out, looked at the sky, recited the same verses, and returned, brushed his teeth, performed the ablution then stood up and prayed'.**

حَدَّثَنَا عَبْدُ بْنُ حُمَيْدٍ، حَدَّثَنَا أَبُو نُعَيْمٍ، حَدَّثَنَا إِسْمَاعِيلُ بْنُ مُسْلِمٍ، حَدَّثَنَا أَبُو الْمُتَوَكِّلِ، أَنَّ ابْنَ عَبَّاسٍ حَدَّثَهُ أَنَّهُ بَاتَ عِنْدَ النَّبِيِّ صَلَّى اللهُ عَلَيْهِ وَسَلَّمَ ذَاتَ لَيْلَةٍ « فَقَامَ نَبِيُّ اللهِ صَلَّى اللهُ عَلَيْهِ وَسَلَّمَ مِنْ آخِرِ اللَّيْلِ، فَخَرَجَ فَنَظَرَ فِي السَّمَاءِ، ثُمَّ تَلَا هَذِهِ الْآيَةَ فِي آلِ عِمْرَانَ «إِنَّ فِي خَلْقِ السَّمَاوَاتِ وَالْأَرْضِ وَاخْتِلَافِ اللَّيْلِ وَالنَّهَارِ» حَتَّى بَلَغَ «فَقِنَا عَذَابَ النَّارِ» [آل عمران: ١٩٠-١٩١] ثُمَّ رَجَعَ إِلَى الْبَيْتِ فَتَسَوَّكَ وَتَوَضَّأَ، ثُمَّ قَامَ فَصَلَّى ثُمَّ اضْطَجَعَ ثُمَّ قَامَ، فَخَرَجَ فَنَظَرَ إِلَى السَّمَاءِ فَتَلَا هَذِهِ الْآيَةَ، ثُمَّ رَجَعَ فَتَسَوَّكَ فَتَوَضَّأَ، ثُمَّ قَامَ فَصَلَّى.

Text Explanation

Note: The Arabs used to clean their teeth with a *miswāk* or *siwāk*. The two words mean the same thing, but the second also refers to the action of using a *miswāk* to clean one's teeth. Both words refer to a small stick that is taken from the thin branches of a desert tree with a gentle refreshing smell called an *arāk*. The stick could be of any length, and if it is cut into small pieces, each piece is suitable for the purpose. The bark of the top part of the piece is peeled off, revealing numerous threads, just like a toothbrush. If it is regularly used and washed, it may last for a long time. The *miswāk* is referred to as a 'tooth stick', and a toothbrush is equally adequate.

Imam al-Nawawī wrote: The cleaning of one's teeth is a recommended practice, i.e. Sunnah, and it is not obligatory at any time of prayer or other times. This is unanimously agreed upon by scholars who are worth considering for the purpose of unanimity. Imam Abū Ḥāmid Ahmad al-Isfarāyīnī, the leading Shāfiʿī scholar in Iraq, reports that Dāwūd al-Ẓahirī considered it a duty before prayer. Also, al-Māwardī mentions that Dāwūd considered it a duty, but if one omits doing it, one's prayer remains valid. It is also reported that Isḥāq ibn Rāhawayh said that it is a duty and that a deliberate omission of it makes a prayer invalid. Our later Shāfiʿī scholars disagree with Imam al-Isfarāyīnī's report of Dāwūd's and other scholars' view, stating that Dāwūd agreed with the unanimous view that the use of a *siwāk* is recommended. If it is true that Dāwūd considered it a duty, his disagreement with the other scholars does not detract from the validity of their unanimity. As for Isḥāq, the report of his disagreement is not authentic, but God knows best.

The use of a tooth stick, or toothbrush, is desirable at all times, but even more so at five particular times: 1) just before prayer, whether one has performed water ablution or a dry ablution or even without any ablution, as in the case of one who cannot find water or dust; 2) during ablution; 3) just before starting to recite from the Qur'an; 4) when one wakes up; and 5) when one's mouth starts to give off a smell as a result of not having had food or drink for a long while, or as a result of eating something that gives a bad smell, or remaining silent or speaking for a long time. Al-Shāfiʿī's view is that a fasting person is discouraged from using a tooth stick after midday, so that he does not remove the smell of fasting, which is desirable to retain.

It is desirable to clean one's teeth with a tooth stick taken from an *arāk* tree, but the use of anything that removes the mouth smell is adequate. Using one's soft finger is unacceptable, but if the finger is rough, then three views are expressed: 1) it is adequate; 2) it is inadequate; and 3) it is adequate if nothing better is available but not adequate otherwise. It is also recommended to choose a suitable tooth stick that is neither too hard so as to cause a cut nor too soft that leaves no good effect. One should also move the tooth stick horizontally, so as not to cut one's gum. However, using it vertically is acceptable. Moreover, one should gently clean the edges of one's teeth, molars and palate, starting generally with the right side.[i]

i. Al-Nawawī mentions here what was desirable according to the common knowledge during his time. Certain things have now been established to be preferable and it is appropriate to conform to these, unless there is a specific authentic text suggesting something different.

The Prophet says: 'Were it not that I may be setting the believers, or my community, a task that is too hard, I would have commanded them to brush their teeth at the time of every prayer'. This statement serves as evidence confirming that brushing one's teeth is not obligatory. Al-Shāfiʿī said: 'Had it been obligatory, the Prophet would have issued an order to this effect, whether the task would be hard or not'.

Many scholars say that this hadith indicates that an order constitutes obligation. This is the view of most *fiqh* and legal theory [i.e. *uṣūl al-fiqh*] scholars as well as scholars of theology. They say that the use of a tooth stick is generally agreed to be recommended. Therefore, what is left out makes it obligatory. Yet, to arrive perfectly at this conclusion requires evidence that the use of a tooth stick was recommended at the time the Prophet mentioned this hadith. Other scholars said that this hadith also indicates that what is recommended is not subject to an order, but this is also debatable according to scholars of legal theory. Furthermore, what we said earlier about the obligation also applies in this case, but God knows best. The hadith also indicates that the Prophet may use his own discretion where no specific instruction is given by God. This is the view of most scholars of *fiqh* and legal theory, and it is the correct view. Furthermore, the hadith shows how the Prophet was always caring for his community, eager to show them what was good and easy for them. It furthermore shows the desirability of using the tooth stick, or toothbrush, before every prayer. We have already explained the times when it is desirable.

Hadith No. 447 mentions that when the Prophet entered his own home, he started with brushing his teeth. This indicates the desirability of using the tooth stick or toothbrush at all times. The Prophet was keen to use it repeatedly and at all times, but God knows best.

Hadith No. 449 mentions that the Prophet used to have a quick brush of his teeth when he woke up. The hadith uses the word *yashūṣ* to describe the Prophet's action. This is an unfamiliar word to which scholars attach different meanings. It means rubbing the teeth horizontally, according to Ibn al-Aʿrābi, Ibrāhīm al-Ḥarbī, al-Khaṭṭābī and others, while al-Harawī and others say that it means washing.

According to Abū 'Ubayd and al-Dāwūdī, it means cleansing, and Ibn ʿAbd al-Barr says it means rubbing. All these interpretations are not widely different, but the first is perhaps more correct, but God knows best.

The last hadith is given here in a shorter version, while its longer version occurs in the Book of Prayer. It includes some very useful and interesting points. We shall discuss it at length later, God willing. However, we may point out here that it is recommended to recite the two verses mentioned in the hadith when one wakes up at night and to look at the sky, as this enables one to contemplate the meanings of these verses. If someone wakes up more than once and goes out, it is recommended that he recite these verses anew, but God knows best.

Transmission

The chain of transmission of hadith No. 448 features: 'Yaḥyā ibn Ḥabīb al-Ḥārithī narrated: Ḥammād ibn Zayd narrated; from Ghaylān (who is Ibn Jarīr al-Maʿwalī); from Abū Burdah; from Abū Mūsā'. All the narrators in this chain, apart from Abū Burdah, belonged to Basrah. Abū Burdah, whose name is ʿĀmir, or al-Ḥārith according to some scholars, was from Kufah, while Abū Mūsā is considered to be from both Kufah and Basrah.

Abū al-Mutawakkil, who features in the chain of the last hadith, is called ʿAlī ibn Dāwūd, and he may be defined as al-Baṣrī.

CHAPTER 16

PRACTICES OF SOUND HUMAN NATURE

[453–49]. (Dār al-Salām 0495) Abū Bakr ibn Abī Shaybah, ʿAmr al-Nāqid and Zuhayr ibn Ḥarb narrated:[i] all from Sufyān. Abū Bakr said: Ibn ʿUyaynah narrated; from al-Zuhrī; from Saʿīd ibn al-Musayyib; from Abū Hurayrah; from the Prophet (peace be upon him): **'Sound human nature includes five (or five practices are aspects of sound human nature): circumcision, shaving pubic hair, clipping one's nails, plucking armpit hair and trimming one's moustache'**.

حَدَّثَنَا أَبُو بَكْرِ بْنُ أَبِي شَيْبَةَ، وَعَمْرٌو النَّاقِدُ، وَزُهَيْرُ بْنُ حَرْبٍ، جَمِيعًا عَنْ سُفْيَانَ، قَالَ أَبُو بَكْرٍ: حَدَّثَنَا ابْنُ عُيَيْنَةَ، عَنِ الزُّهْرِيِّ، عَنْ سَعِيدِ بْنِ الْمُسَيَّبِ، عَنْ أَبِي هُرَيْرَةَ، عَنِ النَّبِيِّ صَلَّى اللهُ عَلَيْهِ وَسَلَّمَ قَالَ: «الْفِطْرَةُ خَمْسٌ - أَوْ خَمْسٌ مِنَ الْفِطْرَةِ - الْخِتَانُ، وَالِاسْتِحْدَادُ، وَتَقْلِيمُ الْأَظْفَارِ، وَنَتْفُ الْإِبِطِ، وَقَصُّ الشَّارِبِ»

[454–50]. (Dār al-Salām 0496) Abū al-Ṭāhir and Ḥarmalah ibn Yaḥyā narrated to me:[ii] Ibn Wahb reported; Yūnus reported to me; from Ibn Shihāb; from Saʿīd ibn al-Musayyib; from Abū Hurayrah; from God's Messenger (peace be upon him): **'Sound human nature includes five [practices]: circumcision,**

---

i. Related by al-Bukhārī, 5889, 5891 and 6297; Abū Dāwūd, 4198; al-Nasāʾī, 11; Ibn Mājah, 292.

ii. Related by al-Nasāʾī, 9.

shaving pubic hair, trimming one's moustache, clipping one's nails and plucking armpit hair'.

حَدَّثَنِي أَبُو الطَّاهِرِ، وَحَرْمَلَةُ بْنُ يَحْيَى، قَالَا: أَخْبَرَنَا ابْنُ وَهْبٍ، أَخْبَرَنِي يُونُسُ، عَنِ ابْنِ شِهَابٍ، عَنْ سَعِيدِ بْنِ الْمُسَيِّبِ، عَنْ أَبِي هُرَيْرَةَ، عَنْ رَسُولِ اللهِ صَلَّى اللهُ عَلَيْهِ وَسَلَّمَ أَنَّهُ قَالَ: «الْفِطْرَةُ خَمْسٌ الِاخْتِتَانُ، وَالِاسْتِحْدَادُ، وَقَصُّ الشَّارِبِ، وَتَقْلِيمُ الْأَظْفَارِ، وَنَتْفُ الْإِبِطِ»

[455–51]. (Dār al-Salām 0497) Yaḥyā ibn Yaḥyā and Qutaybah ibn Saʿīd narrated:[i] both from Jaʿfar, Yaḥyā said: Jaʿfar ibn Sulaymān reported; from Abū ʿImrān al-Jawnī; from Anas ibn Mālik. Anas said: **'We have been instructed not to exceed forty nights in attending to trimming moustaches, clipping nails, plucking armpit hair and shaving pubic hair'**.

حَدَّثَنَا يَحْيَى بْنُ يَحْيَى، وَقُتَيْبَةُ بْنُ سَعِيدٍ، كِلَاهُمَا عَنْ جَعْفَرٍ، قَالَ: يَحْيَى، أَخْبَرَنَا جَعْفَرُ بْنُ سُلَيْمَانَ، عَنْ أَبِي عِمْرَانَ الْجَوْنِيِّ، عَنْ أَنَسِ بْنِ مَالِكٍ، قَالَ: - قَالَ أَنَسٌ - «وُقِّتَ لَنَا فِي قَصِّ الشَّارِبِ، وَتَقْلِيمِ الْأَظْفَارِ، وَنَتْفِ الْإِبِطِ، وَحَلْقِ الْعَانَةِ، أَنْ لَا نَتْرُكَ أَكْثَرَ مِنْ أَرْبَعِينَ لَيْلَةً»

[456–52]. (Dār al-Salām 0498) Muhammad ibn al-Muthannā narrated:[ii] Yaḥyā (meaning Ibn Saʿīd) narrated [H]. Also, Ibn Numayr narrated; my father narrated; all from ʿUbaydillāh; from Nāfiʿ; from Ibn ʿUmar; from the Prophet: **'Trim the moustache but leave the beard'**.

---

i. Related by Abū Dāwūd, 4200; al-Tirmidhī, 2758 and 2759; al-Nasāʾī, 14; Ibn Mājah, 295.

ii. Related by al-Nasāʾī, 15 and 5241.

حَدَّثَنَا مُحَمَّدُ بْنُ الْـمُثَنَّى، حَدَّثَنَا يَحْيَى يَعْنِي ابْنَ سَعِيدٍ ح، وَحَدَّثَنَا ابْنَ نُمَيْرٍ، حَدَّثَنَا أَبِي، جَمِيعًا عَنْ عُبَيْدِ اللهِ، عَنْ نَافِعٍ، عَنِ ابْنِ عُمَرَ، عَنِ النَّبِيِّ صَلَّى اللهُ عَلَيْهِ وَسَلَّمَ قَالَ: «أَحْفُوا الشَّوَارِبَ وَأَعْفُوا اللِّحَى»

[457–53]. (Dār al-Salām 0499) Qutaybah ibn Saʿīd narrated:[i] from Mālik ibn Anas; from Abū Bakr ibn Nāfiʿ; from his father; from Ibn ʿUmar; from the Prophet (peace be upon him): **'He ordered that moustaches should be trimmed and beards be left'**.

وَحَدَّثَنَاهُ قُتَيْبَةُ بْنُ سَعِيدٍ، عَنْ مَالِكِ بْنِ أَنَسٍ، عَنْ أَبِي بَكْرِ بْنِ نَافِعٍ، عَنْ أَبِيهِ، عَنِ ابْنِ عُمَرَ عَنِ النَّبِيِّ صَلَّى اللهُ عَلَيْهِ وَسَلَّمَ أَنَّهُ: «أَمَرَ بِإِحْفَاءِ الشَّوَارِبِ، وَإِعْفَاءِ اللِّحْيَةِ»

[458–54]. (Dār al-Salām 0500) Sahl ibn ʿUthmān narrated:[ii] Yazīd ibn Zurayʿ narrated; from ʿUmar ibn Muhammad; Nāfiʿ narrated; from Ibn ʿUmar: **'God's Messenger (peace be upon him) said: "Do the opposite of the idolaters: trim moustaches and leave beards"**.'

حَدَّثَنَا سَهْلُ بْنُ عُثْمَانَ، حَدَّثَنَا يَزِيدُ بْنُ زُرَيْعٍ، عَنْ عُمَرَ بْنِ مُحَمَّدٍ، حَدَّثَنَا نَافِعٌ، عَنِ ابْنِ عُمَرَ، قَالَ: قَالَ رَسُولُ اللهِ صَلَّى اللهُ عَلَيْهِ وَسَلَّمَ: «خَالِفُوا الْـمُشْرِكِينَ أَحْفُوا الشَّوَارِبَ، وَأَوْفُوا اللِّحَى»

[459–55]. (Dār al-Salām 0501) Abū Bakr ibn Isḥāq narrated to me: Ibn Abī Maryam reported; Muhammad ibn Jaʿfar reported; al-ʿAlā' ibn ʿAbd al-Raḥmān ibn Yaʿqūb, al-Ḥuraqah's *mawlā*, reported to me; from his father; from Abū Hurayrah: **'God's**

i. Related by Abū Dāwūd, 4199; al-Nasā'ī, 2764.

ii. Related by al-Bukhārī, 5892.

Messenger (peace be upon him) said: "Cut [your] moustaches and leave beards: do the opposite of the Mageans".'

حَدَّثَنِي أَبُو بَكْرِ بْنُ إِسْحَاقَ، أَخْبَرَنَا ابْنُ أَبِي مَرْيَمَ، أَخْبَرَنَا مُحَمَّدُ بْنُ جَعْفَرٍ، أَخْبَرَنِي الْعَلَاءُ بْنُ عَبْدِ الرَّحْمَنِ بْنِ يَعْقُوبَ، مَوْلَى الْحُرَقَةِ، عَنْ أَبِيهِ، عَنْ أَبِي هُرَيْرَةَ، قَالَ: قَالَ رَسُولُ اللهِ صَلَّى اللهُ عَلَيْهِ وَسَلَّمَ: «جُزُّوا الشَّوَارِبَ، وَأَرْخُوا اللِّحَى خَالِفُوا الْـمَجُوسَ»

[460–56]. (Dār al-Salām 0502) Qutaybah ibn Sa'īd, Abū Bakr ibn Abī Shaybah and Zuhayr ibn Ḥarb narrated: Wakī' narrated; from Zakariyyā' ibn Abī Zā'idah; from Muṣ'ab ibn Shaybah; from Ṭalq ibn Ḥabīb; from 'Abdullāh ibn al-Zubayr; from 'Ā'ishah: **'God's Messenger (peace be upon him) said: "Ten practices are [aspects of] sound human nature: trimming one's moustache, leaving one's beard, brushing teeth, inhaling water, clipping nails, washing finger joints, plucking armpit hair, shaving pubic hair and reducing water".'**

Zakariyyā' said: **Muṣ'ab said: 'I have forgotten the tenth, but perhaps it is rinsing one's mouth'. Qutaybah adds: Wakī' said: 'Reducing water means washing one's private parts'.**

حَدَّثَنَا قُتَيْبَةُ بْنُ سَعِيدٍ، وَأَبُو بَكْرِ بْنُ أَبِي شَيْبَةَ، وَزُهَيْرُ بْنُ حَرْبٍ، قَالُوا: حَدَّثَنَا وَكِيعٌ، عَنْ زَكَرِيَّا بْنِ أَبِي زَائِدَةَ، عَنْ مُصْعَبِ بْنِ شَيْبَةَ، عَنْ طَلْقِ بْنِ حَبِيبٍ، عَنْ عَبْدِ اللهِ بْنِ الزُّبَيْرِ، عَنْ عَائِشَةَ، قَالَتْ: قَالَ رَسُولُ اللهِ صَلَّى اللهُ عَلَيْهِ وَسَلَّمَ: «عَشْرٌ مِنَ الْفِطْرَةِ: قَصُّ الشَّارِبِ، وَإِعْفَاءُ اللِّحْيَةِ، وَالسِّوَاكُ، وَاسْتِنْشَاقُ الْـمَاءِ، وَقَصُّ الْأَظْفَارِ، وَغَسْلُ الْبَرَاجِمِ، وَنَتْفُ الْإِبِطِ، وَحَلْقُ الْعَانَةِ، وَانْتِقَاصُ الْـمَاءِ»

قَالَ زَكَرِيَّا: قَالَ مُصْعَبٌ: وَنَسِيتُ الْعَاشِرَةَ إِلَّا أَنْ تَكُونَ الْـمَضْمَضَةَ. زَادَ قُتَيْبَةُ، قَالَ وَكِيعٌ: « انْتِقَاصُ الْـمَاءِ: يَعْنِي الِاسْتِنْجَاءَ»

[000–000]. (Dār al-Salām 0503) Abū Kurayb reported: Ibn Abī Zā'idah reported; from his father; from Mus'ab ibn Shaybah; with the same chain of transmission: **the same text. However, he said that his father said: 'I forgot the tenth'**.

وَحَدَّثَنَاهُ أَبُو كُرَيْبٍ، أَخْبَرَنَا ابْنُ أَبِي زَائِدَةَ، عَنْ أَبِيهِ، عَنْ مُصْعَبِ بْنِ شَيْبَةَ، فِي هَذَا الْإِسْنَادِ مِثْلَهُ. غَيْرَ أَنَّهُ قَالَ: قَالَ أَبُوهُ وَنَسِيتُ الْعَاشِرَةَ.

Text Explanation

The first version starts with, 'Sound human nature includes five (or five practices are aspects of sound human nature)'. This reflects a doubt by the narrator as to the exact wording. The second version has no such doubt. It states the first wording, 'sound human nature includes five practices'. The hadith then states the five practices: 'circumcision, shaving pubic hair, clipping one's nails, plucking armpit hair and trimming one's moustache'. In the last hadith, ten practices are stated to be aspects of sound human nature: 'trimming one's moustache, leaving one's beard, brushing teeth, inhaling water, clipping nails, washing finger joints, plucking armpit hair, shaving pubic hair and reducing water. Muṣ'ab said: 'I have forgotten the tenth, but perhaps it is rinsing one's mouth'. These hadiths state certain practices as belonging to sound human nature, but they make clear that sound nature is not limited to these five or ten hygiene functions. In this hadith, the Prophet uses the word *fiṭrah*, which is translated as 'sound human nature'. Al-Nawawī mentions that scholars express different views as to what this word refers to in this context. Abu Sulaymān Ḥamad ibn Muhammad al-Khaṭṭābī says that most scholars are of the view that it means the Sunnah. Other scholars agree, saying that it means the way chosen by all prophets (peace be upon them all). It is also stated to mean 'religion'.

Most of these practices are not obligatory, according to scholars. They differ concerning some practices, such as circumcision, rinsing one's mouth and inhaling water. It is perfectly acceptable that an obligatory duty is joined with a practice of a different status. God says in the Qur'an: *'Eat of their fruit when they come to fruition, and give (to the poor) what is due to them on harvest day'*. (6: 141) Giving the poor their due is obligatory, but eating of the fruit is not, but God knows best. We will now discuss these practices in detail.

Circumcision is a duty, according to al-Shāfiʿī and a large number of scholars, but it is recommended, i.e. Sunnah, according to Mālik and the majority of scholars. Al-Shāfiʿī makes it a duty, however, the correct view of our Shāfiʿī school of *fiqh*, which is shared by the great majority of our scholars, is that circumcision is permissible, not a duty, in childhood. My view is that the child's guardian has a duty to have a boy circumcised before he attains puberty. Another view is that it is forbidden to circumcise a child before he is ten years of age. If we take the authentic hadiths, it is desirable to circumcise a boy on the seventh day of his birth. There are two contending views about whether the day when the child is born should be the first of the seven days, or whether they are seven days after the day of birth. The preferable view is that the day of birth is the first of the seven. Our scholars differ with regard to the circumcision of a child whose sex is problematic.[i] A child born with both types of sexual organs should be circumcised in both, but the more correct view is that the child should be circumcised only when its sex is ascertained. If a child is born with two penises, and both are active, then both should be circumcised, but if only one is active, then that is the one to be circumcised; it is known to be active either by urination or copulation when he is an adult. Our scholars express three views concerning a person who dies without being circumcised. The best-known, which is the correct view, is that he should not be circumcised, whether he be a young boy or an adult male. The second view is that an adult is circumcised, but not a young boy, but God knows best.

Shaving pubic hair means removing the hair that is on and around a man's penis or around a woman's vagina. It is reported that Abū al-ʿAbbās ibn Surayj said that it includes the hair that may be around

---

i. This is an example of the theoretical exercises *fiqh* scholars discuss so as to cover even unrealistic situations.

the anus. Thus, together these views make it desirable to remove all the hair around and on the genitals. The timing depends on the need when the hair becomes long. The same applies to trimming one's moustache, plucking armpit hair and clipping nails. The hadith narrated by Anas mentioned in this chapter states: 'We have been instructed not to exceed forty nights in attending to trimming moustaches, clipping nails, plucking armpit hair and shaving pubic hair'. This does not mean that these actions should be done every forty days, as some people suggest; rather, they should not be left for forty days without attending to them, but God knows best.

Clipping one's nails is a recommended practice, not a duty. It is recommended to start with one's hands, before one's feet. It is preferable to start with the forefinger of one's right hand, then the middle finger, then the one next to it, then the little finger, then the right thumb. Then one clips the nails of the left hand, starting with the little finger and finishing with the thumb. Then one moves to clip the nails on one's toes, starting with the little toe of the right foot, and finishing with the little toe of the left foot.

Plucking armpit hair is agreed to be a Sunnah, i.e. recommended. It is preferable to pluck it out, if one is able to do so. However, it may be shaved or removed with a hair remover. Yūnus ibn ʿAbd al-Aʿlā is quoted as saying: 'I visited al-Shāfiʿī and I found the barber with him, shaving his armpit hair. Al-Shāfiʿī said: "I know that the Sunnah is to pluck it, but I cannot tolerate the pain".' It is also recommended to start with the right side.

Trimming one's moustache is also a Sunnah, and it is also desirable that one starts with the right side. One may choose to do it oneself or let someone else do it, because this can be done without any embarrassment or prohibition, unlike shaving one's pubic hair. How far back should the moustache be trimmed? The answer is that it is enough to reveal the edge of one's upper lip. It need not be shaved altogether. The narrations that require trimming the moustache mean cutting what extends lower than the lip, but God knows best.

Leaving the beard means to let it grow. The Persians used to cut or shave their beards and Islam ordered not to do like them. Scholars mention ten ugly practices regarding beards, but some of these are uglier than others: (1) dying one's beard black for a reason other than jihad; (2) dying it with a yellow colour in imitation of devout people, not as a Sunnah; (3) giving it a white colour to pretend that one is of an age that gives one a position of respectability; (4) plucking or shaving it when it starts to appear, to give oneself a younger appearance; (5) plucking grey hair; (6) arranging it in one layer over another so as to win women's admiration; (7) increasing it with long whiskers or decreasing it by shaving part of one's whiskers along with one's head and similar action; (8) excessive combing of one's beard for people's sake; (9) leaving it uncombed and dishevelled to give an impression of carelessness about worldly comfort; and (10) examining its black hairs in admiration of one's youth and vigour or its grey hairs taking pride in one's age. Al-Nawawī adds two more practices: (11) arranging it in plaits; and (12) shaving it, unless a woman finds herself growing a beard. In this case it is desirable for the woman to shave it, but God knows best.

We have already discussed inhaling water and the different views on whether it is obligatory or desirable.

Washing finger joints is a separate Sunnah which is not related to ablution. Scholars say that they should be washed to remove any dirt that may gather in skin folds. Likewise, it is desirable to wipe off any dirt that may gather on one's ears or in one's nose or on any part of one's body because of perspiration or dust or anything else, but God knows best.

Reducing water is interpreted by Wakīʿ as meaning washing one's private parts. Abū ʿUbaydah and others say that it means removing the traces of urine by using water to wash one's genital organ. A different version of this hadith uses a word that means sprinkling water over the area of one's private parts so as to remove any doubts about removing impurities. There are other views on the meaning of this expression, but what we have stated is the correct view, but God knows best.

The narrator says that he forgot the tenth practice, but it may be rinsing one's mouth. This expresses a doubt by the narrator. *Qāḍī* ʿIyāḍ suggests that it may be circumcision, which is mentioned in the first hadith that specifies five practices.

This is the sum explanation of the practices of sound human nature. I have explained them in greater detail, citing the evidence supporting each, in *Sharḥ al-Muhadhdhab*, but God knows best.

Hadith No. 455 quotes Anas ibn Mālik: 'We have been instructed ...'. Scholars agree that hadiths using such formulae are attributed directly to the Prophet himself. Instructions concerning religious matters could not come from another source. The hadith is entered in other authentic anthologies: 'God's Messenger (peace be upon him) instructed us ...'.

The hadiths use different words concerning beards, but all these have the same meaning, which is to grow one's beard. The apparent meaning of all these narrations is to leave the beard as it grows. This is agreed by many scholars, including a number of our Shafiʿī school.

Qāḍī ʿIyāḍ said:

> To shave, cut or burn one's beard is strongly discouraged, i.e. *makrūh*, but to trim its length or breadth is desirable. It is discouraged to use it as a means to gain status, either by making it too long or too short. Early scholars differ as to whether there is a limit to the length of the beard. Some of them did not mention any limit, but stated that it should not be left too long so as to attract people's attention. Mālik made clear that leaving the beard too long is discouraged. Other scholars say that it should not be longer than one's fist when one holds one's chin. Whatever extends lower than one's fist as one holds one's chin should be removed, except during the pilgrimage and the *ʿumrah*.
>
> As for the moustache, many early scholars were of the view that it should be shaved, as this is indicated by the apparent meaning of the Prophet's hadith: 'trim it hard'. This is the view of the Kufi scholars. Many other scholars objected to total shaving of one's moustache. Indeed, Imam Mālik considered this to be a type of disfigurement that deserved punishment. He also disliked that trimming should include the top of the moustache. Scholars of this view considered that all the words

used in the hadiths concerning the moustache have the same meaning, which is to trim it so that the edge of the upper lip is visible. Other scholars considered that the two options of trimming and shaving are equally good.

My own view is that the beard should be left without shortening, but the moustache should not be shaved. It should be trimmed, leaving the edge of the upper lip clearly visible, but God knows best.

Transmission

The chain of transmission of hadith No. 455 features: 'Ja'far ibn Sulaymān reported; from Abū 'Imrān al-Jawnī; from Anas'. *Qāḍī* 'Iyāḍ said: 'Al-'Uqaylī says that this hadith narrated by Ja'far is questionable. He adds that Ibn 'Abd al-Barr says that it is reported only by Ja'far ibn Sulaymān and he is not highly graded because of his poor memorization and frequent errors'. In reply I may say that many of the early scholars grade Ja'far ibn Sulaymān as reliable. It is sufficient that Muslim grades him as such, and many other scholars of Hadith follow his lead.

CHAPTER 17

CORRECT BEHAVIOUR IN THE TOILET

[461–57]. (Dār al-Salām 0504) Abū Bakr ibn Abī Shaybah narrated:[i] Abū Mu'āwiyah narrated and Wakī' narrated; from al-A'mash [H]. Also, Yaḥyā ibn Yaḥyā narrated (his text); Mu'āwiyah reported; from al-A'mash; from Ibrāhīm; from 'Abd al-Raḥmān ibn Yazīd; from Salmān: '**He was asked: "Your Prophet had taught you everything, even defecation?" He said: "Yes, he instructed us not to face the direction of prayer when urinating or defecating; not to clean ourselves with our right hands; not to use fewer than three stones; and not to clean ourselves with stools or bones".**'

حَدَّثَنَا أَبُو بَكْرِ بْنُ أَبِي شَيْبَةَ، حَدَّثَنَا أَبُو مُعَاوِيَةَ، وَوَكِيعٌ، عَنِ الْأَعْمَشِ ح، وحَدَّثَنَا يَحْيَى بْنُ يَحْيَى، - وَاللَّفْظُ لَهُ - أَخْبَرَنَا أَبُو مُعَاوِيَةَ، عَنِ الْأَعْمَشِ، عَنْ إِبْرَاهِيمَ، عَنْ عَبْدِ الرَّحْمَنِ بْنِ يَزِيدَ، عَنْ سَلْمَانَ، قَالَ: قِيلَ لَهُ: قَدْ عَلَّمَكُمْ نَبِيُّكُمْ صَلَّى اللهُ عَلَيْهِ وَسَلَّمَ كُلَّ شَيْءٍ حَتَّى الْخِرَاءَةَ قَالَ: فَقَالَ: أَجَلْ «لَقَدْ نَهَانَا أَنْ نَسْتَقْبِلَ الْقِبْلَةَ لِغَائِطٍ، أَوْ بَوْلٍ، أَوْ أَنْ نَسْتَنْجِيَ بِالْيَمِينِ، أَوْ أَنْ نَسْتَنْجِيَ بِأَقَلَّ مِنْ ثَلَاثَةِ أَحْجَارٍ، أَوْ أَنْ نَسْتَنْجِيَ بِرَجِيعٍ أَوْ بِعَظْمٍ»

[462–000]. (Dār al-Salām 0505) Muhammad ibn al-Muthannā narrated: 'Abd al-Raḥmān narrated; Sufyān narrated; from al-A'mash and Manṣūr; from Ibrāhīm; from 'Abd al-Raḥmān ibn

i. Related by Abū Dāwūd, 7 (in a longer version); al-Tirmidhī, 16; al-Nasā'ī, 41 and 49; Ibn Mājah, 316.

Yazīd; from Salmān who said: '**The unbelievers said to us: "I see your crony teaching you. He even teaches you defecation". I said: "Yes. He instructed us not to clean ourselves with our right hands; not to face the direction of prayer; and not to use stools or bones. He added: 'Let none of you clean yourself with fewer than three stones'"**.'

حَدَّثَنَا مُحَمَّدُ بْنُ الْـمُثَنَّى، حَدَّثَنَا عَبْدُ الرَّحْمَنِ، حَدَّثَنَا سُفْيَانُ، عَنِ الْأَعْمَشِ، وَمَنْصُورٍ، عَنْ إِبْرَاهِيمَ، عَنْ عَبْدِ الرَّحْمَنِ بْنِ يَزِيدَ، عَنْ سَلْمَانَ، قَالَ: قَالَ لَنَا الْـمُشْرِكُونَ إِنِّي أَرَى صَاحِبَكُمْ يُعَلِّمُكُمْ حَتَّى يُعَلِّمَكُمُ الْخِرَاءَةَ، فَقَالَ: أَجَلْ «إِنَّهُ نَهَانَا أَنْ يَسْتَنْجِيَ أَحَدُنَا بِيَمِينِهِ، أَوْ يَسْتَقْبِلَ الْقِبْلَةَ، وَنَهَى عَنِ الرَّوْثِ وَالْعِظَامِ» وَقَالَ: «لَا يَسْتَنْجِي أَحَدُكُمْ بِدُونِ ثَلَاثَةِ أَحْجَارٍ»

[463–58]. (Dār al-Salām 0506) Zuhayr ibn Ḥarb narrated:[i] Rawḥ ibn ʿUbādah narrated; Zakariyyā' ibn Isḥāq narrated; Abū al-Zubayr narrated; that he heard Jabir say: '**God's Messenger (peace be upon him) prohibited that anyone may rub off [his dirt] with a bone or animal droppings**'.

حَدَّثَنَا زُهَيْرُ بْنُ حَرْبٍ، حَدَّثَنَا رَوْحُ بْنُ عُبَادَةَ، حَدَّثَنَا زَكَرِيَّا بْنُ إِسْحَاقَ، حَدَّثَنَا أَبُو الزُّبَيْرِ، أَنَّهُ سَمِعَ جَابِرًا يَقُولُ: «نَهَى رَسُولُ اللهِ صَلَّى اللهُ عَلَيْهِ وَسَلَّمَ أَنْ يُتَمَسَّحَ بِعَظْمٍ، أَوْ بِبَعْرٍ»

[464–59]. (Dār al-Salām 0507) Zuhayr bin Ḥarb and Ibn Numayr narrated:[ii] Sufyān ibn ʿUyaynah narrated [H]. Also, Yaḥyā ibn Yaḥyā narrated (his text): 'I said to Sufyān ibn ʿUyaynah: Did

i. Related by Abū Dāwūd, 38.

ii. Related by al-Bukhārī, 144, and 394 in a longer version; Abū Dāwūd, 9 (in a longer version); al-Tirmidhī, 8 (in a longer version); al-Nasā'ī, 21 and 22; Ibn Mājah, 318 (in similar wording).

you hear al-Zuhrī mention to ʿAṭā' ibn Yazīd al-Laythī; from Abū Ayyūb; that the Prophet (peace be upon him) said: **"When you go to stools, do not face or turn your back to the direction of prayer, neither in urination nor defecation. Rather, turn eastwards or westwards"**.'

Abū Ayyūb said: 'When we came to Syria, we found toilets built facing the direction of prayer. We turn away from that direction and pray for forgiveness'. He said: 'Yes'.

وَحَدَّثَنَا زُهَيْرُ بْنُ حَرْبٍ، وَابْنُ نُمَيْرٍ، قَالَا: حَدَّثَنَا سُفْيَانُ بْنُ عُيَيْنَةَ ح، قَالَ: وَحَدَّثَنَا يَحْيَى بْنُ يَحْيَى، - وَاللَّفْظُ لَهُ - قَالَ: قُلْتُ لِسُفْيَانَ بْنِ عُيَيْنَةَ، سَمِعْتَ الزُّهْرِيَّ، يَذْكُرُ عَنْ عَطَاءِ بْنِ يَزِيدَ اللَّيْثِيِّ، عَنْ أَبِي أَيُّوبَ، أَنَّ النَّبِيَّ صَلَّى اللهُ عَلَيْهِ وَسَلَّمَ قَالَ: «إِذَا أَتَيْتُمُ الْغَائِطَ فَلَا تَسْتَقْبِلُوا الْقِبْلَةَ، وَلَا تَسْتَدْبِرُوهَا بِبَوْلٍ وَلَا غَائِطٍ، وَلَكِنْ شَرِّقُوا أَوْ غَرِّبُوا»

قَالَ أَبُو أَيُّوبَ: « فَقَدِمْنَا الشَّامَ فَوَجَدْنَا مَرَاحِيضَ قَدْ بُنِيَتْ قِبَلَ الْقِبْلَةِ، فَنَنْحَرِفُ عَنْهَا وَنَسْتَغْفِرُ اللهَ؟ قَالَ: نَعم»

[465–60]. (Dār al-Salām 0508) Ahmad ibn al-Ḥasan ibn Khirāsh narrated: ʿUmar ibn ʿAbd al-Wahhāb narrated; Yazīd—meaning Ibn Zurayʿ—narrated; Rawḥ narrated; from Suhayl; from al-Qaʿqāʿ; from Abū Sāliḥ; from Abū Hurayrah; from God's Messenger (peace be upon him): **'When any of you sits to answer the call of nature, he should neither face nor turn his back to the direction of prayer'**.

وَحَدَّثَنَا أَحْمَدُ بْنُ الْحَسَنِ بْنِ خِرَاشٍ، حَدَّثَنَا عُمَرُ بْنُ عَبْدِ الْوَهَّابِ، حَدَّثَنَا يَزِيدُ، يَعْنِي ابْنَ زُرَيْعٍ، حَدَّثَنَا رَوْحٌ، عَنْ سُهَيْلٍ، عَنِ الْقَعْقَاعِ، عَنْ أَبِي صَالِحٍ، عَنْ أَبِي هُرَيْرَةَ، عَنْ رَسُولِ اللهِ صَلَّى اللهُ عَلَيْهِ وَسَلَّمَ قَالَ: «إِذَا جَلَسَ أَحَدُكُمْ عَلَى حَاجَتِهِ، فَلَا يَسْتَقْبِلِ الْقِبْلَةَ، وَلَا يَسْتَدْبِرْهَا»

[466–61]. (Dār al-Salām 0509) ʿAbdullāh ibn Maslamah ibn Qaʿnab narrated:[i] Sulaymān (meaning Ibn Bilāl) narrated; from Yaḥyā ibn Saʿīd; from Muhammad ibn Yaḥyā; from his uncle, Wāsiʿ ibn Ḥabbān: **'I was praying in the mosque, and ʿAbdullāh ibn ʿUmar was sitting with his back to the wall of the Kaʿbah. When I had finished my prayer, I turned towards him. ʿAbdullāh said: "Some people say that when you sit to answer the call of nature, do not sit facing either the direction of prayer or Jerusalem. I once went up on the roof of a house and I saw God's Messenger (peace be upon him) sitting on two bricks, facing Jerusalem and answering the call of nature".'**

حَدَّثَنَا عَبْدُ اللهِ بْنُ مَسْلَمَةَ بْنِ قَعْنَبٍ، حَدَّثَنَا سُلَيْمَانُ يَعْنِي ابْنَ بِلَالٍ، عَنْ يَحْيَى بْنِ سَعِيدٍ، عَنْ مُحَمَّدِ بْنِ يَحْيَى، عَنْ عَمِّهِ وَاسِعِ بْنِ حَبَّانَ، قَالَ: كُنْتُ أُصَلِّي فِي الْمَسْجِدِ وَعَبْدُ اللهِ بْنُ عُمَرَ مُسْنِدٌ ظَهْرَهُ إِلَى الْقِبْلَةِ، فَلَمَّا قَضَيْتُ صَلَاتِي انْصَرَفْتُ إِلَيْهِ مِنْ شِقِّي، فَقَالَ عَبْدُ اللهِ: يَقُولُ نَاسٌ: إِذَا قَعَدْتَ لِلْحَاجَةِ تَكُونُ لَكَ، فَلَا تَقْعُدْ مُسْتَقْبِلَ الْقِبْلَةِ وَلَا بَيْتَ الْمَقْدِسِ، قَالَ عَبْدُ اللهِ: وَلَقَدْ رَقِيتُ عَلَى ظَهْرِ بَيْتٍ، فَرَأَيْتُ رَسُولَ اللهِ صَلَّى اللهُ عَلَيْهِ وَسَلَّمَ قَاعِدًا عَلَى لَبِنَتَيْنِ مُسْتَقْبِلًا بَيْتَ الْمَقْدِسِ، لِحَاجَتِهِ.

[467–62]. (Dār al-Salām 0510) Abū Bakr ibn Abī Shaybah narrated: Muhammad ibn Bishr al-ʿAbdī; ʿUbaydillāh ibn ʿUmar narrated; from Muhammad ibn Yaḥyā ibn Ḥabbān; from his uncle Wāsiʿ ibn Ḥabbān; from Ibn ʿUmar: **'I went up on the roof of my sister Ḥafṣah's home, and I saw God's Messenger (peace be upon him) seated answering the call of nature, facing Syria and with his back to the direction of prayer'.**

حَدَّثَنَا أَبُو بَكْرِ بْنُ أَبِي شَيْبَةَ، حَدَّثَنَا مُحَمَّدُ بْنُ بِشْرٍ الْعَبْدِيُّ، حَدَّثَنَا عُبَيْدُ اللهِ بْنُ عُمَرَ، عَنْ مُحَمَّدِ بْنِ يَحْيَى بْنِ حَبَّانَ، عَنْ عَمِّهِ وَاسِعِ بْنِ حَبَّانَ، عَنِ ابْنِ عُمَرَ، قَالَ: رَقِيتُ عَلَى

i. Related by al-Bukhārī, 145, 148, 149 and 3102 (in longer versions); Abū Dāwūd, 12; al-Tirmidhī, 11; al-Nasāʾī, 23; Ibn Mājah, 322 (in a longer version).

بَيْتِ أُخْتِي حَفْصَةَ، «فَرَأَيْتُ رَسُولَ اللهِ صَلَّى اللهُ عَلَيْهِ وَسَلَّمَ قَاعِدًا لِحَاجَتِهِ، مُسْتَقْبِلَ الشَّامِ، مُسْتَدْبِرَ الْقِبْلَةِ»

Text Explanation

The hadiths included in this chapter and the following ones give instruction that people should not face the *qiblah* or the direction of prayer when they are in the desert and they answer a call of nature. They should not hold their genitals with their right hands, defecate by the roadside or in the shade. They should not use fewer than three stones, or solid objects such as toilet paper, to clean themselves after urination or defecation, or use animal droppings or bones for this purpose. However, they may use water.

The first hadith speaks about the instruction not to face the *qiblah* or the direction of prayer when urinating or defecating. Scholars give different verdicts on this point. Imam Mālik and Imam al-Shāfiʿī say that it is forbidden, i.e. haram, to face the *qiblah* when one is relieving oneself of either need if one is in the desert, but not forbidden within buildings. This view is reported from al-ʿAbbās ibn ʿAbd al-Muṭṭalib, ʿAbdullāh ibn ʿUmar, al-Shaʿbī, Isḥāq ibn Rāhawayh, and in one version from Ahmad ibn Ḥanbal. The second view is that facing the *qiblah* is not permissible either in buildings or open spaces. This is the view of Abū Ayyūb al-Anṣārī, Mujāhid, Ibrāhīm al-Nakhaʿī, Sufyān al-Thawrī, Abū Thawr and in another version from Ahmad. Another view is that it is permissible both in buildings and in the desert and open spaces. This is expressed by ʿUrwah ibn al-Zubayr, Rabīʿah, Mālik's teacher and Dāwūd al-Ẓāhirī. A fourth view is that facing the *qiblah* is prohibited in both buildings and the desert, but turning one's back towards them is permissible in both situations. This view is also expressed by Abū Ḥanīfah and Ahmad.

Scholars who say that facing the *qiblah* is prohibited in these situations, in all places, cite in evidence some authentic hadiths that give general instructions, such as the first hadith narrated by Salmān and hadith Nos 464 and 465 narrated by Abū Ayyūb and Abū Hurayrah respectively, as well as similar hadiths. They argue that the prohibition is due to the sanctity of the Ka'bah, which is the *qiblah*. This applies to both open spaces and within buildings. Had a barrier been sufficient to remove the prohibition, it would have applied in the desert and open spaces, because there are hills, valleys and other barriers between us and the Ka'bah.

Scholars who maintain that it is permissible to face it in all situations base their argument on hadith No. 467, in which Ibn 'Umar says that he saw the Prophet 'facing Jerusalem and with his back to the direction of prayer'. They also cite a hadith narrated by 'Ā'ishah, stating that the Prophet was informed that some people dislike facing the *qiblah* with their private parts exposed. The Prophet said: 'Have they done it? Turn my seat', meaning turning it so that it faces the *qiblah*. This hadith is related by Ahmad in his *al-Musnad*, and by Ibn Mājah, with a sound chain of transmission.

Scholars who permit turning one's back towards the *qiblah* but not facing it cite in support of their argument hadith Nos 461 and 462, narrated by Salmān. On the other hand, scholars who prohibit both facing and turning one's back to the *qiblah* in the desert and open spaces, permitting it in buildings, base their argument on hadith Nos 466, 467 and the above-mentioned hadith narrated by 'Ā'ishah. In addition, they quote the hadith narrated by Jābir: 'God's Messenger (peace be upon him) instructed us that we must not face the *qiblah* when urinating, but I saw him facing it a year before he passed away'. This hadith is related by Abū Dāwūd, al-Tirmidhī and others, with a sound chain of transmission. They add a hadith narrated by Marwān al-Aṣfar who said: 'I saw Ibn 'Umar sitting his camel down, facing the *qiblah*, and then he sat to urinate facing it. I said: "Abū 'Abd al-Raḥmān, is it not true that this was prohibited?" He said: "Yes; but this applies when you are in the open. If there is between you and the *qiblah* something to screen you, there is no harm".' This hadith is related by Abū Dāwūd and others. All these hadiths are authentic and clear in meaning, allowing facing the *qiblah* in buildings. The hadiths narrated by Abū Ayyūb, Salmān and Abū Hurayrah, Nos 464, 461 and 465 respectively, state the prohibition. Therefore, this prohibition may be understood to refer to doing so in the desert and open spaces in order to accept all the relevant hadiths together. There is no disagreement among scholars that whenever it is possible to apply all the hadiths relevant to a particular issue, this should be done. It is not allowed to ignore any. Indeed, all should be implemented. In this case, we are able to combine the hadiths and implement them as we have just suggested. Hence, this should be done. Scholars have distinguished between the desert and buildings in their understanding of these hadiths, stating that making it obligatory not to face the *qiblah* in buildings may be too hard for people, while it is perfectly easy in the desert. Rejection of the view that permits turning one's back to the *qiblah* is based on hadith No. 464, narrated by Abū Ayyūb, and similar hadiths that clearly state the prohibition of facing and turning one's back to the *qiblah*, but God knows best.

Here are certain points related to facing the *qiblah* when answering the call of nature according to al-Shāfiʿī School of *fiqh*:

Firstly: The view preferred by our scholars is that facing and turning one's back to the *qiblah* in buildings is permissible when a person is close to a sort of screen, such as a wall. There should be no more than three arm's lengths between a person and such a screen. Another condition is that the screen should be high enough to cover the lower parts of one's body. Its height is estimated to be not less than two-thirds of an arm's length. If the distance between one and the screen is more than three arm's lengths and its height is less than what has been mentioned, then facing the *qiblah* or turning one's back to it when answering the call of nature is forbidden, just like in the desert, unless it is in a place that is specifically used for this purpose, such as a lavatory, in which case there is no restriction. They add that if a person is doing his toilet in the desert and puts up some sort of screen, meeting the above two conditions, the prohibition is removed. The point is the presence or absence of a screen. When a screen is there, in either a building or the desert, it is permissible, and when there is no screen the prohibition applies. This is the correct and well-known view of our scholars. However, some of our scholars give no consideration to the presence of a screen in any case, permitting facing the *qiblah* when answering the call of nature in a building and prohibiting it in the desert and open spaces. The first view is the correct one. They give further details, saying that any type of screen is acceptable: it may be an animal, a wall, a sand dune or a hill. If a person places some of his clothes as a screen between him and the *qiblah,* our scholars give two opposite views on whether this is sufficient. The better known and more correct view is that it is, but God knows best.

Secondly, where we consider it permissible to face and turn one's back to the *qiblah,* some of our scholars say that it is *makrūh,* or offensive; but the majority do not mention offensiveness. The preferable view is that if a person finds himself in a situation where moving away from the direction of the *qiblah* causes difficulty or inconvenience then there is no discouragement. If there is no inconvenience, then it is better to move away from that direction so as not to be entangled with the different views of scholars. No *makrūh* ruling may be attached to such action because the authentic hadiths mentioning this case do not state it.

Thirdly, sexual intercourse is permissible if the couple are facing the *qiblah,* whether in the desert or in a built place. This is the view of our school, the Ḥanafi and Ḥanbalī Schools of *fiqh,* as well as Dāwūd al-Ẓāhirī, but Mālik's disciples differ, with Abū al-Qāsim ruling that it is permissible and Ibn Ḥabīb saying that it is offensive. The correct view is that it is permissible, because prohibition may be based only on religious text. No text prohibiting it is there, but God knows best.

Fourthly, to face the direction of Jerusalem when urinating or defecating is not forbidden, but discouraged.

Fifthly, if one moves away so as not to face or turn one's back to the *qiblah* at the time of urinating or defecating, but then faces it when cleaning oneself, this is permissible, but God knows best.[i]

---

i. In his voluminous work of commentary on Muslim's *Ṣaḥīḥ,* the late scholar, Mūsā Shāhīn Lāshīn says: 'I believe that the order not to face the *qiblah* when one answers the call of nature is intended to stress the sanctity of the Kaʿbah in people's minds. The point is not to deliberately face it with what is dirty or disgusting … . No one may say that we let our genitals be in its direction. If this is meant when there is some sort of cover, we perform the *ṭawāf* during the pilgrimage, going around the Kaʿbah having only a piece of cloth covering our bodies. If it is meant when our genitals are exposed, all scholars agree that it is permissible to take a bath, in the nude, facing the direction of the *qiblah*'. (Lāshīn, *Fatḥ al-Munʿim fī Sharḥ Ṣaḥīḥ Muslim* (Cairo, 2002), Vol. 2, p. 191)

The hadith mentions that we are required not to use our right hands when we clean ourselves after answering the call of nature. Scholars are unanimous that we are ordered not to do so, and the overwhelming majority of scholars are of the view that this is not an order of prohibition, but rather a question of preferability. Some scholars of the Ẓāhirī School, which takes every statement at its face value, argue that it is forbidden to use the right hand for this purpose. The same is mentioned by some scholars of our own school, but their view is insupportable. Our scholars say: 'It is desirable that a person does not use his right hand to clean himself after answering the call of nature, except for a reason. If he is washing with water, he should pour it with his right hand and wipe it off with his left. If he is using a stone or a solid object,[i] he holds it in his left hand to wipe off his anus, and if he is using it after urination, he holds the solid object in his right hand without moving it and holds his penis in his left hand to dry it. This is the proper way. Some of our scholars say that he may hold his organ in his right hand and the solid object in his left hand which is the one to be moved, but this is incorrect, because it means that he unnecessarily holds his genital organ in his right hand, which is discouraged, but God knows best. Moreover, the ruling against using the right hand to clean oneself confirms the need to keep it free from all dirt. We shall presently be speaking further about this rule, God willing.

The first hadith, No. 461, mentions that the Prophet instructed his companions to use no fewer than three stones to clean themselves after answering the call of nature. This is an authentic and clear statement that wiping the dirty area three times is obligatory. Yet scholars have different views on this point. Our Shāfiʿī School of *fiqh* makes clear that when solid objects, such as toilet paper, are used for cleansing, it is obligatory to remove the impurity and wipe it off three times. If one wipes it off once or twice and it is fully removed, a third wipe remains necessary. This is also the view of Ahmad ibn Ḥanbal,

---

i. Nowadays it is better to use toilet paper for all purposes of cleaning oneself. Imam al-Nawawī wrote his book at a time when paper was still a precious commodity, used only for writing.

Isḥāq ibn Rāhawayh and Abū Thawr. On the other hand, Mālik and Dāwūd say that what is obligatory is to achieve full cleansing. If it happens with wiping with one solid object, it is sufficient. This view is accepted by some scholars of our Shāfiʿī School, but the more widely held view of our school is the one we have already explained. Our scholars add that if one is using a stone with three sides, wiping once on each side, this is sufficient, because the important thing is the number of wipes, but using three different stones is better. When one is cleaning oneself from both urine and stools, then six wipes are needed, three for each place. It is preferable to use six different solid objects, but if one is using one solid object with six sides, and one wipes once on each side, this is good enough. The same applies to a thick piece of cloth which when used on one side remains dry on the other: it may be used on both sides, but God knows best.

It is most important to ensure that the cleansing is full. If it is achieved by using three stones, or solid objects, that is sufficient. If it is not, then using a fourth is obligatory. If full cleansing is achieved with a fourth, this is sufficient, but it remains preferable to use a fifth in order to maintain an odd number. The same process goes on: if five wipes do not achieve full cleansing, a sixth is necessary, and if seven wipes do not achieve it, an eighth is obligatory, and so on. Moreover, it is always preferable to use an odd number, even though full cleansing occurs after an even number of wipes. The rule is that full cleansing is obligatory and an odd number is desirable, but God knows best.

Some scholars of the Ẓāhirī School, which takes statements at their face value, consider that the Prophet's mention of stones means that it is obligatory to use stones, and that nothing else may be used to clean oneself. All scholars of all schools of *fiqh* disagree, saying that cloth, wood or any other object is equally good.[i] What is necessary is to use something that removes the dirt and the impurity. Other objects achieve this and they may be used. The Prophet mentioned

---

i. As explained earlier, toilet paper is better than any such material, but it was not known during the Prophet's lifetime, or even later when al-Nawawī wrote his commentary.

stones because they were the object most readily available at the time. There is nothing peculiar about their use. The same applies to the Qur'anic injunction: *'Do not kill your children because of your poverty'*.[i] (6: 151) That the use of stones is not specifically required is further indicated by the fact that the Prophet prohibited the use of bones and animal droppings. Had the use of stones been specifically required, the Prophet would have made the prohibition applicable to everything else, instead of specifying these particular objects. Our scholars say: 'What may be used instead of stones is any clean solid object that can remove the impurity and has no sanctity, provided that it is not part of an animal. It is not necessary that it should be of the same type.' This means that one may use stones for urine and cloth for defecation, or use one stone and two pieces of cloth, or one cloth and a piece of wood, etc.

The Prophet also forbids cleaning oneself with 'stools or bones'. This means that no impurity may be used for cleaning oneself after answering the call of nature. The Prophet uses the word *'rajī''*, which means animal droppings or stools to refer to every type of impurity. The use of bones is also prohibited because bones are eaten by the jinn. Thus the Prophet indicates that whatever is edible may not be used for this purpose. This prohibition also covers everything that is used for a good purpose, such as any part of an animal, paper from books, etc. When we speak of impurities, there is no difference between solid and fluid impurities. If a person cleans himself with an impurity, this cleaning is improper and he must clean himself again using water. To use stones or other solid objects for removing the impurity he used to clean himself is insufficient, because the place has become stained with the additional impurity which is different from his own. If one cleans oneself with an edible object or some other object that carries some sanctity, the correct view is that his cleaning is improper and he must clean himself again, but using a solid object in this case is acceptable, provided that his first action

i. The point of comparison is that the verse mentions killing one's child because of poverty, but killing one's child is a grave crime, regardless of the cause.

did not cause the removal of the impurity from its initial position. Some scholars say that his first cleaning is sufficient, but he has incurred a sin for using such objects, but God knows best.

In the second hadith, No. 462, Salmān, the Prophet's companion, says: 'The unbelievers said to us: "I see ..."'. This is how the hadith is entered in the original copies, and it is correct to put it in this way. It means that a spokesman of the unbelievers, or a particular person among them said to us, but he referred to them in the plural because they all agreed with that person.

In hadith No. 464, the Prophet tells us to 'turn eastwards or westwards' in order to avoid the direction of the prayer. Scholars say that this is an address to the people of Madinah and others to whom this applies. They should turn either to the east or to the west so that they would not be facing the *qiblah* or turning their backs to it. In this hadith, Abū Ayyūb mentions that in Syria they had to use toilets that were built facing the *qiblạh*, and they were keen to turn away from that direction as much as possible. This is followed in the hadith by the words: 'He said: "Yes".' This is the answer to Yaḥyā's question which occurs in the chain of transmission as follows: 'I said to Sufyān ibn ʿUyaynah: Did you hear al-Zuhrī mention to ʿAṭā'?'

In hadith Nos 466 and 467, Ibn ʿUmar mentions that he went onto the roof of his sister's home and he saw the Prophet performing his toilet. This was accidental, not deliberate. His sister was Ḥafṣah, the Prophet's wife.

Transmission

The chain of transmission of hadith No. 465 goes as follows: 'Ahmad ibn al-Ḥasan ibn Khirāsh narrated: ʿUmar ibn ʿAbd al-Wahhāb narrated; Yazīd—meaning Ibn Zurayʿ—narrated; Rawḥ narrated; from Suhayl; from al-Qaʿqāʿ; from Abu Sāliḥ; from Abū Hurayrah'. Al-Dāraquṭnī said: 'This is not learnt from Suhayl. It is a hadith narrated by Ibn ʿAjlān from Rawḥ and others'. Abū al-Faḍl, the grandson of Abū Saʿīd al-Harawī said: 'The error in this hadith belongs to ʿUmar ibn ʿAbd al-Wahhāb, because this hadith is known as reported by Muhammad ibn ʿAjlān from al-Qaʿqāʿ while Suhayl has no mention in this chain of transmission. It is correctly reported by Umayyah ibn Bisṭām from Yazīd ibn Zurayʿ from Rawḥ from Ibn ʿAjlān from al-Qaʿqāʿ from Abū Sāliḥ from Abū Hurayrah from the Prophet (peace be upon him). Moreover, ʿUmar ibn ʿAbd al-Wahhāb's narration is shorter'.

To me, these objections do not seem valid. It may well be that both Suhayl and Ibn ʿAjlān learnt it from al-Qaʿqāʿ, but its reporting by Ibn ʿAjlān was widely circulated while the report by Suhayl remained in limited circulation. Indeed Abū Dāwūd, al-Nasā'ī and Ibn Mājah report it only from Ibn ʿAjlān. Abū Dāwūd enters it from Ibn al-Mubārak from Ibn ʿAjlān from al-Qaʿqāʿ; al-Nasā'ī enters it from Ibn ʿAjlān; and Ibn Mājah enters it from Sufyān ibn ʿUyaynah, al-Mughīrah ibn ʿAbd al-Raḥmān and ʿAbdullāh ibn Rajā': all three from Ibn ʿAjlān; but God knows best.

CHAPTER 18

DO NOT USE THE RIGHT HAND WHEN CLEANING ONESELF

[468–63]. (Dār al-Salām 0511) Yaḥyā ibn Yaḥyā narrated: ʿAbd al-Raḥmān ibn Mahdī reported; from Hammām; from Yaḥyā ibn Abī Kathīr; from ʿAbdullāh ibn Abī Qatādah; from his father: **'God's Messenger (peace be upon him) said: "Let none of you hold his genital organ with his right hand when urinating. Let none clean oneself after defecating with one's right hand. Do not breathe into a water jug".'**

حَدَّثَنَا يَحْيَى بْنُ يَحْيَى أَخْبَرَنَا عَبْدُ الرَّحْمَنِ بْنُ مَهْدِيٍّ، عَنْ هَمَّامٍ، عَنْ يَحْيَى بْنِ أَبِي كَثِيرٍ، عَنْ عَبْدِ اللهِ بْنِ أَبِي قَتَادَةَ، عَنْ أَبِيهِ، قَالَ: قَالَ رَسُولُ اللهِ صَلَّى اللهُ عَلَيْهِ وَسَلَّمَ: «لَا يُمْسِكَنَّ أَحَدُكُمْ ذَكَرَهُ بِيَمِينِهِ وَهُوَ يَبُولُ، وَلَا يَتَمَسَّحْ مِنَ الْخَلَاءِ بِيَمِينِهِ، وَلَا يَتَنَفَّسْ فِي الْإِنَاءِ»

[469–64]. (Dār al-Salām 0512) Yaḥyā ibn Yaḥyā narrated: Wakīʿ reported; from Hishām al-Dastawā'ī; from Yaḥyā ibn Abī Kathīr; from ʿAbdullāh ibn Abī Qatādah; from his father: **'God's Messenger (peace be upon him) said: "When any of you goes into the toilet, he should not hold his genital organ in his right hand".'**

حَدَّثَنَا يَحْيَى بْنُ يَحْيَى، أَخْبَرَنَا وَكِيعٌ، عَنْ هِشَامٍ الدَّسْتَوَائِيِّ، عَنْ يَحْيَى بْنِ أَبِي كَثِيرٍ، عَنْ عَبْدِ اللهِ بْنِ أَبِي قَتَادَةَ، عَنْ أَبِيهِ، قَالَ: قَالَ رَسُولُ اللهِ صَلَّى اللهُ عَلَيْهِ وَسَلَّمَ: «إِذَا دَخَلَ أَحَدُكُمُ الْخَلَاءَ فَلَا يَمَسَّ ذَكَرَهُ بِيَمِينِهِ»

[470–65]. (Dār al-Salām 0513) Ibn Abī ʿUmar narrated: al-Thaqafī narrated; from Ayyūb; from Yaḥyā ibn Abī Kathīr; from ʿAbdullāh ibn Abī Qatādah; from Abū Qatādah: **'The Prophet ordered that one should not breathe into a water jug; hold his genital organ in his right hand; or clean himself [after defection] with his right hand'**.

حَدَّثَنَا ابْنُ أَبِي عُمَرَ، حَدَّثَنَا الثَّقَفِيُّ، عَنْ أَيُّوبَ، عَنْ يَحْيَى بْنِ أَبِي كَثِيرٍ، عَنْ عَبْدِ اللهِ بْنِ أَبِي قَتَادَةَ، عَنْ أَبِي قَتَادَةَ: «أَنَّ النَّبِيَّ صَلَّى اللهُ عَلَيْهِ وَسَلَّمَ نَهَى أَنْ يَتَنَفَّسَ فِي الْإِنَاءِ، وَأَنْ يَمَسَّ ذَكَرَهُ بِيَمِينِهِ، وَأَنْ يَسْتَطِيبَ بِيَمِينِهِ»

Text Explanation

The Prophet says: 'Let none of you hold his genital organ with his right hand when urinating. Let none clean oneself after defecating with one's right hand'. As we have explained earlier, when we discussed how to clean oneself after going to the toilet, holding one's genital organ with one's right hand is discouraged, but this discouragement is of the milder type, not the one close to prohibition. We have also already explained that one should not use one's right hand in any way related to cleansing. The Prophet's statement: 'Let none clean oneself after defecation with one's right hand' applies to both types of relieving oneself, but God knows best.

The Prophet's other instruction is not to breathe into a jug of water. This means that after drinking one should not hold the water container close to one's mouth and breathe into it. To take three breaths away from the water container after having had a drink is a well-known Sunnah, but the order is not to breathe directly at the jug. This is an aspect of good manners, to ensure that whatever is used for drinking is kept clean, with nothing dropping into it out of the drinker's mouth or nose, but God knows best.

Transmission

The chain of transmission of the first hadith, No. 468, mentions Yaḥyā ibn Yaḥyā from ʿAbd al-Raḥmān ibn Mahdī from Hammām, while the second hadith, No. 469, has a chain of Yaḥyā from Wakīʿ from Hishām al-Dastawā'ī. This is how these hadiths are stated in the original manuscripts we have seen, giving the name Hammām in the first and Hishām in the second.[i] I think that the first is merely a typo by one or another of the copiers from Muslim. Al-Bukhārī, al-Nasā'ī and other famous scholars narrate the hadith from Hishām al-Dastawā'ī, just like it is in the second version given by Muslim. Imam Abū Muhammad Khalaf al-Wāsiṭī illustrates what I have just said. He said: 'Muslim narrates this hadith from Yaḥyā ibn Yaḥyā, from ʿAbd al-Raḥmān ibn Mahdī, from Hishām, and he also narrates it from Yaḥyā ibn Yaḥyā from Wakīʿ from Hishām from Yaḥyā ibn Abi Kathīr.' Thus Imam Khalaf clearly states that Muslim narrates it in both chains from Hishām al-Dastawā'ī, which clearly indicates that the use of the name Hammām is merely a typo that has occurred in our manuscripts that were copied after Muslim's time, but God knows best.

i. In Arabic these two names look very similar, particularly because diacritics and short vowels are rarely entered. Thus the first vowel in both names is not shown, and the doubled 'm' is written as a single one, leaving the difference between them to be that of a single letter.

CHAPTER 19

PREFERENCE FOR THE RIGHT SIDE

[471–66]. (Dār al-Salām 0514) Yaḥyā ibn Yaḥyā al-Tamīmī narrated:[i] Abū al-Aḥwaṣ reported; from Ashʿath; from his father; from Masrūq; from ʿĀ'ishah: **'Indeed, God's Messenger preferred to start with the right side whenever he performed ablution; in combing his hair when he did; and in wearing his shoes when he put them on'**.

وحَدَّثَنَا يَحْيَى بْنُ يَحْيَى التَّمِيمِيُّ، أَخْبَرَنَا أَبُو الْأَحْوَصِ، عَنْ أَشْعَثَ، عَنْ أَبِيهِ، عَنْ مَسْرُوقٍ، عَنْ عَائِشَةَ، قَالَتْ: إِنْ كَانَ رَسُولُ اللهِ صَلَّى اللهُ عَلَيْهِ وَسَلَّمَ: «لَيُحِبُّ التَّيَمُّنَ فِي طُهُورِهِ إِذَا تَطَهَّرَ، وَفِي تَرَجُّلِهِ، إِذَا تَرَجَّلَ، وَفِي انْتِعَالِهِ إِذَا انْتَعَلَ»

[472–67]. (Dār al-Salām 0515) ʿUbaydillāh ibn Muʿādh narrated: my father narrated; Shuʿbah narrated; from al-Ashʿath; from his father; from Masrūq; from ʿĀ'ishah: **'God's Messenger (peace be upon him) used to love to start with the right side in all matters: wearing his shoes, combing his hair and performing the ablution'**.

وَحَدَّثَنَا عُبَيْدُ اللهِ بْنُ مُعَاذٍ، حَدَّثَنَا أَبِي، حَدَّثَنَا شُعْبَةُ، عَنِ الْأَشْعَثِ، عَنْ أَبِيهِ، عَنْ مَسْرُوقٍ، عَنْ عَائِشَةَ، قَالَتْ: «كَانَ رَسُولُ اللهِ صَلَّى اللهُ عَلَيْهِ وَسَلَّمَ يُحِبُّ التَّيَمُّنَ فِي شَأْنِهِ كُلِّهِ، فِي نَعْلَيْهِ، وَتَرَجُّلِهِ، وَطُهُورِهِ»

---

i. Related by al-Bukhārī, 168, 446, 5380, 5854 and 5926; Abū Dāwūd, 4140; al-Tirmidhī, 608; al-Nasā'ī, 112, 419 and 5255; Ibn Mājah, 401.

Text Explanation

This is an Islamic rule that applies in all situations. It means that in whatever is conducive to good appearance or manners, such as wearing clothes or shoes, entering the mosque, brushing one's teeth, applying kohl, clipping one's nails, trimming one's moustache, combing one's hair, plucking armpit hair, cutting hair, finishing prayer, washing body organs, coming out of the toilet, eating, drinking, shaking hands and kissing the Black Stone, etc. starting with the right side is preferable. In whatever is the opposite, such as going to the toilet, leaving the mosque, blowing one's nose, cleaning oneself in the toilet, undressing, taking off one's shoes, etc. it is preferable to start with the left side. All this is because the right hand is given a higher status, but God knows best. Scholars are unanimous that starting with the right hand and leg when performing the ablution is recommended. If one does the opposite, one misses out on the preferable but one's ablution remains valid. The Shia say that starting with the right side is obligatory, but their disagreement is not rated.

It should be understood that to start with the left side is discouraged, even though it is valid. This is stated by al-Shāfiʿī, and it is very clear. It is entered in Abū Dāwūd's and al-Tirmidhī's *Sunan*, with sound chains of transmission that the Prophet said: 'When you put on your clothes or perform the ablution, start with your right side'. This is a clear statement ordering us to start with the right side. To go against it is either discouraged or prohibited. Scholars are unanimous that it is not forbidden; hence, it must be discouraged, or *makrūh*. Moreover, some parts that are included in the ablution should not be started with the right side before the left. These are the two ears, hands and cheeks. In all three, both sides are washed or wiped at the same time. If this is not possible, as in the case of a person who has only one hand, then such a person starts with the right side, but God knows best.

In some versions of these hadiths as narrated by al-Bukhārī, we see the phrase 'as much as possible' added to the Prophet's preference of the right side. This indicates that he was always keen to do this, but God knows best.

CHAPTER 20

PROHIBITION OF DEFECATION BY THE ROADSIDE AND IN THE SHADE

[473–68]. (Dār al-Salām 0516) Yaḥyā ibn Ayyūb, Qutaybah and Ibn Ḥujr narrated: all from Ismāʿīl ibn Jaʿfar. Ibn Ayyūb said: Ismāʿīl narrated: al-ʿAlāʾ reported to me; from his father, from Abu Hurayrah: **'God's Messenger (peace be upon him) said: "Avoid the two cursers". People asked: "What are the two cursers, Messenger of God?" He said: "A person who defecates by people's roadside or in their shade".'**

حَدَّثَنَا يَحْيَى بْنُ أَيُّوبَ، وَقُتَيْبَةُ، وَابْنُ حُجْرٍ، جَمِيعًا عَنْ إِسْمَاعِيلَ بْنِ جَعْفَرٍ، قَالَ: ابْنُ أَيُّوبَ، حَدَّثَنَا إِسْمَاعِيلُ، أَخْبَرَنِي الْعَلَاءُ، عَنْ أَبِيهِ، عَنْ أَبِي هُرَيْرَةَ، أَنَّ رَسُولَ اللهِ صَلَّى اللهُ عَلَيْهِ وَسَلَّمَ قَالَ: «اتَّقُوا اللَّعَّانَيْنِ» قَالُوا: وَمَا اللَّعَّانَانِ يَا رَسُولَ اللهِ؟ قَالَ: «الَّذِي يَتَخَلَّى فِي طَرِيقِ النَّاسِ، أَوْ فِي ظِلِّهِمْ»

Text Explanation

Imam Abū Sulaymān Ḥamad ibn Muhammad al-Khaṭṭābī said: 'What is meant by the two cursers is the two actions that incur people's curses, or cause people to curse the one who does them. These are deeds that make people curse the doer. Since these actions are the cause of cursing, the curses are thus attributed to them'. As such, the hadith means, according to Abū Dāwūd's version: 'Avoid the two actions whose doer is cursed', but according to Muslim's version it means: 'Stay away from those whom people normally curse', but God knows best.

Al-Khaṭṭābī and other scholars said: 'in their shade' means the places where people choose to sit and rest. It is not every shade that is included in this prohibition. The Prophet went into a thick palm date plantation to answer the call of nature, and this was undoubtedly an area with shade, but God knows best.

'A person who defecates by people's roadside' refers to the one who does so at a place where people pass by. The prohibition of doing this in the shade and by the roadside is because it irritates people and it is disgusting, but God knows best.

CHAPTER 21

CLEANING ONESELF WITH WATER

[474–69]. (Dār al-Salām 0517) Yaḥyā ibn Yaḥyā narrated:[i] Khālid ibn ʿAbdullāh reported; from Khālid; from ʿAṭāʾ ibn Abī Maymūnah; from Anas ibn Mālik: **'God's Messenger (peace be upon him) entered a farm, followed by a young lad who was carrying a water container. He was our youngest. He placed the container near a tree. Having relieved himself, God's Messenger came back to us after cleaning himself with water.'**

حَدَّثَنَا يَحْيَى بْنُ يَحْيَى، أَخْبَرَنَا خَالِدُ بْنُ عَبْدِ اللهِ، عَنْ خَالِدٍ، عَنْ عَطَاءِ بْنِ أَبِي مَيْمُونَةَ، عَنْ أَنَسِ بْنِ مَالِكٍ أَنَّ رَسُولَ اللهِ صَلَّى اللهُ عَلَيْهِ وَسَلَّمَ: «دَخَلَ حَائِطًا وَتَبِعَهُ غُلَامٌ مَعَهُ مِيضَأَةٌ، هُوَ أَصْغَرُنَا، فَوَضَعَهَا عِنْدَ سِدْرَةٍ، فَقَضَى رَسُولُ اللهِ صلَّى اللهِ عليْهِ وسلَّم حَاجَتَهُ، فَخَرَجَ عَلَيْنَا وَقَدِ اسْتَنْجَى بِالْمَاءِ»

[475–70]. (Dār al-Salām 0518) Abū Bakr ibn Abī Shaybah narrated: Wakīʿ and Ghundar narrated; from Shuʿbah [H]. Also, Muhammad ibn al-Muthannā narrated (his text): Muhammad ibn Jaʿfar narrated; Shuʿbah narrated; from ʿAṭāʾ ibn Abī Maymūnah; that he heard Anas ibn Mālik say: **'God's Messenger (peace be upon him) would go for stools. I and a lad like me would carry a water container and a stick, and he would clean himself with water.'**

i. Related by al-Bukhārī, 150, 151, 152, 217 and 500; Abū Dāwūd, 43; al-Nasāʾī, 45.

وَحَدَّثَنَا أَبُو بَكْرِ بْنُ أَبِي شَيْبَةَ، حَدَّثَنَا وَكِيعٌ، وَغُنْدَرٌ، عَنْ شُعْبَةَ ح، وَحَدَّثَنَا مُحَمَّدُ بْنُ الْمُثَنَّى، وَاللَّفْظُ لَهُ حَدَّثَنَا مُحَمَّدُ بْنُ جَعْفَرٍ، حَدَّثَنَا شُعْبَةُ، عَنْ عَطَاءِ بْنِ أَبِي مَيْمُونَةَ، أَنَّهُ سَمِعَ أَنَسَ بْنَ مَالِكٍ، يَقُولُ: «كَانَ رَسُولُ اللهِ صَلَّى اللهُ عَلَيْهِ وَسَلَّمَ يَدْخُلُ الْخَلَاءَ فَأَحْمِلُ أَنَا، وَغُلَامٌ نَحْوِي، إِدَاوَةً مِنْ مَاءٍ، وَعَنَزَةً فَيَسْتَنْجِي بِالْمَاءِ»

[476–71]. (Dār al-Salām 0519) Zuhayr ibn Ḥarb and Abū Kurayb narrated to me (Zuhayr's text): Ismāʿīl (meaning Ibn ʿUlayyah) narrated: Rawḥ ibn al-Qāsim narrated to me; from ʿAṭā' ibn Abī Maymūnah; from Anas ibn Mālik: **'God's Messenger used to go far to relieve himself. I would bring him water and he would clean himself with it'**.

وَحَدَّثَنِي زُهَيْرُ بْنُ حَرْبٍ، وَأَبُو كُرَيْبٍ، - وَاللَّفْظُ لِزُهَيْرٍ -، حَدَّثَنَا إِسْمَاعِيلُ يَعْنِي ابْنَ عُلَيَّةَ، حَدَّثَنِي رَوْحُ بْنُ الْقَاسِمِ، عَنْ عَطَاءِ بْنِ أَبِي مَيْمُونَةَ، عَنْ أَنَسِ بْنِ مَالِكٍ، قَالَ: «كَانَ رَسُولُ اللهِ صَلَّى اللهُ عَلَيْهِ وَسَلَّمَ يَتَبَرَّزُ لِحَاجَتِهِ، فَآتِيهِ بِالْمَاءِ، فَيَتَغَسَّلُ بِهِ»

Text Explanation

These hadiths speak of the Prophet's practice when he wanted to relieve himself. He would go to a place which was sure to give him shelter, because at that time the Arabs did not have toilets in their homes.[i] He would have some water brought for him and he would take a stick with a sharp metal end. He needed this because when he performed the ablution, the Prophet always offered a prayer, and he needed the stick to place before him as a mark of his praying space.

These hadiths tell us that if one is answering the call of nature out of doors it is desirable to go away from people so as not to be seen. They indicate that it is permissible to use some of one's subordinates

i. The Arabs did not have any sewerage system, and water was not plentiful in their towns and cities. With their hot weather, to have indoor toilets in such conditions would give off a very bad smell.

to attend to one's needs. Further, it is good to serve honourable and devout people and to seek God's blessing for doing so. The hadiths make clear that it is perfectly in order to use water to clean oneself after answering the call of nature, and it is indeed preferable to using only stones or solid objects for this purpose. Indeed, this is a point on which people differ. However, the overwhelming majority of scholars of early and recent days, as well as prominent scholars in all countries, are of the view that the most preferable practice is to use both water and a solid object, using the latter first to reduce the impurity and lessen its contact with one's hand, and then one uses the water. To use only one of the two is acceptable, whether the other is available or not. In other words, it is permissible to use only a solid object, [or toilet paper], when water is also available, or to opt for the opposite. However, if one is using only one of the two, then water is preferable because it cleans the area perfectly well. Solid objects can only reduce the impurity enough to make prayer valid, despite the presence of light traces of impurity. A small number of early scholars expressed the view that stones are preferable, and indeed the words of some of these may give the impression that water is not enough on its own. Ibn Ḥabīb, a Mālikī scholar, said that stones are only sufficient when one has no access to water. However, this is contrary to what early and later scholars say, and contrary to the apparent meaning of the Sunnah, but God knows best.

Some scholars suggest on the basis of these hadiths that it is desirable to use a water container for ablution, and that this is preferable to water from ponds or basins or similar places, because the Prophet is not reported to have performed the ablution from such water sources. This view is unacceptable and we do not know that anyone has agreed to it. *Qāḍī* 'Iyāḍ said: 'There is no basis for this opinion. It has not been reported that such water sources were available to the Prophet but he left them in preference for water from jugs or flagons, but God knows best'.

CHAPTER 22

WIPING ON FOOTWEAR

[477–72]. (Dār al-Salām 0520) Yaḥyā ibn Yaḥyā al-Tamīmī, Isḥāq ibn Ibrāhīm and Abū Kurayb narrated:[i] all from Abū Muʿāwiyah [H]. Also Abū Bakr ibn Abī Shaybah narrated: Abū Muʿāwiyah and Wakīʿ narrated (but this is Yaḥyā's text) he said: Abū Muʿāwiyah reported; from al-Aʿmash; from Ibrāhīm; from Hammām: **'Jarīr urinated, then performed the ablution but he wiped his *khuffs*.[ii] He was asked: "Do you do this?" He said: "Yes. I saw God's Messenger (peace be upon him) when he urinated. He then performed the ablution and wiped his *khuffs*'.**

Al-Aʿmash said that Ibrāhīm said: 'They liked this hadith because Jarīr embraced Islam after the revelation of [the surah] *Al-Mā'idah*'.

حَدَّثَنَا يَحْيَى بْنُ يَحْيَى التَّمِيمِيُّ، وَإِسْحَاقُ بْنُ إِبْرَاهِيمَ، وَأَبُو كُرَيْبٍ، جَمِيعًا عَنْ أَبِي مُعَاوِيَةَ ح، وَحَدَّثَنَا أَبُو بَكْرِ بْنُ أَبِي شَيْبَةَ، حَدَّثَنَا أَبُو مُعَاوِيَةَ، وَوَكِيعٌ - وَاللَّفْظُ لِيَحْيَى

i. Related by al-Bukhārī, 387 (in similar wording); al-Tirmidhī , 93 (in similar wording); al-Nasā'ī, 118 and 773; Ibn Mājah, 543 (in similar wording).

ii. The *khuffs* are a type of thin leather shoe worn like socks. Hence, we translated the title of this chapter as wiping on footwear, because what applies to *khuffs* in this regard applies to other types of footwear, such as socks and stockings, provided that they cover the ankles.

Wiping one's *khuffs* replaces washing one's feet when performing the ablution. This is a concession to make it easier for people to perform the ablution for prayer. There are certain conditions for this concession to apply. It is essential that one should wear the *khuffs* when one has performed the ablution, i.e. *wuḍū'*, and his ablution is still valid. When he needs to have a fresh ablution, he may wipe his *khuffs* instead of washing his feet. This concession extends for five prayers after wearing one's *khuffs*, i.e. for 24-hours.

- قَالَ: أَخْبَرَنَا أَبُو مُعَاوِيَةَ، عَنِ الْأَعْمَشِ، عَنْ إِبْرَاهِيمَ، عَنْ هَمَّامٍ، قَالَ: بَالَ جَرِيرٌ، ثُمَّ تَوَضَّأَ، وَمَسَحَ عَلَى خُفَّيْهِ، فَقِيلَ: تَفْعَلُ هَذَا؟ فَقَالَ: نَعَمْ، «رَأَيْتُ رَسُولَ اللهِ صَلَّى اللهُ عَلَيْهِ وَسَلَّمَ بَالَ، ثُمَّ تَوَضَّأَ وَمَسَحَ عَلَى خُفَّيْهِ»

قَالَ الْأَعْمَشُ: قَالَ إِبْرَاهِيمُ: «كَانَ يُعْجِبُهُمْ هَذَا الْحَدِيثُ لِأَنَّ إِسْلَامَ جَرِيرٍ، كَانَ بَعْدَ نُزُولِ الْمَائِدَةِ»

[478–000]. (Dār al-Salām 0521) Isḥāq ibn Ibrāhīm and ʿAlī ibn Khashram narrated: ʿĪsā ibn Yūnus reported [H]. Also, Muhammad ibn Abī ʿUmar narrated: Sufyān narrated [H]. Minjab ibn al-Ḥārith al-Tamīmī narrated: Ibn Mushīr reported; all of them from al-Aʿmash, with this chain of transmission, reporting the same meaning as the [previous] hadith of Abū Muʿāwiyah. **However, ʿĪsā's and Sufyān's narration includes: 'ʿAbdullāh's companions liked this hadith because Jarīr embraced Islam after the revelation of [the surah]** ***Al-Mā'idah***'.

وَحَدَّثَنَاهُ إِسْحَاقُ بْنُ إِبْرَاهِيمَ، وَعَلِيُّ بْنُ خَشْرَمٍ، قَالَا: أَخْبَرَنَا عِيسَى بْنُ يُونُسَ، ح، وَحَدَّثَنَاهُ مُحَمَّدُ بْنُ أَبِي عُمَرَ، قَالَ: حَدَّثَنَا سُفْيَانُ، ح، وَحَدَّثَنَا مِنْجَابُ بْنُ الْحَارِثِ التَّمِيمِيُّ، أَخْبَرَنَا ابْنُ مُسْهِرٍ، كُلُّهُمْ عَنِ الْأَعْمَشِ، فِي هَذَا الْإِسْنَادِ بِمَعْنَى حَدِيثِ أَبِي مُعَاوِيَةَ، غَيْرَ أَنَّ فِي حَدِيثِ عِيسَى، وَسُفْيَانَ قَالَ: فَكَانَ أَصْحَابُ عَبْدِ اللهِ يُعْجِبُهُمْ هَذَا الْحَدِيثُ لِأَنَّ إِسْلَامَ جَرِيرٍ كَانَ بَعْدَ نُزُولِ الْمَائِدَةِ.

[479–73]. (Dār al-Salām 0522) Yaḥyā ibn Yaḥyā al-Tamīmī narrated:[i] Abū Khaythamah reported; from al-Aʿmash; from Shaqīq; from Ḥudhayfah: **'I was with the Prophet (peace be upon him) when he came to the rubbish heap of some people. He urinated standing. I moved away, but he said:**

i. Related by al-Bukhārī, 225 (in a shorter version), 224, 226 and 2471; Abū Dāwūd, 23; al-Tirmidhī, 13; al-Nasā'ī, 26, 27, 28 and 18; Ibn Mājah, 305, 306 and 544.

"Come near". I stepped forward until I was close to his feet. He performed the ablution, wiping his *khuffs*.'

حَدَّثَنَا يَحْيَى بْنُ يَحْيَى التَّمِيمِيُّ، أَخْبَرَنَا أَبُو خَيْثَمَةَ، عَنِ الْأَعْمَشِ، عَنْ شَقِيقٍ، عَنْ حُذَيْفَةَ، قَالَ: «كُنْتُ مَعَ النَّبِيِّ صَلَّى اللهُ عَلَيْهِ وَسَلَّمَ فَانْتَهَى إِلَى سُبَاطَةِ قَوْمٍ، فَبَالَ قَائِمًا» فَتَنَحَّيْتُ فَقَالَ: «ادْنُهْ» فَدَنَوْتُ حَتَّى قُمْتُ عِنْدَ عَقِبَيْهِ «فَتَوَضَّأَ فَمَسَحَ عَلَى خُفَّيْهِ»

[480–74]. (Dār al-Salām 0523) Yaḥyā ibn Yaḥyā narrated: Jarīr reported; from Manṣūr; from Abū Wā'il: **'Abū Mūsā used to be strict about urine and he would urinate in a bottle. He used to say: "If urine dropped onto the skin of a person from the Children of Israel, he would cut it off with scissors". Ḥudhayfah said: "I wish that your friend is not so strict. I could see myself walking with God's Messenger (peace be upon him). He came to a heap of rubbish behind a wall. He stood as any of you would stand and urinated. I stood away from him. He then signalled me and I came forward, and stood close to his feet until he finished".'**

حَدَّثَنَا يَحْيَى بْنُ يَحْيَى، أَخْبَرَنَا جَرِيرٌ، عَنْ مَنْصُورٍ، عَنْ أَبِي وَائِلٍ، قَالَ: كَانَ أَبُو مُوسَى، يُشَدِّدُ فِي الْبَوْلِ، وَيَبُولُ فِي قَارُورَةٍ وَيَقُولُ: إِنَّ بَنِي إِسْرَائِيلَ كَانَ إِذَا أَصَابَ جِلْدَ أَحَدِهِمْ بَوْلٌ قَرَضَهُ بِالْمَقَارِيضِ، فَقَالَ حُذَيْفَةُ: «لَوَدِدْتُ أَنَّ صَاحِبَكُمْ لَا يُشَدِّدُ هَذَا التَّشْدِيدَ، فَلَقَدْ رَأَيْتُنِي أَنَا وَرَسُولُ اللهِ صَلَّى اللهُ عَلَيْهِ وَسَلَّمَ نَتَمَاشَى، فَأَتَى سُبَاطَةً خَلْفَ حَائِطٍ، فَقَامَ كَمَا يَقُومُ أَحَدُكُمْ، فَبَالَ، فَانْتَبَذْتُ مِنْهُ، فَأَشَارَ إِلَيَّ فَجِئْتُ، فَقُمْتُ عِنْدَ عَقِبِهِ حَتَّى فَرَغَ»

Text Explanation

It is universally agreed by all who may be considered in questions requiring unanimity that when a person is performing the ablution, it is perfectly permissible to wipe one's footwear when a person is travelling, whether this is for a particular need or not. It is indeed permissible for a woman who is staying at home and for a person who is ill and does not walk. It is only denied by the Shiah and the Khawārij, but their disagreement is discarded. Different reports have been attributed to Mālik concerning this issue, but what is well-known in the Mālikī School of *fiqh* is the same as the view of the great majority of scholars. Indeed, wiping the *khuffs* or footwear is reported by a countless number of the Prophet's companions. Al-Ḥasan al-Baṣrī said: 'Seventy of the Prophet's companions narrated to me that God's Messenger (peace be upon him) used to wipe on his *khuffs*.' I mentioned the names of a large number of the Prophet's companions who reported it in *Sharḥ al-Muhadhdhab*, I also added some very interesting points concerning it. May God guide us to what is best.

Scholars have different views regarding whether in ablution it is better to wipe on footwear or to wash one's feet. Our scholars are of the view that washing one's feet is preferable because it is the original requirement. A number of the Prophet's companions are of this view, including ʿUmar ibn al-Khaṭṭāb and his son, ʿAbdullāh and Abū Ayyūb al-Anṣārī. A number of scholars of the Tābiʿīn generation express the view that wiping footwear is preferable. This is the view of al-Shaʿbī, al-Ḥakam and Ḥammād. Both views are reported to have been expressed by Ahmad, but the more authentic one is that wiping footwear is preferable, and this is the choice of Ibn al-Mundhir. The other view is that both options are equal, but God knows best.

In the first hadith, al-Aʿmash quotes Ibrāhīm: 'They liked this hadith because Jarīr embraced Islam after the revelation of [the surah] *Al-Mā'idah*'. This refers to the sixth verse in Surah 5, *Al-Mā'idah*, or The Repast, which gives detailed requirements in ablution: '*Believers, when you are about to pray, wash your faces, and your hands and arms up to the elbows, and pass your wet hands lightly over your heads, and wash your feet up to the ankles*'. (5: 6) Had Jarīr embraced Islam before the revelation of this surah, his hadith might have been abrogated by this verse. Since he became a Muslim later than its revelation, we realize that his hadith remains valid. It makes clear that the verse applies to a person who is not wearing *khuffs*, and thus the hadith limits the application of the verse, but God knows best.

In al-Bayhaqī's *Sunan*, Ibrāhīm ibn Adham is quoted: 'I have not heard anything better than Jarīr's hadith on the subject of wiping on the *khuffs*, but God knows best'.

In hadith No. 479, Ḥudhayfah, the narrator, said: 'I was with the Prophet (peace be upon him) when he came to the rubbish heap of some people. He urinated standing. I moved away, but he said: "Come near". I stepped forward until I was close to his feet. He performed the ablution wiping his *khuffs*'. The rubbish heap used to be outside people's homes and al-Khaṭṭābī explains that it was normally soft and would absorb the urine and not let it splash back. Scholars give different reasons for the Prophet's standing up as he urinated, and these have been reported by al-Khaṭṭābī, al-Bayhaqī and other eminent scholars. The first, which is attributed to al-Shāfiʿī, is that Arabs used to believe that it helped to cure pain in one's loins. This hadith suggests that the Prophet complained of such pain at the time. A second view attributes this to what is mentioned that the Prophet was at the time complaining of pain in his knees, but this report is not highly authentic. A third view suggests that the side of the rubbish heap was too high for the Prophet to squat. Imam al-Māzarī and *Qāḍī* ʿIyāḍ mention a fourth view, which is that standing when urinating ensures that nothing is discharged through the anus, while squatting makes this possible. Hence, ʿUmar said: 'Urinating standing up gives more back security'. A fifth explanation is also possible, suggesting that the Prophet did it on this occasion to show that it is permissible, but his normal practice was to squat when urinating. This is further indicated by the hadith reported by ʿĀ'ishah: 'Do not believe anyone who tells you that the Prophet used to stand up when urinating. He always did it squatting'. [This hadith is related by Ahmad ibn Ḥanbal, al-Tirmidhī, al-Nasā'ī and others, with a sound chain of transmission], but God knows best.

Some hadiths prohibiting urination in the standing position have been reported, but none of these aspires to any degree of authenticity. However, ʿĀ'ishah's hadith mentioned above is authentic. Hence, scholars say that to urinate while standing is discouraged, but this discouragement is of the milder type. Ibn al-Mundhir said in *al-Ishrāf ʿalā Madhāhib al-ʿUlamā'*:

> Scholars differ concerning standing when urinating. It is authentically reported to have been done by 'Umar ibn al-Khaṭṭāb, Zayd ibn Thābit, Ibn 'Umar and Sahl ibn Sa'd. It is also reported of Anas, 'Alī and Abū Hurayrah. Likewise, it was done by Ibn Sīrīn and 'Urwah ibn al-Zubayr. It is stated to be discouraged by Ibn Mas'ūd, al-Sha'bī and Ibrāhīm ibn Sa'd. Indeed, Ibrāhīm ibn Sa'd considered a person who stands up when urinating to be unacceptable as a witness. A third view is that if the person is at a place that causes the urine to splash, then to urinate standing is discouraged, but if it does not splash, then it is acceptable. This is Mālik's view. Personally, I prefer that it should be done squatting, but to do it standing is permissible. All this is authentically reported from God's Messenger (peace be upon him).

The Prophet is stated to have urinated on the rubbish heap of some people. This admits different explanations, and the most apparent is that people liked that and even preferred it. If it is known that a person prefers or likes something that may be done by others, such as urinating in their place, or eating of their food, then this is perfectly permissible. Similar situations are plentiful in the Prophet's guidance. We have referred to this rule when we discussed hadith No. 53, in the Book of Faith, where Abū Hurayrah mentions that he shrank himself like a fox does. The second explanation is that this rubbish heap did not belong to a particular family, but was available to all people. It is described as belonging to some people because of its proximity to their homes. A third explanation is that those people had permitted others to relieve themselves there, giving either an express or implied permission, but God knows best.[i]

The Prophet was known to move well away from people and habitation in order to relieve himself. Hence, a question arises as to why on this occasion he did it on the rubbish heap that was close to some people's homes. *Qāḍī* 'Iyāḍ explains: 'It is well known that the Prophet was always busy with people's affairs, considering what

i. Urinating on vegetable matter assists in the formation of good compost for growing crops. It also reminds vermin and larger animals, e.g. foxes that humans are around.

serves their interests. It may be that on this occasion he stayed at a particular place for some time and he urgently needed to relieve himself. He could not walk a long distance this time, and had he done so it might have caused him some harm. Therefore, he went to the rubbish heap because it was convenient. He placed Ḥudhayfah close to him to shield him from other people'. *Qāḍī* 'Iyāḍ's explanation is certainly good, but God knows best.

Ḥudhayfah, the narrator of this hadith, said: 'I moved away, but he said: "Come near". I stepped forward until I was close to his feet'. Scholars say that the Prophet asked him to come closer to him so that he would be shielding the Prophet and so would not be seen urinating, because people do not like to be seen in this predicament. As the Prophet was only urinating in the standing position, there was little chance of breaking wind or giving off a bad smell. Hence, he told Ḥudhayfah to come closer. In a different hadith the Prophet told his companion to move away when he wanted to relieve himself. On that occasion, he was squatting and perhaps relieving both needs, which would have caused a bad smell. Hence, some scholars say in their comments on this hadith that it is desirable to be close to a person urinating in the standing position and to move away from him if he is squatting, but God knows best.

This hadith gives us a number of useful points and we have already explained most of them, but we will add them again in brief. It confirms the permissibility of wiping on footwear, and that it is permissible to do it at home. It confirms that it is permissible to urinate in the standing position; to be close to a person who is urinating; to request a close friend to come close so as to be a sort of a shield; to seek to be shielded; to relieve oneself at a place close to people's homes; and other points, but God knows best.

In hadith No. 480, Ḥudhayfah expresses his feeling that Abū Mūsā was too strict concerning urination. He considers that such strictness is contrary to the Sunnah. The Prophet urinated in the standing position, and it is clear that in this position some splashing may occur. Yet the Prophet did not bother about this possibility and did not go to the extent of urinating in a bottle, as Abū Mūsā used to do, but God knows best.

[481–75]. (Dār al-Salām 0524) Qutaybah ibn Sa῾īd narrated:[i] Layth narrated [H]. Also, Muhammad ibn Rumḥ ibn al-Muhājir narrated: al-Layth reported; from Yaḥyā ibn Sa῾īd; from Sa῾d ibn Ibrāhīm; from Nāfi῾ ibn Jubayr; from ῾Urwah ibn al-Mughīrah; from his father al-Mughīrah ibn Shu῾bah; from God's Messenger (peace be upon him): **'He went out for his need and al-Mughīrah followed him holding a bottle containing water. He poured for him when he finished his need. He performed the ablution and wiped on his *khuffs*'**.

In Ibn Rumḥ's narration of the word 'when' is replaced by 'until'.

حَدَّثَنَا قُتَيْبَةُ بْنُ سَعِيدٍ، حَدَّثَنَا لَيْثٌ ح، وَحَدَّثَنَا مُحَمَّدُ بْنُ رُمْحِ بْنُ الْـمُهَاجِرِ، أَخْبَرَنَا اللَّيْثُ، عَنْ يَحْيَى بْنِ سَعِيدٍ، عَنْ سَعْدِ بْنِ إِبْرَاهِيمَ، عَنْ نَافِعِ بْنِ جُبَيْرٍ، عَنْ عُرْوَةَ بْنِ الْـمُغِيرَةِ، عَنْ أَبِيهِ الْـمُغِيرَةِ بْنِ شُعْبَةَ: عَنْ «رَسُولِ اللهِ صَلَّى اللهُ عَلَيْهِ وَسَلَّمَ أَنَّهُ خَرَجَ لِحَاجَتِهِ فَاتَّبَعَهُ الْـمُغِيرَةُ بِإِدَاوَةٍ فِيهَا مَاءٌ فَصَبَّ عَلَيْهِ حِينَ فَرَغَ مِنْ حَاجَتِهِ، فَتَوَضَّأَ وَمَسَحَ عَلَى الْخُفَّيْنِ»

وَفِي رِوَايَةِ ابْنِ رُمْحٍ: مَكَانَ حِينَ حَتَّى.

[482–000]. (Dār al-Salām 0525) Muhammad ibn al-Muthannā narrated: ῾Abd al-Wahhāb narrated saying: I heard Yaḥyā ibn Sa῾īd … giving the same chain of transmission, but said: **'He washed his face and hands, wiped his head then wiped on his *khuffs*'**.

وَحَدَّثَنَاهُ مُحَمَّدُ بْنُ الْـمُثَنَّى، حَدَّثَنَا عَبْدُ الْوَهَّابِ، قَالَ، سَمِعْتُ يَحْيَى بْنَ سَعِيدٍ بِهَذَا الْإِسْنَادِ وَقَالَ: فَغَسَلَ وَجْهَهُ وَيَدَيْهِ وَمَسَحَ بِرَأْسِهِ ثُمَّ مَسَحَ عَلَى الْخُفَّيْنِ.

---

i. Related by al-Bukhārī, 182, 203, 206 (in similar wording), and 4421 and 5799 in longer versions; Abū Dāwūd, 149, and 151 in a longer version; al-Nasā'ī, 79, 124, and 82 in a longer version; Ibn Mājah, 545.

[483–76]. (Dār al-Salām 0526) Yaḥyā ibn Yaḥyā al-Tamīmī narrated: Abū al-Aḥwaṣ reported; from Ashʿath; from al-Aswad ibn Hilāl; from al-Mughīrah ibn Shuʿbah: **'I was with God's Messenger one night when he went down and relieved himself. He came back and I poured water for him from a bottle I had with me. He performed the ablution and wiped on his *khuffs*'.**

وَحَدَّثَنَا يَحْيَى بْنُ يَحْيَى التَّمِيمِيُّ، أَخْبَرَنَا أَبُو الْأَحْوَصِ، عَنْ أَشْعَثَ، عَنِ الْأَسْوَدِ بْنِ هِلَالٍ، عَنِ الْمُغِيرَةِ بْنِ شُعْبَةَ، قَالَ: «بَيْنَا أَنَا مَعَ رَسُولِ اللهِ صَلَّى اللهُ عَلَيْهِ وَسَلَّمَ ذَاتَ لَيْلَةٍ إِذْ نَزَلَ فَقَضَى حَاجَتَهُ، ثُمَّ جَاءَ فَصَبَبْتُ عَلَيْهِ مِنْ إِدَاوَةٍ كَانَتْ مَعِي، فَتَوَضَّأَ وَمَسَحَ عَلَى خُفَّيْهِ»

[484–77]. (Dār al-Salām 527) Abū Bakr ibn Abī Shaybah and Abū Kurayb narrated.[i] Abū Bakr said: Abū Muʿāwiyah narrated; from al-Aʿmash; from Muslim; from Masrūq; from al-Mughīrah ibn Shuʿbah: **'I was travelling with the Prophet when he said: "Mughīrah, bring the bottle". I picked it up and went out with him. God's Messenger then went alone until I could not see him. He relieved himself, then came back. He was wearing a Syrian overcoat with narrow sleeves. He tried to bring his hand out of the sleeve but it was too tight. He brought out his hand from the bottom. I poured water for him and he performed the ablution as he would do for prayer, then he wiped on his *khuffs*, and prayed'.**

وَحَدَّثَنَا أَبُو بَكْرِ بْنُ أَبِي شَيْبَةَ، وَأَبُو كُرَيْبٍ، قَالَ: أَبُو بَكْرٍ، حَدَّثَنَا أَبُو مُعَاوِيَةَ، عَنِ الْأَعْمَشِ، عَنْ مُسْلِمٍ، عَنْ مَسْرُوقٍ، عَنِ الْمُغِيرَةِ بْنِ شُعْبَةَ، قَالَ: كُنْتُ مَعَ النَّبِيِّ صَلَّى اللهُ عَلَيْهِ وَسَلَّمَ فِي سَفَرٍ فَقَالَ: «يَا مُغِيرَةُ خُذِ الْإِدَاوَةَ» فَأَخَذْتُهَا، ثُمَّ خَرَجْتُ مَعَهُ،

i. Related by al-Bukhārī, 363 (in similar wording), and 388 (in a shorter version), 2918, and 5798; al-Nasāʾī, 123; Ibn Mājah, 389.

فَانْطَلَقَ رَسُولُ اللهِ صَلَّى اللهُ عَلَيْهِ وَسَلَّمَ حَتَّى تَوَارَى عَنِّي، «فَقَضَى حَاجَتَهُ، ثُمَّ جَاءَ وَعَلَيْهِ جُبَّةٌ شَامِيَّةٌ ضَيِّقَةُ الْكُمَّيْنِ، فَذَهَبَ يُخْرِجُ يَدَهُ مِنْ كُمِّهَا فَضَاقَتْ عَلَيْهِ فَأَخْرَجَ يَدَهُ مِنْ أَسْفَلِهَا، فَصَبَبْتُ عَلَيْهِ فَتَوَضَّأَ وُضُوءَهُ لِلصَّلَاةِ، ثُمَّ مَسَحَ عَلَى خُفَّيْهِ ثُمَّ صَلَّى»

[485–78]. (Dār al-Salām 0528) Isḥāq ibn Ibrāhīm and ʿAlī ibn Khashram narrated: both from ʿĪsā ibn Yūnus, Isḥāq said: ʿĪsā reported; al-Aʿmash narrated; from Muslim; from Masrūq; from al-Mughīrah ibn Shuʿbah: **'God's Messenger (peace be upon him) went out to relieve himself. When he came back I held the bottle for him and poured him water. He washed his hands, then washed his face. He wanted to wash his arms, but the coat was too narrow, and he brought his arms out from underneath the coat, and washed them. He wiped his head and wiped on his *khuffs*, then led us in prayer'**.

وَحَدَّثَنَا إِسْحَاقُ بْنُ إِبْرَاهِيمَ، وَعَلِيُّ بْنُ خَشْرَمٍ، جَمِيعًا عَنْ عِيسَى بْنِ يُونُسَ، قَالَ: إِسْحَاقُ، أَخْبَرَنَا عِيسَى، حَدَّثَنَا الْأَعْمَشُ، عَنْ مُسْلِمٍ، عَنْ مَسْرُوقٍ، عَنِ الْمُغِيرَةِ بْنِ شُعْبَةَ، قَالَ: «خَرَجَ رَسُولُ اللهِ صَلَّى اللهُ عَلَيْهِ وَسَلَّمَ لِيَقْضِيَ حَاجَتَهُ، فَلَمَّا رَجَعَ تَلَقَّيْتُهُ بِالْإِدَاوَةِ فَصَبَبْتُ عَلَيْهِ، فَغَسَلَ يَدَيْهِ ثُمَّ غَسَلَ وَجْهَهُ، ثُمَّ ذَهَبَ لِيَغْسِلَ ذِرَاعَيْهِ فَضَاقَتِ الْجُبَّةُ، فَأَخْرَجَهُمَا مِنْ تَحْتِ الْجُبَّةِ فَغَسَلَهُمَا، وَمَسَحَ رَأْسَهُ، وَمَسَحَ عَلَى خُفَّيْهِ ثُمَّ صَلَّى بِنَا»

[486–79]. (Dār al-Salām 0529) Muhammad ibn ʿAbdullāh ibn Numayr narrated: my father narrated; Zakariyyā' narrated; from ʿĀmir; ʿUrwah ibn al-Mughīrah reported to me; from his father: **'I was with the Prophet (peace be upon him) one night travelling. He said to me: "Do you have some water?" I said: "Yes". He dismounted and walked away until he disappeared in the darkness of the night. When he came back, I poured water for him from the bottle. He washed his face. He was wearing a woollen coat, and he could not bring his**

arms out, so he brought them out from the bottom of the coat. He washed his arms and wiped his head. I went down to take off his *khuffs*, but he said: "Leave them. I put them on in a state of purity". He wiped on them'.

حَدَّثَنَا مُحَمَّدُ بْنُ عَبْدِ اللهِ بْنِ نُمَيْرٍ، حَدَّثَنَا أَبِي، حَدَّثَنَا زَكَرِيَّا، عَنْ عَامِرٍ، قَالَ: أَخْبَرَنِي عُرْوَةُ بْنُ الْمُغِيرَةِ، عَنْ أَبِيهِ، قَالَ: كُنْتُ مَعَ النَّبِيِّ صَلَّى اللهُ عَلَيْهِ وَسَلَّمَ ذَاتَ لَيْلَةٍ فِي مَسِيرٍ، فَقَالَ لِي: «أَمَعَكَ مَاءٌ» قُلْتُ: نَعَمْ «فَنَزَلَ عَنْ رَاحِلَتِهِ، فَمَشَى حَتَّى تَوَارَى فِي سَوَادِ اللَّيْلِ، ثُمَّ جَاءَ فَأَفْرَغْتُ عَلَيْهِ مِنَ الْإِدَاوَةِ، فَغَسَلَ وَجْهَهُ، وَعَلَيْهِ جُبَّةٌ مِنْ صُوفٍ، فَلَمْ يَسْتَطِعْ أَنْ يُخْرِجَ ذِرَاعَيْهِ مِنْهَا حَتَّى أَخْرَجَهُمَا مِنْ أَسْفَلِ الْجُبَّةِ فَغَسَلَ ذِرَاعَيْهِ وَمَسَحَ بِرَأْسِهِ ثُمَّ أَهْوَيْتُ لِأَنْزِعَ خُفَّيْهِ» فَقَالَ: «دَعْهُمَا فَإِنِّي أَدْخَلْتُهُمَا طَاهِرَتَيْنِ وَمَسَحَ عَلَيْهِمَا»

[487–80]. (Dār al-Salām 0530) Muhammad ibn Ḥātim narrated to me: Isḥāq ibn Manṣūr narrated; 'Umar ibn Abī Zā'idah narrated; from al-Sha'bī; from 'Urwah ibn al-Mughīrah; from his father: **'He [helped] the Prophet doing his ablution. He performed the ablution and wiped on his *khuffs*. He asked him and he [the Prophet] said: "I put them on in a state of purity".'**

وَحَدَّثَنِي مُحَمَّدُ بْنُ حَاتِمٍ، حَدَّثَنَا إِسْحَاقُ بْنُ مَنْصُورٍ، حَدَّثَنَا عُمَرُ بْنُ أَبِي زَائِدَةَ، عَنِ الشَّعْبِيِّ، عَنْ عُرْوَةَ بْنِ الْمُغِيرَةِ، عَنْ أَبِيهِ، أَنَّهُ وَضَّأَ النَّبِيَّ صَلَّى اللهُ عَلَيْهِ وَسَلَّمَ فَتَوَضَّأَ وَمَسَحَ عَلَى خُفَّيْهِ، فَقَالَ لَهُ: فَقَالَ: «إِنِّي أَدْخَلْتُهُمَا طَاهِرَتَيْنِ»

Text Explanation

Hadith No. 481 mentions 'Urwah's report from his father al-Mughīrah: 'He went out for his need and al-Mughīrah followed him …'. This is how 'Urwah reported his father's words. This mode occurs often in hadith reporting, with a narrator quoting the first narrator but using the third person pronoun in reference to himself, in place of the first person. The hadith states: 'He poured for him when he finished his need'. This means that the action of pouring the water took place after the Prophet came back from where he relieved himself and moved to another place. Al-Mughīrah poured the water for him so that he performed the ablution.

The version which replaces 'when' with 'until' means that he poured the water for him from his bottle until he finished his ablution. Thus 'his need' in this case means his need to perform the ablution. Another narration stated above makes clear that al-Mughīrah poured water for the Prophet's ablution after he returned from answering the call of nature, but God knows best.

This hadith shows that it is permissible to have help in performing the ablution. It is also confirmed in a hadith narrated by Usāmah ibn Zayd that he poured water for the Prophet when he performed the ablution after he left Arafat during his pilgrimage. Some hadiths give instructions against seeking others' help in performing the ablution but these hadiths are not confirmed to be authentic. Our scholars say: 'Seeking help is of three kinds: 1) to ask others to bring the water. This is not discouraged and the ablution is perfect; 2) to seek help in washing one's organs, and the other person actually washes them for him. This is discouraged, unless there is specific need for it; and 3) having another person pour water. It is preferable not to have this. The question is whether this third type is offensive, i.e. *makrūh*? There are two views on this point. Our scholars also said: 'If someone is pouring water for another to perform the ablution, the one pouring the water should stand to the left of the one performing it, but God knows best.'

The Prophet brought out his arms from the bottom of his coat. This shows that this is permissible when needed and in a secluded area. If people are around, it should not be done unless there is clear need for it, because it is unbecoming.

Hadith No. 487 mentions that al-Mughīrah helped the Prophet doing his ablution and mentions that the Prophet performed the ablution and wiped his *khuffs* instead of washing his feet. The Prophet said: 'When I put them on I was in a state of purity'.

The Prophet thus explains wiping his footwear, stating that he 'put them on in a state of purity'. This makes clear that it is not permissible to wipe on the *khuffs* or footwear unless one has worn them after having performed the ablution fully. Only if he has done this and then put on his footwear may he wipe on it instead of washing his feet when he needs a fresh ablution. That both are put on in a state of purity means that each one of them is put on with the foot having been in a state of purity. Scholars differ on this point, and our school of *fiqh* makes it a condition that they should be worn when one is in a complete state of purity. Thus, if one washes one's right foot and puts on its *khuff* then washes one's left foot and puts on its *khuff*, wearing it on the right foot is incorrect. One must take the *khuff* of the right foot and put it on again. He need not take off the *khuff* of the left foot because he put it on after his ablution was complete. Some of our scholars take the odd view requiring taking off both *khuffs*. The view of our Shāfiʿī School is also the view of Mālik, Ahmad and Isḥāq. On the other hand, Abū Ḥanīfah, Sufyān al-Thawrī, Yaḥyā ibn Adam, al-Muzanī, Abū Thawr and Dāwūd said: 'It is permissible to wear the *khuff* and then complete one's ablution', but God knows best.

Transmission

The chain of transmission of hadith No. 481 features: 'al-Layth reported; from Yaḥyā ibn Saʿīd; from Saʿd ibn Ibrāhīm; from Nāfiʿ ibn Jubayr; from ʿUrwah ibn al-Mughīrah; from his father al-Mughīrah'. This chain includes four narrators from the Tābiʿīn generation reporting from each other. These are Yaḥyā ibn Saʿīd al-Anṣārī, Saʿd, Nāfiʿ and ʿUrwah.

The chain of transmission of hadith No. 486 mentions: 'Muhammad ibn ʿAbdullāh ibn Numayr narrated: my father narrated; Zakariyyā' narrated; from ʿĀmir; ʿUrwah ibn al-Mughīrah reported to me from his father'. All narrators in this chain belonged to Kufah.

Hadith No. 487 begins with the following chain of transmission: 'Muhammad ibn Ḥātim narrated to me: Isḥāq ibn Manṣūr narrated; ʿUmar ibn Abī Zā'idah narrated; from al-Shaʿbī; from ʿUrwah ibn al-Mughīrah; from his father'. Imam Abū ʿAlī al-Ḥusayn ibn ʿAlī al-Naisabūrī said:

> This is how this chain of transmission has been reported to us from Muslim, with all its versions featuring ʿUmar ibn Abī Zā'idah directly from al-Shaʿbī, with no one else between them. Abū Masʿūd mentions that Muslim ibn al-Ḥajjāj enters it from Ibn Ḥātim from Isḥāq from ʿUmar ibn Abī Zā'idah from ʿAbdullāh ibn Abī al-Safar from al-Shaʿbī. The same is stated by Abu Bakr al-Jawraqī in his larger book *al-Kabīr*. Al-Bukhārī mentions in his book that ʿUmar ibn Abī Zā'idah heard from al-Shaʿbī, and he also used to send Ibn Abī al-Safar and Zakariyyā' to al-Shaʿbī, putting questions to him.

Abū Muhammad Khalaf al-Wāsiṭī, an eminent Hadith scholar, mentions in his *al-Aṭrāf* that Muslim reports it from Ibn Ḥātim from Isḥāq from ʿUmar ibn Abī Zā'idah from al-Shaʿbī, as it appears in original manuscripts, without mentioning Ibn Abī al-Safar, but God knows best.

CHAPTER 23

WIPING THE FOREHEAD AND ON THE TURBAN

[488–81]. (Dār al-Salām 0531) Muhammad ibn ʿAbdullāh ibn Bazīʿ narrated to me:[i] Yazīd (meaning Ibn Zurayʿ) narrated; Ḥumayd al-Ṭawīl narrated; Bakr ibn ʿAbdullāh al-Muzanī narrated; from ʿUrwah ibn al-Mughīrah ibn Shuʿbah; from his father: **'God's Messenger stayed behind and I stayed behind with him. When he had answered the call of nature, he said: "Do you have water?" I brought him a bottle and he washed his hands and face. He then tried to roll back his sleeves but the sleeve of his coat was too tight. He stretched his arms from under his coat, throwing the coat over his shoulders. He washed his arms and wiped his forehead, his turban and his *khuffs*. He then rode and I rode. We caught up with the people after they had started the prayer. ʿAbd al-Raḥmān ibn ʿAwf was leading the prayer and they had completed one *rakʿah*. As he felt the Prophet's presence, he wanted to step back, but [the Prophet] signalled him and he continued to lead the prayer. When he finished, the Prophet stood up and I did the same. We prayed the *rakʿah* that we had missed'.**

حَدَّثَنِي مُحَمَّدُ بْنُ عَبْدِ اللهِ بْنِ بَزِيعٍ، حَدَّثَنَا يَزِيدُ يَعْنِي ابْنَ زُرَيْعٍ، حَدَّثَنَا حُمَيْدٌ الطَّوِيلُ، حَدَّثَنَا بَكْرُ بْنُ عَبْدِ اللهِ الْمُزَنِيُّ، عَنْ عُرْوَةَ بْنِ الْمُغِيرَةِ بْنِ شُعْبَةَ، عَنْ أَبِيهِ، قَالَ: تَخَلَّفَ رَسُولُ اللهِ صَلَّى اللهُ عَلَيْهِ وَسَلَّمَ وَتَخَلَّفْتُ مَعَهُ فَلَمَّا قَضَى حَاجَتَهُ قَالَ: «أَمَعَكَ مَاءٌ؟»

i. Related by Muslim, 952; al-Nasāʾī, 108 and 125.

فَأَتَيْتُهُ بِمِطْهَرَةٍ، «فَغَسَلَ كَفَّيْهِ وَوَجْهَهُ، ثُمَّ ذَهَبَ يَحْسِرُ عَنْ ذِرَاعَيْهِ فَضَاقَ كُمُّ الْجُبَّةِ، فَأَخْرَجَ يَدَهُ مِنْ تَحْتِ الْجُبَّةِ، وَأَلْقَى الْجُبَّةَ عَلَى مَنْكِبَيْهِ، وَغَسَلَ ذِرَاعَيْهِ، وَمَسَحَ بِنَاصِيَتِهِ وَعَلَى الْعِمَامَةِ وَعَلَى خُفَّيْهِ، ثُمَّ رَكِبَ وَرَكِبْتُ فَانْتَهَيْنَا إِلَى الْقَوْمِ، وَقَدْ قَامُوا فِي الصَّلَاةِ، يُصَلِّي بِهِمْ عَبْدُ الرَّحْمَنِ بْنُ عَوْفٍ وَقَدْ رَكَعَ بِهِمْ رَكْعَةً، فَلَمَّا أَحَسَّ بِالنَّبِيِّ صَلَّى اللهُ عَلَيْهِ وَسَلَّمَ ذَهَبَ يَتَأَخَّرُ، فَأَوْمَأَ إِلَيْهِ، فَصَلَّى بِهِمْ، فَلَمَّا سَلَّمَ قَامَ النَّبِيُّ صَلَّى اللهُ عَلَيْهِ وَسَلَّمَ وَقُمْتُ، فَرَكَعْنَا الرَّكْعَةَ الَّتِي سَبَقَتْنَا»

[489–82]. (Dār al-Salām 0532) Umayyah ibn Bisṭām and Muhammad ibn ʿAbd al-Aʿlā narrated:[i] al-Muʿtamir narrated; from his father; Bakr ibn ʿAbdullāh narrated to me; from Ibn al-Mughīrah; from his father that: '**the Prophet (peace be upon him) wiped on his *khuffs*, the front of his head and his turban**'.

حَدَّثَنَا أُمَيَّةُ بْنُ بِسْطَامَ، وَمُحَمَّدُ بْنُ عَبْدِ الْأَعْلَى، قَالَا: حَدَّثَنَا الْـمُعْتَمِرُ، عَنْ أَبِيهِ، قَالَ: حَدَّثَنِي بَكْرُ بْنُ عَبْدِ اللهِ، عَنِ ابْنِ الْـمُغِيرَةِ، عَنْ أَبِيهِ، أَنَّ النَّبِيَّ صَلَّى اللهُ عَلَيْهِ وَسَلَّمَ: «مَسَحَ عَلَى الْخُفَّيْنِ، وَمُقَدَّمِ رَأْسِهِ وَعَلَى عِمَامَتِهِ»

[000–000]. (Dār al-Salām 0533) Muhammad ibn ʿAbd al-Aʿlā narrated: al-Muʿtamir narrated; from his father; from Bakr; from al-Ḥasan, from Ibn al-Mughīrah; from his father; from the Prophet: **the same text**.

وحَدَّثَنَا مُحَمَّدُ بْنُ عَبْدِ الْأَعْلَى، حَدَّثَنَا الْـمُعْتَمِرُ، عَنْ أَبِيهِ، عَنْ بَكْرٍ، عَنِ الْحَسَنِ، عَنِ ابْنِ الْـمُغِيرَةِ، عَنْ أَبِيهِ، عَنِ النَّبِيِّ صَلَّى اللهُ عَلَيْهِ وَسَلَّمَ بِمِثْلِهِ.

[490–83]. (Dār al-Salām 0534) Muhammad ibn Bashshār and Muhammad ibn Ḥātim narrated: both from Yaḥyā al-Qaṭṭān.

---

i. Related by Abu Dāwūd, 150; al-Tirmidhī, 100; al-Nasāʾī, 107.

Ibn Ḥātim said: Yaḥyā ibn Saʿīd narrated; from al-Taymī; from Bakr ibn ʿAbdullāh; from al-Ḥasan; from Ibn al-Mughīrah ibn Shuʿbah; from his father. Bakr said: **'And I heard from Ibn al-Mughīrah that the Prophet performed the ablution, wiping his forehead, turban and *khuffs*.**

وَحَدَّثَنَا مُحَمَّدُ بْنُ بَشَّارٍ، وَمُحَمَّدُ بْنُ حَاتِمٍ، جَمِيعًا عَنْ يَحْيَى الْقَطَّانِ، قَالَ: ابْنُ حَاتِمٍ، حَدَّثَنَا يَحْيَى بْنُ سَعِيدٍ، عَنِ التَّيْمِيِّ، عَنْ بَكْرِ بْنِ عَبْدِ اللهِ، عَنِ الْحَسَنِ، عَنِ ابْنِ الْمُغِيرَةِ بْنِ شُعْبَةَ، عَنْ أَبِيهِ، قَالَ: بَكْرٌ، وَقَدْ سَمِعْتُ مِنَ ابْنِ الْمُغِيرَةِ، أَنَّ النَّبِيَّ صَلَّى اللهُ عَلَيْهِ وَسَلَّمَ: «تَوَضَّأَ فَمَسَحَ بِنَاصِيَتِهِ، وَعَلَى الْعِمَامَةِ وَعَلَى الْخُفَّيْنِ»

[491– 84]. (Dār al-Salām 0535) Abū Bakr ibn Abī Shaybah and Muhammad ibn al-ʿAlā' narrated:[i] Abū Muʿāwiyah narrated [H]. Also, Isḥāq narrated: ʿĪsā ibn Yūnus reported; both from al-Aʿmash; from al-Ḥakam; from ʿAbd al-Raḥmān ibn Abī Laylā; from Kaʿb ibn ʿUjrah; from Bilāl: **'that God's Messenger (peace be upon him) wiped on the *khuffs* and the head cover'**.

وَحَدَّثَنَا أَبُو بَكْرِ بْنُ أَبِي شَيْبَةَ، وَمُحَمَّدُ بْنُ الْعَلَاءِ، قَالَا: حَدَّثَنَا أَبُو مُعَاوِيَةَ ح، وَحَدَّثَنَا إِسْحَاقُ، أَخْبَرَنَا عِيسَى بْنُ يُونُسَ، كِلَاهُمَا عَنِ الْأَعْمَشِ، عَنِ الْحَكَمِ، عَنْ عَبْدِ الرَّحْمَنِ بْنِ أَبِي لَيْلَى، عَنْ كَعْبِ بْنِ عُجْرَةَ، عَنْ بِلَالٍ: «أَنَّ رَسُولَ اللهِ صَلَّى اللهُ عَلَيْهِ وَسَلَّمَ مَسَحَ عَلَى الْخُفَّيْنِ وَالْخِمَارِ».

[000–000]. (Dār al-Salām 0536) In ʿĪsā's narration: al-Ḥakam narrated to me; Bilāl narrated to me; and it was narrated to me by Suwayd ibn Saʿīd. ʿAlī (meaning Ibn Mushīr) narrated; from al-Aʿmash, with this chain of transmission. **He said in his narration: 'I saw God's Messenger (peace be upon him) ...'**.

i. Related by al-Tirmidhī, 101; al-Nasā'ī, 104; Ibn Mājah, 561.

وَفِي حَدِيثِ عِيسَى، حَدَّثَنِي الْحَكَمُ، حَدَّثَنِي بِلَالٌ. وَحَدَّثَنِيهِ سُوَيْدُ بْنُ سَعِيدٍ، حَدَّثَنَا عَلِيٌّ يَعْنِي ابْنَ مُسْهِرٍ، عَنِ الْأَعْمَشِ، بِهَذَا الْإِسْنَادِ وَقَالَ فِي الْحَدِيثِ: «رَأَيْتُ رَسُولَ اللهِ صَلَّى اللهُ عَلَيْهِ وَسَلَّمَ ...».

Text Explanation

Hadith No. 488 mentions that the Prophet 'wiped the front of his head and on his turban'. This constitutes some of the argument of our scholars in support of their view that wiping a part of one's head during ablution is sufficient, and that it is not a condition to wipe over one's whole head. Had it been a requirement that one should wipe one's entire head, the Prophet would not have made it enough to wipe his turban instead of the rest of his head. To combine a part of an original requirement and its substitute is not permissible, such as wiping on the *khuff* of one foot and washing the other. As for complementing wiping the front of one's head by wiping on one's turban so that the ablution covers all one's head this is desirable. There is no difference if one has put on one's turban after or before one's earlier ablution. The same applies if one is wearing some sort of a cap and does not wish to remove it: one should wipe the front of one's head. It is desirable for such a person to complement with wiping the cap, just like wiping on one's turban. To only wipe one's turban without wiping any part of one's head is not sufficient according to our Shāfiʿī School, without any disagreement. The same is the view of Mālik, Abū Ḥanīfah and the majority of scholars. Ahmad ibn Ḥanbal is of the view that to limit oneself to wiping over one's turban is sufficient, and his view is agreed by a number of early scholars, but God knows best.

After giving the details of how the Prophet performed his ablution, hadith No. 488 adds: 'We caught up with the people after they had started the prayer. ʿAbd al-Raḥmān ibn ʿAwf was leading the prayer and they had completed one *rakʿah*. As he felt the Prophet's presence, he wanted to step back, but [the Prophet] signalled him and he continued to lead the prayer. When he finished, the Prophet stood up and I did the same. We prayed the *rak'ah* that we had missed'. This hadith includes several very useful points. These include that it is permissible that a better qualified person prays behind a lesser person, and it is permissible for the Prophet (peace be upon him) to pray behind one of his followers.

Another useful point is that it is preferable to offer the prayer at the beginning of its time range, when it falls due. In this hadith, the Prophet's companions offered the prayer at the beginning of the time, without waiting for the Prophet to arrive. Hence, if the regular imam is delayed it is desirable that the congregation should choose one of their number to lead the prayer, provided that they know the imam is reasonable and would not be upset, and no problem would ensue. If they are unsure of what the regular imam would feel, they should offer their prayers individually at the beginning of the time range. If they find a congregation afterwards, it would be desirable for them to repeat their prayer.

A further useful point is that the person who joins congregational prayer when it is in progress, and the imam has completed a part of it, should complete his prayer, adding the part he missed after the imam has finished. The missed part is not waived, except for the recitation of al-Fātiḥah, or the opening surah, which it is required to recite in every *rak'ah*. If a person joins the imam when he is in the bowing position, that *rak'ah* is considered complete. Furthermore, the hadith indicates that a latecomer who joins congregational prayer must follow the imam in bowing, prostration and sitting down, even though the latecomer has missed earlier parts. Only when the imam has finished his prayer should latecomers complete their prayer individually, but God knows best.

'Abd al-Raḥmān ibn 'Awf continued to lead the prayer, but when Abū Bakr was leading the prayer in the mosque during the Prophet's illness and the Prophet came over, Abu Bakr moved behind so that the Prophet stepped forward and took over. The difference between the two cases was that 'Abd al-Raḥmān had completed one *rak'ah* with his congregation. Had the Prophet taken over, the prayer of the congregation would have become confused and its order problematic. In the case of Abū Bakr, there was no possibility of that because the congregation was still in the first *rak'ah*, but God knows best.

In hadith No. 491, Bilāl reports that 'God's Messenger (peace be upon him) wiped on the *khuffs* and the head cover'. By 'head cover' he meant the turban because it covers one's head.

Transmission

Abū 'Alī al-Ḥusayn ibn Muhammad al-Ghassānī quotes Abū Mas'ūd Ibrāhīm ibn Muhammad al-Dimashqī who said: 'Such says Muslim in the chain of transmission of the hadith narrated by Ibn Bazī' from Yazīd ibn Zuray' from 'Urwah ibn al-Mughīrah. Others disagree, mentioning Ḥamzah ibn al-Mughīrah instead of 'Urwah. Abū al-Ḥasan al-Dāraquṭnī attributes the inaccuracy to Muhammad ibn 'Abdullāh ibn Bazī', not to Muslim'. *Qāḍī* 'Iyāḍ said:

> To them the accurate reporting of this hadith is from Ḥamzah ibn al-Mughīrah, while 'Urwah is the one in the other hadiths. Ḥamzah and 'Urwah are two sons of al-Mughīrah and the hadith is reported from both of them. However, the version reported by Bakr ibn 'Abdullāh ibn al-Muzanī includes Ḥamzah ibn al-Mughīrah, or Ibn al-Mughīrah without mentioning his name. Bakr does not mention 'Urwah, and whoever attributes Bakr's reporting as 'from 'Urwah' is confused. Differences also occur in reporting from Bakr: in one version Mu'tamir reports it from Bakr from al-Ḥasan from Ibn al-Mughīrah. The same is reported by Yaḥyā ibn Sa'īd from al-Taymī. Muslim mentions this. Others say: 'from Bakr from al-Mughīrah'. Al-Dāraquṭnī said that this is the result of confusion.

This is what *Qāḍī* 'Iyāḍ said, but God knows best.

The chain of transmission of hadith No. 489 features: 'al-Mu'tamir narrated; from his father; Bakr ibn 'Abdullāh narrated to me; from Ibn al-Mughīrah'. This chain includes four from the Tābi'īn generation reporting from each other. These are Abū al-Mu'tamir

Sulaymān ibn Ṭarkhān, Bakr ibn ʿAbdullāh, al-Ḥasan al-Baṣrī and Ḥamzah ibn al-Mughīrah. The first three belonged to Basrah while Ibn al-Mughīrah was from Kufah.

In hadith No. 490, Bakr says: 'And I heard from Ibn al-Mughīrah ...'. This is how we have checked it in the original manuscripts available in our cities: 'I heard from ...' without the pronoun 'it' after the word 'heard'. *Qāḍī* ʿIyāḍ said: 'According to all our teachers the hadith says: 'I heard it from Ibn al-Mughīrah', with the pronoun 'it' included after 'heard'. It is also mentioned as such by Ibn Abī Khaythamah and al-Dāraquṭnī and others. However, it occurs with some of them without the pronoun 'it', but I have not reported it so'.

The chain of transmission of hadith No. 491 is stated as follows: 'Abū Bakr ibn Abī Shaybah and Muhammad ibn al-ʿAlā' narrated: Abū Muʿāwiyah narrated [H]. Also, Isḥāq narrated: ʿĪsā ibn Yūnus reported; both from al-Aʿmash; from al-Ḥakam; from ʿAbd al-Raḥmān ibn Abī Laylā; from Kaʿb ibn ʿUjrah; from Bilāl: "that God's Messenger (peace be upon him) wiped on the *khuffs* and the head cover". In ʿĪsā's narration: al-Ḥakam narrated to me; Bilāl narrated to me ...'. What Muslim mentions here belongs to the finer aspects of the study of Hadith transmission. What it means is two scholars, Abū Muʿāwiyah and ʿĪsā ibn Yūnus, narrate this hadith from al-Aʿmash. However, in his narration Abū Muʿāwiyah says: 'from al-Aʿmash from al-Ḥakam', while ʿĪsā ibn Yūnus said: 'from al-Aʿmash; al-Ḥakam narrated to me'. Ibn Yūnus thus replaces 'from' by 'narrated', and the latter form is certainly more accurate, particularly when someone like al-Aʿmash is involved because al-Aʿmash is known to make misleading errors. Furthermore, Abū Muʿāwiyah says in his reporting from al-Aʿmash: 'from al-Ḥakam; from ʿAbd al-Raḥmān ibn Abī Laylā; from Kaʿb ibn ʿUjrah; from Bilāl', while ʿĪsā's narration from al-Aʿmash: 'al-Ḥakam narrated to me; from Ibn Abī Laylā; from Kaʿb ibn ʿUjrah; Bilāl narrated to me'. Thus, he replaces 'from Bilāl' in Abū Muʿāwiyah's narration with 'Bilāl narrated to me'.

In his book *al-ʿIlal*, al-Dāraquṭnī discusses the chain of transmission of hadith No. 491, pointing out the disagreement on its sequence and the difference of reporting from al-A'mash. He points out that some reporters drop Bilāl from its transmitters, stopping at Ka'b ibn 'Ujrah, while others add al-Barā' in between Bilāl and Ibn Abī Laylā. However, the majority of scholars reporting this hadith give it in the same way as Muslim. Some also report it from 'Alī ibn Abī Ṭālib from Bilāl, but God knows best.

CHAPTER 24

TIME LIMIT FOR WIPING ON FOOTWEAR

[492–85]. (Dār al-Salām 0537) Isḥāq ibn Ibrāhīm al-Ḥanẓalī narrated:[i] ʿAbd al-Razzāq reported; al-Thawrī reported; from ʿAmr ibn Qays al-Mullāʾī; from al-Ḥakam ibn ʿUtaybah; from al-Qāsim ibn Mukhaymirah; from Shurayḥ ibn Hāniʾ: **'I went to ʿĀʾishah to ask her about wiping on the *khuffs*. She said: "You better ask Ibn Abī Ṭālib, because he used to travel with God's Messenger (peace be upon him)". We asked him and he said: "The Prophet defined three days and nights for a traveller, and one day and night for a person in residence".'**

He added: Sufyān praised ʿAmr whenever he mentioned him.

وَحدَّثَنَا إِسْحَاقُ بْنُ إِبْرَاهِيمَ الْحَنْظَلِيُّ، أَخْبَرَنَا عَبْدُ الرَّزَّاقِ، أَخْبَرَنَا الثَّوْرِيُّ، عَنْ عَمْرِو بْنِ قَيْسٍ الْمُلَائِيِّ، عَنِ الْحَكَمِ بْنِ عُتَيْبَةَ، عَنِ الْقَاسِمِ بْنِ مُخَيْمِرَةَ، عَنْ شُرَيْحِ بْنِ هَانِئٍ، قَالَ: أَتَيْتُ عَائِشَةَ أَسْأَلُهَا عَنِ الْمَسْحِ عَلَى الْخُفَّيْنِ، فَقَالَتْ: عَلَيْكَ بِابْنِ أَبِي طَالِبٍ، فَسَلْهُ فَإِنَّهُ كَانَ يُسَافِرُ مَعَ رَسُولِ اللهِ صَلَّى اللهُ عَلَيْهِ وَسَلَّمَ فَسَأَلْنَاهُ فَقَالَ: «جَعَلَ رَسُولُ اللهِ صَلَّى اللهُ عَلَيْهِ وَسَلَّمَ ثَلَاثَةَ أَيَّامٍ وَلَيَالِيَهُنَّ لِلْمُسَافِرِ، وَيَوْمًا وَلَيْلَةً لِلْمُقِيمِ»

قَالَ: وَكَانَ سُفْيَانُ، إِذَا ذَكَرَ عَمْرًا، أَثْنَى عَلَيْهِ.

[000–000]. (Dār al-Salām 0538) Isḥāq narrated: Zakariyyāʾ ibn ʿAdī reported; from ʿUbaydillāh ibn ʿAmr; from Zayd ibn Abī

i. Related by al-Nasāʾī, 128 and 129; Ibn Mājah, 552.

Unaysah; from al-Ḥakam; with this chain of transmission: **the same text**.

وَحَدَّثَنَا إِسْحَاقُ، أَخْبَرَنَا زَكَرِيَّا بْنُ عَدِيٍّ، عَنْ عُبَيْدِ اللهِ بْنِ عَمْرٍو، عَنْ زَيْدِ بْنِ أَبِي أُنَيْسَةَ، عَنِ الْحَكَمِ، بِهَذَا الْإِسْنَادِ مِثْلَهُ.

[493–000]. (Dār al-Salām 0539) Zuhayr ibn Ḥarb narrated to me: Abū Muʿāwiyah narrated; from al-Aʿmash; from al-Ḥakam; from al-Qāsim ibn Mukhaymirah; from Shurayḥ ibn Hāni': **'I asked ʿĀ'ishah about wiping on the *khuffs*. She said: "Go to ʿAlī, because he knows this better than me". I went to ʿAlī'. He reported the same from the Prophet (peace be upon him)**.'

وحَدَّثَنِي زُهَيْرُ بْنُ حَرْبٍ، حَدَّثَنَا أَبُو مُعَاوِيَةَ، عَنِ الْأَعْمَشِ، عَنِ الْحَكَمِ، عَنِ الْقَاسِمِ بْنِ مُخَيْمِرَةَ، عَنْ شُرَيْحِ بْنِ هَانِئٍ، قَالَ سَأَلْتُ عائشةَ، عَنِ الْمَسْحِ عَلَى الْخُفَّيْنِ، فَقَالَتْ: ائْتِ عَلِيًّا فَإِنَّهُ أَعْلَمُ بِذَلِكَ مِنِّي فَأَتَيْتُ عَلِيًّا فَذَكَرَ عَنِ النَّبِيِّ صَلَّى اللهُ عَلَيْهِ وَسَلَّمَ بِمِثْلِهِ.

Text Explanation

In all its versions, this hadith provides clear and definitive evidence in support of the view of the majority of scholars, which gives a time limit for wiping footwear, which is three days when travelling and one day for people in residence. This is the view of Abū Ḥanīfah, al-Shāfiʿī, Ahmad and the great majority of scholars from the time of the Prophet's companions and all succeeding generations. The best known view of Mālik is that there is no time limit. This is also an old view of al-Shāfiʿī, relying on no solid evidence. Those who subscribe to this view cite in evidence the hadith narrated by Ibn Abī ʿImārah which abandons time limitation. The hadith is related by Abū Dāwūd and others, but it remains lacking in authenticity according to the general agreement of scholars of Hadith.

The evidence provided by this hadith is very clear, according to scholars who consider the general meaning of the statement. As for scholars who pay no consideration to the general meaning, the basis is that wiping on footwear instead of washing one's feet is disallowed when the time limit is exceeded. Al-Shāfiʿī and many others say that the period begins from the first time one's ablution is invalidated after one has put on one's *khuffs* or footwear. It does not start either at the time when the footwear is put on or when one is wiping the footwear for the first time. Moreover, the event that invalidates ablution is general, applicable to all types, with a limitation specified in a hadith narrated by Ṣafwān ibn ʿAssāl: 'God's Messenger (peace be upon him) instructed us that when we are travelling we need not take off our *khuffs* for three days and nights, except due to *janābah,* i.e. major ritual impurity. Our scholars say that if a person is in a state of major ritual impurity before the time allowed for wiping one's footwear is over, such wiping is not permissible for him. If he performs the major ritual ablution, i.e. *ghusl,* including washing his feet, while wearing his *khuffs,* his major ritual impurity is removed and his subsequent prayer is valid. If he subsequently invalidates his ablution, wiping on his *khuffs* is not available to him. He must take off his *khuffs* and perform the full ablution, washing his feet, then he wears his *khuffs* and starts anew. This is different from a situation whereby his foot is contaminated with some impurity while he is wearing the *khuffs* and he washes his foot while wearing it. He may continue to wipe his *khuffs* afterwards, but God knows best.

Scholars stress an aspect of good manners pointed out in this hadith: if a teacher, a scholar, or a *muftī* is asked about something which he knows to be better understood by someone else he should direct his questioner to that person. If he is asked something which he does not know, he should say: 'Put your question to so-and-so'.

Transmission

The chain of transmission of hadith No. 492 includes ʿAmr ibn Qays al-Mullāʾī, who is known as al-Mullāʾī because he used to sell a type of clothing called al-Mullāʾ, and he was known to be a highly virtuous person. Al-Aʿmash, al-Ḥakam, al-Qāsim and Shurayḥ are all from the Tābiʿīn generation and from Kufah.

Abū ʿUmar ibn ʿAbd al-Barr said: 'Narrators differ as to whether the transmission of this hadith stops at ʿAlī or goes all the way to the Prophet'. Those who take it to the Prophet are more accurate and better memorizers, but God knows best.

CHAPTER 25

OFFERING ALL FIVE PRAYERS WITH ONE MINOR RITUAL ABLUTION

[494–86]. (Dār al-Salām 0540) Muhammad ibn ʿAbdullāh ibn Numayr narrated:[i] my father narrated; Sufyān narrated; from ʿAlqamah ibn Marthad [H]. Also, Muhammad ibn Ḥātim narrated to me (his text); Yaḥyā ibn Saʿīd narrated; from Sufyān who said: ʿAlqamah ibn Marthad narrated to me; from Sulaymān ibn Buraydah; from his father: **'On the day of the conquest, the Prophet offered all prayers with one minor ritual ablution, wiping on his *khuffs*. ʿUmar said to him: "You have done today something you used not to do". He said: "I have done it deliberately, ʿUmar".'**

حَدَّثَنَا مُحَمَّدُ بْنُ عَبْدِ اللهِ بْنِ نُمَيْرٍ، حَدَّثَنَا أَبِي، حَدَّثَنَا سُفْيَانُ، عَنْ عَلْقَمَةَ بْنِ مَرْثَدٍ ح، وَحَدَّثَنِي مُحَمَّدُ بْنُ حَاتِمٍ، وَاللَّفْظُ لَهُ حَدَّثَنَا يَحْيَى بْنُ سَعِيدٍ، عَنْ سُفْيَانَ، قَالَ: حَدَّثَنِي عَلْقَمَةُ بْنُ مَرْثَدٍ، عَنْ سُلَيْمَانَ بْنِ بُرَيْدَةَ، عَنْ أَبِيهِ، أَنَّ النَّبِيَّ صَلَّى اللهُ عَلَيْهِ وَسَلَّمَ: «صَلَّى الصَّلَوَاتِ يَوْمَ الْفَتْحِ بِوُضُوءٍ وَاحِدٍ، وَمَسَحَ عَلَى خُفَّيْهِ» فَقَالَ لَهُ عُمَرُ: لَقَدْ صَنَعْتَ الْيَوْمَ شَيْئًا لَمْ تَكُنْ تَصْنَعُهُ، قَالَ: «عَمْدًا صَنَعْتُهُ يَا عُمَرُ»

Text Explanation

This hadith gives us very useful and interesting points, including the permissibility of wiping on *khuffs* or footwear, and the permissibility

i. Related by Abū Dāwūd, 172 (in a shorter version); al-Tirmidhī, 61; al-Nasāʾī, 133; Ibn Mājah, 510.

of offering all obligatory and recommended prayers with one ablution, unless a person invalidates such ablution. This is acceptable, according to the unanimous view of all scholars of note. Abū Ja'far Ahmad ibn Muhammad al-Ṭaḥāwī mentions, as does Abū al-Ḥasan 'Alī ibn Khalaf ibn Baṭṭāl in his commentary on al-Bukhārī's *Ṣaḥīḥ* anthology that a number of scholars express the view that performing the ablution is obligatory before every prayer, even if a person has not invalidated his earlier ablution. They make their argument on the basis of the verse that gives the details of ablution starting with the order: '*Believers, when you are about to pray, wash your faces, and your hands and arms …*' (5: 6) I believe that this view is not upheld by anyone. Perhaps they mean that it is desirable to renew one's ablution at the time of every prayer. The evidence cited by the majority of scholars in support of their view is a number of authentic hadiths including this present hadith and the one narrated by Anas and related by al-Bukhārī in his *Ṣaḥīḥ*: 'God's Messenger (peace be upon him) used to perform the ablution for every prayer, but for any one of us one ablution was sufficient unless invalidated'. Another hadith related by al-Bukhārī is narrated by Suwayd ibn al-Nu'mān: 'God's Messenger (peace be upon him) prayed 'Aṣr then he ate *sawīq* then prayed Maghrib without performing a fresh ablution'. Many other hadiths give the same import, such as offering two prayers together at Arafat and Muzdalifah, as well as during all types of travel, and the Prophet's combination of all the day's prayers during the Encounter of the Moat, and other situations. The aforementioned Qur'anic verse means—but God knows best—'when you are about to pray and you have no valid ablution'. It is said that this verse is abrogated by the Prophet's action, but this view lacks proper evidence to support it, but God knows best.

Our scholars said: 'It is desirable to renew one's ablution, which means to perform a fresh ablution, even when one has already performed the ablution and it is still valid'. This desirability has different situations: 1) it is desirable for a person who has already offered a prayer, whether obligatory or recommended; 2) it is not desirable except for one who has already offered an obligatory prayer; 3) it is desirable for one who has done something that should be done after an ablution, such as holding the Qur'an or prostrating oneself during a recitation of the Qur'an; and 4) it is desirable even though one has not done any of these, provided that there is a time gap between the first and the second ablution. The correct and well known view is that it is not desirable to renew the major ritual ablution, i.e. *ghusl*. There are two views regarding renewing the dry ablution, i.e. *tayammum*, but the better known one is that it is not desirable. This applies to a person who is wounded or ill and needs to perform the *tayammum* despite the availability of water. In other cases, it is not desirable that a person who has performed the *tayammum* do it again in the same place, but God knows best.

ʿUmar said to the Prophet that he did something on that occasion that he used not to do. This makes clear that the Prophet used to perform the ablution for every prayer, choosing the better and preferable option. Yet this time, he offered all obligatory prayers for the day with one ablution, so as to make clear that this is perfectly acceptable. Hence, he said: 'I have done it deliberately, ʿUmar'.

This hadith shows that it is permissible for a person to enquire from his superior about some of his actions that appear to be unusual. This may be due to forgetting, and his enquiry would be a reminder, or it may be deliberate and the enquiry teaches the questioner something useful, but God knows best.

Transmission

The chain of transmission of this hadith is as follows: 'Muhammad ibn ʿAbdullāh ibn Numayr narrated: my father narrated; Sufyān narrated; from ʿAlqamah ibn Marthad'. The other route mentions Muhammad ibn Ḥātim narrated to me; Yaḥyā ibn Saʿīd narrated; from Sufyān who said: 'Alqamah ibn Marthad narrated to me …'. Muslim puts it in this way, repeating mentioning Sufyān and ʿAlqamah to indicate some useful points. Sufyān was graded as 'misleading' and in the first chain he reports 'from ʿAlqamah'. It is agreed that when a 'misleading' narrator reports 'from' his teacher, this way of reporting is not accepted unless he makes clear in a different way that he actually heard the hadith from that teacher. Hence, Muslim adds the second chain of transmission because Sufyān clearly states that ʿAlqamah narrated to him.

Another useful point is that in the first chain, Ibn Numayr states: 'Sufyān narrated', but in the second, Yaḥyā ibn Saʿīd reports 'from Sufyān'. Therefore, Muslim felt that he could not report from both of them in the same wording. As we explained in the Introduction, 'narrated' is agreed by all scholars to mean direct and personal contact between the two reporters. But 'from' is subject to controversy.

CHAPTER 26

WHEN RITUAL IMPURITY IS SUSPECTED, DIPPING ONE'S HAND IN WATER IS DISCOURAGED

[495–87]. (Dār al-Salām 0541) Naṣr ibn ʿAlī al-Jahḍamī and Ḥāmid ibn ʿUmar al-Bakrāwī narrated: both said: Bishr ibn al-Mufaḍḍal narrated; from Khālid; from ʿAbdullāh ibn Shaqīq; from Abū Hurayrah that the Prophet (peace be upon him) said: **'When any of you wakes up from sleep, let him not dip his hand in the ewer until he has washed it three times. He does not know where his hand was during the night'**.

وَحَدَّثَنَا نَصْرُ بْنُ عَلِيٍّ الْجَهْضَمِيُّ، وَحَامِدُ بْنُ عُمَرَ الْبَكْرَاوِيُّ، قَالَا: حَدَّثَنَا بِشْرُ بْنُ الْمُفَضَّلِ، عَنْ خَالِدٍ، عَنْ عَبْدِ اللهِ بْنِ شَقِيقٍ، عَنْ أَبِي هُرَيْرَةَ، أَنَّ النَّبِيَّ صَلَّى اللهُ عَلَيْهِ وَسَلَّمَ قَالَ: «إِذَا اسْتَيْقَظَ أَحَدُكُمْ مِنْ نَوْمِهِ، فَلَا يَغْمِسْ يَدَهُ فِي الْإِنَاءِ حَتَّى يَغْسِلَهَا ثَلَاثًا، فَإِنَّهُ لَا يَدْرِي أَيْنَ بَاتَتْ يَدُهُ»

[000–000]. (Dār al-Salām 0542) Abū Kurayb and Abū Saʿīd al-Ashajj narrated saying:[i] Wakīʿ narrated [H]. Also, Abū Kurayb narrated; Abū Muʿāwiyah narrated; both from al-Aʿmash; from Abū Razīn and Abū Sāliḥ; from Abū Hurayrah. In Abū Muʿāwiyah's narration: 'God's Messenger (peace be upon him) said', and in Wakīʿ's narration: 'He attributes it to God's Messenger'. **The same text.**

i. Related by Abū Dāwūd, 103.

حَدَّثَنَا أَبُو كُرَيْبٍ، وَأَبُو سَعِيدٍ الْأَشَجُّ، قَالَا: حَدَّثَنَا وَكِيعٌ، ح، وَحَدَّثَنَا أَبُو كُرَيْبٍ، حَدَّثَنَا أَبُو مُعَاوِيَةَ، كِلَاهُمَا عَنِ الْأَعْمَشِ، عَنْ أَبِي رَزِينٍ، وَأَبِي صَالِحٍ، عَنْ أَبِي هُرَيْرَةَ، فِي حَدِيثِ أَبِي مُعَاوِيَةَ، قَالَ: قَالَ رَسُولُ اللهِ صَلَّى اللهُ عَلَيْهِ وَسَلَّمَ وَفِي حَدِيثِ وَكِيعٍ، قَالَ: يَرْفَعُهُ بِمِثْلِهِ.

[000–000]. (Dār al-Salām 0543) Abū Bakr ibn Abī Shaybah, ʿAmr al-Nāqid and Zuhayr ibn Ḥarb narrated: Sufyān narrated; from al-Zuhrī; from Abū Salamah [H]. Also, ʿAbd al-Razzāq narrated; Maʿmar reported; from al-Zuhrī; from Ibn al-Musayyib; both from Abū Hurayrah; from the Prophet (peace be upon him): **the same text**.

وَحَدَّثَنَا أَبُو بَكْرِ بْنُ أَبِي شَيْبَةَ، وَعَمْرٌو النَّاقِدُ، وَزُهَيْرُ بْنُ حَرْبٍ، قَالُوا: حَدَّثَنَا سُفْيَانُ بْنُ عُيَيْنَةَ، عَنِ الزُّهْرِيِّ، عَنْ أَبِي سَلَمَةَ ح، وَحَدَّثَنِيهِ مُحَمَّدُ بْنُ رَافِعٍ، حَدَّثَنَا عَبْدُ الرَّزَّاقِ، أَخْبَرَنَا مَعْمَرٌ، عَنِ الزُّهْرِيِّ، عَنِ ابْنِ الْـمُسَيِّبِ، كِلَاهُمَا عَنْ أَبِي هُرَيْرَةَ، عَنِ النَّبِيِّ صَلَّى اللهُ عَلَيْهِ وَسَلَّمَ بِمِثْلِهِ.

[496–88]. (Dār al-Salām 0544) Salamah ibn Shabīb narrated to me: al-Ḥasan ibn Aʿyan narrated; Maʿqil narrated; from Abū al-Zubayr; from Jābir; from Abū Hurayrah who told him that the Prophet (peace be upon him) said: ‘**When any of you wakes up, let him pour water over his hand three times before he dips his hand in his ewer. He does not know what his hand did during the night**’.

وَحَدَّثَنِي سَلَمَةُ بْنُ شَبِيبٍ، قَالَ: حَدَّثَنَا الْحَسَنُ بْنُ أَعْيَنَ، حَدَّثَنَا مَعْقِلٌ، عَنْ أَبِي الزُّبَيْرِ، عَنْ جَابِرٍ، عَنْ أَبِي هُرَيْرَةَ، أَنَّهُ أَخْبَرَهُ أَنَّ النَّبِيَّ صَلَّى اللهُ عَلَيْهِ وَسَلَّمَ قَالَ: «إِذَا اسْتَيْقَظَ أَحَدُكُمْ فَلْيُفْرِغْ عَلَى يَدِهِ ثَلَاثَ مَرَّاتٍ قَبْلَ أَنْ يُدْخِلَ يَدَهُ فِي إِنَائِهِ، فَإِنَّهُ لَا يَدْرِي فِيمَ بَاتَتْ يَدُهُ»

[000–000]. (Dār al-Salām 0545) Qutaybah ibn Sa'īd narrated: al-Mughīrah (meaning al-Ḥizāmī) narrated; from Abū al-Zinād; from al-A'raj; from Abū Hurayrah [H]. Also, Naṣr ibn 'Alī narrated; 'Abd al-A'lā narrated; from Hishām; from Muhammad; from Abū Hurayrah [H]. And Abū Kurayb narrated to me; Khālid (meaning Ibn Makhlad) narrated; from Muhammad ibn Ja'far; from al-'Alā'; from his father; from Abū Hurayrah [H]. Also, Muhammad ibn Rāfi' narrated; 'Abd al-Razzāq narrated; Ma'mar narrated; from Hammām ibn Munabbih; from Abū Hurayrah [H]. Also, al-Ḥulwānī and Ibn Rāfi' narrated, both said: 'Abd al-Razzāq narrated; both said: Ibn Jurayj reported; Ziyād reported to me; that Thābit, 'Abd al-Raḥmān's *mawlā*, reported to him; that he heard Abū Hurayrah; in all their narrations from the Prophet (peace be upon him) they state this hadith. All of them said: 'until he has washed it', but none of them said 'three times', except in the earlier narrations by Jābir, Ibn al-Musayyib, Abū Salamah, 'Abdullāh ibn Shaqīq, Abū Sāliḥ and Abū Razīn. In the narrations of these, three times is stated.

وَحَدَّثَنَا قُتَيْبَةُ بْنُ سَعِيدٍ، حَدَّثَنَا الْـمُغِيرَةُ يَعْنِي الْحِزَامِيَّ، عَنْ أَبِي الزِّنَادِ، عَنِ الْأَعْرَجِ، عَنْ أَبِي هُرَيْرَةَ، ح، وَحَدَّثَنَا نَصْرُ بْنُ عَلِيٍّ، حَدَّثَنَا عَبْدُ الْأَعْلَى، عَنْ هِشَامٍ، عَنْ مُحَمَّدٍ، عَنْ أَبِي هُرَيْرَةَ، ح، وَحَدَّثَنِي أَبُو كُرَيْبٍ، حَدَّثَنَا خَالِدٌ يَعْنِي ابْنَ مَخْلَدٍ، عَنْ مُحَمَّدِ بْنِ جَعْفَرٍ، عَنِ الْعَلَاءِ، عَنْ أَبِيهِ، عَنْ أَبِي هُرَيْرَةَ، ح، وَحَدَّثَنَا مُحَمَّدُ بْنُ رَافِعٍ، حَدَّثَنَا عَبْدُ الرَّزَّاقِ، حَدَّثَنَا مَعْمَرٌ، عَنْ هَمَّامِ بْنِ مُنَبِّهٍ، عَنْ أَبِي هُرَيْرَةَ، ح، وَحَدَّثَنِي مُحَمَّدُ بْنُ حَاتِمٍ، حَدَّثَنَا مُحَمَّدُ بْنُ بَكْرٍ، ح، وَحَدَّثَنَا الْحُلْوَانِيُّ، وَابْنُ رَافِعٍ قَالَا: حَدَّثَنَا عَبْدُ الرَّزَّاقِ قَالَا جَمِيعًا: أَخْبَرَنَا ابْنُ جُرَيْجٍ، أَخْبَرَنِي زِيَادٌ، أَنَّ ثَابِتًا، مَوْلَى عَبْدِ الرَّحْمَنِ بْنِ زَيْدٍ، أَخْبَرَهُ أَنَّهُ سَمِعَ أَبَا هُرَيْرَةَ فِي رِوَايَتِهِمْ جَمِيعًا عَنِ النَّبِيِّ صَلَّى اللهُ عَلَيْهِ وَسَلَّمَ بِهَذَا الْحَدِيثِ كُلُّهُمْ يَقُولُ حَتَّى يَغْسِلَهَا، وَلَمْ يَقُلْ وَاحِدٌ مِنْهُمْ ثَلَاثًا إِلَّا مَا قَدَّمْنَا مِنْ رِوَايَةِ

جَابِرٍ، وَابْنِ الْـمُسَيَّبِ، وَأَبِي سَلَمَةَ، وَعَبْدِ اللهِ بْنِ شَقِيقٍ، وَأَبِي صَالِحٍ، وَأَبِي رَزِينٍ فَإِنَّ فِي حَدِيثِهِمْ ذِكْرَ الثَّلَاثِ.

Text Explanation

In this hadith, the Prophet says: 'When any of you wakes up from sleep, let him not dip his hand in the ewer until he has washed it three times. He does not know where his hand was during the night'. Al-Shāfiʿī and other scholars explain what the Prophet meant by 'He does not know where his hand was during the night', saying that the people of Arabia used to clean themselves with stones and theirs was a very hot climate. When they slept, they might perspire. During sleep a person may touch a spot of impurity, or some puss, or other dirt.

This hadith provides evidence for many questions in our school of *fiqh* and the views of the majority of scholars. These include that if impurity comes into a small quantity of water, it makes the water impure, even if it is little and produces no visible change in the water. The impurity that stains one's hand may be very little, and the people of Arabia used to have small water containers, none of which comes anywhere near the quantity that is not affected by a small impurity, which is two *qullahs*.[i] The hadith shows the difference between water coming over an impurity and the impurity coming into the water. If it is brought into the water, the impurity is transmitted to the water and it becomes impure, but when water is poured over the impurity, it removes it. Another point is that washing seven times does not apply to all types of impurity. It applies particularly to the case of a dog drinking from a water container. The hadith also indicates that the anus is not purified when cleaned with stones, [or a solid object such as toilet paper]. The impurity remains, but it is little and overlooked in respect of the validity of prayer. Furthermore,

---

i. The *qullah* was a volume measure, but it differed from one area to another. According to different contemporary scholars, two *qullahs* are equivalent to 203 litres, but some put it higher than this.

the hadith shows that it is desirable to wash off any impurity three times. Since it clearly orders washing three times to remove a doubtful impurity, this applies even more clearly to real impurity. Moreover, it is desirable to wash doubtful impurity three times, and that it should be washed, not sprinkled. The Prophet said: 'until he has washed it', without adding 'or sprinkled it'. It is also desirable in questions of worship to take precautions, provided that these do not become excessive bordering on obsession. The difference between precaution and obsession is discussed at length and I have explained it in the chapter on containers in my book *Sharḥ al-Muhadhdhab*.

The hadith also suggests that it is desirable to use figurative speech to say what is better left implied. In this hadith the Prophet said: 'He does not know where his hand was during the night'. He did not say anything like: 'His hand might have touched his anus or genitals or some impurity', but this is exactly what he meant. There are many similar cases in the Qur'an and the Prophet's hadiths. The only proviso is that the listener is expected to clearly understand what is meant. If this is doubtful, then clear expression is required, so that no confusion occurs. This is the reason behind the instances where clear and unambiguous wording is preferred, even though they are normally avoided, but God knows best.

These are useful points that are understood from this hadith in addition to its main purpose, which is the instruction not to put one's hand in water before washing it. This is unanimously agreed, though the overwhelming majority of scholars of old and recent days agree that the instruction is one of discouragement not prohibition. If a person does not observe the instruction and dips his hand into water before washing it, the water is not considered impure and the person who dips his hand in it is not ruled as having committed a sin. Our scholars report that al-Ḥasan al-Baṣri expressed the view that if a person wakes up after a night's sleep and dips his hand into a water container without first washing it, the water is deemed impure. They also report this to be expressed by Isḥāq ibn Rāhawayh and Muhammad ibn Jarīr al-Ṭabarī, but this view is considered very weak because the original state of water and a person's hand is that both are pure. Therefore, they cannot be ruled impure on the basis of doubt and plenty of Islamic rules confirm this. It cannot be said that the sleeper's hand is apparently contaminated with impurity, the hadith is understood to mean discouragement. Moreover, our school shares the view of meticulous scholars who say that this ruling is not restricted to the case of waking up from sleep. It refers to the case of doubtful impurity. If one suspects that one's hand is contaminated with impurity, one is discouraged from dipping it into a water container, whether one was asleep during the night or during the day, or if the suspicion is due to some reason other than sleep. This is the view of the majority of scholars.

It is mentioned that one version expressed by Imam Ahmad ibn Ḥanbal says that if one wakes up from a night's sleep, then dips one's hand in a water container without first washing, it is very strongly discouraged, but it is only mildly discouraged after sleeping during the day. This is also agreed by Dāwūd al-Ẓāhirī, because the hadith mentions the night. Again this is very weak. The Prophet's statement, 'He does not know where his hand was during the night', points out the reason, which means that such a person cannot be certain of not touching an impurity. Such uncertainty is a general condition, because the presence of impurity is there in night or day sleep, and when one is awake. The Prophet mentions the night first because it is the time when most sleep occurs, but he does not limit the ruling to it, so his statement is not taken to relate only to night. He follows its mention by explaining the reason, but God knows best.

All this applies if a person suspects his hand to be impure. If he is certain that it has no impurity and wanted to put his hand into the water before washing it, some of our scholars say that the same ruling as that of doubtful impurity applies here. They argue that causes of contaminating impurity may remain unheeded by most people. Therefore, they prefer to give a general ruling so that people do not take a lax attitude based on no certain knowledge. The view that is more accurate and endorsed by the large majority of our scholars is that there is no discouragement to dipping one's hand into water without first washing it when one is certain that it touched no impurity. The choice is his whether to wash it first or not, because the Prophet mentioned sleep and pointed out the reason, which is the doubt. If the reason does not apply, the ruling based on it does not apply as well. Had the ruling been general, the Prophet would have said: 'When you wish to use water, do not dip your hand into it before washing it'. That would have been applicable to all situations, but God knows best.

If the water is in a large container or in a pond and the person cannot pour some out of it, and does not have a cup or a similar article to take a little water to wash his hand with, then he may take some water with his mouth and wash his hands with it. Alternatively, he may ask someone else to help him, or he may take some water with the end of his clean robe or shirt and use it to wash his hand, but God knows best.

Transmission

The chain of transmission of the first narration of this hadith includes Ḥāmid al-Bakrāwī, whose full name is Ḥāmid ibn ʿUmar ibn Ḥafṣ ibn ʿUmar ibn ʿAbdullāh ibn Abī Bakrah Nufayʿ ibn al-Ḥārith, the Prophet's companion. Thus, al-Bakrāwī means affiliation to his ancestor, who was honoured by being a companion of the Prophet. The chain of transmission of the second hadith includes Abū Razīn, whose name is Masʿūd ibn Mālik. He was a well established scholar from Kufah and formerly a *mawlā* of Abū Wā'il Shaqīq ibn Salamah.

After mentioning the chain of transmission of the second hadith, with its two different routes, Muslim says: 'In Abū Muʿāwiyah's narration: "God's Messenger (peace be upon him) said", and in Wakīʿ's narration: "He attributes it to God's Messenger".' This reflects Muslim's meticulous approach, attention to detail, rich knowledge and perfect understanding. What it tells us is that Abū Muʿāwiyah and Wakīʿ differ in the way they narrated the hadith. One of them said: 'Abū Hurayrah said: God's Messenger said ...', while the other said: 'Abū Hurayrah said attributing to God's Messenger ...'.

According to scholars, the two have the same meaning, as we have explained in the Notes in our Introduction. However, Muslim did not wish to relate the hadith reporting its meaning, because some scholars consider reporting by meaning to be forbidden, while the majority consider it permissible but better avoided, but God knows best.

The chain of transmission of this hadith includes Ma'qil reporting from Abū al-Zubayr. Abū al-Zubayr is Muhammad ibn Muslim ibn Tadrus. We have mentioned him earlier.

CHAPTER 27

WHEN A DOG DRINKS FROM A WATER CONTAINER

[497–89]. (Dār al-Salām 0546) ʿAlī ibn Ḥujr al-Saʿdī narrated to me:[i] ʿAlī ibn Mushīr narrated; al-Aʿmash reported; from Abū Razīn and Abū Ṣāliḥ; from Abū Hurayrah: **'God's Messenger (peace be upon him) said: "If a dog drinks out of anyone's water container, he should pour it out, then he should wash it seven times"**.'

وَحَدَّثَنِي عَلِيُّ بْنُ حُجْرٍ السَّعْدِيُّ، حَدَّثَنَا عَلِيُّ بْنُ مُسْهِرٍ، أَخْبَرَنَا الْأَعْمَشُ، عَنْ أَبِي رَزِينٍ، وَأَبِي صَالِحٍ، عَنْ أَبِي هُرَيْرَةَ، قَالَ: قَالَ رَسُولُ اللهِ صَلَّى اللهُ عَلَيْهِ وَسَلَّمَ: «إِذَا وَلَغَ الْكَلْبُ فِي إِنَاءِ أَحَدِكُمْ فَلْيُرِقْهُ ثُمَّ لِيَغْسِلْهُ سَبْعَ مِرَارٍ»

[498–000]. (Dār al-Salām 0547)) Muhammad ibn al-Ṣabbāḥ narrated to me: Ismāʿīl ibn Zakariyyā' narrated; from al-Aʿmash, with the same chain of transmission: **The same text, but did not say 'he should pour it out'**.

حَدَّثَنِي مُحَمَّدُ بْنُ الصَّبَّاحِ، حَدَّثَنَا إِسْمَاعِيلُ بْنُ زَكَرِيَّا، عَنِ الْأَعْمَشِ، بِهَذَا الْإِسْنَادِ مِثْلَهُ وَلَمْ يَقُلْ فَلْيُرِقْهُ.

i. Related by al-Nasāʾī, 66; Ibn Mājah, 363.

[499–90]. (Dār al-Salām 0548) Yaḥyā ibn Yaḥyā narrated, saying:[i] I read out to Mālik from Abū al-Zinād; from al-Aʿraj; from Abū Hurayrah that God's Messenger (peace be upon him) said: **'If a dog drinks out of anyone's water container, he should wash it seven times'**.

حَدَّثَنَا يَحْيَى بْنُ يَحْيَى، قَالَ: قَرَأْتُ عَلَى مَالِكٍ، عَنْ أَبِي الزِّنَادِ، عَنِ الْأَعْرَجِ، عَنْ أَبِي هُرَيْرَةَ، أَنَّ رَسُولَ اللهِ صَلَّى اللهُ عَلَيْهِ وَسَلَّمَ قَالَ: «إِذَا شَرِبَ الْكَلْبُ فِي إِنَاءِ أَحَدِكُمْ، فَلْيَغْسِلْهُ سَبْعَ مَرَّاتٍ»

[500–91]. (Dār al-Salām 0549) Zuhayr ibn Ḥarb narrated to me: Ismāʿīl ibn Ibrāhīm narrated; from Hishām ibn Ḥassān; from Muhammad ibn Sīrīn; from Abū Hurayrah: '**God's Messenger (peace be upon him) said: "The cleansing of anyone's water container, if a dog drinks out of it, is for him to wash it seven times, the first of which is using fine soil"**.'

وَحَدَّثَنَا زُهَيْرُ بْنُ حَرْبٍ، حَدَّثَنَا إِسْمَاعِيلُ بْنُ إِبْرَاهِيمَ، عَنْ هِشَامِ بْنِ حَسَّانَ، عَنْ مُحَمَّدِ بْنِ سِيرِينَ، عَنْ أَبِي هُرَيْرَةَ، قَالَ: قَالَ رَسُولُ اللهِ صَلَّى اللهُ عَلَيْهِ وَسَلَّمَ: «طَهُورُ إِنَاءِ أَحَدِكُمْ إِذَا وَلَغَ فِيهِ الْكَلْبُ، أَنْ يَغْسِلَهُ سَبْعَ مَرَّاتٍ أُولَاهُنَّ بِالتُّرَابِ»

[501–92]. (Dār al-Salām 0550) Muhammad ibn Rāfiʿ narrated: ʿAbd al-Razzāq narrated; Maʿmar narrated; from Hammām ibn Munabbih: he said: 'This is what Abū Hurayrah narrated to us from Muhammad, God's Messenger (peace be upon him): He mentioned a number of hadiths, including: **"And God's Messenger (peace be upon him) said: 'The cleansing of anyone's water container, if a dog drinks out of it, is for him to wash it seven times'"**.'

---

i. Related by al-Bukhārī, 172; al-Nasā'ī 63; Ibn Mājah, 364.

حَدَّثَنَا مُحَمَّدُ بْنُ رَافِعٍ، حَدَّثَنَا عَبْدُ الرَّزَّاقِ، حَدَّثَنَا مَعْمَرٌ، عَنْ هَمَّامِ بْنِ مُنَبِّهٍ، قَالَ: هَذَا مَا حَدَّثَنَا أَبُو هُرَيْرَةَ، عَنْ مُحَمَّدٍ رَسُولِ اللهِ صَلَّى اللهُ عَلَيْهِ وَسَلَّمَ - فَذَكَرَ أَحَادِيثَ مِنْهَا - وَقَالَ رَسُولُ اللهِ صَلَّى اللهُ عَلَيْهِ وَسَلَّمَ: «طَهُورُ إِنَاءِ أَحَدِكُمْ إِذَا وَلَغَ الْكَلْبُ فِيهِ، أَنْ يَغْسِلَهُ سَبْعَ مَرَّاتٍ»

[502–93]. (Dār al-Salām 0551) ʿUbaydillāh ibn Muʿādh narrated:[i] my father narrated; Shuʿbah narrated; from Abu al-Tayyāḥ; that he heard Muṭarrif ibn ʿAbdullāh narrating from Ibn al-Mughaffal; who said: '**God's Messenger (peace be upon him) ordered that dogs be killed. He then said: "What have they got to do with dogs?" He subsequently made a concession [to own] a hunting dog or a sheep dog. He also said: "If a dog drinks out of a water container, wash the container seven times, and use fine soil in the eighth wash"**.'

وَحَدَّثَنَا عُبَيْدُ اللهِ بْنُ مُعَاذٍ، حَدَّثَنَا أَبِي، حَدَّثَنَا شُعْبَةُ، عَنْ أَبِي التَّيَّاحِ، سَمِعَ مُطَرِّفَ بْنَ عَبْدِ اللهِ عَنِ ابْنِ الْمُغَفَّلِ، قَالَ: أَمَرَ رَسُولُ اللهِ صَلَّى اللهُ عَلَيْهِ وَسَلَّمَ بِقَتْلِ الْكِلَابِ، ثُمَّ قَالَ: «مَا بَالُهُمْ وَبَالُ الْكِلَابِ؟» ثُمَّ رَخَّصَ فِي كَلْبِ الصَّيْدِ وَكَلْبِ الْغَنَمِ، وَقَالَ: «إِذَا وَلَغَ الْكَلْبُ فِي الْإِنَاءِ فَاغْسِلُوهُ سَبْعَ مَرَّاتٍ، وَعَفِّرُوهُ الثَّامِنَةَ فِي التُّرَابِ»

[503–000]. (Dār al-Salām 0552) Yaḥyā ibn Ḥabīb al-Ḥārithī narrated it to me: Khālid (meaning Ibn al-Ḥārith) narrated [H]. Also, Muhammad ibn Ḥātim narrated to me: Yaḥyā ibn Saʿīd narrated [H]. And, Muhammad ibn al-Walīd narrated to me: Muhammad ibn Jaʿfar narrated: all of them from Shuʿbah, with this chain of transmission: **The same, but Yaḥyā ibn Saʿīd's**

---

i. Related by Muslim, Book of Sharing Irrigation Water; al-Nasāʾī, 67, 335 and 336; Ibn Mājah, 365 (in a shorter version) and 3200, 3201.

narration adds: 'He made a concession [to own] a hunting dog or a sheep dog or a farm dog'. None other than Yaḥyā mentions a farm dog.

وَحَدَّثَنِيهِ يَحْيَى بْنُ حَبِيبٍ الْحَارِثِيُّ، حَدَّثَنَا خَالِدٌ يَعْنِي ابْنَ الْحَارِثِ، ح، وَحَدَّثَنِي مُحَمَّدُ بْنُ حَاتِمٍ، حَدَّثَنَا يَحْيَى بْنُ سَعِيدٍ، ح، وَحَدَّثَنِي مُحَمَّدُ بْنُ الْوَلِيدِ، حَدَّثَنَا مُحَمَّدُ بْنُ جَعْفَرٍ، كُلُّهُمْ عَنْ شُعْبَةَ، فِي هَذَا الْإِسْنَادِ بِمِثْلِهِ غَيْرَ أَنَّ فِي رِوَايَةِ يَحْيَى بْنِ سَعِيدٍ، مِنَ الزِّيَادَةِ: وَرَخَّصَ فِي كَلْبِ الْغَنَمِ وَالصَّيْدِ وَالزَّرْعِ، وَلَيْسَ ذَكَرَ الزَّرْعَ فِي الرِّوَايَةِ غَيْرُ يَحْيَى.

Text Explanation

The Prophet uses the word *walagha* to indicate a dog's drinking, a word that denotes that dogs use the edge of their tongue to drink. Ritual purification is required because of either a discharge of wind, urine or stools, or because of ritual impurity. Since these hadiths do not mention any discharge, then the cleansing must be due to an impurity. Hence, these hadiths provide clear evidence in support of the view of the Shāfiʿī school and others, stating that a dog is impure. If it is suggested that what is meant here is abstract cleansing, we say that taking words as they mean in reality takes precedence over giving them abstract meanings.

The hadiths make clear that should a dog drink out of one's container, that container becomes impure. If it contains liquid food, it becomes forbidden to eat. This is understood from the order to pour it out. Had it not been impure, the Prophet would not have ordered us to pour it out, because that means wasting it, and wasting useful things is forbidden. This is the view of our school and the great majority of scholars. There is no difference between dogs that are permitted to be owned or others, nor between urban dogs and dogs in the wild, because the wording of the hadith is general.

The Mālikī school of *fiqh* provides four different views concerning the impurity or otherwise of dogs. Three views are attributed to Imam Mālik himself, stating that a dog is pure, impure, and that dogs permitted to be owned are pure, but not other dogs. The fourth view differentiates between urban dogs and those living in the wild, and it is stated by ʿAbd al-Malik ibn al-Mājishūn of the Mālikī School.

The hadiths include the order to pour out whatever is in the water container. This is agreed by all scholars. However, scholars differ as to whether such pouring out of the contents is obligatory in all situations, or if it is required if one wants to use the container. Most of our scholars are of the view that pouring out the contents is not obligatory for its own sake; rather, it is recommended. But when we want to use the container, then it must be emptied and washed. Some of our scholars, however, consider that pouring out the contents is obligatory straight away, even if one does not wish to use the container. This view is stated by al-Māwardī, who belongs to the Shāfiʿī school, in his book *al-Ḥāwī*, citing in support the fact that the order is general, which means that it places an obligation. This is the view of the majority of scholars. The first view is argued on the basis of analogy with other types of water contaminated with impurity. These need not be poured out, and this is agreed by all scholars. In answer, it may be said that with regard to a dog drinking out of a container, the Prophet's intention is to confirm the prohibition and to stress the need to keep dogs away, but God knows best.

The hadiths in this chapter make it clear that it is obligatory to wash seven times the impurity resulting from a dog drinking out of a water container. This is the view of our Shāfiʿī school of *fiqh*, as well as the Mālikī and Ḥanbalī schools. Abū Ḥanīfah says that it is sufficient to wash it three times, but God knows best.

The different narrations mention washing this impurity seven times, or seven but the first or the last wash should use fine soil as well, and one narration says seven times but the seventh is mixed with fine soil. One narration mentioned above says that the eighth is mixed with fine soil. Al-Bayhaqī and other scholars mention all these narrations. They provide evidence that specifying the first wash or a different one is not a condition that must be adhered to, but what is required is that one of them is sufficient. One narration mentions seven times and the eighth is mixed with fine soil. The view of our school and the large majority of scholars is that washing is required seven times, one of which is with fine soil and water together. This suggests that the fine soil stands for a wash, and this is why it is described in the hadith as the eighth, but God knows best.

It must be clear that to us there is no difference between a dog drinking or any other part of the dog. This means that if its urine, stools, blood, perspiration, hair, saliva or any organ touches some clean object, and either the clean object or the part of the dog that gets in contact with it is wet, that object must be washed seven times, one of which should be mixed with fine soil. If two dogs drink out of the same container, or one dog drinks out of it several times, our scholars express three views in this case, but the correct view is that it is sufficient to wash it seven times to clear the total impurity. The other view is that seven washes are required for each drink. The third view is that seven washes are needed for all the drinks of one dog, but each dog requires seven washes. If a different type of a dog's impurity falls in the container, seven washes are enough for all. The eighth wash is not adequate if it uses water only. Nor is it appropriate to immerse the contaminated container in a large amount of water and leaving it there for the length of seven washes; this cannot replace the wash with fine soil. This is the right view, even though some say that it does. The more correct view is that soap and similar products may not be used instead of fine soil; and there is no difference if the fine soil is added or not. Also, using fine soil contaminated with impurity is unacceptable. If the dog's impurity is its blood or stools and it is not fully removed except, say, after the sixth wash, do these count as one wash or six, or does it count as one of the seven? There are three different views on this point, and the more correct one is that they all count as one wash. What applies to dogs in all this also applies to pigs and wild boars. This is the view of our school of *fiqh*. Most scholars are of the view that the pig impurity does not require to be washed off seven times. This is al-Shāfiʿī's view, and it is supported by strong evidence.

Our scholars say that mixing one wash with water means that fine soil should be mixed with the water so that the water becomes unclear. Either the fine soil should be added to the water or the water should be poured over the soil. Alternatively, soil-bearing water may be taken from a suitable place to wash the impurity. To wipe the place contaminated by the impurity with fine soil is not sufficient. It is not necessary to put one's hand into the container, but it is enough to pour the water into it and stir it. It is preferable that the wash that is mixed with soil should be before the last one, and more preferable to be the first wash, so that the container is thoroughly cleansed.

If a dog drinks out of a large quantity of water, and what is left is over two *qullahs*, the water remains clean, uncontaminated with impurity. [A *qullah* was a known measure of volume. Scholars estimate two *qullahs* to be equivalent to approximately 203 litres.] If a dog drinks out of a small quantity of water, or eats some liquid food, and the water or the food then falls on a garment of clothing, or some other object or container, the contaminated garment or object must be washed seven times, one of which should be mixed with dust. If the dog eats from a plate containing some solid food, the food where it ate and that around it should be thrown away. The remainder may be used normally, as it continues to be clean. This is the same as in the case of a mouse falling into a jar of solid fat and dying there: it is removed with the fat around it, so that the rest is used for human consumption, but God knows best.

Hadith No. 502 mentions that the Prophet 'ordered that dogs be killed. He then said: "What have they got to do with dogs?" He subsequently made a concession [to own] a hunting dog or a sheep dog'. The next narration adds farm dogs. This hadith is clear in prohibiting owning dogs. Our scholars and others agree that it is forbidden to own a dog unless it is needed for a particular purpose. Thus, to own a dog because one likes its appearance, or to boast of owning it, is agreed by all scholars to be forbidden. The need that permits owning a dog is specified in this hadith to be one of three types: farming, tending sheep and hunting.[i] To own a dog for any of these three purposes is permissible, but there is disagreement on this. Our scholars differ concerning owning a guard dog for a home or a street, and also concerning owning a young dog to train

i. Contemporary scholars have used analogy to rule that it is also permissible to own dogs for useful purposes, such as a guide dog for a blind person, or dogs used in tracing criminal suspects or bombs, etc.

it for these purposes. Some scholars consider it forbidden, because the concession is made only in the three specified purposes. Others make it permissible, because the purpose is the same as those mentioned in the concession. This is the more correct view. Scholars also differ with regard to the permissibility of owning a hunting dog by a person who does not hunt, but God knows best.

As for the order to kill dogs, our scholars say that a biting dog should be killed, otherwise, a dog must not be killed, whether it can be used for any of the useful purposes already mentioned or not. Imam al-Ḥaramayn said: 'The order to kill dogs has been annulled. It is confirmed that God's Messenger ordered the killing of dogs on one occasion, and it is confirmed that he subsequently ordered not to kill them. This is the last religious verdict on this issue, as we have clarified. The Prophet also ordered the killing of black wild dogs, but this was at the beginning and subsequently annulled'. Nothing may be added to what Imam al-Ḥaramayn has explained, but God knows best.

Transmission

The chains of transmission of these hadiths include Abū al-Tayyāḥ, whose name is Yazīd ibn Ḥumayd al-Duba'i, who was a devout person from Basrah. Shu'bah said: we used to call him Abū Ḥammād, but I learnt that when he was still a teenager he was called Abū al-Tayyāḥ.

Ibn al-Mughaffal mentioned in the transmission of the hadith No. 502 is 'Abdullāh ibn al-Mughaffal al-Muzanī, a companion of the Prophet.

The transmission of the last hadith provides several branches of its chain, but all reporters in these branches, as well as those in hadith No. 502, were from Basrah. We have mentioned, on more than one occasion, that Shu'bah belonged originally to Wāsiṭ, but he then moved to Basrah and settled there. As such he belonged to Basrah. Yaḥyā ibn Sa'īd mentioned in the transmission of the last hadith is also known as al-Qaṭṭān.

CHAPTER 28

PROHIBITION OF URINATING IN STAGNANT WATER

[504–94]. (Dār al-Salām 0553) Yaḥyā ibn Yaḥyā and Muhammad ibn Rumḥ narrated:[i] both said: al-Layth reported [H]. Also, Qutaybah narrated; al-Layth narrated; from Abū al-Zubayr; from Jābir; from God's Messenger (peace be upon him): '**He prohibited urination in stagnant water**'.

وَحَدَّثَنَا يَحْيَى بْنُ يَحْيَى، وَمُحَمَّدُ بْنُ رُمْحٍ، قَالَا: أَخْبَرَنَا اللَّيْثُ، ح، وَحَدَّثَنَا قُتَيْبَةُ، حَدَّثَنَا اللَّيْثُ، عَنْ أَبِي الزُّبَيْرِ، عَنْ جَابِرٍ: «عَنْ رَسُولِ اللهِ صَلَّى اللهُ عَلَيْهِ وَسَلَّمَ أَنَّهُ نَهَى أَنْ يُبَالَ فِي الْمَاءِ الرَّاكِدِ»

[505–95]. (Dār al-Salām 0554) Zuhayr ibn Ḥarb narrated to me: Jarīr narrated; from Hishām; from Ibn Sīrīn; from Abū Hurayrah; from the Prophet (peace be upon him). He said: '**Let none of you urinate in stagnant water then use it to wash himself**'.

وَحَدَّثَنِي زُهَيْرُ بْنُ حَرْبٍ، حَدَّثَنَا جَرِيرٌ، عَنْ هِشَامٍ، عَنِ ابْنِ سِيرِينَ، عَنْ أَبِي هُرَيْرَةَ، عَنِ النَّبِيِّ صَلَّى اللهُ عَلَيْهِ وَسَلَّمَ قَالَ: «لَا يَبُولَنَّ أَحَدُكُمْ فِي الْمَاءِ الدَّائِمِ ثُمَّ يَغْتَسِلُ مِنْهُ»

[506–96]. (Dār al-Salām 0555) Muhammad ibn Rāfiʿ narrated:[ii] ʿAbd al-Razzāq narrated; Maʿmar narrated; from Hammām

i. Related by al-Nasāʾī, 35; Ibn Mājah, 343.

ii. Related by al-Tirmidhī, 68.

ibn Munabbih who said: This is what Abū Hurayrah narrated to us from Muhammad, God's Messenger (peace be upon him). He mentioned a number of hadiths, including: **'And God's Messenger (peace be upon him) said: "Do not urinate in stagnant water that is not running, then wash yourself with it".'**

وَحَدَّثَنَا مُحَمَّدُ بْنُ رَافِعٍ، حَدَّثَنَا عَبْدُ الرَّزَّاقِ، حَدَّثَنَا مَعْمَرٌ، عَنْ هَمَّامِ بْنِ مُنَبِّهٍ، قَالَ: هَذَا مَا حَدَّثَنَا أَبُو هُرَيْرَةَ، عَنْ مُحَمَّدٍ رَسُولِ اللهِ صَلَّى اللهُ عَلَيْهِ وَسَلَّمَ - فَذَكَرَ أَحَادِيثَ مِنْهَا - وَقَالَ رَسُولُ اللهِ صَلَّى اللهُ عَلَيْهِ وَسَلَّمَ: «لَا تَبُلْ فِي الْمَاءِ الدَّائِمِ الَّذِي لَا يَجْرِي ثُمَّ تَغْتَسِلُ مِنْهُ»

Text Explanation

What is meant in these hadiths is a prohibition of urinating in stagnant water. Although the Prophet mentions washing oneself with such water, the prohibition applies to urination in such water, whether a person intends to use the same water to wash any part of one's body or not. To suggest that the prohibition applies only when urination is combined with washing oneself with the same water is wrong according to all scholars. In the last of these three hadiths the Prophet clarifies stagnant water by adding 'that is not running', so as to include water that is partly running, as in the case of some ponds and pools.

This order signifies total prohibition in some cases and strong discouragement in others, which is understood from the applicable rulings on this question. If the water is plentiful and running, urination in it is not prohibited according to the hadith, but it should be avoided. If the water is little but running, some of our scholars say that urination in it is reprehensible, but the preferred view is that it is forbidden, because according to the well-known view of the Shāfiʿī school and other scholars, urine makes it dirty and impure.

Moreover, other people will unwittingly use such water although it is contaminated with impurity. If the water is plentiful but not running, some of our scholars say that it is strongly reprehensible, not forbidden, to urinate in it, but to say that it is forbidden is better, because an order not to do something means that it is forbidden, according to meticulous scholars. Undoubtedly, urination makes it dirty and probably impure as it changes the water. Indeed, according to Abū Ḥanīfah and scholars who share his view, a stream which runs because one side of it is running is rendered impure when contaminated with impurity, then such stagnant and plentiful water becomes impure when someone urinates in it. If the stagnant water is of a small amount, some of our scholars consider urination in it to be discouraged, but the correct view is that it is forbidden, because urine makes it impure and unusable; other people might need to use it, but God knows best.

Our scholars and most other scholars consider defecation in water in the same way as urinating in it, and even worse. The same rulings apply to urinating in a bowl and then pouring this into water, and to urinating close to a river and allowing the urine to run towards it. All this is strongly reprehensible and prohibited, as we have mentioned in detail. No scholar disagrees with this, except what has been reported of the views of Dāwūd ibn ʿAlī, who claims that the prohibition applies only to actual urination in water, and that defecation is not the same. As such, he says that the prohibition does not apply to urinating in a bowl and then pouring it into the water, nor to urinating close to water. These views are contrary to the unanimous views of scholars. Indeed, these are the worst cases of his rigid adherence to the literal meaning of texts, but God knows best.

Scholars say that it is reprehensible to urinate or defecate close to water, even though it does not reach the water. This is based on the general meaning of the Prophet's prohibition of defecation in places that are frequented by people, because it is disgusting to passers-by. Moreover, it may get into the water, but God knows best.

If a person who has not cleansed himself takes a dip in water to remove the impurity and clean himself, then different rulings apply. If the water is of a small amount, which means that it becomes impure when it is contaminated with impurity, then to take a dip in it is forbidden, because the water becomes impure. If the water is plentiful and will not become impure as a result, this is acceptable if it is running water. If it is stagnant but plentiful water, it is not forbidden. Nor does it appear to be reprehensible, because it is not the same or similar to urination, but to avoid this altogether is much better, but God knows best.

CHAPTER 29

DO NOT BATHE IN STAGNANT WATER

[507–97]. (Dār al-Salām 0556) Hārūn ibn Sa'īd al-Aylī, Abū al-Ṭāhir and Ahmad ibn 'Īsā narrated: all from Ibn Wahb. Hārūn said Ibn Wahb narrated; 'Amr ibn al-Ḥārith reported to me; from Bukayr ibn al-Ashajj; that Abū al-Sā'ib, the *mawlā* of Hishām ibn Zuhrah, narrated to him; that he heard Abū Hurayrah say: **'Let none of you take a bath in stagnant water when he is in a state of major ritual impurity'. He asked: 'What he should do then, Abū Hurayrah?' He said: 'He picks from it'.**

وَحَدَّثَنَا هَارُونُ بْنُ سَعِيدٍ الْأَيْلِيُّ، وَأَبُو الطَّاهِرِ، وَأَحْمَدُ بْنُ عِيسَى، جَمِيعًا عَنِ ابْنِ وَهْبٍ، قَالَ هَارُونُ: حَدَّثَنَا ابْنُ وَهْبٍ، أَخْبَرَنِي عَمْرُو بْنُ الْحَارِثِ، عَنْ بُكَيْرِ بْنِ الْأَشَجِّ، أَنَّ أَبَا السَّائِبِ، مَوْلَى هِشَامِ بْنِ زُهْرَةَ، حَدَّثَهُ أَنَّهُ سَمِعَ أَبَا هُرَيْرَةَ، يَقُولُ: قَالَ رَسُولُ اللهِ صَلَّى اللهُ عَلَيْهِ وَسَلَّمَ: «لَا يَغْتَسِلْ أَحَدُكُمْ فِي الْمَاءِ الدَّائِمِ وَهُوَ جُنُبٌ» فَقَالَ: كَيْفَ يَفْعَلُ يَا أَبَا هُرَيْرَةَ، قَالَ: «يَتَنَاوَلُهُ تَنَاوُلًا»

Text Explanation

According to scholars of our school and others, this hadith makes clear that bathing in stagnant water is reprehensible, whether it is plentiful or small in amount. Likewise, it is reprehensible to take a bath at a running spring. As quoted by al-Buwayṭī, al-Shāfi'ī said: 'I dislike for a person in a state of major ritual impurity, i.e. *janābah*, to do his major ritual ablution, i.e. *ghusl*, in a well, whether it is with running or stagnant water, and in stagnant water that is not running'. Al-Shāfi'ī adds: 'Whether it is little or plentiful, I dislike anyone bathing in it'. This is his statement, and our scholars, like others, express the same view. All this expresses mild reprehensibility, rather than one that is close to prohibition.

If a person performs the major ritual ablution in stagnant water to remove a state of major ritual impurity, does the water become 'used'? Our scholars provide well-known details, stating that if the volume of the water is two *qullahs* or more, i.e. more than 203 litres, it does not technically become 'used', even though several people do the major ritual ablution in it at different times. If it is less than two *qullahs*, then if a person who is in a state of major ritual impurity dips himself in it without intending to do the major ritual ablution, then when he is under the water he decides to do it, his *janābah*, or major ritual impurity, is removed and the water is considered 'used'. If such a person gets into stagnant water which is less than two *qullahs* up to his knees, then intends to do the major ritual ablution before the rest of his body gets under the water, the water immediately becomes 'used' in respect of other people. The state of *janābah* is removed from the part of his body which is already in the water, and also from the rest of his body if he dips himself in the water, according to the correct, preferred and well-known view. The water becomes 'used' in respect of this person when he gets out of it. Abū 'Abdullāh al-Khiḍrī, a scholar of our school, said that the state of *janābah* is not removed from the rest of his body, but the correct view is the first one, which speaks of dipping the rest of one's body without leaving the water. If he leaves the water then dips himself in it later, his major ritual ablution is not valid. There is no disagreement on this point.

If two people dip themselves in stagnant water that is less than 160 litres in volume, making the intention to do the major ritual ablution at the same time, their state of *janābah* is removed and the water becomes 'used' water. If one makes his intention before the other, the *janābah* of that person is removed, but the water becomes 'used' in respect of the other and it is no longer usable to remove the state of *janābah*. Yet there is an odd view which suggests that it is removed. If they go into the water up to, say, their knees then intend to perform the major ritual ablution, the state of *janābah* is removed for the part in the water, but not the rest of their bodies, except according to the odd view, but God knows best.

CHAPTER 30

IMPURITIES IN THE MOSQUE MUST BE WASHED; IMPURITY IS REMOVED FROM THE GROUND BY WASHING

[508–98]. (Dār al-Salām 0557) Qutaybah ibn Saʿīd narrated: Ḥammād (who is Ibn Zayd) narrated; from Thābit; from Anas that '**A bedouin urinated in the mosque. Some people went up to stop him. God's Messenger (peace be upon him) said: "Leave him alone; do not stop him". When the man had finished, [the Prophet] called for a bucket of water and poured it over the place**'.

وَحَدَّثَنَا قُتَيْبَةُ بْنُ سَعِيدٍ، حَدَّثَنَا حَمَّادٌ وَهُوَ ابْنُ زَيْدٍ، عَنْ ثَابِتٍ، عَنْ أَنَسٍ، أَنَّ أَعْرَابِيًّا بَالَ فِي الْمَسْجِدِ، فَقَامَ إِلَيْهِ بَعْضُ الْقَوْمِ، فَقَالَ رَسُولُ اللهِ صَلَّى اللهُ عَلَيْهِ وَسَلَّمَ: «دَعُوهُ وَلَا تُزْرِمُوهُ» قَالَ: فَلَمَّا فَرَغَ دَعَا بِدَلْوٍ مِنْ مَاءٍ فَصَبَّهُ عَلَيْهِ.

[509–99]. (Dār al-Salām 0558) Muhammad ibn al-Muthannā narrated: Yaḥyā ibn Saʿīd al-Qaṭṭān narrated; from Yaḥyā in Saʿīd al-Anṣārī [H]. Also, Yaḥyā ibn Yaḥyā and Qutaybah ibn Saʿīd narrated, both from al-Darāwardī, but Yaḥyā ibn Yaḥyā said: ʿAbd al-ʿAzīz ibn Muhammad al-Madanī reported; from Yaḥyā ibn Saʿīd; that he heard Anas ibn Mālik say: '**A bedouin went to a corner of the mosque where he urinated. People shouted at him, but God's Messenger (peace be upon him) said: "Leave him alone". When the man had finished, God's**

Messenger (peace be upon him) ordered that a bucket of water should be brought and poured over the man's urine'.

حَدَّثَنَا مُحَمَّدُ بْنُ الْـمُثَنَّى، حَدَّثَنَا يَحْيَى بْنُ سَعِيدٍ الْقَطَّانُ، عَنْ يَحْيَى بْنِ سَعِيدٍ الأَنْصَارِيِّ، ح، وَحَدَّثَنَا يَحْيَى بْنُ يَحْيَى، وَقُتَيْبَةُ بْنُ سَعِيدٍ، جَمِيعًا عَنِ الدَّرَاوَرْدِيِّ، قَالَ يَحْيَى بْنُ يَحْيَى: أَخْبَرَنَا عَبْدُ الْعَزِيزِ بْنُ مُحَمَّدٍ الْـمَدَنِيُّ، عَنْ يَحْيَى بْنِ سَعِيدٍ، أَنَّهُ سَمِعَ أَنَسَ بْنَ مَالِكٍ، يَذْكُرُ أَنَّ أَعْرَابِيًّا قَامَ إِلَى نَاحِيَةٍ فِي الْـمَسْجِدِ فَبَالَ فِيهَا، فَصَاحَ بِهِ النَّاسُ، فَقَالَ رَسُولُ اللهِ صَلَّى اللهُ عَلَيْهِ وَسَلَّمَ: «دَعُوهُ» فَلَمَّا فَرَغَ أَمَرَ رَسُولُ اللهِ صَلَّى اللهُ عَلَيْهِ وَسَلَّمَ بِذَنُوبٍ فَصُبَّ عَلَى بَوْلِهِ.

[510–100]. (Dār al-Salām 0559) Zuhayr ibn Ḥarb narrated: ʿUmar ibn Yūnus al-Ḥanafī narrated; ʿIkrimah ibn ʿAmmār narrated; Isḥāq ibn Abī Ṭalḥah narrated; Anas ibn Mālik (who is Isḥāq's own uncle) narrated to me: **'Once we were in the mosque with God's Messenger (peace be upon him) when a bedouin came in. He then went to urinate in the mosque. The Prophet's companions said: "What is this? What are you doing?" God's Messenger said: "Do not stop him. Leave him". They let him finish. Then the Prophet called [the bedouin] to come over, and said to him: "Mosques are places where no urine or dirt can be left. They are places for the glorification of God, the Mighty and Exalted, and for prayer and reciting the Qur'an", or whatever God's Messenger said. He then ordered one of his companions and he brought a bucket of water and poured it over the urine'.**

حَدَّثَنَا زُهَيْرُ بْنُ حَرْبٍ، حَدَّثَنَا عُمَرُ بْنُ يُونُسَ الْحَنَفِيُّ، حَدَّثَنَا عِكْرِمَةُ بْنُ عَمَّارٍ، حَدَّثَنَا إِسْحَاقُ بْنُ أَبِي طَلْحَةَ، حَدَّثَنِي أَنَسُ بْنُ مَالِكٍ – وَهُوَ عَمُّ إِسْحَاقَ –، قَالَ: بَيْنَمَا نَحْنُ فِي الْـمَسْجِدِ مَعَ رَسُولِ اللهِ صَلَّى اللهُ عَلَيْهِ وَسَلَّمَ. إِذْ جَاءَ أَعْرَابِيٌّ فَقَامَ يَبُولُ فِي الْـمَسْجِدِ، فَقَالَ أَصْحَابُ رَسُولِ اللهِ صَلَّى اللهُ عَلَيْهِ وَسَلَّمَ: مَهْ مَهْ، قَالَ: قَالَ رَسُولُ

اللهِ صَلَّى اللهُ عَلَيْهِ وَسَلَّمَ: «لَا تُزْرِمُوهُ دَعُوهُ» فَتَرَكُوهُ حَتَّى بَالَ، ثُمَّ إِنَّ رَسُولَ اللهِ صَلَّى اللهُ عَلَيْهِ وَسَلَّمَ دَعَاهُ فَقَالَ لَهُ: «إِنَّ هَذِهِ الْمَسَاجِدَ لَا تَصْلُحُ لِشَيْءٍ مِنْ هَذَا الْبَوْلِ، وَلَا الْقَذَرِ إِنَّمَا هِيَ لِذِكْرِ اللهِ عَزَّ وَجَلَّ، وَالصَّلَاةِ وَقِرَاءَةِ الْقُرْآنِ» أَوْ كَمَا قَالَ رَسُولُ اللهِ صَلَّى اللهُ عَلَيْهِ وَسَلَّمَ قَالَ: فَأَمَرَ رَجُلًا مِنَ الْقَوْمِ فَجَاءَ بِدَلْوٍ مِنْ مَاءٍ فَشَنَّهُ عَلَيْهِ.

Text Explanation

The hadiths in this chapter make clear that human urine is impure. This is universally agreed by scholars, and there is no difference between young people and adults according to the unanimous view, but a child's urine is cleansed by sprinkling water over it, as will be explained in the next chapter, God willing. These hadiths also make clear that a mosque must be respected and cleaned of all dirt. They explain that the ground is cleansed by pouring water over it, and need not be dug. This is the view of our school and the majority of scholars. Abū Ḥanīfah, however, maintains that it should be dug.

It is also clear that water that washes away impurity is pure. This is subject to different views among scholars. Our scholars hold three different views: the first is that it is pure, and the second considers it impure. The third view, which is the correct one, is that if it splits after the place of the impurity has been cleansed, then it is clean, but if it splits when the place has not yet been cleansed, it is impure. These different views apply if the water splits and it is clear, unchanged. If it is changed in colour, taste or smell when it splits, it is impure, regardless of whether the change is marginal or substantial. This is agreed by all Muslims, but God knows best.

These hadiths make clear that an uneducated person should be treated kindly and taught what he needs to know without rebuke or harshness, as long as it is clear that his unlawful action is not meant to show carelessness or stubbornness. The hadith also suggests that a lesser harm is to be tolerated in order to prevent a greater harm. Scholars said that the Prophet's order to his companions to leave the man alone ensured two benefits. One of these was that if the man was suddenly stopped when some impurity had already fallen, he might have suffered some harm. To allow more impurity was better than causing the man harm. The other benefit was that the impurity only affected a small part of the mosque. Had people caused the man to rise while he was urinating, the impurity might have affected his clothes, body and several places in the mosque, but God knows best.

The Prophet said to the man: 'Mosques are places where no urine or dirt can be left. They are places for the glorification of God, the Mighty and Exalted, and for prayer and reciting the Qur'an'. This statement by the Prophet makes clear that mosques must be kept clean of all dirt, litter, spitting, noise, loud voices, verbal disputes, buying and selling as well as all types of contracts and similar matters. This gives us several points which I will mention briefly:

1. All Muslims are in agreement that it is permissible for a person who has not performed the ablution to sit in the mosque. If he is staying there for any type of worship, including devotion, religious study, listening to a sermon or admonition, or waiting for prayer, etc. then such stay is recommended. If a person stays in the mosque for no such reason, that is permissible. Some of our scholars say that it is discouraged, but this view lacks clear evidence in support.
2. According to our school, it is permissible to sleep in the mosque, and this is stated by al-Shāfiʿī in *al-Umm*. In his book *al-Ishrāq*, Ibn al-Mundhir says: 'Ibn al-Musayyib, al-Ḥasan, ʿAṭā' and al-Shāfiʿī agree that it is permissible to sleep in a mosque, but Ibn ʿAbbās said: "Do not make it a sleeping place". He is also reported to have said: "If you sleep there awaiting prayer, this is acceptable". Al-Awzāʿī said that sleeping in the mosque is discouraged. Mālik said that it is acceptable for travellers, but not for residents. Ahmad said that if a traveller or someone in a similar situation sleeps in the mosque, it is acceptable, but to make the mosque a place where people take a nap or stay the night is unacceptable. This is also Isḥāq's view'. Scholars who say that it is permissible to sleep in the mosque cite in evidence

the facts that during the Prophet's lifetime, ʿAlī ibn Abī Ṭālib, Ibn ʿUmar, the people of al-Ṣuffah, the woman accused of stealing jewellery, the two strangers, Thumāmah ibn Athāl, Ṣafwān ibn Umayyah and others slept in the mosque. Hadiths mentioning these are well-known and entered in the *Ṣaḥīḥ* anthologies, but God knows best. It is permissible to allow an unbeliever to enter a mosque, but unbelievers may not enter a mosque without permission.

3. Ibn al-Mundhir said that all well-known scholars permit performing the ablution in a mosque, provided that this is not done where other people find it inconvenient or where the place is left wet. Imam Abū al-Ḥasan ibn Baṭṭāl of the Mālikī School attributes this to Ibn ʿUmar, Ibn ʿAbbās, ʿAṭā', Ṭāwūs, al-Ḥanafī, Ibn al-Qāsim and most scholars. However, Ibn Sīrīn, Mālik and Saḥnūn are reported to have discouraged it so as to keep mosques clean, but God knows best.
4. A number of our scholars maintain that it is reprehensible to allow animals, mad people and young children into a mosque except for a particular purpose, because they may stain the mosque with an impurity. However, it is not forbidden to allow them in, because the Prophet performed his *ṭawāf* riding a camel. Yet this does not contradict saying that their entry into the mosque is discouraged or reprehensible, because the Prophet did this to show that it is permissible, or to show people what to do when they perform the *ṭawāf*, but God knows best.
5. It is forbidden to bring any impurity into the mosque. If a person who is carrying an impurity on his body wants to enter a mosque and he fears that he may let that impurity affect the mosque, then he cannot enter. If he has no fear of this, he may go in. A person may not bleed himself in a mosque. If he does this ensuring that his blood drips into a bowl, this is reprehensible, but if it drips onto the floor of the mosque, it is forbidden. If a person urinates into a bowl in a mosque, two verdicts are stated about his action. The more correct one is that

it is forbidden to do so and the other is that it is reprehensible.

6. It is permissible to recline in the mosque, shake one's leg and cross one's fingers. Several authentic hadiths make clear that the Prophet did all this.
7. It is strongly recommended to use a broom to clean the mosque and remove dust from it and keep it clean and tidy. This is stated in several well-known and authentic hadiths, but God knows best.

CHAPTER 31

A SUCKLING CHILD'S URINE AND HOW TO WASH IT

[511–101]. (Dār al-Salām 0560) Abū Bakr ibn Abī Shaybah and Abū Kurayb narrated:[i] both said: ʿAbdullāh ibn Numayr narrated; Hishām narrated; from his father; from ʿĀ'ishah, the Prophet's wife: **'Young children were brought to God's Messenger (peace be upon him) and he would bless them and rub their jaws [with dates]. Once, he was brought a young boy and the boy urinated on him. He called for some water and he poured it over the child's urine, but did not wash it'**.

حَدَّثَنَا أَبُو بَكْرِ بْنُ أَبِي شَيْبَةَ، وَأَبُو كُرَيْبٍ، قَالَا: حَدَّثَنَا عَبْدُ اللهِ بْنُ نُمَيْرٍ، حَدَّثَنَا هِشَامٌ، عَنْ أَبِيهِ، عَنْ عَائِشَةَ زَوْجِ النَّبِيِّ صَلَّى اللهُ عَلَيْهِ وَسَلَّمَ: «أَنَّ رَسُولَ اللهِ صَلَّى اللهُ عَلَيْهِ وَسَلَّمَ كَانَ يُؤْتَى بِالصِّبْيَانِ فَيُبَرِّكُ عَلَيْهِمْ وَيُحَنِّكُهُمْ، فَأُتِيَ بِصَبِيٍّ فَبَالَ عَلَيْهِ، فَدَعَا بِمَاءٍ، فَأَتْبَعَهُ بَوْلَهُ وَلَمْ يَغْسِلْهُ»

[512–102]. (Dār al-Salām 0561) Zuhayr ibn Ḥarb narrated: Jarīr narrated; from Hishām; from his father; from ʿĀ'ishah: **'God's Messenger was brought a suckling boy and the boy urinated in his lap. He called for some water and poured it over it'**.

وَحَدَّثَنَا زُهَيْرُ بْنُ حَرْبٍ، حَدَّثَنَا جَرِيرٌ، عَنْ هِشَامٍ، عَنْ أَبِيهِ، عَنْ عَائِشَةَ، قَالَتْ: «أُتِيَ رَسُولُ اللهِ صَلَّى اللهُ عَلَيْهِ وَسَلَّمَ بِصَبِيٍّ يَرْضَعُ فَبَالَ فِي حَجْرِهِ فَدَعَا بِمَاءٍ فَصَبَّهُ عَلَيْهِ»

i. Related by Muslim in the Book of Good Manners.

[000–000]. (Dār al-Salām 0562) Isḥāq ibn Ibrāhīm narrated: ʿĪsā reported; Hishām narrated with the same chain of transmission: **the same text as the hadith narrated by Ibn Numayr**.

حَدَّثَنَا إِسْحَاقُ بْنُ إِبْرَاهِيمَ، أَخْبَرَنَا عِيسَى، حَدَّثَنَا هِشَامٌ، بِهَذَا الإِسْنَادِ مِثْلَ حَدِيثِ ابْنِ نُمَيْرٍ.

[513–103]. (Dār al-Salām 0563) Muhammad ibn Rumḥ ibn al-Muhājir narrated:[i] al-Layth reported; from Ibn Shihāb; from ʿUbaydillāh ibn ʿAbdullāh; from Umm Qays bint Miḥṣan: **'She brought a son of hers who had not yet eaten food to God's Messenger (peace be upon him) and placed the child in his lap. He urinated. [The Prophet] did no more than soak it with water'**.

حَدَّثَنَا مُحَمَّدُ بْنُ رُمْحِ بْنِ الْمُهَاجِرِ، أَخْبَرَنَا اللَّيْثُ، عَنِ ابْنِ شِهَابٍ، عَنْ عُبَيْدِ اللهِ بْنِ عَبْدِ اللهِ، عَنْ أُمِّ قَيْسٍ بِنْتِ مِحْصَنٍ، أَنَّهَا أَتَتْ رَسُولَ اللهِ صَلَّى اللهُ عَلَيْهِ وَسَلَّمَ بِابْنٍ لَهَا لَمْ يَأْكُلِ الطَّعَامَ فَوَضَعَتْهُ فِي حَجْرِهِ فَبَالَ، قَالَ: «فَلَمْ يَزِدْ عَلَى أَنْ نَضَحَ بِالْمَاءِ»

[514–000]. (Dār al-Salām 0564) Yaḥyā ibn Yaḥyā, Abū Bakr ibn Abī Shaybah, ʿAmr al-Nāqid and Zuhayr ibn Ḥarb narrated the same: all of them from Ibn ʿUyaynah; from al-Zuhrī; with the same chain of transmission. **He said: 'He called for some water and sprinkled it'**.

وَحَدَّثَنَاهُ يَحْيَى بْنُ يَحْيَى، وَأَبُو بَكْرِ بْنُ أَبِي شَيْبَةَ، وَعَمْرٌو النَّاقِدُ، وَزُهَيْرُ بْنُ حَرْبٍ، جَمِيعًا عَنِ ابْنِ عُيَيْنَةَ، عَنِ الزُّهْرِيِّ، بِهَذَا الإِسْنَادِ. وَقَالَ فَدَعَا بِمَاءٍ فَرَشَّهُ.

---

i. Related by al-Bukhārī, 223; Abū Dāwūd, 374; al-Tirmidhī, 71; al-Nasāʾī, 301; Ibn Mājah, 524.

[515–104]. (Dār al-Salām 0565) Ḥarmalah ibn Yaḥyā narrated it to me: Ibn Wahb reported; Yūnus ibn Yazīd reported to me; that Ibn Shihāb reported to him, saying: 'Ubaydillāh ibn 'Abdullāh ibn 'Utbah ibn Mas'ūd reported to me; of Umm Qays bint Miḥṣan (She was one of the early women Muhājirīn who gave their pledges to God's Messenger (peace be upon him) and she was the sister of 'Ukkāshah ibn Miḥṣan who belonged to the clan of Asad ibn Khuzaymah). **He said: 'She told me that she took a son of hers who was not old enough to eat food'. 'Ubaydillāh said: 'She told me that this child of hers urinated on God's Messenger's lap. The Prophet called for some water and soaked his robe, but did not wash it thoroughly'**.

وَحَدَّثَنِيهِ حَرْمَلَةُ بْنُ يَحْيَى، أَخْبَرَنَا ابْنُ وَهْبٍ، أَخْبَرَنِي يُونُسُ بْنُ يَزِيدَ، أَنَّ ابْنَ شِهَابٍ، أَخْبَرَهُ قَالَ: أَخْبَرَنِي عُبَيْدُ اللهِ بْنُ عَبْدِ اللهِ بْنِ عُتْبَةَ بْنِ مَسْعُودٍ، أَنَّ أُمَّ قَيْسٍ بِنْتَ مِحْصَنٍ، - وَكَانَتْ مِنَ الْـمُهَاجِرَاتِ الْأُوَلِ اللَّاتِي بَايَعْنَ رَسُولَ اللهِ صَلَّى اللهُ عَلَيْهِ وَسَلَّمَ وَهِيَ أُخْتُ عُكَّاشَةَ بْنِ مِحْصَنٍ أَحَدُ بَنِي أَسَدِ بْنِ خُزَيْمَةَ - قَالَ: أَخْبَرَتْنِي أَنَّهَا أَتَتْ رَسُولَ اللهِ صَلَّى اللهُ عَلَيْهِ وَسَلَّمَ بِابْنٍ لَهَا لَمْ يَبْلُغْ أَنْ يَأْكُلَ الطَّعَامَ قَالَ: عُبَيْدُ اللهِ أَخْبَرَتْنِي «أَنَّ ابْنَهَا ذَاكَ بَالَ فِي حَجْرِ رَسُولِ اللهِ صَلَّى اللهُ عَلَيْهِ وَسَلَّمَ، فَدَعَا رَسُولُ اللهِ صَلَّى اللهُ عَلَيْهِ وَسَلَّمَ بِمَاءٍ فَنَضَحَهُ عَلَى ثَوْبِهِ وَلَمْ يَغْسِلْهُ غَسْلاً».

Text Explanation

The first hadith mentions that when young children were brought to the Prophet he would bless them and rub their jaws. This means that he would say some prayers for the child and then chew a date a little and rub the child's jaws with it.

These hadiths show that it is recommended to take newborn children to people who are known to be devout and learned to bless them. This applies to the child who has just been born or at some later time. The hadiths also encourage kindly behaviour, easy interaction and humility with people and gentility with children.

The main point in this chapter is that the impurity of a young boy's urine is removed by soaking with water. Scholars have different views concerning the cleansing of a young boy's and a young girl's urine, with our scholars expressing three views. The correct and preferred view is that soaking is enough for a boy's urine, but not enough for a young girl's urine. The latter must be washed like all similar impurities. The second view is that soaking is sufficient in both cases, and the third view is that soaking is not sufficient in either case. These last two views are stated by ʿAbd al-Raḥmān ibn Ma'mūn al-Mutawallī, the author of *al-Tatimmah,* who belonged to the Shāfiʿī school, but neither is well-founded. Among those scholars who differentiate between a boy and a girl in this connection are ʿAlī ibn Abī Ṭālib, ʿAṭā' ibn Abī Rabāḥ, al-Ḥasan al-Baṣrī, Ahmad ibn Ḥanbal, Isḥāq ibn Rāhawayh, a number of early scholars, scholars of Hadith and Ibn Wahb, who was close to Mālik (may God be pleased with them all). This view is also reported to have been mentioned by Abu Ḥanīfah.

Scholars who maintain that the urine of both young boys and girls must be washed include Abū Ḥanīfah and Mālik, according to what is best known of their views, and the scholars of Kufah. It should be understood that this difference among scholars is merely concerned with how to cleanse an object if a young child's urine falls on it. There is no difference in belief that such urine is impure. Some of our scholars assert that there is unanimity among scholars that a young boy's urine is impure, and the only one who dissents on this point is Dāwūd al-Ẓāhirī. Al-Khaṭṭābī and others said: 'Those scholars who say that it is sufficient to soak the place where a young boy's urine has fallen merely make it easier to cleanse it, but they agree that it is impure. What Ibn Baṭṭāl and *Qāḍī* ʿIyāḍ attribute to al-Shāfiʿī and others of saying that the urine of a young boy is not impure, and therefore, it is soaked, is certainly false'.

What does soaking mean? Our scholars give different explanations. Abū Muhammad al-Juwaynī, *Qāḍī* Ḥusayn and al-Baghawī suggest that it means that an object where urine has fallen should be immersed in water, like all other impurities, but if it is wrung no water need be forced out. It differs from other impurities in that in this case, no wringing is needed. Imam al-Ḥaramayn and other meticulous scholars say that soaking means to drench it with water up to a point where water does not drip from it. In the case of other impurities, water is supposed to run off the contaminated object, even though it is not required to wring it. This is the correct and preferred view. The evidence is Umm Miḥṣan's statement that he soaked it but did not wash it, but God knows best.

It must be understood that soaking is sufficient to remove the impurity as long as the young boy is breastfed. If he has started to eat food, his urine must be washed off, and there is no disagreement on this point, but God knows best.

CHAPTER 32

ON SEMEN

[516–105]. (Dār al-Salām 0566) Yaḥyā ibn Yaḥyā narrated: Khālid ibn ʿAbdullāh reported; from Khālid; from Abū Maʿshar; from Ibrāhīm; from ʿAlqamah and al-Aswad that: '**A man who was a guest at ʿĀ'ishah's home was washing his robe in the morning. ʿĀ'ishah said: "If you see it, it is enough to wash the place. If you do not see it, you soak the area. I used to rub it off God's Messenger's robe and he would then offer his prayers wearing it"**.'

حَدَّثَنَا يَحْيَى بْنُ يَحْيَى، أَخْبَرَنَا خَالِدُ بْنُ عَبْدِ اللهِ، عَنْ خَالِدٍ، عَنْ أَبِي مَعْشَرٍ، عَنْ إِبْرَاهِيمَ، عَنْ عَلْقَمَةَ، وَالْأَسْوَدِ، أَنَّ رَجُلًا نَزَلَ بِعَائِشَةَ، فَأَصْبَحَ يَغْسِلُ ثَوْبَهُ فَقَالَتْ عَائِشَةُ: «إِنَّمَا كَانَ يُجْزِئُكَ إِنْ رَأَيْتَهُ أَنْ تَغْسِلَ مَكَانَهُ، فَإِنْ لَمْ تَرَ نَضَحْتَ حَوْلَهُ وَلَقَدْ رَأَيْتُنِي أَفْرُكُهُ مِنْ ثَوْبِ رَسُولِ اللهِ صَلَّى اللهُ عَلَيْهِ وَسَلَّمَ فَرْكًا فَيُصَلِّي فِيهِ»

[517–106]. (Dār al-Salām 0567) ʿUmar ibn Ḥafṣ ibn Ghiyāth narrated: my father narrated; from al-Aʿmash; from Ibrāhīm; from al-Aswad and Hammām; from ʿĀ'ishah: '**In reference to semen, she said: "I used to rub it off God's Messenger's robe"**.'

وَحَدَّثَنَا عُمَرُ بْنُ حَفْصِ بْنِ غِيَاثٍ، حَدَّثَنَا أَبِي، عَنِ الْأَعْمَشِ، عَنْ إِبْرَاهِيمَ، عَنِ الْأَسْوَدِ، وَهَمَّامٍ، عَنْ عَائِشَةَ فِي الْمَنِيِّ قَالَتْ: «كُنْتُ أَفْرُكُهُ مِنْ ثَوْبِ رَسُولِ اللهِ صَلَّى اللهُ عَلَيْهِ وَسَلَّمَ»

[000–107]. (Dār al-Salām 0568) Qutaybah ibn Saʿīd narrated: Ḥammād (meaning Ibn Zayd) narrated; from Hishām ibn Ḥassān [H]. Also, Isḥāq ibn Ibrāhīm narrated; ʿAbdah ibn Sulaymān reported; Ibn Abī ʿArūbah narrated: all of them from Abū Maʿshar [H]. Further, Abū Bakr ibn Abī Shaybah narrated; Hushaym narrated; from Mughīrah [H]. And, ʿAbd al-Raḥmān ibn Mahdī narrated; from Mahdī ibn Maymūn; from Wāṣil al-Aḥdab [H]. Also, Ibn Ḥātim narrated to me: Isḥāq ibn Manṣūr narrated; Isrā'īl narrated from Manṣūr and Mughīrah: all these from Ibrāhīm; from al-Aswad; from ʿĀ'ishah, concerning rubbing semen off God's Messenger's robe: **a very similar text to the narration of Khālid from Abu Maʿshar**.

حَدَّثَنَا قُتَيْبَةُ بْنُ سَعِيدٍ، حَدَّثَنَا حَمَّادٌ يَعْنِي ابْنَ زَيْدٍ، عَنْ هِشَامِ بْنِ حَسَّانَ ح، وَحَدَّثَنَا إِسْحَاقُ بْنُ إِبْرَاهِيمَ، أَخْبَرَنَا عَبْدَةُ بْنُ سُلَيْمَانَ، حَدَّثَنَا ابْنُ أَبِي عَرُوبَةَ جَمِيعًا عَنْ أَبِي مَعْشَرٍ ح، وَحَدَّثَنَا أَبُو بَكْرِ بْنُ أَبِي شَيْبَةَ، حَدَّثَنَا هُشَيْمٌ، عَنْ مُغِيرَةَ، ح، وَحَدَّثَنِي مُحَمَّدُ بْنُ حَاتِمٍ، حَدَّثَنَا عَبْدُ الرَّحْمَنِ بْنُ مَهْدِيٍّ، عَنْ مَهْدِيِّ بْنِ مَيْمُونٍ، عَنْ وَاصِلٍ الْأَحْدَبِ، ح، وَحَدَّثَنِي ابْنُ حَاتِمٍ، حَدَّثَنَا إِسْحَاقُ بْنُ مَنْصُورٍ، حَدَّثَنَا إِسْرَائِيلُ، عَنْ مَنْصُورٍ، وَمُغِيرَةَ، كُلُّ هَؤُلَاءِ عَنْ إِبْرَاهِيمَ، عَنِ الْأَسْوَدِ، عَنْ عَائِشَةَ فِي حَتِّ الْمَنِيِّ مِنْ ثَوْبِ رَسُولِ اللهِ صَلَّى اللهُ عَلَيْهِ وَسَلَّمَ نَحْوَ حَدِيثِ خَالِدٍ، عَنْ أَبِي مَعْشَرٍ.

[000–000]. (Dār al-Salām 0569) Muhammad ibn Ḥātim narrated to me: Ibn ʿUyaynah narrated; from Manṣūr; from Ibrāhīm; from Hammām; from ʿĀ'ishah: **The same text as their narration**.

وَحَدَّثَنِي مُحَمَّدُ بْنُ حَاتِمٍ، حَدَّثَنَا ابْنُ عُيَيْنَةَ، عَنْ مَنْصُورٍ، عَنْ إِبْرَاهِيمَ، عَنْ هَمَّامٍ، عَنْ عَائِشَةَ بِنَحْوِ حَدِيثِهِمْ.

[518–108]. (Dār al-Salām 0570) Abū Bakr ibn Abī Shaybah narrated:[i] Muhammad ibn Bishr narrated; from ʿAmr ibn Maymūn;

he said: **'I asked Sulaymān ibn Yasār about semen falling on one's robe: should one wash it off or should one wash the robe? He said: "ʿĀ'ishah told me that God's Messenger (peace be upon him) used to wash off the semen and then go out to pray wearing the same robe. I could see the trace of the washing on the robe".'**

وَحَدَّثَنَا أَبُو بَكْرِ بْنُ أَبِي شَيْبَةَ، حَدَّثَنَا مُحَمَّدُ بْنُ بِشْرٍ، عَنْ عَمْرِو بْنِ مَيْمُونٍ، قَالَ: سَأَلْتُ سُلَيْمَانَ بْنَ يَسَارٍ، عَنِ الْمَنِيِّ يُصِيبُ ثَوْبَ الرَّجُلِ أَيَغْسِلُهُ أَمْ يَغْسِلُ الثَّوْبَ؟ فَقَالَ: أَخْبَرَتْنِي عَائِشَةُ، أَنَّ رَسُولَ اللهِ صَلَّى اللهُ عَلَيْهِ وَسَلَّمَ كَانَ يَغْسِلُ الْمَنِيَّ ثُمَّ يَخْرُجُ إِلَى الصَّلَاةِ فِي ذَلِكَ الثَّوْبِ، وَأَنَا أَنْظُرُ إِلَى أَثَرِ الْغَسْلِ فِيهِ.

[000–000]. (Dār al-Salām 0571) Abū Kāmil al-Jaḥdarī narrated: ʿAbd al-Wāḥid (meaning Ibn Ziyād) narrated [H]. Also, Abū Kurayb narrated: Ibn al-Mubārak and Ibn Abi Zā'idah reported; all from ʿAmr ibn Maymūn, with this same chain of transmission. **Ibn Abī Zā'idah's narration is the same as Ibn Bishr's, stating that God's Messenger (peace be upon him) used to wash the semen off. Ibn al-Mubārak and ʿAbd al-Wāḥid's narration mentions that she said: 'I used to wash it off God's Messenger's robe'**.

وَحَدَّثَنَا أَبُو كَامِلٍ الْجَحْدَرِيُّ، حَدَّثَنَا عَبْدُ الْوَاحِدِ يَعْنِي ابْنَ زِيَادٍ ح، وَحَدَّثَنَا أَبُو كُرَيْبٍ، أَخْبَرَنَا ابْنُ الْمُبَارَكِ، وَابْنُ أَبِي زَائِدَةَ كُلُّهُمْ عَنْ عَمْرِو بْنِ مَيْمُونٍ، بِهَذَا الْإِسْنَادِ أَمَّا ابْنُ أَبِي زَائِدَةَ فَحَدِيثُهُ كَمَا قَالَ ابْنُ بِشْرٍ، أَنَّ رَسُولَ اللهِ صَلَّى اللهُ عَلَيْهِ وَسَلَّمَ كَانَ يَغْسِلُ الْمَنِيَّ وَأَمَّا ابْنُ الْمُبَارَكِ، وَعَبْدُ الْوَاحِدِ فَفِي حَدِيثِهِمَا قَالَتْ: «كُنْتُ أَغْسِلُهُ مِنْ ثَوْبِ رَسُولِ اللهِ صَلَّى اللهُ عَلَيْهِ وَسَلَّمَ»

---

i. Related by al-Bukhārī, 229, 230, 231 and 232; Abū Dāwūd, 373; al-Tirmidhī, 117 (in a shorter version); al-Nasā'ī, 294; Ibn Mājah, 536 (in a similar but longer version).

[519–109]. (Dār al-Salām 0572) Ahmad ibn Jawwās al-Ḥanafī Abū ʿĀṣim narrated: Abū al-Aḥwaṣ narrated; from Shabīb ibn Gharqadah; from ʿAbdullāh ibn Shihāb al-Khawlānī: '**I was a guest at ʿĀ'ishah's and I had a wet dream [leaving marks] on my two garments. I drenched them in water. I was seen by ʿĀ'ishah's maid and she told her. ʿĀ'ishah sent, asking me: "Why have you done this with your two garments?" I said: "I saw what a sleeping person may see in his dream". She asked: "Have you seen anything on them?" I said: "No". She said: "If you see something, wash it off. I used to rub it off God's Messenger's robe when it dried, using my nail".**'

وَحَدَّثَنَا أَحْمَدُ بْنُ جَوَّاسٍ الْحَنَفِيُّ أَبُو عَاصِمٍ، حَدَّثَنَا أَبُو الْأَحْوَصِ، عَنْ شَبِيبِ بْنِ غَرْقَدَةَ، عَنْ عَبْدِ اللهِ بْنِ شِهَابٍ الْخَوْلَانِيِّ، قَالَ: كُنْتُ نَازِلًا عَلَى عَائِشَةَ فَاحْتَلَمْتُ فِي ثَوْبَيَّ فَغَمَسْتُهُمَا فِي الْمَاءِ، فَرَأَتْنِي جَارِيَةٌ لِعَائِشَةَ فَأَخْبَرَتْهَا فَبَعَثَتْ إِلَيَّ عَائِشَةُ فَقَالَتْ: مَا حَمَلَكَ عَلَى مَا صَنَعْتَ بِثَوْبَيْكَ؟ قَالَ قُلْتُ: رَأَيْتُ مَا يَرَى النَّائِمُ فِي مَنَامِهِ، قَالَتْ: هَلْ رَأَيْتَ فِيهِمَا شَيْئًا؟ قُلْتُ: لَا، قَالَتْ: «فَلَوْ رَأَيْتَ شَيْئًا غَسَلْتَهُ. لَقَدْ رَأَيْتُنِي وَإِنِّي لَأَحُكُّهُ مِنْ ثَوْبِ رَسُولِ اللهِ صَلَّى اللهُ عَلَيْهِ وَسَلَّمَ يَابِسًا بِظُفُرِي»

Text Explanation

ʿĀ'ishah objected to the man washing his robe, stating that she used to rub semen off with her nail. Had it been ritually impure, the Prophet would not have deemed it enough to so rub it off, he would have required its being washed off and would not have used his robe before it was washed.

Scholars differ as to whether human semen is ritually impure or not. Mālik and Abū Ḥanīfah consider it impure, but Abū Ḥanīfah says that if it is dry, it is sufficient to rub it off to cleanse the garment. The same for one report attributed to Ahmad. Mālik considers that it must be washed off, whether it is wet or dry. Al-Layth considers it impure, but if one prays without having washed it, one does not need to repeat one's prayer. Al-Ḥasan said that prayer need not be repeated if one prayed with semen on one's clothes, even if there is plenty of it, but if it is on one's body, then the prayer must be repeated after it is washed off, even if there is only a little of it. Many scholars consider semen to be pure. This is reported to be the view of ʿAlī ibn Abī Ṭālib, Saʿd ibn Abī Waqqāṣ, Ibn ʿUmar, ʿĀ'ishah, Dāwūd and Ahmad, according to the more accurate of the two views attributed to him. It is also the view of the Shāfiʿī school of *fiqh* and Hadith scholars. Those who claimed that al-Shāfiʿī was the only scholar who considered it pure made a clear error.

The evidence cited by scholars who consider semen to be impure is the hadith that requires it to be washed off. The evidence cited by those who consider it pure is the hadith that mentions that it was rubbed off. Had it been impure, rubbing it off would not have been enough, as is the case with blood and other impurities. They add that the narration mentioning washing it suggests preference and opting for what is cleaner, but God knows best.

Such is the ruling concerning human semen. We add an odd and weak view that a woman's semen is impure, unlike man's semen.[i] An even weaker view is that the semen of both is impure. The correct view is that both are pure. Another question is: since semen is pure, is it permissible to eat? There are two views on this point, but the more correct one is that it is forbidden because it is dirty. As such, it belongs to the category of foul stuffs that are forbidden for Muslims to eat. The semen of other animals, such as dogs and pigs or a cross between either one of these two and another animal, is impure, and there is no difference of views on this point. As for other animals, there are three different views, and the more correct of these is that their semen is all pure, whether such animals are permissible to eat

---

i. This paragraph is an example of the theoretical details scholars of old times considered and provided rulings for. The point about 'eating' semen is a detail that follows from its being ritually pure or impure. I considered deleting this paragraph, as it is irrelevant. These points were not considered by scholars like Mūsā Shāhīn Lāshīn, a twentieth century scholar who wrote a full commentary on Muslim's *Ṣaḥīḥ* anthology in ten large volumes. I ultimately decided to retain it, as an example of the sort of academic question requiring an answer.

or not. The second view is that they are all impure, and the third view is that the semen of animals that may be eaten is pure, but that of other animals is impure, but God knows best.

A number of scholars consider this hadith to provide evidence that the wetness of a woman's vagina is pure. This is subject to well-known differences of view among scholars, both of our school and others. It is more likely that it is not impure. Those who take this view cite this hadith as evidence, saying that the Prophet could not have a wet dream, because a wet dream involved Satan manipulating a sleeping person, and this could not happen to God's Messenger (peace be upon him). Therefore, the semen on his robe could only be the result of sexual intercourse. As such, the semen must have touched the wetness of the woman's vagina. If this wetness were impure, the semen would have become impure, and the Prophet would not have allowed that it remained on his robe and merely rubbed it off. Those who take the opposite view and consider the wetness of the woman's vagina impure give two answers. The first is that a wet dream has nothing to do with Satan; rather, it is a discharge of the excess of semen in one's body. As such, the Prophet could have wet dreams like all men. (Note: sounds like the addressees are only intended to be male?) The other answer is that the semen on his robe could be the result of foreplay, rather than actual intercourse. But God knows best.

Transmission

The chain of transmission of the first hadith in this chapter features: 'Yaḥyā ibn Yaḥyā narrated: Khālid ibn ʿAbdullāh reported; from Khālid; from Abū Maʿshar'. The first named Khālid in this chain was a miller from the city of Wāsiṭ, and the second of this name was Khālid ibn Mahrān, whose appellation was Abū al-Munāzil. He was best known as Khālid al-Ḥadhdhā', which means the shoemaker. He was not a shoemaker but he used to sit in the shoemakers' market place.

CHAPTER 33

THE RITUAL IMPURITY OF BLOOD AND HOW IT SHOULD BE WASHED

[520–110]. (Dār al-Salām 0573) Abū Bakr ibn Abī Shaybah narrated:[i] Wakīʿ narrated; Hishām ibn ʿUrwah narrated [H]. Also, Muhammad ibn Ḥātim narrated to me (his text); Yaḥyā ibn Saʿīd narrated; from Hishām ibn ʿUrwah; Fāṭimah narrated to me; from Asmā': '**A woman came to the Prophet and asked: "Anyone of us may have her dress stained by her blood as she is in her period. What should she do?" He said: "She should rub it off, then clean it with water, then soak it, then she may pray wearing it".**'

وَحَدَّثَنَا أَبُو بَكْرِ بْنُ أَبِي شَيْبَةَ، حَدَّثَنَا وَكِيعٌ، حَدَّثَنَا هِشَامُ بْنُ عُرْوَةَ ح، وَحَدَّثَنِي مُحَمَّدُ بْنُ حَاتِمٍ - وَاللَّفْظُ لَهُ - حَدَّثَنَا يَحْيَى بْنُ سَعِيدٍ، عَنْ هِشَامِ بْنِ عُرْوَةَ قَالَ: حَدَّثَتْنِي فَاطِمَةُ، عَنْ أَسْمَاءَ قَالَتْ: جَاءَتِ امْرَأَةٌ إِلَى النَّبِيِّ صَلَّى اللهُ عَلَيْهِ وَسَلَّمَ، فَقَالَتْ: إِحْدَانَا يُصِيبُ ثَوْبَهَا مِنْ دَمِ الْحَيْضَةِ، كَيْفَ تَصْنَعُ بِهِ، قَالَ: «تَحُتُّهُ، ثُمَّ تَقْرُصُهُ بِالْمَاءِ، ثُمَّ تَنْضَحُهُ، ثُمَّ تُصَلِّي فِيهِ»

[000–000]. (Dār al-Salām 0574) Abū Kurayb narrated: Ibn Numayr narrated [H]. Also, Abū al-Ṭāhir narrated to me; Ibn Wahb reported to me; Yaḥyā ibn ʿAbdullāh ibn Sālim, Mālik ibn Anas and ʿAmr ibn al-Ḥārith reported to me; all of them

i. Related by al-Bukhārī, 227 and 307 (in similar wording); Abū Dāwūd, 361 and 362; al-Tirmidhī, 138; al-Nasā'ī, 292 and 293; Ibn Mājah, 629.

from Hishām ibn ʿUrwah; with this chain of transmission: **the same text as the narration by Yaḥyā ibn Saʿīd**.

حَدَّثَنَا أَبُو كُرَيْبٍ، حَدَّثَنَا ابْنُ نُمَيْرٍ ح، وَحَدَّثَنِي أَبُو الطَّاهِرِ، أَخْبَرَنِي ابْنُ وَهْبٍ، أَخْبَرَنِي يَحْيَى بْنُ عَبْدِ اللهِ بْنِ سَالِمٍ، وَمَالِكُ بْنُ أَنَسٍ، وَعَمْرُو بْنُ الْحَارِثِ، كُلُّهُمْ عَنْ هِشَامِ بْنِ عُرْوَةَ بِهَذَا الإِسْنَادِ مِثْلَ حَدِيثِ يَحْيَى بْنِ سَعِيدٍ.

Text Explanation

What the Prophet told his questioner was that she should rub her dry blood then use water and wet the blood with the tips of her fingers to dilute it, then wash it off. This hadith makes clear that impurity must be washed off with water. It means that washing it with, say, vinegar or some other liquid is not good enough to cleanse it, because by doing so one disobeys what the Prophet has ordered. The hadith also makes clear that blood is impure. This is unanimously agreed by all Muslims. Further, the hadith tells us that there is no specified number of washes for removing impurity, but complete cleansing is required.

If the impurity cannot be seen with one's eye, such as dried urine, the requirement is to wash it once. To wash more than once is not obligatory, but washing it three times is recommended, on the basis of the hadith: 'When any of you wakes up, he should not dip his hand in a water container before washing it three times'. We have already explained this hadith. If the impurity is visible, such as blood, it must be physically removed. It is recommended to wash the place twice or three times after removing it. As to whether a garment should be wrung, there are two views, and the more correct one is that it is not obligatory. If one washes off a physical impurity, but its colour remains, there is no harm, because cleansing has been accomplished. If its taste remains, it is still impure and the taste must be removed. If its smell remains, there are two views expressed by al-Shāfiʿī and the more correct one is that the impurity is removed. The other view is that it is not, but God knows best.

CHAPTER 34

CONFIRMATION OF THE RITUAL IMPURITY OF URINE AND THE CLEANSING OBLIGATION

[521–111]. (Dār al-Salām 0575) Abū Saʿīd al-Ashajj, Abū Kurayb Muhammad ibn al-ʿAlā' and Isḥāq ibn Ibrāhīm narrated:[i] Isḥāq said 'Wakīʿ reported' and the other two said Wakīʿ narrated; al-Aʿmash narrated, saying: I heard Mujāhid narrating from Ṭāwūs; from Ibn ʿAbbās: **'God's Messenger (peace be upon him) passed by two graves. He said: "These two are suffering torment, and their torment is for nothing so serious. One of them was a habitual tale-bearer, and the other did not take precautions when urinating". He then called for a fresh palm branch and split it in two. He planted one on each of the two graves, then said: "Perhaps their torment will be reduced, until these [branches] have dried".'**

حَدَّثَنَا أَبُو سَعِيدٍ الْأَشَجُّ، وَأَبُو كُرَيْبٍ مُحَمَّدُ بْنُ الْعَلَاءِ، وَإِسْحَاقُ بْنُ إِبْرَاهِيمَ، - قَالَ إِسْحَاقُ: أَخْبَرَنَا وَقَالَ الْآخَرَانِ - حَدَّثَنَا وَكِيعٌ، حَدَّثَنَا الْأَعْمَشُ، قَالَ: سَمِعْتُ مُجَاهِدًا، يُحَدِّثُ عَنْ طَاوُسٍ، عَنِ ابْنِ عَبَّاسٍ قَالَ: مَرَّ رَسُولُ اللهِ صَلَّى اللهُ عَلَيْهِ وَسَلَّمَ عَلَى قَبْرَيْنِ فَقَالَ: «أَمَا إِنَّهُمَا لَيُعَذَّبَانِ وَمَا يُعَذَّبَانِ فِي كَبِيرٍ، أَمَّا أَحَدُهُمَا فَكَانَ يَمْشِي بِالنَّمِيمَةِ، وَأَمَّا الْآخَرُ فَكَانَ لَا يَسْتَتِرُ مِنْ بَوْلِهِ»، قَالَ فَدَعَا بِعَسِيبٍ رَطْبٍ فَشَقَّهُ بِاثْنَيْنِ ثُمَّ غَرَسَ عَلَى هَذَا وَاحِدًا وَعَلَى هَذَا وَاحِدًا ثُمَّ قَالَ: «لَعَلَّهُ أَنْ يُخَفَّفُ عَنْهُمَا مَا لَمْ يَيْبَسَا».

---

i. Related by al-Bukhārī, 218, 1361, 1378 and 6052; Abū Dāwūd, 20; al-Tirmidhī, 70; al-Nasā'ī, 31, 2067 and 2068; Ibn Mājah, 347.

[522–000]. (Dār al-Salām 0576) Ahmad ibn Yūsuf al-Azdī narrated the same to me: Muʿallā ibn Asad narrated; ʿAbd al-Wāḥid narrated; from Sulaymān al-Aʿmash; with this chain of transmission, except that he said: **'The other did not protect himself from urine'**.

حَدَّثَنِيهِ أَحْمَدُ بْنُ يُوسُفَ الْأَزْدِيُّ، حَدَّثَنَا مُعَلَّى بْنُ أَسَدٍ، حَدَّثَنَا عَبْدُ الْوَاحِدِ، عَنْ سُلَيْمَانَ الْأَعْمَشِ، بِهَذَا الْإِسْنَادِ غَيْرَ أَنَّهُ قَالَ: وَكَانَ الْآخَرُ لَا يَسْتَنْزِهُ عَنِ الْبَوْلِ - أَوْ مِنَ الْبَوْلِ.

Text Explanation

'Tale-bearing' in the hadith means in particular to report to people what others say about them, with the intention of spoiling relations. We explained this in the Book of Faith, making clear that tale-bearing is strictly forbidden.

The Prophet describes the reason for the two buried in those two graves suffering torment as 'nothing so serious'. However, in al-Bukhārī's narration the hadith says: 'for nothing so serious, but it is certainly serious: one of them did not take precautions when urinating ...'. Al-Bukhārī mentions this added sentence in two places where he enters this hadith. This addition clearly states that the sins those two people committed were indeed serious. Therefore, we need to interpret the Prophet's words: 'for nothing so serious'.

Scholars give these words two meanings. The first is that they did not think that what they did was serious, and the other interpretation is that it was not difficult for them to refrain from what they did. *Qāḍī* ʿIyāḍ gives a third interpretation, saying that the Prophet meant that their sins were not the gravest or most serious. According to these interpretations, the Prophet meant his words as a warning to all people that they must not imagine that God's punishment applies only for the most serious of sins. It could be for lesser ones as well, but God knows best.

That these two sins were serious is very clear. To allow urine to splash on one's clothes or body means that one's prayer becomes invalid. Therefore, such complacency is certainly a grave sin.

Tale-bearing with the intention of spoiling people's relations and creating enmity between them is a very nasty habit, particularly when the person concerned did so repeatedly, as was the case here.

The Prophet placed the two palm branches on the two graves. Scholars say that this is understood to mean that the Prophet sought to intercede with God for the two dead people, and God accepted his intercession, reducing or withholding the torment until the two branches had become completely dry. In a long hadith narrated by Jābir, which Muslim enters towards the end of his book, the Prophet says about these two people: 'My intercession was answered as the torment will be stopped while the two branches remain fresh'. It is also said that the Prophet prayed for them during that period, and another suggestion relates stopping the torment because the two branches glorify God while they are fresh, but a dry branch does not. This is the view of most commentators on the Qur'an in relation to the verse that says: '*Indeed every single thing extols His glory and praise, but you cannot understand their praises*'. (17: 44) They say that the verse refers to 'every living thing', and add that the life of every thing relates to its nature: wood is alive until it is dry, and stone is alive unless cut off. Scrupulous commentators and other scholars say that this statement should be understood in its general meaning. They differ as to whether such things do actually glorify God or simply bear evidence of the Creator, and as such glorify God by being His creation. Meticulous scholars believe that they actually glorify God. God tells us in the Qur'an: '*Some other rocks fall down for fear of God*'. (2: 74) Since the human mind does not consider it impossible that different objects can distinguish things, and since clear texts state it, then it must be accepted as real, but God knows best.

Scholars encourage reciting the Qur'an near a grave, basing their view on this hadith, arguing that if reduction of punishment is hoped for on account of a tree branch glorifying God, reciting the Qur'an is a better reason, but God knows best. Al-Bukhārī mentions in his *Ṣaḥīḥ* that Buraydah ibn al-Ḥuṣayb al-Aslamī, a companion of the Prophet, requested that two palm branches should be placed in his grave when he died. In this, he was seeking the blessing of doing as the Prophet did. Al-Khaṭṭābī rejects what people do, placing tree branches on graves, on the basis of this hadith. He says that there is nothing to suggest that this is acceptable, but God knows best.

The hadith confirms the fact of torment in the grave for those who deserve it. This is the correct view, contrary to the view of the Muʿtazilah. The hadith also confirms that urine is impure, as this is clear in the second narration. It also makes clear that tale-bearing is strictly forbidden, but God knows best.

BOOK OF MENSTRUATION

CHAPTER 1

FOREPLAY DURING MENSTRUATION

[523–1]. (Dār al-Salām 0577) Abū Bakr ibn Abī Shaybah, Zuhayr ibn Ḥarb and Isḥāq ibn Ibrāhīm narrated: Isḥāq said Jarīr reported and the other two said Jarīr narrated; from Manṣūr; from Ibrāhīm; from al-Aswad; from ʿĀ'ishah: **'When any of us [the Prophet's wives] was in menstruation, God's Messenger (peace be upon him) would tell her to cover her lower parts with a robe, then he would foreplay with her'**.

حَدَّثَنَا أَبُو بَكْرِ بْنُ أَبِي شَيْبَةَ، وَزُهَيْرُ بْنُ حَرْبٍ، وَإِسْحَاقُ بْنُ إِبْرَاهِيمَ، - قَالَ إِسْحَاقُ: أَخْبَرَنَا، وَقَالَ الْآخَرَانِ - حَدَّثَنَا جَرِيرٌ، عَنْ مَنْصُورٍ، عَنْ إِبْرَاهِيمَ، عَنِ الْأَسْوَدِ، عَنْ عَائِشَةَ قَالَتْ: «كَانَ إِحْدَانَا إِذَا كَانَتْ حَائِضًا أَمَرَهَا رَسُولُ اللهِ صَلَّى اللهُ عَلَيْهِ وَسَلَّمَ فَتَأْتَزِرُ بِإِزَارٍ ثُمَّ يُبَاشِرُهَا»

[524–2]. (Dār al-Salām 0578) Abū Bakr ibn Abī Shaybah narrated: ʿAlī ibn Mushir narrated; from al-Shaybānī [H]. Also, ʿAlī ibn Ḥujr al-Saʿdī narrated to me (his text); ʿAlī ibn Mushir reported; Abū Isḥāq reported; from ʿAbd al-Raḥmān ibn al-Aswad; from his father; from ʿĀ'ishah: **'When any of us [the Prophet's wives] was in menstruation, God's Messenger (peace be upon him) would tell her to cover her lower part even if she was at the height of her period, then he would have foreplay with her'. She added: 'Who of you can control his desire as God's Messenger (peace be upon him) controlled his desire?'**

وَحَدَّثَنَا أَبُو بَكْرِ بْنُ أَبِي شَيْبَةَ، حَدَّثَنَا عَلِيُّ بْنُ مُسْهِرٍ، عَنِ الشَّيْبَانِيِّ ح، وَحَدَّثَنِي عَلِيُّ بْنُ حُجْرٍ السَّعْدِيُّ، - وَاللَّفْظُ لَهُ - أَخْبَرَنَا عَلِيُّ بْنُ مُسْهِرٍ، أَخْبَرَنَا أَبُو إِسْحَاقَ، عَنْ عَبْدِ الرَّحْمَنِ بْنِ الْأَسْوَدِ، عَنْ أَبِيهِ، عَنْ عَائِشَةَ قَالَتْ: «كَانَ إِحْدَانَا إِذَا كَانَتْ حَائِضًا أَمَرَهَا رَسُولُ اللهِ صَلَّى اللهُ عَلَيْهِ وَسَلَّمَ أَنْ تَأْتَزِرَ فِي فَوْرِ حَيْضَتِهَا، ثُمَّ يُبَاشِرُهَا» قَالَتْ: «وَأَيُّكُمْ يَمْلِكُ إِرْبَهُ كَمَا كَانَ رَسُولُ اللهِ صَلَّى اللهُ عَلَيْهِ وَسَلَّمَ يَمْلِكُ إِرْبَهُ»

[525–3]. (Dār al-Salām 0579) Yaḥyā ibn Yaḥyā narrated: Khālid ibn ʿAbdullāh reported; from al-Shaybānī; from ʿAbdullāh ibn Shaddād; from Maymūnah: **'God's Messenger (peace be upon him) used to have foreplay with his wives when they had their periods, but above their lower garments'**.

حَدَّثَنَا يَحْيَى بْنُ يَحْيَى، أَخْبَرَنَا خَالِدُ بْنُ عَبْدِ اللهِ، عَنِ الشَّيْبَانِيِّ، عَنْ عَبْدِ اللهِ بْنِ شَدَّادٍ، عَنْ مَيْمُونَةَ قَالَتْ: «كَانَ رَسُولُ اللهِ صَلَّى اللهُ عَلَيْهِ وَسَلَّمَ يُبَاشِرُ نِسَاءَهُ فَوْقَ الْإِزَارِ وَهُنَّ حُيَّضٌ»

Text Explanation

The second hadith mentions that this happened when any of the Prophet's wives was at the height of her period, which refers to the time when the discharge of blood was at its most frequent and plentiful. The Prophet would tell his wife to tighten her lower garment, i.e. *izār*, so as to cover herself from her waistline down to lower than her knees. In the second hadith, ʿĀ'ishah asks a rhetorical question: 'Who of you can control his desire as the Prophet did?' This makes clear that the Prophet never went beyond what is permissible. She is actually giving a warning, hinting that when a person does this, he should be in full control of himself, making sure not to do what is forbidden, which is sexual intercourse. Al-Khaṭṭābī prefers the second narration, which includes ʿĀ'ishah's rhetorical question. He discounts the first one and criticizes Hadith scholars for including it, but God knows best.

What a man may do with his wife during her menstrual period may be of several types. One of these is to have a full, penetrative intercourse. This is unanimously agreed by all Muslims to be strictly forbidden, as it is clearly stated in the Qur'an and authentic Sunnah. Our scholars say that a Muslim who believes that it is permissible to have full intercourse during a woman's period is an apostate unbeliever. If a man does so, believing that it is unlawful, then if he has forgotten, or does not know that his wife is having her period, or does not know that it is unlawful, or if he is under duress, then he incurs no sin and owes no atonement. On the other hand, if he chooses to have full intercourse with his wife, knowing that she is having her period and that such intercourse is forbidden, he commits a grave sin. Al-Shāfiʿī states that it is grave and that he must repent.

As to whether he owes an atonement, al-Shāfiʿī expressed two views, the more correct of them is the later one which confirms that no atonement is due. This is also the view of Mālik, Abū Ḥanīfah and Ahmad in one of his two reports, as well as the majority of early scholars. Among the early scholars who expressed this view of no atonement are ʿAṭa', Ibn Abī Mulaykah, al-Shaʿbī, al-Nakhaʿī, Makḥūl, al-Zuhrī, Abū al-Zinād, Rabīʿah, Ḥammād ibn Abī Sulaymān, Ayyūb al-Sakhtiyāni, Sufyān al-Thawrī and al-Layth ibn Saʿd (may God bestow mercy on them all). The earlier view of al-Shāfiʿī is less correct, stating that an atonement is due for intercourse during a woman's period, when one is aware of the fact and that it is forbidden. This view is reported to have been expressed by Ibn ʿAbbās, al-Ḥasan al-Basrī, Saʿīd ibn Jubayr, al-Awzāʿī, Isḥāq and Ahmad in his second view. Yet these scholars differ as to what should be given in atonement. Al-Ḥasan and Saʿīd said that it takes the form of setting a slave free. The others suggest that it is to give to charity a dinar or half a dinar. [The dinar was the gold currency of the time.] They also differed as to when it should be one dinar and when it is half that amount. Some suggest that a dinar is payable at the beginning of the period and half a dinar towards the end. Others say that a dinar should be paid at any time during the discharge and half of it when the discharge has stopped. They all rely on a hadith narrated by Ibn ʿAbbās and attributed to the

Prophet: 'Whoever has intercourse with his wife when she is having her period should give to charity one dinar or half a dinar'. This hadith is agreed by all reliable Hadith scholars to be very poor in authenticity. Therefore, the correct view is that no atonement need be made, but God knows best.

The second type limits foreplay to the parts of the body above the waistline and below the knees, with any part of the husband's body, including kissing, embracing, caressing, etc. This is perfectly permissible according to all scholars. Shaykh Abū Ḥāmid Ahmad ibn Muhammad al-Isfarāyīnī and many others report that this is unanimously agreed upon. However, it is reported that ʿUbaydah al-Salamānī and others said that no foreplay that involves bodily contact is permissible. This is odd and unacceptable. If this report is true, it contradicts several authentic hadiths that are entered in the two *Ṣaḥīḥ* and other Hadith anthologies. These hadiths mention that the Prophet had foreplay with his wives provided that they covered the lower parts of their bodies. The hadiths also mention his permission of doing so. This is agreed by all Muslims, before and after the time of those who give a different view.

It is also correct to say that the presence of menses on the part of the woman's body that is touched or caressed does not affect the permissibility. This is the well-known view stated by all scholars of our Shāfiʿī school and other scholars. They express this view on the basis of the clear hadiths stating that it is permissible. However, al-Muḥāmilī, a Shāfiʿī scholar, mentions a view attributed to some of our scholars suggesting that if there is some menstruation blood on a part of the woman's body, above her waistline or lower than her knees, then it is forbidden to touch that part. This view is undoubtedly wrong, but God knows best.

The third type is to have foreplay between the wife's waistline and her knees, without touching her genital area. Scholars of our Shāfiʿī school express three different views on this. The best-known and most correct of the three, according to the majority, is that it is forbidden. The second view is that it is only discouraged. This view is supported by the stronger and more correct evidence, and it is the preferred one. The third view is that if the man is sure of himself, confident that he will not touch his wife's vagina, either because his desire is not too strong or because his piety stops him short of this, then it is permissible. Otherwise it is not. This is a reasonable view, expressed by Abū al-ʿAbbās al-Baṣrī of our school.

Scholars who subscribe to the first view of total prohibition include Mālik, Abū Ḥanīfah and most scholars, such as Saʿīd ibn al-Musayyib, Sharīḥ, Ṭāwūs, ʿAṭā', Sulaymān ibn Yasār and Qatādah. Others who maintain that it is permissible include ʿIkrimah, Mujāhid, al-Shaʿbī, al-Nakhaʿī, al-Ḥakam, al-Thawrī, al-Awzāʿī, Ahmad ibn Ḥanbal, Muhammad ibn al-Ḥasan, Asbagh, Isḥāq ibn Rāhawayh, Abū Thawr, Ibn al-Mundhir and Dāwūd. As we mentioned earlier, this view enjoys the better evidence, citing the hadith narrated by Anas and quoting the Prophet: 'You may do everything short of intercourse'. They argue that the fact that the Prophet limited foreplay to what is above the lower garment indicates what is preferable, but God knows best.

The prohibition of intercourse and foreplay, according to scholars who say that both are prohibited, extends throughout the period of menstrual discharge and after its end until the woman has taken a bath, or performed dry ablution if water is not available. This is the view of our school, as well as the view of Mālik, Ahmad and the great majority of earlier and later scholars. Abū Ḥanīfah, on the other hand, said that if the blood discharge stops after most of the woman's regular period,[i] intercourse becomes permissible. The majority of scholars express their view on the basis of the Qur'anic verse that says: *'They ask you about menstruation. Say: "It is an unclean condition; so keep aloof from women during menstruation, and do not draw near to them until they are cleansed. When they have cleansed themselves, you may go in unto them in the proper way, as God has bidden you"'*. (2: 222)

i. This view is concerned with the case of a woman whose normal period is seven full days but on some occasions she stops bleeding after six days.

CHAPTER 2

IN BED WITH ONE'S WIFE DURING HER PERIOD

[526–4]. (Dār al-Salām 0580) Abū al-Ṭāhir narrated to me: Ibn Wahb reported; from Makhramah [H]. Also, Hārūn ibn Saʿīd al-Aylī and Ahmad ibn ʿĪsā narrated; both said: Ibn Wahb narrated; Makhramah reported to me; from his father; from Kurayb, Ibn ʿAbbās's *mawlā*: **'I heard Maymūnah, the Prophet's wife, say: "God's Messenger used to lie with me when I had my period, with a robe between us".'**

حَدَّثَنِي أَبُو الطَّاهِرِ، أَخْبَرَنَا ابْنُ وَهْبٍ، عَنْ مَخْرَمَةَ، ح، وَحَدَّثَنَا هَارُونُ بْنُ سَعِيدٍ الْأَيْلِيُّ، وَأَحْمَدُ بْنُ عِيسَى، قَالَا: حَدَّثَنَا ابْنُ وَهْبٍ، أَخْبَرَنِي مَخْرَمَةُ، عَنْ أَبِيهِ، عَنْ كُرَيْبٍ مَوْلَى ابْنِ عَبَّاسٍ، قَالَ: سَمِعْتُ مَيْمُونَةَ زَوْجَ النَّبِيِّ صَلَّى اللهُ عَلَيْهِ وَسَلَّمَ قَالَتْ: «كَانَ رَسُولُ اللهِ صَلَّى اللهُ عَلَيْهِ وَسَلَّمَ يَضْطَجِعُ مَعِي وَأَنَا حَائِضٌ، وَبَيْنِي وَبَيْنَهُ ثَوْبٌ»

[527–5]. (Dār al-Salām 0581) Muhammad ibn al-Muthannā narrated: Muʿādh ibn Hishām narrated; my father narrated to me; from Yaḥyā ibn Abī Kathīr; Abū Salamah ibn ʿAbd al-Raḥmān narrated that Zaynab bint Umm Salamah; that Umm Salamah narrated to her: **'I was lying with God's Messenger (peace be upon him) under a velvet bed cover when I started my period. I crept out quietly and took my period's underwear. God's Messenger said to me: "Have you started your period?" I said: "Yes". He called me back and I lay with him under the velvet cover'.**

Zaynab said: 'She and God's Messenger (peace be upon him) used to take a bath together, to cleanse themselves from the state of major ritual impurity, using the same water container'.

حَدَّثَنَا مُحَمَّدُ بْنُ الْمُثَنَّى، حَدَّثَنَا مُعَاذُ بْنُ هِشَامٍ، حَدَّثَنِي أَبِي، عَنْ يَحْيَى بْنِ أَبِي كَثِيرٍ، حَدَّثَنَا أَبُو سَلَمَةَ بْنُ عَبْدِ الرَّحْمَنِ، أَنَّ زَيْنَبَ بِنْتَ أُمِّ سَلَمَةَ حَدَّثَتْهُ أَنَّ أُمَّ سَلَمَةَ، حَدَّثَتْهَا قَالَتْ: بَيْنَمَا أَنَا مُضْطَجِعَةٌ مَعَ رَسُولِ اللهِ صَلَّى اللهُ عَلَيْهِ وَسَلَّمَ فِي الْخَمِيلَةِ، إِذْ حِضْتُ، فَانْسَلَلْتُ، فَأَخَذْتُ ثِيَابَ حِيضَتِي فَقَالَ لِي رَسُولُ اللهِ صَلَّى اللهُ عَلَيْهِ وَسَلَّمَ: «أَنَفِسْتِ؟» قُلْتُ: نَعَمْ، فَدَعَانِي فَاضْطَجَعْتُ مَعَهُ فِي الْخَمِيلَةِ. قَالَتْ: وَكَانَتْ هِيَ وَرَسُولُ اللهِ صَلَّى اللهُ عَلَيْهِ وَسَلَّمَ يَغْتَسِلَانِ فِي الْإِنَاءِ الْوَاحِدِ، مِنَ الْجَنَابَةِ»

Text Explanation

Umm Salamah, the Prophet's wife, mentions that she crept out of bed when she realized that she had started her period, perhaps because she feared that some blood might drop on the Prophet's body, or perhaps she felt herself unclean. She might have felt that she could not stay in that position or feared that he might wish to be more intimate with her without realizing she had started her period, knowing that intercourse was unlawful at that time, but God knows best.

Hence, she put on her underwear that was only used during her period. The Prophet wished to know whether her period had commenced and she confirmed that it had.

The two hadiths confirm that it is perfectly permissible to sleep in one bed with one's wife during her period, and to share the same cover, provided that there is something that prevents skin-to-skin contact between the woman's waistline and her knees, or prevents genital contact according to scholars who say that only genital contact is forbidden during the woman's period. Scholars say that lying in bed with one's wife during her period, kissing her, and foreplay confined to above her waistline and lower than her knees is permissible. It is perfectly appropriate at this time for her to put her hand into any liquid stuff, or for her to wash her husband's head or that of her immediate relatives whom she cannot marry. Likewise, her cooking, breadmaking, etc. is perfectly wholesome, and the remainder of her food or drink and her perspiration are perfectly clean. All this is agreed by all scholars. Muhammad ibn Jarīr al-Ṭabarī mentions in his book *Madhāhib al-Ulamā'*, that all Muslims are agreed on all this, and the evidence supporting it from the Prophet's Sunnah is very clear and well known. The Qur'an says: '*Keep aloof from women during menstruation, and do not draw near to them until they are cleansed*'. (2: 222) This clearly refers to sexual intercourse. This is what a Muslim should remain aloof from when his wife has her period, but God knows best.

CHAPTER 3

A WOMAN IN MENSTRUATION MAY WASH HER HUSBAND'S HEAD, AND HE MAY LEAN ON HER LAP AND RECITE THE QUR'AN

[528–6]. (Dār al-Salām 0582) Yaḥyā ibn Yaḥyā narrated:[i] I read out to Mālik; from Ibn Shihāb; from ʿUrwah; from ʿAmrah; from ʿĀ'ishah: **'When the Prophet was in his sojourn in the mosque, i.e. *iʿtikāf*, he would put his head forward to me and I would comb his hair. He did not come into the house except to answer the call of nature'**.

حَدَّثَنَا يَحْيَى بْنُ يَحْيَى، قَالَ: قَرَأْتُ عَلَى مَالِكٍ، عَنِ ابْنِ شِهَابٍ، عَنْ عُرْوَةَ، عَنْ عَمْرَةَ، عَنْ عَائِشَةَ، قَالَتْ: «كَانَ النَّبِيُّ صَلَّى اللهُ عَلَيْهِ وَسَلَّمَ، إِذَا اعْتَكَفَ، يُدْنِي إِلَيَّ رَأْسَهُ فَأُرَجِّلُهُ، وَكَانَ لَا يَدْخُلُ الْبَيْتَ إِلَّا لِحَاجَةِ الْإِنْسَانِ»

[529–7]. (Dār al-Salām 0583) Qutaybah ibn Saʿīd narrated:[ii] Al-Layth narrated [H]. Also, Muhammad ibn Rumḥ narrated; al-Layth reported; from Ibn Shihāb; from ʿUrwah and ʿAmrah bint ʿAbd al-Raḥmān; that ʿA'ishah the Prophet's wife said: **'I used to enter my home only for necessity, and if an ill person was inside, I would only enquire about him while going through. God's Messenger used to put his head inside for me**

i. Related by Abū Dāwūd, 2467 and 2468.
ii. Related by al-Bukhārī, 2029; Abū Dāwūd, 2468; al-Tirmidhī, 804; Ibn Mājah, 1776.

while he was in the mosque and I would comb his hair.[i] **If he was in *iʿtikāf* he would only come into the house to answer the call of nature'. Ibn Rumḥ said: 'If they were in *iʿtikāf*'.**

وَحَدَّثَنَا قُتَيْبَةُ بْنُ سَعِيدٍ، حَدَّثَنَا لَيْثٌ، ح، وَحَدَّثَنَا مُحَمَّدُ بْنُ رُمْحٍ، قَالَ: أَخْبَرَنَا اللَّيْثُ، عَنِ ابْنِ شِهَابٍ، عَنْ عُرْوَةَ، وَعَمْرَةَ بِنْتِ عَبْدِ الرَّحْمَنِ، أَنَّ عَائِشَةَ زَوْجَ النَّبِيِّ صَلَّى اللهُ عَلَيْهِ وَسَلَّمَ قَالَتْ: «إِنْ كُنْتُ لَأَدْخُلُ الْبَيْتَ لِلْحَاجَةِ، وَالْمَرِيضُ فِيهِ، فَمَا أَسْأَلُ عَنْهُ إِلَّا وَأَنَا مَارَّةٌ، وَإِنْ كَانَ رَسُولُ اللهِ صَلَّى اللهُ عَلَيْهِ وَسَلَّمَ لَيُدْخِلُ عَلَيَّ رَأْسَهُ وَهُوَ فِي الْمَسْجِدِ فَأُرَجِّلُهُ، وَكَانَ لَا يَدْخُلُ الْبَيْتَ إِلَّا لِحَاجَةٍ، إِذَا كَانَ مُعْتَكِفًا» وَقَالَ ابْنُ رُمْحٍ: «إِذَا كَانُوا مُعْتَكِفِينَ»

[530–8]. (Dār al-Salām 0584) Hārūn ibn Saʿīd al-Aylī narrated to me:[ii] Ibn Wahb narrated; ʿAmr ibn al-Ḥārith reported to me; from Muhammad ibn ʿAbd al-Raḥmān ibn Nawfal; from ʿUrwah ibn al-Zubayr; that ʿĀ'ishah the Prophet's wife said: **'God's Messenger would put inside his head to me from the mosque when he was in *iʿtikāf* and I would wash it when I was in menstruation'.**

وَحَدَّثَنِي هَارُونُ بْنُ سَعِيدٍ الْأَيْلِيُّ، حَدَّثَنَا ابْنُ وَهْبٍ، أَخْبَرَنِي عَمْرُو بْنُ الْحَارِثِ، عَنْ مُحَمَّدِ بْنِ عَبْدِ الرَّحْمَنِ بْنِ نَوْفَلٍ، عَنْ عُرْوَةَ بْنِ الزُّبَيْرِ، عَنْ عَائِشَةَ زَوْجِ النَّبِيِّ صَلَّى اللهُ عَلَيْهِ وَسَلَّمَ أَنَّهَا قَالَتْ: «كَانَ رَسُولُ اللهِ صَلَّى اللهُ عَلَيْهِ وَسَلَّمَ يُخْرِجُ إِلَيَّ رَأْسَهُ مِنَ الْمَسْجِدِ، وَهُوَ مُجَاوِرٌ، فَأَغْسِلُهُ وَأَنَا حَائِضٌ»

---

i. It is clear that ʿĀ'ishah is speaking about a time when she had her period, but the Prophet was staying in the mosque for a period of *iʿtikāf*, which means an extended stay in the mosque for worship. The Prophet did this to show in practice what was permissible to do between a woman and her husband when she had her period. It should be remembered that ʿĀ'ishah's home was next to the mosque, and the Prophet would be in the mosque but he would put his head inside through the door or a window.

ii. Related by al-Nasā'ī, 275 (in a shorter version).

[531–9]. (Dār al-Salām 0585) Yaḥyā ibn Yaḥyā narrated: Abū Khaythamah reported; from Hishām; 'Urwah reported; from 'Ā'ishah that she said: **'God's Messenger used to put his head inside for me when I was in my home, and I would comb his hair when I had my period'**.

وَحَدَّثَنَا يَحْيَى بْنُ يَحْيَى، أَخْبَرَنَا أَبُو خَيْثَمَةَ، عَنْ هِشَامٍ، أَخْبَرَنَا عُرْوَةُ، عَنْ عَائِشَةَ أَنَّهَا قَالَتْ: «كَانَ رَسُولُ اللهِ صَلَّى اللهُ عَلَيْهِ وَسَلَّمَ يُدْنِي إِلَيَّ رَأْسَهُ وَأَنَا فِي حُجْرَتِي، فَأُرَجِّلُ رَأْسَهُ وَأَنَا حَائِضٌ»

[532–10]. (Dār al-Salām 0586) Abū Bakr ibn Abī Shaybah narrated:[i] Ḥusayn ibn 'Alī narrated; from Zā'idah; from Manṣūr; from Ibrāhīm; from al-Aswad; from 'Ā'ishah. She said: **'I used to wash God's Messenger's head when I was in menstruation'**.

حَدَّثَنَا أَبُو بَكْرِ بْنُ أَبِي شَيْبَةَ، حَدَّثَنَا حُسَيْنُ بْنُ عَلِيٍّ، عَنْ زَائِدَةَ، عَنْ مَنْصُورٍ، عَنْ إِبْرَاهِيمَ، عَنِ الْأَسْوَدِ، عَنْ عَائِشَةَ قَالَتْ: «كُنْتُ أَغْسِلُ رَأْسَ رَسُولِ اللهِ صَلَّى اللهُ عَلَيْهِ وَسَلَّمَ وَأَنَا حَائِضٌ»

[533–11]. (Dār al-Salām 0587) Yaḥyā ibn Yaḥyā, Abū Bakr ibn Abī Shaybah and Abu Kurayb narrated:[ii] Abū Mu'āwiyah (Yaḥyā said 'reported', while the other two said 'narrated'): from al-A'mash; from Thābit ibn 'Ubayd; from al-Qāsim ibn Muhammad; from 'Ā'ishah. She said: **'God's Messenger said to me from the mosque: "Bring me the mat". I said: "I am in menstruation". He said: "Your menstruation is not in your hand".'**

---

i. Related by al-Bukhārī, 301, 299, 2031; Abū Dāwūd, 77; al-Nasā'ī, 274, 234, 235, 411 and 385.

ii. Related by Abū Dāwūd, 261; al-Tirmidhī, 134; al-Nasā'ī, 271 and 382.

وَحَدَّثَنَا يَحْيَى بْنُ يَحْيَى، وَأَبُو بَكْرِ بْنُ أَبِي شَيْبَةَ، وَأَبُو كُرَيْبٍ، - قَالَ: يَحْيَى، أَخْبَرَنَا وَقَالَ الْآخَرَانِ - حَدَّثَنَا أَبُو مُعَاوِيَةَ، عَنِ الْأَعْمَشِ، عَنْ ثَابِتِ بْنِ عُبَيْدٍ، عَنِ الْقَاسِمِ بْنِ مُحَمَّدٍ، عَنْ عَائِشَةَ قَالَتْ: قَالَ لِي رَسُولُ اللهِ صَلَّى اللهُ عَلَيْهِ وَسَلَّمَ: «نَاوِلِينِي الْخُمْرَةَ مِنَ الْمَسْجِدِ»، قَالَتْ فَقُلْتُ: إِنِّي حَائِضٌ، فَقَالَ: «إِنَّ حَيْضَتَكِ لَيْسَتْ فِي يَدِكِ».

[534–12]. (Dār al-Salām 0588) Abū Kurayb narrated: Ibn Abī Zā'idah narrated; from Ḥajjāj and Ibn Abī Ghāniyyah; from Thābit ibn ʿUbayd; from al-Qāsim ibn Muhammad; from ʿĀ'ishah. She said: **'God's Messenger (peace be upon him) told me from the mosque to hand him the mat. I said: "I am in menstruation". He said: "Bring it. Menstruation is not in your hand".'**

حَدَّثَنَا أَبُو كُرَيْبٍ، حَدَّثَنَا ابْنُ أَبِي زَائِدَةَ، عَنْ حَجَّاجٍ، وَابْنِ أَبِي غَنِيَّةَ، عَنْ ثَابِتِ بْنِ عُبَيْدٍ، عَنِ الْقَاسِمِ بْنِ مُحَمَّدٍ، عَنْ عَائِشَةَ قَالَتْ: أَمَرَنِي رَسُولُ اللهِ صَلَّى اللهُ عَلَيْهِ وَسَلَّمَ أَنْ أُنَاوِلَهُ الْخُمْرَةَ مِنَ الْمَسْجِدِ، فَقُلْتُ: إِنِّي حَائِضٌ، فَقَالَ: «تَنَاوَلِيهَا فَإِنَّ الْحَيْضَةَ لَيْسَتْ فِي يَدِكِ»

[535–13]. (Dār al-Salām 0589) Zuhayr ibn Ḥarb, Abu Kāmil and Muhammad ibn Ḥātim narrated to me:[i] all from Yaḥyā ibn Saʿīd. Zuhayr said: Yaḥyā narrated from Yazīd ibn Kaysān; from Abū Ḥāzim; from Abū Hurayrah. He said: **'God's Messenger (peace be upon him) was in the mosque when he said: "ʿĀ'ishah, hand me the garment". She said: "I am in the period". He said: "Your period is not in your hand". She handed it to him'.**

i. Related by al-Nasā'ī, 381.

وَحَدَّثَنِي زُهَيْرُ بْنُ حَرْبٍ، وَأَبُو كَامِلٍ، وَمُحَمَّدُ بْنُ حَاتِمٍ، كُلُّهُمْ عَنْ يَحْيَى بْنِ سَعِيدٍ، قَالَ: زُهَيْرٌ، حَدَّثَنَا يَحْيَى، عَنْ يَزِيدَ بْنِ كَيْسَانَ، عَنْ أَبِي حَازِمٍ، عَنْ أَبِي هُرَيْرَةَ، قَالَ: بَيْنَمَا رَسُولُ اللهِ صَلَّى اللهُ عَلَيْهِ وَسَلَّمَ فِي الْمَسْجِدِ، فَقَالَ: «يَا عَائِشَةُ نَاوِلِينِي الثَّوْبَ» فَقَالَتْ: إِنِّي حَائِضٌ، فَقَالَ: «إِنَّ حَيْضَتَكِ لَيْسَتْ فِي يَدِكِ» فَنَاوَلَتْهُ.

[536–14]. (Dār al-Salām 0590) Abū Bakr ibn Abī Shaybah and Zuhayr ibn Ḥarb narrated: both said:[i] Wakīʿ narrated; from Misʿar and Sufyān; from al-Miqdām ibn Shurayḥ; from his father; from ʿĀʾishah. She said: **'I might drink when I was in menstruation, and then hand [the cup over] to the Prophet. He would put his mouth where I placed my mouth, and would drink. I might eat meat off a bone when I was in menstruation and then hand it over to the Prophet. He would put his mouth where I placed my mouth'. Zuhayr did not mention that [the Prophet] would drink.**

حَدَّثَنَا أَبُو بَكْرِ بْنُ أَبِي شَيْبَةَ، وَزُهَيْرُ بْنُ حَرْبٍ، قَالَا: حَدَّثَنَا وَكِيعٌ، عَنْ مِسْعَرٍ، وَسُفْيَانَ، عَنِ الْمِقْدَامِ بْنِ شُرَيْحٍ، عَنْ أَبِيهِ، عَنْ عَائِشَةَ قَالَتْ: «كُنْتُ أَشْرَبُ وَأَنَا حَائِضٌ، ثُمَّ أُنَاوِلُهُ النَّبِيَّ صَلَّى اللهُ عَلَيْهِ وَسَلَّمَ فَيَضَعُ فَاهُ عَلَى مَوْضِعِ فِيَّ، فَيَشْرَبُ، وَأَتَعَرَّقُ الْعَرْقَ وَأَنَا حَائِضٌ، ثُمَّ أُنَاوِلُهُ النَّبِيَّ صَلَّى اللهُ عَلَيْهِ وَسَلَّمَ فَيَضَعُ فَاهُ عَلَى مَوْضِعِ فِيَّ» وَلَمْ يَذْكُرْ زُهَيْرٌ فَيَشْرَبُ.

[537–15]. (Dār al-Salām 0591) Yaḥyā ibn Yaḥyā narrated:[ii] Dāwūd ibn ʿAbd al-Raḥmān al-Makkī reported; from Manṣūr; from his mother; from ʿĀʾishah that she said: **'God's Messenger**

---

i. Related by Abū Dāwūd, 259; al-Nasāʾī, 70, 278, 279, 280, 281, 340, 375, 376, 377 and 378; Ibn Mājah, 643.

ii. Related by al-Bukhārī, 297 and 7549; Abū Dāwūd, 260; al-Nasāʾī, 273 and 379; Ibn Mājah, 634.

(peace be upon him) would recline on my lap when I had my period and he would recite the Qur'an'.

حَدَّثَنَا يَحْيَى بْنُ يَحْيَى، أَخْبَرَنَا دَاوُدُ بْنُ عَبْدِ الرَّحْمَنِ الْـمَكِّيُّ، عَنْ مَنْصُورٍ، عَنْ أُمِّهِ، عَنْ عَائِشَةَ، أَنَّهَا قَالَتْ: «كَانَ رَسُولُ اللهِ صَلَّى اللهُ عَلَيْهِ وَسَلَّمَ يَتَّكِئُ فِي حِجْرِي وَأَنَا حَائِضٌ، فَيَقْرَأُ الْقُرْآنَ»

[538–16]. (Dār al-Salām 0592) Zuhayr ibn Ḥarb narrated to me:[i] ʿAbd al-Raḥmān ibn Mahdī narrated; Ḥammād ibn Salamah narrated; Thābit narrated; from Anas that: **'When one of their women was in menstruation, the Jews would not sit to eat with her and they would not mix with their [menstruating] women in their homes. The Prophet's companions asked him about this, and God revealed the verse that says: "*They ask you about menstruation. Say: 'It is an unclean condition; so keep aloof from women during menstruation, and do not draw near to them until they are cleansed. When they have cleansed themselves, you may go in unto them in the proper way, as God has bidden you. God loves those who turn to Him in repentance, and He loves those who keep themselves pure'.*" (2: 222) God's Messenger said [to his companions]: "You may do everything apart from sexual intercourse". The Jews came to know of this and they said: This man would not stop until he has differed with every practice we do. Usayd ibn Ḥudayr and ʿAbbād ibn Bishr came over and said: "Messenger of God, the Jews have said so-and-so. May we have intercourse with them?" The Prophet's face changed colour to the extent that they felt that he was angry with them. They left, and they saw a gift of milk coming to the Prophet. He sent [someone]**

i. Related by Abū Dāwūd, 258 and 2165; al-Tirmidhī, 2977 and 2878; al-Nasā'ī, 287 and 367; Ibn Mājah, 644.

to call them back, and he gave them a drink. They realized that he was not angry with them'.

وَحَدَّثَنِي زُهَيْرُ بْنُ حَرْبٍ، حَدَّثَنَا عَبْدُ الرَّحْمَنِ بْنُ مَهْدِيٍّ، حَدَّثَنَا حَمَّادُ بْنُ سَلَمَةَ، حَدَّثَنَا ثَابِتٌ، عَنْ أَنَسٍ أَنَّ الْيَهُودَ كَانُوا إِذَا حَاضَتِ الْمَرْأَةُ فِيهِمْ لَمْ يُؤَاكِلُوهَا، وَلَمْ يُجَامِعُوهُنَّ فِي الْبُيُوتِ فَسَأَلَ أَصْحَابُ النَّبِيِّ صَلَّى اللهُ عَلَيْهِ وَسَلَّمَ النَّبِيَّ صَلَّى اللهُ عَلَيْهِ وَسَلَّمَ فَأَنْزَلَ اللهُ تَعَالَى «وَيَسْأَلُونَكَ عَنِ الْمَحِيضِ قُلْ هُوَ أَذًى فَاعْتَزِلُوا النِّسَاءَ فِي الْمَحِيضِ» [البقرة: 222] إِلَى آخِرِ الْآيَةِ، فَقَالَ رَسُولُ اللهِ صَلَّى اللهُ عَلَيْهِ وَسَلَّمَ: «اصْنَعُوا كُلَّ شَيْءٍ إِلَّا النِّكَاحَ» فَبَلَغَ ذَلِكَ الْيَهُودَ، فَقَالُوا: مَا يُرِيدُ هَذَا الرَّجُلُ أَنْ يَدَعَ مِنْ أَمْرِنَا شَيْئًا إِلَّا خَالَفَنَا فِيهِ، فَجَاءَ أُسَيْدُ بْنُ حُضَيْرٍ، وَعَبَّادُ بْنُ بِشْرٍ فَقَالَا يَا رَسُولَ اللهِ، إِنَّ الْيَهُودَ تَقُولُ: كَذَا وَكَذَا، فَلَا نُجَامِعُهُنَّ؟ فَتَغَيَّرَ وَجْهُ رَسُولِ اللهِ صَلَّى اللهُ عَلَيْهِ وَسَلَّمَ حَتَّى ظَنَنَّا أَنْ قَدْ وَجَدَ عَلَيْهِمَا، فَخَرَجَا فَاسْتَقْبَلَهُمَا هَدِيَّةٌ مِنْ لَبَنٍ إِلَى النَّبِيِّ صَلَّى اللهُ عَلَيْهِ وَسَلَّمَ، فَأَرْسَلَ فِي آثَارِهِمَا فَسَقَاهُمَا، فَعَرَفَا أَنْ لَمْ يَجِدْ عَلَيْهِمَا.

Text Explanation

The main points of this chapter have been discussed in the previous one. We note here that 'Ā'ishah mentions that she used to comb the Prophet's hair when she was menstruating. *I'tikāf* means to stay in the mosque for worship. The linguistic meaning of the term is to restrict oneself, and in the religious sense it means to restrict oneself to stay in a mosque for worship. The hadiths of this chapter include many useful points about *i'tikāf*, but we will discuss these in detail in the relevant chapter. We may point out, however, that if a person in *i'tikāf* puts a part of his body, such as his hand, leg or head, out of the mosque, his sojourn in the mosque, i.e. *i'tikāf*, is not invalidated. Thus, if someone says an oath that he shall not enter or leave a place, but then he puts a part of his body inside or outside that place, his action does not constitute breaking his oath, but God knows best.

These hadiths show that it is permissible for a wife to do the cooking, washing, baking, etc. provided that she agrees. If she does not agree, then it is not permissible to force her to do any such thing. Her marital duties are only to enable her husband to have sex with her and to stay in his home,[i] but God knows best.

In hadith No. 533, the Prophet asks his wife to give him a mat. The hadith uses the word *khumrah* for mat, which refers to a small mat on which a worshipper puts his head when prostrating in prayer. Some scholars insist that it is only a small mat, but al-Khaṭṭābī said that it means a prayer mat. A hadith in Abū Dāwūd's *Sunan* mentions that 'a mouse drew a wick [of a lantern] and left it in front of God's Messenger on the *khumrah* on which he was sitting, and it burnt a small part of it, equal to the size of a small coin'. This is clear that the word is also used to refer to a usual sized prayer mat. The word is derived from a root that means 'to cover', because it covers the worshipper's face. From the same root we derive the word *khamr*, which means wine and intoxicant drinks, because they place a cover on one's mind.

Qāḍī ʿIyāḍ said: 'The hadith means that the Prophet was in the mosque when he asked ʿĀ'ishah to hand him the mat, not that the mat was in the mosque and he wanted her to bring it from there. He was in his *iʿtikāf* in the mosque, while ʿĀ'ishah was in her home and she was in the period. She thought that she should not put her hand into the mosque when she was having her period. Hence, he said to her: "Your period is not in your hand". Had he told her to come inside the mosque, he would not have specified her hand, but God knows best'.

The hadiths make clear that it is perfectly permissible to recite the Qur'an when one is lying down, reclining or leaning on one's wife when she is menstruating, or when one is close to a place where there is impurity, but God knows best.

Note: This is what al-Nawawī wrote about these hadiths, except for some explanation of a few Arabic words used in them, and these are already taken care of in the translation. We may add, however,

---

i. This means that a wife's marital duties do not include any housework, unless she agrees to do it out of good will.

that these hadiths indicate that the Prophet was keen to correct some practices which were prevalent in different communities concerning menstruation and how women were treated during their menstrual period. We note that during the Prophet's time, the Jews did not allow their menstruating women to mix with them in their homes. The Arabs had some similar restrictions. ʿĀ'ishah was reluctant to hand the Prophet the mat because he was in the mosque. The best way to correct such practices was for the Prophet himself to do the right thing and for that to be reported and explained. Hence, he wanted his wife to hand him the prayer mat when he was in the mosque, and he would put his head on her lap while reciting the Qur'an. He knew that recting the Qur'an in the mosque earned greater reward, but he wanted to show what is permissible. He would eat and drink with her, and put his lips at the same spot she put her lips. All this was to indicate that the discharge of menses did not mean that the woman herself became impure or unclean.

CHAPTER 4

PROSTATIC FLUID (*MADHĪ*)

[539–17]. (Dār al-Salām 0593) Abū Bakr ibn Abī Shaybah narrated:[i] Wakīʿ, Abū Muʿāwiyah and Hushaym narrated; from al-Aʿmash; from Mundhir ibn Yaʿlā (whose appellation was Abū Yaʿlā); from Ibn al-Ḥanafiyyah; from ʿAlī. He said: **'I used to frequently discharge prostatic fluid (*madhī*), and I was too shy to ask the Prophet about it, because of his daughter's position with me. I told al-Miqdād ibn al-Aswad and he asked him. [The Prophet] said: "Such a person should wash his genital organ and perform the ablution".'**

حَدَّثَنَا أَبُو بَكْرِ بْنُ أَبِي شَيْبَةَ، حَدَّثَنَا وَكِيعٌ، وَأَبُو مُعَاوِيَةَ، وَهُشَيْمٌ، عَنِ الْأَعْمَشِ، عَنْ مُنْذِرِ بْنِ يَعْلَى، - وَيُكْنَى أَبَا يَعْلَى - عَنِ ابْنِ الْحَنَفِيَّةِ، عَنْ عَلِيٍّ قَالَ: كُنْتُ رَجُلًا مَذَّاءً وَكُنْتُ أَسْتَحْيِي أَنْ أَسْأَلَ النَّبِيَّ صَلَّى اللهُ عَلَيْهِ وَسَلَّمَ لِمَكَانِ ابْنَتِهِ فَأَمَرْتُ الْمِقْدَادَ بْنَ الْأَسْوَدِ فَسَأَلَهُ فَقَالَ: «يَغْسِلُ ذَكَرَهُ وَيَتَوَضَّأُ»

[540–18]. (Dār al-Salām 0594) Yaḥyā ibn Ḥabīb al-Ḥārithī narrated: Khālid (meaning Ibn al-Ḥārith) narrated; Shuʿbah narrated; Sulyamān reported to me: I heard Mundhir narrating from Muhammad ibn ʿAlī; from ʿAlī. He said: **'I felt very shy to ask the Prophet about the prostatic fluid because of Fāṭimah. I told al-Miqdād and he asked him. [The Prophet] said: "From such [discharge] ablution is needed".'**

i. Related by al-Bukhārī, 132 and 178; al-Nasāʾī, 157.

وَحَدَّثَنَا يَحْيَى بْنُ حَبِيبٍ الْحَارِثِيُّ، حَدَّثَنَا خَالِدٌ يَعْنِي ابْنَ الْحَارِثِ، حَدَّثَنَا شُعْبَةُ، أَخْبَرَنِي سُلَيْمَانُ، قَالَ: سَمِعْتُ مُنْذِرًا، عَنْ مُحَمَّدِ بْنِ عَلِيٍّ، عَنْ عَلِيٍّ أَنَّهُ قَالَ: اسْتَحْيَيْتُ أَنْ أَسْأَلَ النَّبِيَّ صَلَّى اللهُ عَلَيْهِ وَسَلَّمَ عَنِ الْمَذْيِ مِنْ أَجْلِ فَاطِمَةَ، فَأَمَرْتُ الْمِقْدَادَ فَسَأَلَهُ فَقَالَ: «مِنْهُ الْوُضُوءُ»

[541–19]. (Dār al-Salām 0595) Ḥārūn ibn Saʿīd al-Aylī and Ahmad ibn ʿĪsā narrated to me:[i] both said: Ibn Wahb narrated; Makhramah ibn Bukayr reported to me; from his father; from Sulaymān ibn Yasār; from Ibn ʿAbbās: ʿAlī ibn Abī Ṭālib said: **'We sent al-Miqdād ibn al-Aswad to God's Messenger (peace be upon him) and he asked him about the discharge of the prostatic fluid, and what to do about it? The Prophet said: "Wash your gential organ and perform the ablution".'**

وَحَدَّثَنِي هَارُونُ بْنُ سَعِيدٍ الْأَيْلِيُّ، وَأَحْمَدُ بْنُ عِيسَى، قَالَا: حَدَّثَنَا ابْنُ وَهْبٍ، أَخْبَرَنِي مَخْرَمَةُ بْنُ بُكَيْرٍ، عَنْ أَبِيهِ، عَنْ سُلَيْمَانَ بْنِ يَسَارٍ، عَنِ ابْنِ عَبَّاسٍ، قَالَ: قَالَ عَلِيُّ بْنُ أَبِي طَالِبٍ: أَرْسَلْنَا الْمِقْدَادَ بْنَ الْأَسْوَدِ إِلَى رَسُولِ اللهِ صَلَّى اللهُ عَلَيْهِ وَسَلَّمَ فَسَأَلَهُ عَنِ الْمَذْيِ يَخْرُجُ مِنَ الْإِنْسَانِ كَيْفَ يَفْعَلُ بِهِ؟ فَقَالَ رَسُولُ اللهِ صَلَّى اللهُ عَلَيْهِ وَسَلَّمَ: «تَوَضَّأْ وَانْضَحْ فَرْجَكَ»

Text Explanation

These hadiths are about the discharge of prostatic fluid, which is called *madhī* in Arabic. It is a thin, sticky, white fluid which is discharged with arousal, not due to an orgasm. It is not strongly discharged and is not followed by a state of langure. In fact, a man may not feel its discharge. It is discharged by both men and women, and it is more frequent in the case of women, but God knows best.

i. Related by al-Nasā'ī, 434, 435, 437 and 438.

Scholars are unanimous that the discharge of the prostatic fluid does not require a major ritual ablution, i.e. *ghusl*. However, Abū Ḥanīfah, al-Shāfiʿī, Ahmad and the great majority of scholars say that it requires a minor ritual ablution, i.e. *wuḍū'*. The hadiths make clear that it is impure, and it is because of this impurity that one must wash one's genital organ. According to al-Shāfiʿī and the majority of scholars, what is required is to wash the area which is touched by it, not necessarily the entire organ, but one report mentions that Mālik and Ahmad say that washing the entire organ is required.

The hadiths also imply that the use of a solid matter, such as toilet paper or a stone, for cleansing is permissible in the case of the discharge of normal impurities, i.e. urine and stools. In the case of other discharges, such as blood and prostatic fluid, washing with water is necessary. This is the more correct view of our school of *fiqh*. A scholar who takes a different view, making it permissible to use only a solid object, drawing an analogy with the normal case, may argue that this hadith refers to the more frequent cases of people living in a town where the majority use water for such cleansing. Alternatively, he may suggest that this hadith only gives a preference.

The hadiths make clear that it is perfectly permissible to ask someone else to request a fatwa in place of oneself. They also suggest that it is permissible to rely on information by others, even though one is able to make absolutely sure. This is the case of ʿAlī, who relied on al-Miqdād's reporting of the Prophet's answer even though ʿAlī was able to ask the question himself. However, this may be countered by suggesting that ʿAlī might have been present when the question was put by al-Miqdād. He was simply too shy to put the question himself. The hadith further suggests that it is recommended to maintain good relations with one's in-laws. A man is recommended not to mention anything related to his private conduct with his wife in front of her father, brother or son, or her other relatives. ʿAlī did not wish to put the question himself to the Prophet because such discharge often occurs during foreplay with one's wife. But God knows best.

Transmission

The chain of transmission of the last hadith, No. 541, features 'Ḥārūn ibn Saʿīd al-Aylī and Ahmad ibn ʿĪsā narrated to me: Ibn Wahb narrated; Makhramah ibn Bukayr reported to me; from his father; from Sulaymān ibn Yasār; from Ibn ʿAbbās', and goes on to report what ʿAlī said. Al-Dāraquṭnī questions this chain, saying: 'Ḥammād ibn Khālid said: "I asked Makhramah: Did you listen to your father narrating hadiths? He said: No". Al-Layth differs with this narration from Bukayr, as he does not mention Ibn ʿAbbās. Mālik does the same narrating from Abū al-Naḍr'. This is what al-Dāraquṭnī says in his objection.

Al-Nasā'ī also said in his *Sunan* anthology that Makhramah did not listen to anything his father narrated. Al-Nasā'ī relates this hadith with different chains of transmission, some of which take up the same chain entered by Muslim, and some feature: 'al-Layth ibn Saʿd from Bukayr from Sulaymān ibn Yasār, who said: ʿAlī sent al-Miqdād ...'. He thus leaves it incomplete, making the hadith a *mursal*.

Scholars differ on this point of whether Makhramah listend to narrations by his father. Mālik said: 'I asked Makhramah: did you actually hear your father narrating what you report from him? He swore by God that he heard it from his father'. Mālik added that Makhramah was a pious person. The same is mentioned by Maʿn ibn ʿĪsā confirming that Makhramah heard from his father. Yet several scholars are of the view that Makhramah heard no narrations from his father. Ahmad ibn Ḥanbal said that Makhramah did not hear anything directly from his father, but he used to narrate from his father's book. Yaḥyā ibn Maʿīn and Ibn Abī Khaythamah mention that it is said that he had his father's book but he did not actually listen to his father. Mūsā ibn Salamah reports: 'I asked Makhramah: Did your father narrate to you? He said: I did not attend my father, but here are his books'. Abū Ḥātim said: 'Makhramah is reliable if he had heard from his father'. ʿAlī ibn al-Madīnī said: 'I do not think that Makhramah heard from his father the book containing hadiths narrated by Sulaymān ibn Yasār, but he might have heard a few. I never saw anyone in Madinah reporting from Makhramah that he used to say in any hadith he reported that he heard it from his father, but God knows best'. These are the statements of the leading scholars of Hadith transmission. However, the hadith is authentic, as it is reported with the other chains of transmission mentioned by Muslim before this last hadith, and reported with other chains of transmission mentioned by other scholars, but God knows best.

CHAPTER 5

WASHING ONE'S FACE AND HANDS WHEN ONE WAKES UP

[542–20]. (Dār al-Salām 0596) Abū Bakr ibn Abī Shaybah and Abū Kurayb narrated:[i] Wakīʿ narrated from Sufyān; from Salamah ibn Kuhayl; from Kurayb; from Ibn ʿAbbās that: **'The Prophet (peace be upon him) woke up, attended to his need, then washed his face and hands, then went back to sleep'**.

حَدَّثَنَا أَبُو بَكْرِ بْنُ أَبِي شَيْبَةَ، وَأَبُو كُرَيْبٍ، قَالَا: حَدَّثَنَا وَكِيعٌ، عَنْ سُفْيَانَ، عَنْ سَلَمَةَ بْنِ كُهَيْلٍ، عَنْ كُرَيْبٍ، عَنِ ابْنِ عَبَّاسٍ: «أَنَّ النَّبِيَّ صَلَّى اللهُ عَلَيْهِ وَسَلَّمَ قَامَ مِنَ اللَّيْلِ، فَقَضَى حَاجَتَهُ، ثُمَّ غَسَلَ وَجْهَهُ وَيَدَيْهِ، ثُمَّ نَامَ»

Text Explanation

It appears, but God knows best, that what is meant by 'attended to his need' is answering the call of nature. This is confirmed by *Qāḍī* ʿIyāḍ. The purpose of washing one's face is to refresh oneself and remove the effects of sleep. As for washing one's hands, it might have been for having touched something. This is what the *Qāḍī* mentioned.

The hadith shows that going back to sleep is perfectly permissible. Some particularly devout people in the early generations of Islam expressed disapproval. Perhaps they meant this with regard to a person who may oversleep and miss his regular practice. The Prophet did not fear oversleeping. He always attended to his night worship, but God knows best.

---

i. Related by al-Bukhārī, 6316; Abū Dāwūd, 5043; al-Nasāʾī, 1120; Ibn Mājah, 508.

CHAPTER 6

GOING TO BED IN A STATE OF JANABAH AND THE RECOMMENDATION OF MINOR RITUAL ABLUTION BEFORE DOING CERTAIN THINGS

[543–21]. (Dār al-Salām 0597) Yaḥyā ibn Yaḥyā al-Tamīmī and Muhammad ibn Rumḥ narrated:[i] al-Layth reported [H]. Also, Qutaybah ibn Saʿīd narrated; Layth narrated; from Ibn Shihāb; from Abū Salamah ibn ʿAbd al-Raḥmān; from ʿĀʾishah that: **'If God's Messenger (peace be upon him) wished to sleep and he was in a state of major ritual impurity [i.e. *janābah*], he would perform minor ritual ablution before he slept, in the same way as he would for prayer'**.

حَدَّثَنَا يَحْيَى بْنُ يَحْيَى التَّمِيمِيُّ، وَمُحَمَّدُ بْنُ رُمْحٍ، قَالَا: أَخْبَرَنَا اللَّيْثُ، ح، وَحَدَّثَنَا قُتَيْبَةُ بْنُ سَعِيدٍ، حَدَّثَنَا لَيْثٌ، عَنِ ابْنِ شِهَابٍ، عَنْ أَبِي سَلَمَةَ بْنِ عَبْدِ الرَّحْمَنِ، عَنْ عَائِشَةَ: «أَنَّ رَسُولَ اللهِ صَلَّى اللهُ عَلَيْهِ وَسَلَّمَ كَانَ إِذَا أَرَادَ أَنْ يَنَامَ، وَهُوَ جُنُبٌ، تَوَضَّأَ وُضُوءَهُ لِلصَّلَاةِ، قَبْلَ أَنْ يَنَامَ»

[544–22]. (Dār al-Salām 0598) Abū Bakr ibn Abī Shaybah narrated:[ii] Ibn ʿUlayyah, Wakīʿ and Ghudar narrated; from Shuʿbah; from al-Ḥakam; from Ibrāhīm; from al-Aswad; from

i. Related by Abū Dāwūd, 222 and 223; al-Nasāʾī, 256, 257 and 258; Ibn Mājah, 593 and 584.

ii. Related by Abū Dāwūd, 224; al-Nasāʾī, 255; Ibn Mājah, 591 and 467.

ʿĀ'ishah. She said: **'If God's Messenger (peace be upon him) was in a state of major ritual impurity and he wished to eat or go to sleep, he would first perform minor ritual ablution, as he would for prayer'**.

حَدَّثَنَا أَبُو بَكْرِ بْنُ أَبِي شَيْبَةَ، حَدَّثَنَا ابْنُ عُلَيَّةَ، وَوَكِيعٌ، وَغُنْدَرٌ، عَنْ شُعْبَةَ، عَنِ الْحَكَمِ، عَنْ إِبْرَاهِيمَ، عَنِ الْأَسْوَدِ، عَنْ عَائِشَةَ قَالَتْ: «كَانَ رَسُولُ اللهِ صَلَّى اللهُ عَلَيْهِ وَسَلَّمَ إِذَا كَانَ جُنُبًا، فَأَرَادَ أَنْ يَأْكُلَ أَوْ يَنَامَ، تَوَضَّأَ وُضُوءَهُ لِلصَّلَاةِ»

[000–000]. (Dār al-Salām 0599) Muhammad ibn al-Muthannā and Ibn Bashshār narrated: both said: Muhammad ibn Jaʿfar narrated [H]. Also, ʿUbaydullāh ibn Muʿādh narrated: my father narrated; Shuʿbah narrated, with the same chain of transmission. Ibn al-Muthannā, however, said in his narration: 'al-Ḥakam narrated: I heard Ibrāhīm narrating …'.

حَدَّثَنَا مُحَمَّدُ بْنُ الْمُثَنَّى، وَابْنُ بَشَّارٍ، قَالَا: حَدَّثَنَا مُحَمَّدُ بْنُ جَعْفَرٍ، ح، وَحَدَّثَنَا عُبَيْدُ اللهِ بْنُ مُعَاذٍ، قَالَ: حَدَّثَنَا أَبِي، قَالَا: حَدَّثَنَا شُعْبَةُ بِهَذَا الْإِسْنَادِ. قَالَ ابْنُ الْمُثَنَّى: فِي حَدِيثِهِ حَدَّثَنَا الْحَكَمُ، سَمِعْتُ إِبْرَاهِيمَ يُحَدِّثُ.

[545–23]. (Dār al-Salām 0600) Muhammad ibn Abī Bakr al-Muqaddamī and Zuhayr ibn Ḥarb narrated to me:[i] both said: Yaḥyā (who is Ibn Saʿīd) narrated; from ʿUbaydillāh [H]. Also, Abū Bakr ibn Abī Shaybah and Ibn Numayr narrated (their text): Ibn Numayr said: my father narrated, while Abū Bakr said: Abū Usāmah narrated. Both said: ʿUbaydullāh narrated; from Nāfiʿ; from Ibn ʿUmar: that ʿUmar said: **'Messenger of God, may anyone go to sleep when he is in a state of major ritual impurity?' He said: 'Yes, if he performs the ablution'**.

i. Related by al-Nasāʾī, 259; al-Tirmidhī, 120.

وَحَدَّثَنِي مُحَمَّدُ بْنُ أَبِي بَكْرٍ الْـمُقَدَّمِيُّ، وَزُهَيْرُ بْنُ حَرْبٍ قَالَا: حَدَّثَنَا يَحْيَى وَهُوَ ابْنُ سَعِيدٍ، عَنْ عُبَيْدِ اللهِ، ح، وَحَدَّثَنَا أَبُو بَكْرِ بْنُ أَبِي شَيْبَةَ، وَابْنُ نُمَيْرٍ، - وَاللَّفْظُ لَـهُمَا - قَالَ ابْنُ نُمَيْرٍ: حَدَّثَنَا أَبِي، وَقَالَ: أَبُو بَكْرٍ، حَدَّثَنَا أَبُو أُسَامَةَ، قَالَا: حَدَّثَنَا عُبَيْدُ اللهِ، عَنْ نَافِعٍ، عَنِ ابْنِ عُمَرَ، أَنَّ عُمَرَ، قَالَ: يَا رَسُولَ اللهِ أَيَرْقُدُ أَحَدُنَا وَهُوَ جُنُبٌ؟ قَالَ: «نَعَمْ إِذَا تَوَضَّأَ»

[546–24]. (Dār al-Salām 0601) Muhammad ibn Rāfiʿ narrated: ʿAbd al-Razzāq narrated; from Ibn Jurayj; Nāfiʿ reported to me; from Ibn ʿUmar that '**ʿUmar asked the Prophet (peace be upon him): "May a person go to sleep when he is in a state of major ritual impurity?" The Prophet said: "Yes. He may perform the ablution, then go to sleep. He may take a bath when he wishes"**.'

وَحَدَّثَنَا مُحَمَّدُ بْنُ رَافِعٍ، حَدَّثَنَا عَبْدُ الرَّزَّاقِ، عَنِ ابْنِ جُرَيْجٍ، أَخْبَرَنِي نَافِعٌ، عَنِ ابْنِ عُمَرَ، أَنَّ عُمَرَ اسْتَفْتَى النَّبِيَّ صَلَّى اللهُ عَلَيْهِ وَسَلَّمَ فَقَالَ: هَلْ يَنَامُ أَحَدُنَا وَهُوَ جُنُبٌ؟ قَالَ: «نَعَمْ، لِيَتَوَضَّأْ ثُمَّ لِيَنَمْ، حَتَّى يَغْتَسِلَ إِذَا شَاءَ»

[547–25]. (Dār al-Salām 0602) Yaḥyā ibn Yaḥyā narrated to me:[i] I read out to Mālik; from ʿAbdullāh ibn Dīnār; from Ibn ʿUmar: '**ʿUmar ibn al-Khaṭṭāb mentioned to God's Messenger (peace be upon him) that he might be in a state of major ritual impurity at night. The Prophet said to him: "Wash your gentials and perform the ablution, then go to sleep"**.'

وَحَدَّثَنِي يَحْيَى بْنُ يَحْيَى، قَالَ: قَرَأْتُ عَلَى مَالِكٍ، عَنْ عَبْدِ اللهِ بْنِ دِينَارٍ، عَنِ ابْنِ عُمَرَ، قَالَ: ذَكَرَ عُمَرُ بْنُ الْخَطَّابِ، لِرَسُولِ اللهِ صَلَّى اللهُ عَلَيْهِ وَسَلَّمَ أَنَّهُ تُصِيبُهُ جَنَابَةٌ مِنَ اللَّيْلِ، فَقَالَ لَهُ رَسُولُ اللهِ صَلَّى اللهُ عَلَيْهِ وَسَلَّمَ: «تَوَضَّأْ وَاغْسِلْ ذَكَرَكَ، ثُمَّ نَمْ»

---

i. Related by al-Bukhārī, 290; Abū Dāwūd, 221; al-Nasāʾī, 260.

[548–26]. (Dār al-Salām 0603) Qutaybah ibn Saʿīd narrated:[i] Layth narrated; from Muʿāwiyah ibn Ṣāliḥ; from ʿAbdullāh ibn Abī Qays. He said: **'I asked ʿĀ'ishah about the Prophet's Witr Prayer and he mentioned the [relevant] hadith. I said: "How did he do regarding the state of major ritual impurity? Did he take a bath before going to sleep, or did he sleep before taking a bath?" She said: "He did both: He might take a bath before going to bed, and he might only perform minor ritual ablution and go to bed". I said: "All praise be to God for making it easy".'**

حَدَّثَنَا قُتَيْبَةُ بْنُ سَعِيدٍ، حَدَّثَنَا لَيْثٌ، عَنْ مُعَاوِيَةَ بْنِ صَالِحٍ، عَنْ عَبْدِ اللهِ بْنِ أَبِي قَيْسٍ، قَالَ: سَأَلْتُ عَائِشَةَ، عَنْ وِتْرِ رَسُولِ اللهِ صَلَّى اللهُ عَلَيْهِ وَسَلَّمَ فَذَكَرَ الْحَدِيثَ قُلْتُ: كَيْفَ كَانَ يَصْنَعُ فِي الْجَنَابَةِ؟ أَكَانَ يَغْتَسِلُ قَبْلَ أَنْ يَنَامَ؟ أَمْ يَنَامُ قَبْلَ أَنْ يَغْتَسِلَ؟ قَالَتْ: «كُلُّ ذَلِكَ قَدْ كَانَ يَفْعَلُ، رُبَّمَا اغْتَسَلَ فَنَامَ، وَرُبَّمَا تَوَضَّأَ فَنَامَ، قُلْتُ: الْحَمْدُ للهِ الَّذِي جَعَلَ فِي الْأَمْرِ سَعَةً»

[000–000]. (Dār al-Salām 0604) Zuhayr ibn Ḥarb narrated it to me: ʿAbd al-Raḥmān ibn Mahdī narrated [H]. Also, Ḥārūn ibn Saʿīd al-Aylī narrated it to me: Ibn Wahb narrated; all from Muʿāwiyah ibn Ṣāliḥ, with the same chain of transmission: **the same text**.

وَحَدَّثَنِيهِ زُهَيْرُ بْنُ حَرْبٍ، حَدَّثَنَا عَبْدُ الرَّحْمَنِ بْنُ مَهْدِيٍّ، ح، وَحَدَّثَنِيهِ هَارُونُ بْنُ سَعِيدٍ الْأَيْلِيُّ، حَدَّثَنَا ابْنُ وَهْبٍ جَمِيعًا عَنْ مُعَاوِيَةَ بْنِ صَالِحٍ بِهَذَا الْإِسْنَادِ مِثْلَهُ.

[549–27]. (Dār al-Salām 0605) Abū Bakr ibn Abī Shaybah narrated:[ii] Ḥafṣ ibn Ghiyāth narrated [H]. Also, Abū Kurayb

i. Related by Abū Dāwūd, 1437; al-Tirmidhī, 449 (in a shorter version), and 2924.
ii. Related by Abū Dāwūd, 220; al-Tirmidhī, 141; al-Nasā'ī, 262; Ibn Mājah, 587.

narrated: Ibn Abī Zā'idah reported [H]. And, ʿAmr al-Nāqid and Ibn Numayr narrated to me; both said: Marwān ibn Muʿāwiyah al-Fazārī narrated: all of them from ʿĀṣim; from Abū al-Mutawkkil; from Abū Saʿīd al-Khudrī: **'God's Messenger (peace be upon him) said: "If any of you has had sexual intercourse with his wife, then he wished for a repeat, let him perform the ablution".'**

Abu Bakr added in his narration: 'Let him perfrom minor ritual ablution between the two times'.

وَحَدَّثَنَا أَبُو بَكْرِ بْنُ أَبِي شَيْبَةَ، حَدَّثَنَا حَفْصُ بْنُ غِيَاثٍ، ح، وَحَدَّثَنَا أَبُو كُرَيْبٍ، أَخْبَرَنَا ابْنُ أَبِي زَائِدَةَ ح، وَحَدَّثَنِي عَمْرٌو النَّاقِدُ، وَابْنُ نُمَيْرٍ، قَالَا: حَدَّثَنَا مَرْوَانُ بْنُ مُعَاوِيَةَ الْفَزَارِيُّ، كُلُّهُمْ عَنْ عَاصِمٍ، عَنْ أَبِي الْمُتَوَكِّلِ، عَنْ أَبِي سَعِيدٍ الْخُدْرِيِّ، قَالَ: قَالَ رَسُولُ اللهِ صَلَّى اللهُ عَلَيْهِ وَسَلَّمَ: «إِذَا أَتَى أَحَدُكُمْ أَهْلَهُ، ثُمَّ أَرَادَ أَنْ يَعُودَ، فَلْيَتَوَضَّأْ»

زَادَ أَبُو بَكْرٍ فِي حَدِيثِهِ: بَيْنَهُمَا وُضُوءًا، وَقَالَ: ثُمَّ أَرَادَ أَنْ يُعَاوِدَ.

[550–28]. (Dār al-Salām 0606) Al-Ḥasan ibn Ahmad ibn Abī Shuʿayb al-Ḥarrānī narrated: Miskīn (meaning Ibn Bukayr al-Hadhdhā') narrated; from Shuʿbah; from Hishām ibn Zayd; from Anas that **'The Prophet might go round to his wives, performing only one major ritual ablution [at the end]'**.

وَحَدَّثَنَا الْحَسَنُ بْنُ أَحْمَدَ بْنِ أَبِي شُعَيْبٍ الْحَرَّانِيُّ، حَدَّثَنَا مِسْكِينٌ يَعْنِي ابْنَ بُكَيْرٍ الْحَذَّاءَ، عَنْ شُعْبَةَ، عَنْ هِشَامِ بْنِ زَيْدٍ، عَنْ أَنَسٍ: «أَنَّ النَّبِيَّ صَلَّى اللهُ عَلَيْهِ وَسَلَّمَ كَانَ يَطُوفُ عَلَى نِسَائِهِ بِغُسْلٍ وَاحِدٍ»

Text Explanation

All these hadiths confirm that a person in a state of major ritual impurity, or *janābah*, may go to sleep, eat, drink, or have sexual intercourse before he takes a bath or *ghusl* to be free of *janābah*. This is unanimously agreed upon by scholars. They are also unanimous that the body and sweat of a person in major ritual impurity carries no impurity. The hadiths also make clear that it is recommended or desirable for such a person to wash his genital organs and perform the ablution before doing any such matter, particularly if he wishes to have intercourse with his wife whom he had not been in bed with earlier. In this last case, it is strongly recommended that he wash his genital organs before this. Our scholars state that to go to sleep, eat, drink or have intercourse before performing the ablution is discouraged. This is suggested by these hadiths. There is no disagreement among our scholars that such an ablution is not a duty. This is also the view of Mālik and the majority of scholars, but Ibn Ḥabīb, of the Mālikī School and Dāwūd al-Ẓāhirī consider it a duty. The ablution referred to in these hadiths is the full ablution one normally performs for prayer. The earlier hadith narrated by Ibn ʿAbbās and mentioning that the Prophet washed his face and hands does not relate to a state of major ritual impurity, but rather to urination.

A different hadith, narrated by Abū Isḥāq al-Sabīʿī from al-Aswad from ʿĀ'ishah, mentions that 'the Prophet (peace be upon him) used to go to sleep when he was in a state of major ritual impurity, without touching any water'. This hadith is related by al-Tirmidhī, al-Nasā'ī, Ibn Mājah and others. Abū Dāwūd quotes Yazīd ibn Ḥārūn that the suggestion that the Prophet did not touch any water was a mistake by Abū Isḥāq, and al-Tirmidhī said that scholars considered this to be a mistake by Abū Isḥāq. Al-Bayhaqī said that eminent Hadith scholars discard this word, and this makes clear that the hadith is lacking in authenticity. Since it is so, there is no need to cite it as a point of objection. Indeed, even if it were authentic, it would not provide a counter argument, as it is responded to with two answers. The first is advanced by the two leading scholars, Abū al-ʿAbbās ibn Surayj and Abū Bakr al-Bayhaqī, who said that this means that he did not touch water specifically for a major ritual ablution, i.e. *ghusl*. The second answer, which I find good, is that the Prophet sometimes did not touch water to indicate that it is permissible. Had he always performed an ablution, it might have been thought to be a binding duty.

The last hadith mentions that the Prophet might consort with all his wives and take only one bath at the end. It may be that he performed the ablution in between, or it may mean to show that it is permissible not to perform the ablution. It is also related in Abū Dāwūd's *Sunan* that the Prophet one night went around to his wives, and he took a bath at each one's place. It was said to him: 'Would it not be sufficient that you take only one bath'. He said: 'But this is better, fresher and purer'. Abū Dāwūd said: 'but the first hadith is more authentic'. I may add that if this hadith is also authentic, it may be that the two hadiths speak of two different occasions, but God knows best.

Scholars express different opinions concerning the purpose of performing this ablution. Some of our scholars say that it reduces the effect of the act, as it purifies the body organs that are washed during the ablution. Abū ʿAbdullāh al-Māzarī said that its purpose is given differently by scholars, with some saying that it ensures that the person concerned would thus go to sleep having performed one of the two acts of cleansing. This serves well if he were to die while asleep. It is also suggested that when performing the ablution, he may find himself more willing to go ahead and take a bath to remove the state of major ritual impurity. Al-Māzarī further says that this difference of opinion also applies to a woman in menstruation. Scholars who encourage going to sleep with one act of cleansing also recommend such a woman to perform the ablution before going to bed. This is al-Māzarī's view. Scholars of our Shāfiʿī school are in agreement that performing the ablution before sleep is not recommended for a woman having her period or with postnatal discharge, because the ablution has no effect on her condition. When a woman has finished her period, she is then in the same condition of major ritual impurity as a man, but God knows best.

That the Prophet consorted with all his wives on the same night, taking only one bath at the end, is understood to be by their consent, or by the consent of the one whose turn it was on that night. Such an explanation is needed by scholars who claim that fairness was obligatory on the Prophet in all cases, just as it is with us. Other scholars, who do not make such a claim of fairness, do not need this explanation. It was up to the Prophet to do what he liked. Our scholars have two different views on this point, with some making fairness binding and others not, but God knows best.

These hadiths make clear that taking a bath to perform the major ritual ablution and remove the state of major ritual impurity is not necessarily done immediately. However, it becomes necessary when one needs to offer an obligatory prayer. This is agreed by all Muslims. Our scholars have different views on what makes the major ritual ablution necessary: is it the contact of the genital organs of the man and his wife, or the discharge of semen or the need to offer a prayer, or is it being in major ritual impurity and wanting to offer a prayer? The same lines of difference are upheld on what makes an ablution obligatory: is it the discharge of impurity, or rising to offer a prayer, or both together. Yet the same disagreement applies to what makes taking a bath obligatory for a woman who is in menstruation: is it the discharge of blood, or its cessation at the end of her period? But God knows best.

Transmission

In hadith No. 544, Muslim gives a second chain of transmission and says at the end: 'Ibn al-Muthannā, however, said in his narration: 'al-Ḥakam narrated: I heard Ibrāhīm narrating'. This means that in his reporting from Muhammad ibn Ja'far from Shu'bah, Ibn al-Muthannā said: 'Shu'bah said: al-Ḥakam narrated to us saying: I heard Ibrāhīm narrating …'. The first chain of transmission does not mention this, but says: 'Shu'bah from al-Ḥakam from Ibrāhīm'. This means that the second is stronger than the first, because the first uses 'from … from …' while the second uses 'narrated to us …' and 'I heard …'. These two forms are stronger than 'from'. Indeed, a number of scholars maintain that 'from' does not necessarily mean continuity, even though the narrator is not confused. We have clarified this point in the Notes and in several other places.

The chain of transmission of hadith No. 545 mentions Abū Bakr al-Muqaddamī, who is thus affiliated to his grandfather called Muqaddam. He has been mentioned more than once.

Also, the transmission mentions Abū al-Mutawakkil from Abū Saʿīd. This refers to Abū al-Mutawakkil al-Nājī, whose name was ʿAlī ibn Dāwūd. He belonged to a tribe known as Nājiyah, but God knows best.

CHAPTER 7

WOMEN'S SEMEN REQUIRES MAJOR RITUAL ABLUTION

[551–29]. (Dār al-Salām 0607) Zuhayr ibn Ḥarb narrated to me: ʿUmar ibn Yūnus al-Ḥanafī narrated; ʿIkrimah ibn ʿAmmār narrated: Isḥāq ibn Abī Ṭalḥah said: Anas ibn Mālik narrated to me: '**Umm Sulaym (who was Isḥāq's grandmother) came to God's Messenger (peace be upon him) as ʿĀ'ishah was with him. She said: "Messenger of God, [may I ask about] a woman who sees in her dream what a man sees, seeing of herself what a man sees of himself"? ʿĀ'ishah said: "Umm Sulaym, you have shamed women! How shameful!" The Prophet said to ʿĀ'ishah: "Rather shame to you! Yes, Umm Sulaym. She must take a bath if she sees that".**'

وَحَدَّثَنِي زُهَيْرُ بْنُ حَرْبٍ، حَدَّثَنَا عُمَرُ بْنُ يُونُسَ الْحَنَفِيُّ، حَدَّثَنَا عِكْرِمَةُ بْنُ عَمَّارٍ، قَالَ: قَالَ إِسْحَاقُ بْنُ أَبِي طَلْحَةَ، حَدَّثَنِي أَنَسُ بْنُ مَالِكٍ، قَالَ: جَاءَتْ أُمُّ سُلَيْمٍ - وَهِيَ جَدَّةُ إِسْحَاقَ -، إِلَى رَسُولِ اللهِ صَلَّى اللهُ عَلَيْهِ وَسَلَّمَ فَقَالَتْ لَهُ، وَعَائِشَةُ عِنْدَهُ: يَا رَسُولَ اللهِ، الْمَرْأَةُ تَرَى مَا يَرَى الرَّجُلُ فِي الْمَنَامِ، فَتَرَى مِنْ نَفْسِهَا مَا يَرَى الرَّجُلُ مِنْ نَفْسِهِ، فَقَالَتْ عَائِشَةُ: يَا أُمَّ سُلَيْمٍ، فَضَحْتِ النِّسَاءَ، تَرِبَتْ يَمِينُكِ، فَقَالَ لِعَائِشَةَ: «بَلْ أَنْتِ، فَتَرِبَتْ يَمِينُكِ، نَعَمْ، فَلْتَغْتَسِلْ يَا أُمَّ سُلَيْمٍ، إِذَا رَأَتْ ذَاكِ»

[552–30]. (Dār al-Salām 0608) ʿAbbās ibn al-Walīd narrated:[i] Yazīd ibn Zurayʿ narrated; Saʿīd narrated; from Qatādah; that

i. Related by al-Nasā'ī, 195 and 200; Ibn Mājah, 1181.

Anas ibn Mālik narrated; that Umm Sulaym narrated that '**She asked the Prophet about a woman seeing in a dream what a man sees. The Prophet said: "If a woman sees that, she should take a bath". Umm Sulaym said: I felt shy having asked that, and I said: Does this happen? The Prophet said: "Yes. How else does similarity happen? The man's fluid is thick and white, while the woman's is thin and yellow. Whichever fluid is on top, or ahead [of the other], the [child's] similarity is due to it"**.'

حَدَّثَنَا عَبَّاسُ بْنُ الْوَلِيدِ، حَدَّثَنَا يَزِيدُ بْنُ زُرَيْعٍ، حَدَّثَنَا سَعِيدٌ، عَنْ قَتَادَةَ، أَنَّ أَنَسَ بْنَ مَالِكٍ، حَدَّثَهُمْ أَنَّ أُمَّ سُلَيْمٍ، حَدَّثَتْ أَنَّهَا سَأَلَتْ نَبِيَّ اللهِ صَلَّى اللهُ عَلَيْهِ وَسَلَّمَ عَنِ الْمَرْأَةِ تَرَى فِي مَنَامِهَا مَا يَرَى الرَّجُلُ، فَقَالَ رَسُولُ اللهِ صَلَّى اللهُ عَلَيْهِ وَسَلَّمَ: «إِذَا رَأَتْ ذَلِكَ الْمَرْأَةُ فَلْتَغْتَسِلْ» فَقَالَتْ أُمُّ سُلَيْمٍ: وَاسْتَحْيَيْتُ مِنْ ذَلِكَ، قَالَتْ: وَهَلْ يَكُونُ هَذَا؟ فَقَالَ نَبِيُّ اللهِ صَلَّى اللهُ عَلَيْهِ وَسَلَّمَ: «نَعَمْ، فَمِنْ أَيْنَ يَكُونُ الشَّبَهُ؟ إِنَّ مَاءَ الرَّجُلِ غَلِيظٌ أَبْيَضُ، وَمَاءَ الْمَرْأَةِ رَقِيقٌ أَصْفَرُ، فَمِنْ أَيِّهِمَا عَلَا، أَوْ سَبَقَ، يَكُونُ مِنْهُ الشَّبَهُ»

[553–31]. (Dār al-Salām 0609) Dāwūd ibn Rushayd narrated: Ṣāliḥ ibn ʿUmar narrated; Abū Mālik al-Ashjaʿī narrated; from Anas ibn Mālik: '**A woman asked God's Messenger (peace be upon him) if a woman saw in her dream what a man sees in his dream? He said: "If she has the same experience as a man, she must take a bath"**.'

حَدَّثَنَا دَاوُدُ بْنُ رُشَيْدٍ، حَدَّثَنَا صَالِحُ بْنُ عُمَرَ، حَدَّثَنَا أَبُو مَالِكٍ الْأَشْجَعِيُّ، عَنْ أَنَسِ بْنِ مَالِكٍ، قَالَ: سَأَلَتِ امْرَأَةٌ رَسُولَ اللهِ صَلَّى اللهُ عَلَيْهِ وَسَلَّمَ عَنِ الْمَرْأَةِ تَرَى فِي مَنَامِهَا مَا يَرَى الرَّجُلُ فِي مَنَامِهِ، فَقَالَ: «إِذَا كَانَ مِنْهَا مَا يَكُونُ مِنَ الرَّجُلِ فَلْتَغْتَسِلْ»

[554–32]. (Dār al-Salām 0610) Yaḥyā ibn Yaḥyā al-Tamīmī narrated:[i] Abū Mu'āwiyah reported from Hishām ibn 'Urwah; from his father; from Zaynab bint Abū Salamah; from Umm Salamah: '**Umm Sulaym came to the Prophet and said: "God does not shy of stating what is right. Must a woman take a bath if she sees a wet dream?" The Prophet said: "Yes, if she discharges the fluid". Umm Salamah said: "Messenger of God, do women see wet dreams?" He said: "Indeed; how else does her child resemble her?"**'

وَحَدَّثَنَا يَحْيَى بْنُ يَحْيَى التَّمِيمِيُّ، أَخْبَرَنَا أَبُو مُعَاوِيَةَ، عَنْ هِشَامِ بْنِ عُرْوَةَ، عَنْ أَبِيهِ، عَنْ زَيْنَبَ بِنْتِ أَبِي سَلَمَةَ، عَنْ أُمِّ سَلَمَةَ قَالَتْ: جَاءَتْ أُمُّ سُلَيْمٍ إِلَى النَّبِيِّ صَلَّى اللهُ عَلَيْهِ وَسَلَّمَ فَقَالَتْ: يَا رَسُولَ اللهِ، إِنَّ اللهَ لَا يَسْتَحْيِي مِنَ الْحَقِّ، فَهَلْ عَلَى الْمَرْأَةِ مِنْ غُسْلٍ إِذَا احْتَلَمَتْ؟ فَقَالَ رَسُولُ اللهِ صَلَّى اللهُ عَلَيْهِ وَسَلَّمَ: «نَعَمْ، إِذَا رَأَتِ الْمَاءَ» فَقَالَتْ أُمُّ سَلَمَةَ: يَا رَسُولَ اللهِ، وَتَحْتَلِمُ الْمَرْأَةُ؟ فَقَالَ: «تَرِبَتْ يَدَاكِ، فَبِمَ يُشْبِهُهَا وَلَدُهَا»

[555–000]. (Dār al-Salām 0611) Abū Bakr ibn Abī Shaybah and Zuhayr ibn Ḥarb narrated: both said: Wakī' narrated [H]. Also, Ibn Abī 'Umar narrated: Sufyān narrated; all of them from Hishām ibn 'Urwah, with the same chain of transmission, a similar hadith, but added: '**I said: You have shamed women**'.

حَدَّثَنَا أَبُو بَكْرِ بْنُ أَبِي شَيْبَةَ، وَزُهَيْرُ بْنُ حَرْبٍ، قَالَا: حَدَّثَنَا وَكِيعٌ، ح، وَحَدَّثَنَا ابْنُ أَبِي عُمَرَ، حَدَّثَنَا سُفْيَانُ، جَمِيعًا عَنْ هِشَامِ بْنِ عُرْوَةَ بِهَذَا الْإِسْنَادِ، مِثْلَ مَعْنَاهُ وَزَادَ قَالَتْ: قُلْتُ: فَضَحْتِ النِّسَاءَ.

[556–000]. (Dār al-Salām 0612) 'Abd Mālik ibn Shu'ayb ibn al-Layth narrated:[ii] my father narrated to me; from my grandfather;

---

i. Related by al-Bukhārī, 130, 282, 3328, 6091 and 6121; al-Tirmidhī, 122; Ibn Mājah, 600.
ii. Related by Abū Dāwūd, 237; al-Nasā'ī, 196.

ʿUqayl ibn Khālid narrated to me; from Ibn Shihāb that he said: ʿUrwah ibn al-Zubayr reported to me; that ʿĀ'ishah the Prophet's wife reported to him that: **'Umm Sulaym (Abū Ṭalḥah's children's mother) entered the Prophet's home. She said a similar hadith to that narrated by Hishām, except that it included that ʿĀ'ishah said: "I said to her: Ugh to you! Do women see that?"'**

وَحَدَّثَنَا عَبْدُ الْـمَلِكِ بْنُ شُعَيْبِ بْنِ اللَّيْثِ، حَدَّثَنِي أَبِي، عَنْ جَدِّي، حَدَّثَنِي عَقِيلُ بْنُ خَالِدٍ، عَنِ ابْنِ شِهَابٍ أَنَّهُ قَالَ: أَخْبَرَنِي عُرْوَةُ بْنُ الزُّبَيْرِ، أَنَّ عَائِشَةَ زَوْجَ النَّبِيِّ صَلَّى اللهُ عَلَيْهِ وَسَلَّمَ أَخْبَرَتْهُ أَنَّ أُمَّ سُلَيْمٍ، أُمَّ بَنِي أَبِي طَلْحَةَ، دَخَلَتْ عَلَى رَسُولِ اللهِ صَلَّى اللهُ عَلَيْهِ وَسَلَّمَ بِمَعْنَى حَدِيثِ هِشَامٍ غَيْرَ أَنَّ فِيهِ قَالَ: قَالَتْ عَائِشَةُ «فَقُلْتُ لَهَا أُفٍّ لَكِ أَتَرَى الْـمَرْأَةُ ذَلِكِ»

[557–33]. (Dār al-Salām 0613) Ibrāhīm ibn Mūsā al-Rāzī, Sahl ibn ʿUthmān and Abū Kurayb narrated but the text is Abū Kurayb's: Ibn Abī Zā'idah (Sahl said 'narrated' and the other two said 'reported'); from his father; from Muṣʿab ibn Shaybah; from Musāfiʿ ibn ʿAbdullāh; from ʿUrwah ibn al-Zubayr; from ʿĀ'ishah that **'A woman said to God's Messenger (peace be upon him): "Should a woman take a bath if she has a wet dream and sees the fluid?" He said: "Yes". ʿĀ'ishah said to her: "How shameful!" The Prophet said to her: "Leave her alone. Is [the child's] similarity due to anything other than this? If her fluid rises above the man's fluid, the child will resemble its maternal uncles, and if the man's fluid rises above her fluid, the child will resemble his paternal uncles".'**

حَدَّثَنَا إِبْرَاهِيمُ بْنُ مُوسَى الرَّازِيُّ، وَسَهْلُ بْنُ عُثْمَانَ، وَأَبُو كُرَيْبٍ، - وَاللَّفْظُ لِأَبِي كُرَيْبٍ قَالَ سَهْلٌ: حَدَّثَنَا، وقَالَ الْآخَرَانِ - أَخْبَرَنَا ابْنُ أَبِي زَائِدَةَ، عَنْ أَبِيهِ، عَنْ

مُصْعَبِ بْنِ شَيْبَةَ، عَنْ مُسَافِعِ بْنِ عَبْدِ اللهِ، عَنْ عُرْوَةَ بْنِ الزُّبَيْرِ، عَنْ عَائِشَةَ، أَنَّ امْرَأَةً قَالَتْ لِرَسُولِ اللهِ صَلَّى اللهُ عَلَيْهِ وَسَلَّمَ: هَلْ تَغْتَسِلُ الْمَرْأَةُ إِذَا احْتَلَمَتْ وَأَبْصَرَتِ الْمَاءَ؟ فَقَالَ: «نَعَمْ» فَقَالَتْ لَهَا عَائِشَةُ: تَرِبَتْ يَدَاكِ وَأُلَّتْ، قَالَتْ: فَقَالَ رَسُولُ اللهِ صَلَّى اللهُ عَلَيْهِ وَسَلَّمَ: «دَعِيهَا. وَهَلْ يَكُونُ الشَّبَهُ إِلَّا مِنْ قِبَلِ ذَلِكِ، إِذَا عَلَا مَاؤُهَا مَاءَ الرَّجُلِ، أَشْبَهَ الْوَلَدُ أَخْوَالَهُ، وَإِذَا عَلَا مَاءُ الرَّجُلِ مَاءَهَا أَشْبَهَ أَعْمَامَهُ»

Text Explanation

The different versions of this hadith make clear that if semen is discharged by a woman, she must take a bath, just as a man must do as a result of such a discharge. Muslims are unanimous that a major ritual ablution, i.e. *ghusl*, or a bath in which a person washes oneself from head to foot with water is required of both man and woman for a discharge of semen, or for penetrative intercourse between man and woman. They are also unanimous that a woman must have a major ritual ablution after menstruation and postnatal discharge. They differ as to whether it is required of a woman who gives birth but has no blood discharged at all. The more correct view of our scholars is that she must have it. The same difference of opinion applies in the case of a woman who has a miscarriage at any stage of pregnancy, with the more correct view being that a bath is required. Scholars who do not see it as obligatory say that she must have an ablution, i.e. *wuḍū'*, but God knows best. Moreover, our school's view is that a major ritual ablution is required as a result of a discharge of semen, whether with desire and ejaculation, or because of merely looking at someone or something, when one is awake or asleep, feels its discharge or not, and whether he is sane or insane.

What is meant by a discharge of semen is that it should come out of one's body. If it remains inside the body, it does not require anything. Suppose a man sees in his dream that he is having intercourse and an orgasm, but when he wakes up, he finds no trace of this. In this case all Muslims agree that he is not required to take a bath. Likewise, if he feels the shiver that combines ejaculation but does not ejaculate, or if the semen reaches the top or the middle of his genital organ, but does not come out. We may cite the case of one who is praying and feels about to ejaculate, but holds his organ above his clothes and the semen is not discharged until he has finished praying, his prayer is valid, as he has remained in a state of cleansing until the discharge took place.[i]

The same applies to women, but if the woman is not a virgin and the semen reaches the surface of her vagina, she must have a major ritual ablution, i.e. a bath, because the fluid is deemed to have been fully discharged. If she is a virgin, the major ritual ablution is not required unless the fluid is discharged out of her body, but God knows best.

Umm Sulaym, who is at the centre of all these hadiths, was Anas ibn Mālik's mother, but scholars report her name differently as Sahlah, Mulaykah, Rumaythah, Anīfah, al-Rumayṣā or al-Ghumayṣā. She was one of the best known and most honoured of the women Companions of the Prophet. Her sister was Umm Ḥarām bint Milḥān. 'Ā'ishah said to her that she shamed women. This means that she mentioned something that they would rather have remained secret and not be mentioned about them, because such a discharge suggests that they are lusty.

'Ā'ishah also said: 'How shameful'! In fact, 'Ā'ishah used a phrase that literally meant 'may your hands be dusty', but the phrase, which used to be frequently said by the Arabs at the time, was never used in this sense. It is used merely to express disapproval of what a person might have said or done, with perhaps more than one degree of disapproval. The Prophet used the same phrase to indicate to 'Ā'ishah that she was more deserving of disapproval because Umm Sulaym was enquiring about a religious point. As such, she should be encouraged.

The second hadith, No. 552, quotes Umm Sulaym saying: 'I felt shy having asked that'. This is how the hadith is recorded in the

---

i. This sounds extremely unusual, but I suppose that it refers to some physical disorder.

original copies. However, the leading Hadith scholar, Abū ʿAlī al-Ghassānī mentions that whilst it is so in most copies it is changed in some to put Umm Salamah instead of Umm Sulaym as the one who said this. What is learnt in memory with different chains of transmission is that it was Umm Salamah. *Qāḍī* ʿIyāḍ said: 'This is the correct version, because the question was put by Umm Sulaym and the one who replied to her in this version was Umm Salamah, while it was ʿĀ'ishah in the first version. It might have been that both ʿĀ'ishah and Umm Salamah took issue with her. However, Hadith scholars say that the one concerned in this hadith was Umm Salamah, not ʿĀ'ishah, but God knows best.

The Prophet answers the question about whether this happens by saying: 'How else does similarity happen?' What this means is that both parents are involved in the creation of a child and the resemblance a child carries is determined by whose fluid is stronger. If the woman produces semen, then its discharge is possible. The Prophet then explains: 'The man's fluid is thick and white, while the woman's is thin and yellow'. This is a clear statement of the condition of semen in the great majority of healthy people. Scholars say that the man's semen is white, thick and emitted with force by a healthy person, and comes out with pleasure, followed then by a feeling of relaxation. It has a smell similar to the pollen of the date tree, which is similar to the smell of dough. It is said that when it dries, its smell becomes similar to the smell of urine. Such is the man's semen, but some of these descriptions may change if a man has some illness. In this case, his semen may become thin or yellow, or it may be discharged without pleasure or desire. Alternatively, a man may have intercourse too frequently, and his semen may become reddish, similar to the water that comes out of meat. If it is red it is not impure but requires taking a bath, in the same way as when it is white. Three characteristics determine whether the discharge is semen: 1) it is discharged with desire and followed by relaxation; 2) its smell is like pollen; and 3) it comes out in spurts and with force. Any one of these is sufficient to consider the discharge to be semen. They need not be present all together. If the discharge has none of these, it is most probably not semen. All this applies to the man's semen. The woman's semen is yellow and thin, but it may tend to be whitish, if she is physically strong. It is recognized by two characteristics: it has a similar smell to the man's semen, and it is discharged with pleasure and followed by relaxation. Taking a bath is required for the discharge of semen in any condition or situation, but God knows best.

The Prophet further adds: 'Whichever fluid is on top, or ahead [of the other], the [child's] similarity is due to it'. 'Being on top' perhaps means ahead, or perhaps means more in quantity or force, according to how strong each partner's desire is.

In hadith No. 553, the Prophet says in answer to Umm Sulaym's question: 'If she has the same experience as a man, she must take a bath'. This means that if she discharges semen, she must have a bath, just like a man must do. This is a case of fine speech, referring implicitly to what people may feel shy to state openly.

In the following hadith, No. 554, Umm Sulaym starts by saying: 'God does not shy of stating what is right'. Scholars say that it means that God does not refrain from stating the truth, just like He does not shy of giving an example, using something trivial, like a gnat or some similar thing. He says: '*God does not disdain to give a parable of a gnat, or a higher creature*'. (2: 26) What she means is that she is not reluctant to put her question because she needs to know. It is also suggested that it means that God does not order or permit shyness which prevents stating or learning the truth. This is stated by way of apology for having to ask a question that women normally feel too shy to express in the presence of men. This hadith makes clear that whoever needs to know about a certain situation or case, should ask about it. They need not hesitate out of shyness or modesty. To do so is not real modesty, because modesty is all good and brings nothing but good. To refrain from asking in such a situation is not good; it is bad. How can it then be described as modesty? We explained this earlier, at the beginning of the Book of Faith. 'Ā'ishah said: 'Good women are the Anṣārī women. Shyness does not prevent them from learning about their faith'.

In hadith No. 556, 'Ā'ishah says to Umm Sulaym: 'Ugh to you'. This is a phrase that expresses disgust at what has been said. Al-Bājī said: It is meant here as a word of disapproval.

Transmission

The second hadith, No. 552, mentions the narrator as 'Abbās ibn al-Walīd. Some reporters of Muslim's anthology mention him differently, calling him 'Ayyāsh ibn al-Walīd. This is a clear mistake, due to the fact that in old writing, letters were not dotted and the difference between the two Arabic spellings is in this way. 'Ayyāsh ibn al-Walīd is not one from whom Muslim narrated anything, but al-Bukhārī does, while 'Abbās ibn al-Walīd is quoted by both al-Bukhārī and Muslim. The mistake is also due to the fact that both had fathers who had the same name and they lived in the same city, Basrah, and were contemporaries.

CHAPTER 8

DESCRIPTION OF MEN'S AND WOMEN'S SEMEN; A CHILD IS CREATED OF BOTH THEIR FLUIDS

[558–34]. (Dār al-Salām 0614) al-Ḥasan ibn ʿAlī al-Ḥulwānī narrated to me: Abū Tawbah (al-Rabīʿ ibn Nāfiʿ) narrated; Muʿāwiyah (meaning Ibn Sallām) narrated; from Zayd (meaning his brother) that he heard Abū Sallām say: Abū Asmā' al-Raḥabī narrated to me; that Thawbān, God's Messenger's *mawlā*, narrated to him: **'I was standing at God's Messenger's place when a Jewish rabbi came over. He said: "Peace be to you, Muhammad". I pushed him hard and he almost fell. He said: "Why are you pushing me?" I said: "Should you not address him as God's Messenger?" He said: "We only call him by the name his family gave him". The Prophet (peace be upon him) said: "My name which my family gave me is Muhammad". The Jew said: "I have come to ask you some questions". The Prophet said to him: "Will anything I tell benefit you?" He said: "I shall listen with my ears". The Prophet poked the earth with a short stick he had and said: "Put your question". The Jew said: "Where will people be on the day when the earth shall be changed into another earth as shall be the heavens?" The Prophet said: "They will be in the darkness below the bridge". He asked: "Who will be the first to cross?" The Prophet said: "The poor among the migrants". The Jew said: "What will be their gift when they enter Heaven?" The Prophet said: "The end of the whale's liver". He said: "What**

food will they have after that?" The Prophet said: "The ox of heaven who used to eat from its edges will be slaughtered for them". The Jew said: "What drink will they have with it?" The Prophet said: "They will drink from a spring called Salsabīl". The man said: "You have told the truth. I have come to ask you also about something that no one on earth knows except a prophet or one or two men". The Prophet said: "Will it benefit you if I tell you?" The man said: "I shall listen with my ears. I want to ask you about the creation of a child". The Prophet said: "Man's fluid is white and the woman's fluid is yellow. When they mix, if the man's semen is on top of the woman's fluid, they will have a male child by God's will. But if the woman's fluid is on top of the man's semen, they will have a female child by God's will". The Jew said: "You are right, and indeed you are a prophet". He then left.

'God's Messenger (peace be upon him) said: "This man has asked me these questions and I knew nothing about them, until God informed me".'

حَدَّثَنِي الْحَسَنُ بْنُ عَلِيٍّ الْحُلْوَانِيُّ، حَدَّثَنَا أَبُو تَوْبَةَ وَهُوَ الرَّبِيعُ بْنُ نَافِعٍ، حَدَّثَنَا مُعَاوِيَةُ، يَعْنِي ابْنَ سَلَّامٍ، عَنْ زَيْدٍ، يَعْنِي أَخَاهُ أَنَّهُ سَمِعَ أَبَا سَلَّامٍ، قَالَ: حَدَّثَنِي أَبُو أَسْمَاءَ الرَّحَبِيُّ، أَنَّ ثَوْبَانَ مَوْلَى رَسُولِ اللهِ صَلَّى اللهُ عَلَيْهِ وَسَلَّمَ حَدَّثَهُ قَالَ: كُنْتُ قَائِمًا عِنْدَ رَسُولِ اللهِ صَلَّى اللهُ عَلَيْهِ وَسَلَّمَ فَجَاءَ حِبْرٌ مِنْ أَحْبَارِ الْيَهُودِ فَقَالَ: السَّلَامُ عَلَيْكَ يَا مُحَمَّدُ فَدَفَعْتُهُ دَفْعَةً كَادَ يُصْرَعُ مِنْهَا فَقَالَ: لِمَ تَدْفَعُنِي؟ فَقُلْتُ: أَلَا تَقُولُ يَا رَسُولَ اللهِ، فَقَالَ الْيَهُودِيُّ: إِنَّمَا نَدْعُوهُ بِاسْمِهِ الَّذِي سَمَّاهُ بِهِ أَهْلُهُ. فَقَالَ رَسُولُ اللهِ صَلَّى اللهُ عَلَيْهِ وَسَلَّمَ: «إِنَّ اسْمِي مُحَمَّدٌ الَّذِي سَمَّانِي بِهِ أَهْلِي»، فَقَالَ الْيَهُودِيُّ: جِئْتُ أَسْأَلُكَ، فَقَالَ لَهُ رَسُولُ اللهِ صَلَّى اللهُ عَلَيْهِ وَسَلَّمَ: «أَيَنْفَعُكَ شَيْءٌ إِنْ حَدَّثْتُكَ؟» قَالَ: أَسْمَعُ بِأُذُنَيَّ، فَنَكَتَ رَسُولُ اللهِ صَلَّى اللهُ عَلَيْهِ وَسَلَّمَ بِعُودٍ مَعَهُ، فَقَالَ: «سَلْ» فَقَالَ الْيَهُودِيُّ: أَيْنَ يَكُونُ النَّاسُ يَوْمَ تُبَدَّلُ الْأَرْضُ غَيْرَ الْأَرْضِ وَالسَّمَاوَاتُ؟ فَقَالَ رَسُولُ اللهِ صَلَّى اللهُ

عَلَيْهِ وَسَلَّمَ: «هُمْ فِي الظُّلْمَةِ دُونَ الْجِسْرِ» قَالَ: فَمَنْ أَوَّلُ النَّاسِ إِجَازَةً؟ قَالَ: «فُقَرَاءُ الْـمُهَاجِرِينَ» قَالَ الْيَهُودِيُّ: فَمَا تُحْفَتُهُمْ حِينَ يَدْخُلُونَ الْجَنَّةَ؟ قَالَ: «زِيَادَةُ كَبِدِ النُّونِ»، قَالَ: فَمَا غِذَاؤُهُمْ عَلَى إِثْرِهَا؟ قَالَ: «يُنْحَرُ لَهُمْ ثَوْرُ الْجَنَّةِ الَّذِي كَانَ يَأْكُلُ مِنْ أَطْرَافِهَا» قَالَ: فَمَا شَرَابُهُمْ عَلَيْهِ؟ قَالَ: «مِنْ عَيْنٍ فِيهَا تُسَمَّى سَلْسَبِيلًا» قَالَ: صَدَقْتَ. قَالَ: وَجِئْتُ أَسْأَلُكَ عَنْ شَيْءٍ لَا يَعْلَمُهُ أَحَدٌ مِنْ أَهْلِ الْأَرْضِ إِلَّا نَبِيٌّ أَوْ رَجُلٌ أَوْ رَجُلَانِ. قَالَ: «يَنْفَعُكَ إِنْ حَدَّثْتُكَ؟» قَالَ: أَسْمَعُ بِأُذُنَيَّ. قَالَ: جِئْتُ أَسْأَلُكَ عَنِ الْوَلَدِ؟ قَالَ: «مَاءُ الرَّجُلِ أَبْيَضُ، وَمَاءُ الْـمَرْأَةِ أَصْفَرُ، فَإِذَا اجْتَمَعَا، فَعَلَا مَنِيُّ الرَّجُلِ مَنِيَّ الْـمَرْأَةِ، أَذْكَرَا بِإِذْنِ اللهِ، وَإِذَا عَلَا مَنِيُّ الْـمَرْأَةِ مَنِيَّ الرَّجُلِ، آنَثَا بِإِذْنِ اللهِ». قَالَ الْيَهُودِيُّ: لَقَدْ صَدَقْتَ، وَإِنَّكَ لَنَبِيٌّ، ثُمَّ انْصَرَفَ فَذَهَبَ. فَقَالَ رَسُولُ اللهِ صَلَّى اللهُ عَلَيْهِ وَسَلَّمَ: «لَقَدْ سَأَلَنِي هَذَا عَنِ الَّذِي سَأَلَنِي عَنْهُ، وَمَا لِي عِلْمٌ بِشَيْءٍ مِنْهُ، حَتَّى أَتَانِيَ اللهُ بِهِ»

[559–000]. (Dār al-Salām 0615) ʿAbdullāh ibn ʿAbd al-Raḥmān al-Dārimī narrated it to me: Yaḥyā ibn Ḥassān reported; Muʿāwiyah ibn Sallām narrated, with this chain of transmission: **The same text, except that [Thawbān] said: 'I was sitting at God's Messenger's, and [in reply to the question about the gift] said *'Zā'idat kabid al-Nūn'*, and said 'the child will be male' or 'female', instead of 'they will have a male or female child'**.

وَحَدَّثَنِيهِ عَبْدُ اللهِ بْنُ عَبْدِ الرَّحْمَنِ الدَّارِمِيُّ، أَخْبَرَنَا يَحْيَى بْنُ حَسَّانَ، حَدَّثَنَا مُعَاوِيَةُ بْنُ سَلَّامٍ فِي هَذَا الْإِسْنَادِ، بِمِثْلِهِ غَيْرَ أَنَّهُ، قَالَ: كُنْتُ قَاعِدًا عِنْدَ رَسُولِ اللهِ صَلَّى اللهُ عَلَيْهِ وَسَلَّمَ وَقَالَ: زَائِدَةُ كَبِدِ النُّونِ، وَقَالَ: أَذْكَرَ وَآنَثَ وَلَمْ يَقُلْ أَذْكَرَا وَآنَثَا.

Text Explanation

Al-Nawawī confines himself to explaining the words used in this hadith, as the dialogue needs no further comment; this is taken care of in the translation. However, he added as he explained the

Prophet's action of poking the earth with a short stick. It means that the Prophet drew lines on the ground, and this is normally an action by a person deep in thought. It shows that it is perfectly acceptable to do so, and that it does not detract from a person's status.

In reference to the spring which provides the dwellers of Heaven with their drink, al-Nawawī said: 'A number of linguists and commentators said that Salsabīl is the name of that water spring. Mujāhid and others said that it means that it flows speedily, and it is also said that it is soft, pleasant water'.

Transmission

Abū Asmā' al-Raḥabī is mentioned in the chain of transmission. His name is ʿAmr ibn Marthad and he belonged to Damascus. Abū Sulaymān ibn Zayd said: 'Abū Asmā' was from the Raḥabah, a village which is only one mile away from Damascus. I saw it and it was a flourishing place'.

CHAPTER 9

A BATH TO REMOVE THE STATE OF *JANĀBAH*

[560–35]. (Dār al-Salām 0616) Yaḥyā ibn Yaḥyā al-Tamīmī narrated: Abū Muʿāwiyah narrated; from Hishām ibn ʿUrwah; from his father; from ʿĀʾishah. She said: **'When God's Messenger (peace be upon him) took a bath to remove the state of major ritual impurity, he started by washing his hands, then he would pour water with his right hand over his left, washing his genital organ. He then performed the ablution, as he did for prayer. He then took water with his hand and penetrated with his fingers to wipe the ends of his hair. When he was sure that he had cleansed it, he would pour three handfills of water over his head, and would then pour water over all his body. He then washed his feet'**.

حَدَّثَنَا يَحْيَى بْنُ يَحْيَى التَّمِيمِيُّ، حَدَّثَنَا أَبُو مُعَاوِيَةَ، عَنْ هِشَامِ بْنِ عُرْوَةَ، عَنْ أَبِيهِ، عَنْ عَائِشَةَ، قَالَتْ: «كَانَ رَسُولُ اللهِ صَلَّى اللهُ عَلَيْهِ وَسَلَّمَ إِذَا اغْتَسَلَ مِنَ الْجَنَابَةِ يَبْدَأُ فَيَغْسِلُ يَدَيْهِ. ثُمَّ يُفْرِغُ بِيَمِينِهِ عَلَى شِمَالِهِ فَيَغْسِلُ فَرْجَهُ. ثُمَّ يَتَوَضَّأُ وُضُوءَهُ لِلصَّلَاةِ. ثُمَّ يَأْخُذُ الْمَاءَ فَيُدْخِلُ أَصَابِعَهُ فِي أُصُولِ الشَّعْرِ. حَتَّى إِذَا رَأَى أَنْ قَدِ اسْتَبْرَأَ حَفَنَ عَلَى رَأْسِهِ ثَلَاثَ حَفَنَاتٍ. ثُمَّ أَفَاضَ عَلَى سَائِرِ جَسَدِهِ. ثُمَّ غَسَلَ رِجْلَيْهِ»

[000–000]. (Dār al-Salām 0617) Qutaybah ibn Saʿīd and Zuhayr ibn Ḥarb narrated: both said: Jarīr narrated [H]. Also, ʿAlī ibn Ḥujr narrated; ʿAlī ibn Mushir narrated [H]. And Abū Kurayb narrated; Ibn Numayr narrated: all of them from Hishām, with this chain of transmission. **'Their narration does not include washing the feet'**.

وَحَدَّثَنَاهُ قُتَيْبَةُ بْنُ سَعِيدٍ، وَزُهَيْرُ بْنُ حَرْبٍ، قَالَا: حَدَّثَنَا جَرِيرٌ، ح، وَحَدَّثَنَا عَلِيُّ بْنُ حُجْرٍ، حَدَّثَنَا عَلِيُّ بْنُ مُسْهِرٍ، ح، وحَدَّثَنَا أَبُو كُرَيْبٍ، حَدَّثَنَا ابْنُ نُمَيْرٍ، كُلُّهُمْ عَنْ هِشَامٍ فِي هَذَا الْإِسْنَادِ، وَلَيْسَ فِي حَدِيثِهِمْ غَسْلُ الرِّجْلَيْنِ.

[561–36]. (Dār al-Salām 0618) Abū Bakr ibn Abī Shaybah narrated: Wakīʿ narrated; Hishām narrated; from his father; from ʿĀ'ishah: **'The Prophet took a bath to remove the state of major ritual impurity. He started by washing his hands three times. He then mentioned a similar narration to that of Abū Muʿāwiyah, but did not mention washing his feet'**.

وَحَدَّثَنَا أَبُو بَكْرِ بْنُ أَبِي شَيْبَةَ، حَدَّثَنَا وَكِيعٌ، حَدَّثَنَا هِشَامٌ، عَنْ أَبِيهِ، عَنْ عَائِشَةَ أَنَّ النَّبِيَّ صَلَّى اللهُ عَلَيْهِ وَسَلَّمَ «اغْتَسَلَ مِنَ الْجَنَابَةِ، فَبَدَأَ فَغَسَلَ كَفَّيْهِ ثَلَاثًا، ثُمَّ ذَكَرَ نَحْوَ حَدِيثِ أَبِي مُعَاوِيَةَ وَلَمْ يَذْكُرْ غَسْلَ الرِّجْلَيْنِ»

[562–000]. (Dār al-Salām 0619) ʿAmr al-Nāqid also narrated it: Muʿāwiyah ibn ʿAmr narrated; Zā'idah narrated; from Hishām, who said: ʿUrwah reported to me; from ʿĀ'ishah that: **'When God's Messenger (peace be upon him) took a bath to remove the state of major ritual impurity, he started by washing his hand before putting his hand in the water vessel. He then performed the ablution as he normally did for prayer'**.

وَحَدَّثَنَاهُ عَمْرٌو النَّاقِدُ، حَدَّثَنَا مُعَاوِيَةُ بْنُ عَمْرٍو، حَدَّثَنَا زَائِدَةُ، عَنْ هِشَامٍ، قَالَ: أَخْبَرَنِي عُرْوَةُ، عَنْ عَائِشَةَ: «أَنَّ رَسُولَ اللهِ صَلَّى اللهُ عَلَيْهِ وَسَلَّمَ كَانَ إِذَا اغْتَسَلَ مِنَ الْجَنَابَةِ بَدَأَ فَغَسَلَ يَدَيْهِ قَبْلَ أَنْ يُدْخِلَ يَدَهُ فِي الْإِنَاءِ. ثُمَّ تَوَضَّأَ مِثْلَ وُضُوئِهِ لِلصَّلَاةِ»

[563–37]. (Dār al-Salām 0620) ʿAlī ibn Ḥujr al-Saʿdī narrated to me:[i] ʿĪsā ibn Yūnus narrated to me; al-Aʿmash narrated; from Sālim ibn Abī al-Jaʿd; from Kurayb; from Ibn ʿAbbās: **'Maymūnah, my maternal aunt, narrated to me: I brought God's Messenger water for his bath to remove major ritual impurity. He washed his hands twice or three times, then he put his hand in the water vessel, taking water with his hand to pour over his genital organ which he washed with his left hand. He then struck the ground with his left hand and rubbed it hard. He performed the ablution as he did for prayer. He then poured on his head three fills of his cupped hands, then he washed the rest of his body. He then moved from his place and washed his feet. I brought him the towel but he gave it back'**.

وَحَدَّثَنِي عَلِيُّ بْنُ حُجْرٍ السَّعْدِيُّ، حَدَّثَنِي عِيسَى بْنُ يُونُسَ، حَدَّثَنَا الْأَعْمَشُ، عَنْ سَالِمِ بْنِ أَبِي الْجَعْدِ، عَنْ كُرَيْبٍ، عَنِ ابْنِ عَبَّاسٍ، قَالَ: حَدَّثَتْنِي خَالَتِي مَيْمُونَةُ، قَالَتْ: «أَدْنَيْتُ لِرَسُولِ اللهِ صَلَّى اللهُ عَلَيْهِ وَسَلَّمَ غُسْلَهُ مِنَ الْجَنَابَةِ، فَغَسَلَ كَفَّيْهِ مَرَّتَيْنِ أَوْ ثَلَاثًا، ثُمَّ أَدْخَلَ يَدَهُ فِي الْإِنَاءِ، ثُمَّ أَفْرَغَ بِهِ عَلَى فَرْجِهِ، وَغَسَلَهُ بِشِمَالِهِ، ثُمَّ ضَرَبَ بِشِمَالِهِ الْأَرْضَ، فَدَلَكَهَا دَلْكًا شَدِيدًا، ثُمَّ تَوَضَّأَ وُضُوءَهُ لِلصَّلَاةِ، ثُمَّ أَفْرَغَ عَلَى رَأْسِهِ ثَلَاثَ حَفَنَاتٍ مِلْءَ كَفِّهِ، ثُمَّ غَسَلَ سَائِرَ جَسَدِهِ، ثُمَّ تَنَحَّى عَنْ مَقَامِهِ ذَلِكَ، فَغَسَلَ رِجْلَيْهِ، ثُمَّ أَتَيْتُهُ بِالْمِنْدِيلِ فَرَدَّهُ»

[564–000]. (Dār al-Salām 0621) Muhammad ibn al-Ṣabbāḥ, Abū Bakr ibn Abī Shaybah, Abū Kurayb, al-Ashajj and Isḥāq narrated: all of them from Wakīʿ [H]. Also Yaḥyā ibn Yaḥyā and Abū Kurayb narrated: Abū Muʿāwiyah narrated; both from al-Aʿmash, with this chain of transmission: **'Their narration**

i. Related by al-Bukhārī, 249, 257, 259, 260, 265, 266, 274, 276 and 281; Abū Dāwūd, 245; al-Tirmidhī, 103; al-Nasāʾī, 253, 406, 416 and 417; Ibn Mājah, 467.

does not include pouring three handfulls over one's head. Wakī''s narration includes a full description of the ablution, including rinsing one's mouth and blowing one's nose. Abū Mu'āwiyah's narration does not mention the towel.'

وَحَدَّثَنَا مُحَمَّدُ بْنُ الصَّبَّاحِ، وَأَبُو بَكْرِ بْنُ أَبِي شَيْبَةَ، وَأَبُو كُرَيْبٍ، وَالْأَشَجُّ، وَإِسْحَاقُ، كُلُّهُمْ عَنْ وَكِيعٍ ح، وَحَدَّثَنَاهُ يَحْيَى بْنُ يَحْيَى، وَأَبُو كُرَيْبٍ، قَالَا: حَدَّثَنَا أَبُو مُعَاوِيَةَ كِلَاهُمَا عَنِ الْأَعْمَشِ بِهَذَا الْإِسْنَادِ، وَلَيْسَ فِي حَدِيثِهِمَا إِفْرَاغُ ثَلَاثِ حَفَنَاتٍ عَلَى الرَّأْسِ. وَفِي حَدِيثِ وَكِيعٍ وَصْفُ الْوُضُوءِ كُلِّهِ يَذْكُرُ الْمَضْمَضَةَ وَالِاسْتِنْشَاقَ فِيهِ. وَلَيْسَ فِي حَدِيثِ أَبِي مُعَاوِيَةَ ذِكْرُ الْمِنْدِيلِ.

[565–38]. (Dār al-Salām 0622) Abū Bakr ibn Abī Shaybah narrated: 'Abdullāh ibn Idrīs narrated; from al-A'mash; from Sālim; from Kurayb; from Ibn 'Abbās; from Maymūnah: **'The Prophet was brought a towel, but he did not touch it. He just shook the water off his body'**.

وَحَدَّثَنَا أَبُو بَكْرِ بْنُ أَبِي شَيْبَةَ، حَدَّثَنَا عَبْدُ اللهِ بْنُ إِدْرِيسَ، عَنِ الْأَعْمَشِ، عَنْ سَالِمٍ، عَنْ كُرَيْبٍ، عَنِ ابْنِ عَبَّاسٍ، عَنْ مَيْمُونَةَ: «أَنَّ النَّبِيَّ صَلَّى اللهُ عَلَيْهِ وَسَلَّمَ أُتِيَ بِمِنْدِيلٍ فَلَمْ يَمَسَّهُ وَجَعَلَ يَقُولُ: بِالْمَاءِ هَكَذَا يَعْنِي يَنْفُضُهُ»

[566–39]. (Dār al-Salām 0623) Muhammad ibn al-Muthannā al-'Anazī narrated:[i] Abū 'Āṣim narrated to me; from Ḥanẓalah ibn Abī Sufyān; from al-Qāsim; from 'Ā'ishah: **'When the Prophet wanted to take a bath to remove major ritual impurity, he would call for a [middle-sized] vessel of water and he would take water from it by his hand. He started with the right side**

i. Related by al-Bukhārī, 258; Abū Dāwūd, 240; al-Nasā'ī, 422.

of his head, then the left side. He would then take water with his two hands and pour it over his head'.

وَحَدَّثَنَا مُحَمَّدُ بْنُ الْمُثَنَّى الْعَنَزِيُّ، حَدَّثَنِي أَبُو عَاصِمٍ، عَنْ حَنْظَلَةَ بْنِ أَبِي سُفْيَانَ، عَنِ الْقَاسِمِ، عَنْ عَائِشَةَ، قَالَتْ: «كَانَ رَسُولُ اللهِ صَلَّى اللهُ عَلَيْهِ وَسَلَّمَ إِذَا اغْتَسَلَ مِنَ الْجَنَابَةِ، دَعَا بِشَيْءٍ نَحْوَ الْحِلَابِ فَأَخَذَ بِكَفِّهِ، بَدَأَ بِشِقِّ رَأْسِهِ الْأَيْمَنِ، ثُمَّ الْأَيْسَرِ، ثُمَّ أَخَذَ بِكَفَّيْهِ، فَقَالَ بِهِمَا عَلَى رَأْسِهِ»

Text Explanation

Scholars of our Shāfiʿī school of *fiqh* say that the perfect way to take a bath to remove the state of major ritual impurity, i.e. *janābah*, is to start by washing one's hands three times, before putting one's hand in the water vessel.[i] He should then wash his genital organ and remove what traces may be there or on the rest of his body. Then he should perform the complete ablution, as he does for prayer. One then puts one's fingers into the water, takes a handful of water and penetrates with his fingers through his hair, on both his head and beard. He then pours over his head three fills of his cupped hands and ensures that the water reaches covered and depression areas of his body such as armpits, navel, abdomen, buttocks, toes, etc. making sure that all these parts are washed. He then pours water three times over his head, and over all his body three times, rubbing with his hands whatever he can reach of his body. Water should reach all of his skin as well as through thick and light hair, and one should thoroughly wash one's hair. It is desirable to always begin with the right side and the top part of one's body, and also to take a position so that one is facing the *qiblah*. When finished, one should say: 'I bear witness that there is no deity other than God, the One God who has no partners, and I bear witness that Muhammad is God's servant

---

i. It should be remembered that generally speaking water was in short supply in Arabia during the Prophet's time. It was brought into homes from wells or springs and kept in barrels and vessels of different sizes. The Prophet always recommended economy in the use of water.

and Messenger'. It is important to form the intention to perform the *ghusl*, i.e. major ritual ablution or ritual bath, at the beginning and to be mindful of one's intention throughout. This is the perfect *ghusl*.

What is required as a duty in all of this is intention, from the first moment of touching the water, and to wash all of one's body and hair with water once. A condition of the validity of the ritual bath is to remove any impurity that might have attached to one's body. Everything else we have mentioned is a Sunnah, or recommended.

A person who is using a water vessel for his major ritual ablution should remember a subtle point that people may overlook: if one has gone to the toilet and washed the area before starting his bath, he should wash it again as part of his bath, or *ghusl*. If he does not do so straightaway, he may overlook washing it later. If he remembers, he will need to hold his organ and this invalidates his ablution. Otherwise, he needs to wrap his hand with something before holding his organ so as not to touch it, but God knows best. This is the view of our school and many other leading scholars.

The only scholars who say that rubbing one's body as one performs the ablution, whether *ghusl* or *wuḍū'*, is a duty are Mālik and al-Muzanī. Everyone else says that it is recommended or Sunnah, which means that if omitted, the act of cleansing is correct and valid. The only scholar who says that ablution is a duty when peforming the major ritual ablution is Dāwūd al-Ẓāhirī. All others say that it is a Sunnah. This means that if a person pours water over all his body, without doing the ablution, his *ghusl* is valid and sufficient for offering prayers, even though performing the ablution is better, whether it is done before or after the *ghusl*. If a person performs the ablution first, he should not repeat it at the end, for scholars are in agreement that it is not desirable to have two ablutions, but God knows best.

This is, in brief, all that needs be said about *ghusl* and how it is done. The hadiths in this chapter indicate most of what we have said. The rest is supported by well-known evidence.

The narrations attributed to 'Ā'ishah in both al-Bukhārī's and Muslim's anthologies suggest that the Prophet performed his ablution as he did for prayer, before pouring the water over all his body.

The apparent meaning is that he completed his ablution, washing his feet. The majority of narrations attributed to Maymūnah suggest that he performed the ablution then poured the water over his body and then moved and washed his feet. In one of her narrations, related by al-Bukhārī, she said that he performed the ablution as he did for prayer except washing his feet, then he poured the water over his body before moving his feet and washing them. This is a clear indication that washing one's feet is delayed to the end. Al-Shāfiʿī gives two views, the more authentic and better known of which is that one should start by completing one's ablution by washing one's feet. The other view is that one delays washing them. If we take this latter and weaker view, we interpret ʿĀ'ishah's narrations and most of Maymūnah's to mean that by saying 'as he performed the ablution for prayer' they meant 'most of the ablution, i.e. all except the feet'. This is what Maymūnah states in al-Bukhārī's version which is clear while the other reports allow interpretations that reconcile all narrations.

The well-known and correct way is to follow the numerous narrations stated by the Prophet's wives, ʿĀ'ishah and Maymūnah, and perform the ablution for prayer at the beginning. The apparent meaning of these narrations is that the ablution the Prophet did was complete. This was his practice on most occasions, and it was his normal habit. He would repeat washing his feet at the end to remove any mud attached to them, not as part of the *ghusl*. Thus, his feet would be washed twice and this is the best way that he normally did. The situation mentioned in al-Bukhārī's hadith narrated by Maymūnah took place on one or two occasions to indicate permissibility. This is the same as confirmed by how the Prophet performed his ablution, sometimes washing the required organs three times each, but also on occasions once only. The three times was the regular practice in most cases, because it is better, and the one time was done only rarely to show that it is permissible and adequate. There are numerous similar situations and practices by the Prophet, but God knows best.

The intention that precedes the ablution should be that of cleansing, except when a person is in a state of major ritual impurity without having gone to the toilet. In this latter case, the intention is that the ablution is performed as a Sunnah before *ghusl*, but God knows best.

The phraseology of these narrations suggests that when the Prophet put his wet fingers through his head, he wanted to wet his hair so that the water easily runs through it, and when he felt that he had done so, he would pour over his head three fills of his cupped hands. The hadiths mention that the Prophet hit the ground with his hand and rubbed it hard. This indicates that when we cleanse ourselves with water after going to the toilet, it is recommended that we wash our hands with fine soil, or cleansing material, or soap to make them absolutely clean.

Maymūnah mentions that she brought a towel to the Prophet but he gave it back to her. This suggests that it is desirable not to dry one's body with a towel of any material. Our scholars differ concerning drying one's body after ablution or *ghusl*, expressing five different views: 1) the best known view is that it is desirable not to dry one's body, but doing it is neither discouraged nor reprehensible; 2) to dry with a towel is reprehensible, i.e. *makrūh*; 3) it is permissible, which means that doing it or leaving it are the same. This is the view of our choice because to consider something desirable or undesirable needs clear evidence; 4) it is desirable because it is cleaner; and 5) it is discouraged in summer but not in winter. This is what our Shāfiʿī scholars have mentioned. The Prophet's companions and others expressed three views concerning drying one's body: 1) it is acceptable in both ablution and *ghusl*, which is the view of Anas ibn Mālik and al-Thawrī; 2) it is discouraged in both, which is the view of Ibn ʿUmar and Ibn Abī Laylā; and 3) it is discouraged for ablution but not *ghusl*, which is the view of Ibn ʿAbbās. Omitting drying one's body is mentioned in this hadith and in another authentic hadith that mentions that the Prophet took a bath and came out with his head dripping. That the Prophet dried himself is reported by a number of his companions, but these reports have chains of transmission suggesting they are lacking in authenticity. Al-Tirmidhī said: 'Nothing on this point is authentically reported from the Prophet'. Some scholars argue that drying is permissible on the basis that Maymūnah said in this hadith that the Prophet shook his hands and body to remove the water from his body. If shaking is permissible, using a towel to dry oneself is also permissible, because the two actions are for the same purpose, but God knows best.

Maymūnah mentioned the Prophet shaking water off with his arms. This suggests that doing so after ablution and *ghusl* is acceptable. Our scholars express different views, the best known of which is that it is undesirable but not discouraged. The second view is that it is discouraged and the third is that it is equally permissible to do so or not. This is the more correct view, but God knows best.

CHAPTER 10

HOW MUCH WATER FOR GHUSL; USING THE SAME VESSEL AND WATER BY MAN AND WOMAN

[567–40]. (Dār al-Salām 0624) Yaḥyā ibn Yaḥyā narrated:[i] I read out to Mālik; from Ibn Shihāb; from ʿUrwah ibn al-Zubayr; from ʿĀ'ishah: **'God's Messenger (peace be upon him) used to perform the *ghusl* to remove the state of major ritual impurity using a vessel, which is called *al-faraq*'**.

وَحَدَّثَنَا يَحْيَى بْنُ يَحْيَى، قَالَ: قَرَأْتُ عَلَى مَالِكٍ، عَنِ ابْنِ شِهَابٍ، عَنْ عُرْوَةَ بْنِ الزُّبَيْرِ، عَنْ عَائِشَةَ: «أَنَّ رَسُولَ اللهِ صَلَّى اللهُ عَلَيْهِ وَسَلَّمَ كَانَ يَغْتَسِلُ مِنْ إِنَاءٍ هُوَ الْفَرَقُ، مِنَ الْجَنَابَةِ»

[568–41]. (Dār al-Salām 0625) Qutabybah ibn Saʿīd narrated:[ii] Layth narrated [H]. Ibn Rumḥ narrated; al-Layth reported [H]. Also, Qutaybah ibn Saʿīd, Abū Bakr ibn Abī Shaybah, ʿAmr al-Nāqid and Zuhayr ibn Ḥarb narrated: They said: Sufyān narrated; both from al-Zuhrī; from ʿUrwah; from ʿĀ'ishah. She said: **'God's Messenger used to perform the *ghusl* using a water vessel, which is called *al-faraq*. I used to perform the *ghusl* with him using the same vessel'.**

In Sufyān's narration: 'from one vessel'. Qutaybah said: Sufyān said: '*Al-faraq* is equal to three *ṣā*ʿ*s*'.

i. Related by Abū Dāwūd, 238.
ii. Related by Ibn Mājah, 376.

حَدَّثَنَا قُتَيْبَةُ بْنُ سَعِيدٍ، حَدَّثَنَا لَيْثٌ، ح، وَحَدَّثَنَا ابْنُ رُمْحٍ، أَخْبَرَنَا اللَّيْثُ، ح، وَحَدَّثَنَا قُتَيْبَةُ بْنُ سَعِيدٍ، وأَبُو بكرِ بْنُ أَبِي شَيْبَةَ، وَعَمْرٌو النَّاقِدُ، وَزُهَيْرُ بْنُ حَرْبٍ قَالُوا: حَدَّثَنَا سُفْيَانُ كِلَاهُمَا عَنِ الزُّهْرِيِّ، عَنْ عُرْوَةَ، عَنْ عَائِشَةَ، قَالَتْ: «كَانَ رَسُولُ اللهِ صَلَّى اللهُ عَلَيْهِ وَسَلَّمَ يَغْتَسِلُ فِي الْقَدَحِ وَهُوَ الْفَرَقُ، وَكُنْتُ أَغْتَسِلُ أَنَا وَهُوَ فِي الْإِنَاءِ الْوَاحِدِ» وَفِي حَدِيثِ سُفْيَانَ مِنْ إِنَاءٍ وَاحِدٍ، قَالَ قُتَيْبَةُ: قَالَ سُفْيَانُ: «وَالْفَرَقُ ثَلَاثَةُ آصُعٍ»

[569–42]. (Dār al-Salām 0626) ʿUbaydullāh ibn Muʿādh al-ʿAnbarī narrated to me:[i] my father narrated: Shuʿbah narrated; from Abū Bakr ibn Ḥafṣ; from Abū Salamah ibn ʿAbd al-Raḥmān: **'I visited ʿĀ'ishah in the company of her brother-through-breastfeeding. He asked her about the Prophet's *ghusl* to remove the state of major ritual impurity. She called for a vessel that is close to one *ṣāʿ* and she performed the *ghusl*, with a screen between us and her. She poured water three times on her head. The Prophet's wives used to cut their hair so that it would be ear-length'**.

وَحَدَّثَنِي عُبَيْدُ اللهِ بْنُ مُعَاذٍ الْعَنْبَرِيُّ، قَالَ: حَدَّثَنَا أَبِي، قَالَ: حَدَّثَنَا شُعْبَةُ، عَنْ أَبِي بَكْرِ بْنِ حَفْصٍ، عَنْ أَبِي سَلَمَةَ بْنِ عَبْدِ الرَّحْمنِ، قَالَ: دَخَلْتُ عَلَى عَائِشَةَ أَنَا وَأَخُوهَا مِنَ الرَّضَاعَةِ. فَسَأَلَهَا عَنْ غُسْلِ النَّبِيِّ صَلَّى اللهُ عَلَيْهِ وَسَلَّمَ مِنَ الْجَنَابَةِ؟ «فَدَعَتْ بِإِنَاءٍ قَدْرِ الصَّاعِ فَاغْتَسَلَتْ وَبَيْنَنَا وَبَيْنَهَا سِتْرٌ وَأَفْرَغَتْ عَلَى رَأْسِهَا ثَلَاثًا» قَالَ: «وَكَانَ أَزْوَاجُ النَّبِيِّ صَلَّى اللهُ عَلَيْهِ وَسَلَّمَ يَأْخُذْنَ مِنْ رُءُوسِهِنَّ حَتَّى تَكُونَ كَالْوَفْرَةِ»

[570–43]. (Dār al-Salām 0627) Hārūn ibn Saʿīd al-Aylī narrated: Ibn Wahb narrated; Makhramah ibn Bukayr reported to me; from his father; from Abū Salamah ibn ʿAbd al-Raḥmān:

---

i. Related by al-Bukhārī, 251; al-Nasā'ī, 227.

'Ā'ishah said: **'When God's Messenger performed the *ghusl*, he would start with his right hand pouring water over it to wash it. He would then pour water with his right hand on any dirt on his body to wash it off with his left hand. When he had done that, he would pour water over his head'.**

'Ā'ishah added: 'I and God's Messenger (peace be upon him) used to perform the *ghusl* using water from one vessel, and both of us would be in a state of major ritual impurity'.

حَدَّثَنَا هَارُونُ بْنُ سَعِيدٍ الْأَيْلِيُّ، حَدَّثَنَا ابْنُ وَهْبٍ، أَخْبَرَنِي مَخْرَمَةُ بْنُ بُكَيْرٍ، عَنْ أَبِيهِ، عَنْ أَبِي سَلَمَةَ بْنِ عَبْدِ الرَّحْمَنِ، قَالَ: قَالَتْ عَائِشَةُ: «كَانَ رَسُولُ اللهِ صَلَّى اللهُ عَلَيْهِ وَسَلَّمَ إِذَا اغْتَسَلَ بَدَأَ بِيَمِينِهِ، فَصَبَّ عَلَيْهَا مِنَ الْمَاءِ، فَغَسَلَهَا، ثُمَّ صَبَّ الْمَاءَ عَلَى الْأَذَى الَّذِي بِهِ بِيَمِينِهِ، وَغَسَلَ عَنْهُ بِشِمَالِهِ، حَتَّى إِذَا فَرَغَ مِنْ ذَلِكَ صَبَّ عَلَى رَأْسِهِ»

قَالَتْ عَائِشَةُ: «كُنْتُ أَغْتَسِلُ أَنَا وَرَسُولُ اللهِ صَلَّى اللهُ عَلَيْهِ وَسَلَّمَ مِنْ إِنَاءٍ وَاحِدٍ وَنَحْنُ جُنُبَانِ»

[571–44]. (Dār al-Salām 0628) Muhammad ibn Rāfiʿ narrated to me: Shabābah narrated; Layth narrated; from Yazīd; from ʿIrāk; from Ḥafṣah bint ʿAbd al-Raḥmān ibn Abī Bakr (she was al-Mundhir ibn al-Zubayr's wife) that 'Ā'ishah reported to her that: **'She and the Prophet would perform the *ghusl* using one vessel that takes three *mudds*, or close to that'.**

وَحَدَّثَنِي مُحَمَّدُ بْنُ رَافِعٍ، حَدَّثَنَا شَبَابَةُ، حَدَّثَنَا لَيْثٌ، عَنْ يَزِيدَ، عَنْ عِرَاكٍ عَنْ حَفْصَةَ بِنْتِ عَبْدِ الرَّحْمَنِ بْنِ أَبِي بَكْرٍ، - وَكَانَتْ تَحْتَ الْمُنْذِرِ بْنِ الزُّبَيْرِ - أَنَّ عَائِشَةَ أَخْبَرَتْهَا: «أَنَّهَا كَانَتْ تَغْتَسِلُ هِيَ وَالنَّبِيُّ صَلَّى اللهُ عَلَيْهِ وَسَلَّمَ فِي إِنَاءٍ وَاحِدٍ، يَسَعُ ثَلَاثَةَ أَمْدَادٍ أَوْ قَرِيبًا مِنْ ذَلِكَ»

[572–45]. (Dār al-Salām 0629) ʿAbdullāh ibn Maslamah ibn Qaʿnab narrated:[i] Aflaḥ ibn Ḥumayd narrated; from al-Qāsim ibn Muhammad; from ʿĀʾishah: **'I used to perform the *ghusl* with God's Messenger (peace be upon him) using the same vessel, and we put our hands in it, [and that was] to remove the state of major ritual impurity'**.

حَدَّثَنَا عَبْدُ اللهِ بْنُ مَسْلَمَةَ بْنِ قَعْنَبٍ، قَالَ: حَدَّثَنَا أَفْلَحُ بْنُ حُمَيْدٍ، عَنِ الْقَاسِمِ بْنِ مُحَمَّدٍ، عَنْ عَائِشَةَ، قَالَتْ: «كُنْتُ أَغْتَسِلُ أَنَا وَرَسُولُ اللهِ صَلَّى اللهُ عَلَيْهِ وَسَلَّمَ مِنْ إِنَاءٍ وَاحِدٍ، تَخْتَلِفُ أَيْدِينَا فِيهِ مِنَ الْجَنَابَةِ»

[573–46]. (Dār al-Salām 0630) Yaḥyā ibn Yaḥyā narrated:[ii] Abū Khaythamah reported; from ʿĀṣim al-Aḥwal; from Muʿādhah; from ʿĀʾishah. She said: **'I used to perform the *ghusl* with God's Messenger using one vessel between me and him. He would beat me to it and I would say: "Leave some for me; leave some for me". She said: Both of us were in a state of major ritual impurity'**.

وَحَدَّثَنَا يَحْيَى بْنُ يَحْيَى، أَخْبَرَنَا أَبُو خَيْثَمَةَ، عَنْ عَاصِمٍ الْأَحْوَلِ، عَنْ مُعَاذَةَ، عَنْ عَائِشَةَ، قَالَتْ: «كُنْتُ أَغْتَسِلُ أَنَا وَرَسُولُ اللهِ صَلَّى اللهُ عَلَيْهِ وَسَلَّمَ مِنْ إِنَاءٍ بَيْنِي وَبَيْنَهُ وَاحِدٍ، فَيُبَادِرُنِي حَتَّى أَقُولَ: دَعْ لِي، دَعْ لِي. قَالَتْ: وَهُمَا جُنُبَانِ»

[574–47]. (Dār al-Salām 0631) Qutaybah ibn Saʿīd and Abū Bakr ibn Abī Shaybah narrated:[iii] both from Ibn ʿUyaynah. Qutaybah said: Sufyān narrated; from ʿAmr; from Abū al-Shaʿthāʾ; from Ibn ʿAbbās. He said: **'Maymūnah told me that she and the Prophet used to perform the *ghusl* using one vessel'**.

---

i. Related by al-Bukhārī, 261.
ii. Related by al-Nasāʾī, 238 and 412.
iii. Related by al-Tirmidhī, 62; al-Nasāʾī, 236; Ibn Mājah, 377.

وَحَدَّثَنَا قُتَيْبَةُ بْنُ سَعِيدٍ، وَأَبُو بَكْرِ بْنُ أَبِي شَيْبَةَ، جَمِيعًا عَنِ ابْنِ عُيَيْنَةَ، قَالَ قُتَيْبَةُ: حَدَّثَنَا سُفْيَانُ، عَنْ عَمْرٍو، عَنْ أَبِي الشَّعْثَاءِ، عَنِ ابْنِ عَبَّاسٍ، قَالَ: أَخْبَرَتْنِي مَيْمُونَةُ: «أَنَّهَا كَانَتْ تَغْتَسِلُ هِيَ وَالنَّبِيُّ صَلَّى اللهُ عَلَيْهِ وَسَلَّمَ فِي إِنَاءٍ وَاحِدٍ»

[575–48]. (Dār al-Salām 0632) Isḥāq ibn Ibrāhīm and Muhammad ibn Ḥātim narrated:[i] Muhammad ibn Bakr (Isḥāq said 'reported' and Ibn Ḥātim said 'narrated'); Ibn Jurayj reported; 'Amr ibn Dīnār reported to me saying: to the best of my knowledge and what is clear in my mind is that Abū al-Sha'thā' reported to me; that Ibn 'Abbās told him **'God's Messenger (peace be upon him) used to perform the *ghusl* with water left over by Maymūnah'**.

وَحَدَّثَنَا إِسْحَاقُ بْنُ إِبْرَاهِيمَ، وَمُحَمَّدُ بْنُ حَاتِمٍ، - قَالَ إِسْحَاقُ، أَخْبَرَنَا وَقَالَ ابْنُ حَاتِمٍ -، حَدَّثَنَا مُحَمَّدُ بْنُ بَكْرٍ، أَخْبَرَنَا ابْنُ جُرَيْجٍ، أَخْبَرَنِي عَمْرُو بْنُ دِينَارٍ، قَالَ: أَكْبَرُ عِلْمِي، وَالَّذِي يَخْطِرُ عَلَى بَالِي أَنَّ أَبَا الشَّعْثَاءِ، أَخْبَرَنِي أَنَّ ابْنَ عَبَّاسٍ، أَخْبَرَهُ: «أَنَّ رَسُولَ اللهِ صَلَّى اللهُ عَلَيْهِ وَسَلَّمَ كَانَ يَغْتَسِلُ بِفَضْلِ مَيْمُونَةَ»

[576–49]. (Dār al-Salām 0633) Muhammad ibn al-Muthannā narrated:[ii] Mu'ādh ibn Hishām narrated; my father narrated to me; from Yaḥyā ibn Abi Kathīr; Abu Salamah ibn 'Abd al-Raḥmān narrated; that Zaynab bint Umm Salamah narrated to him; that Umm Salamah narrated to her: **'She and God's Messenger (peace be upon him) used to perform the *ghusl* using one vessel to remove a state of major ritual impurity'**.

حَدَّثَنَا مُحَمَّدُ بْنُ الْمُثَنَّى، حَدَّثَنَا مُعَاذُ بْنُ هِشَامٍ، قَالَ: حَدَّثَنِي أَبِي، عَنْ يَحْيَى بْنِ أَبِي كَثِيرٍ، حَدَّثَنَا أَبُو سَلَمَةَ بْنُ عَبْدِ الرَّحْمَنِ، أَنَّ زَيْنَبَ بِنْتَ أُمِّ سَلَمَةَ حَدَّثَتْهُ، أَنَّ أُمَّ سَلَمَةَ

---

i. Related by al-Bukhārī, 253.
ii. Related by al-Bukhārī, 322 and 1929; Ibn Mājah, 380.

حَدَّثَتْهَا قَالَتْ: «كَانَتْ هِيَ وَرَسُولُ اللهِ صَلَّى اللهُ عَلَيْهِ وَسَلَّمَ يَغْتَسِلَانِ فِي الْإِنَاءِ الْوَاحِدِ مِنَ الْجَنَابَةِ»

[577–50]. (Dār al-Salām 0634) ʿAbdullāh ibn Muʿādh narrated:[i] my father narrated [H]. Also, Muhammad ibn al-Muthannā narrated; ʿAbd al-Raḥmān (meaning Ibn Mahdī) narrated; both said: Shuʿbah narrated from ʿAbdullāh ibn ʿAbdullāh ibn Jabr. He said: I heard Anas say: **'God's Messenger (peace be upon him) used to perform the *ghusl* with five *makkūks* and he performed the ablution with one *makkūk*'. Ibn al-Muthannā used a different plural form of *makkūk*, while Ibn Muʿādh said: 'from ʿAbdullāh ibn ʿAbdullāh' without mentioning Ibn Jabr**.

حَدَّثَنَا عُبَيْدُ اللهِ بْنُ مُعَاذٍ، حَدَّثَنَا أَبِي، ح، وَحَدَّثَنَا مُحَمَّدُ بْنُ الْـمُثَنَّى، حَدَّثَنَا عَبْدُ الرَّحْمَنِ يَعْنِي ابْنَ مَهْدِيٍّ قَالَا: حَدَّثَنَا شُعْبَةُ، عَنْ عَبْدِ اللهِ بْنِ عَبْدِ اللهِ بْنِ جَبْرٍ، قَالَ: سَمِعْتُ أَنَسًا، يَقُولُ: «كَانَ رَسُولُ اللهِ صَلَّى اللهُ عَلَيْهِ وَسَلَّمَ يَغْتَسِلُ بِخَمْسِ مَكَاكِيكَ وَيَتَوَضَّأُ بِمَكُّوكٍ» وَقَالَ ابْنُ الْـمُثَنَّى: بِخَمْسِ مَكَاكِيَّ، وَقَالَ ابْنُ مُعَاذٍ، عَنْ عَبْدِ اللهِ بْنِ عَبْدِ اللهِ وَلَمْ يَذْكُرِ ابْنَ جَبْرٍ.

[578–51]. (Dār al-Salām 0635) Qutaybah ibn Saʿīd narrated: Wakīʿ narrated; from Misʿar; from Ibn Jabr; from Anas: **'The Prophet used to perform the ablution with one *mudd* and the *ghusl* with one *ṣāʿ* up to five *mudds*'**.

حَدَّثَنَا قُتَيْبَةُ بْنُ سَعِيدٍ، حَدَّثَنَا وَكِيعٌ، عَنْ مِسْعَرٍ، عَنِ ابْنِ جَبْرٍ، عَنْ أَنَسٍ، قَالَ: «كَانَ النَّبِيُّ صَلَّى اللهُ عَلَيْهِ وَسَلَّمَ يَتَوَضَّأُ بِالْـمُدِّ، وَيَغْتَسِلُ بِالصَّاعِ، إِلَى خَمْسَةِ أَمْدَادٍ»

---

i. Related by al-Bukhārī, 201; Abū Dāwūd, 95; al-Tirmidhī, 609; al-Nasā'ī, 73, 229 and 344.

[579–52]. (Dār al-Salām 0636) Abū Kāmil al-Jaḥdarī and ʿAmr ibn ʿAlī narrated:[i] both from Bishr ibn al-Mufaḍḍal. Abu Kāmil said: Bishr narrated; Abū Rayḥānah narrated; from Safīnah: **'One *ṣāʿ* of water used to be sufficient for God's Messenger (peace be upon him) to perform the *ghusl* to remove the state of major ritual impurity, and one *mudd* was enough for his ablution'**.

وَحَدَّثَنَا أَبُو كَامِلٍ الْجَحْدَرِيُّ، وَعَمْرُو بْنُ عَلِيٍّ، كِلَاهُمَا عَنْ بِشْرِ بْنِ الْمُفَضَّلِ، قَالَ: أَبُو كَامِلٍ، حَدَّثَنَا بِشْرٌ، حَدَّثَنَا أَبُو رَيْحَانَةَ، عَنْ سَفِينَةَ، قَالَ: «كَانَ رَسُولُ اللهِ صَلَّى اللهُ عَلَيْهِ وَسَلَّمَ يُغَسِّلُهُ الصَّاعُ مِنَ الْمَاءِ مِنَ الْجَنَابَةِ، وَيُوَضِّئُهُ الْمُدُّ»

[580–53]. (Dār al-Salām 0637) Abū Bakr ibn Abī Shaybah narrated: Ibn ʿUlayyah narrated [H]. ʿAlī ibn Ḥujr narrated to me: Ismāʿīl narrated; from Abū Rayḥānah; from Safīnah (Abū Bakr added, the Prophet's companion). He said: **'God's Messenger used to perform the *ghusl* with one *ṣāʿ* and perform the ablution with one *mudd*'. In Ibn Ḥujr's narration: 'Or he might have said: one *mudd* was sufficient for his ablution'. He had grown old and I did not trust his narrations**.

وَحَدَّثَنَا أَبُو بَكْرِ بْنُ أَبِي شَيْبَةَ، حَدَّثَنَا ابْنُ عُلَيَّةَ، ح، وَحَدَّثَنِي عَلِيُّ بْنُ حُجْرٍ، حَدَّثَنَا إِسْمَاعِيلُ، عَنْ أَبِي رَيْحَانَةَ، عَنْ سَفِينَةَ قَالَ أَبُو بَكْرٍ صَاحِبُ رَسُولِ اللهِ صَلَّى اللهُ عَلَيْهِ وَسَلَّمَ - قَالَ: «كَانَ رَسُولُ اللهِ صَلَّى اللهُ عَلَيْهِ وَسَلَّمَ يَغْتَسِلُ بِالصَّاعِ وَيَتَطَهَّرُ بِالْمُدِّ» وَفِي حَدِيثِ ابْنِ حُجْرٍ، أَوْ قَالَ: وَيُطَهِّرُهُ الْمُدُّ، وَقَالَ: وَقَدْ كَانَ كَبِرَ وَمَا كُنْتُ أَثِقُ بِحَدِيثِهِ.

Text Explanation

Muslims are unanimous that the quantity of water that is sufficient to perform the ablution or the major ritual ablution, i.e. *ghusl*, is not

i. Related by al-Tirmidhī, 56; Ibn Mājah, 267.

specified. A small or large amount is appropriate if the condition of *ghusl* is met, which is that water runs over all one's body. Al-Shāfiʿī said: 'A person may use a small amount wisely and it will be sufficient and he may use a large amount unwisely and it will not be sufficient'. Scholars said: 'It is desirable that one does not use for the major ritual ablution less than one *ṣāʿ* or less than one *mudd* for ablution'. The *ṣāʿ* and the *mudd* were standard volume measures.[i] Scholars are unanimous that using water in an extravagant way is unacceptable, even if one is at the seashore. Perhaps it is more correct to say that it is only discouraged. Yet, some of our scholars say that extravagant use of water is forbidden, but God knows best.

That both man and wife should use one vessel for ablution, of either type, is permissible according to the unanimous view of all Muslims, based on the hadiths of the present chapter. For a woman to use the water left over by her husband for ablution is perfectly permissible, and this is also unanimous. For the man to use his wife's left over water for his ablution is also permissible according to our school, the Mālikī and Ḥanafī schools as well as the great majority of scholars, whether she was alone when using it or not. Some of our Shāfiʿī scholars say: 'No discouragement applies here, since some authentic hadiths mention it'. Ahmad ibn Ḥanbal and Dāwūd are of the view that if the woman is on her own when using the water, the man may not use what she has left of it. This is also reported to have been expressed by ʿAbdullāh ibn Sirjis and al-Ḥasan al-Baṣrī. Yet it is also reported that Ahmad expressed the same view as that of our Shāfiʿī school. It is also reported that al-Ḥasan and Saʿīd ibn al-Musayyib consider using the water left over by a woman to be discouraged in all cases. The view of choice is that expressed by the great majority of scholars based on these authentic hadiths, reporting that the Prophet used to do the cleansing, of both types of ablution,

i. Four *mudds* equal one *ṣāʿ* and the *ṣāʿ* is calculated to be approximately equal to 2.25 litres. These measures seem frugal for the purposes of ablution and *ghusl* but this seems to apply to the situation of minimum need, when water is very scarce. The Prophet perhaps wanted to show that even with such limited amounts, duties may be performed.

with any one of his wives, with each of them using what the other had left over, and there was no effect on whether the wife was on her own or not. It is also mentioned in another authentic hadith that he performed the *ghusl* using the water left over by one or other of his wives. This hadith is related by Abū Dāwūd, al-Tirmidhī and al-Nasā'ī as well as other Hadith scholars, with al-Tirmidhī stating that it is of the grade of good and authentic. A different hadith narrated by al-Ḥakam ibn 'Umar prohibits using a woman's left over water, but scholars give the following views on this: 1) this hadith is poor in authenticity, according to al-Bukhārī and other leading Hadith scholars; 2) it refers to the water dripping off her body, because it is used water; 3) the hadith merely states what is preferable, but God knows best.

The first two hadiths mention *al-faraq*, which was a type of water vessel with a capacity of three *ṣā*' which is approximately seven litres. It is clear that the Prophet used all types of water vessels for his ablution.

Hadith No. 569 quotes Abū Salamah ibn 'Abd al-Raḥmān mentioning that he visited 'Ā'ishah with her brother and she called for a vessel and performed the *ghusl* with a screen between her and them. *Qāḍī* 'Iyāḍ said: 'The apparent meaning is that they saw what she did washing her head and the top of her body, which is permissible to be seen by a relative whom she is forbidden to marry. One of them was her brother through breastfeeding, named 'Abdullāh ibn Yazīd, while Abū Salamah ibn 'Abd al-Raḥmān, the narrator of the hadith, was her nephew through breastfeeding, as he was breastfed when a child by her sister, Umm Kulthūm bint Abū Bakr … . Had they not seen this, her call for the water and performance of the *ghusl* in their presence would have been meaningless. She would have had to describe it for them. She put up the screen so that they could only see the top of her body, but God knows best'. What 'Ā'ishah did on this occasion clearly indicates that it is preferable to teach through action, because it is better than giving merely verbal description. Such action is better understood and longer retained in memory.

The same hadith mentions that the Prophet's wives used to have their hair cut short, so that it was only ear-length. *Qāḍī* ʿIyāḍ said: 'It is well known that Arab women used to have plaits and long hair. Perhaps the Prophet's wives did this after he had passed away because they no longer used makeup or kept long hair'. What *Qāḍī* ʿIyāḍ mentions of this being done only after the Prophet had passed away is correct. They could not have done it during his lifetime. It indicates that it is permissible for women to wear their hair short, but God knows best.

These hadiths mention different quantities of water used by the Prophet and his wives for performing the major ritual ablution, or *ghusl*. ʿĀ'ishah mentions that she and the Prophet performed the major ritual ablution using one vessel, and it held three *mudds*. In another hadith, she mentions that they both put their hands into the vessel. Commenting on the first of these narrations, *Qāḍī* ʿIyāḍ suggests two explanations, the first is that each of them used three *mudds* for the *ghusl*. Three *mudds* is a very small quantity, a little over 1.5 litres. The second explanation is that in this instance the *mudd* is meant as the *ṣāʿ*, and this would make the hadith consistent with that mentioning they used a vessel called *al-faraq*, which held three *ṣāʿ*s. It may also be that in some cases they used a small vessel that held three *mudds* and then refilled it when it became empty, but God knows best.

Various other ways are used to estimate the quantity of water the Prophet used for his ablution, including five *makkūks*. A *makkūk* is another name for the *mudd*. Imam al-Shāfiʿī and other scholars say: 'These reports may be reconciled as speaking of different situations and they describe the larger and smaller amounts of water the Prophet used for his cleansing. This clearly shows that there is no fixed quantity that must be used in ritual cleansing', but God knows best.

In the last hadith, No. 580, Muslim mentions in the chain of transmission: 'Abū Bakr added, the Prophet's companion'. The one who mentions this is Abū Bakr ibn Abī Shaybah. What Muslim means by stating this is that Abū Bakr ibn Abī Shaybah described Safīnah, and that the other narrator of this hadith, ʿAlī ibn Ḥujr, did not describe him as such, only mentioning his nickname.

The same hadith mentions what Safīnah reported about the Prophet's ablution, and adds the narrator's words: 'He had grown old and I did not trust his narrations'. This statement is by Abū Rayḥānah, and the one who grew old was Safīnah. Muslim did not mention this hadith as the main evidence, but he entered it by way of endorsement of the other hadiths, but God knows best.

Transmission

The chains of transmission mention Abū al-Sha'thā'. His name was Jābir ibn Zayd and he belonged to the Tābi'īn generation. Another narrator is 'Abdullāh ibn 'Abdullāh ibn Jabr, who is also mentioned as Ibn Jabr. This is all correct, although some leading scholars questioned this name and claimed that the correct form is Jābir, rather than Jabr. Indeed the objection is incorrect because the name is mentioned in both forms, Jabr and Jābir, and the full name of this narrator is 'Abdullāh ibn 'Abdullāh ibn Jābir ibn 'Atīk. Al-Bukhārī himself mentions both versions of his name and that Mus'ir, Abū al-'Umays, Shu'bah and 'Abdullāh ibn 'Īsā report him as Jabr.

Abū Rayḥānah's name is 'Abdullāh ibn Maṭar, but his name was also reported as Ziyād ibn Maṭar. Safīnah was a companion of the Prophet and his servant. It is said that his name was Mahrān ibn Farrūkh, but he is also said to be named Baḥrān, or Rawmān, or Qays, or 'Umayr, or Shanbah. His best known appellation is Abū 'Abd al-Raḥmān, but he is also known as Abu al-Bakhtarī. It is reported that he was given the nickname because he carried a great deal of luggage for some friends when they were going on jihad, and when the Prophet saw him doing this, he said to him: 'You are a *safīnah*', which means 'ship' or 'boat'.

CHAPTER 11

THE DESIRABILITY OF POURING WATER THREE TIMES ON ONE'S HEAD AND OTHER PARTS

[581–54]. (Dār al-Salām 0638) Yaḥyā ibn Yaḥyā, Qutaybah ibn Sa'īd and Abū Bakr ibn Abī Shaybah narrated:[i] Abū al-Aḥwaṣ (Yaḥyā said 'reported', but the other two said 'narrated'); from Abū Isḥāq; from Sulaymān ibn Ṣurad; from Jubayr ibn Muṭ'im. He said: '**People argued about the major ritual ablution in the Prophet's presence. Some of them said: "As for myself, I pour on my head and this and that". The Prophet (peace be upon him) said: "But as for myself, I pour on my head three handfuls"**.'

حَدَّثَنَا يَحْيَى بْنُ يَحْيَى، وَقُتَيْبَةُ بْنُ سَعِيدٍ، وَأَبُو بَكْرِ بْنُ أَبِي شَيْبَةَ، - قَالَ: يَحْيَى أَخْبَرَنَا وَقَالَ الْآخَرَانِ - حَدَّثَنَا أَبُو الْأَحْوَصِ، عَنْ أَبِي إِسْحَاقَ، عَنْ سُلَيْمَانَ بْنِ صُرَدٍ، عَنْ جُبَيْرِ بْنِ مُطْعِمٍ، قَالَ: تَمَارَوْا فِي الْغُسْلِ عِنْدَ رَسُولِ اللهِ صَلَّى اللهُ عَلَيْهِ وَسَلَّمَ. فَقَالَ بَعْضُ الْقَوْمِ: أَمَّا أَنَا فَإِنِّي أَغْسِلُ رَأْسِي كَذَا وَكَذَا. فَقَالَ رَسُولُ اللهِ صَلَّى اللهُ عَلَيْهِ وَسَلَّمَ: «أَمَّا أَنَا فَإِنِّي أُفِيضُ عَلَى رَأْسِي ثَلَاثَ أَكُفٍّ»

[582–55]. (Dār al-Salām 0639) Muhammad ibn Bashshār narrated: Muhammad ibn Ja'far narrated; Shu'bah narrated; from Abū Isḥāq; from Sulaymān ibn Ṣurad; from Jubayr ibn

i. Related by al-Bukhārī, 254; Abū Dāwūd, 239; al-Nasā'ī, 250 and 423; Ibn Mājah, 575.

Muṭʿim; from the Prophet that **'People mentioned the major ritual ablution in his presence. He said: "As for me, I pour [water] on my head three times".'**

وَحَدَّثَنَا مُحَمَّدُ بْنُ بَشَّارٍ، حَدَّثَنَا مُحَمَّدُ بْنُ جَعْفَرٍ، حَدَّثَنَا شُعْبَةُ، عَنْ أَبِي إِسْحَاقَ، عَنْ سُلَيْمَانَ بْنِ صُرَدٍ، عَنْ جُبَيْرِ بْنِ مُطْعِمٍ، عَنِ النَّبِيِّ صَلَّى اللهُ عَلَيْهِ وَسَلَّمَ أَنَّهُ ذُكِرَ عِنْدَهُ الْغُسْلُ مِنَ الْجَنَابَةِ فَقَالَ: «أَمَّا أَنَا فَأُفْرِغُ عَلَى رَأْسِي ثَلَاثًا»

[583–56]. (Dār al-Salām 0640) Yaḥyā ibn Yaḥyā and Ismāʿīl ibn Sālim narrated: both said: Hushaym reported; from Abū Bishr; from Abū Sufyān; from Jābir ibn ʿAbdullāh: **'The Thaqīf delegation asked the Prophet, and said: "Our land is cold. How do we do the major ritual ablution?" He said: "As for me, I pour on my head three times".'**

(Dār al-Salām 0641) Ibn Sālim said in his narration: 'Hushaym narrated; Abū Bishr reported: **"The Thaqīf delegation said: God's Messenger ...".**

وَحَدَّثَنَا يَحْيَى بْنُ يَحْيَى، وَإِسْمَاعِيلُ بْنُ سَالِمٍ قَالَا: أَخْبَرَنَا هُشَيْمٌ، عَنْ أَبِي بِشْرٍ، عَنْ أَبِي سُفْيَانَ، عَنْ جَابِرِ بْنِ عَبْدِ اللهِ، أَنَّ وَفْدَ ثَقِيفٍ سَأَلُوا النَّبِيَّ صَلَّى اللهُ عَلَيْهِ وَسَلَّمَ فَقَالُوا: إِنَّ أَرْضَنَا أَرْضٌ بَارِدَةٌ فَكَيْفَ بِالْغُسْلِ؟ فَقَالَ: «أَمَّا أَنَا فَأُفْرِغُ عَلَى رَأْسِي ثَلَاثًا»

قَالَ ابْنُ سَالِمٍ: فِي رِوَايَتِهِ حَدَّثَنَا هُشَيْمٌ، أَخْبَرَنَا أَبُو بِشْرٍ وَقَالَ: «إِنَّ وَفْدَ ثَقِيفٍ قَالُوا: يَا رَسُولَ اللهِ»

[584–57]. (Dār al-Salām 0642) Muhammad ibn al-Muthannā narrated:[i] ʿAbd al-Wahhāb (meaning al-Thaqafī) narrated; Jaʿfar narrated; from his father; from Jābir ibn ʿAbdullāh:

i. Related by Ibn Mājah, 577.

'When God's Messenger performed the major ritual ablution to remove the state of major ritual impurity, he would pour three handfuls of water over his head'. Al-Ḥasan ibn Muhammad said to him: 'I have much hair'. Jābir said: 'I said to him: my nephew, God's Messenger's hair was more plentiful and better than your hair'.

وَحَدَّثَنَا مُحَمَّدُ بْنُ الْمُثَنَّى، حَدَّثَنَا عَبْدُ الْوَهَّابِ يَعْنِي الثَّقَفِيَّ، حَدَّثَنَا جَعْفَرٌ، عَنْ أَبِيهِ، عَنْ جَابِرِ بْنِ عَبْدِ اللهِ، قَالَ: كَانَ رَسُولُ اللهِ صَلَّى اللهُ عَلَيْهِ وَسَلَّمَ إِذَا اغْتَسَلَ مِنْ جَنَابَةٍ صَبَّ عَلَى رَأْسِهِ ثَلَاثَ حَفَنَاتٍ مِنْ مَاءٍ » فَقَالَ لَهُ: الْحَسَنُ بْنُ مُحَمَّدٍ إِنَّ شَعْرِي كَثِيرٌ. قَالَ جَابِرٌ فَقُلْتُ لَهُ: يَا ابْنَ أَخِي «كَانَ شَعْرُ رَسُولِ اللهِ صَلَّى اللهُ عَلَيْهِ وَسَلَّمَ أَكْثَرَ مِنْ شَعْرِكَ وَأَطْيَبَ»

Text Explanation

The Prophet's companions argued about how the major ritual ablution, or *ghusl*, should be done. Some said it should be done in this way and others suggested another way. This makes clear that it is permissible to debate questions. It is also permissible for people of lesser rank to conduct such debate in the presence of one of higher rank, or for colleagues to debate in the presence of their leader or teacher.

The Prophet said that he poured on his head three handfuls of water. This means that each one was the fill of his two cupped hands. The hadith makes clear that it is desirable to pour water on one's head three times. This is agreed by all. Our scholars add that the same applies to the rest of the body, basing their argument on analogy with one's head and how the minor ritual ablution, i.e. *wuḍū'*, is done. Needless to say, washing three times is more important in the major ritual ablution than in the ordinary ablution. The latter is meant to be easy and it is done frequently. If it is recommended to wash one's parts three times in *wuḍū'*, then there is more reason to do the same in the major ritual ablution. We do not know of any different view except that the Chief Justice Abū al-Ḥasan al-Māwardī said that repeating is not recommended in *ghusl*. This view is abandoned. We spoke in the last chapter about the minimum that is needed in *ghusl*, but God knows best.

Transmission

The chain of transmission of the third hadith, No. 583 goes as follows: 'Yaḥyā ibn Yaḥyā and Ismāʿīl ibn Sālim narrated: Hushaym reported; from Abū Bishr; from Abū Sufyān; from Jābir'. At the end, Muslim says that Ibn Sālim said in his narration: 'Hushaym narrated; Abū Bishr reported'. This highlights an important point, which is one of the most interesting and subtle aspects of the study of Hadith transmission, and also reflects the richness of Muslim's knowledge and his sharpness. The point is that Hushaym is graded as 'misleading'. In the first narration, he reports 'from Abū Bishr'. When a misleading narrator reports 'from' his teacher, his narration is not accepted, unless his listening to that hadith from his teacher is confirmed in another way. Here, Muslim establishes the fact that Hushaym did so. This is clearly stated in Ibn Sālim's narration which states: 'Husaym narrated; Abū Bishr reported'. We have already highlighted such cases earlier. Abū Bishr's name is Jaʿfar ibn Iyās, and he is also called Jaʿfar ibn Abī Waḥshiyyah. Abū Sufyān's name is Ṭalḥah ibn Nāfiʿ, whose details we gave earlier.

CHAPTER 12

WOMEN'S PLAITS

[585–58]. (Dār al-Salām 0643) Abū Bakr ibn Abī Shaybah, ʿAmr al-Nāqid, Isḥāq ibn Ibrāhīm and Ibn Abī ʿUmar narrated:[i] all from Ibn ʿUyaynah. Isḥāq said: Sufyān reported; from Ayyūb ibn Mūsā; from Saʿīd ibn Abī Saʿīd al-Maqburī; from ʿAbdullāh ibn Rāfiʿ, Umm Salamah's *mawlā*; from Umm Salamah: I said: **'Messenger of God, I am a woman who tightens my hair plaits. Should I undo my hair when I do the major ritual ablution?' He said: 'No. It is sufficient that you pour three fills of your hands over your head, then pour water over your body and you have done your cleansing'**.

حَدَّثَنَا أَبُو بَكْرِ بْنُ أَبِي شَيْبَةَ، وَعَمْرٌو النَّاقِدُ، وَإِسْحَاقُ بْنُ إِبْرَاهِيمَ، وَابْنُ أَبِي عُمَرَ، كُلُّهُمْ عَنِ ابْنِ عُيَيْنَةَ - قَالَ إِسْحَاقُ: أَخْبَرَنَا سُفْيَانُ - عَنْ أَيُّوبَ بْنِ مُوسَى، عَنْ سَعِيدِ بْنِ أَبِي سَعِيدٍ الْمَقْبُرِيِّ، عَنْ عَبْدِ اللهِ بْنِ رَافِعٍ مَوْلَى أُمِّ سَلَمَةَ، عَنْ أُمِّ سَلَمَةَ، قَالَتْ: قُلْتُ يَا رَسُولَ اللهِ إِنِّي امْرَأَةٌ أَشُدُّ ضَفْرَ رَأْسِي فَأَنْقُضُهُ لِغُسْلِ الْجَنَابَةِ؟ قَالَ: «لَا. إِنَّمَا يَكْفِيكِ أَنْ تَحْثِي عَلَى رَأْسِكِ ثَلَاثَ حَثَيَاتٍ ثُمَّ تُفِيضِينَ عَلَيْكِ الْمَاءَ فَتَطْهُرِينَ»

[586–000]. (Dār al-Salām 0644) ʿAmr al-Nāqid narrated: Yazīd ibn Hārūn narrated [H]. ʿAbd ibn Ḥumayd narrated; ʿAbd al-Razzāq reported. Both said: al-Thawrī reported; from Ayyūb ibn Mūsā, with this chain of transmission. In ʿAbd al-Razzāq's narration: **'Should I undo my hair for [major ritual ablution**

i. Related by Abū Dāwūd, 251; al-Tirmidhī, 105; al-Nasāʾī, 241; Ibn Mājah, 603.

from] menstruation and major ritual impurity?' He said: 'No'. He then added the same meaning as the narration by Ibn ʿUyaynah.

وَحَدَّثَنَا عَمْرٌو النَّاقِدُ، حَدَّثَنَا يَزِيدُ بْنُ هَارُونَ، ح، وَحَدَّثَنَا عَبْدُ بْنُ حُمَيْدٍ، أَخْبَرَنَا عَبْدُ الرَّزَّاقِ، قَالَا: أَخْبَرَنَا الثَّوْرِيُّ، عَنْ أَيُّوبَ بْنِ مُوسَى، فِي هَذَا الْإِسْنَادِ. وَفِي حَدِيثِ عَبْدِ الرَّزَّاقِ فَأَنْقُضُهُ لِلْحَيْضَةِ وَالْجَنَابَةِ، فَقَالَ: «لَا.» ثُمَّ ذَكَرَ بِمَعْنَى حَدِيثِ ابْنِ عُيَيْنَةَ.

[587–000]. (Dār al-Salām 0645) Ahmad al-Dārimī narrated it to me: Zakariyyā' ibn ʿAdī narrated; Yazīd (meaning Ibn Zurayʿ) narrated; from Rawḥ ibn al-Qāsim; Ayyūb ibn Mūsā narrated; with this chain of transmission. He said: **'Should I undo it and wash it for major ritual impurity?' He did not mention menstruation.**

وَحَدَّثَنِيهِ أَحْمَدُ الدَّارِمِيُّ، حَدَّثَنَا زَكَرِيَّا بْنُ عَدِيٍّ، حَدَّثَنَا يَزِيدُ يَعْنِي ابْنَ زُرَيْعٍ، عَنْ رَوْحِ بْنِ الْقَاسِمِ، حَدَّثَنَا أَيُّوبُ بْنُ مُوسَى بِهَذَا الْإِسْنَادِ. وَقَالَ: أَفَأَحُلُّهُ فَأَغْسِلُهُ مِنَ الْجَنَابَةِ وَلَمْ يَذْكُرِ الْحَيْضَةَ.

[588–59]. (Dār al-Salām 0646) Yaḥyā ibn Yaḥyā, Abū Bakr ibn Abī Shaybah and ʿAlī ibn Ḥujr narrated:[i] all from Ibn ʿUlayyah. Yaḥyā said: Ismāʿīl ibn ʿUlayyah reported; from Ayyūb; from Abū al-Zubayr; from ʿUbayd ibn ʿUmayr: **'ʿĀ'ishah was informed that ʿAbdullāh ibn ʿAmr ordered women to undo their hair when taking a major ritual bath. She said: "How odd this Ibn ʿAmr is! He orders women to undo their hair when they take a bath. Would he order them to shave their heads? I used to take a bath together with God's Messenger**

i. Related by al-Nasāʾī, 414; Ibn Mājah, 604.

(peace be upon him), using one vessel, and I would do no more than pour three fills of my hands on my head".'

وَحَدَّثَنَا يَحْيَى بْنُ يَحْيَى، وَأَبُو بَكْرِ بْنُ أَبِي شَيْبَةَ، وَعَلِيُّ بْنُ حُجْرٍ، جَمِيعًا عَنِ ابْنِ عُلَيَّةَ، قَالَ يَحْيَى: أَخْبَرَنَا إِسْمَاعِيلُ ابْنُ عُلَيَّةَ، عَنْ أَيُّوبَ، عَنْ أَبِي الزُّبَيْرِ، عَنْ عُبَيْدِ بْنِ عُمَيْرٍ، قَالَ: بَلَغَ عَائِشَةَ، أَنَّ عَبْدَ اللهِ بْنَ عَمْرٍو يَأْمُرُ النِّسَاءَ إِذَا اغْتَسَلْنَ أَنْ يَنْقُضْنَ رُءُوسَهُنَّ. فَقَالَتْ: يَا عَجَبًا لِابْنِ عَمْرٍو هَذَا يَأْمُرُ النِّسَاءَ إِذَا اغْتَسَلْنَ أَنْ يَنْقُضْنَ رُءُوسَهُنَّ. أَفَلَا يَأْمُرُهُنَّ أَنْ يَحْلِقْنَ رُءُوسَهُنَّ، «لَقَدْ كُنْتُ أَغْتَسِلُ أَنَا وَرَسُولُ اللهِ صَلَّى اللهُ عَلَيْهِ وَسَلَّمَ مِنْ إِنَاءٍ وَاحِدٍ. وَلَا أَزِيدُ عَلَى أَنْ أُفْرِغَ عَلَى رَأْسِي ثَلَاثَ إِفْرَاغَاتٍ»

Text Explanation

The Prophet tells Umm Salamah, whose name was Hind, that it is sufficient that she should pour three handfuls of water over her head. This means the fill of her two hands when they are cupped together. The appropriate ruling on this point according to our school and the majority of scholars is that if the woman's plaits allow the water to reach all her hair, top and bottom, then she need not undo her plaits. If the water does not reach all her hair unless she undoes them, then she must undo them. The hadith is understood to mean that the water should wet all her hair without having to undo it. That all the hair should be wet with water is obligatory. It is reported that al-Nakhaʿī said that a woman must undo her hair in all situations. Al-Ḥasan and Ṭāwūs say that undoing a woman's hair is obligatory when she takes a bath after she finishes menstruation, but not for major ritual impurity. Our view is based on this hadith narrated by Umm Salamah. If a man has long hair and he makes it into a plait, the same ruling as for a woman applies to him, but God knows best.

It should be clear that the *ghusl*, or the major ritual ablution, is the same for both man and woman, whether it is to remove the state of major ritual impurity, or after menstruation, or at the end of postnatal discharge and other types of *ghusl* that is done for religious purpose. The only exception is that a woman taking a bath when her menstrual period or postnatal discharge is over is recommended to use a piece of cotton or wool, perfumed with musk, to apply to the place of discharge, so as to remove the remaining smell of blood. We have described how the *ghusl* is done in the previous chapter. However, if the woman is a virgin, she does not need to let the water inside her vagina, but if she is not a virgin, she should wash with water the area that appears when she sits at toilet, because the ruling concerning her apparent body applies to this area. This is stated by al-Shāfiʿī and the great majority of our scholars. However, a number of our scholars say that it is not obligatory for any woman to wash the inside of her vagina. Some say it is necessary to wash it after the period and postnatal discharge, but not for major ritual impurity. The first view is the correct one, but God knows best.

That ʿAbdullāh ibn ʿAmr ordered women to undo their hair may be understood that he meant to make it obligatory for them. This applies to hair that the water does not reach. Alternatively, it may be his view that undoing the hair is obligatory in all cases, as we have mentioned of al-Nakhaʿī's view. He might not have heard of the hadiths narrated by Umm Salamah or ʿĀ'ishah. It may also be that he ordered them to do so as something preferable, not obligatory, but God knows best.

CHAPTER 13

PURIFICATION WITH MUSK AFTER MENSTRUATION

[589–60]. (Dār al-Salām 0647) ʿAmr ibn Muhammad al-Nāqid and Ibn Abī ʿUmar narrated:[i] both from Ibn ʿUyaynah. ʿAmr said: Sufyān ibn ʿUyaynah narrated; from Manṣūr ibn Ṣafiyyah; from his mother; from ʿĀ'ishah: '**A woman asked the Prophet (peace be upon him) how she should take a bath after her menstruation. She mentioned that he taught her how to wash herself. "Then she takes a piece perfumed with musk and cleans herself with it". She said: "How do I purify myself with it". He said: "Purify yourself with it. All glory be to God!" He hid his face (Sufyān ibn ʿUyaynah pointed to his face with his hand). ʿĀ'ishah said: "I pulled her towards me, as I realized what the Prophet wanted. I said: 'Rub with it any traces of blood'. Ibn Abī ʿUmar said in his narration: I said: 'Rub with it all traces of blood'."**'

حَدَّثَنَا عَمْرُو بْنُ مُحَمَّدٍ النَّاقِدُ، وَابْنُ أَبِي عُمَرَ، جَمِيعًا عَنِ ابْنِ عُيَيْنَةَ، قَالَ عَمْرٌو: حَدَّثَنَا سُفْيَانُ بْنُ عُيَيْنَةَ، عَنْ مَنْصُورِ بْنِ صَفِيَّةَ، عَنْ أُمِّهِ، عَنْ عَائِشَةَ قَالَتْ: سَأَلَتِ امْرَأَةٌ النَّبِيَّ صَلَّى اللهُ عَلَيْهِ وَسَلَّمَ. كَيْفَ تَغْتَسِلُ مِنْ حَيْضَتِهَا؟ قَالَ: فَذَكَرَتْ أَنَّهُ عَلَّمَهَا كَيْفَ تَغْتَسِلُ. ثُمَّ تَأْخُذُ فِرْصَةً مِنْ مِسْكٍ فَتَطَهَّرُ بِهَا. قَالَتْ: كَيْفَ أَتَطَهَّرُ بِهَا؟ قَالَ: «تَطَهَّرِي بِهَا سُبْحَانَ اللهِ» وَاسْتَتَرَ – وَأَشَارَ لَنَا سُفْيَانُ بْنُ عُيَيْنَةَ بِيَدِهِ عَلَى وَجْهِهِ – قَالَ: قَالَتْ

---

i. Related by Abū Dāwūd, 314, 315 and 316; Ibn Mājah, 642.

عَائِشَةُ: وَاجْتَذَبْتُهَا إِلَيَّ وَعَرَفْتُ مَا أَرَادَ النَّبِيُّ صَلَّى اللهُ عَلَيْهِ وَسَلَّمَ. فَقُلْتُ: تَتَبَّعِي بِهَا أَثَرَ الدَّمِ وَقَالَ ابْنُ أَبِي عُمَرَ فِي رِوَايَتِهِ، فَقُلْتُ: تَتَبَّعِي بِهَا آثَارَ الدَّمِ.

[590–000]. (Dār al-Salām 0648) Ahmad ibn Sa'īd al-Dārimī narrated to me: Ḥabbān narrated; Wuhayb narrated; Manṣūr narrated; from his mother; from 'Ā'ishah: **'A woman asked the Prophet: "How do I take a bath for purifying myself?" He said: "Take a piece perfumed with musk and purify yourself with it".' He went on to narrate what is similar to the hadith narrated by Sufyān.**

وَحَدَّثَنِي أَحْمَدُ بْنُ سَعِيدٍ الدَّارِمِيُّ، حَدَّثَنَا حَبَّانُ، حَدَّثَنَا وُهَيْبٌ، حَدَّثَنَا مَنْصُورٌ، عَنْ أُمِّهِ، عَنْ عَائِشَةَ أَنَّ امْرَأَةً سَأَلَتِ النَّبِيَّ صَلَّى اللهُ عَلَيْهِ وَسَلَّمَ. كَيْفَ أَغْتَسِلُ عِنْدَ الطُّهْرِ؟ فَقَالَ: خُذِي فِرْصَةً مُمَسَّكَةً فَتَوَضَّئِي بِهَا ثُمَّ ذَكَرَ نَحْوَ حَدِيثِ سُفْيَانَ.

[591–61]. (Dār al-Salām 0649) Muhammad ibn al-Muthannā and Ibn Bashshār narrated:[i] Ibn al-Muthannā said: Muhammad ibn Ja'far narrated; Shu'bah narrated; from Ibrāhīm ibn al-Muhājir: **'I heard Ṣafiyyah narrating from 'Ā'ishah that Asmā' asked the Prophet about the bath necessary after menstruation. He said: "Any woman of you should take her water and *sidr* and perform the minor ritual ablution [i.e. *wuḍū'*]. She then pours water over her head and rubs it well so as to penetrate to the skin of her head. She then pours water over her body. Then she takes a piece of cotton, perfumed with musk, and purify herself with it". Asmā' said: "How does she purify herself with it?" The Prophet said: "All glory be to God! Purify yourself with it". 'Ā'ishah said (as though to keep it secret):**

i. Related by al-Bukhārī, 228; al-Tirmidhī, 125; al-Nasā'ī, 357; Ibn Mājah, 621.

"Follow the traces of blood". She then asked him about taking a bath to remove the state of major ritual impurity. He said: "She takes water and performs the ablution well, or complete, then pours water over her head and rubs it so as to reach the skin of her head. She then pours water over her body". ʿĀ'ishah said: "Good women are the Anṣār women. Modesty has not prevented them from learning about their religion".'

حَدَّثَنَا مُحَمَّدُ بْنُ الْـمُثَنَّى، وَابْنُ بَشَّارٍ، قَالَ ابْنُ الْـمُثَنَّى: حَدَّثَنَا مُحَمَّدُ بْنُ جَعْفَرٍ، حَدَّثَنَا شُعْبَةُ، عَنْ إِبْرَاهِيمَ بْنِ الْـمُهَاجِرِ، قَالَ: سَمِعْتُ صَفِيَّةَ، تُحَدِّثُ عَنْ عَائِشَةَ، أَنَّ أَسْمَاءَ سَأَلَتِ النَّبِيَّ صَلَّى اللهُ عَلَيْهِ وَسَلَّمَ عَنْ غُسْلِ الْـمَحِيضِ؟ فَقَالَ: «تَأْخُذُ إِحْدَاكُنَّ مَاءَهَا وَسِدْرَتَهَا، فَتَطَهَّرُ فَتُحْسِنُ الطُّهُورَ، ثُمَّ تَصُبُّ عَلَى رَأْسِهَا فَتَدْلُكُهُ دَلْكًا شَدِيدًا حَتَّى تَبْلُغَ شُؤُونَ رَأْسِهَا، ثُمَّ تَصُبُّ عَلَيْهَا الْـمَاءَ، ثُمَّ تَأْخُذُ فِرْصَةً مُمَسَّكَةً فَتَطَهَّرُ بِهَا» فَقَالَتْ أَسْمَاءُ: وَكَيْفَ تَطَهَّرُ بِهَا؟ فَقَالَ: «سُبْحَانَ اللهِ، تَطَهَّرِينَ بِهَا» فَقَالَتْ عَائِشَةُ: كَأَنَّهَا تُخْفِي ذَلِكَ تَتَبَّعِينَ أَثَرَ الدَّمِ، وَسَأَلَتْهُ عَنْ غُسْلِ الْجَنَابَةِ؟ فَقَالَ: «تَأْخُذُ مَاءً فَتَطَهَّرُ فَتُحْسِنُ الطُّهُورَ أَوْ تُبْلِغُ الطُّهُورَ، ثُمَّ تَصُبُّ عَلَى رَأْسِهَا فَتَدْلُكُهُ حَتَّى تَبْلُغَ شُؤُونَ رَأْسِهَا، ثُمَّ تُفِيضُ عَلَيْهَا الْـمَاءَ» فَقَالَتْ عَائِشَةُ: «نِعْمَ النِّسَاءُ نِسَاءُ الْأَنْصَارِ لَمْ يَكُنْ يَمْنَعُهُنَّ الْحَيَاءُ أَنْ يَتَفَقَّهْنَ فِي الدِّينِ»

[592–000]. (Dār al-Salām 0650) ʿUbaydillāh ibn Muʿādh narrated: my father narrated; Shuʿbah narrated; with this chain of transmission: a similar narration, but said: **the Prophet said: 'All glory be to God! Clean yourself with it', and he covered his face.**

وَحَدَّثَنَا عُبَيْدُ اللهِ بْنُ مُعَاذٍ، حَدَّثَنَا أَبِي، حَدَّثَنَا شُعْبَةُ فِي هَذَا الْإِسْنَادِ نَحْوَهُ، وَقَالَ: قَالَ: «سُبْحَانَ اللهِ، تَطَهَّرِي بِهَا وَاسْتَتَرَ»

[593–000]. (Dār al-Salām 0651) Yaḥyā ibn Yaḥyā and Abū Bakr ibn Abī Shaybah narrated: both from Abū al-Aḥwaṣ; from Ibrāhīm ibn Muhājir; from Ṣafiyyah bint Shaybah; from ʿĀ'ishah. She said: **'Asmā' bint Shakal came to the Prophet (peace be upon him) and said: "Messenger of God, how does a woman take a bath when her period is over?" He narrated the hadith, but did not mention the *ghusl* to remove major ritual impurity'**.

وَحَدَّثَنَا يَحْيَى بْنُ يَحْيَى، وَأَبُو بَكْرِ بْنُ أَبِي شَيْبَةَ، كِلَاهُمَا عَنْ أَبِي الْأَحْوَصِ، عَنْ إِبْرَاهِيمَ بْنِ مُهَاجِرٍ، عَنْ صَفِيَّةَ بِنْتِ شَيْبَةَ، عَنْ عَائِشَةَ، قَالَتْ: دَخَلَتْ أَسْمَاءُ بِنْتُ شَكَلٍ عَلَى رَسُولِ اللهِ صَلَّى اللهُ عَلَيْهِ وَسَلَّمَ. فَقَالَتْ: يَا رَسُولَ اللهِ، كَيْفَ تَغْتَسِلُ إِحْدَانَا إِذَا طَهُرَتْ مِنَ الْحَيْضِ؟ وَسَاقَ الْحَدِيثَ وَلَمْ يَذْكُرْ فِيهِ غُسْلَ الْجَنَابَةِ.

Text Explanation

In the previous chapter we explained in full that the major ritual ablution, or *ghusl*, is the same for both men and women. In this chapter, the emphasis is on a woman taking a bath at the end of her menstruation period and how it is recommended she use a small amount of musk, putting it on a piece of cotton, or cloth, so as to wipe her vagina with it after she has taken her bath. The same applies to a woman who is cleansing herself after the end of her postnatal discharge, because their discharge is of the same nature. Al-Maḥāmilī, a scholar of our school, mentions in his book, *al-Muqni*ʿ, that a woman taking a bath after her menstrual or postnatal period is recommended to perfume all parts of her body where the blood fell at one point or another. What he mentions of its application to all parts where blood fell is strange, I have researched this but did not find anyone sharing this view.

Scholars differ as to the purpose of using musk. The correct view, to which most scholars of our and other schools subscribe, is that it is to remove the bad odour and give the area a more pleasant smell. Al-

Māwardī, of our school, mentions two alternative reasons: the first is what we have just mentioned, while the second is that it facilitates conception. If we take the first view and musk is unavailable, then whatever gives a good smell is good enough. If we take the second view, then anything that helps conception may be used. He added that scholars differ as to the time when musk is to be used. The ones who claim that the purpose is to give a pleasant smell say that the musk should be used after the bath, while those who opt for the second purpose say it should be used before taking the bath. This is what al-Māwardī said, but what he said about using the musk before the bath should be disounted. The third hadith in this chapter, No. 591, clearly states that the musk should be used after the bath.

The suggestion that the purpose of using musk is to facilitate conception has no strong foundation. Had it been correct, it should have been limited to a woman whose husband was present and expected to have intercourse with her soon. This is not suggested by anyone we know. Indeed, the general drift of the hadiths is enough to refute this suggestion. The correct purpose is to clean the area and remove the bad smell. It should be used after the bath and is desirable for every woman who takes such a bath, whether married or unmarried. If she does not find musk, then any perfume is good enough. If this is also unavailable to her, she may use anything that removes the bad smell. If not, then water is sufficient. However, if she can use some perfume and she does not, her action, or lack of it, is discouraged. If she has none, no reprehension applies to her, but God knows best.

When the Anṣārī lady asked the Prophet how she should clean herself with the piece of cotton, he said: 'All glory be to God! Clean yourself with it'. The Arabic equivalent of 'all glory be to God' is *subḥān Allah.* In such a situation, it is said as an exclamatory sentence. Another sentence that is similarly used is *lā ilāh illā Allāh,* which means 'there is no deity other than God'. Such usage is perfectly appropriate. In such a case as the hadith mentions, it means that the matter is so clear that it does not need a thought. Thus, to utter a glorification of God to express surprise or exclamation and also to express certainty of something is acceptable. The hadith also indicates the desirability of using figurative speech when referring to private parts, but God knows best.

ʿĀ'ishah explains to the questioner that she should 'follow the traces of blood' with the perfumed piece of cotton. The majority of scholars say that this is a reference to the place of discharge of the menstruation blood. We mentioned earlier al-Maḥāmilī's view that she should perfume every spot of her body touched by blood. The wording of the hadith gives some endorsement of this view.

In hadith No. 591, the Prophet gives this description of how to perform the major ritual ablution: 'Any woman of you should take her water and *sidr* and perform the complete ablution. She then pours water over her head and rubs it well so as to penetrate to the skin of her head. She then pours water over her body'. The wording of the hadith admits more than one interpretation. The Prophet actually said: 'perform her purification well and complete'. *Qāḍī* ʿIyāḍ said: 'This refers to removing any impurity and any blood left on her body'. This is his view. However, the clearer meaning—but God knows best—is that it means that she performs a complete *wuḍū'*, as this was mentioned in describing his *ghusl*. We mentioned earlier that 'doing the ablution well' means making it complete and doing all its parts well.

ʿĀ'ishah explained it to the questioner, speaking to her in a whisper, so that no one else could hear her. In his book on unmentioned names, al-Khaṭīb al-Baghdādī mentions that the woman who asked the Prophet was Asmā' bint Yazīd ibn al-Sakan. She was known as the 'women's orator', as she often put their case to the Prophet.

CHAPTER 14

WOMEN'S PROLONGED BLEEDING AND ITS EFFECT ON PRAYER

[594–62]. (Dār al-Salām 0652) Abū Bakr ibn Abī Shaybah and Abū Kurayb narrated:[i] Wakīʿ narrated; from Hishām ibn ʿUrwah; from his father; from ʿĀʾishah. She said: ʻ**Fāṭimah bint Abī Ḥubaysh came to the Prophet. She said: "Messenger of God, I am a woman who continues in menstruation without an end. Am I to leave off prayer?" The Prophet said: "No. This is [haemorrhage from] a blood vessel, not menstruation. When your period comes, stop praying, and when it is over, wash the blood off yourself and resume praying"**.ʼ

وَحَدَّثَنَا أَبُو بَكْرِ بْنُ أَبِي شَيْبَةَ، وَأَبُو كُرَيْبٍ، قَالَا: حَدَّثَنَا وَكِيعٌ، عَنْ هِشَامِ بْنِ عُرْوَةَ، عَنْ أَبِيهِ، عَنْ عَائِشَةَ قَالَتْ، جَاءَتْ فَاطِمَةُ بِنْتُ أَبِي حُبَيْشٍ، إِلَى النَّبِيِّ صَلَّى اللهُ عَلَيْهِ وَسَلَّمَ فَقَالَتْ: يَا رَسُولَ اللهِ، إِنِّي امْرَأَةٌ أُسْتَحَاضُ فَلَا أَطْهُرُ. أَفَأَدَعُ الصَّلَاةَ؟ فَقَالَ: «لَا. إِنَّمَا ذَلِكِ عِرْقٌ وَلَيْسَ بِالْحَيْضَةِ فَإِذَا أَقْبَلَتِ الْحَيْضَةُ فَدَعِي الصَّلَاةَ، وَإِذَا أَدْبَرَتْ فَاغْسِلِي عَنْكِ الدَّمَ وَصَلِّي»

[595–000]. (Dār al-Salām 0653) Yaḥyā ibn Yaḥyā narrated:[ii] ʿAbd al-ʿAzīz ibn Muhammad and Abū Muʿāwiyah reported [H]. Qutaybah ibn Saʿīd narrated; Jarīr narrated [H]. Also, Ibn

i. Related by al-Bukhārī, 228; al-Tirmidhī, 125; al-Nasāʾī, 357; Ibn Mājah, 621.

ii. The version by Khalaf ibn Hishām is related by al-Nasāʾī, 217 and 362; Ibn Mājah, 621. The version by Abū Muʿāwiyah is related by al-Bukhārī, 228; al-Tirmidhī, 125; al-Nasāʾī, 212 and 257.

Numayr narrated; my father narrated [H]. Further, Khalaf ibn Hishām narrated; Ḥammād ibn Zayd narrated. All of them from Hishām ibn ʿUrwah: The same as Wakīʿ's narration and his chain of transmission. **In Qutaybah's narration from Jarīr: 'Fāṭimah bint Abī Ḥubaysh ibn 'Abd al-Muṭṭalib ibn Asad came to the Prophet. She is one of our women ...' And in Ḥammād's narration a word is added, but we have left it out.**

حَدَّثَنَا يَحْيَى بْنُ يَحْيَى، أَخْبَرَنَا عَبْدُ الْعَزِيزِ بْنُ مُحَمَّدٍ، وَأَبُو مُعَاوِيَةَ ح، وَحَدَّثَنَا قُتَيْبَةُ بْنُ سَعِيدٍ، حَدَّثَنَا جَرِيرٌ ح، وَحَدَّثَنَا ابْنُ نُمَيْرٍ، حَدَّثَنَا أَبِي ح، وَحَدَّثَنَا خَلَفُ بْنُ هِشَامٍ، حَدَّثَنَا حَمَّادُ بْنُ زَيْدٍ، كُلُّهُمْ عَنْ هِشَامِ بْنِ عُرْوَةَ، بِمِثْلِ حَدِيثِ وَكِيعٍ، وَإِسْنَادِهِ. وَفِي حَدِيثِ قُتَيْبَةَ، عَنْ جَرِيرٍ جَاءَتْ فَاطِمَةُ بِنْتُ أَبِي حُبَيْشِ بْنِ عَبْدِ الْمُطَّلِبِ بْنِ أَسَدٍ وَهِيَ امْرَأَةٌ مِنَّا، قَالَ: وَفِي حَدِيثِ حَمَّادِ بْنِ زَيْدٍ زِيَادَةُ حَرْفٍ تَرَكْنَا ذِكْرَهُ.

[596–63]. (Dār al-Salām 0654) Qutaybah ibn Saʿīd narrated:[i] Layth narrated [H]. Also, Muhammad ibn Rumḥ narrated; al-Layth narrated; from Ibn Shihāb; from ʿUrwah; from ʿĀ'ishah. She said: **'Umm Ḥabībah bint Jaḥsh requested a ruling from God's Messenger (peace be upon him). She said to him: "I have a prolonged period'. He said: "That is only haemorrhage from a blood vessel. Take a bath and then offer your prayers". She used to take a bath before every prayer'.**

Al-Layth ibn Saʿd said: **'Ibn Shihāb did not mention that God's Messenger (peace be upon him) ordered Umm Ḥabībah bint Jaḥsh to take a bath before every prayer, but this was something of her own initiative, which she did. Ibn Rumḥ only said in his narration, 'Bint Jaḥsh' without mentioning 'Umm Ḥabībah' before it.**

i. Related by Abū Dāwūd, 290; al-Tirmidhī, 129; al-Nasā'ī, 206 and 350.

حَدَّثَنَا قُتَيْبَةُ بْنُ سَعِيدٍ، حَدَّثَنَا لَيْثٌ، ح، وَحَدَّثَنَا مُحَمَّدُ بْنُ رُمْحٍ، أَخْبَرَنَا اللَّيْثُ، عَنِ ابْنِ شِهَابٍ، عَنْ عُرْوَةَ، عَنْ عَائِشَةَ، أَنَّهَا قَالَتْ: اسْتَفْتَتْ أُمُّ حَبِيبَةَ بِنْتُ جَحْشٍ رَسُولَ اللهِ صَلَّى اللهُ عَلَيْهِ وَسَلَّمَ فَقَالَتْ: إِنِّي أُسْتَحَاضُ فَقَالَ: «إِنَّمَا ذَلِكِ عِرْقٌ فَاغْتَسِلِي ثُمَّ صَلِّي» فَكَانَتْ تَغْتَسِلُ عِنْدَ كُلِّ صَلَاةٍ.

قَالَ اللَّيْثُ بْنُ سَعْدٍ: «لَمْ يَذْكُرِ ابْنُ شِهَابٍ، أَنَّ رَسُولَ اللهِ صَلَّى اللهُ عَلَيْهِ وَسَلَّمَ أَمَرَ أُمَّ حَبِيبَةَ بِنْتَ جَحْشٍ أَنْ تَغْتَسِلَ عِنْدَ كُلِّ صَلَاةٍ وَلَكِنَّهُ شَيْءٌ فَعَلَتْهُ هِيَ»، وَقَالَ ابْنُ رُمْحٍ فِي رِوَايَتِهِ ابْنَةُ جَحْشٍ وَلَمْ يَذْكُرْ أُمَّ حَبِيبَةَ.

[597–64]. (Dār al-Salām 0655) Muhammad ibn Salamah al-Murādī narrated:[i] ʿAbdullāh ibn Wahb narrated; from ʿAmr ibn al-Ḥārith; from Ibn Shihāb; from ʿUrwah ibn al-Zubayr and ʿAmrah bint ʿAbd al-Raḥmān; from ʿĀʾishah, the Prophet's wife: **'Umm Ḥabībah bint Jaḥsh (God's Messenger's sister-in-law and ʿAbd al-Raḥmān ibn ʿAwf's wife) continued to have a discharge for seven years. She asked God's Messenger about this. He said: "This is not menstruation, but haemorrhage from a blood vessel. Wash yourself and pray".'**

ʿĀʾishah said: **'She used to perform the *ghusl* using a tub in Zaynab's, her sister's compartment, and the water would become red because of the blood'.**

Ibn Shihāb said: **'I narrated this to Abū Bakr ibn ʿAbd al-Raḥmān ibn al-Ḥārith ibn Hishām. He said: "May God bestow mercy on Hind. Would that Hind had heard this fatwa. By God, she used to cry, because she did not pray".'**

وَحَدَّثَنَا مُحَمَّدُ بْنُ سَلَمَةَ الْمُرَادِيُّ، حَدَّثَنَا عَبْدُ اللهِ بْنُ وَهْبٍ، عَنْ عَمْرِو بْنِ الْحَارِثِ، عَنِ ابْنِ شِهَابٍ، عَنْ عُرْوَةَ بْنِ الزُّبَيْرِ، وَعَمْرَةَ بِنْتِ عَبْدِ الرَّحْمَنِ، عَنْ عَائِشَةَ، زَوْجِ

i. Related by al-Bukhārī, 327; Abū Dāwūd, 285; al-Nasāʾī, 203, 204 and 205; Ibn Mājah, 626.

النَّبِيِّ صَلَّى اللهُ عَلَيْهِ وَسَلَّمَ أَنَّ أُمَّ حَبِيبَةَ بِنْتَ جَحْشٍ - خَتَنَةَ رَسُولِ اللهِ صَلَّى اللهُ عَلَيْهِ وَسَلَّمَ وَتَحْتَ عَبْدِ الرَّحْمَنِ بْنِ عَوْفٍ - اسْتُحِيضَتْ سَبْعَ سِنِينَ. فَاسْتَفْتَتْ رَسُولَ اللهِ صَلَّى اللهُ عَلَيْهِ وَسَلَّمَ فِي ذَلِكَ. فَقَالَ رَسُولُ اللهِ صَلَّى اللهُ عَلَيْهِ وَسَلَّمَ: «إِنَّ هَذِهِ لَيْسَتْ بِالْحَيْضَةِ وَلَكِنَّ هَذَا عِرْقٌ فَاغْتَسِلِي وَصَلِّي»

قَالَتْ عَائِشَةُ: «فَكَانَتْ تَغْتَسِلُ فِي مِرْكَنٍ فِي حُجْرَةِ أُخْتِهَا زَيْنَبَ بِنْتِ جَحْشٍ حَتَّى تَعْلُوَ حُمْرَةُ الدَّمِ الْمَاءَ»

قَالَ ابْنُ شِهَابٍ: فَحَدَّثْتُ بِذَلِكَ أَبَا بَكْرِ بْنَ عَبْدِ الرَّحْمَنِ بْنِ الْحَارِثِ بْنِ هِشَامٍ، فَقَالَ: «يَرْحَمُ اللهُ هِنْدًا لَوْ سَمِعَتْ بِهَذِهِ الْفُتْيَا وَاللهِ إِنْ كَانَتْ لَتَبْكِي لِأَنَّهَا كَانَتْ لَا تُصَلِّي»

[598–000]. (Dār al-Salām 0656) Abū ʿImrān Muhammad ibn Jaʿfar ibn Ziyād narrated to me: Ibrāhīm (meaning Ibn Saʿd) reported; from Ibn Shihāb; from ʿAmrah bint ʿAbd al-Raḥmān; from ʿĀ'ishah: **'Umm Ḥabībah bint Jaḥsh came to see God's Messenger (peace be upon him). She used to bleed for seven years. She added the same as the narration of ʿAmr ibn al-Ḥārith, up to "the water would become red because of the blood", but did not mention what came after that'**.

وَحَدَّثَنِي أَبُو عِمْرَانَ مُحَمَّدُ بْنُ جَعْفَرِ بْنِ زِيَادٍ، أَخْبَرَنَا إِبْرَاهِيمُ يَعْنِي ابْنَ سَعْدٍ، عَنِ ابْنِ شِهَابٍ، عَنْ عَمْرَةَ بِنْتِ عَبْدِ الرَّحْمَنِ، عَنْ عَائِشَةَ، قَالَتْ: جَاءَتْ أُمُّ حَبِيبَةَ بِنْتُ جَحْشٍ إِلَى رَسُولِ اللهِ صَلَّى اللهُ عَلَيْهِ وَسَلَّمَ، وَكَانَتِ اسْتُحِيضَتْ سَبْعَ سِنِينَ. بِمِثْلِ حَدِيثِ عَمْرِو بْنِ الْحَارِثِ إِلَى قَوْلِهِ: تَعْلُوَ حُمْرَةُ الدَّمِ الْمَاءَ وَلَمْ يَذْكُرْ مَا بَعْدَهُ.

[599–000]. (Dār al-Salām 0657) Muhammad ibn al-Muthannā narrated to me: Sufyān ibn ʿUyaynah narrated; from al-Zuhrī; from ʿAmrah; from ʿĀ'ishah that: **Bint Jaḥsh continued to bleed for seven years, adding a similar hadith**.

وَحَدَّثَنِي مُحَمَّدُ بْنُ الْـمُثَنَّى، حَدَّثَنَا سُفْيَانُ بْنُ عُيَيْنَةَ، عَنِ الزُّهْرِيِّ، عَنْ عَمْرَةَ، عَنْ عَائِشَةَ أَنَّ ابْنَةَ جَحْشٍ كَانَتْ تُسْتَحَاضُ سَبْعَ سِنِينَ. بِنَحْوِ حَدِيثِهِمْ.

[600–65]. (Dār al-Salām 0658) Muhammad ibn Rumḥ narrated:[i] al-Layth reported [H]. Also Qutaybah ibn Saʿīd narrated; Layth narrated; from Yazīd ibn Abī Ḥabīb; from Jaʿfar; from ʿIrāk; from ʿUrwah; from ʿĀ'ishah. She said: **'Umm Ḥabībah asked God's Messenger about bleeding. ʿĀ'ishah said: I saw her tub full of blood. God's Messenger said to her: "Stay [without praying] for the length you used to have your period, then take a bath and offer your prayers".'**

وَحَدَّثَنَا مُحَمَّدُ بْنُ رُمْحٍ، أَخْبَرَنَا اللَّيْثُ، ح، وَحَدَّثَنَا قُتَيْبَةُ بْنُ سَعِيدٍ، حَدَّثَنَا لَيْثٌ، عَنْ يَزِيدَ بْنِ أَبِي حَبِيبٍ، عَنْ جَعْفَرٍ، عَنْ عِرَاكٍ، عَنْ عُرْوَةَ، عَنْ عَائِشَةَ، أَنَّهَا قَالَتْ: إِنَّ أُمَّ حَبِيبَةَ، سَأَلَتْ رَسُولَ اللهِ صَلَّى اللهُ عَلَيْهِ وَسَلَّمَ عَنِ الدَّمِ؟ فَقَالَتْ عَائِشَةُ: رَأَيْتُ مِرْكَنَهَا مَلْآنَ دَمًا. فَقَالَ لَهَا رَسُولُ اللهِ صَلَّى اللهُ عَلَيْهِ وَسَلَّمَ: «امْكُثِي قَدْرَ مَا كَانَتْ تَحْبِسُكِ حَيْضَتُكِ، ثُمَّ اغْتَسِلِي وَصَلِّي»

[601–66]. (Dār al-Salām 0659) Mūsā ibn Quraysh al-Tamīmī narrated to me: Isḥāq ibn Bakr ibn Muḍar narrated; my father narrated to me; Jaʿfar ibn Rabīʿah narrated to me; from ʿIrāk ibn Mālik; from ʿUrwah ibn al-Zubayr; from ʿĀ'ishah, the Prophet's wife. She said: **'Umm Ḥabībah bint Jaḥsh, who was ʿAbd al-Raḥmān ibn ʿAwf's wife, complained to God's Messenger about her bleeding. He said to her: "Stay [without praying] for the length you used to have your period, then perform the major ritual ablution". She used to take a bath for every prayer'.**

i. Related by Abū Dāwūd, 279; al-Nasā'ī, 207 and 351.

حَدَّثَنِي مُوسَى بْنُ قُرَيْشٍ التَّمِيمِيُّ، حَدَّثَنَا إِسْحَاقُ بْنُ بَكْرِ بْنِ مُضَرَ، حَدَّثَنِي أَبِي، حَدَّثَنِي جَعْفَرُ بْنُ رَبِيعَةَ، عَنْ عِرَاكِ بْنِ مَالِكٍ، عَنْ عُرْوَةَ بْنِ الزُّبَيْرِ، عَنْ عَائِشَةَ زَوْجِ النَّبِيِّ صَلَّى اللهُ عَلَيْهِ وَسَلَّمَ أَنَّهَا قَالَتْ: إِنَّ أُمَّ حَبِيبَةَ بِنْتَ جَحْشٍ الَّتِي كَانَتْ تَحْتَ عَبْدِ الرَّحْمَنِ بْنِ عَوْفٍ شَكَتْ إِلَى رَسُولِ اللهِ صَلَّى اللهُ عَلَيْهِ وَسَلَّمَ الدَّمَ. فَقَالَ لَهَا: «امْكُثِي قَدْرَ مَا كَانَتْ تَحْبِسُكِ حَيْضَتُكِ ثُمَّ اغْتَسِلِي» فَكَانَتْ تَغْتَسِلُ عِنْدَ كُلِّ صَلَاةٍ.

Text Explanation

These hadiths speak about vaginal blood discharge, which is different from menstruation as it is haemorrhage from a particular blood vessel. Thus, it has a different source from that of menses. The rulings applicable to a woman who suffers from this condition is spelled out in detail in books of *fiqh*, but I will mention certain points of it here. The first thing to explain in this regard is that such a sufferer is considered in the same position as women free from menstruation, and most rulings applicable to such women apply to her. It is permissible for her to have sexual intercourse with her husband, even at the time she is bleeding. This is the view of our school and the majority of scholars. In his book *al-Ishrāq*, Ibn al-Mundhir reports that this is the view of Ibn ʿAbbās, Saʿīd ibn al-Musayyib, al-Ḥasan al-Baṣrī, ʿAṭā', Saʿīd ibn Jubayr, Qatādah, Ḥammād ibn Abī Sulaymān, Bakr ibn ʿAbdullāh al-Muzanī, al-Awzāʿī, al-Thawrī, Mālik, Isḥāq and Abū Thawr. Ibn al-Mundhir confirms that he shares this view. He then adds that ʿĀ'ishah is reported to have said that she may not have sexual intercourse with her husband. This is the view of al-Nakhaʿī and al-Ḥakam. Ibn Sīrīn considers intercourse in such a condition to be reprehensible. Ahmad said: 'Her husband may not have sexual intercourse with her unless he fears to be in distress'.

Choice in the matter, as we said earlier, is the view of the majority of scholars. The evidence in support of this view is the hadith narrated by ʿIkrimah, from Ḥamnah bint Jaḥsh that she used to be in this condition and her husband used to have intercourse with her. This hadith is related by Abū Dāwūd and al-Bayhaqī, and by others in the same wording and a good chain of transmission. In his *Ṣaḥīḥ* anthology, al-Bukhārī mentions that 'Ibn 'Abbās said: A woman who is in prolonged bleeding, *istiḥāḍah,* may have sexual intercourse with her husband when she resumes prayer. Prayer is of a much higher standing and such a woman prays and fasts, and she does other types of worship. The same ruling applies to sexual intercourse. Besides, prohibition must be based on a legal statement, but no such statement of prohibition is made, but God knows best. As for prayer, fasting, *i'tikāf,* which is to stay in a mosque for worship, reciting and holding the Qur'an, prostration when reading certain verses of the Qur'an, or to give thanks to God and other types of worship: they are all binding on her in the same way as on a woman who does not have such a condition. This is unanimously agreed. When a woman who suffers from *istiḥāḍah* wishes to pray, she is required to take precautions with regards to her ablutions. She must wash her vagina before she performs the ablution or dry ablution, i.e. *tayammum.* She also applies a piece of cotton or some pad to stop the discharge, or to lessen it. If her discharge is light and can be stopped in this way, this is all she has to do. If it does not stop, then she has to take further precautions. She puts a napkin in between her legs and ties it from the front and back to a belt on her waist, ensuring that this napkin is well stuck on the piece of cotton on her vagina. This precaution is required except in two situations: if it becomes painful or harmful, and if she is fasting. Our scholars say that she takes these precautions and follows it with performing the ablution, without delay. If she delays the ablution for a length of time, scholars have two different views about the validity of her ablution, and the more correct view is that it is not valid. If she has tightened the napkin and then some blood is discharged, without any negligence on her part, her ablution and prayer remain valid. She may pray any number of voluntary prayers after she has done the obligatory prayer, without need to renew her precautions. This is in consideration of the fact that she is not at fault and cannot do more. On the other hand, if blood is discharged because her precautions are loose, or she did not tie the napkin well, or because the napkin moved, and thus more blood is discharged, her ablution becomes invalid. If this happens during the prayer, then the prayer is invalid. If after the prayer, she may not pray voluntary or Sunnah prayers.

Does this procedure of washing the vagina and blocking the discharge with a piece of cotton or pad and tying a napkin need to be repeated for every obligatory prayer? Here we need to look at details. If the napkin has effectively moved from its original place or some drops of blood appear on its edges, then the procedure should be renewed. If none of this has occurred, our Shāfiʿī scholars express two views. The more correct view is that it should be renewed, as also the ablution. The view of our school is that a woman who suffers from *istiḥāḍah* may not offer more than one obligatory prayer with one procedure of cleansing. This applies to any obligatory prayer, whether offered during its right time or after it has lapsed. She may add whatever she wants of voluntary prayers, before or after the obligatory prayer. My own view[i] is that she should not add any voluntary prayer because she does not need it. The correct view is the first one. The same view has been reported to have been expressed by ʿUrwah ibn al-Zubayr, Sufyān al-Thawrī, Aḥmad and Abū Thawr. Abū Ḥanīfah said that her purification is related to time. She may offer with one purification any number of missed obligatory prayers. Rabīʿah, Mālik and Dāwūd said: *istiḥāḍah* blood does not invalidate the ablution. She may offer with the same cleansing and ablution any number of obligatory prayers until she has invalidated her ablution in some way other than the *istiḥāḍah* blood discharge, but God knows best.

Our Shāfiʿī scholars say: The minor ritual ablution, or *wuḍū'*, of a woman suffering *istiḥāḍah* intended for offering an obligatory prayer is invalid if it is performed before the time range of that prayer has started. Abū Ḥanīfah says it is valid. Our evidence is that this is an ablution done to meet a necessity, and therefore it cannot be valid before that necessity arises. Our scholars say that she must offer the prayer shortly after she has done her ablution. If she delays it, as in

i. This is al-Nawawī's own view.

performing the ablution at the beginning of the time range, and prays in the middle of that time range, different rulings apply. If the delay is for some reason that is related to the prayer, such as dressing for prayer, awaiting the start of the congregational prayer, determining the direction of the *qiblah*, walking to the mosque or to other blessed places, looking for a cover, awaiting the Friday Prayer, etc. her prayer is valid according to the correct and best-known view. I have a different view, which is that it is not valid. If the delay is for a reason other than these or similar ones, three different rulings have been expressed. The first and most correct is that her ablution is invalid and she may not offer the prayer with that ablution. The second view is that her ablution remains valid and the delay is permissible. She may offer her prayer even if its time has lapsed. The third view is that she may delay offering the prayer within its time range. If the time range has lapsed, she may not pray with that ablution.

On the basis of the more correct ruling, which means that if she delays praying then she cannot offer her obligatory prayer with that ablution, we say that if she proceeds without delay and offers the obligatory prayer, she may offer Sunnah prayers for the remaining time range of the same obligatory prayer. When the time range lapses she may not offer more voluntary prayer with that ablution. This is the more correct of two views, but God knows best.

Our scholars say that when a woman suffering *istiḥāḍah* starts her ablution her intention should be to validate her prayer, not merely to remove the state of uncleansing. My own view is that it is sufficient for her to intend the removal of uncleansing. A third view is that she must combine the two things: to validate her prayer and remove her uncleansing. The first view is the correct one. When the woman has performed her ablution, she validates her prayer. Is she considered, however, to have removed the state of uncleansing? Our scholars express different views; the most correct of these is that nothing of her uncleansing is removed, but she merely validates her prayer with this ablution, despite uncleansing. This is the same as with dry ablution. For the person who needs to resort to dry ablution, i.e. *tayammum*, their uncleansing remains but they may pray, but God knows best. The second view is that her earlier uncleansing, as well as the one that occurs at the time of her ablution is removed, but not the one that follows. The third is that only the past condition of uncleansing is removed.

A woman suffering *istiḥāḍah* is not required to perform the major ritual ablution as a duty for any prayer, or at any time, except once when her menstruation period is finished.[i] This is the view expressed by the majority of scholars of the early and later generations. It is reported to have been expressed by ʿAlī, Ibn Masʿūd, Ibn ʿAbbās, ʿĀ'ishah, ʿUrwah ibn al-Zubayr, Abū Salamah ibn ʿAbd al-Raḥmān, Mālik, Abū Ḥanīfah and Ahmad. It is reported that Ibn ʿUmar, ʿAbdullāh ibn al-Zubayr and ʿAṭā' ibn Abī Rabāḥ said it is a duty that she should perform the *ghusl* for every prayer. This is also reported to have been said by ʿAlī and Ibn ʿAbbās. Furthermore, it is reported that ʿĀ'ishah said she should perform the *ghusl* once every day. Also, al-Musayyib and al-Ḥasan said that she should perform the *ghusl* at the time of Ẓuhr, or midday, prayer every day, but God knows best. The evidence in support of the majority view is that the normal case is that a *ghusl* is not obligatory. Therefore, it does not become obligatory unless an order is given to make it so. The only authentic report of an order by the Prophet is that which requires such a woman to perform the major ritual ablution, or *ghusl*, once only when her menstruation ceases. He said to her: 'When your period comes, stop praying, and when it is over, wash the blood off yourself and resume praying'. This does not imply repeating the *ghusl*. There are hadiths entered in the anthologies of Abū Dāwūd and al-Bayhaqī, as well as other anthologies, suggesting that the Prophet ordered her to repeat the *ghusl*, but these hadiths do not include anything that is confirmed to be authentic. Indeed, al-Bayhaqī and earlier scholars proved them to be lacking in authenticity. What is authentic is what is related by both al-Bukhārī and Muslim in their anthologies, stating that Umm Ḥabībah bint Jaḥsh suffered from *istiḥāḍah* and the Prophet said

i. She determines the end of her period either by the colour of the blood being discharged or by completing the number of days of her period, as she used to have before the onset of her *istiḥāḍah*.

to her: 'This is only haemorrhage from a blood vessel. Take a bath and then pray'. She used to do the *ghusl* for every prayer. Al-Shāfiʿī (may God bestow mercy on him) said: 'God's Messenger (peace be upon him) ordered her to do the *ghusl* and then pray. It does not include any order to her to do the *ghusl* for every prayer. There is no doubt, God willing, that her further *ghusls* were voluntary, in addition to the order given to her. This is something open to her'. This is the exact statement by al-Shāfiʿī. The same was said by his teacher Sufyān ibn ʿUyaynah, al-Layth ibn Saʿd and other scholars, and their view is expressed in similar wording.

A woman in *istiḥāḍah* may be in one of two situations: the first is that her discharge is not menses and not mixed with menses, as in the case when her discharge is for less than one day and night. The second situation is that her discharge is some menses and some blood which is not menses. This is the situation of a woman whose discharge is continuous, or lasts for more than the maximum length of the period of menstruation. There are three cases in this situation. The first is that of a young woman who has the discharge for the first time ever. Al-Shāfiʿī gives two rulings on this case, the more correct one is that she is treated as one whose discharge lasts one day and night. The other ruling is that she is treated as one with a period of six or seven nights. The second case is that of a woman who has a regular period. She allows for her menstruation the same number of days as her period in the month previous to her *istiḥāḍah*. The third case is that of one who can differentiate her discharge, which means that at times she discharges dark and strong blood, while at others the discharged blood is light and thinner. Her period of menstruation is in this case on the days of the dark blood, provided that it lasts not less than one day and night and not more than fifteen days, while the red and lighter discharge is not less than fifteen days. There are further details on all these situations which we need not go into, because discussion of such details is beyond the scope of this book. Hence I have limited myself to some aspects of the general question of *istiḥāḍah*, while I have discussed these issues in detail, and cited the evidence for each ruling in my other work, *Sharḥ al-Muhadhdhab*, but God knows best.

The first two hadiths mention the case of Fāṭimah bint Abī Ḥubaysh. Abū Ḥubaysh's name is Qays ibn al-Muṭṭalib ibn Asad ibn ʿAbd al-ʿUzzā ibn Quṣay. In the second hadith the name occurs as Fāṭimah bint Abī Ḥubaysh ibn ʿAbd al-Muṭṭalib ibn Asad. In the original manuscripts it occurs as 'ibn ʿAbd al-Muṭṭalib', but scholars agree that this is due to confusion and the correct name is without ʿAbd. In the second hadith, her name is followed by 'one of our women'. The one who says it is either Hishām ibn ʿUrwah or his father, ʿUrwah ibn al-Zubayr ibn al-ʿAwwām, ibn Khuwaylid, ibn Asad ibn ʿAbd al-ʿUzzā, but God knows best.

In the first hadith, No. 594, Fāṭimah tells the Prophet: 'Messenger of God, I am a woman who continues in menstruation without an end. Am I to leave off prayer?' The Prophet tells her that she must not. This is a clear statement that a woman who suffers from *istiḥāḍah* continues to pray normally, except for the time when her discharge is considered menstruation. As stated earlier, this is unanimously agreed. The hadith also shows that a person who has a problem may enquire about it, and that a woman may ask about questions of purification and ablution, as well as other feminine needs, and that she may put her questions to men.

The Prophet tells her that this discharge is from a blood vessel and that it is not menstruation. In many books of *fiqh*, it is said that this is a blood vessel that is split and causes a gush of blood. However, this is not mentioned in any hadith but it may be correct.

The Prophet tells her: 'When your period comes, stop praying'. This is an order by the Prophet to stop prayer during menstruation. This is a full prohibition that means that, if offered, prayer during menstruation is invalid, whether it is obligatory or voluntary, and this is unanimously agreed by all Muslims. It is also forbidden for a woman in menstruation to perform the *ṭawāf*, offer the prayer for a deceased person, do a prostration for the recitation of certain verses of the Qur'an, or a prostration of gratitude to God. All this is agreed by all Muslims. Scholars are also unanimous that a woman in menstruation is not required to pray, and that she does not pray later in compensation for the prayers she has missed during her period, but God knows best.

The Prophet also tells his questioner: 'And when it is over, wash the blood off yourself and resume praying'. His words, 'when it is over', mean when menstruation is at an end. It is important to know the sign of the ending of menstruation, but it is rarely discussed. A number of our scholars say that the sign that the period of menstruation is over is the cession of the discharge of blood, yellow or cloudy discharge, whether this is followed by a white discharge or not. Al-Bayhaqī and Ibn al-Ṣabbāgh, and other scholars of our school, said that there may be some slight wetness that is neither yellow nor slightly dark. It just leaves a colourless trace on the pad. This is how it is after the woman's period is over. Al-Bukhārī enters an authentic hadith that 'Ā'ishah said to women: 'Do not precipitate things; wait until you see the whiteness'. She meant that they should be sure that menstruation has completely ceased.

Our scholars say: when the time of her normal period is over, she must take a bath immediately so that she can offer the first prayer due of her. Thereafter, she may not omit any prayer or fasting. Her husband need not abstain from having sexual intercourse with her. She need not stop anything a woman does in her time of cleanliness from menstruation. Nor does she need to add a period of reassurance. It is mentioned that Mālik said that she leaves a period for reassurance lasting three days after the end of her menstruation, but God knows best.

This hadith includes an order to remove impurities, and that blood is impure, and that prayer becomes obligatory once menstruation has ceased, but God knows best.

In hadith No. 595, Muslim says at the end: 'In Ḥammād's narration, a word is added but we have left it out'. *Qāḍī* 'Iyāḍ said: 'The word Muslim left out is that he said to her: "Wash the blood off yourself and do the *wuḍū'*." Al-Nasā'ī and other Hadith scholars mentioned this, but Muslim left it out because only Ḥammād reported it. Al-Nasā'ī said: "We do not know of anyone other than Ḥammād who said 'do the *wuḍū'*,'" meaning saying it as part of Hishām's narrated hadith'. Abū Dāwūd and others mention the *wuḍū'* in the narration of 'Adī ibn Thābit, Ḥabīb ibn Abī Thābit and Ayyūb ibn Abī Makīn.

Abū Dāwūd said that all these narrations are poor in authenticity, but God knows best.

The hadiths refer to Umm Ḥabībah bint Jaḥsh, and in some her appellation is not mentioned but she is referred to as Jaḥsh's daughter. All these are acceptable. However, *Qāḍī* 'Iyāḍ mentions that in one narration in Abū al-'Abbās al-Rāzī's manuscript, the name is mentioned as Zaynab bint Jaḥsh. He adds:

> The reporters of *al-Muwaṭṭa'* from Mālik differ on this point, but most of them mention Zaynab bint Jaḥsh, but many narrators only mention 'Bint Jaḥsh,' which is the correct form. The mistake is clear as the fourth hadith, number 597, mentions that she was ''Abd al-Raḥmān ibn 'Awf's wife'. Zaynab bint Jaḥsh, the Mother of the Believers, was never married to 'Abd al-Raḥ mān ibn 'Awf. Her first husband was Zayd ibn Ḥārithah, and she was subsequently married to the Prophet. The one who was married to 'Abd al-Raḥmān was her sister, Umm Ḥabībah, and this is clear in the hadith, as it describes her as 'God's Messenger's sister-in-law and 'Abd al-Raḥmān ibn 'Awf's wife'. Further clarification occurs in the same hadith as it mentions that she used to do her bath in her sister Zaynab's home.
>
> Ibn 'Abd al-Barr mentions that it has been reported that all three daughters of Jaḥsh: Zaynab, Umm Ḥabībah and Ḥamnah used to suffer from *istiḥāḍah*. It is also mentioned that the only one of them that so suffered was Umm Ḥabībah. In his book *al-Mū'ib*, which is a commentary on *al-Muwaṭṭa'*, *Qāḍī* Yūnus bin Mughīth mentions something like this. He adds that every one of them was called Zaynab, but one of them was given the nickname Ḥamnah and the other was known by her appellation Umm Ḥabībah. If this is so, then Mālik did not err in calling her Umm Ḥabībah Zaynab.
>
> Al-Bukhārī enters in his *Ṣaḥīḥ* anthology a hadith narrated by 'Ā'ishah that 'one of the Prophet's wives' or 'one of the Mothers of the Believers' or 'some of his wives' joined him in *i'tikāf* when she was experiencing *istiḥāḍah*.

Concerning Umm Ḥabībah, al-Dāraquṭnī mentions that Ibrāhīm al-Ḥarbī said: 'Her correct appellation is Umm Ḥabīb, without the 'ah', and that her own name was Ḥabībah'. Al-Dāraquṭnī said: 'Al-Ḥarbī's statement is correct and he was one of the best authorities on this. Others said that it is reported from ʿAmrah from ʿĀ'ishah that her appellation was Umm Ḥabīb'. Abū ʿAlī al-Ghassanī said: 'The correct thing is that her name was Ḥabībah'. The same is said by al-Ḥumaydī from Sufyān. Ibn al-Athīr said: She is called Umm Ḥabībah, but she is also called Umm Ḥabīb, but the first version is more frequently used. She experienced *istiḥāḍah,* but specialists in the Sirah say that the one who suffered this condition of *istiḥāḍah* was her sister Ḥamnah bint Jaḥsh. Ibn ʿAbd al-Barr said that the correct thing is that both suffered from this condition.

In the last two hadiths, Nos 600 and 601, the Prophet tells her: 'Stay [without praying] for the length you used to have your period, then take a bath and offer your prayers'. The two instructions given by the Prophet make clear that a woman experiencing *istiḥāḍah* must do the major ritual ablution when the time of menstruation is over, even though the blood discharge continues. As stated earlier, this is unanimously agreed upon. The woman in question is reported to have done the *ghusl* in a tub in her sister's home. She would sit in the tub and pour water over herself, and the water was then mixed with the blood, giving the water a red colour. Undoubtedly, she cleaned herself, removing the coloured water and its traces, but God knows best.

Transmission

In hadith No. 597, the chain of transmission features: 'Muhammad ibn Salamah al-Murādī narrated:[i] ʿAbdullāh ibn Wahb narrated; from ʿAmr ibn al-Ḥārith; from Ibn Shihāb; from ʿUrwah ibn al-Zubayr and ʿAmrah bint ʿAbd al-Raḥmān; from ʿĀ'ishah'. This narration mentions that both ʿUrwah and ʿAmrah bint ʿAbd al-Raḥmān reported from

---

i. Related by al-Bukhārī, 327; Abū Dāwūd, 285; al-Nasā'ī, 203, 204 and 205; Ibn Mājah, 626.

ʿĀ'ishah. This is the correct way. Ibn Abi Dhi'b narrates it in the same manner from al-Zuhrī from ʿUrwah and ʿAmrah. The same is done by Yaḥyā ibn Saʿīd al-Anṣārī who, like al-Zuhrī, reports it from ʿĀ'ishah and ʿAmrah. However, al-Awzāʿī differs, reporting the hadith from al-Zuhrī, from ʿUrwah from ʿAmrah, which means that ʿUrwah reported from ʿAmrah, not directly from ʿĀ'ishah.

After that Muslim says: 'Muhammad ibn al-Muthannā narrated; from Sufyān; from al-Zuhrī; from ʿAmrah; from ʿĀ'ishah'. This is how it occurs in the original manuscripts, and thus it has been reported by *Qāḍī* ʿIyāḍ from all Muslim's reporters except al-Samarqandī, who replaces ʿAmrah by ʿUrwah, but God knows best.

CHAPTER 15

MAKING UP FASTING IS OBLIGATORY, BUT NOT PRAYER

[602–67]. (Dār al-Salām 0660) Abū al-Rabīʿ al-Zahrānī narrated:[i] Ḥammād narrated; from Ayyūb; from Abū Qilābah; from Muʿādhah [H]. Also, Ḥammād narrated; from Yazīd al-Rishk; from Muʿādhah; that a woman asked ʿĀ'ishah: **'Should any of us make up for missed prayers during her period of menstruation?' ʿĀ'ishah said: 'Are you Ḥarūrī? Every one of us used to have her period during the Prophet's lifetime, but none was ordered to make up'**.

حَدَّثَنَا أَبُو الرَّبِيعِ الزَّهْرَانِيُّ، حَدَّثَنَا حَمَّادٌ، عَنْ أَيُّوبَ، عَنْ أَبِي قِلَابَةَ، عَنْ مُعَاذَةَ ح، وَحَدَّثَنَا حَمَّادٌ، عَنْ يَزِيدَ الرِّشْكِ، عَنْ مُعَاذَةَ، أَنَّ امْرَأَةً سَأَلَتْ عَائِشَةَ فَقَالَتْ: أَتَقْضِي إِحْدَانَا الصَّلَاةَ أَيَّامَ مَحِيضِهَا؟ فَقَالَتْ عَائِشَةُ: أَحَرُورِيَّةٌ أَنْتِ؟ قَدْ «كَانَتْ إِحْدَانَا تَحِيضُ عَلَى عَهْدِ رَسُولِ اللهِ صَلَّى اللهُ عَلَيْهِ وَسَلَّمَ، ثُمَّ لَا تُؤْمَرُ بِقَضَاءٍ»

[603–68]. (Dār al-Salām 0661) Muhammad ibn al-Muthannā narrated: Muhammad ibn Jaʿfar narrated; Shuʿbah narrated; from Yazīd. He said: I heard Muʿādhah say that she asked ʿĀ'ishah: **'Should a woman who had her period offer compensatory prayers?' ʿĀ'ishah said: 'Are you Ḥarūrī? God's Messenger's wives used to have their periods of menstruation.**

---

i. Related by al-Bukhārī, 321; Abū Dāwūd, 262 and 263; al-Tirmidhī, 130; al-Nasā'ī, 380 and 2317; Ibn Mājah, 631.

Did he ever order them to make up?' Muhammad ibn Ja'far said: 'She meant to make up the missed prayers'.

وَحَدَّثَنَا مُحَمَّدُ بْنُ الْـمُثَنَّى، حَدَّثَنَا مُحَمَّدُ بْنُ جَعْفَرٍ، حَدَّثَنَا شُعْبَةُ، عَنْ يَزِيدَ، قَالَ: سَمِعْتُ مُعَاذَةَ، أَنَّهَا سَأَلَتْ عَائِشَةَ أَتَقْضِي الْحَائِضُ الصَّلَاةَ؟ فَقَالَتْ: عَائِشَةُ أَحَرُورِيَّةٌ أَنْتِ؟ «قَدْ كُنَّ نِسَاءُ رَسُولِ اللهِ صَلَّى اللهُ عَلَيْهِ وَسَلَّمَ يَحِضْنَ أَفَأَمَرَهُنَّ أَنْ يَجْزِينَ؟» قَالَ مُحَمَّدُ بْنُ جَعْفَرٍ: «تَعْنِي يَقْضِينَ»

[604–69]. (Dār al-Salām 0662) 'Abd ibn Ḥumayd narrated: 'Abd al-Razzāq reported; Ma'mar reported; from 'Āṣim; from Mu'ādhah. She said: **'I asked 'Ā'ishah: How is it that we make up for missed fasting but not for missed prayer? She said: "Are you Ḥarūrī?" I said: I am not a Ḥarūrī; I am only asking. She said: "We used to have that and we were ordered to make up for fasting but not ordered to make up for prayer".'**

وَحَدَّثَنَا عَبْدُ بْنُ حُمَيْدٍ، أَخْبَرَنَا عَبْدُ الرَّزَّاقِ، أَخْبَرَنَا مَعْمَرٌ، عَنْ عَاصِمٍ، عَنْ مُعَاذَةَ، قَالَتْ: سَأَلْتُ عَائِشَةَ فَقُلْتُ: مَا بَالُ الْحَائِضِ تَقْضِي الصَّوْمَ، وَلَا تَقْضِي الصَّلَاةَ. فَقَالَتْ: أَحَرُورِيَّةٌ أَنْتِ؟ قُلْتُ: لَسْتُ بِحَرُورِيَّةٍ، وَلَكِنِّي أَسْأَلُ. قَالَتْ: «كَانَ يُصِيبُنَا ذَلِكَ، فَنُؤْمَرُ بِقَضَاءِ الصَّوْمِ، وَلَا نُؤْمَرُ بِقَضَاءِ الصَّلَاةِ»

Text Explanation

This ruling is agreed by all. Muslims are unanimous that any woman having her period or postnatal discharge is not required to offer prayers or fast during that time. They are also unanimous that she is not required to make up for missed prayers but that she must make up missed fasting. Scholars say that the difference is that the prayer is large in number and frequent, which makes its compensation difficult. Fasting, on the other hand, is once a year, and the menstruation period may be as short as one or two days. Our scholars say that the two *rak'ahs* of prayer offered after performing the *ṭawāf* are the only prayer that needs to be offered in compensation if missed due to menstruation.

The majority of scholars, including our Shāfi'ī scholars, say that a woman who has her period is not addressed by the order to fast, but she must make up on the basis of another order. Some of our scholars say that she is addressed by the order to fast during her period, but at the same time she is ordered to delay her fasting. They give the analogy of a person who has invalidated his ablution. He is ordered to pray, but his prayer will not be valid until he has performed the ablution. This analogy is not valid. How can fasting be obligatory on her and at the same time forbidden for a reason she can do nothing about? This is unlike a person with no valid ablution. He can change this condition at any time by performing ablution.

In all three hadiths, 'Ā'ishah asks the questioner: Are you a Ḥarūrī? This refers to a village called Ḥarūrā', close to Kufah, which witnessed the first meeting of the Khawārij who rebelled against 'Alī ibn Abī Ṭālib. They made their pledges there and started their rebellion. Hence, they were called the Ḥarūrīs. 'Ā'ishah's question implies that a group of them make it obligatory for women to make up for prayers they miss due to being in menstruation. This is contrary to the unanimous view of all Muslims. 'Ā'ishah's question: are you a Ḥarūrī, is one of disapproval. It means: this is the way followed by those people, and it is very wrong.

'Ā'ishah's answer was: 'Every one of us used to have her period during the Prophet's lifetime, but none was ordered to make up'. This means that the Prophet ordered none of his wives to offer compensatory prayers, despite being aware of their experiencing a period, and they did not pray while it lasted. Had compensation been needed, he would have told them to do so.

Transmission

Abū Qilābah's name is 'Abdullāh ibn Zayd, and we gave some details about him earlier. Yazīd al-Rishk is Abū al-Azharī Yazīd ibn Abī Yazīd, who belonged to Basrah. Scholars give different reasons for giving him the nickname 'al-Rishk'. It is said that it is a Persian word that means 'the divider', or 'the one who protects what belongs to him'. It is also said that it means 'one with a thick beard'. It is further said that the word means 'scorpion', and he was given this name because a scorpion got into his beard and stayed there for three days without him noticing, because his beard was long and very thick. All these explanations have been stated by Ibn Qaraqūl, the author of *Maṭāliʿ al-Anwār*, as well as other scholars. They were also mentioned by Abū ʿAlī al-Ḥusayn ibn Muhammad al-Ghassānī, and given a chain of transmission for the last of these explanations.

CHAPTER 16

A WOMAN MAY HOLD A ROBE TO SCREEN A PERSON TAKING A BATH

[605–70]. (Dār al-Salām 0663) Yaḥyā ibn Yaḥyā narrated:[i] I read out to Mālik; from Abū al-Naḍr; that Abū Murrah, Umm Hāni' bint Abū Ṭālib's *mawlā* reported to him that he heard Umm Hāni' bint Abū Ṭālib say: '**I went to God's Messenger (peace be upon him) during the year of the takeover of Makkah, and I found him taking a bath, with Fāṭimah, his daughter, screening him with a robe**'.

وَحَدَّثَنَا يَحْيَى بْنُ يَحْيَى، قَالَ: قَرَأْتُ عَلَى مَالِكٍ، عَنْ أَبِي النَّضْرِ، أَنَّ أَبَا مُرَّةَ مَوْلَى أُمِّ هَانِئٍ بِنْتِ أَبِي طَالِبٍ، أَخْبَرَهُ أَنَّهُ سَمِعَ أُمَّ هَانِئٍ بِنْتَ أَبِي طَالِبٍ، تَقُولُ: «ذَهَبْتُ إِلَى رَسُولِ اللهِ صَلَّى اللهُ عَلَيْهِ وَسَلَّمَ عَامَ الْفَتْحِ فَوَجَدْتُهُ يَغْتَسِلُ وَفَاطِمَةُ ابْنَتُهُ تَسْتُرُهُ بِثَوْبٍ»

[606–71]. (Dār al-Salām 0664) Muhammad ibn Rumḥ ibn al-Muhājir narrated: al-Layth reported; from Yazīd ibn Abī Ḥabīb; from Sa'īd ibn Abī Hind; that Abū Murrah, 'Aqīl's *mawlā*, reported to him; that Umm Hāni' bint Abū Ṭālib narrated to him that '**At the time when Makkah fell to Islam, she went to God's Messenger when he was at the higher end of Makkah. The Prophet was taking his bath, with Fāṭimah screening him. He then took his robe and wore it. He then offered eight *rak'ahs*, the mid-morning Sunnah prayer**'.

---

i. Related by al-Bukhārī, 280, and 357, 3171 and 6158 in longer versions; al-Tirmidhī, 2734 and 1579; al-Nasā'ī, 225; Ibn Mājah, 465.

حَدَّثَنَا مُحَمَّدُ بْنُ رُمْحِ بْنِ الْـمُهَاجِرِ، أَخْبَرَنَا اللَّيْثُ، عَنْ يَزِيدَ بْنِ أَبِي حَبِيبٍ، عَنْ سَعِيدِ بْنِ أَبِي هِنْدَ، أَنَّ أَبَا مُرَّةَ، مَوْلَى عَقِيلٍ، حَدَّثَهُ أَنَّ أُمَّ هَانِئٍ بِنْتَ أَبِي طَالِبٍ، حَدَّثَتْهُ أَنَّهُ لَـمَّا كَانَ عَامُ الْفَتْحِ. أَتَتْ رَسُولَ اللهِ صَلَّى اللهُ عَلَيْهِ وَسَلَّمَ وَهُوَ بِأَعْلَى مَكَّةَ «قَامَ رَسُولُ اللهِ صَلَّى اللهُ عَلَيْهِ وَسَلَّمَ إِلَى غُسْلِهِ، فَسَتَرَتْ عَلَيْهِ فَاطِمَةُ ثُمَّ أَخَذَ ثَوْبَهُ فَالْتَحَفَ بِهِ، ثُمَّ صَلَّى ثَمَانَ رَكَعَاتٍ سُبْحَةَ الضُّحَى»

[607–72]. (Dār al-Salām 0665) Abū Kurayb narrated it: Abū Usāmah narrated; from al-Walīd ibn Kathīr; from Sa'īd ibn Abī Hind, with this chain of transmission, stating: '**His daughter, Fāṭimah, screened him with a robe. When he finished his bath, he took the robe and covered himself with it. He then prayed eight *rak'ahs*. That was in mid-morning**'.

وَحَدَّثَنَاهُ أَبُو كُرَيْبٍ، حَدَّثَنَا أَبُو أُسَامَةَ، عَنِ الْوَلِيدِ بْنِ كَثِيرٍ، عَنْ سَعِيدِ بْنِ أَبِي هِنْدَ، بِهَذَا الْإِسْنَادِ، وَقَالَ: فَسَتَرَتْهُ ابْنَتُهُ فَاطِمَةُ بِثَوْبِهِ فَلَمَّا اغْتَسَلَ أَخَذَهُ فَالْتَحَفَ بِهِ، ثُمَّ قَامَ فَصَلَّى ثَمَانَ سَجَدَاتٍ، وَذَلِكَ ضُحًى.

[608–73]. (Dār al-Salām 0666) Isḥaq ibn Ibrāhīm al-Ḥanẓalī narrated: Mūsā al-Qāri' reported; Zā'idah narrated; from al-A'mash; from Sālim ibn Abī al-Ja'd; from Kurayb; from Ibn 'Abbās; from Maymūnah. She said: '**I placed water for the Prophet and screened him as he took a bath**'.

حَدَّثَنَا إِسْحَاقُ بْنُ إِبْرَاهِيمَ الْحَنْظَلِيُّ، أَخْبَرَنَا مُوسَى الْقَارِئُ، حَدَّثَنَا زَائِدَةُ، عَنِ الْأَعْمَشِ، عَنْ سَالِمِ بْنِ أَبِي الْجَعْدِ، عَنْ كُرَيْبٍ، عَنِ ابْنِ عَبَّاسٍ، عَنْ مَيْمُونَةَ قَالَتْ: «وَضَعْتُ لِلنَّبِيِّ صَلَّى اللهُ عَلَيْهِ وَسَلَّمَ مَاءً، وَسَتَرْتُهُ فَاغْتَسَلَ»

Text Explanation

The hadith mentions that when she went to see the Prophet, she found him taking a bath and screened by his daughter. This makes it clear that it is permissible for a man to take a bath while a close female relative, whom it is not permissible for him to marry, is present, provided that he is screened with a curtain or a robe or something similar.

She said: 'He then offered eight *rak'ahs*, the mid-morning Sunnah prayer'. This statement gives a useful point, which is that the mid-morning, or Ḍuḥā, prayer consists of eight *rak'ahs*. The fact that she describes it as the 'mid-morning Sunnah prayer' means that this is an established Sunnah, or recommended, prayer, and that the Prophet offered it with this intention. This is contrary to the other report that mentions that 'the Prophet offered eight *rak'ahs*; and this was in mid-morning'. Some people understand this wrongly, claiming that there is no evidence in this hadith to suggest that the mid-morning prayer is eight *rak'ahs*. They claim that the Prophet offered this prayer at that time by way of gratitude for the takeover of Makkah, not as an established Sunnah at mid-morning. Such understanding does not fit with the wording used by Umm Hāni', as she says 'the mid-morning sunnah'. People of earlier and recent generations continued to cite this hadith in confirmation of the mid-morning prayer as consisting of eight *rak'ahs*, but God knows best.

Transmission

The chain of transmission of the first hadith includes Abū al-Naḍr reported that 'Abū Murrah, Umm Hāni's *mawlā* ...', while the next hadith describes Abu Murrah as 'Aqīl's *mawlā*. Abū al-Naḍr was Sālim ibn Abū Umayyah, who belonged to the Taym branch of the Quraysh and was from Madinah. He was a *mawlā* of 'Umar ibn 'Abdullāh al-Taymī. Abū Murrah was Yazīd, a *mawlā* of Umm Hāni', the Prophet's cousin. He was very close to her brother 'Aqīl. Hence, he is mentioned in this second narration as his *mawlā*. Umm Hāni's name was Fākhitah, but other reports say that she was Fāṭimah, or Hind. Hāni' ibn Habīrah ibn 'Amr was her son. She embraced Islam at the time Makkah fell to Islam.

One of the narrators mentioned is Mūsā al-Qāri'. Al-Qāri' means 'the reciter'.

CHAPTER 17

PROHIBITION OF LOOKING AT SOMEONE ELSE'S PRIVATE PARTS

[609–74]. (Dār al-Salām 0667) Abū Bakr ibn Abī Shaybah narrated:[i] Zayd ibn al-Ḥubāb narrated; from al-Ḍaḥḥāk ibn ʿUthmān; Zayd ibn Aslam reported to me; from ʿAbd al-Raḥmān ibn Abū Saʿīd al-Khudrī; from his father; that God's Messenger (peace be upon him) said: '**Let no man look at the private parts [i.e. the *ʿawrah*] of another man; nor a woman at the private parts of another woman. Let no man be with another man covered with one robe; nor a woman with another woman covered with one dress**'.

حَدَّثَنَا أَبُو بَكْرِ بْنُ أَبِي شَيْبَةَ، حَدَّثَنَا زَيْدُ بْنُ الْحُبَابِ، عَنِ الضَّحَّاكِ بْنِ عُثْمَانَ، قَالَ: أَخْبَرَنِي زَيْدُ بْنُ أَسْلَمَ، عَنْ عَبْدِ الرَّحْمَنِ بْنِ أَبِي سَعِيدٍ الْخُدْرِيِّ، عَنْ أَبِيهِ، أَنَّ رَسُولَ اللهِ صَلَّى اللهُ عَلَيْهِ وَسَلَّمَ قَالَ: «لَا يَنْظُرُ الرَّجُلُ إِلَى عَوْرَةِ الرَّجُلِ، وَلَا الْمَرْأَةُ إِلَى عَوْرَةِ الْمَرْأَةِ، وَلَا يُفْضِي الرَّجُلُ إِلَى الرَّجُلِ فِي ثَوْبٍ وَاحِدٍ، وَلَا تُفْضِي الْمَرْأَةُ إِلَى الْمَرْأَةِ فِي الثَّوْبِ الْوَاحِدِ»

[610–000]. (Dār al-Salām 0668) The same hadith was narrated to me by Hārūn ibn ʿAbdullāh and Muhammad ibn Rāfiʿ: They said: Ibn Abū Fudayk narrated; al-Ḍaḥḥāk ibn ʿUthmān reported; with the same chain of transmission. However, they replaced the word *ʿawrah*, meaning 'private parts', with its variant *ʿuryah*, in both places.

---

i. Related by Abū Dāwūd, 4018; al-Tirmidhī, 2793; Ibn Mājah, 661.

وَحَدَّثَنِيهِ هَارُونُ بْنُ عَبْدِ اللهِ، وَمُحَمَّدُ بْنُ رَافِعٍ، قَالَا: حَدَّثَنَا ابْنُ أَبِي فُدَيْكٍ، أَخْبَرَنَا الضَّحَّاكُ بْنُ عُثْمَانَ، بِهَذَا الْإِسْنَادِ، وَقَالَا: - مَكَانَ عَوْرَةِ - عُرْيَةِ الرَّجُلِ، وَعُرْيَةِ الْمَرْأَةِ.

Text Explanation

The hadith makes clear that it is forbidden for a man to look at the private parts of another man, and this applies to a woman looking at the private parts of another woman. This is unanimously agreed upon, and there is no difference of opinion on this point. Likewise, for a man to look at the private parts of a woman, or a woman to look at the private parts of a man, is unanimously agreed to be strictly forbidden. The Prophet mentions the prohibition of a man looking at the private parts of another man, pointing to the other, and more important, prohibition of a man looking at a woman's private parts. Needless to say, this prohibition applies to a man looking at a woman who is not his wife. As for married couples, they may look at the private areas of their spouses, except the genital organs. With regard to genital organs, scholars of our school express three different views, the most correct of which is that it is offensive, i.e. *makrūh*, but not prohibited for either spouse to look at the other's genital organ unless there is need. The second view is that it is forbidden for both, while the third view is that it is forbidden for the man, whilst reprehensible for the woman. To look at the inside of her vagina is more strictly reprehensible or forbidden. As for a man looking at women whom he is forbidden to marry, such as his sister, aunt or niece, or their looking at him, the correct view is that it is permissible for them to look at what is above the waistline and below the knees. However, some scholars say that only what appears normally as people go about their needs and work is permissible to see, but God knows best.

The private area covered by this prohibition is between the waistline at the navel and the knees, when we are speaking about men among themselves, or women among themselves. As for the navel and the knees themselves, there are three different views expressed by our Shāfiʿī scholars. The most correct of these is that they are not part of the private area. The second view is that they are within it, and the third says that the navel is part of the private area, but not the knees.

For a man to look at a woman's body, or a woman to look at a man's body, is forbidden, whether the look is with desire or not. Some of our scholars say that it is not forbidden for a woman to look at a man's face without desire, but this view is insupportable. Likewise, it is forbidden for a man to look at the hairless face of a handsome boy, whether with desire or not, even when one is sure of having no stir of desire. This is the correct view of scrupulous scholars. It is stated by al-Shāfiʿī and the most learned of his disciples. He applies the same evidence as that applicable to women, because such a boy may be the subject of sexual desire like women. Many boys of this type are even prettier than many women. Indeed, looking at such boys is more likely to be forbidden because it is easier for a man to perpetrate a forbidden action with such a boy than it is with a woman, but God knows best.

All that we have mentioned of prohibitons applies when there is no need for looking. If there is a legitimate need, such as in the case of shopping, medical examination, giving testimony, etc. then looking is not forbidden. However, if the look is accompanied by desire in such cases, then it becomes forbidden. The point is that a legitimate need makes looking permissible, but desire is not a need. Our scholars say that a look with desire is forbidden to anyone other than a woman's husband. Indeed, it is forbidden for a man to look at his mother or daughter with desire, but God knows best.

The hadith also mentions that no man should be with another covered with the same robe or covering. The same applies to women. This is a strict prohibition when there is no personal covering between them. The hadith provides evidence of the prohibiton of any part of one's body touching another person's private area. This is agreed by all scholars. Yet it is frequently done and many people are lax or careless in this respect, particularly when they are in a public bath.

It is a duty of anyone who goes there to make sure not to touch or look at the private area of another, and to ensure that his own private area is covered. If one sees something amiss in this area, one must speak out against it. Scholars say that one cannot be exempted from speaking out against such practice for merely thinking that his word will not be heeded. Only if the person fears an adverse outcome for himself or for others may he be exempted, but God knows best.

To expose one's private parts when alone, unseen by any human being, is permissible if there is need for it. If there is no need, scholars express different opinions ranging from offensive, or *makrūh*, to forbidden. The view which we find more correct is that it is forbidden.

All these points have more details and conditions that are discussed at length in books of *fiqh*. We have briefly referred to them here so that this book includes the basic rulings concerning them.

CHAPTER 18

TAKING A BATH IN THE NUDE

[611–75]. (Dār al-Salām 0669) Muhammad ibn Rāfiʿ narrated:[i] ʿAbd al-Razzāq narrated; Maʿmar narrated; from Hammām ibn Munabbih, who said: This is what Abū Hurayrah narrated to us from Muhammad, God's Messenger (peace be upon him). He mentioned some hadiths including: **'And God's Messenger said: "The Children of Israel used to bathe naked, and they would look at one another's genitals. Moses (peace be upon him) used to bathe alone. They said: 'By God, nothing prevents Moses from bathing with us except that he is deformed'. He went to bathe one day, and he placed his garment on a stone. The stone moved away carrying his garment. Moses ran after it and shouted: 'O stone; my garment! O stone; my garment!' Thus the Children of Israel could see Moses' genitals, and they said: 'By God, there is nothing wrong with Moses'. The stone stopped until Moses was seen. He then took his garment and started to beat the stone".'**

Abū Hurayrah said: **'By God, the stone has six or seven dents, as a result of Moses' beating it'**.

وَحَدَّثَنَا مُحَمَّدُ بْنُ رَافِعٍ، حَدَّثَنَا عَبْدُ الرَّزَّاقِ، حَدَّثَنَا مَعْمَرٌ، عَنْ هَمَّامِ بْنِ مُنَبِّهٍ، قَالَ: هَذَا مَا حَدَّثَنَا أَبُو هُرَيْرَةَ، عَنْ مُحَمَّدٍ رَسُولِ اللهِ صَلَّى اللهُ عَلَيْهِ وَسَلَّمَ. فَذَكَرَ أَحَادِيثَ مِنْهَا. وَقَالَ رَسُولُ اللهِ صَلَّى اللهُ عَلَيْهِ وَسَلَّمَ: «كَانَتْ بَنُو إِسْرَائِيلَ يَغْتَسِلُونَ عُرَاةً،

i. Related by al-Bukhārī, 278.

يَنْظُرُ بَعْضُهُمْ إِلَى سَوْأَةِ بَعْضٍ. وَكَانَ مُوسَى عَلَيْهِ السَّلَامُ يَغْتَسِلُ وَحْدَهُ، فَقَالُوا: وَاللهِ مَا يَمْنَعُ مُوسَى أَنْ يَغْتَسِلَ مَعَنَا إِلَّا أَنَّهُ آدَرُ قَالَ: فَذَهَبَ مَرَّةً يَغْتَسِلُ فَوَضَعَ ثَوْبَهُ عَلَى حَجَرٍ، فَفَرَّ الْحَجَرُ بِثَوْبِهِ. قَالَ: فَجَمَحَ مُوسَى بِإِثْرِهِ يَقُولُ: ثَوْبِي حَجَرُ، ثَوْبِي حَجَرُ، حَتَّى نَظَرَتْ بَنُو إِسْرَائِيلَ إِلَى سَوْأَةِ مُوسَى قَالُوا: وَاللهِ، مَا بِمُوسَى مِنْ بَأْسٍ، فَقَامَ الْحَجَرُ حَتَّى نُظِرَ إِلَيْهِ، قَالَ: فَأَخَذَ ثَوْبَهُ فَطَفِقَ بِالْحَجَرِ ضَرْبًا»

قَالَ أَبُو هُرَيْرَةَ: «وَاللهِ إِنَّهُ بِالْحَجَرِ نَدَبٌ سِتَّةٌ، أَوْ سَبْعَةٌ، ضَرْبُ مُوسَى بِالْحَجَرِ»

Text Explanation

The hadith mentions a story about Moses (peace be upon him). We stated in the previous chapter that it is permissible to expose one's private area when alone for a real need, such as taking a bath, urination, having intercourse with one's wife, etc. In all such cases, it is permissible to uncover one's private parts when alone. If other people are present, then it is forbidden to uncover this area, even for such purposes. Scholars say that to have a piece of cloth around one's waist when taking a bath alone is better than not having it. However, to be in the nude is permissible for the duration of the need when taking a bath, etc. but to go beyond the duration of need is prohibited, according to the more correct view. As we mentioned in the previous chapter, to cover one's private parts when alone is a duty according to the more correct view, except as needed, but God knows best. The evidence derived from this hadith is that Moses bathed in the nude in a secluded area. This is correct according to scholars of legal theory, i.e. *uṣūl al-fiqh*, who say that laws given to earlier communities are binding on us, but God knows best.

The hadith mentions that the Children of Israel used to bathe in the nude, and were able to look at one another's genitals. It may be that this was permissible in their religion but Moses refrained from doing so out of decorum or shyness. On the other hand, it might have been forbidden in their religion, as it is in ours, but they were lax in implementing this, as many of us are lax.

Those Children of Israel suggested that Moses kept bathing alone, in seclusion, because he was deformed. The hadith uses the Arabic word *ādar*, which according to linguists means 'having disproportionately large testes'.

When the stone rolled away with Moses' garment, he ran quickly after it trying to catch up. The stone then stopped and Moses was seen. When Moses took his garment, he beat the stone. Perhaps he wanted to show his people a miracle in the form of a dent on the stone caused by his beating, or it might have been that God revealed to him to beat the stone so that it would have a dent and the miracle would be clear, but God knows best.

CHAPTER 19

TAKING CARE TO COVER ONE'S PRIVATE PARTS

[612–76]. (Dār al-Salām 0670) Isḥāq ibn Ibrāhīm al-Ḥanẓalī and Muhammad ibn Ḥātim ibn Maymūn narrated:[i] both from Muhammad ibn Bakr; Ibn Jurayj reported [H]. Also, Isḥāq ibn Manṣūr and Muhammad ibn Rāfiʿ narrated to me (their text). ʿAbd al-Razzāq (Isḥāq said 'reported' but Ibn Rāfiʿ said 'narrated'); Ibn Jurayj reported; ʿAmr ibn Dīnār reported to me that he listened to Jābir ibn ʿAbdullāh when he said: **'When the Kaʿbah was being rebuilt, the Prophet and ʿAbbās worked carrying stones. Al-ʿAbbās said to the Prophet (peace be upon him): "Place your lower garment on your shoulder [to protect it] from the stones". He did so, but he fell to the ground, with his eyes staring up to the sky. He then rose and said: "My garment! My garment!" He put it on securely'.**

In his narration, Ibn Rāfiʿ said 'on your neck' not 'on your shoulder'.

وَحَدَّثَنَا إِسْحَاقُ بْنُ إِبْرَاهِيمَ الْحَنْظَلِيُّ، وَمُحَمَّدُ بْنُ حَاتِمِ بْنِ مَيْمُونٍ جَمِيعًا عَنْ مُحَمَّدِ بْنِ بَكْرٍ، قَالَ: أَخْبَرَنَا ابْنُ جُرَيْجٍ ح، وَحَدَّثَنِي إِسْحَاقُ بْنُ مَنْصُورٍ، وَمُحَمَّدُ بْنُ رَافِعٍ - وَاللَّفْظُ لَهُمَا قَالَ: إِسْحَاقُ، أَخْبَرَنَا وَقَالَ: ابْنُ رَافِعٍ - حَدَّثَنَا عَبْدُ الرَّزَّاقِ، أَخْبَرَنَا ابْنُ جُرَيْجٍ، أَخْبَرَنِي عَمْرُو بْنُ دِينَارٍ، أَنَّهُ سَمِعَ جَابِرَ بْنَ عَبْدِ اللهِ، يَقُولُ: لَمَّا بُنِيَتِ الْكَعْبَةُ ذَهَبَ النَّبِيُّ صَلَّى اللهُ عَلَيْهِ وَسَلَّمَ وَعَبَّاسٌ يَنْقُلَانِ حِجَارَةً. فَقَالَ الْعَبَّاسُ، لِلنَّبِيِّ

i. Related by al-Bukhārī, 1582 and 3829.

صَلَّى اللهُ عَلَيْهِ وَسَلَّمَ اجْعَلْ إِزَارَكَ عَلَى عَاتِقِكَ مِنَ الْحِجَارَةِ، فَفَعَلَ فَخَرَّ إِلَى الْأَرْضِ وَطَمَحَتْ عَيْنَاهُ إِلَى السَّمَاءِ، ثُمَّ قَامَ فَقَالَ: «إِزَارِي إِزَارِي» فَشَدَّ عَلَيْهِ إِزَارَهُ.

قَالَ ابْنُ رَافِعٍ فِي رِوَايَتِهِ: «عَلَى رَقَبَتِكَ» وَلَمْ يَقُلْ: عَلَى عَاتِقِكَ.

[613–77]. (Dār al-Salām 0671) Zuhayr ibn Ḥarb narrated:[i] Rawḥ ibn ʿUbādah narrated; Zakariyyā' ibn Isḥāq narrated; ʿAmr ibn Dīnār narrated. He said: I heard Jābir ibn ʿAbdullāh narrating that **'God's Messenger (peace be upon him) carried stones with them for the rebuilding of the Kaʿbah, wearing his lower garment. Al-ʿAbbās, his uncle, said to him: "Nephew, you may untie your lower garment and place it on your shoulder below the stones". He untied it and placed it on his shoulder. He fell unconscious. He was never again seen naked'**.

وَحَدَّثَنَا زُهَيْرُ بْنُ حَرْبٍ، حَدَّثَنَا رَوْحُ بْنُ عُبَادَةَ، حَدَّثَنَا زَكَرِيَّا بْنُ إِسْحَاقَ، حَدَّثَنَا عَمْرُو بْنُ دِينَارٍ، قَالَ: سَمِعْتُ جَابِرَ بْنَ عَبْدِ اللهِ، يُحَدِّثُ أَنَّ رَسُولَ اللهِ صَلَّى اللهُ عَلَيْهِ وَسَلَّمَ كَانَ يَنْقُلُ مَعَهُمُ الْحِجَارَةَ لِلْكَعْبَةِ وَعَلَيْهِ إِزَارُهُ. فَقَالَ لَهُ الْعَبَّاسُ عَمُّهُ يَا ابْنَ أَخِي لَوْ حَلَلْتَ إِزَارَكَ فَجَعَلْتَهُ عَلَى مَنْكِبِكَ دُونَ الْحِجَارَةِ. قَالَ: «فَحَلَّهُ. فَجَعَلَهُ عَلَى مَنْكِبِهِ فَسَقَطَ مَغْشِيًّا عَلَيْهِ»، قَالَ: «فَمَا رُئِيَ بَعْدَ ذَلِكَ الْيَوْمِ عُرْيَانًا»

[614–78]. (Dār al-Salām 0672) Saʿīd ibn Yaḥyā al-Umawī narrated:[ii] my father narrated to me; ʿUthmān ibn Ḥakīm ibn ʿAbbād ibn Ḥunayf al-Anṣārī narrated; Abū Umāmah ibn Sahl ibn Ḥunayf reported to me; from al-Miswar ibn Makhramah. He said: **'I came forward carrying a heavy stone, wearing a light lower garment. My garment became loose, but I had the stone and I could not drop it until I reached the place where it was**

i. Related by al-Bukhārī, 364.
ii. Related by Abū Dāwūd, 4016.

to go. God's Messenger (peace be upon him) said [to me]: "Go back and put on your garment. Never walk about naked".'

حَدَّثَنَا سَعِيدُ بْنُ يَحْيَى الْأُمَوِيُّ، حَدَّثَنِي أَبِي، حَدَّثَنَا عُثْمَانُ بْنُ حَكِيمِ بْنِ عَبَّادِ بْنِ حُنَيْفٍ الْأَنْصَارِيُّ، أَخْبَرَنِي أَبُو أُمَامَةَ بْنُ سَهْلِ بْنِ حُنَيْفٍ، عَنِ الْمِسْوَرِ بْنِ مَخْرَمَةَ، قَالَ: أَقْبَلْتُ بِحَجَرٍ أَحْمِلُهُ ثَقِيلٍ وَعَلَيَّ إِزَارٌ خَفِيفٌ، قَالَ: فَانْحَلَّ إِزَارِي وَمَعِي الْحَجَرُ لَمْ أَسْتَطِعْ أَنْ أَضَعَهُ حَتَّى بَلَغْتُ بِهِ إِلَى مَوْضِعِهِ. فَقَالَ رَسُولُ اللهِ صَلَّى اللهُ عَلَيْهِ وَسَلَّمَ: «ارْجِعْ إِلَى ثَوْبِكَ فَخُذْهُ، وَلَا تَمْشُوا عُرَاةً»

Text Explanation

The first hadith is narrated by Jābir ibn ʿAbdullāh, and he does not attribute it to the Prophet. As such, it is classified as *mursal*, or incomplete. We have stated earlier that a *mursal* by a companion of the Prophet is accepted by all scholars as valid evidence, except by Abu Isḥāq al-Farāyīnī, who does not accept such hadiths as valid for deducing rulings. We have outlined the view of the majority of scholars on this point in the Notes in our Introduction.

The Kaʿbah is given this name because of its height, but some say because of its shape, as a cube, and its height, but God knows best. When the Prophet was taking part in the work to rebuild the Kaʿbah, his uncle al-ʿAbbās was with him and he suggested that he should place his lower garment on his shoulder as protection. When the Prophet did so, he fell to the ground with his eyes staring to the sky. This explains some aspects of the care God took of His future messenger, protecting him from unbecoming behaviour that was acceptable in pre-Islamic days. We have discussed the infallibility of prophets in the Book of Faith.

In a different version entered in Hadith anthologies other than the two *Ṣaḥīḥ*s, it is stated that an angel came down and tied up the Prophet's lower garment for him, but God knows best.

In the last hadith, the Prophet tells his companion not to walk about naked. This is an order of prohibition, as we have explained in the previous chapter, but God knows best.

CHAPTER 20

WHAT COVER TO USE WHEN RELIEVING ONESELF

[615–79]. (Dār al-Salām 0673) Shaybān ibn Farrūkh and ʿAbdullāh ibn Muhammad ibn Asmā' al-Ḍubaʿī narrated:[i] both said: Mahdī (who is Ibn Maymūn) narrated; Muhammad ibn ʿAbdullāh ibn Abī Yaʿqūb narrated; from al-Ḥasan ibn Saʿd, who is al-Ḥasan ibn ʿAlī's *mawlā*; from ʿAbdullāh ibn Jaʿfar: **'One day God's Messenger (peace be upon him) took me behind him on his mount, and he told me a secret I would never mention to any human being. The screen God's Messenger preferred to have when he relieved himself was a knoll or [an area of] palm date trees'.**

حَدَّثَنَا شَيْبَانُ بْنُ فَرُّوخَ، وَعَبْدُ اللهِ بْنُ مُحَمَّدِ بْنِ أَسْمَاءَ الضُّبَعِيُّ، قَالَا: حَدَّثَنَا مَهْدِيٌّ وَهُوَ ابْنُ مَيْمُونٍ، حَدَّثَنَا مُحَمَّدُ بْنُ عَبْدِ اللهِ بْنِ أَبِي يَعْقُوبَ، عَنِ الْحَسَنِ بْنِ سَعْدٍ، مَوْلَى الْحَسَنِ بْنِ عَلِيٍّ، عَنْ عَبْدِ اللهِ بْنِ جَعْفَرٍ، قَالَ: أَرْدَفَنِي رَسُولُ اللهِ صَلَّى اللهُ عَلَيْهِ وَسَلَّمَ ذَاتَ يَوْمٍ خَلْفَهُ. فَأَسَرَّ إِلَيَّ حَدِيثًا لَا أُحَدِّثُ بِهِ أَحَدًا مِنَ النَّاسِ «وَكَانَ أَحَبَّ مَا اسْتَتَرَ بِهِ رَسُولُ اللهِ صَلَّى اللهُ عَلَيْهِ وَسَلَّمَ لِحَاجَتِهِ، هَدَفٌ أَوْ حَائِشُ نَخْلٍ» قَالَ ابْنُ أَسْمَاءَ فِي حَدِيثِهِ: «يَعْنِي حَائِطَ نَخْلٍ»

Text Explanation

The hadith mentions that the screen behind which the Prophet preferred to answer the call of nature was a knoll, or any rise in

i. Related by Abū Dāwūd, 2549; Ibn Mājah, 340 (in a shorter version).

the ground to give him such shelter, so as not to be seen from any distance. Alternatively, in a date farm where the thick trees give complete cover. The hadith shows that a covering that gives one full screening, so as not to be seen at all, is most preferable. This applies to a rise or slope in the ground, as well as to thick trees in a farm. This is a well established Sunnah, but God knows best.

CHAPTER 21

WHAT REQUIRES TAKING A BATH

[616–80]. (Dār al-Salām 0674) Yaḥyā ibn Yaḥyā, Yaḥyā ibn Ayyūb, Qutaybah and Ibn Ḥujr narrated: Ismāʿīl (who is Ibn Jaʿfar) (Yaḥyā ibn Yaḥyā said 'reported' while the others said 'narrated'); from Sharīk (meaning Ibn Abī Namir); from ʿAbd al-Raḥmān ibn Abī Saʿīd al-Khudrī; from his father who said: **'I went with God's Messenger (peace be upon him) on a Monday to Quba'. When we were at the quarters of Banī Sālim, the Prophet stopped at ʿItbān's door and called out to him. He came out dragging his lower garment. The Prophet said: "We have hastened the man". ʿItbān said: "Messenger of God, suppose a man withdraws from his wife without having discharged semen. What is required of him?" The Prophet said: "The use of water is required only for [the discharge of] the fluid".'**

وَحَدَّثَنَا يَحْيَى بْنُ يَحْيَى، وَيَحْيَى بْنُ أَيُّوبَ، وَقُتَيْبَةُ، وَابْنُ حُجْرٍ، - قَالَ يَحْيَى بْنُ يَحْيَى: أَخْبَرَنَا، وَقَالَ الآخَرُونَ - حَدَّثَنَا إِسْمَاعِيلُ وَهُوَ ابْنُ جَعْفَرٍ، عَنْ شَرِيكٍ يَعْنِي ابْنَ أَبِي نَمِرٍ، عَنْ عَبْدِ الرَّحْمَنِ بْنِ أَبِي سَعِيدٍ الْخُدْرِيِّ، عَنْ أَبِيهِ، قَالَ خَرَجْتُ مَعَ رَسُولِ اللهِ صَلَّى اللهُ عَلَيْهِ وَسَلَّمَ يَوْمَ الاِثْنَيْنِ إِلَى قُبَاءَ حَتَّى إِذَا كُنَّا فِي بَنِي سَالِمٍ. وَقَفَ رَسُولُ اللهِ صَلَّى اللهُ عَلَيْهِ وَسَلَّمَ عَلَى بَابِ عِتْبَانَ فَصَرَخَ بِهِ، فَخَرَجَ يَجُرُّ إِزَارَهُ، فَقَالَ رَسُولُ اللهِ صَلَّى اللهُ عَلَيْهِ وَسَلَّمَ: «أَعْجَلْنَا الرَّجُلَ» فَقَالَ عِتْبَانُ: يَا رَسُولَ اللهِ، أَرَأَيْتَ الرَّجُلَ يُعْجَلُ عَنِ امْرَأَتِهِ وَلَمْ يُمْنِ، مَاذَا عَلَيْهِ؟ قَالَ رَسُولُ اللهِ صَلَّى اللهُ عَلَيْهِ وَسَلَّمَ: «إِنَّمَا الْمَاءُ مِنَ الْمَاءِ»

[617–81]. (Dār al-Salām)[i] Hārūn ibn Saʿīd al-Aylī narrated:[ii] Ibn Wahb narrated; ʿAmr ibn al-Ḥārith reported to me; from Ibn Shihāb that he narrated to him that Abū Salamah ibn ʿAbd al-Raḥmān narrated to him; from Abū Saʿīd al-Khudrī that the Prophet said: **'The use of water is required only for [the discharge of] the fluid'**.

حَدَّثَنَا هَارُونُ بْنُ سَعِيدٍ الْأَيْلِيُّ، حَدَّثَنَا ابْنُ وَهْبٍ، أَخْبَرَنِي عَمْرُو بْنُ الْحَارِثِ، عَنِ ابْنِ شِهَابٍ حَدَّثَهُ، أَنَّ أَبَا سَلَمَةَ بْنَ عَبْدِ الرَّحْمَنِ حَدَّثَهُ، عَنْ أَبِي سَعِيدٍ الْخُدْرِيِّ، عَنِ النَّبِيِّ صَلَّى اللهُ عَلَيْهِ وَسَلَّمَ أَنَّهُ قَالَ: «إِنَّمَا الْمَاءُ مِنَ الْمَاءِ»

[618–82]. (Dār al-Salām 0675) ʿUbaydullāh ibn Muʿādh al-ʿAnbarī narrated: al-Muʿtamir narrated; my father narrated; Abū al-ʿAlāʾ ibn al-Shikhkhīr narrated: **'Some hadiths of the Prophet qualified others, just like verses of the Qur'an qualified others'**.

حَدَّثَنَا عُبَيْدُ اللهِ بْنُ مُعَاذٍ الْعَنْبَرِيُّ، حَدَّثَنَا الْمُعْتَمِرُ، حَدَّثَنَا أَبِي، حَدَّثَنَا أَبُو الْعَلَاءِ بْنُ الشِّخِّيرِ، قَالَ: «كَانَ رَسُولُ اللهِ صَلَّى اللهُ عَلَيْهِ وَسَلَّمَ يَنْسَخُ حَدِيثُهُ بَعْضُهُ بَعْضًا، كَمَا يَنْسَخُ الْقُرْآنُ بَعْضُهُ بَعْضًا»

[619–83]. (Dār al-Salām 0676) Abū Bakr ibn Abī Shaybah narrated:[iii] Ghundar narrated; from Shuʿbah [H]. Also, Muhammad ibn al-Muthannā and Ibn Bashshār narrated; Muhammad ibn Jaʿfar narrated; Shuʿbah narrated; from al-Ḥakam; from Dhakwān; from Abū Saʿīd al-Khudrī: **'God's Messenger (peace be upon him) passed by [the house of] a**

i. This hadith is not included in Dār al-Salām's edition.
ii. Related by Abū Dāwūd, 217.
iii. Related by al-Bukhārī, 180; Ibn Mājah, 606.

man from the Anṣār. He sent someone to call him. The man came out, with his head dripping. [The Prophet] said: "Have we hastened you?" He said: "Yes, Messenger of God". The Prophet said: "If you are hastened or failed [to discharge] then you need not take a bath. You are only required to perform minor ritual ablution [i.e. *wuḍū'*].'

Ibn Bashshār said: **'If you are hastened or deprived …'.**

حَدَّثَنَا أَبُو بَكْرِ بْنُ أَبِي شَيْبَةَ، حَدَّثَنَا غُنْدَرٌ، عَنْ شُعْبَةَ، ح، وَحَدَّثَنَا مُحَمَّدُ بْنُ الْـمُثَنَّى، وَابْنُ بَشَّارٍ، قَالَا: حَدَّثَنَا مُحَمَّدُ بْنُ جَعْفَرٍ، حَدَّثَنَا شُعْبَةُ، عَنِ الْحَكَمِ، عَنْ ذَكْوَانَ، عَنْ أَبِي سَعِيدٍ الْخُدْرِيِّ، أَنَّ رَسُولَ اللهِ صَلَّى اللهُ عَلَيْهِ وَسَلَّمَ مَرَّ عَلَى رَجُلٍ مِنَ الْأَنْصَارِ. فَأَرْسَلَ إِلَيْهِ. فَخَرَجَ وَرَأْسُهُ يَقْطُرُ، فَقَالَ: «لَعَلَّنَا أَعْجَلْنَاكَ؟» قَالَ: نَعَمْ يَا رَسُولَ اللهِ، قَالَ: «إِذَا أُعْجِلْتَ أَوْ أَقْحَطْتَ فَلَا غُسْلَ عَلَيْكَ، وَعَلَيْكَ الْوُضُوءُ»

وَقَالَ ابْنُ بَشَّارٍ: «إِذَا أُعْجِلْتَ، أَوْ أُقْحِطْتَ ...»

[620–84]. (Dār al-Salām 0677) Abū al-Rabī' al-Zahrānī:[i] Ḥammād narrated; Hishām ibn 'Urwah narrated [H]. Also, Abū Kurayb Muhammad ibn al-'Alā' narrated (his text); Abū Mu'āwiyah narrated; Hishām narrated; from his father; from Abu Ayyūb; from Ubayy ibn Ka'b: **'I asked God's Messenger (peace be upon him) about the case of a man who makes love with his wife but stops short. He said: "He should wash off what has dropped on him from his wife then perform the ablution and pray".'**

حَدَّثَنَا أَبُو الرَّبِيعِ الزَّهْرَانِيُّ، حَدَّثَنَا حَمَّادٌ، حَدَّثَنَا هِشَامُ بْنُ عُرْوَةَ ح، وَحَدَّثَنَا أَبُو كُرَيْبٍ مُحَمَّدُ بْنُ الْعَلَاءِ، - وَاللَّفْظُ لَهُ -، حَدَّثَنَا أَبُو مُعَاوِيَةَ، حَدَّثَنَا هِشَامٌ، عَنْ أَبِيهِ، عَنْ أَبِي

i. Related by al-Bukhārī, 293.

أَيُّوبَ، عَنْ أُبَيِّ بْنِ كَعْبٍ، قَالَ: سَأَلْتُ رَسُولَ اللهِ صَلَّى اللهُ عَلَيْهِ وَسَلَّمَ عَنِ الرَّجُلِ يُصِيبُ مِنَ الْمَرْأَةِ ثُمَّ يُكْسِلُ؟ فَقَالَ: «يَغْسِلُ مَا أَصَابَهُ مِنَ الْمَرْأَةِ ثُمَّ يَتَوَضَّأُ، وَيُصَلِّي»

[621–85]. (Dār al-Salām 0678) Muhammad ibn al-Muthannā narrated: Muhammad ibn Jaʿfar narrated; Shuʿbah narrated; from Hishām ibn ʿUrwah; my father narrated to me; from al-Malī; from al-Malī (as he says al-Malī from al-Malī, he means Abū Ayyūb); from Ubayy ibn Kaʿb; from God's Messenger (peace be upon him), speaking about a man having intercourse with his wife but without discharging semen. He said: **'He should wash his genital organ and perform the ablution'**.

وَحَدَّثَنَا مُحَمَّدُ بْنُ الْمُثَنَّى، حَدَّثَنَا مُحَمَّدُ بْنُ جَعْفَرٍ، حَدَّثَنَا شُعْبَةُ، عَنْ هِشَامِ بْنِ عُرْوَةَ، حَدَّثَنِي أَبِي، عَنْ - الْمَلِيِّ عَنِ الْمَلِيِّ يَعْنِي بِقَوْلِهِ الْمَلِيِّ عَنِ الْمَلِيِّ - أَبُو أَيُّوبَ، عَنْ أُبَيِّ بْنِ كَعْبٍ، عَنْ رَسُولِ اللهِ صَلَّى اللهُ عَلَيْهِ وَسَلَّمَ أَنَّهُ قَالَ: فِي الرَّجُلِ يَأْتِي أَهْلَهُ ثُمَّ لَا يُنْزِلُ قَالَ: «يَغْسِلُ ذَكَرَهُ، وَيَتَوَضَّأُ»

[622–86]. (Dār al-Salām 0680)[i] Zuhayr ibn Ḥarb and ʿAbd ibn Ḥumayd narrated to me:[ii] ʿAbd al-Ṣamad ibn ʿAbd al-Wārith [H]. Also, ʿAbd al-Wārith ibn ʿAbd al-Ṣamad narrated (his text); my father narrated to me; from my grandfather; from al-Ḥusayn ibn Dhakwān; from Yaḥyā ibn Abī Kathīr; Abū Salamah reported to me; that ʿAṭā' ibn Yasār reported to him; that Zayd ibn Khālid al-Juhanī reported to him; that he asked ʿUthmān ibn ʿAffān: **'Suppose that a man has sexual intercourse with his wife but without discharging semen'. ʿUthmān said: 'He**

i. Dār al-Salām's translation includes a short hadith, giving it number 0679, but this hadith is not included in Arabic copies with al-Nawawī's commentary, and it merely mentions that ejaculation requires taking a full bath.

ii. Related by al-Bukhārī, 179 and 292.

performs the ablution as he would do for prayer, after having washed his genital organ'. 'Uthmān added: 'I heard this from God's Messenger (peace be upon him)'.

وَحَدَّثَنِي زُهَيْرُ بْنُ حَرْبٍ، وَعَبْدُ بْنُ حُمَيْدٍ قَالَا: حَدَّثَنَا عَبْدُ الصَّمَدِ بْنُ عَبْدِ الْوَارِثِ ح، وَحَدَّثَنَا عَبْدُ الْوَارِثِ بْنُ عَبْدِ الصَّمَدِ - وَاللَّفْظُ لَهُ - حَدَّثَنِي أَبِي، عَنْ جَدِّي، عَنِ الْحُسَيْنِ بْنِ ذَكْوَانَ، عَنْ يَحْيَى بْنِ أَبِي كَثِيرٍ، أَخْبَرَنِي أَبُو سَلَمَةَ، أَنَّ عَطَاءَ بْنَ يَسَارٍ، أَخْبَرَهُ أَنَّ زَيْدَ بْنَ خَالِدٍ الْجُهَنِيَّ، أَخْبَرَهُ أَنَّهُ سَأَلَ عُثْمَانَ بْنَ عَفَّانَ، قَالَ: قُلْتُ: أَرَأَيْتَ إِذَا جَامَعَ الرَّجُلُ امْرَأَتَهُ، وَلَمْ يُمْنِ؟ قَالَ عُثْمَانُ: «يَتَوَضَّأُ كَمَا يَتَوَضَّأُ لِلصَّلَاةِ، وَيَغْسِلُ ذَكَرَهُ» قَالَ عُثْمَانُ سَمِعْتُهُ مِنْ رَسُولِ اللهِ صَلَّى اللهُ عَلَيْهِ وَسَلَّمَ.

[000–000]. (Dār al-Salām 0681) ʿAbd al-Wārith ibn ʿAbd al-Ṣamad narrated: my father narrated to me; from my grandfather; from al-Ḥusayn. Yaḥyā said: And Abū Salamah reported to me; that ʿUrwah ibn al-Zubayr reported to him; that Abū Ayyub reported to him; that he heard that from God's Messenger (peace be upon him).

وَحَدَّثَنَا عَبْدُ الْوَارِثِ بْنُ عَبْدِ الصَّمَدِ، حَدَّثَنِي أَبِي، عَنْ جَدِّي، عَنِ الْحُسَيْنِ، قَالَ يَحْيَى: وَأَخْبَرَنِي أَبُو سَلَمَةَ، أَنَّ عُرْوَةَ بْنَ الزُّبَيْرِ، أَخْبَرَهُ أَنَّ أَبَا أَيُّوبَ، أَخْبَرَهُ أَنَّهُ سَمِعَ ذَلِكَ مِنْ رَسُولِ اللهِ صَلَّى اللهُ عَلَيْهِ وَسَلَّمَ.

Text Explanation

It must be clear that the entire Muslim community is unanimous that taking a full bath is obligatory after sexual intercourse, even if such intercourse is not accompanied by ejaculation. It is also obligatory in the case of ejaculation. A number of the Prophet's companions were of the view that taking a bath is not obligatory unless ejaculation has taken place, but some of them changed their view. Unanimity was achieved after the others had passed away.

This chapter starts with the hadith that says: 'The use of water is required only for [the discharge of] the fluid'. It also includes the hadith narrated by Ubayy ibn Kaʿb from the Prophet, concerning the situation of a man who has intercourse with his wife but without ejaculation. He said: 'He washes his genital organ then performs the ablution'. There is also the hadith in the next chapter which says: 'If he sits between her four limbs and exerts his effort with her, he incurs the duty of taking a bath even if without ejaculation'. Scholars say that this is the definitive hadith. They maintain that the first hadith has been qualified. This is the hadith that says: 'The use of water is required only for [the discharge of] the fluid'. This is the view of the majority of the Prophet's companions and later scholars. What they mean by the ruling being qualified is that it was not in force, but was subsequently made binding. Ibn ʿAbbās and others are of the view that it was not qualified. It only meant that taking a bath is not obligatory for seeing a sexual dream unless it is coupled with ejaculation. This ruling remains valid without doubt. As for the hadith narrated by Ubayy ibn Kaʿb, which speaks of intercourse without ejaculation, it is understood in two ways. The first is that it is abrogated, and the second understands it as meaning foreplay without actual penetration, but God knows best.

Muslim includes hadith No. 618, which says that some of the Prophet's hadiths qualified others in the same way as Qur'anic verses qualified earlier ones. Muslim's purpose of including this hadith is to show that the earlier hadith that says 'The use of water is required only for [the discharge of] the fluid', has been qualified[i] by later hadiths.

Scholars say that qualifying hadiths by later ones takes four different ways. The first is that a recurrent [i.e. *mutawātir*] hadith is qualified by a similarly recurrent one. The second is a singly-reported hadith

---

i. It should be pointed out that although most translations of the word *nasakha* and its derivatives use the term 'abrogated', I am using here the term 'qualified'. My preference for 'qualified' is that in practically all cases, the earlier ruling is not annulled altogether, but rather it is modified. It may even remain applicable in certain conditions which mirror the time when it was in force during the Prophet's lifetime.

[i.e. *āḥād*] is qualified by a similarly singly-reported one. The third is the case of a singly-reported hadith is qualified by a recurrent hadith and the fourth is that a recurrent hadith qualified by a singly-reported one. The first three are generally agreed to be valid, but the fourth is invalid according to the vast majority of scholars, even though some scholars of the Ẓāhirī School allow it, but God knows best.

In hadith No. 620, the Prophet gives the instruction, 'he should wash off what has dropped on him from his wife'. This is clear evidence that the wetness of a woman's vagina is impure. However, this is subject to well-known differences of opinion among scholars. The more correct view, according to some of our scholars, is that it is impure, i.e. *najis*. However, scholars who disagree, maintaining that it is not impure, understand the hadith as giving a preference, rather than an obligation. This is the more correct view according to the majority of our scholars, but God knows best.

Transmission

Hadith No. 618 features in its chain of transmission: 'Ubaydullāh ibn Mu'ādh al-'Anbarī, al-Mu'tamir and his father as well as Abū al-'Alā' ibn al-Shikhkhīr. This chain of transmission consists of narrators who all belonged to Basrah except for Abū al-'Alā' who was from Kufah. His name is Yazīd ibn 'Abdullāh ibn al-Shikhkhīr, and he belonged to the Tābi'īn generation.

The chain of transmission of hadith No. 621 mentions 'from al-Malī; from al-Malī'. Al-Malī is a description, and this is why Muslim identifies him as Abū Ayyūb. The description means 'the reliable who is to be trusted'.

CHAPTER 22

WHEN THE TWO GENITALS MEET, A BATH IS OBLIGATORY

[623–87]. (Dār al-Salām 0682) Zuhayr ibn Ḥarb and Abū Ghassān al-Mismaʿī narrated to me [H].[i] Also, Muhammad ibn al-Muthannā and Ibn Bashshār narrated it. They all said: Muʿādh ibn Hishām narrated; my father narrated to me; from Qatādah; and also Maṭar narrated from al-Ḥasan; from Abū Rāfiʿ; from Abū Hurayrah that the Prophet said: **'If the man takes his position between her four limbs and works himself over her, taking a bath is obligatory to him'**.

Maṭar adds in his narration: **'Even if he does not ejaculate'**. Only Zuhayr uses the word *ashʿub* instead of *shuʿab*, both of which mean 'limbs', and both are derived from the same root.

وَحَدَّثَنِي زُهَيْرُ بْنُ حَرْبٍ، وَأَبُو غَسَّانَ الْمِسْمَعِيُّ، ح، وَحَدَّثَنَاهُ مُحَمَّدُ بْنُ الْمُثَنَّى، وَابْنُ بَشَّارٍ قَالُوا: حَدَّثَنَا مُعَاذُ بْنُ هِشَامٍ، قَالَ: حَدَّثَنِي أَبِي، عَنْ قَتَادَةَ، وَمَطَرٌ، عَنِ الْحَسَنِ، عَنْ أَبِي رَافِعٍ، عَنْ أَبِي هُرَيْرَةَ، أَنَّ نَبِيَّ اللهِ صَلَّى اللهُ عَلَيْهِ وَسَلَّمَ قَالَ: «إِذَا جَلَسَ بَيْنَ شُعَبِهَا الْأَرْبَعِ ثُمَّ جَهَدَهَا، فَقَدْ وَجَبَ عَلَيْهِ الْغُسْلُ» وَفِي حَدِيثِ مَطَرٍ وَإِنْ لَمْ يُنْزِلْ قَالَ زُهَيْرٌ: مِنْ بَيْنِهِمْ بَيْنَ أَشْعُبِهَا الْأَرْبَعِ.

[624–000]. (Dār al-Salām 0683) Muhammad ibn ʿAmr ibn ʿAbbād ibn Jabalah narrated: Muhammad ibn Abī ʿAdī narrated [H]. Also, Muhammad ibn al-Muthannā narrated; Wahb ibn

i. Related by al-Bukhārī, 291; Abū Dāwūd, 216; al-Nasāʾī, 191; Ibn Mājah, 610.

Jarīr narrated to me; both from Shu'bah; from Qatādah; with this same chain of transmission: **The same text**, except that Shu'bah uses another variant of the word meaning 'works himself', and does not say 'even if he does not ejaculate'.

حَدَّثَنَا مُحَمَّدُ بْنُ عَمْرِو بْنِ عَبَّادِ بْنِ جَبَلَةَ، حَدَّثَنَا مُحَمَّدُ بْنُ أَبِي عَدِيٍّ، ح، وَحَدَّثَنَا مُحَمَّدُ بْنُ الْمُثَنَّى، حَدَّثَنِي وَهْبُ بْنُ جَرِيرٍ، كِلَاهُمَا عَنْ شُعْبَةَ، عَنْ قَتَادَةَ بِهَذَا الْإِسْنَادِ مِثْلَهُ، غَيْرَ أَنَّ فِي حَدِيثِ شُعْبَةَ ثُمَّ اجْتَهَدَ وَلَمْ يَقُلْ «وَإِنْ لَمْ يُنْزِلْ»

[625–88]. (Dār al-Salām 0684) Muhammad ibn al-Muthannā narrated: Muhammad ibn 'Abdullāh al-Anṣārī narrated; Hishām ibn Ḥassān narrated; Ḥumayd ibn Hilāl narrated; from Abū Burdah; from Abū Mūsā al-Ash'arī [H]. Also, Muhammad ibn al-Muthannā narrated; 'Abd al-A'lā narrated (this is his text); Hishām narrated; from Ḥumayd ibn Hilāl. He said: 'I do not know it except from Abū Burdah); from Abū Mūsā who said: '**A number of the Muhājirīn and the Anṣār differed on this point. The Anṣār said: "A bath becomes obligatory only in the case of ejaculation", but the Muhājirīn said: "If intercourse takes place, taking a bath becomes obligatory". Abū Mūsā said to them: "I will bring you the definitive answer". I left them and sought permission to enter 'Ā'ishah's place, and permission was granted. I said to her: "Mother, (or Mother of the Believers), I want to put a question to you but I feel embarrassed". She said: "Do not be embarrassed to ask me what you would have asked your mother who gave birth to you. I am your mother". I said: "What makes taking a bath obligatory"? She said: "You are asking the expert. God's Messenger (peace be upon him) said: 'If the man takes his position between her four limbs and the two genitals meet, a bath becomes obligatory'"**.'

وَحَدَّثَنَا مُحَمَّدُ بْنُ الْـمُثَنَّى، حَدَّثَنَا مُحَمَّدُ بْنُ عِبْدِ اللهِ الْأَنْصَارِيُّ، حَدَّثَنَا هِشَامُ بْنُ حَسَّانَ، حَدَّثَنَا حُمَيْدُ بْنُ هِلَالٍ، عَنْ أَبِي بُرْدَةَ، عَنْ أَبِي مُوسَى الْأَشْعَرِيِّ ح، وَحَدَّثَنَا مُحَمَّدُ بْنُ الْـمُثَنَّى، حَدَّثَنَا عَبْدُ الْأَعْلَى، وَهَذَا حَدِيثُهُ حَدَّثَنَا هِشَامٌ، عَنْ حُمَيْدِ بْنِ هِلَالٍ، قَالَ: - وَلَا أَعْلَمُهُ إِلَّا عَنْ أَبِي بُرْدَةَ، عَنْ أَبِي مُوسَى، قَالَ: اخْتَلَفَ فِي ذَلِكَ رَهْطٌ مِنَ الْـمُهَاجِرِينَ، وَالْأَنْصَارِ فَقَالَ الْأَنْصَارِيُّونَ: لَا يَجِبُ الْغُسْلُ إِلَّا مِنَ الدَّفْقِ أَوْ مِنَ الْـمَاءِ. وَقَالَ الْـمُهَاجِرُونَ: بَلْ إِذَا خَالَطَ فَقَدْ وَجَبَ الْغُسْلُ، قَالَ: قَالَ أَبُو مُوسَى: فَأَنَا أَشْفِيكُمْ مِنْ ذَلِكَ فَقُمْتُ فَاسْتَأْذَنْتُ عَلَى عَائِشَةَ فَأُذِنَ لِي، فَقُلْتُ لَهَا: يَا أُمَّاهْ - أَوْ يَا أُمَّ الْـمُؤْمِنِينَ - إِنِّي أُرِيدُ أَنْ أَسْأَلَكِ عَنْ شَيْءٍ وَإِنِّي أَسْتَحْيِيكِ، فَقَالَتْ: لَا تَسْتَحْيِي أَنْ تَسْأَلَنِي عَمَّا كُنْتَ سَائِلًا عَنْهُ أُمَّكَ الَّتِي وَلَدَتْكَ، فَإِنَّمَا أَنَا أُمُّكَ، قُلْتُ: فَمَا يُوجِبُ الْغُسْلَ؟ قَالَتْ عَلَى الْخَبِيرِ سَقَطْتَ، قَالَ رَسُولُ اللهِ صَلَّى اللهُ عَلَيْهِ وَسَلَّمَ: «إِذَا جَلَسَ بَيْنَ شُعَبِهَا الْأَرْبَعِ وَمَسَّ الْخِتَانُ الْخِتَانَ فَقَدْ وَجَبَ الْغُسْلُ»

[626–89]. (Dār al-Salām 0685) Hārūn ibn Maʿrūf and Hārūn ibn Saʿīd al-Aylī narrated: Ibn Wahb narrated; ʿIyāḍ ibn ʿAbdullāh reported to me; from Abū al-Zubayr; from Jābir ibn ʿAbdullāh; from Umm Kulthūm; from ʿĀʾishah, the Prophet's wife. She said: **'A man asked God's Messenger (peace be upon him) about the case of a man who has sexual intercourse with his wife but does not ejaculate. Are they required to take a bath? ʿĀʾishah was present. God's Messenger (peace be upon him) said to him: "I do that, with this one, then we take a bath".'**

حَدَّثَنَا هَارُونُ بْنُ مَعْرُوفٍ، وَهَارُونُ بْنُ سَعِيدٍ الْأَيْلِيُّ، قَالَا: حَدَّثَنَا ابْنُ وَهْبٍ، أَخْبَرَنِي عِيَاضُ بْنُ عَبْدِ اللهِ، عَنْ أَبِي الزُّبَيْرِ، عَنْ جَابِرِ بْنِ عَبْدِ اللهِ، عَنْ أُمِّ كُلْثُومٍ، عَنْ عَائِشَةَ، زَوْجِ النَّبِيِّ صَلَّى اللهُ عَلَيْهِ وَسَلَّمَ قَالَتْ: إِنَّ رَجُلًا سَأَلَ رَسُولَ اللهِ صَلَّى اللهُ عَلَيْهِ وَسَلَّمَ عَنِ الرَّجُلِ يُجَامِعُ أَهْلَهُ ثُمَّ يُكْسِلُ هَلْ عَلَيْهِمَا الْغُسْلُ؟ وَعَائِشَةُ جَالِسَةٌ. فَقَالَ رَسُولُ اللهِ صَلَّى اللهُ عَلَيْهِ وَسَلَّمَ: «إِنِّي لَأَفْعَلُ ذَلِكَ، أَنَا وَهَذِهِ، ثُمَّ نَغْتَسِلُ»

Text Explanation

The first hadith in this chapter refers to a man taking his position between his wife's four limbs. The Arabic word used here is *shuʿab*, which literally means exterior parts. Scholars differ as to what the word's usage in this instance means. It is said that it means her arms and legs, or legs and thighs, and other meanings are suggested. *Qāḍī* ʿIyāḍ says it refers to the four sides of her vagina. Al-Khaṭṭābī said that 'works himself over her' refers to penetration. Others said that it means 'he tires her'. *Qāḍī* ʿIyāḍ said: 'It is better to say that it means that he exerts his effort over her. The Arabic word refers to straining oneself, which means movement and the ability to do it … Otherwise, what strain is there?' but God knows best.

The hadith means that taking a bath does not become obligatory only if ejaculation takes place and semen is discharged. Once the tip of the man's genital enters the woman's vagina, taking a bath becomes obligatory for both man and wife. There is no disagreement on this point now. There was some disagreement among the Prophet's companions and their successors, but now the unanimous view is the one we have mentioned. We have already explained this.

Our scholars say: If a man puts the top of his genital organ in the back passage of a woman or a man or in the vagina or back passage of an animal, taking a bath is obligatory, whether that person or animal is alive or dead, young or old, and whether it is deliberate or unconsciously done, by choice or under duress, or even if the woman places it in her vagina while he is asleep, or whether an erection takes place or not, and whether the man is circumcised or not. In all such situations, taking a bath is obligatory for both parties, except in the case of either one being a young boy or girl. In this case we do not say that the bath is obligatory on him or her, but we say that they are now in a state of major ritual impurity. If the child is of an age when he can take action, his or her guardian must tell him to take a bath, just like he tells them to perform the ablution. If they pray without taking a bath, their prayer is invalid. If either does not take a bath until they attain puberty, taking a bath becomes obligatory. If they take a bath when they are still children, this is sufficient and no repeat of the bath is necessary.

Our scholars say that sexual intercourse is deemed to have taken place when the top part of the man's genital organ has been inserted into the woman's vagina. Once the whole of that top part has been inserted, all rulings related to intercourse apply. Scholars are in agreement that it is not conditional that the whole of the man's organ is inserted in the vagina. However, if only a portion of the top part is inserted, then none of the rulings apply, according to all scholars, except for an odd view that mentions that even a small part is like the whole of the top part. This view is both strange and wrong. If a portion of the man's genital organ has been cut off, then if the remaining part is less than the length of the top part, then its insertion in the vagina is meaningless and none of the rulings related to intercourse applies. If the remaining part is longer than the top part, there are two views expressed by our Shāfiʿī scholars. The more correct one is that rulings apply when a portion of it equal to the top part has been inserted, and the other view is that none of the rulings applies unless all of the remaining part is inserted, but God knows best.

If the man wraps his genital organ with a piece of cloth or some other covering before inserting it in a woman's vagina, our scholars give three different views: the best-known and correct one is that both must take a bath.[i] The second view is that no bath is obligatory to them because of the covering. The third says that if the covering is thick enough to prevent sensation and pleasure, then taking a bath is not required. Otherwise, it is obligatory, but God knows best. If the woman deliberately inserts in her vagina the gential organ of an animal, she must take a bath. If she inserts an organ that has been cut off, there are two views, the more correct of which is that she must take a bath.

When Abū Mūsā put his question to ʿĀ'ishah, she told him that he asked an expert. She meant that she was well aware of the case in question and knew its details. She quoted the Prophet who said: 'When … and the two genitals meet, a bath becomes obligatory'.

i. This makes clear that if the man uses a condom, a bath is obligatory to both man and wife.

Scholars say this means that penetration of the man's organ in the woman's vagina has taken place, not the mere touch of the two genitals. Scholars are unanimous that if the man places his genital organ on the woman's vagina, without insertion, no obligatory bath is required of either.

In the last hadith, No. 626, the Prophet answers his questioner by saying: 'I do that, with this one, then we take a bath'. This suggests that it is permissible to talk about such matters in the presence of one's wife, if such is beneficial and no harm is caused. The Prophet said this so as to make his answer clearer to his questioner. Moreover, it suggests that it is obligatory. Otherwise, the man would not have received a full answer.

Transmission

In the chain of transmission of the first hadith we have Abū Ghassān al-Misma'ī, whose name is Mālik ibn 'Abd al-Wāḥid. I have mentioned him several times earlier, but I am repeating it here for easier reference, as I promised in the Introduction. Abu Rāfi''s name is Nufay', and he was also mentioned earlier.

The chain of transmission of the last hadith in this chapter, No. 626, includes 'Jābir ibn 'Abdullāh; from Umm Kulthūm; from 'Ā'ishah'. Umm Kulthūm was the daughter of Abū Bakr, but she belonged to the Tābi'īn generation. Thus, we have here an example of seniors reporting from their juniors. Jābir was a companion of the Prophet and he was older and of higher rank than Umm Kulthūm. May God be pleased with them and all the Prophet's companions and their successors.

CHAPTER 23

THE REQUIREMENT OF ABLUTION FOR EATING COOKED FOOD

[627–90]. (Dār al-Salām 0686) ʿAbd al-Malik ibn Shuʿayb ibn al-Layth narrated:[i] my father narrated to me; from my grandfather; from ʿUqayl ibn Khālid; Ibn Shihāb said: ʿAbd al-Malik ibn Abī Bakr ibn ʿAbd al-Raḥmān ibn al-Ḥārith ibn Hishām reported to me; that Khārijah ibn Zayd al-Anṣārī reported to him; that his father Zayd ibn Thābit said: I heard God's Messenger (peace be upon him) say: **'Ablution is required for eating what is cooked on fire'**.

وَحَدَّثَنَا عَبْدُ الْمَلِكِ بْنُ شُعَيْبِ بْنِ اللَّيْثِ، قَالَ: حَدَّثَنِي أَبِي، عَنْ جَدِّي، حَدَّثَنِي عُقَيْلُ بْنُ خَالِدٍ، قَالَ: قَالَ ابْنُ شِهَابٍ: أَخْبَرَنِي عَبْدُ الْمَلِكِ بْنُ أَبِي بَكْرِ بْنِ عَبْدِ الرَّحْمَنِ بْنِ الْحَارِثِ بْنِ هِشَامٍ، أَنَّ خَارِجَةَ بْنَ زَيْدٍ الْأَنْصَارِيَّ، أَخْبَرَهُ أَنَّ أَبَاهُ زَيْدَ بْنَ ثَابِتٍ قَالَ: سَمِعْتُ رَسُولَ اللهِ صَلَّى اللهُ عَلَيْهِ وَسَلَّمَ يَقُولُ: «الْوُضُوءُ مِمَّا مَسَّتِ النَّارُ»

[628–000]. (Dār al-Salām 0687) Ibn Shihāb said: ʿUmar ibn ʿAbd al-ʿAzīz reported to me; that ʿAbdullāh ibn Ibrāhīm ibn Qāriẓ reported to him; that he found Abū Hurayrah performing the ablution in the mosque. He said: I am only doing the ablution because I ate some pieces of *aqṭ* and I had heard the Prophet say: **'Perform the ablution after eating what is cooked on fire'**.

i. Related by al-Nasāʾī, 179.

قَالَ ابْنُ شِهَابٍ: أَخْبَرَنِي عُمَرُ بْنُ عَبْدِ الْعَزِيزِ، أَنَّ عَبْدَ اللهِ بْنَ إِبْرَاهِيمَ بْنِ قَارِظٍ، أَخْبَرَهُ أَنَّهُ وَجَدَ أَبَا هُرَيْرَةَ يَتَوَضَّأُ عَلَى الْمَسْجِدِ، فَقَالَ: إِنَّمَا أَتَوَضَّأُ مِنْ أَثْوَارِ أَقِطٍ أَكَلْتُهَا لِأَنِّي سَمِعْتُ رَسُولَ اللهِ صَلَّى اللهُ عَلَيْهِ وَسَلَّمَ يَقُولُ: «تَوَضَّئُوا مِمَّا مَسَّتِ النَّارُ»

[629–000]. (Dār al-Salām 0688) Ibn Shihāb said: Saʿīd ibn Khālid ibn ʿAmr ibn ʿUthmān reported to me as I was narrating this hadith to him that he asked ʿUrwah ibn al-Zubayr about ablution for eating cooked food. ʿUrwah said: I heard ʿĀ'ishah, the Prophet's wife, say: **'God's Messenger (peace be upon him) said: "Perform the ablution after eating what is cooked on fire".'**

قَالَ ابْنُ شِهَابٍ: أَخْبَرَنِي سَعِيدُ بْنُ خَالِدِ بْنِ عَمْرِو بْنِ عُثْمَانَ، وَأَنَا أُحَدِّثُهُ هَذَا الْحَدِيثَ أَنَّهُ سَأَلَ عُرْوَةَ بْنَ الزُّبَيْرِ، عَنِ الْوُضُوءِ مِمَّا مَسَّتِ النَّارُ؟ فَقَالَ: عُرْوَةُ، سَمِعْتُ عَائِشَةَ زَوْجَ النَّبِيِّ صَلَّى اللهُ عَلَيْهِ وَسَلَّمَ تَقُولُ: قَالَ رَسُولُ اللهِ صَلَّى اللهُ عَلَيْهِ وَسَلَّمَ: «تَوَضَّئُوا مِمَّا مَسَّتِ النَّارُ»

Text Explanation

Muslim (may God bestow mercy on him) devotes this chapter to the hadiths that require the performance of ablution after eating cooked food. He devotes the next chapter to the hadiths that make such ablution unnecessary. He thus implies that the requirement has been cancelled or abrogated. This is the practice of Muslim and other leading Hadith scholars. They list the hadiths that they consider to have been subsequently cancelled and follow them with the hadiths that annul the earlier rulings.

Scholars differ as to the import of the Prophet's instruction: 'Perform the ablution after eating what is cooked on fire'. The large majority of scholars of the early and later generations are of the view that eating such food does not invalidate an earlier ablution. This view is upheld by Abū Bakr, 'Umar ibn al-Khaṭṭāb, 'Uthmān ibn 'Affān, 'Alī ibn Abī Ṭālib, 'Abdullāh ibn Mas'ūd, Abū al-Dardā', Ibn 'Abbās, 'Abdullāh ibn 'Umar, Anas ibn Mālik, Jābir ibn Samurah, Zayd ibn Thābit, Abū Mūsā, Abū Hurayrah, Ubayy ibn Ka'b, 'Āmir ibn Rabī'ah, Abū Umāmah and 'Ā'ishah (may God be pleased with them all). All of these were companions of the Prophet. The same view is upheld by the great majority of the Tābi'īn generation. It is the view of Mālik, Abū Ḥanīfah, al-Shāfi'ī, Ahmad, Isḥāq ibn Rāhawayh, Yaḥyā ibn Yaḥyā, Abū Thawr and Abū Khaythamah (may God bestow mercy on them all). Others maintain that an ablution is required as a duty for eating cooked food, just like the ablution for prayer. This is reported to be the view of 'Umar ibn 'Abd al-'Azīz, al-Ḥasan al-Baṣrī, al-Zuhrī, Abū Qilābah and Abū Mijliz. They cite in evidence the hadith that says: 'Perform the ablution after eating what is cooked on fire'.

The majority of scholars who take the opposite view base their argument on the hadiths that make clear that no ablution is required for eating cooked food. Muslim cites here some of these hadiths and the rest are available in the well-known Hadith anthologies composed by leading scholars. They give two answers when citation is made of the hadith that says, 'Ablution is required for eating what is cooked on fire'. The first is that this hadith has been annulled by another hadith narrated by Jābir: 'The last of the two practices during the Prophet's lifetime was that ablution was not required of a person who ate cooked food'. This is an authentic hadith related by Abū Dāwūd and al-Nasā'ī as well as other hadith scholars, and enjoys good chains of transmission. The other answer is that ablution in this instance means rinsing one's mouth and washing one's hands. Moreover, this difference of views, as we have explained, took place in the early days of Islam, then scholars were unanimous that performing the ablution is not required of any person who eats cooked food, but God knows best.

Abū Hurayrah performed his ablution at the top of the mosque, which makes clear that it is permissible to do so. Ibn al-Mundhir states that scholars are all in agreement that it is permissible as long as it does not bother anyone.

Transmission

In the chain of transmission of the first hadith, No. 627, we read: 'Ibn Shihāb said: ʿAbd al-Malik ibn Abī Bakr ibn ʿAbd al-Raḥmān ibn al-Ḥārith ibn Hishām'. This is how it occurs in all original manuscripts, ʿAbd al-Malik ibn Abī Bakr. This is also how Abū ʿAlī al-Ghassānī reports it quoting all scholars transmitting the book. Abū ʿAlī further said:

> Ibn al-Ḥadhdhā' makes another one of the corrections that result in an error. He thus makes it: 'Ibn Shihāb said: ʿAbdullāh ibn Abī Bakr reports ...'. Thus he replaces ʿAbd al-Malik's name by ʿAbdullāh, but the narrator's correct name is ʿAbd al-Malik. Thus it is reported by al-Julūdī, and written in Abū Zakarriyā' ibn Māhān's copy. It is also reported in the same way by al-Zubaydī, from al-Zuhrī, from ʿAbd al-Malik ibn Abī Bakr who was the brother of ʿAbdullāh ibn Abi Bakr', but God knows best.

The chain of transmission of hadith No. 628 includes 'ʿUmar ibn ʿAbd al-ʿAzīz reported to me that ʿAbdullāh ibn Ibrāhīm ibn Qāriẓ reported to him ...'. This is how the narrator's name is entered here as well as in the chapter on Friday and Sales in Muslim's book. Also in the chapter on Friday in Muslim's book, the name of the reporter as given by Ibn Jurayj is: Ibrāhīm ibn ʿAbdullāh ibn Qāriẓ. Both versions of the narrator's name have been given and learned scholars have differed as to which is the correct one. Each is supported by a large number of scholars.

CHAPTER 24

ANNULMENT OF THE REQUIREMENT OF ABLUTION AFTER EATING COOKED FOOD

[630–91]. (Dār al-Salām 0689) ʿAbdullāh ibn Maslamah ibn Qaʿnab narrated:[i] Mālik narrated; from Zayd ibn Aslam; from ʿAṭāʾ ibn Yasār; from Ibn ʿAbbās: **ʿGod's Messenger (peace be upon him) ate of a lamb's shoulder then offered his prayer without performing a fresh ablution**ʾ.

حَدَّثَنَا عَبْدُ اللهِ بْنُ مَسْلَمَةَ بْنِ قَعْنَبٍ، حَدَّثَنَا مَالِكٌ، عَنْ زَيْدِ بْنِ أَسْلَمَ، عَنْ عَطَاءِ بْنِ يَسَارٍ، عَنِ ابْنِ عَبَّاسٍ: «أَنَّ رَسُولَ اللهِ صَلَّى اللهُ عَلَيْهِ وَسَلَّمَ أَكَلَ كَتِفَ شَاةٍ ثُمَّ صَلَّى وَلَمْ يَتَوَضَّأْ»

[631–000]. (Dār al-Salām 0690) Zuhayr ibn Ḥarb narrated:[ii] Yaḥyā ibn Saʿīd narrated; from Hishām ibn ʿUrwah; Wahb ibn Kaysān reported to me; from Muhammad ibn ʿAmr ibn ʿAṭāʾ; from Ibn ʿAbbās [H]. Also, Muhammad ibn ʿAlī narrated to me; from his father; from Ibn ʿAbbās: **ʿThe Prophet (peace be upon him) ate meat off a bone (or meat), then prayed without performing a fresh ablution, or washing with water**ʾ.

وَحَدَّثَنَا زُهَيْرُ بْنُ حَرْبٍ، حَدَّثَنَا يَحْيَى بْنُ سَعِيدٍ، عَنْ هِشَامِ بْنِ عُرْوَةَ، أَخْبَرَنِي وَهْبُ بْنُ كَيْسَانَ، عَنْ مُحَمَّدِ بْنِ عَمْرِو بْنِ عَطَاءٍ، عَنِ ابْنِ عَبَّاسٍ، ح، وَحَدَّثَنِي الزُّهْرِيُّ، عَنْ

i. Related by al-Bukhārī, 207; Abū Dāwūd, 187.
ii. Related by Ibn Mājah, 490 with the chain of transmission featuring Muhammad ibn ʿAlī.

عَلِيِّ بْنِ عَبْدِ اللهِ بْنِ عَبَّاسٍ، عَنِ ابْنِ عَبَّاسٍ، ح، وَحَدَّثَنِي مُحَمَّدُ بْنُ عَلِيٍّ، عَنْ أَبِيهِ، عَنِ ابْنِ عَبَّاسٍ: «أَنَّ النَّبِيَّ صَلَّى اللهُ عَلَيْهِ وَسَلَّمَ أَكَلَ عَرْقًا، أَوْ لَحْمًا، ثُمَّ صَلَّى وَلَمْ يَتَوَضَّأْ، وَلَمْ يَمَسَّ مَاءً»

[632–92]. (Dār al-Salām 0691) Muhammad ibn al-Ṣabbāḥ narrated:[i] Ibrāhīm ibn Saʿd narrated; al-Zuhrī narrated; from Jaʿfar ibn ʿAmr ibn Umayyah al-Ḍamrī; from his father that: **'He saw God's Messenger (peace be upon him) cutting [meat] off a shoulder he was eating. He then offered prayers without performing a fresh ablution'**.

وَحَدَّثَنَا مُحَمَّدُ بْنُ الصَّبَّاحِ، حَدَّثَنَا إِبْرَاهِيمُ بْنُ سَعْدٍ، حَدَّثَنَا الزُّهْرِيُّ، عَنْ جَعْفَرِ بْنِ عَمْرِو بْنِ أُمَيَّةَ الضَّمْرِيِّ، عَنْ أَبِيهِ، «أَنَّهُ رَأَى رَسُولَ اللهِ صَلَّى اللهُ عَلَيْهِ وَسَلَّمَ يَحْتَزُّ مِنْ كَتِفٍ يَأْكُلُ مِنْهَا، ثُمَّ صَلَّى وَلَمْ يَتَوَضَّأْ»

[633–93]. (Dār al-Salām 0692) Ahmad ibn ʿĪsā narrated to me: Ibn Wahb narrated; ʿAmr ibn al-Ḥārith reported to me; from Ibn Shihāb; from Jaʿfar ibn ʿAmr ibn Umayyah al-Ḍamrī; from his father, who said: **'I saw God's Messenger (peace be upon him) cutting [meat] off a lamb shoulder and eating of it. He was then called for the prayer. He stood up, put down the knife and prayed without performing a fresh ablution'**.

Ibn Shihāb said: This was also narrated to me by ʿAlī ibn ʿAbdullāh ibn ʿAbbās; from his father; from God's Messenger.

حَدَّثَنِي أَحْمَدُ بْنُ عِيسَى، حَدَّثَنَا ابْنُ وَهْبٍ، أَخْبَرَنِي عَمْرُو بْنُ الْحَارِثِ، عَنِ ابْنِ شِهَابٍ، عَنْ جَعْفَرِ بْنِ عَمْرِو بْنِ أُمَيَّةَ الضَّمْرِيِّ، عَنْ أَبِيهِ، قَالَ: «رَأَيْتُ رَسُولَ اللهِ صَلَّى اللهُ عَلَيْهِ

i. Related by al-Bukhārī, 208, 675, 2923, 5408, 5422 and 5462; al-Tirmidhī, 1836; Ibn Mājah, 490.

وَسَلَّمَ يَحْتَزُّ مِنْ كَتِفِ شَاةٍ، فَأَكَلَ مِنْهَا، فَدُعِيَ إِلَى الصَّلَاةِ، فَقَامَ وَطَرَحَ السِّكِّينَ، وَصَلَّى وَلَمْ يَتَوَضَّأْ» قَالَ ابْنُ شِهَابٍ: وَحَدَّثَنِي عَلِيُّ بْنُ عَبْدِ اللهِ بْنِ عَبَّاسٍ، عَنْ أَبِيهِ عَنْ رَسُولِ اللهِ صَلَّى اللهُ عَلَيْهِ وَسَلَّمَ.

[634–000]. (Dār al-Salām 0693) ʿAmr said: Bukayr ibn al-Ashajj narrated to me:[i] from Kurayb, Ibn ʿAbbās's *mawlā*; from Maymūnah, the Prophet's wife: **'The Prophet ate a lamb shoulder at her place, then offered his prayer without performing a fresh ablution'**.

قَالَ عَمْرٌو: وَحَدَّثَنِي بُكَيْرُ بْنُ الْأَشَجِّ، عَنْ كُرَيْبٍ، مَوْلَى ابْنِ عَبَّاسٍ، عَنْ مَيْمُونَةَ، زَوْجِ النَّبِيِّ صَلَّى اللهُ عَلَيْهِ وَسَلَّمَ: «أَنَّ النَّبِيَّ صَلَّى اللهُ عَلَيْهِ وَسَلَّمَ أَكَلَ عِنْدَهَا كَتِفًا، ثُمَّ صَلَّى وَلَمْ يَتَوَضَّأْ»

[000–000]. (Dār al-Salām 0694) ʿAmr said: Jaʿfar ibn Rabīʿah narrated to me; from Yaʿqūb ibn al-Ashajj; from Kurayb, Ibn ʿAbbās's *mawlā*; from Maymūnah, the Prophet's wife: **the same text**.

قَالَ عَمْرٌو، وَحَدَّثَنِي جَعْفَرُ بْنُ رَبِيعَةَ، عَنْ يَعْقُوبَ بْنِ الْأَشَجِّ، عَنْ كُرَيْبٍ، مَوْلَى ابْنِ عَبَّاسٍ، عَنْ مَيْمُونَةَ زَوْجِ النَّبِيِّ صَلَّى اللهُ عَلَيْهِ وَسَلَّمَ بِذَلِكَ.

[635–94]. (Dār al-Salām 0695) ʿAmr said: Saʿīd ibn Abī Hilāl narrated to me; from ʿAbdullāh ibn ʿUbaydillāh ibn Abi Rāfiʿ; from Abū Ghaṭafān; from Abū Rāfiʿ: **'I testify that I used to roast the lamb's liver for God's Messenger (peace be upon him). He then offered his prayer without performing a fresh ablution'**.

---

i. Related by al-Bukhārī, 210.

قَالَ عَمْرٌو، وَحَدَّثَنِي سَعِيدُ بْنُ أَبِي هِلَالٍ، عَنْ عَبْدِ اللهِ بْنِ عُبَيْدِ اللهِ بْنِ أَبِي رَافِعٍ، عَنْ أَبِي غَطَفَانَ، عَنْ أَبِي رَافِعٍ، قَالَ: «أَشْهَدُ لَكُنْتُ أَشْوِي لِرَسُولِ اللهِ صَلَّى اللهُ عَلَيْهِ وَسَلَّمَ بَطْنَ الشَّاةِ، ثُمَّ صَلَّى وَلَمْ يَتَوَضَّأْ»

[636–95]. (Dār al-Salām 0696) Qutaybah ibn Saʿīd narrated:[i] Layth narrated; from ʿUqayl; from al-Zuhrī; from ʿUbaydillāh ibn ʿAbdullāh; from Ibn ʿAbbās: ʻ**The Prophet (peace be upon him) drank some milk, then he called for some water and rinsed his mouth. He then said: "It is fatty"**.ʼ

حَدَّثَنَا قُتَيْبَةُ بْنُ سَعِيدٍ، حَدَّثَنَا لَيْثٌ، عَنْ عُقَيْلٍ، عَنِ الزُّهْرِيِّ، عَنْ عُبَيْدِ اللهِ بْنِ عَبْدِ اللهِ، عَنِ ابْنِ عَبَّاسٍ: «أَنَّ النَّبِيَّ صَلَّى اللهُ عَلَيْهِ وَسَلَّمَ شَرِبَ لَبَنًا، ثُمَّ دَعَا بِمَاءٍ فَتَمَضْمَضَ»، وَقَالَ: «إِنَّ لَهُ دَسَمًا»

[000–000]. (Dār al-Salām 0697) Ahmad ibn ʿĪsā narrated to me: Ibn Wahb narrated; and ʿAmr reported to me [H]. Also, Zuhayr ibn Ḥarb narrated to me; Yaḥyā ibn Saʿīd narrated; from al-Awzāʿī [H]. Ḥarmalah ibn Yaḥyā narrated to me; Ibn Wahb reported; Yūnus narrated to me: all from Ibn Shihāb, with ʿUqayl's chain of transmission from al-Zuhrī: **the same text**.

وَحَدَّثَنِي أَحْمَدُ بْنُ عِيسَى، حَدَّثَنَا ابْنُ وَهْبٍ وَأَخْبَرَنِي عَمْرٌو ح، وَحَدَّثَنِي زُهَيْرُ بْنُ حَرْبٍ، حَدَّثَنَا يَحْيَى بْنُ سَعِيدٍ، عَنِ الْأَوْزَاعِيِّ، ح، وَحَدَّثَنِي حَرْمَلَةُ بْنُ يَحْيَى، أَخْبَرَنَا ابْنُ وَهْبٍ، حَدَّثَنِي يُونُسُ كُلُّهُمْ عَنِ ابْنِ شِهَابٍ بِإِسْنَادِ عَقِيلٍ، عَنِ الزُّهْرِيِّ مِثْلَهُ.

[637–96]. (Dār al-Salām 0698) ʿAlī ibn Ḥujr narrated to me: Ismāʿīl ibn Jaʿfar narrated; Muhammad ibn ʿAmr ibn Ḥalḥalah

i. Related by al-Bukhārī, 211 and 5609; Abū Dāwūd, 196; al-Tirmidhī, 89; al-Nasāʾī, 187; Ibn Mājah, 498.

narrated; from Muhammad ibn ʿAmr ibn ʿAṭā'; from Ibn ʿAbbās: **'God's Messenger (peace be upon him) tidied his clothes and went out for the prayer. He was brought a gift of bread and meat. He ate three bites then led the congregational prayer without touching any water'**.

وَحَدَّثَنِي عَلِيُّ بْنُ حُجْرٍ، حَدَّثَنَا إِسْمَاعِيلُ بْنُ جَعْفَرٍ، حَدَّثَنَا مُحَمَّدُ بْنُ عَمْرِو بْنِ حَلْحَلَةَ، عَنْ مُحَمَّدِ بْنِ عَمْرِو بْنِ عَطَاءٍ، عَنِ ابْنِ عَبَّاسٍ: «أَنَّ رَسُولَ اللهِ صَلَّى اللهُ عَلَيْهِ وَسَلَّمَ جَمَعَ عَلَيْهِ ثِيَابَهُ ثُمَّ خَرَجَ إِلَى الصَّلَاةِ، فَأُتِيَ بِهَدِيَّةٍ خُبْزٍ وَلَحْمٍ، فَأَكَلَ ثَلَاثَ لُقَمٍ، ثُمَّ صَلَّى بِالنَّاسِ، وَمَا مَسَّ مَاءً»

[638–000]. (Dār al-Salām 0699) Abū Kurayb narrated the same: Abū Usāmah narrated; from al-Walīd ibn Kathīr; from Muhammad ibn ʿAmr ibn ʿAṭā'; He said: **'I was with Ibn ʿAbbās. He narrated the hadith with the same meaning as Ibn Ḥalḥalah's narration. It includes that Ibn ʿAbbās saw the Prophet doing so, and he said: "He prayed", not "led the congregational prayer"**.'

وَحَدَّثَنَاهُ أَبُو كُرَيْبٍ، حَدَّثَنَا أَبُو أُسَامَةَ، عَنِ الْوَلِيدِ بْنِ كَثِيرٍ، حَدَّثَنَا مُحَمَّدُ بْنُ عَمْرِو بْنِ عَطَاءٍ، قَالَ: كُنْتُ مَعَ ابْنِ عَبَّاسٍ، وَسَاقَ الْحَدِيثَ بِمَعْنَى حَدِيثِ ابْنِ حَلْحَلَةَ، وَفِيهِ أَنَّ ابْنَ عَبَّاسٍ، شَهِدَ ذَلِكَ مِنَ النَّبِيِّ صَلَّى اللهُ عَلَيْهِ وَسَلَّمَ وَقَالَ صَلَّى وَلَمْ يَقُلْ بِالنَّاسِ.

Text Explanation

Hadith No. 633 mentions that the Prophet put down the knife with which he was cutting the meat. This makes clear that it is perfectly permissible to cut meat with a knife, but some scholars say that it is discouraged if there is no need for it. The Prophet was called for prayer. This indicates that it is permissible, indeed desirable, to call the imam to prayer when it falls due. The hadiths in this chapter make clear that testifying a negative is acceptable if what is denied is well defined, as in this case. The hadiths also make clear that performing the ablution is not obligatory for merely eating cooked food.

Hadith No. 635 says: 'I testify that I used to roast the lamb's liver for God's Messenger (peace be upon him). He then offered his prayer without performing a fresh ablution'. A literal translation would give the meaning as roasting 'the lamb's belly', and al-Nawawī explains that it means 'the liver and other parts next to it'. He adds: There is some omission in the wording, and it means: I would roast the parts inside the lamb's belly, and the Prophet would eat from it, then offer his prayer without performing a fresh ablution', but God knows best.

Hadith No. 636 mentions that the Prophet rinsed his mouth after drinking some milk. This shows that rinsing of one's mouth is desirable after drinking milk. Scholars say that it is also desirable after eating or drinking generally, so that no particles of food remain in one's mouth which may be swallowed during prayer. Also, rinsing one's mouth ensures that the fattiness and traces of food and drink are removed and one's mouth is clean.

Scholars hold different views concerning the desirability or otherwise of washing one's hands before and after eating. It appears that it is desirable before eating, unless one is certain that one's hands are clean. It is also desirable after finishing a meal, unless there are no traces of food left on one's hands or one did not touch the food directly. Mālik said that it is not recommended to wash one's hands unless it is unclean before one starts eating, or smelling of the food after one finishes, but God knows best.

Transmission

Hadith No. 635 includes in its chain of transmission 'Abū Ghaṭafān; from Abū Rāfi'.' Abū Ghaṭafān is Ibn Ṭarīf al-Murrī. He was from Madinah, but al-Ḥākim Abū Ahmad said: 'His name is unknown'. His appellation is variously given as Abū Mālik.

Abū Rāfi' was the Prophet's own *mawlā*, and his name was Aslam, but it is variously stated as Ibrāhīm, Hurmuz or Thābit.

In the second transmission of hadith No. 636, the wording goes like this: 'Ahmad ibn ʿĪsā narrated to me: Ibn Wahb narrated; and ʿAmr reported to me'. This is how it appears in the original manuscripts, 'and ʿAmr reported ...'. It is Ibn Wahb who said 'and ʿAmr reported'. He adds the conjunction 'and' because he heard several hadiths from ʿAmr and reported them, stating them in order and adding the conjunction 'and' between them. Thus, Ahmad ibn ʿĪsā, the next narrator, listened to Ibn Wahb as he reported these with the conjunction, and he transmitted each hadith exactly as he heard it, but God knows best.

Hadith No. 638 states: 'It includes that Ibn ʿAbbās saw the Prophet doing so'. This is another version of the preceding hadith in which it is stated that the Prophet was brought a gift and meat, from which he ate three bites then proceeded to pray without performing a fresh ablution. The first version mentions that the Prophet 'tidied his clothes' before proceeding to the prayer. It does not say that Ibn ʿAbbās saw him doing it. Thus, he might have seen it or might have heard it reported by someone else. If the second possibility was the case, the hadith would be of the *mursal* type, which is transmitted by a companion of the Prophet. The scholar Abū Isḥāq al-Isfarāyīnī does not accept such hadiths as evidence. He disagrees with the majority of scholars on this point, but the correct view is that of the majority. Because the first version, stated in hadith No. 637, allows this possibility, Muslim included the second version to dispel any doubt, stating that 'Ibn ʿAbbās saw the Prophet doing so', but God knows best.

CHAPTER 25

THE REQUIREMENT OF ABLUTION FOR EATING CAMEL MEAT

[639–97]. (Dār al-Salām 0700) Abū Kāmil Fuḍayl ibn Ḥusayn al-Jaḥdarī narrated:[i] Abū ʿAwānah narrated; from ʿUthmān ibn ʿAbdullāh ibn Mawhab; from Jaʿfar ibn Abī Thawr; from Jābir ibn Samurah that '**a man asked God's Messenger (peace be upon him): "Should I perform the ablution if I eat lamb meat?" The Prophet said: "You may perform the ablution if you wish and you may not if you choose". The man asked: "Should I perform the ablution if I eat camel meat?" The Prophet said: "Yes. Do perform the ablution after eating camel meat". The man asked: "May I pray in a sheep barn?" The Prophet said: "Yes". The man asked: "May I pray in a camel stable?" The Prophet said: "No".**'

حَدَّثَنَا أَبُو كَامِلٍ فُضَيْلُ بْنُ حُسَيْنٍ الْجَحْدَرِيُّ، حَدَّثَنَا أَبُو عَوَانَةَ، عَنْ عُثْمَانَ بْنِ عَبْدِ اللهِ بْنِ مَوْهَبٍ، عَنْ جَعْفَرِ بْنِ أَبِي ثَوْرٍ، عَنْ جَابِرِ بْنِ سَمُرَةَ، أَنَّ رَجُلًا سَأَلَ رَسُولَ اللهِ صَلَّى اللهُ عَلَيْهِ وَسَلَّمَ أَأَتَوَضَّأُ مِنْ لُحُومِ الْغَنَمِ؟ قَالَ: «إِنْ شِئْتَ فَتَوَضَّأْ، وَإِنْ شِئْتَ فَلَا تَوَضَّأْ» قَالَ أَتَوَضَّأُ مِنْ لُحُومِ الْإِبِلِ؟ قَالَ: «نَعَمْ فَتَوَضَّأْ مِنْ لُحُومِ الْإِبِلِ» قَالَ: أُصَلِّي فِي مَرَابِضِ الْغَنَمِ؟ قَالَ: «نَعَمْ» قَالَ: أُصَلِّي فِي مَبَارِكِ الْإِبِلِ؟ قَالَ: «لَا»

[000–000]. (Dār al-Salām 0701) Abū Bakr ibn Abī Shaybah narrated: Muʿāwiyah ibn ʿAmr narrated; Zā'idah narrated;

---

i. Related by Ibn Mājah, 495 (in a shorter version).

from Simāk [H]. Also, al-Qāsim ibn Zakariyyā' narrated to me; 'Ubaydullāh ibn Mūsā; from Shaybān; from 'Uthmān ibn 'Abdullāh ibn Mawhab and Ash'ath ibn Abī al-Sha'thā'; all of them from Ja'far ibn Abī Thawr; from Jābir ibn Samurah; from the Prophet: the same text as the narration of Abū Kāmil from Abū 'Awānah.

حَدَّثَنَا أَبُو بَكْرِ بْنُ أَبِي شَيْبَةَ، حَدَّثَنَا مُعَاوِيَةُ بْنُ عَمْرٍو، حَدَّثَنَا زَائِدَةُ، عَنْ سِمَاكٍ، ح وَحَدَّثَنِي الْقَاسِمُ بْنُ زَكَرِيَّا، حَدَّثَنَا عُبَيْدُ اللهِ بْنُ مُوسَى، عَنْ شَيْبَانَ، عَنْ عُثْمَانَ بْنِ عَبْدِ اللهِ بْنِ مَوْهَبٍ، وَأَشْعَثَ بْنِ أَبِي الشَّعْثَاءِ، كُلُّهُمْ عَنْ جَعْفَرِ بْنِ أَبِي ثَوْرٍ، عَنْ جَابِرِ بْنِ سَمُرَةَ، عَنِ النَّبِيِّ صَلَّى اللهُ عَلَيْهِ وَسَلَّمَ بِمِثْلِ حَدِيثِ أَبِي كَامِلٍ، عَنْ أَبِي عَوَانَةَ.

Text Explanation

Scholars differ in their views concerning the eating of camel meat. The majority are of the view that it does not invalidate ablution. This view is agreed by the four Rightly-Guided Caliphs, Abū Bakr, 'Umar, 'Uthmān and 'Alī, as well as Ibn Mas'ūd, Ubayy ibn Ka'b, Ibn 'Abbās, Abū al-Dardā', Abū Ṭalḥah, 'Āmir ibn Rabī'ah and Abū Umāmah, as well as the large majority of the Tābi'īn, and also Mālik, Abū Ḥanīfah and al-Shāfi'ī. Other scholars who adopt the view that eating camel meat invalidates the ablution include Ahmad ibn Ḥanbal, Isḥāq ibn Rāhawayh, Yaḥyā ibn Yaḥyā, Abū Bakr ibn al-Mundhir and Ibn Khuzaymah. This is the view chosen by Abū Bakr al-Bayhaqī. It is thus reported from most Hadith scholars, and a number of the Prophet's companions. Their argument is the hadith mentioned in this chapter, quoting the Prophet as saying: 'Do perform the ablution after eating camel meat'.

Al-Barā' ibn 'Āzib, a companion of the Prophet, said: 'The Prophet was asked about the need to perform the ablution after eating camel meat and he ordered that it should be performed. Ahmad ibn Ḥanbal and Isḥāq ibn Rāhawayh said that two authentic hadiths have been reported from the Prophet, one narrated by Jābir and the other by al-Barā'. This view enjoys the stronger evidence, even though the majority of scholars support the opposite view. These scholars respond by citing the hadith narrated by Jābir: 'The last of the two views endorsed by God's Messenger (peace be upon him) was that the performance of a fresh ablution after eating cooked food was not required'. However, this hadith is of general import, while the hadith requiring the performance of ablution after eating camel meat is specific. What is specific is given preference over what is general, but God knows best.

The Prophet permitted offering prayer in a sheep barn but not in a camel stable. This is agreed by all scholars. The order not to pray in camel stables is one of discouragement, not total prohibition. The reason being that camels may become irritated and disturb the person who is offering worship, but God knows best.

Transmission

Abū al-Sha'thā' mentioned in the chain of narration of this hadith is named Sulaym ibn Aswad.

CHAPTER 26

DOUBT ABOUT INVALIDATING ABLUTION

[640–98]. (Dār al-Salām 0702) ʿAmr al-Nāqid and Zuhayr ibn Ḥarb narrated to me:[i] [H]. Also, Abū Bakr ibn Abī Shaybah narrated; all of them from Ibn ʿUyaynah; ʿAmr said: Sufyān ibn ʿUyaynah narrated; from al-Zuhrī; from Saʿīd and ʿAbbād ibn Tamīm; from his uncle. ʻ**A complaint was put to the Prophet (peace be upon him): Suppose that a man imagines that something has taken place while he is offering his prayer. He said: "He should not abandon his prayer unless he hears a sound or finds a smell"**.ʼ

In their narrations, Abū Bakr and Zuhayr said: 'He was ʿAbdullāh ibn Zayd'.

وَحَدَّثَنِي عَمْرٌو النَّاقِدُ، وَزُهَيْرُ بْنُ حَرْبٍ، ح، وَحَدَّثَنَا أَبُو بَكْرِ بْنُ أَبِي شَيْبَةَ جَمِيعًا عَنِ ابْنِ عُيَيْنَةَ - قَالَ عَمْرٌو: حَدَّثَنَا سُفْيَانُ بْنُ عُيَيْنَةَ، عَنِ الزُّهْرِيِّ، عَنْ سَعِيدٍ، وَعَبَّادِ بْنِ تَمِيمٍ، عَنْ عَمِّهِ شُكِيَ إِلَى النَّبِيِّ صَلَّى اللهُ عَلَيْهِ وَسَلَّمَ: الرَّجُلُ، يُخَيَّلُ إِلَيْهِ أَنَّهُ يَجِدُ الشَّيْءَ فِي الصَّلَاةِ، قَالَ: «لَا يَنْصَرِفُ حَتَّى يَسْمَعَ صَوْتًا، أَوْ يَجِدَ رِيحًا»

قَالَ أَبُو بَكْرٍ: وَزُهَيْرُ بْنُ حَرْبٍ فِي رِوَايَتِهِمَا هُوَ عَبْدُ اللهِ بْنُ زَيْدٍ.

[641–99]. (Dār al-Salām 0703) Zuhayr ibn Ḥarb narrated to me: Jarīr narrated; from Suhayl; from his father; from Abū

---

i. Related by al-Bukhārī, 137, 177 (in a shorter version) and 2056; Abū Dāwūd, 176; al-Nasāʾī, 160; Ibn Mājah, 513.

Hurayrah: God's Messenger (peace be upon him) said: **'If any of you hears something in his belly and he is uncertain whether he made a discharge or not, he need not leave the mosque unless he hears a sound or finds a smell'**.

وَحَدَّثَنِي زُهَيْرُ بْنُ حَرْبٍ، حَدَّثَنَا جَرِيرٌ، عَنْ سُهَيْلٍ، عَنْ أَبِيهِ، عَنْ أَبِي هُرَيْرَةَ، قَالَ: قَالَ رَسُولُ اللهِ صَلَّى اللهُ عَلَيْهِ وَسَلَّمَ: «إِذَا وَجَدَ أَحَدُكُمْ فِي بَطْنِهِ شَيْئًا، فَأَشْكَلَ عَلَيْهِ أَخَرَجَ مِنْهُ شَيْءٌ أَمْ لَا، فَلَا يَخْرُجَنَّ مِنَ الْمَسْجِدِ حَتَّى يَسْمَعَ صَوْتًا، أَوْ يَجِدَ رِيحًا»

Text Explanation

The hadith says that 'a man imagines that something has taken place'. This means that he imagines that he has invalidated his ablution by breaking wind. The Prophet says that such a person should remain in prayer 'unless he hears a sound or finds a smell', which means until he is certain that either has taken place. Muslims are unanimous that it is not a condition that he hears or smells anything.

This hadith states a very important Islamic principle and an essential rule of *fiqh*, which is that things remain in their original condition until the opposite becomes certain. An incidental doubt does not affect this. An example is the question stated in this chapter about the one who is certain that he performed the required act of cleansing, but doubts whether he invalidated his ablution. Such a person is ruled to still have a valid ablution. There is no difference if the doubt occurs while he is praying or not. This is the view of our school and the great majority of scholars of older and more recent generations. However, two views are reported to have been stated by Imam Mālik: the first is that such a person need not perform a fresh ablution if his doubt occurs during his prayer, but must have a new ablution if his doubt is not during prayer. The second view is that he must perform a new ablution in all cases. The first view is also reported from al-Ḥasan al-Baṣrī. Yet, it is an odd view that is also attributed to some of our scholars, but it need not be considered.

Scholars of our Shāfiʿī school say that there is no difference if the two possibilities of having invalidated one's ablution or not are equal or one of them is stronger, or even much stronger. Such a person need not have a fresh ablution in any case. Our scholars, however, say that it is desirable for such a person to perform a fresh ablution, in order to be on the safe side. If he does, and continues to have doubts, he has nothing to worry about. A question may arise here: if the person subsequently realizes for certain that his original ablution was invalidated, is his ablution, which he performed as a precaution to stay on the safe side, valid and sufficient? Our scholars express two views, and the more correct of the two is that it is not sufficient, because it was done with an uncertain intention, but God knows best.

In the reverse case, of one who is certain that he invalidated his ablution and doubts whether he subsequently performed a fresh ablution, Muslims are unanimous that he must have a fresh ablution. Let us take the example of one who is certain that he performed an ablution and made a discharge that invalidated it, with both taking place after sunrise, but he is uncertain which of the two was first. If such a person does not know what his condition was before sunrise, he is required to perform a fresh ablution. Yet what if he is well aware of his condition before sunrise? Our scholars express different views on this case. The first is that his present condition is ruled to be the opposite of what it was before sunrise. Thus, if he is certain to have been in ablution before sunrise, he is now without ablution, and the reverse is true. The second, which is the more correct according to the majority of scrupulous scholars, is that he must perform a fresh ablution. The third view is that he applies what he believes to be more correct. The fourth is that he applies what his condition was before sunrise, discarding the two events that occurred after sunrise. This view is obviously wrong, and need not be considered or discussed. I am only mentioning it here so as to explain that it is wrong, lest anyone may think that it could be considered. How can anyone imagine that the condition that was before sunrise remains valid when it is certain that it was invalidated? But God knows best.

Other examples of the rule we have stated include doubts of divorcing one's wife, freeing one's slave, impurity falling in clean water, cleansing something that was contaminated with impurity, an impurity falling on one's clothes or food, how many *rakʿahs* one has performed, performing certain parts of one's prayer, having intended to fast or pray, etc. If such doubts occur while one is performing any such act of worship, or if a doubt about these or similar things occurs, the rule is that none of such doubts has any effect. The rule is that the doubt is dismissed as though it did not occur.

Scholars make certain exceptions to this rule, and these are well known and discussed in books of *fiqh*. They are beyond the scope of this book, because they are amply discussed with views and counter views, and some are subject to different opinions. Therefore, I am not discussing them here but I have clarified them in the chapters discussing the wiping of one's footwear during ablution and the chapter of doubt about the impurity of water in *al-Majmūʿ: Sharḥ al-Muhadhdhab*. There, I summed up the views of our scholars and all that is needed on this point, but God knows best.

Transmission

Muslim says at the end of the hadith: 'Abū Bakr and Zuhayr said in their narration that he is ʿAbdullāh ibn Zayd'. This means that in their narrations, both Abū Bakr ibn Abī Shaybah and Zuhayr ibn Ḥarb named ʿAbbād ibn Tamīm's uncle. He reported it first from Saʿīd, who is Ibn al-Musayyib, and from ʿAbbād ibn Tamīm, from his uncle, without naming the uncle. Thus, in this narration, he named the uncle as ʿAbdullāh ibn Zayd ibn ʿĀṣim, who also narrated the hadith describing the ablution and the one describing the prayer for rain, as well as other hadiths. He is different from ʿAbdullāh ibn Zayd ibn ʿAbd Rabbih, who saw the call to prayer, i.e. the *adhān*, in his dream.

In al-Bukhārī's narration, the one who asked the question was the narrator, ʿAbdullāh ibn Zayd.

CHAPTER 27

TANNING PURIFIES THE HIDE OF DEAD ANIMALS

[642–100]. (Dār al-Salām 0704) Yaḥyā ibn Yaḥyā, Abū Bakr ibn Abī Shaybah, ʿAmr al-Nāqid and Ibn Abī ʿUmar narrated:[i] all from Ibn ʿUyaynah. Yaḥyā said: Sufyān ibn ʿUyaynah reported; from al-Zuhrī; from ʿUbaydullāh ibn ʿAbdullāh; from Ibn ʿAbbās, who said: '**A slave woman belonging to Maymūnah was given a lamb as a *ṣadaqah* [i.e. a charitable gift], but the lamb died. God's Messenger (peace be upon him) passed by and said: "Why do you not take its hide, tan it and make use of it?" They said: "It is carrion". He said: "It is only forbidden to eat"**.'

In their narration, Abū Bakr and Ibn Abī ʿUmar said: '**from Maymūnah, may God be pleased with her**'.

وَحَدَّثَنَا يَحْيَى بْنُ يَحْيَى، وَأَبُو بَكْرِ بْنُ أَبِي شَيْبَةَ، وَعَمْرٌو النَّاقِدُ، وَابْنُ أَبِي عُمَرَ، جَمِيعًا عَنِ ابْنِ عُيَيْنَةَ، قَالَ يَحْيَى: أَخْبَرَنَا سُفْيَانُ بْنُ عُيَيْنَةَ، عَنِ الزُّهْرِيِّ، عَنْ عُبَيْدِ اللهِ بْنِ عَبْدِ اللهِ، عَنِ ابْنِ عَبَّاسٍ، قَالَ: تُصُدِّقَ عَلَى مَوْلَاةٍ لِمَيْمُونَةَ بِشَاةٍ فَمَاتَتْ فَمَرَّ بِهَا رَسُولُ اللهِ صَلَّى اللهُ عَلَيْهِ وَسَلَّمَ فَقَالَ: «هَلَّا أَخَذْتُمْ إِهَابَهَا فَدَبَغْتُمُوهُ فَانْتَفَعْتُمْ بِهِ؟» فَقَالُوا: إِنَّهَا مَيْتَةٌ فَقَالَ: «إِنَّمَا حَرُمَ أَكْلُهَا»

قَالَ أَبُو بَكْرٍ، وَابْنُ أَبِي عُمَرَ، فِي حَدِيثِهِمَا: «عَنْ مَيْمُونَةَ رَضِيَ اللهُ عَنْهَا»

---

i. Related by al-Bukhārī, 1492, and in 2221 and 5531 in shorter versions; Abū Dāwūd, 4120 and 4121; al-Nasāʾī, 4245, 4246 and 4247; Ibn Mājah, 3610.

[643–101]. (Dār al-Salām 0705) Abū al-Ṭāhir and Ḥarmalah narrated to me: Ibn Wahb narrated; Yūnus reported to me; from Ibn Shihāb; from 'Ubaydullāh ibn 'Abdullāh ibn 'Utbah; from Ibn 'Abbās that '**God's Messenger (peace be upon him) saw a dead lamb which was given to a maid of Maymūnah, and it was originally a *ṣadaqah*. The Prophet said: "Why do you not make use of its hide?" They said: "It is carrion". He said: "It is only forbidden to eat"**.'

وَحَدَّثَنِي أَبُو الطَّاهِرِ، وَحَرْمَلَةُ، قَالَا: حَدَّثَنَا ابْنُ وَهْبٍ، أَخْبَرَنِي يُونُسُ، عَنِ ابْنِ شِهَابٍ، عَنْ عُبَيْدِ اللهِ بْنِ عَبْدِ اللهِ بْنِ عُتْبَةَ، عَنِ ابْنِ عَبَّاسٍ، أَنَّ رَسُولَ اللهِ صَلَّى اللهُ عَلَيْهِ وَسَلَّمَ وَجَدَ شَاةً مَيْتَةً أُعْطِيَتْهَا مَوْلَاةٌ لِمَيْمُونَةَ مِنَ الصَّدَقَةِ. فَقَالَ رَسُولُ اللهِ صَلَّى اللهُ عَلَيْهِ وَسَلَّمَ: «هَلَّا انْتَفَعْتُمْ بِجِلْدِهَا» قَالُوا: إِنَّهَا مَيْتَةٌ. فَقَالَ: «إِنَّمَا حَرُمَ أَكْلُهَا»

[000–000]. (Dār al-Salām 0706) Ḥasan al-Ḥulwānī and 'Abd ibn Ḥumayd narrated: from Ya'qūb ibn Ibrāhīm ibn Sa'd; my father narrated; from Ṣāliḥ; from Ibn Shihāb; with the same transmission: **similar to Yūnus's narration**.

حَدَّثَنَا حَسَنٌ الْحُلْوَانِيُّ، وَعَبْدُ بْنُ حُمَيْدٍ، جَمِيعًا عَنْ يَعْقُوبَ بْنِ إِبْرَاهِيمَ بْنِ سَعْدٍ، حَدَّثَنِي أَبِي، عَنْ صَالِحٍ، عَنِ ابْنِ شِهَابٍ، بِهَذَا الْإِسْنَادِ بِنَحْوِ رِوَايَةِ يُونُسَ.

[644–102]. (Dār al-Salām 0707) Ibn Abī 'Umar and 'Abdullāh ibn Muhammad al-Zuhrī narrated (Ibn Abī 'Umar's text):[i] both said: Sufyān narrated; from 'Amr; from 'Aṭā'; from Ibn 'Abbās: '**God's Messenger (peace be upon him) passed by a thrown-away dead lamb which had been given as charity to a maid of Maymūnah. The Prophet said: "Why do they not take its hide, tan it and put it to good use?"**'

---

i. Related by al-Nasā'ī, 4249.

وَحَدَّثَنَا ابْنُ أَبِي عُمَرَ، وَعَبْدُ اللهِ بْنُ مُحَمَّدٍ الزُّهْرِيُّ - وَاللَّفْظُ لِابْنِ أَبِي عُمَرَ - قَالَا: حَدَّثَنَا سُفْيَانُ، عَنْ عَمْرٍو، عَنْ عَطَاءٍ، عَنِ ابْنِ عَبَّاسٍ، أَنَّ رَسُولَ اللهِ صَلَّى اللهُ عَلَيْهِ وَسَلَّمَ مَرَّ بِشَاةٍ مَطْرُوحَةٍ أُعْطِيَتْهَا مَوْلَاةٌ لِمَيْمُونَةَ مِنَ الصَّدَقَةِ، فَقَالَ النَّبِيُّ صَلَّى اللهُ عَلَيْهِ وَسَلَّمَ: «أَلَّا أَخَذُوا إِهَابَهَا فَدَبَغُوهُ فَانْتَفَعُوا بِهِ؟»

[645–103]. (Dār al-Salām 0708) Ahmad ibn ʿUthmān al-Nawfalī narrated: Abū ʿĀṣim narrated; Ibn Jurayj narrated; ʿAmr ibn Dīnār reported to me; ʿAṭā' reported to me a while ago, saying: Ibn ʿAbbās reported to me; that Maymūnah reported to him that: '**a domestic lamb belonged to a woman of the Prophet's household and it died. The Prophet said: "Why do you not take its hide and make use of it?"**'

حَدَّثَنَا أَحْمَدُ بْنُ عُثْمَانَ النَّوْفَلِيُّ، حَدَّثَنَا أَبُو عَاصِمٍ، حَدَّثَنَا ابْنُ جُرَيْجٍ، أَخْبَرَنِي عَمْرُو بْنُ دِينَارٍ، أَخْبَرَنِي عَطَاءٌ، مُنْذُ حِينٍ قَالَ: أَخْبَرَنِي ابْنُ عَبَّاسٍ، أَنَّ مَيْمُونَةَ، أَخْبَرَتْهُ أَنَّ دَاجِنَةً كَانَتْ لِبَعْضِ نِسَاءِ رَسُولِ اللهِ صَلَّى اللهُ عَلَيْهِ وَسَلَّمَ. فَمَاتَتْ. فَقَالَ رَسُولُ اللهِ صَلَّى اللهُ عَلَيْهِ وَسَلَّمَ: «أَلَّا أَخَذْتُمْ إِهَابَهَا فَاسْتَمْتَعْتُمْ بِهِ؟»

[646–104]. (Dār al-Salām 0709) Abū Bakr ibn Abī Shaybah narrated: ʿAbd al-Raḥīm ibn Sulaymān narrated; from ʿAbd al-Malik ibn Abī Sulaymān; from ʿAṭā'; from Ibn ʿAbbās, that '**the Prophet passed by a [dead] lamb belonging to a maid of Maymūnah. He said: "Why do you not take its hide and make use of it?"**'

حَدَّثَنَا أَبُو بَكْرِ بْنُ أَبِي شَيْبَةَ، حَدَّثَنَا عَبْدُ الرَّحِيمِ بْنُ سُلَيْمَانَ، عَنْ عَبْدِ الْمَلِكِ بْنِ أَبِي سُلَيْمَانَ، عَنْ عَطَاءٍ، عَنِ ابْنِ عَبَّاسٍ أَنَّ النَّبِيَّ صَلَّى اللهُ عَلَيْهِ وَسَلَّمَ مَرَّ بِشَاةٍ لِمَوْلَاةٍ لِمَيْمُونَةَ. فَقَالَ: «أَلَّا انْتَفَعْتُمْ بِإِهَابِهَا؟»

[647–105]. (Dār al-Salām 0710) Yaḥyā ibn Yaḥyā narrated:[i] Sulaymān ibn Bilāl reported; from Zayd ibn Aslam; that ʿAbd al-Raḥmān ibn Waʿlah reported to him; from ʿAbdullāh ibn ʿAbbās: **ʻI heard God's Messenger (peace be upon him) say: "When a hide has been tanned, it has been cleansed"**.'

حَدَّثَنَا يَحْيَى بْنُ يَحْيَى، أَخْبَرَنَا سُلَيْمَانُ بْنُ بِلَالٍ، عَنْ زَيْدِ بْنِ أَسْلَمَ، أَنَّ عَبْدَ الرَّحْمَنِ بْنَ وَعْلَةَ، أَخْبَرَهُ عَنْ عَبْدِ اللهِ بْنِ عَبَّاسٍ، قَالَ: سَمِعْتُ رَسُولَ اللهِ صَلَّى اللهُ عَلَيْهِ وَسَلَّمَ يَقُولُ: «إِذَا دُبِغَ الْإِهَابُ فَقَدْ طَهُرَ»

[000–000]. (Dār al-Salām 0711) Abū Bakr ibn Abī Shaybah and ʿAmr al-Nāqid narrated: both said: Ibn ʿUyaynah narrated [H]. Also, Qutaybah ibn Saʿīd narrated; ʿAbd al-ʿAzīz (meaning Ibn Muhammad al-Darāwardī) narrated [H]. And, Abū Kurayb and Isḥāq ibn Ibrāhīm narrated; all from Wakīʿ; from Sufyān; all of them from Zayd ibn Aslam; from ʿAbd al-Raḥmān ibn Waʿlah; from Ibn ʿAbbās; from the Prophet: **the same**; meaning the same text as the hadith narrated by Yaḥyā ibn Yaḥyā.

وَحَدَّثَنَا أَبُو بَكْرِ بْنُ أَبِي شَيْبَةَ، وَعَمْرٌو النَّاقِدُ، قَالَا: حَدَّثَنَا ابْنُ عُيَيْنَةَ، ح، وَحَدَّثَنَا قُتَيْبَةُ بْنُ سَعِيدٍ، حَدَّثَنَا عَبْدُ الْعَزِيزِ يَعْنِي ابْنَ مُحَمَّدٍ، ح، وَحَدَّثَنَا أَبُو كُرَيْبٍ، وَإِسْحَاقُ بْنُ إِبْرَاهِيمَ جَمِيعًا عَنْ وَكِيعٍ، عَنْ سُفْيَانَ، كُلُّهُمْ عَنْ زَيْدِ بْنِ أَسْلَمَ، عَنْ عَبْدِ الرَّحْمَنِ بْنِ وَعْلَةَ، عَنِ ابْنِ عَبَّاسٍ، عَنِ النَّبِيِّ صَلَّى اللهُ عَلَيْهِ وَسَلَّمَ بِمِثْلِهِ يَعْنِي حَدِيثَ يَحْيَى بْنِ يَحْيَى.

[648–106]. (Dār al-Salām 0712) Isḥāq ibn Manṣūr and Abū Bakr ibn Isḥāq narrated to me: ʿAmr ibn al-Rabīʿ (Abū Bakr said 'narrated' and Ibn Manṣūr said 'reported'); Yaḥyā ibn

i. Related by Abū Dāwūd, 4123; al-Tirmidhī, 1728; al-Nasāʾī, 4252, and 4235 in a longer version; Ibn Mājah, 3609.

Ayyūb reported; from Yazīd ibn Abī Ḥabīb; that Abū al-Khayr narrated to him: **'I saw Ibn Waʿlah al-Sabaʾī wearing a fur, and I touched it. He said: "How come you touched it?" He said: "I asked ʿAbdullāh ibn ʿAbbās about it and said: 'We may be in the Maghrib, and with us are some of the Berber and Magians. We may be brought a lamb they might have slaughtered, but we do not eat what they slaughter. They bring us a water container in which they may put some fat'. Ibn ʿAbbās said: 'We asked God's Messenger (peace be upon him) about this and he said: "Tanning purifies it"'".'**

حَدَّثَنِي إِسْحَاقُ بْنُ مَنْصُورٍ، وَأَبُو بَكْرِ بْنُ إِسْحَاقَ، - قَالَ: أَبُو بَكْرٍ، حَدَّثَنَا وَقَالَ ابْنُ مَنْصُورٍ: - أَخْبَرَنَا عَمْرُو بْنُ الرَّبِيعِ، أَخْبَرَنَا يَحْيَى بْنُ أَيُّوبَ، عَنْ يَزِيدَ بْنِ أَبِي حَبِيبٍ، أَنَّ أَبَا الْخَيْرِ، حَدَّثَهُ قَالَ: رَأَيْتُ عَلَى ابْنِ وَعْلَةَ السَّبَئِيِّ، فَرْوًا فَمَسِسْتُهُ، فَقَالَ: مَا لَكَ تَمَسُّهُ؟ قَدْ سَأَلْتُ عَبْدَ اللهِ بْنَ عَبَّاسٍ قُلْتُ: إِنَّا نَكُونُ بِالْمَغْرِبِ. وَمَعَنَا الْبَرْبَرُ وَالْمَجُوسُ نُؤْتَى بِالْكَبْشِ قَدْ ذَبَحُوهُ، وَنَحْنُ لَا نَأْكُلُ ذَبَائِحَهُمْ، وَيَأْتُونَا بِالسِّقَاءِ يَجْعَلُونَ فِيهِ الْوَدَكَ، فَقَالَ: ابْنُ عَبَّاسٍ، قَدْ سَأَلْنَا رَسُولَ اللهِ صَلَّى اللهُ عَلَيْهِ وَسَلَّمَ عَنْ ذَلِكَ؟ فَقَالَ: «دِبَاغُهُ طَهُورُهُ»

[649–107]. (Dār al-Salām 0713) Isḥāq ībn Manṣūr and Abū Bakr ibn Isḥāq narrated to me: from ʿAmr ibn al-Rabīʿ; Yaḥyā ibn Ayyūb reported; from Jaʿfar ibn Rabīʿah; from Abū al-Khayr who narrated to him: Ibn Waʿlah al-Sabaʾī narrated to me: he said: **'I asked ʿAbdullāh ibn ʿAbbās, saying: We may be in the Maghrib and some Magians may bring containers full of water and fat. He said: "Drink of it". I said: Is this your own view? He said: "I heard God's Messenger (peace be upon him) say: Tanning cleanses it".'**

وَحَدَّثَنِي إِسْحَاقُ بْنُ مَنْصُورٍ، وَأَبُو بَكْرِ بْنُ إِسْحَاقَ، عَنْ عَمْرِو بْنِ الرَّبِيعِ، أَخْبَرَنَا يَحْيَى بْنُ أَيُّوبَ، عَنْ جَعْفَرِ بْنِ رَبِيعَةَ، عَنْ أَبِي الْخَيْرِ، حَدَّثَهُ قَالَ: حَدَّثَنِي ابْنُ وَعْلَةَ

السَّبَإِيُّ، قَالَ: سَأَلْتُ عَبْدَ اللهِ بْنَ عَبَّاسٍ، قُلْتُ: إِنَّا نَكُونُ بِالْـمَغْرِبِ فَيَأْتِينَا الْـمَجُوسُ بِالْأَسْقِيَةِ فِيهَا الْـمَاءُ وَالْوَدَكُ، فَقَالَ: اشْرَبْ. فَقُلْتُ: أَرَأْيٌ تَرَاهُ؟ فَقَالَ: ابْنُ عَبَّاسٍ سَمِعْتُ رَسُولَ اللهِ صَلَّى اللهُ عَلَيْهِ وَسَلَّمَ يَقُولُ: «دِبَاغُهُ طَهُورُهُ»

Text Explanation

In all these hadiths, the Prophet encourages people to make use of the hide of dead animals, provided that the hide is tanned. It is made clear that tanning cleanses the hide and makes it appropriate for use.

Scholars have different views concerning the tanning of the hide of dead animals and whether they are cleansed by this process. They express seven different views: The first is that the hide of all dead animals is cleansed by tanning, except that of dogs, pigs and whatever is crossed between a dog or a pig and some other animal. This is the view of the Shāfiʿī school, which makes clear that both the outside and the inside of the hide is thus cleansed so as to make it usable for dry and fluid substances. According to this view, there is no difference between animals that are permissible to eat and forbidden ones. This view is reported to have been stated by ʿAlī ibn Abī Ṭālib and ʿAbdullāh ibn Masʿūd. The second view is stated by ʿUmar ibn al-Khaṭṭāb, his son ʿAbdullāh and ʿĀ'ishah, the Prophet's wife. They state that no animal hide is cleansed by tanning. This is the best known of the two reported views of Ahmad and one of two views stated by Mālik. The third view says only the hides of animals that are permissible to eat is cleansed by tanning, but not other animals. This view is shared by al-Awzāʿī, Ibn al-Mubārak, Abū Thawr and Isḥāq ibn Rāhawayh. The fourth view considers that the hide of all dead animals other than the pig is cleansed by tanning. This is the view of Abū Ḥanīfah. The fifth view considers all hides to be cleansed by tanning, but that only the outside is cleansed, not the inside. It may thus be used for dry things, but not wet ones, and prayer on it is valid but it may not be worn during prayer. This is the well-known view of Mālik, as stated by his disciples. The sixth view is that of Dāwūd and the Ẓāhirī School and it considers that all hide is cleansed by tanning including the hide of dogs and pigs, and its cleansing is on the outside and the inside. This view is also reported to be expressed by Abū Yūsuf. The seventh view considers that it is permissible to use the hide of dead animals, even if not tanned, and that it may be used for dry and wet things. This is the view of al-Zuhrī. It is an odd view of some of our scholars, but no discussion or details are provided for it and it should be discounted.

Scholars provide arguments in support of their views, and some of them reply to the evidence cited by other scholars. I have explained the evidence given by them all in some pages of my book, *Sharḥ al-Muhadhdhab*, but my purpose here is to outline the rulings and how they are deduced from the hadiths. The hadith narrated by Ibn Waʿlah from Ibn ʿAbbās provides clear evidence in support of the view of the majority of scholars that tanning cleanses the outside and inside of animal hide, making it usable with dry and wet stuff. The hide of animals slaughtered by Magians is impure, and the hadith states that it is cleansed by tanning and that it may be used as containers for water and fat. Al-Zuhrī cites in support of his view the hadith that quotes the Prophet saying: 'Why do you not take its hide and make use of it?' He does not mention tanning. The answer to this argument is that it is general, while other versions state the tanning and also mention that tanning cleanses the hide, but God knows best.

Tanning may be done with any stuff that dries up the hide, changes its smell and prevents rotting, such as alum, anethum graveolens, acacia nilotica, the peel of pomegranate or similar pure medical stuff. According to our Shāfiʿī school, it is not done by drying the hide in the sun, but the Ḥanafī school says that it is done so. Nor is it done with soil, ashes or salt. This is the more correct view. A question is raised as to whether tanning is done by the use of impure stuff, such as pigeon droppings or alum contaminated with impurity. Two opposite views are expressed on this point, the more correct according to our scholars is that it is done, but the hide must be washed after tanning. Should the hide tanned with clean stuff be washed after it has been tanned? Two answers are given: a positive and a negative one. Again, two answers are given to the question of whether water should be used at the beginning of the tanning process. Our scholars add that tanning need not be done by a person. Suppose that a hide is lifted by wind and it falls in a tanning plant or factory. It is, then, deemed to have been cleansed, but God knows best.

When a hide has been cleansed by tanning, it becomes permissible to use. There is no disagreement on this point. However, is it permissible to sell the same? Two answers are given by al-Shāfiʿī, and the more correct one is that it is permissible to sell. Is it permissible to eat? To this question three answers are given, the most correct of which is that it is not permissible in any way. The second is that it is permissible and the third view is that it is permissible to eat the hide of animals that are permissible to eat but not other animals, but God knows best. When hide is cleansed by tanning, is its hair cleansed as well? If we uphold the more widely held view among scholars of our Shāfiʿī school, which considers the hair of a dead animal to be impure, then two views are quoted from al-Shāfiʿī, the more correct of which is that the hair remains impure because, unlike the hide, it is unaffected by tanning. Moreover, our scholars say that it is not permissible to use the hide of dead animals with wet stuff before it is tanned. As for using it with dry stuff, it is permissible, but discouraged, but God knows best.

Transmission

At the end of hadith No. 642, Muslim mentions that 'Abū Bakr and Ibn Abī ʿUmar say in their narration: 'From Maymūnah, may God be pleased with her'. He means that they mention that Ibn ʿAbbās reports the hadith from Maymūnah, the Prophet's wife.

Abū al-Khayr is mentioned in the chains of transmission of hadiths Nos 648 and 649. His name is Marthad ibn ʿAbdullāh al-Yazanī.

CHAPTER 28

DRY ABLUTION [i.e. *TAYAMMUM*]

[650–108]. (Dār al-Salām 0714) Yaḥyā ibn Yaḥyā narrated:[i] he said: I read out to Mālik; from ʿAbd al-Raḥmān ibn al-Qāsim; from his father; from ʿĀ'ishah; that she said: '**We went out with God's Messenger (peace be upon him) on one of his travels. When we were out in the desert (or at Dhat al-Jaysh) my necklace was broken. The Prophet stopped while it was looked for, and people stopped with him. They were not [encamped] near a spring of water, and they did not have water. People came to Abū Bakr and said: "Are you aware what ʿĀ'ishah has done? She stopped God's Messenger (peace be upon him) and the people with him, and they are not near a spring of water and do not have water". Abū Bakr came over, but God's Messenger (peace be upon him) was asleep with his head placed on my thigh. [Abū Bakr] said to me: "You have detained God's Messenger (peace be upon him) and the people. They are not near a spring of water and they do not have water". He remonstrated with me, saying whatever God willed him to say. He poked my side with his hand, but nothing stopped me from moving away except the fact that God's Messenger (peace be upon him) was asleep on my thigh. He remained asleep until he woke up in the**

i. Related by al-Bukhārī, 334, 3672, 4607, 5250 and 6844 in a shorter version; al-Nasā'ī, 309.

morning, having no water. God revealed the verse permitting dry ablution, and the people resorted to dry ablution. Usayd ibn Ḥuḍayr (one of the leading figures [of the Anṣār]) said: "This is not the first blessing you, Abū Bakr's family, bring about". 'Ā'ishah added: We rose the camel I was riding and we found the necklace under it'.

حَدَّثَنَا يَحْيَى بْنُ يَحْيَى، قَالَ: قَرَأْتُ عَلَى مَالِكٍ، عَنْ عَبْدِ الرَّحْمَنِ بْنِ الْقَاسِمِ، عَنْ أَبِيهِ، عَنْ عَائِشَةَ، أَنَّهَا قَالَتْ: خَرَجْنَا مَعَ رَسُولِ اللهِ صَلَّى اللهُ عَلَيْهِ وَسَلَّمَ فِي بَعْضِ أَسْفَارِهِ، حَتَّى إِذَا كُنَّا بِالْبَيْدَاءِ - أَوْ بِذَاتِ الْجَيْشِ - انْقَطَعَ عِقْدٌ لِي، «فَأَقَامَ رَسُولُ اللهِ صَلَّى اللهُ عَلَيْهِ وَسَلَّمَ عَلَى الْتِمَاسِهِ، وَأَقَامَ النَّاسُ مَعَهُ، وَلَيْسُوا عَلَى مَاءٍ، وَلَيْسَ مَعَهُمْ مَاءٌ»، فَأَتَى النَّاسُ إِلَى أَبِي بَكْرٍ فَقَالُوا: أَلَا تَرَى إِلَى مَا صَنَعَتْ عَائِشَةُ؟ «أَقَامَتْ بِرَسُولِ اللهِ صَلَّى اللهُ عَلَيْهِ وَسَلَّمَ وَبِالنَّاسِ مَعَهُ، وَلَيْسُوا عَلَى مَاءٍ، وَلَيْسَ مَعَهُمْ مَاءٌ»، فَجَاءَ أَبُو بَكْرٍ «وَرَسُولُ اللهِ صَلَّى اللهُ عَلَيْهِ وَسَلَّمَ وَاضِعٌ رَأْسَهُ عَلَى فَخِذِي قَدْ نَامَ، فَقَالَ: حَبَسْتِ رَسُولَ اللهِ صَلَّى اللهُ عَلَيْهِ وَسَلَّمَ وَالنَّاسَ وَلَيْسُوا عَلَى مَاءٍ، وَلَيْسَ مَعَهُمْ مَاءٌ»، قَالَتْ فَعَاتَبَنِي أَبُو بَكْرٍ، وَقَالَ مَا شَاءَ اللهُ أَنْ يَقُولَ، وَجَعَلَ يَطْعُنُ بِيَدِهِ فِي خَاصِرَتِي» فَلَا يَمْنَعُنِي مِنَ التَّحَرُّكِ إِلَّا مَكَانُ رَسُولِ اللهِ صَلَّى اللهُ عَلَيْهِ وَسَلَّمَ عَلَى فَخِذِي، فَنَامَ رَسُولُ اللهِ صَلَّى اللهُ عَلَيْهِ وَسَلَّمَ حَتَّى أَصْبَحَ عَلَى غَيْرِ مَاءٍ، فَأَنْزَلَ اللهُ آيَةَ التَّيَمُّمِ فَتَيَمَّمُوا «فَقَالَ أُسَيْدُ بْنُ الْحُضَيْرِ: - وَهُوَ أَحَدُ النُّقَبَاءِ - «مَا هِيَ بِأَوَّلِ بَرَكَتِكُمْ يَا آلَ أَبِي بَكْرٍ» فَقَالَتْ عَائِشَةُ: «فَبَعَثْنَا الْبَعِيرَ الَّذِي كُنْتُ عَلَيْهِ فَوَجَدْنَا الْعِقْدَ تَحْتَهُ»

[651–109]. (Dār al-Salām 0715) Abū Bakr ibn Abī Shaybah narrated:[i] Abū Usāmah narrated [H]. Also, Abū Kurayb narrated; Abū Usāmah and Ibn Bishr narrated; from Hishām; from

i. Related by al-Bukhārī, 5164 and 3773; Ibn Mājah, 568.

his father; from ʿĀʾishah; that **'She borrowed a necklace from Asmā', but it was lost. God's Messenger (peace be upon him) sent some of his companions to look for it, and it was time for prayer. They prayed without performing the ablution. When they came back to the Prophet they reported this to him. God revealed the verse permitting dry ablution. Usayd ibn Ḥuḍayr said: "May God reward you well. By God, whenever you are facing a problem, God will open a way out for you, and make of it a blessing for Muslims".'**

حَدَّثَنَا أَبُو بَكْرِ بْنُ أَبِي شَيْبَةَ، حَدَّثَنَا أَبُو أُسَامَةَ ح، وَحَدَّثَنَا أَبُو كُرَيْبٍ، حَدَّثَنَا أَبُو أُسَامَةَ، وَابْنُ بِشْرٍ، عَنْ هِشَامٍ، عَنْ أَبِيهِ، عَنْ عَائِشَةَ، أَنَّهَا اسْتَعَارَتْ مِنْ أَسْمَاءَ قِلَادَةً فَهَلَكَتْ، «فَأَرْسَلَ رَسُولُ اللهِ صَلَّى اللهُ عَلَيْهِ وَسَلَّمَ نَاسًا مِنْ أَصْحَابِهِ فِي طَلَبِهَا، فَأَدْرَكَتْهُمُ الصَّلَاةُ، فَصَلَّوْا بِغَيْرِ وُضُوءٍ، فَلَمَّا أَتَوُا النَّبِيَّ صَلَّى اللهُ عَلَيْهِ وَسَلَّمَ شَكَوْا ذَلِكَ إِلَيْهِ، فَنَزَلَتْ آيَةُ التَّيَمُّمِ» فَقَالَ أُسَيْدُ بْنُ حُضَيْرٍ: «جَزَاكِ اللهُ خَيْرًا، فَوَاللهِ مَا نَزَلَ بِكِ أَمْرٌ قَطُّ، إِلَّا جَعَلَ اللهُ لَكِ مِنْهُ مَخْرَجًا وَجَعَلَ لِلْمُسْلِمِينَ فِيهِ بَرَكَةً»

[652–110]. (Dār al-Salām 0716) Yaḥyā ibn Yaḥyā, Abū Bakr ibn Abī Shaybah and Ibn Numayr narrated:[i] all from Abū Muʿāwiyah. Abū Bakr said: Abū Muʿāwiyah narrated; from al-Aʿmash; from Shaqīq, who said: **'I was sitting with ʿAbdullāh and Abū Mūsā when Abū Mūsā said: "Abū ʿAbd al-Raḥmān, suppose a man happens to be in a state of major ritual impurity but cannot find water for a month. What will he do regarding his prayer?" ʿAbdullāh said: "He may not perform the dry ablution even though he does not find water for a month". Abū Mūsā said: "Then how about this verse in**

i. Related by al-Bukhārī, 345 (in a similar but shorter version), 346 and 347; Abū Dāwūd, 321; al-Nasāʾī, 319 (in a shorter version).

Surah 5, The Repast, which says: *'[If you] can find no water, then have recourse to pure dust'*?" (5: 6) ʿAbdullāh said: "Had they been given this concession, they would almost resort to dry ablution when the water is too cold for them". Abū Mūsā said to ʿAbdullāh: "Have you not heard what ʿAmmār said: God's Messenger (peace be upon him) sent me on an errand, and I happened to be in a state of major ritual impurity, but could not find water. I soaked myself with fine soil just like animals do. When I later met the Prophet I mentioned this to him. He said: 'It would have been sufficient for you to do this with your hands', and he then struck the earth with his hands once, and wiped his right hand with his left hand and wiped the back of his hands and face?'" ʿAbdullāh said: "Have you not noted that ʿUmar was not convinced by what ʿAmmār said?"'

حَدَّثَنَا يَحْيَى بْنُ يَحْيَى، وَأَبُو بَكْرِ بْنُ أَبِي شَيْبَةَ، وَابْنُ نُمَيْرٍ، جَمِيعًا عَنْ أَبِي مُعَاوِيَةَ، قَالَ أَبُو بَكْرٍ: حَدَّثَنَا أَبُو مُعَاوِيَةَ، عَنِ الْأَعْمَشِ، عَنْ شَقِيقٍ، قَالَ: كُنْتُ جَالِسًا مَعَ عَبْدِ اللهِ، وَأَبِي مُوسَى، فَقَالَ أَبُو مُوسَى: يَا أَبَا عَبْدِ الرَّحْمَنِ أَرَأَيْتَ لَوْ أَنَّ رَجُلًا أَجْنَبَ فَلَمْ يَجِدِ الْمَاءَ شَهْرًا كَيْفَ يَصْنَعُ بِالصَّلَاةِ؟ فَقَالَ عَبْدُ اللهِ: لَا يَتَيَمَّمُ وَإِنْ لَمْ يَجِدِ الْمَاءَ شَهْرًا. فَقَالَ أَبُو مُوسَى: فَكَيْفَ بِهَذِهِ الْآيَةِ فِي سُورَةِ الْمَائِدَةِ «فَلَمْ تَجِدُوا مَاءً فَتَيَمَّمُوا صَعِيدًا طَيِّبًا» [المائدة 6]. فَقَالَ عَبْدُ اللهِ: لَوْ رُخِّصَ لَهُمْ فِي هَذِهِ الْآيَةِ لَأَوْشَكَ إِذَا بَرَدَ عَلَيْهِمُ الْمَاءُ أَنْ يَتَيَمَّمُوا بِالصَّعِيدِ، فَقَالَ أَبُو مُوسَى، لِعَبْدِ اللهِ: أَلَمْ تَسْمَعْ قَوْلَ عَمَّارٍ بَعَثَنِي رَسُولُ اللهِ صَلَّى اللهُ عَلَيْهِ وَسَلَّمَ فِي حَاجَةٍ فَأَجْنَبْتُ فَلَمْ أَجِدِ الْمَاءَ، فَتَمَرَّغْتُ فِي الصَّعِيدِ كَمَا تَمَرَّغُ الدَّابَّةُ ثُمَّ أَتَيْتُ النَّبِيَّ صَلَّى اللهُ عَلَيْهِ وَسَلَّمَ، فَذَكَرْتُ ذَلِكَ لَهُ فَقَالَ: «إِنَّمَا كَانَ يَكْفِيكَ أَنْ تَقُولَ بِيَدَيْكَ هَكَذَا» ثُمَّ ضَرَبَ بِيَدَيْهِ الْأَرْضَ ضَرْبَةً وَاحِدَةً، ثُمَّ مَسَحَ الشِّمَالَ عَلَى الْيَمِينِ، وَظَاهِرَ كَفَّيْهِ، وَوَجْهَهُ فَقَالَ: عَبْدُ اللهِ أَوَلَمْ تَرَ عُمَرَ لَمْ يَقْنَعْ بِقَوْلِ عَمَّارٍ؟

[653–111]. (Dār al-Salām 0717) Abū Kāmil al-Jaḥdarī narrated: ʿAbd al-Wāḥid narrated; al-Aʿmash narrated; from Shaqīq: **'Abū Mūsā said to ʿAbdullāh: he narrated the hadith in all details, similar to the narration of Abū Muʿāwiyah, except that he said: "It would have been sufficient for you to do like this", and he struck the earth with his two hands, shook his hands and wiped his face and hands'**.

وَحَدَّثَنَا أَبُو كَامِلٍ الْجَحْدَرِيُّ، حَدَّثَنَا عَبْدُ الْوَاحِدِ، حَدَّثَنَا الْأَعْمَشُ، عَنْ شَقِيقٍ، قَالَ: قَالَ أَبُو مُوسَى، لِعَبْدِ اللهِ: وَسَاقَ الْحَدِيثَ بِقِصَّتِهِ نَحْوَ حَدِيثِ أَبِي مُعَاوِيَةَ غَيْرَ أَنَّهُ قَالَ: فَقَالَ رَسُولُ اللهِ صَلَّى اللهُ عَلَيْهِ وَسَلَّمَ: «إِنَّمَا كَانَ يَكْفِيكَ أَنْ تَقُولَ هَكَذَا» وَضَرَبَ بِيَدَيْهِ إِلَى الْأَرْضِ فَنَفَضَ يَدَيْهِ فَمَسَحَ وَجْهَهُ وَكَفَّيْهِ.

[654–112]. (Dār al-Salām 0718) ʿAbdullāh ibn Hāshim al-ʿAbdī narrated to me:[i] Yaḥyā (meaning Ibn Saʿīd al-Qaṭṭān) narrated; from Shuʿbah; he said: al-Ḥakam narrated to me; from Dharr; from Saʿīd ibn ʿAbd al-Raḥmān ibn Abzā; from his father that **'A man came to ʿUmar. He said: "I was in a state of major ritual impurity, but I could not find water". [ʿUmar] said: "Do not pray". ʿAmmār said: "Do you not, *Amīr al-Mu'minīn*, remember when you and I were on an expedition when we both found ourselves in a state of major ritual impurity but could not find water. You did not pray, but I soaked myself in fine soil and prayed. The Prophet said [to me]: 'It would have been sufficient for you to strike the earth with your two hands, blow on them and then wipe with them your face and two hands'?" ʿUmar said: "Fear God, ʿAmmār". He said: "If you wish, I shall not report this".'**

---

i. Related by al-Bukhārī, 338, 339, 340, 341, 342 and 343 in shorter versions; Abū Dāwūd, 322, 323, 324, 325, 326, 327 and 328; al-Tirmidhī, 144; al-Nasā'ī, 311, 315, 316, 317 and 318; Ibn Mājah, 569.

Al-Ḥakam said: Ibn ʿAbd al-Raḥmān ibn Abzā narrated this hadith to me; from his father; the same as Dharr's hadith. And Salamah narrated to me from Dharr; in the same chain of transmission mentioned by al-Ḥakam, adding: '**ʿUmar said: "We hold you responsible for what you say"**.'

حَدَّثَنِي عَبْدُ اللهِ بْنُ هَاشِمٍ الْعَبْدِيُّ، حَدَّثَنَا يَحْيَى يَعْنِي ابْنَ سَعِيدٍ الْقَطَّانَ، عَنْ شُعْبَةَ، قَالَ: حَدَّثَنِي الْحَكَمُ، عَنْ ذَرٍّ، عَنْ سَعِيدِ بْنِ عَبْدِ الرَّحْمَنِ بْنِ أَبْزَى، عَنْ أَبِيهِ، أَنَّ رَجُلًا أَتَى عُمَرَ، فَقَالَ: إِنِّي أَجْنَبْتُ فَلَمْ أَجِدْ مَاءً فَقَالَ: لَا تُصَلِّ. فَقَالَ عَمَّارٌ: أَمَا تَذْكُرُ يَا أَمِيرَ الْمُؤْمِنِينَ، إِذْ أَنَا وَأَنْتَ فِي سَرِيَّةٍ فَأَجْنَبْنَا فَلَمْ نَجِدْ مَاءً، فَأَمَّا أَنْتَ فَلَمْ تُصَلِّ، وَأَمَّا أَنَا فَتَمَعَّكْتُ فِي التُّرَابِ وَصَلَّيْتُ، فَقَالَ النَّبِيُّ صَلَّى اللهُ عَلَيْهِ وَسَلَّمَ: «إِنَّمَا كَانَ يَكْفِيكَ أَنْ تَضْرِبَ بِيَدَيْكَ الْأَرْضَ، ثُمَّ تَنْفُخَ، ثُمَّ تَمْسَحَ بِهِمَا وَجْهَكَ، وَكَفَّيْكَ» فَقَالَ عُمَرُ: «اتَّقِ اللهَ يَا عَمَّارُ» قَالَ: «إِنْ شِئْتَ لَمْ أُحَدِّثْ بِهِ»

قَالَ الْحَكَمُ: وَحَدَّثَنِيهِ ابْنُ عَبْدِ الرَّحْمَنِ بْنُ أَبْزَى، عَنْ أَبِيهِ، مِثْلَ حَدِيثِ ذَرٍّ قَالَ: وَحَدَّثَنِي سَلَمَةُ، عَنْ ذَرٍّ، فِي هَذَا الْإِسْنَادِ الَّذِي ذَكَرَ الْحَكَمُ، فَقَالَ عُمَرُ: نُوَلِّيكَ مَا تَوَلَّيْتَ.

[655–113]. (Dār al-Salām 0719) Isḥāq ibn Manṣūr narrated to me: al-Naḍr ibn Shumayl narrated; Shuʿbah reported; from al-Ḥakam; he said: I heard Dharr reporting from Ibn ʿAbd al-Raḥmān ibn Abzā. Al-Ḥakam said: And I heard it from Ibn ʿAbd al-Raḥmān ibn Abzā; from his father: '**A man came to ʿUmar and said: "I was in a state of major ritual impurity but could not find water". He narrated the hadith, adding that ʿAmmār said: "*Amīr al-Mu'minīn*, due to your right that God has given you, if you wish I shall not narrate this to anyone". He did not mention: Salamah narrated to me from Dharr**'.

وَحَدَّثَنِي إِسْحَاقُ بْنُ مَنْصُورٍ، حَدَّثَنَا النَّضْرُ بْنُ شُمَيْلٍ، أَخْبَرَنَا شُعْبَةُ، عَنِ الْحَكَمِ، قَالَ: سَمِعْتُ ذَرًّا، عَنِ ابْنِ عَبْدِ الرَّحْمَنِ بْنِ أَبْزَى، قَالَ: قَالَ الْحَكَمُ: وَقَدْ سَمِعْتُهُ مِنِ ابْنِ عَبْدِ الرَّحْمَنِ بْنِ أَبْزَى، عَنْ أَبِيهِ، أَنَّ رَجُلًا أَتَى عُمَرَ فَقَالَ: إِنِّي أَجْنَبْتُ فَلَمْ أَجِدْ مَاءً. وَسَاقَ الْحَدِيثَ وَزَادَ فِيهِ، قَالَ عَمَّارٌ: يَا أَمِيرَ الْمُؤْمِنِينَ إِنْ شِئْتَ لِمَا جَعَلَ اللهُ عَلَيَّ مِنْ حَقِّكَ لَا أُحَدِّثُ بِهِ أَحَدًا، وَلَمْ يَذْكُرْ حَدَّثَنِي سَلَمَةُ، عَنْ ذَرٍّ.

Dry Ablution

Linguistically speaking, *tayammum* means 'to aim for'. In its particular Islamic context it means 'dry ablution', and is confirmed in the Qur'an, the Sunnah and by the unanimity of the Muslim community. It is a special favour God has granted to the Muslim community, may God increase its honour. Muslims are unanimous that dry ablution is limited to one's face and hands, whether it is in place of ordinary or major ritual ablution, but God knows best.

Scholars differ as to how dry ablution is performed. The view of our school, which is agreed by the majority of scholars, requires striking the earth twice: one to wipe one's face and the second to wipe one's arms up to the elbows. Scholars who maintain that this is the correct method include ʿAlī ibn Abī Ṭālib, ʿAbdullāh ibn ʿUmar, al-Ḥasan al-Baṣrī, al-Shaʿbī, Sālim ibn ʿAbdullāh ibn ʿUmar, Sufyān al-Thawrī, Mālik, Abū Ḥanīfah and many others, may God be pleased with them all. A group of scholars maintain that one strike is sufficient for both one's face and hands. This is the view of 'Aṭā', Makḥūl, al-Awzāʿī, Ahmad, Isḥāq, Ibn al-Mundhir and most Hadith scholars. It is reported that al-Zuhrī says that the arms must be wiped up to the armpits. This is how his view is reported by our scholars in the books of al-Shāfiʿī School. Imam Abū Sulaymān al-Khaṭṭābī said that no scholar disagrees about it being unnecessary to wipe any part beyond the elbows. Our scholars also report that Ibn Sīrīn considers that it is insufficient to use less than three strikes, one to wipe one's face, another to wipe one's hands and the third to wipe one's arms.

Scholars are unanimous that dry ablution is permissible in the case of invalidating one's ablution by a discharge from one's private parts. Likewise, the scholars of recent generations and their predecessors are unanimous that it is permissible for a man in a state of major ritual impurity and a woman who has completed her menstrual or postnatal period. No scholar of a recent or earlier generation disagrees, except for what was reported of ʿUmar ibn al-Khaṭṭāb and ʿAbdullāh ibn Masʿūd. A similar view is attributed to Ibrāhīm al-Nakhaʿī, who was a leading scholar of the Tābiʿīn generation. It is also said that ʿUmar and ʿAbdullāh changed their views. A number of well-known and authentic hadiths confirm that it is permissible for a person who is in a state of major ritual impurity, but God knows best.

If a man in a state of major ritual impurity performs dry ablution and offers his prayer, then finds water, he must take a bath. This is unanimously agreed upon by scholars, except for what is reported of the eminent Tābiʿīn scholar, Abū Salamah ibn ʿAbd al-Raḥmān, who said that it is not required of him to take a bath. This view is abandoned by the unanimity of earlier and later scholars, as authentic and well-known hadiths mention that the Prophet (peace be upon him) ordered a person who was in major ritual impurity to wash himself when he found water, but God knows best. It is also permissible for a man on a journey, or one who is attending to his business away from home, to have sexual intercourse with his wife, even though they may not have water to take a bath. They should subsequently wash their genital organs and perform dry ablution then offer their prayers. The dry ablution is sufficient for them and they do not have to repeat it if they wash their genitals. If the man resorts to dry ablution and prays without washing his genital part or what has fallen on him from his wife's discharge, his case differs. If we say that the wetness of the woman's vagina is impure, he must repeat his prayer when he has cleansed himself with water. If we say that it is not impure, no repeat is required, but God knows best. If some impurity falls on some part of a person and he wants to do the dry ablution to remove it, the view of our school and most scholars is that it is not valid. Imam Ahmad ibn Ḥanbal said that it is appropriate if the impurity is on his body, but inappropriate if it is on his clothes. His disciples differ as to whether he must repeat such prayer. Ibn al-Mundhir said that al-Thawrī, al-Awzāʿī and Abū Thawr used to say that he should wipe the place of impurity with fine soil, and then pray, but God knows best.

Should prayer offered with dry ablution be repeated? Our school say that if the dry ablution is resorted to because of illness, injury or similar, then no repeat is required. If it is caused because of the inavailability of water, then the situation is different: if he is in a place where it is normally difficult to find water, such as being on a journey, then no repeat is required. On the other hand, if he is in a place where water is normally available, then according to the right view, he should repeat the prayer when water is available and he can have his normal ablution, but God knows best.

Which substance is needed for dry ablution? Al-Shāfiʿī, Ahmad, Ibn al-Mundhir, Dāwūd al-Ẓāhirī and most scholars are of the view that dry ablution can only be done with pure earth that has dust which may attach to the body. Abu Ḥanīfah and Mālik say that any part of the earth is good enough for dry ablution, including a washed-off rock surface. Some Mālikī scholars go further, making it valid on whatever is attached to the earth, including wood and other substances. Mālik expresses two views on whether it is permissible on snow. Al-Awzāʿī and Sufyān al-Thawrī say that it is permissible on snow and whatever is on earth, but God knows best.

What ruling applies to dry ablution? The view of our al-Shāfiʿī School and the majority of scholars is that it does not remove the impurity, but permits prayer. Thus, when a person performs dry ablution, he is permitted to offer one obligatory prayer and whatever he wishes to offer of voluntary prayers. He may not offer two obligatory prayers with one dry ablution. If he intends with his dry ablution to offer an obligatory prayer, he may offer it as well as voluntary, or Sunnah, prayers. However, if he intends to offer a

Sunnah prayer, his dry ablution is sufficient only to do voluntary prayers, but not an obligatory one. With one dry ablution a person may offer the prayer for the deceased for several funerals, or for several funerals and one obligatory prayer. One must not do the dry ablution before the time of an obligatory prayer is due. If a person starts his prayer after doing the dry ablution and he sees water during his prayer, his prayer remains valid and he may complete it, unless he is obliged to repeat it. In this case, his prayer is rendered invalid when he sees the water, but God knows best.

Text Explanation

In the first hadith, No. 650, ʿĀ'ishah mentions that she went with the Prophet on one of his travels and when they were out in the desert, or at Dhāt al-Jaysh, she lost her necklace. The desert and Dhāt al-Jaysh are two places between Madinah and Khaybar. In this hadith she describes the necklace as belonging to her, while in the next one she had borrowed it from her sister, Asmā'. Both descriptions are correct, in the sense that the necklace actually belonged to Asmā', but was in ʿĀ'ishah's possession.

This part of the hadith includes several useful points, such as the permissibility of borrowing something, as well as borrowing jewellery. It is also permissible to take a borrowed object when one is travelling, provided that the owner agrees. It is also perfectly permissible for women to have necklaces and jewellery. The hadith also makes clear that it is important to safeguard what is due to other Muslims, even though it may be a small or cheap object. This is why the Prophet stayed for a while to search for the necklace. It is also permissible to stay at a place where no water is available, even though this means that one will have to resort to dry ablution. There are other useful points here, but God knows best.

In the same hadith, No. 650, ʿĀ'ishah mentions that her father, Abū Bakr, remonstrated with her, saying whatever he said and poking her side with his hand. This shows that it is permissible for a father to discipline his children even when they are grown up and married and no longer living in his home.

ʿĀ'ishah mentions that when her camel was made to rise, the necklace was found under it. In al-Bukhārī's narration, it is said that the Prophet sent a man and he found the necklace, and in different versions, he sent two men or a number of people. All this describes the same situation. The man who was sent to look for the necklace was Usayd ibn Ḥuḍayr, and he went with some of his people but they could not find it. When they returned and began to get ready to march, on making the camel rise, Usayd found the necklace as it was hidden under the sitting camel, but God knows best.

In the second hadith, No. 651, it is mentioned that 'they prayed without performing the ablution'. This provides evidence that a person who cannot find either water or fine soil may pray in the condition he is in. This question is subject to different opinions among scholars of earlier and later generations. Four different views are expressed by al-Shāfiʿī, and the most correct according to our scholars is that it is obligatory for such a person to offer the prayer, and then he must repeat it when he finds water. That he should offer the prayer on time is due to the Prophet's order: 'When I give you an order, do it as best you can'. That it should be repeated is because being without both water and soil is a very rare emergency. As such, it is similar to the situation of a person who forgets to wash one of his body parts that must be washed during ablution, and prays. In this case, he must repeat his prayer after renewing his ablution. The second view is that offering the prayer is not obligatory in this condition, but desirable, and he must offer the prayer when he can have his ablution, whether he prayed originally or not. The third view is that he is forbidden to pray because he has no ablution. The fourth view is that it is obligatory for him to pray but a repeat is not obligatory. This is the view of al-Muzanī and it enjoys the strongest evidence, supported by the present hadith and similar ones. It is not reported that the

Prophet ordered repeating such a prayer. The view of choice is that a compensatory prayer becomes obligatory if an order is given, but no order is clearly made in this case. Hence, a repeat is not obligatory. Al-Muzanī applies the same rule to every prayer that is offered on time, with some defect. It need not be repeated. Scholars who are of the view that a repeat is necessary may respond to this hadith saying that the repeat need not be immediate and that it is permissible to delay an explanation until it is needed, but God knows best.

The Qur'anic verse that permits dry ablution says that in a situation of unavailability of water Muslims should turn to an earth surface. Most scholars say that it means 'pure soil', while others make it general and say that it means any surface. Our scholars say that a person should go to the surface, or aim towards it. This means that in windy weather, if the wind bears dust and it falls on his face, and he rubs his face with it, this is not acceptable. The dust must be borne from the earth or some other surface. This question is subject to numerous details which are discussed at length in books of *fiqh*, but God knows best.

In hadith No. 653, the Prophet "tells ʿAmmār: '"It would have been sufficient for you to do like this", and he struck the earth with his two hands, shook his hands and wiped his face and hands'. The hadith provides evidence in support of the view that one strike is sufficient to wipe one's face and hands. Scholars that take the other view, requiring two strikes, may respond by saying that in the present case the Prophet was merely showing his companion how to perform the strike. He did not mean to show him all that the dry ablution included. In normal ablution, God makes it obligatory to wash one's hands up to the elbows. In *tayammum*, or dry ablution, God tells us to wipe our faces and hands. It appears that the 'hand', which is not specified here, is the same that is specified earlier in the verse as it prescribes the ablution. As this is clearly apparent, it may not be ignored without clear instructions, but God knows best.

As the Prophet showed his companion the way to do the dry ablution 'he shook his hands'. This is cited as evidence in support of the view that it is permissible to do the *tayammum* on stones and surfaces that bear no soil. They say: 'Had soil been of essence, the Prophet would not have shaken his hands'. The other scholars respond by saying that he shook his hands to remove some of the soil, because if one's hands bear much soil, it is desirable that one should remove some of it, leaving only what is sufficient to cover the part being wiped, but God knows best.

In the argument between 'Umar and 'Ammār, 'Umar said: 'Fear God', and 'Ammār responds by saying: 'If you wish, I shall not report this'. 'Umar was simply advising 'Ammār to make sure and ascertain that what he was saying was correct, suggesting that he might have forgotten or misunderstood. 'Ammār's response defers to 'Umar, saying that if 'Umar considered that it was better and wiser that 'Ammār should not report what he learnt from the Prophet, he would do so, because he considered it his duty to obey 'Umar, the Caliph, in whatever is permissible. That the knowledge of this Sunnah was already reported and known renders the duty of spreading such knowledge fulfilled. If 'Ammār subsequently stopped reporting it, in deference to the Caliph's wish, he would not be suppressing knowledge. It is also possible that 'Ammār meant that he would not be speaking frequently about it so as to publicize it fully, and would keep it only within limited circles, but God knows best.

The case of 'Ammār explains that it was permissible to exercise *ijtihād*, i.e. using scholarly discretion, during the Prophet's lifetime. 'Ammār exercised his discretion concerning the way the dry ablution is done. Scholars of our school and others differ on this point, expressing three views, the most correct of which is that it was permissible to resort to *ijtihād* during the Prophet's lifetime, in his presence and absence. The second is that it is not permissible at all, and the third view is that it is permissible but not in his presence, but God knows best.

[656–114]. (Dār al-Salām 0720) Muslim said: and al-Layth ibn Sa'd narrated;[i] from Ja'far ibn Rabī'ah; from 'Abd al-Raḥmān ibn Hurmuz; from 'Umayr, Ibn 'Abbās's *mawlā*; that he heard him say: I came with 'Abd al-Raḥmān ibn Yasār, the *mawlā* of Maymūnah, the Prophet's wife and we entered the place of Abū al-Jahm ibn al-Ḥārith ibn al-Ṣimmah al-Anṣārī. Abū al-Jahm said: **'God's Messenger (peace be upon him) came along from the direction of the Jamal Well. A man met him and offered the *salām* greeting to him, but the Prophet did not reply. He first moved to the wall and wiped his face and hand, then he replied to his greeting'**.

قَالَ مُسْلِمٌ، وَرَوَى اللَّيْثُ بْنُ سَعْدٍ، عَنْ جَعْفَرِ بْنِ رَبِيعَةَ، عَنْ عَبْدِ الرَّحْمَنِ بْنِ هُرْمُزَ، عَنْ عُمَيْرٍ، مَوْلَى ابْنِ عَبَّاسٍ، أَنَّهُ سَمِعَهُ يَقُولُ: أَقْبَلْتُ أَنَا وَعَبْدُ الرَّحْمَنِ بْنُ يَسَارٍ، مَوْلَى مَيْمُونَةَ زَوْجِ النَّبِيِّ صَلَّى اللهُ عَلَيْهِ وَسَلَّمَ. حَتَّى دَخَلْنَا عَلَى أَبِي الْجَهْمِ بْنِ الْحَارِثِ بْنِ الصِّمَّةِ الْأَنْصَارِيِّ، فَقَالَ أَبُو الْجَهْمِ: «أَقْبَلَ رَسُولُ اللهِ صَلَّى اللهُ عَلَيْهِ وَسَلَّمَ مِنْ نَحْوِ بِئْرِ جَمَلٍ، فَلَقِيَهُ رَجُلٌ فَسَلَّمَ عَلَيْهِ، فَلَمْ يَرُدَّ رَسُولُ اللهِ صَلَّى اللهُ عَلَيْهِ وَسَلَّمَ عَلَيْهِ، حَتَّى أَقْبَلَ عَلَى الْجِدَارِ فَمَسَحَ وَجْهَهُ وَيَدَيْهِ، ثُمَّ رَدَّ عَلَيْهِ السَّلَامُ»

[657–115]. (Dār al-Salām 0721) Muhammad ibn 'Abdullāh ibn Numayr narrated: my father narrated; Sufyān narrated; from al-Ḍaḥḥāk ibn 'Uthmān; from Nāfi'; from Ibn 'Umar: **'A man passed by when God's Messenger (peace be upon him) was urinating. He offered the greeting of peace, but the Prophet did not reply to him'**.

حَدَّثَنَا مُحَمَّدُ بْنُ عَبْدِ اللهِ بْنِ نُمَيْرٍ، حَدَّثَنَا أَبِي، حَدَّثَنَا سُفْيَانُ، عَنِ الضَّحَّاكِ بْنِ عُثْمَانَ، عَنْ نَافِعٍ، عَنِ ابْنِ عُمَرَ: «أَنَّ رَجُلًا مَرَّ وَرَسُولُ اللهِ صَلَّى اللهُ عَلَيْهِ وَسَلَّمَ يَبُولُ، فَسَلَّمَ، فَلَمْ يَرُدَّ عَلَيْهِ»

i. Related by al-Bukhārī, 337; Abū Dāwūd, 329; al-Nasā'ī, 310.

Text Explanation

Hadith No. 656 mentions that the Prophet came from the direction of the Jamal Well. In this narration, the name of the well is not given the definite article in Arabic, but it has the definite article in al-Nasā'ī's version. This is a place close to Madinah. The hadith mentions that the Prophet did not reply to the greeting of his companion until he had performed the *tayammum,* or dry ablution, at a nearby wall. This is understood as indicating that the Prophet had no water to perform the ablution at that time. If water is available and a person can use it, dry ablution is not an option. This applies in all cases, whether the time for prayer is very short or long, and whether the prayer is obligatory or a collective duty, such as the Funeral or Eid Prayers. This is the view of our school and the majority of scholars. Abū Ḥanīfah said that resort to dry ablution is valid despite the availability of water, if one fears to miss a Funeral or Eid Prayer. Al-Baghawī, a Shāfiʿī scholar, reports that some of our al-Shāfiʿī scholars are of the view that if a person fears that the time of an obligatory prayer should lapse, he may perform the dry ablution and offer it, then he should perform the ordinary ablution with water and repeat the prayer. However, the well-known view is the one mentioned earlier, which considers dry ablution invalid if water is available, even if using the water means that the time of an obligatory prayer has lapsed, but God knows best.

The hadith makes clear that *tayammum,* or dry ablution, may be performed on a wall if the wall is dusty. This is permissible according to our school and the majority of scholars of earlier and later generations. The hadith is cited by some scholars as evidence in support of the view that dry ablution may be performed without soil. Other scholars say that the hadith is understood to mean that the wall used by the Prophet was dusty. The hadith also shows that *tayammum* may be performed for voluntary or recommended acts of worship and other recommended actions, such as the prostration during reciting the Qur'an, or in thanksgiving, or to hold the Qur'an, etc. just as it is valid to perform obligatory prayers. This is the view of all scholars, except those who advance a strange and odd view claiming that it may not be done except to offer an obligatory prayer. This view is discounted. A question may arise: how did the Prophet do the dry ablution on a wall without first having its owner's permission. The answer is that this wall might have been public property or the property of someone he knew and the Prophet was certain that he would not object to the Prophet's action. Such a situation is proper for anyone to do. Needless to say, it is more so for the Prophet, but God knows best.

The last hadith, No. 657, mentions that the Prophet did not reply to the person who greeted him while he was urinating. This makes clear that the one who offers such a greeting does not deserve to be replied to. This is agreed upon by all scholars. Scholars of our school say that it is discouraged to offer a greeting to a person who is answering the call of nature. Should someone so greet him, he should not reply. Scholars also say that it is discouraged for a person answering the call of nature to say any glorification of God, thank Him, state His oneness, bless someone who sneezes, reply to a greeting of peace, etc. He is also discouraged from repeating the phrases of the call to prayer. Likewise, he should not say anything of such glorifications when he is intent on having sexual intercourse with his wife. If he sneezes in any of these situations, he should not praise God verbally, but he may do so silently, without moving his tongue. All this discouragement is of the lesser type, not the stronger which approaches prohibition. As such, it does not represent a sinful act.

Similarly, all conversation is discouraged while one is answering a call of nature, except when it is absolutely necessary, such as seeing a blind person about to fall or seeing a snake or a scorpion heading towards someone who is unaware of it. In such cases, it is a duty to alert the person concerned to the danger.

All such discouragement is agreed upon by our school and most scholars. It is reported by Ibn al-Mundhir from Ibn ʿAbbās, ʿAṭā', Saʿīd al-Juhanī and ʿIkrimah. It is also reported that Ibrāhīm al-Nakhaʿī and Ibn Sīrīn said that it is permissible, but God knows best.

Transmission

The chain of transmission of hadith No. 656 begins as follows: 'Muslim said: and al-Layth ibn Saʿd narrates from Jaʿfar ibn Rabīʿah'. This is how this hadith occurs in all reportings of Muslim's anthology, with the narrators between Muslim and al-Layth missing. This sort of hadith is classified as *munqaṭiʿ*, or discontinued. It is also called *muʿallaq*, i.e. unattached. We have explained this hadith and similar ones in the Notes in our Introduction. We mentioned that there are twelve or fourteen hadiths in the entire anthology of Muslim that are so unattached, but God knows best.

In the chain of transmission of the same hadith, 'I came with ʿAbd al-Raḥmān ibn Yasār ...'. This is how it occurs in all original copies of Muslim's *Ṣaḥīḥ* anthology. Abū ʿAlī al-Ghassānī and all scholars who discuss Muslim's chains of transmission said that giving the name as ʿAbd al-Raḥmān is a clear mistake. The correct name is ʿAbdullāh ibn Yasār. This is how it is reported by al-Bukhārī, Abū Dāwūd, al-Nasā'ī and others. *Qāḍī* ʿIyāḍ said: 'It also occurs correctly as ʿAbdullāh ibn Yasār in our reporting of Muslim's *Ṣaḥīḥ* through al-Samarqandī, from al-Fārisī, from al-Julūdī, from ʿAbdullāh ibn Yasār. These were four brothers: ʿAbdullāh, ʿAbd al-Raḥmān, ʿAbd al-Malik and ʿAṭā', Maymūnah's *mawlā*, but God knows best.

In hadith No. 656, the chain of transmission includes: 'we entered the place of Abū al-Jahm ibn al-Ḥārith ibn al-Ṣimmah'. This is how it occurs in Muslim's anthology, but it is wrong. The correct name is Abū al-Juhaym, which is how it is spelled in al-Bukhārī's *Ṣaḥīḥ* and other anthologies. This is how this narrator's name is spelled and pronounced, as stated in books devoted to names. Furthermore, it is how Muslim himself mentions him in his book of names of narrators, *Asmā' al-Rijāl*, and how al-Bukhārī mentions him in his *Tārīkh*, as well as Abū Dāwūd, al-Nasā'ī and other scholars. Indeed, all scholars who wrote books about names and appellations give him this spelling, Abū al-Juhaym. His name, as stated by Muslim and other scholars, is ʿAbdullāh. He is the well-known narrator of the hadith concerning crossing the path of a person offering prayer. His full name is ʿAbdullāh ibn al-Ḥārith ibn al-Ṣimmah al-Anṣārī al-

Bukhārī. He is different from Abu al-Jahm who is mentioned in the hadith concerning types of clothing. That narrator's name is ʿĀmir ibn Ḥudhayfah ibn Ghānim, who belonged to the ʿAdī branch of the Quraysh. We will speak about him in due course, God willing.

CHAPTER 29

EVIDENCE THAT A MUSLIM IS NEVER RITUALLY IMPURE

[658–000]. (Dār al-Salām 0722) Zuhayr ibn Ḥarb narrated to me:[i] Yaḥyā (meaning Ibn Saʿīd) narrated; Ḥumayd narrated [H]. Also, Abū Bakr ibn Abī Shaybah narrated (his text); Ismāʿīl ibn ʿUlayyah; narrated; from Ḥumayd al-Ṭawīl; from Abū Rāfiʿ; from Abū Hurayrah; that '**the Prophet met him along a road in Madinah when he was in the state of major ritual impurity. He moved away stealthily, went and took a bath. The Prophet looked for him. When he came back, the Prophet asked him: "Where have you been, Abū Hurayrah?" He said: "Messenger of God, when you met me, I was in major ritual impurity. I did not like to sit with you until I had cleansed myself". The Prophet said: "Limitless is God in His glory. A believer is never impure".**'

حَدَّثَنِي زُهَيْرُ بْنُ حَرْبٍ، حَدَّثَنَا يَحْيَى يَعْنِي ابْنَ سَعِيدٍ قَالَ: حُمَيْدٌ حَدَّثَنَا، ح وَحَدَّثَنَا أَبُو بَكْرِ بْنُ أَبِي شَيْبَةَ، - وَاللَّفْظُ لَهُ - حَدَّثَنَا إِسْمَاعِيلُ ابْنُ عُلَيَّةَ، عَنْ حُمَيْدٍ الطَّوِيلِ، قَالَ: حَدَّثَنَا بَكْرُ بْنُ عَبْدِ اللهِ، عَنْ أَبِي رَافِعٍ، عَنْ أَبِي هُرَيْرَةَ، أَنَّهُ لَقِيَهُ النَّبِيُّ صَلَّى اللهُ عَلَيْهِ وَسَلَّمَ فِي طَرِيقٍ مِنْ طُرُقِ الْـمَدِينَةِ، وَهُوَ جُنُبٌ فَانْسَلَّ فَذَهَبَ فَاغْتَسَلَ، فَتَفَقَّدَهُ النَّبِيُّ صَلَّى اللهُ عَلَيْهِ وَسَلَّمَ فَلَمَّا جَاءَهُ قَالَ: «أَيْنَ كُنْتَ يَا أَبَا هُرَيْرَةَ» قَالَ: يَا رَسُولَ اللهِ، لَقِيتَنِي وَأَنَا جُنُبٌ فَكَرِهْتُ أَنْ أُجَالِسَكَ حَتَّى أَغْتَسِلَ، فَقَالَ رَسُولُ اللهِ صَلَّى اللهُ عَلَيْهِ وَسَلَّمَ: «سُبْحَانَ اللهِ إِنَّ الْـمُؤْمِنَ لَا يَنْجُسُ»

---

i. Related by al-Bukhārī, 283 and 285 (in a shorter version); Abū Dāwūd, 231; al-Tirmidhī, 121; al-Nasāʾī, 269; Ibn Mājah, 534.

[659–116]. (Dār al-Salām 0723) Abū Bakr ibn Abī Shaybah and Abū Kurayb narrated:[i] both said: Wakīʿ narrated; from Misʿar; from Wāṣil; from Abū Wā'il; from Ḥudhayfah; that **'God's Messenger met him when he was in a state of major ritual impurity. He moved away and went to take a bath and returned. He said: "I was in a state of major ritual impurity". The Prophet said: "A Muslim is never impure"**.'

وَحَدَّثَنَا أَبُو بَكْرِ بْنُ أَبِي شَيْبَةَ، وَأَبُو كُرَيْبٍ، قَالَا: حَدَّثَنَا وَكِيعٌ، عَنْ مِسْعَرٍ، عَنْ وَاصِلٍ، عَنْ أَبِي وَائِلٍ، عَنْ حُذَيْفَةَ، أَنَّ رَسُولَ اللهِ صَلَّى اللهُ عَلَيْهِ وَسَلَّمَ لَقِيَهُ وَهُوَ جُنُبٌ، فَحَادَ عَنْهُ فَاغْتَسَلَ. ثُمَّ جَاءَ فَقَالَ: كُنْتُ جُنُبًا. قَالَ: «إِنَّ الْمُسْلِمَ لَا يَنْجُسُ»

Text Explanation

In the first hadith, the Prophet says: 'Limitless is God in His glory. A believer is never ritually impure', and in the second: 'A Muslim is never ritually impure'. This hadith sets a great rule, making clear that a Muslim is clean of impurity whether alive or dead. When a Muslim is alive, Muslims are unanimous that he or she is free of impurity. This applies even to a newborn as it is given birth and the wetness of its mother's vagina is still on it. Some of our scholars say that such a newborn is free of impurity according to the unanimous view of the Muslim community, and that the well-known difference of opinion concerning the impurity of the wetness of a woman's vagina does not apply to it. Nor does the difference of opinion mentioned in the books of our scholars concerning the impurity or otherwise of the outside of chicken eggs apply here. This is the ruling concerning a living Muslim person. As for a dead person, scholars, including al-Shāfiʿī, have two views, but the correct one of the two is that the body of a dead person is free of impurity. Therefore, it is washed for burial. This is clear on the basis of the Prophet's statement: 'A Muslim is never

i. Related by Abū Dāwūd, 230; al-Nasā'ī, 268; Ibn Mājah, 535 (in a longer version).

impure'. In his *Ṣaḥīḥ*, al-Bukhārī quotes Ibn 'Abbās's statement that a Muslim is never impure, whether alive or dead. This is the verdict concerning a Muslim person. What about unbelievers? The same verdict as applies to Muslims also applies to unbelievers with regard to freedom of impurity, and this is our view and the view of the overwhelming majority of scholars of earlier and later generations.

How about the Qur'anic statement, *'The idolaters are certainly impure'*? (9: 28) What is meant here is impurity of belief. It does not mean that their bodies are impure like the impurity of urine, faeces and similar things. Indeed, every human being, Muslim or non-Muslim, is free of impurity. As such, then, their sweat, saliva and tears are also pure, even when they have been to the toilet or are in a state of major ritual impurity or a woman is in menstruation or postnatal discharge. All this is unanimously agreed upon by all Muslims, as I explained earlier. The same applies to children: their bodies, clothes and saliva are considered to be pure, unless it is ascertained that they are contaminated with impurity. Therefore, it is perfectly acceptable to pray using their clothes, and to eat with them—including sharing food with them that has plenty of sauce in which they dip their hands. The evidence confirming all this is widely known from the Sunnah and the unanimity of scholars, but God knows best.

This hadith shows the desirability to show respect to honourable people and that a person who is in their company should defer to them and ensure to be in his best condition. Scholars advise their students to be in the best form when they attend them. They should be in a condition of cleanliness, having removed hair that should be removed, clipped their nails and changed any foul smell. They should wear good clothes, etc. All these are aspects of the respect due to scholars and scholarship, but God knows best. The hadith also shows that if a scholar notices that his student does something that is contrary to what is appropriate, he should ask him about it. He should then explain to him what is correct and any ruling that applies to it, but God knows best.

Transmission

The narrators include Abū Rāfiʿ, whose name is Nufayʿ, and Abū Wā'il, whose name is Shaqīq ibn Salamah.

The chain of transmission of hadith No. 659 runs as follows: 'Abū Bakr ibn Abī Shaybah and Abū Kurayb narrated: Wakīʿ narrated; from Misʿar; from Wāṣil; from Abū Wā'il; from Ḥudhayfah'. All these narrators belonged to Kufah, except for Ḥudhayfah who stayed most of his time in al-Madain.

In hadith No. 658, we have the following chain of transmission: 'Zuhayr ibn Ḥarb narrated to me: Yaḥyā (meaning Ibn Saʿīd) narrated; Ḥumayd narrated [H]. Also, Abū Bakr ibn Abī Shaybah narrated (his text); Ismāʿīl ibn ʿUlayyah; narrated; from Ḥumayd al-Ṭawīl; from Abū Rāfiʿ; from Abū Hurayrah'. In the Arabic original, the first of the two chains includes an inversion, which would be reflected in English as 'narrated Ḥumayd'. This may be confusing to some readers, but there is nothing confusing for anyone who studies this discipline. This is a mere inversion and does not alter the meaning in any way.

This chain includes: 'from Ḥumayd al-Ṭawīl from Abū Rāfiʿ,' and this is how it occurs in all copies of Muslim's *Ṣaḥīḥ*. *Qāḍī* ʿIyāḍ said: 'Imam Abū ʿAbdullāh al-Māzarī said that this chain of transmission is incomplete because Ḥumayd narrates the hadith from Bakr ibn ʿAbdullāh al-Muzanī, from Abū Rāfiʿ. This is how al-Bukhārī relates it, as does Abū Bakr ibn Abī Shaybah in his *al-Musnad*.' Also Abū Dāwūd, al-Tirmidhī, al-Nasā'ī, Ibn Mājah and other leading scholars relate the hadith in the same way as al-Bukhārī: Ḥumayd from Bakr from Abū Rāfiʿ. However, the omission that occurs here does not detract from the validity of the text of the hadith because the text is authentic as reported by Abū Hurayrah and Ḥudhayfah, but God knows best.

CHAPTER 30

GLORIFICATION OF GOD WHEN IN MAJOR RITUAL IMPURITY

[660–117]. (Dār al-Salām 0724) Abū Kurayb Muhammad ibn al-ʿAlā' and Ibrāhīm ibn Mūsā narrated:[i] both said: Ibn Abī Zā'idah narrated; from his father; from Khālid ibn Salamah; from al-Bahī; from ʿUrwah; from ʿĀ'ishah. She said: **'God's Messenger (peace be upon him) used to glorify God in all situations'**.

حَدَّثَنَا أَبُو كُرَيْبٍ مُحَمَّدُ بْنُ الْعَلَاءِ، وَإِبْرَاهِيمُ بْنُ مُوسَى، قَالَا: حَدَّثَنَا ابْنُ أَبِي زَائِدَةَ، عَنْ أَبِيهِ، عَنْ خَالِدِ بْنِ سَلَمَةَ، عَنِ الْبَهِيِّ، عَنْ عُرْوَةَ، عَنْ عَائِشَةَ، قَالَتْ: «كَانَ النَّبِيُّ صَلَّى اللهُ عَلَيْهِ وَسَلَّمَ يَذْكُرُ اللهَ عَلَى كُلِّ أَحْيَانِهِ»

Text Explanation

This hadith sets the principle that remembrance and glorification of God and thanking Him, as well as saying similar phrases, is permissible in all situations according to the unanimous view of all Muslims. Scholars held different views concerning the recitation of the Qur'an by a man in a state of major ritual impurity or a woman during her menstruation. The majority of scholars consider that reciting the Qur'an in these two states is forbidden. There is no difference between reciting a complete verse or a part of it: all is forbidden. If the person in a state of major ritual impurity says *Bismillāh*, i.e. in the name of God, or *Alḥamdulillāh*, i.e. praise be

i. Related by al-Bukhārī, 634; Abū Dāwūd, 18; al-Tirmidhī, 3384; Ibn Mājah, 302.

to God, or similar phrases as a part of the Qur'an, he commits a forbidden act, but if he intends it as mere glorification of God, or makes no intention, it is not forbidden. It is also permissible for a man in major ritual impurity or a woman during menstruation to remember verses or surahs of the Qur'an and to be mindful of these, and to look at a copy of the Qur'an. It is desirable for them when they take a bath to say 'in the name of God', as a glorification of Him.

It should be realized that it is reprehensible to glorify God when one goes to the toilet or during intercourse. We mentioned this a short while ago, towards the end of the chapter on *tayammum*, or dry ablution. We explained the situation that is excepted, and mentioned that scholars differ as to its being reprehensible. The majority of scholars confirm that it is reprehensible. On this basis, the present hadith is understood to mean all situations except these particular ones. Thus, the hadith means that the Prophet used to mention God's name and glorify him whether he had performed ablution or not, even in a state of major ritual impurity, seated, standing, reclining or walking, but God knows best.

Transmission

Al-Bahī is one of the narrators of this hadith, reporting from ʿUrwah. Al-Bahī is a nickname, while his actual name is ʿAbdullāh ibn Bashshār. Yaḥyā ibn Maʿīn, Abū ʿAlī al-Ghassānī and others said that he is classified as belonging to the highest class among Hadith narrators from Kufah. He was a *mawlā* of Muṣʿab ibn al-Zubayr and known by his appellation, Abū Muhammad, but God knows best.

CHAPTER 31

EATING WHEN IN A STATE OF MAJOR RITUAL IMPURITY

[661–118]. (Dār al-Salām 0725) Yaḥyā ibn Yaḥyā al-Tamīmī and Abū al-Rabīʿ al-Zahrānī narrated: Yaḥyā said: Ḥammād ibn Zayd reported while Abū al-Rabīʿ said: Ḥammād narrated; from ʿAmr ibn Dīnār; from Saʿīd ibn al-Ḥuwayrith; from Ibn ʿAbbās; that '**The Prophet came out of the toilet and he was brought some food. People mentioned ablution to him, but he said: "Am I about to offer prayer and need to perform ablution?"**'

حَدَّثَنَا يَحْيَى بْنُ يَحْيَى التَّمِيمِيُّ، وَأَبُو الرَّبِيعِ الزَّهْرَانِيُّ، - قَالَ يَحْيَى، أَخْبَرَنَا حَمَّادُ بْنُ زَيْدٍ، وَقَالَ أَبُو الرَّبِيعِ - حَدَّثَنَا حَمَّادٌ، عَنْ عَمْرِو بْنِ دِينَارٍ، عَنْ سَعِيدِ بْنِ الْحُوَيْرِثِ، عَنِ ابْنِ عَبَّاسٍ: «أَنَّ النَّبِيَّ صَلَّى اللهُ عَلَيْهِ وَسَلَّمَ خَرَجَ مِنَ الْخَلَاءِ، فَأُتِيَ بِطَعَامٍ»، فَذَكَرُوا لَهُ الْوُضُوءَ فَقَالَ: «أُرِيدُ أَنْ أُصَلِّيَ فَأَتَوَضَّأَ؟»

[662–119]. (Dār al-Salām 0726) Abū Bakr ibn Abī Shaybah narrated: Sufyān ibn ʿUyaynah narrated; from ʿAmr; from Saʿīd ibn al-Ḥuwayrith: I heard Ibn ʿAbbās say: '**We were at the Prophet's and he came out of the toilet. He was brought some food. He was asked: "Would you do the ablution first?" He said: "What for? Am I going to pray and need to perform the ablution?"**'

وَحَدَّثَنَا أَبُو بَكْرِ بْنُ أَبِي شَيْبَةَ، حَدَّثَنَا سُفْيَانُ بْنُ عُيَيْنَةَ، عَنْ عَمْرٍو، عَنْ سَعِيدِ بْنِ الْحُوَيْرِثِ، سَمِعْتُ ابْنَ عَبَّاسٍ، يَقُولُ: «كُنَّا عِنْدَ النَّبِيِّ صَلَّى اللهُ عَلَيْهِ وَسَلَّمَ، فَجَاءَ مِنَ الْغَائِطِ، وَأُتِيَ بِطَعَامٍ» فَقِيلَ لَهُ: أَلَا تَوَضَّأُ؟ فَقَالَ: «لِمَ؟ أَأُصَلِّي فَأَتَوَضَّأُ؟»

[663–120]. (Dār al-Salām 0727) Yaḥyā ibn Yaḥyā narrated: Muhammad ibn Muslim al-Ṭā'ifī reported; from ʿAmr ibn Dīnār; from Saʿīd ibn al-Ḥuwayrith, the *mawlā* of al-Sā'ib family; that he heard ʿAbdullāh ibn ʿAbbās say: **'God's Messenger (peace be upon him) went to the toilet. When he came back, some food was placed before him. Someone said: "Messenger of God, would you not perform the ablution?" He said: "Why? For prayer?"'**

وَحَدَّثَنَا يَحْيَى بْنُ يَحْيَى، أَخْبَرَنَا مُحَمَّدُ بْنُ مُسْلِمٍ الطَّائِفِيُّ، عَنْ عَمْرِو بْنِ دِينَارٍ، عَنْ سَعِيدِ بْنِ الْحُوَيْرِثِ، مَوْلَى آلِ السَّائِبِ، أَنَّهُ سَمِعَ عَبْدَ اللهِ بْنَ عَبَّاسٍ، قَالَ: «ذَهَبَ رَسُولُ اللهِ صَلَّى اللهُ عَلَيْهِ وَسَلَّمَ إِلَى الْغَائِطِ، فَلَمَّا جَاءَ قُدِّمَ لَهُ طَعَامٌ»، فَقِيلَ: يَا رَسُولَ اللهِ أَلَا تَوَضَّأُ؟ قَالَ: «لِمَ؟ أَلِلصَّلَاةِ؟»

[664–121]. (Dār al-Salām 0728) Muhammad ibn ʿAmr ibn ʿAbbād ibn Jabalah narrated to me: Abū ʿĀṣim narrated; from Ibn Jurayj. He said: Saʿīd ibn Ḥuwayrith narrated; that he heard Ibn ʿAbbās say: **'The Prophet finished his toilet. He was brought some food and he ate without having touched any water'. He said: 'ʿAmr ibn Dīnār added from Saʿīd ibn al-Ḥuwayrith that the Prophet was asked: "You have not performed the ablution?" He said: "I have not intended to offer any prayer so as to perform the ablution". ʿAmr claimed that he heard it from Saʿīd ibn al-Ḥuwayrith'.**

حَدَّثَنِي مُحَمَّدُ بْنُ عَمْرِو بْنِ عَبَّادِ بْنِ جَبَلَةَ، حَدَّثَنَا أَبُو عَاصِمٍ، عَنِ ابْنِ جُرَيْجٍ، قَالَ: حَدَّثَنَا سَعِيدُ بْنُ حُوَيْرِثٍ، أَنَّهُ سَمِعَ ابْنَ عَبَّاسٍ، يَقُولُ: «إِنَّ النَّبِيَّ صَلَّى اللهُ عَلَيْهِ وَسَلَّمَ قَضَى حَاجَتَهُ مِنَ الْخَلَاءِ، فَقُرِّبَ إِلَيْهِ طَعَامٌ فَأَكَلَ وَلَمْ يَمَسَّ مَاءً»، قَالَ: وَزَادَنِي عَمْرُو بْنُ دِينَارٍ، عَنْ سَعِيدِ بْنِ الْحُوَيْرِثِ، أَنَّ النَّبِيَّ صَلَّى اللهُ عَلَيْهِ وَسَلَّمَ قِيلَ لَهُ: إِنَّكَ لَمْ تَوَضَّأْ؟ قَالَ: «مَا أَرَدْتُ صَلَاةً فَأَتَوَضَّأَ» وَزَعَمَ عَمْرٌو، أَنَّهُ سَمِعَ مِنْ سَعِيدِ بْنِ الْحُوَيْرِثِ.

Text Explanation

Scholars are unanimous that a person who has come out of the toilet may eat, drink, glorify God, recite the Qur'an, and have sexual intercourse with his wife. There is nothing to discourage any of this. Numerous evidence from the Sunnah confirms this, and it is all well-known and authentic. In addition, the Muslim community is unanimous on all this. We have already stated that our scholars differed as to the time when ablution becomes a duty: is it just after one has invalidated one's earlier ablution by discharging urine or breaking wind, etc.? In this case, there is ample time for performing the duty. Or does ablution become a duty only when one rises intending to offer prayer? Or is it when one has come out of the toilet and is about to go to prayer? They give three views, the most correct of which is this last one, but God knows best.

When it was suggested to the Prophet that he did not perform the ablution, he asked why he should. This is a rhetorical question, meaning: why should I when I do not intend to offer any prayer at the moment. The ablution meant here is the ritual one which is a duty for prayer. *Qāḍī* ʿIyāḍ suggests that it refers to the general, linguistic meaning of ablution, which is to wash one's hands. He reports that scholars differ as to whether it is desirable or discouraged before eating. He mentions that Mālik and al-Thawrī consider it undesirable. It appears that what we have stated is the one intended, which is the ritual ablution, but God knows best.

CHAPTER 32

WHEN GOING TO THE TOILET

[665–122]. (Dār al-Salām 0729) Yaḥyā ibn Yaḥyā narrated:[i] Ḥammād ibn Zayd reported. Yaḥyā also said: Hushaym reported; both from ʿAbd ʿAzīz ibn Ṣuhayb; from Anas: (In Ḥammād's narration: 'When God's Messenger (peace be upon him) went to the toilet', and in Hushaym's narration: 'When he went to the toilet, God's Messenger (peace be upon him)' said: **'My Lord: I seek Your refuge from all that is wicked and loathsome'**.

حَدَّثَنَا يَحْيَى بْنُ يَحْيَى، أَخْبَرَنَا حَمَّادُ بْنُ زَيْدٍ، وَقَالَ يَحْيَى: أَيْضًا أَخْبَرَنَا هُشَيْمٌ، كِلَاهُمَا عَنْ عَبْدِ الْعَزِيزِ بْنِ صُهَيْبٍ، عَنْ أَنَسٍ - فِي حَدِيثِ حَمَّادٍ كَانَ رَسُولُ اللهِ صَلَّى اللهُ عَلَيْهِ وَسَلَّمَ إِذَا دَخَلَ الْخَلَاءَ وَفِي حَدِيثِ هُشَيْمٍ - أَنَّ رَسُولَ اللهِ صَلَّى اللهُ عَلَيْهِ وَسَلَّمَ كَانَ إِذَا دَخَلَ الْكَنِيفَ قَالَ: «اللهُمَّ إِنِّي أَعُوذُ بِكَ مِنَ الْخُبْثِ وَالْخَبَائِثِ»

[666–000]. (Dār al-Salām 0730) Abū Bakr ibn Abī Shaybah and Zuhayr ibn Ḥarb narrated: they said: Ismāʿīl (meaning Ibn ʿUlayyah) narrated; from ʿAbd al-ʿAzīz; with the same chain of transmission. He said: **'I seek refuge with God from all that is wicked and loathsome'**.

وَحَدَّثَنَا أَبُو بَكْرِ بْنُ أَبِي شَيْبَةَ، وَزُهَيْرُ بْنُ حَرْبٍ، قَالَا: حَدَّثَنَا إِسْمَاعِيلُ وَهُوَ ابْنُ عُلَيَّةَ، عَنْ عَبْدِ الْعَزِيزِ بِهَذَا الْإِسْنَادِ وَقَالَ: «أَعُوذُ بِاللهِ مِنَ الْخُبْثِ وَالْخَبَائِثِ»

i. Ḥammād's and ʿAbd al-ʿAzīz's narration is also related by al-Tirmidhī, 6; Abū Dāwūd, 4.

Text Explanation

The two hadiths use different words for toilet, but they mean the same, which is the place where a person may answer the call of nature. The Prophet used to say this when he approached the place, not when he entered it. This is clear in al-Bukhārī's narration, as it says: 'when he wished to go to the toilet'.

The Arabic words used in the two hadiths and translated as 'wicked and loathsome' are *khubth* and *khabā'ith*. Scholars have suggested different meanings for these words, such as male and female jinns. Abū ʿUbayd, a leading scholar of Arabic said: 'Scholars differ as to their meanings. It is variously said to mean evil and unbelief. It is also said that *khubth* means satans' and *khabā'ith* means sinful actions'. Ibn al-Aʿrābī said: 'In general Arabic usage, *khubth* means what is hated. Thus, if it refers to words, it is slander, and if it refers to beliefs, then it means denial of God. If it is in the context of food, it means what is forbidden, and of drinks it refers to what is harmful'. The Prophet said it is desirable to use this formula wherever one is using the toilet, but God knows best.

CHAPTER 33

SLEEPING WHILE SEATED DOES NOT INVALIDATE MINOR RITUAL ABLUTION

[667–123]. (Dār al-Salām 0731) Zuhayr ibn Ḥarb narrated to me:[i] Ismāʿīl ibn ʿUlayyah narrated [H]. Also, Shaybān ibn Farrūkh narrated; ʿAbd al-Wārith narrated; both from ʿAbd al-ʿAzīz; from Anas. He said: **'The *iqāmah* [i.e. announcement to start prayer] was called when God's Messenger (peace be upon him) was talking privately to a man. (In ʿAbd al-Wārith's narration: when the Prophet was engaged in private talk with a man.) By the time he stood up to pray, the people were asleep'.**

حَدَّثَنِي زُهَيْرُ بْنُ حَرْبٍ، حَدَّثَنَا إِسْمَاعِيلُ ابْنُ عُلَيَّةَ ح، وَحَدَّثَنَا شَيْبَانُ بْنُ فَرُّوخَ، حَدَّثَنَا عَبْدُ الْوَارِثِ كِلَاهُمَا عَنْ عَبْدِ الْعَزِيزِ، عَنْ أَنَسٍ، قَالَ: «أُقِيمَتِ الصَّلَاةُ وَرَسُولُ اللهِ صَلَّى اللهُ عَلَيْهِ وَسَلَّمَ نَجِيٌّ لِرَجُلٍ - وَفِي حَدِيثِ عَبْدِ الْوَارِثِ: وَنَبِيُّ اللهِ صَلَّى اللهُ عَلَيْهِ وَسَلَّمَ يُنَاجِي الرَّجُلَ - فَمَا قَامَ إِلَى الصَّلَاةِ حَتَّى نَامَ الْقَوْمُ»

[668–124]. (Dār al-Salām 0732) ʿUbaydullāh ibn Muʿādh al-ʿAnbarī narrated:[ii] my father narrated; Shuʿbah narrated; from ʿAbd al-ʿAzīz ibn Ṣuhayb; he heard Anas ibn Mālik say:

---

i. Zuhayr's narration is related by al-Nasāʾī, 790; and Shaybān's narration is related by al-Bukhārī, 642; Abū Dāwūd, 544.

ii. Related by al-Bukhārī, 6192.

'The prayer was called when the Prophet was talking to a man. He continued to talk to him until his Companions fell asleep. He then came and led them in prayer'.

حَدَّثَنَا عُبَيْدُ اللهِ بْنُ مُعَاذٍ الْعَنْبَرِيُّ، حَدَّثَنَا أَبِي، حَدَّثَنَا شُعْبَةُ، عَنْ عَبْدِ الْعَزِيزِ بْنِ صُهَيْبٍ، سَمِعَ أَنَسَ بْنَ مَالِكٍ قَالَ: «أُقِيمَتِ الصَّلَاةُ وَالنَّبِيُّ صَلَّى اللهُ عَلَيْهِ وَسَلَّمَ يُنَاجِي رَجُلًا فَلَمْ يَزَلْ يُنَاجِيهِ حَتَّى نَامَ أَصْحَابُهُ ثُمَّ جَاءَ فَصَلَّى بِهِمْ»

[669–125]. (Dār al-Salām 0733) Yaḥyā ibn Ḥabīb al-Ḥārithī narrated to me:[i] Khālid (who is Ibn al-Ḥārith) narrated; Shuʿbah narrated; from Qatādah. He said: I heard Anas say: **'The Prophet's Companions used to fall asleep, then they would pray without performing the ablution'. I said: 'You heard this from Anas?' He said: 'Yes, by God'.**

وَحَدَّثَنِي يَحْيَى بْنُ حَبِيبٍ الْحَارِثِيُّ، حَدَّثَنَا خَالِدٌ وَهُوَ ابْنُ الْحَارِثِ، حَدَّثَنَا شُعْبَةُ، عَنْ قَتَادَةَ، قَالَ: سَمِعْتُ أَنَسًا، يَقُولُ: «كَانَ أَصْحَابُ رَسُولِ اللهِ صَلَّى اللهُ عَلَيْهِ وَسَلَّمَ يَنَامُونَ ثُمَّ يُصَلُّونَ وَلَا يَتَوَضَّئُونَ» قَالَ: قُلْتُ: سَمِعْتَهُ مِنْ أَنَسٍ قَالَ: «إِي وَاللهِ»

[670–126]. (Dār al-Salām 0734) Ahmad ibn Saʿīd ibn Ṣakhr al-Dārimī narrated to me:[ii] Ḥabbān narrated; Ḥammād narrated; from Thābit; from Anas; that he said: **'Ishā' Prayer was called, but a man said: "I have something to say". The Prophet stopped with him talking, and the people fell asleep (or some of them), then they prayed'.**

---

i. Related by al-Tirmidhī, 78.
ii. Related by Abū Dāwūd, 201.

حَدَّثَنِي أَحْمَدُ بْنُ سَعِيدِ بْنِ صَخْرٍ الدَّارِمِيُّ، حَدَّثَنَا حَبَّانُ، حَدَّثَنَا حَمَّادٌ، عَنْ ثَابِتٍ، عَنْ أَنَسٍ، أَنَّهُ قَالَ: «أُقِيمَتْ صَلَاةُ الْعِشَاءِ فَقَالَ رَجُلٌ: لِي حَاجَةٌ فَقَامَ النَّبِيُّ صَلَّى اللهُ عَلَيْهِ وَسَلَّمَ يُنَاجِيهِ حَتَّى نَامَ الْقَوْمُ - أَوْ بَعْضُ الْقَوْمِ - ثُمَّ صَلَّوْا»

Text Explanation

The hadith shows that it is permissible to speak privately to someone when others are present. What is unacceptable is to speak privately when only a third person is present. It also makes clear that it is permissible to speak about important matters after the congregational prayer is called, but this is discouraged if the matter is not so important. When several things are pressing, then the more important should be given priority ahead of the less important. The Prophet spoke privately to the man concerning a matter of religion which he judged to take prioprity ahead of starting the prayer.

The hadiths in this chapter, and its essential theme, confirm that sleeping in the sitting position does not invalidate ablution. Scholars hold widely different opinions on this issue:

1. Sleep does not invalidate the ablution in all cases. This is reported to be the view of Abū Mūsā al-Ashʿarī of the Prophet's companions, Saʿīd ibn al-Musayyib of the Tābiʿīn generation, Abū Mujliz, Ḥumayd al-Aʿraj and Shuʿbah.
2. Sleep invalidates the ablution in all cases. This is the opposite view, which is shared by al-Ḥasan al-Baṣrī, al-Muzanī, Abū ʿUbayd al-Qāsim ibn Sallām, Isḥāq ibn Rāhawayh and an odd view of al-Shāfiʿī. Ibn al-Mundhir said: 'I share this view'. It is also reported to have been implied by Ibn ʿAbbās, Anas and Abū Hurayrah.
3. Long sleep invalidates ablution in all cases while short sleep does not in all cases. This is the view of al-Zuhrī, Rabīʿah, al-Awzāʿī, Mālik and Ahmad in one of his two reports.
4. If a person sleeps taking a position like one in prayer, such as bowing, prostration, standing or seated, then his ablution

remains valid, whether he sleeps during the prayer or not. If he sleeps lying down, his ablution becomes invalid. This is the view of Abū Ḥanīfah and Dāwūd. It is also a strange view attributed to al-Shāfiʿī.

5. Only sleep in the bowing and prostrating positions invalidates the ablution. This is reported to be a view of Ahmad ibn Ḥanbal.
6. Only sleep in prostration invalidates ablution. This is also attributed to Ahmad.
7. Sleep during prayer in any way does not invalidate ablution, while sleep outside prayers invalidates it. This is reported from al-Shāfiʿī, but it is lacking in authenticity.
8. If a person sleeps seated with his bottom firmly positioned, his ablution remains valid. Otherwise, it becomes invalid, whether he remains asleep for a long or short while, and whether he sleeps while praying or not. This is the standard view of al-Shāfiʿī.

According to al-Shāfiʿī, sleep is not in itself something that invalidates ablution; rather it is an indication that wind might be broken by the sleeping person. Therefore, if he sleeps with his bottom not firmly positioned, it is very likely that he breaks wind. Therefore, this strong probability is deemed to be like a certainty. On the other hand, if he sleeps with his bottom firmly positioned, it is unlikely that the ablution becomes invalid. Therefore, the ablution remains valid.

There are numerous hadiths on this point, and they are cited in support of these different views. I have decided to consolidate them and point out their import in *Sharḥ al-Muhadhdhab*. In this present work, I do not intend to speak at length; rather just point out the purposes and intentions, but God knows best.

Scholars agree that loss of reason through madness, fainting, alcoholic drinks, sedatives or medicines invalidates the ablution, whether it is for a long or short while, and seated well or not. Our scholars say that one special privilege given to the Prophet was that his ablution was never invalidated through sleep in the lying position. This is confirmed by the authentic hadith narrated by Ibn ʿAbbās: 'God's Messenger (peace be upon him) slept and I heard his deep breathing, then he prayed without performing the ablution', but God knows best.

Al-Shāfiʿī and his disciples said: ablution is not invalidated by drowsiness. What indicates sleep is that it overpowers one's mind, and the failure of eyesight and other senses. Drowsiness, on the other hand, does not overpower the mind, but weakens the senses without losing them completely. If a person is in doubt as to whether he has been asleep or merely drowsy, he is not required to renew his ablution, but it is better if he does. If he is certain that he was overtaken by sleep, but doubts whether his bottom was firmly positioned during such sleep or not, his ablution remains valid, but to renew it is desirable. If he sleeps in the seated position and one or both of his buttocks move away from the ground, and this happens before he is awake, even by a second, his ablution is invalid, because he slept for a moment without being firmly positioned. If this happens after or during waking up, or if he is in doubt as to when it happened, then his ablution remains valid. If one sleeps seated, but raising his legs to touch his abdomen, then three different verdicts are given by our scholars: 1) his ablution remains valid, like the one seated; 2) his ablution is invalid, like one who is lying down; and 3) if he is thin so that his buttocks cannot close up with the floor, his ablution is invalid, but if he is not thin and his buttocks close up with the floor, his ablution remains valid. But God knows best, and to Him belongs all praise. All blessings come from Him and He is the guide to whom I pray for steering me away from error.

Transmission

The second chain of transmission of hadith No. 667, beginning with Shaybān ibn Farrūkh, as well as the chains of transmission of hadiths Nos 668 and 669, are all composed of narrators from Basrah. We have mentioned on several occasions that Shuʿbah was from Wāsiṭ, but he moved to Basrah and settled there. In hadith No. 669, the narrator says: 'I said: "You heard this from Anas?" He said: "Yes, by God".' This is Shuʿbah asking Qatādah, although Qatādah said initially that he heard it from Anas. Shuʿbah wanted to be absolutely certain, because Qatādah was graded as a 'misleading narrator' and Shuʿbah was very strict about misleading narrations, to the extent that he used to say: 'Even adultery is more tolerable than misleading'. We have already explained that when a misleading narrator says that he is 'reporting from' someone, then his reporting is not acceptable. But if he says 'I heard this from' someone, his reporting is accepted as valid evidence. It appears that Shuʿbah wanted to ascertain that Qatādah actually heard the hadith from Anas, and that Qatādah realized what Shuʿbah was after. Hence, he swore to him that he heard it, but God knows best.

THE BOOK OF PRAYER

CHAPTER 1

THE BEGINNING OF THE *ADHĀN* [i.e. THE CALL TO PRAYER]

[671–1]. (Dār al-Salām 0735) Isḥāq ibn Ibrāhīm al-Ḥanẓalī narrated:[i] Muhammad ibn Bakr narrated [H]. Also, Muhammad ibn Rāfiʿ narrated; ʿAbd al-Razzāq narrated. Both said: Ibn Jurayj reported [H]. And Hārūn ibn ʿAbdullāh narrated to me (his text) saying: Ḥajjāj ibn Muhammad narrated; Ibn Jurayj said; Nāfiʿ, Ibn ʿUmar's *mawlā*, reported to me; from ʿAbdullāh ibn ʿUmar, that he said: **'When Muslims came to Madinah, they would meet and they were keen to be on time for prayer, but no one announced the prayer. They spoke about this one day, and some of them suggested: "Use a bell like that used by the Christians". Others suggested: "Use a horn like the one used by the Jews". ʿUmar said: "Would it not be better to send a man to call out for prayer?" God's Messenger (peace be upon him) said: "Bilāl. Get up and announce the prayer".'**

حَدَّثَنَا إِسْحَاقُ بْنُ إِبْرَاهِيمَ الْحَنْظَلِيُّ، حَدَّثَنَا مُحَمَّدُ بْنُ بَكْرٍ، ح وَحَدَّثَنَا مُحَمَّدُ بْنُ رَافِعٍ، حَدَّثَنَا عَبْدُ الرَّزَّاقِ قَالَا: أَخْبَرَنَا ابْنُ جُرَيْجٍ، ح وَحَدَّثَنِي هَارُونُ بْنُ عَبْدِ اللهِ - وَاللَّفْظُ لَهُ - قَالَ: حَدَّثَنَا حَجَّاجُ بْنُ مُحَمَّدٍ، قَالَ: قَالَ ابْنُ جُرَيْجٍ: أَخْبَرَنِي نَافِعٌ، مَوْلَى ابْنِ عُمَرَ، عَنْ عَبْدِ اللهِ بْنِ عُمَرَ أَنَّهُ قَالَ: كَانَ الْمُسْلِمُونَ حِينَ قَدِمُوا الْمَدِينَةَ يَجْتَمِعُونَ فَيَتَحَيَّنُونَ الصَّلَوَاتِ، وَلَيْسَ يُنَادِي بِهَا أَحَدٌ، فَتَكَلَّمُوا يَوْمًا فِي ذَلِكَ فَقَالَ بَعْضُهُمْ:

i. Related by al-Bukhārī, 604; al-Tirmidhī, 190; al-Nasāʾī, 625.

اتَّخِذُوا نَاقُوسًا مِثْلَ نَاقُوسِ النَّصَارَى، وَقَالَ بَعْضُهُمْ: قَرْنًا مِثْلَ قَرْنِ الْيَهُودِ، فَقَالَ عُمَرُ أَوَلَا تَبْعَثُونَ رَجُلًا يُنَادِي بِالصَّلَاةِ؟ قَالَ رَسُولُ اللهِ صَلَّى اللهُ عَلَيْهِ وَسَلَّمَ: «يَا بِلَالُ قُمْ فَنَادِ بِالصَّلَاةِ»

The Arabic word for prayer is *ṣalāt* and the majority of Arabic linguists and Islamic scholars agree that its original linguistic meaning is *du'ā'*, or supplication, because it includes supplication. There are other suggestions explaining the meaning of the word, but none appears to be very convincing.

Text Explanation

Arabic linguists say that *adhān* means 'announcement of information'. The hadith shows 'Umar's great merit as his suggestion was right on course. The hadith also makes clear that important matters should be decided after discussion and consultation. This is desirable for the Muslim community, according to the unanimous view of scholars. However, our scholars differ as to whether consultation was a duty binding on God's Messenger (peace be upon him) or it was recommended to him, as it is to us. They maintain that the correct view is that it was binding on him. God says: '*Pardon them and pray for them to be forgiven and consult with them in the conduct of public affairs*'. (3: 159) The majority of scholars are of the view that when something is stated in the imperative form, it signifies obligation. The hadith also suggests that when people are in consultation, everyone should express their views and then the person in charge will adopt the view that appears to him to best serve the interests of the community, but God knows best.

The hadith mentions 'Umar's suggestion: 'Would it not be better to send a man to call out for prayer?' *Qāḍī* 'Iyāḍ said: 'This appears to be a mere announcement, not the standard *adhān*. It is just to inform people that prayer is due'. What *Qāḍī* 'Iyāḍ said is probable, or certain. An authentic hadith related in the *Sunan* of both Abū Dāwūd and al-Tirmidhī, as well as other anthologies, mentions that

ʿAbdullāh ibn Zayd ibn ʿAbd Rabbih saw the formal *adhān* in his dream and then went to the Prophet to inform him of it. ʿUmar also went along and said: 'Messenger of God, by Him who sent you with the message of the truth, I have seen the same dream as he saw'. This appears to be on a different occasion. Thus, what happened was that it was first agreed to make an announcement, then ʿAbdullāh ibn Zayd saw the *adhān* in his dream and the Prophet approved it, either through revelation or at his own discretion. The majority of scholars agree that it was permissible for the Prophet to decide something by his own discretion. It was not merely the implementation of a dream. This is agreed without doubt, but God knows best.

The hadith mentions that the Prophet told Bilāl to 'stand up and announce the prayer'. *Qāḍī* ʿIyāḍ said: 'There is evidence here showing that the *adhān* must be done in the standing position and that it is not permissible to do it when seated. This is the view of all scholars, with the exception of Abū Thawr who permits it seated. Abū al-Faraj al-Mālikī endorses this view'. What *Qāḍī* ʿIyāḍ said is not well founded, on two counts. The first is what we have quoted him as saying that this particular announcement is merely meant as a method of information that the prayer is due, not the well-known standard *adhān*. Secondly, what is meant here is that Bilāl should stand on a high place to announce the prayer, so that he would be heard from a further distance. There is nothing here about calling the *adhān* standing. However, there are well known hadiths other than this one which may be cited in support of standing up when calling the *adhān*.

Qāḍī ʿIyāḍ further said that all scholars are of the view that the person calling the *adhān* should be standing when he does it. This is incorrect. Our al-Shāfiʿī School considers this to be recommended, not obligatory. If a person calls the *adhān* while seated, and he has no excuse for being so seated, his action is valid but he has not done it the better way. The same is correct if a person calls the *adhān* when reclining, even though he is able to do it standing. His *adhān* is valid according to the most correct view, because the purpose of the *adhān* is to inform people and this is done. Nothing authentic has been reported to make standing a condition for the validity of the *adhān*, but God knows best.

Why did the Prophet specify Bilāl as the one to make the announcement? This is made clear in the hadith related by Abū Dāwūd, al-Tirmidhī and others and narrated by ʿAbdullāh ibn Zayd. The Prophet said to him: 'Teach it to Bilāl, as his voice is louder than yours'. It is said that it means that Bilāl's voice is sharper, or more melodious. This makes it desirable that a person entrusted with calling the *adhān* should have a loud and fine voice. This is agreed by scholars. Our al-Shāfiʿī scholars say that if we find one person who has a fine voice but requires to have wages for calling the *adhān* regularly, and another who volunteers to do it freely but his voice is not fine: which should we employ? There are two views on this point, but the more correct one is to employ the one who requires wages, because of his fine voice. This is the view of Ibn Shurayḥ, but God knows best.

Scholars mention that the *adhān* serves four purposes: declaring the main aspects of Islam and the oneness of God, announcing that it is time for prayer, informing people of the place where the prayer is held and calling on people to attend the congregational prayer, but God knows best.

Transmission

Al-Tirmidhī said: 'No authentic narration from the Prophet (peace be upon him) is attributed to ʿAbdullāh ibn Zayd ibn ʿAbd Rabbih other than this hadith concerning the *adhān*'. He is different from ʿAbdullāh ibn Zayd ibn ʿĀṣim al-Māzinī, who narrated many hadiths related in the two *Ṣaḥīḥ* anthologies. He was ʿAbbād ibn Tamīm's uncle, but God knows best.

CHAPTER 2

THE ORDER TO REPEAT PHRASES OF THE *ADHĀN* TWICE

[672–2]. (Dār al-Salām 0736) Khalaf ibn Hishām narrated:[i] Ḥammād ibn Zayd narrated [H]. Also, Yaḥyā ibn Yaḥyā narrated; Ismāʿīl ibn ʿUlayyah reported; from Khālid al-Hadhdhā'; from Abū Qilābah; from Anas. He said: **'Bilāl was commanded to repeat [the phrases of] the *adhān* twice and to keep them single in the *iqāmah* [i.e. the announcement that immediately precedes the prayer].'**

Yaḥyā adds in his narration from Ibn ʿUlayyah: **'I narrated it to Ayyūb, and he said: "Except for [the one phrase of] the *iqāmah*".'**

حَدَّثَنَا خَلَفُ بْنُ هِشَامٍ، حَدَّثَنَا حَمَّادُ بْنُ زَيْدٍ، ح وَحَدَّثَنَا يَحْيَى بْنُ يَحْيَى، أَخْبَرَنَا إِسْمَاعِيلُ ابْنُ عُلَيَّةَ، جَمِيعًا عَنْ خَالِدٍ الْحَذَّاءِ، عَنْ أَبِي قِلَابَةَ، عَنْ أَنَسٍ، قَالَ: «أُمِرَ بِلَالٌ أَنْ يَشْفَعَ الْأَذَانَ وَيُوتِرَ الْإِقَامَةَ»

زَادَ يَحْيَى، فِي حَدِيثِهِ عَنِ ابْنِ عُلَيَّةَ، فَحَدَّثْتُ بِهِ أَيُّوبَ فَقَالَ: إِلَّا الْإِقَامَةَ.

[673–3]. (Dār al-Salām 0737) Isḥāq ibn Ibrāhīm al-Ḥanẓalī narrated: ʿAbd al-Wahhāb al-Thaqafī reported; Khālid al-Hadhdhā' narrated; from Abū Qilābah; from Anas ibn Mālik. He said: **'People mentioned the need to announce the time of**

i. Related by al-Bukhārī, 603, 605, 606 (in a longer version), 607 and 3457; Abū Dāwūd, 508 and 509; al-Tirmidhī, 193; al-Nasā'ī, 626; Ibn Mājah, 729 and 730.

prayer by something they could recognize. They mentioned lighting a fire or ringing a bell. Then Bilāl was ordered to repeat the [phrases of the] *adhān* twice and keep the *iqāmah* single'.

وَحَدَّثَنَا إِسْحَاقُ بْنُ إِبْرَاهِيمَ الْحَنْظَلِيُّ، أَخْبَرَنَا عَبْدُ الْوَهَّابِ الثَّقَفِيُّ، حَدَّثَنَا خَالِدٌ الْحَذَّاءُ، عَنْ أَبِي قِلَابَةَ، عَنْ أَنَسِ بْنِ مَالِكٍ، قَالَ: ذَكَرُوا أَنْ يُعْلِمُوا وَقْتَ الصَّلَاةِ بِشَيْءٍ يَعْرِفُونَهُ فَذَكَرُوا أَنْ يُنَوِّرُوا نَارًا، أَوْ يَضْرِبُوا نَاقُوسًا «فَأُمِرَ بِلَالٌ أَنْ يَشْفَعَ الْأَذَانَ وَيُوتِرَ الْإِقَامَةَ»

[674–4]. (Dār al-Salām 0738) Muhammad ibn Ḥātim narrated to me: Bahz narrated; Wuhayb narrated; Khālid al-Hadhdhā' narrated; with the same chain of transmission: **'When people increased in number, they mentioned the need to be informed'. He added the same as al-Thaqafī's narration, except that he said: 'They suggested to kindle a fire**'.

وَحَدَّثَنِي مُحَمَّدُ بْنُ حَاتِمٍ، حَدَّثَنَا بَهْزٌ، حَدَّثَنَا وُهَيْبٌ، حَدَّثَنَا خَالِدٌ الْحَذَّاءُ، بِهَذَا الْإِسْنَادِ: لَـمَّا كَثُرَ النَّاسُ ذَكَرُوا أَنْ يُعْلِمُوا بِمِثْلِ حَدِيثِ الثَّقَفِيِّ، غَيْرَ أَنَّهُ قَالَ: «أَنْ يُورُوا نَارًا»

[675–5]. (Dār al-Salām 0739) 'Ubaydullāh ibn 'Umar al-Qawārīrī narrated to me: 'Abd al-Wārith ibn Sa'īd and 'Abd al-Wahhāb ibn 'Abd al-Majīd narrated; both said: Ayyūb narrated; from Abū Qilābah; from Anas. He said: **'Bilāl was ordered to repeat [the phrases of] the *adhān* twice and to keep the *iqāmah* single**'.

وَحَدَّثَنِي عُبَيْدُ اللهِ بْنُ عُمَرَ الْقَوَارِيرِيُّ، حَدَّثَنَا عَبْدُ الْوَارِثِ بْنُ سَعِيدٍ، وَعَبْدُ الْوَهَّابِ بْنُ عَبْدِ الْـمَجِيدِ، قَالَا: حَدَّثَنَا أَيُّوبُ، عَنْ أَبِي قِلَابَةَ، عَنْ أَنَسٍ، قَالَ: «أُمِرَ بِلَالٌ أَنْ يَشْفَعَ الْأَذَانَ وَيُوتِرَ الْإِقَامَةَ»

Text Explanation

The hadith mentions that Bilāl was given an order to repeat the phrases of the *adhān* twice and to keep those of the *iqāmah* single. This means that the order came from the one who could give such orders, namely God's Messenger (peace be upon him). This is agreed by the great majority of scholars of *fiqh* and Hadith. Indeed, no other explanation is valid. It is like any companion of the Prophet using the formula: 'We were ordered ...' or 'We were prohibited ...' or 'People were given the order that ...'. All such expressions attribute the command to the Prophet himself, whether his companion mentions the order during the Prophet's lifetime or later, but God knows best.

The order given to Bilāl is to repeat the phrases of the *adhān* twice, but he should not do this when he announces the rise to start the congregational prayers. In the first hadith, No. 672, Ayyūb says: 'except for the one phrase of the *iqāmah*'. During the *iqāmah*, that phrase in particular is said twice, not once. Scholars differ with regard to the *iqāmah* and how it is announced. The well-known view in our Shāfiʿī school, which is confirmed by various texts attributed to al-Shāfiʿī and is agreed by Ahmad and the majority of scholars, is that the *iqāmah* consists of eleven phrases: *Allāh-u akbar Allāh-u akbar; ashhud an lā ilāha illā Allāh; ashhad anna Muhammad rasūl Allāh; ḥayy ʿalā al-ṣalāt; ḥayy ʿalā al-falāḥ; qad qāmat al-ṣalāt; qad qāmat al-ṣalāt; Allāh-u akbar Allāh-u akbar; lā ilāha illā Allāh*. These are translated as follows: God is supreme God is supreme; I bear witness that there is no deity other than God; I bear witness that Muhammad is God's Messenger; come to the prayer; come to success; the prayer is about to begin; the prayer is about to begin; God is supreme God is supreme; there is no deity other than God.

Mālik is of the view that the *iqāmah* is only ten phrases, which is the same as the above but does not repeat the phrase of the *iqamah*, which is: *qad qāmat al-ṣalāt*, meaning 'the prayer is about to begin'. This was an old view of al-Shāfiʿī. We also have an odd view that does not repeat any of the phrases, making only eight phrases in total. The correct view is the first. Abū Ḥanīfah said that the *iqāmah* is seventeen phrases, repeating all phrases twice, except the last; this is an odd view. Al-Khaṭṭābī said: 'The view of the great majority of scholars and the practice in the two sacred mosques, Hijaz, Syria, Yemen, Egypt and the Maghrib, right to the end of the Muslim world, is that the phrases of the *iqāmah* are said once only'. Imam Abū Sulaymān al-Khaṭṭābī adds that the view of the majority of scholars is that the phrase, *qad qāmat al-ṣalāt*, is said twice, except for Mālik who is known not to repeat it, but God knows best. The reason for repeating the phrases of the *adhān* and not the *iqāmah* is that the purpose of the *adhān* is to inform people who are not present. Therefore, repetition ensures that they are made aware. On the other hand, the *iqāmah* is for those who are present and, therefore, there is no need to repeat it. Hence, scholars say that the *iqāmah* announcement should not be as loud as the *adhān*. The phrase of the *iqāmah* itself is repeated because it is the central phrase, but God knows best.

It may be said that we have already stated that the *iqāmah* consists of eleven phrases, but it includes *Allāh-u akbar Allāh-u akbar;* and this is a repetition. The fact is that although this appears to repeat a phrase, nonetheless as compared with the *adhān* it is a single phrase. Hence, our scholars say that it is desirable that the person calling the *adhān* should say *Allāh-u akbar Allāh-u akbar*; together, without taking a breath in between, and the same applies to the one at the end, but God knows best.

Transmission

Khālid al-Ḥadhdhā' is named as Khālid ibn Mahrān and his appellation is Abū al-Munāzil. Al-Ḥadhdhā' means 'the shoemaker'. He was not a shoemaker himself but he used to sit at the shoemakers' market place. Other explanations of his nickname are given, and we have mentioned him earlier. We also mentioned Abū Qilābah, whose name is ʿAbdullāh ibn Zayd al-Juramī.

CHAPTER 3

THE CALL TO PRAYER [i.e. THE *ADHĀN*]

[676–6]. (Dār al-Salām 0740) Abū Ghassān al-Misma'ī Mālik ibn 'Abd al-Wāḥid and Isḥāq ibn Ibrāhīm narrated:[i] Abū Ghassān said Mu'ādh narrated, while Isḥāq said Mu'ādh ibn Hishām, al-Dastawā'ī's colleague, reported and my father narrated to me; from 'Āmir al-Aḥwal; from Makḥūl; from 'Abdullāh ibn Muḥayrīz; from Abū Maḥdhūrah; that **God's Messenger (peace be upon him) taught him this *adhān*: *'Allāh-u akbar Allāh-u akbar; ashhadu an lā ilāha illā Allāh; ashhadu an lā ilāha illā Allāh; ashhadu anna Muhammadan rasūlu Allāh; ashhad anna Muhammadan rasūlu Allāh*. He then repeats: *ashhadu an lā ilāha illā Allāh; ashhadu an lā ilāha illā Allāh; ashhadu anna Muhammadan rasūlu Allāh; ashhad anna Muhammadan rasūlu Allāh'*.**

حَدَّثَنِي أَبُو غَسَّانَ الْمِسْمَعِيُّ مَالِكُ بْنُ عَبْدِ الْوَاحِدِ، وَإِسْحَاقُ بْنُ إِبْرَاهِيمَ، قَالَ أَبُو غَسَّانَ: حَدَّثَنَا مُعَاذٌ، وَقَالَ إِسْحَاقُ: أَخْبَرَنَا مُعَاذُ بْنُ هِشَامٍ، صَاحِبِ الدَّسْتُوَائِيِّ، وَحَدَّثَنِي أَبِي، عَنْ عَامِرٍ الْأَحْوَلِ، عَنْ مَكْحُولٍ، عَنْ عَبْدِ اللهِ بْنِ مُحَيْرِيزٍ، عَنْ أَبِي مَحْذُورَةَ، أَنَّ نَبِيَّ اللهِ صَلَّى اللهُ عَلَيْهِ وَسَلَّمَ عَلَّمَهُ هَذَا الْأَذَانَ: «اللهُ أَكْبَرُ اللهُ أَكْبَرُ، أَشْهَدُ أَنْ لَا إِلَهَ إِلَّا اللهُ، أَشْهَدُ أَنْ لَا إِلَهَ إِلَّا اللهُ، أَشْهَدُ أَنَّ مُحَمَّدًا رَسُولُ اللهِ، أَشْهَدُ أَنَّ مُحَمَّدًا

i. Related by Abū Dāwūd, 500, 501, 503 and 505; al-Tirmidhī, 191 (in a shorter version) and 192; al-Nasā'ī, 628, 629, 630 and 632; Ibn Mājah, 708 (in a longer version) and 709.

رَسُولُ اللهِ»، ثُمَّ يَعُودُ فَيَقُولُ: «أَشْهَدُ أَنْ لَا إِلَهَ إِلَّا اللهُ، أَشْهَدُ أَنْ لَا إِلَهَ إِلَّا اللهُ، أَشْهَدُ أَنَّ مُحَمَّدًا رَسُولُ اللهِ، أَشْهَدُ أَنَّ مُحَمَّدًا رَسُولُ اللهِ، حَيَّ عَلَى الصَّلَاةِ مَرَّتَيْنِ، حَيَّ عَلَى الْفَلَاحِ مَرَّتَيْنِ» زَادَ إِسْحَاقُ: «اللهُ أَكْبَرُ اللهُ أَكْبَرُ لَا إِلَهَ إِلَّا اللهُ»

Text Explanation

This is how this hadith is recorded in most original copies of Muslim's *Ṣaḥīḥ*, starting with *Allāh-u akbar* twice. In other anthologies, this occurs four times. *Qāḍī* ʿIyāḍ said that in some of al-Fārisī's narrations of Muslim's *Ṣaḥīḥ*, it occurs four times. The same difference occurs in the hadith narrated by ʿAbdullāh ibn Zayd, mentioning that the glorification *Allāh-u akbar* occurs either twice or four times, but it is more widely known to occur four times. Al-Shāfiʿī, Abū Ḥanīfah, Ahmad and the majority of scholars maintain that it should be said four times, but Mālik opts for saying it twice. Mālik's argument is based on this hadith and the standard practice of the people of Madinah, who are the people most familiar with the Sunnah. The majority of scholars argue that an addition by a reliable reporter is acceptable and that it is the practice of the people of Makkah, where Muslims from all over the world meet during the different seasons. None of the Prophet's companions took issue with them, nor did anyone else, but God knows best.

This hadith provides clear evidence in support of the views of Mālik, al-Shāfiʿī and Ahmad, as well as the majority of scholars that such repetition in the *adhān* is well confirmed. What is meant by repetition is that the person calling the *adhān* says, '*ashhadu an lā ilāha illā Allah; ashhadu anna Muhammadan rasūlu Allāh*', repeating each phrase twice in a low voice, then returning to it and saying each phrase twice aloud. Abū Ḥanīfah and Kufi scholars say that such repetition is not valid, citing in evidence the hadith narrated by ʿAbdullāh ibn Zayd, which mentions no such repetition. The majority who endorse the repetition cite the present hadith in evidence, arguing that the standard rule is that an addition by a reliable narrator is given priority. Moreover, the present hadith, narrated by Abū Maḥdhūrah, was from the chronological point of view much later than the one narrated by ʿAbdullāh ibn Zayd, which took place in the early days of the Muslims' migration to Madinah. Abū Maḥdhūrah's hadith was at the end of year 8 AH, after the Battle of Ḥunayn. Added to all this is the practice of the peoples of Makkah, Madinah and all provinces.

Our scholars hold different views on whether this repetition is an essential requirement, which means that the *adhān* is invalid without it, or if it is it a Sunnah, which makes it preferable and desirable. In the latter case, the *adhān* is valid without it, but less complete. They support one or the other of these two views, but they consider the more correct view to be that the repetition is a Sunnah, or recommended. A number of Hadith scholars say that the caller of the *adhān* has the choice of either doing the repetition or abandoning it, but the correct view is to maintain it, but God knows best.

The *adhān* then includes *Ḥayy ʿalā al-ṣalāt; ḥayy ʿalā al-falāḥ*, repeating each twice. The first phrase means 'come to the prayer, come without delay'. The second phrase means 'come to success and salvation'. It is also suggested that it means 'come to ensure your stay in Heaven'.

Transmission

We have mentioned that al-Mismaʿī refers to Mismaʿ, the great grandfather of a tribe which is called after him.

The chain of transmission mentions Muʿādh ibn Hishām, who was the colleague of al-Dastawā'ī. This is made clear by Muslim towards the end of the Book of Faith. There should never be any confusion suggesting that he was a colleague of Muʿādh. It was Muʿādh's father that was his colleague. I have already explained that the name is after Dastawā, a town in al-Ahwāz.

The chain of transmission of this hadith features ʿĀmir al-Aḥwal; from Makḥūl; from ʿAbdullāh ibn Muḥayrīz. These three reporting from each other belonged to the Tābiʿīn generation. The first of them, ʿĀmir, is Ibn ʿAbd al-Wāḥid of Basrah.

Abū Maḥdhūrah's name is Samurah, but it is also said that he was Aws, or Jābir. In his book *al-Maʿārif*, Ibn Qutaybah says that his name is Sulaymān ibn Samurah, but this is odd. Abū Maḥdhūrah was from the Jumaḥ branch of the Quraysh, and he embraced Islam after the Battle of Ḥunayn. His voice was one of the finest, and he died in Makkah in year 59 AH, 679 CE, but it is also suggested that he died later in 77 AH. He continued to live in Makkah and his offspring continued to call the *adhān* for a long time.

CHAPTER 4

TWO CALLERS IN A MOSQUE

[677–7]. (Dār al-Salām 0741) Ibn Numayr narrated: my father narrated; ʿUbaydullāh narrated; from Nāfiʿ; from Ibn ʿUmar. He said: **'God's Messenger (peace be upon him) had two people to call the *adhān*: Bilāl and Ibn Umm Maktūm, the blind man'**.

حَدَّثَنَا ابْنُ نُمَيْرٍ، حَدَّثَنَا أَبِي، حَدَّثَنَا عُبَيْدُ اللهِ، عَنْ نَافِعٍ، عَنِ ابْنِ عُمَرَ، قَالَ: «كَانَ لِرَسُولِ اللهِ صَلَّى اللهُ عَلَيْهِ وَسَلَّمَ مُؤَذِّنَانِ بِلَالٌ، وَابْنُ أُمِّ مَكْتُومٍ الْأَعْمَى»

[000–000]. (Dār al-Salām 0742) Ibn Numayr narrated:[i] my father narrated; ʿUbaydullāh narrated; al-Qāsim narrated; from ʿĀ'ishah: **the same text**.

وَحَدَّثَنَا ابْنُ نُمَيْرٍ، حَدَّثَنَا أَبِي، حَدَّثَنَا عُبَيْدُ اللهِ، حَدَّثَنَا الْقَاسِمُ، عَنْ عَائِشَةَ مِثْلَهُ.

Text Explanation

This hadith gives us several useful points, including that it is permissible to describe a person by some defect he may have, in order to identify him or for some other useful point, provided that the description is not meant to detract from that person's standing. This is one of six situations in which backbiting is permissible. Backbiting is defined as mentioning someone by a defect or some other thing he might dislike. I explained these six situations, with

i. Related by al-Bukhārī, 622, 623, 1918 and 1919; al-Nasā'ī, 638.

the evidence confirming them, at the end of my book *al-Adhkār*, which is indespensible for any religious person. I shall mention them again, God willing, in the Book of Marriage, in the commentary on the hadith in which the Prophet describes Muʿāwiyah as 'poor', and the hadith that mentions that 'Abū Sufyān is a miser', as well as the hadith in which the Prophet describes one person as 'a bad brother of his tribe'. I will also, God willing, highlight similar cases at their appropriate places.

Ibn Umm Maktūm's name, according to the majority, is ʿAmr ibn Qays ibn Zā'idah ibn al-Aṣamm ibn Harim ibn Rawāḥah. Yet some say that his name is ʿAbdullāh ibn Zā'idah. Umm Maktūm's name is ʿĀtikah. Ibn Umm Maktūm died a martyr in the Battle of al-Qādisiyyah, but God knows best.

The hadith mentions that the Prophet had two people who called the *adhān*. This was in Madinah and at the same time. Abū Maḥdhūrah was the one who called the *adhān* for the Prophet in Makkah, while Saʿd al-Quruz called the *adhān* for the Prophet on several occasions at Qubā', near Madinah. The hadith means that it is desirable to have two people to call the *adhān* in the same mosque, with one of them calling it before the break of dawn and the other at dawn, like Bilāl and Ibn Umm Maktūm did in Madinah. Our scholars say that if there is need to have more than two, then there is no harm in having three or four or more, as the need may be. During ʿUthmān's reign, he appointed four people to call the *adhān*, because there was a need for it as the population of Madinah increased. Our scholars add that it is preferable not to have more than four unless there is clear need for them. They add that if there are two or more people to call the *adhān*, then they should not call it at the same time. If there is time, then they should do it in order, one after the other. If they disagree on who starts, this may be determined by drawing lots. If the time is short, and the mosque is large, they may call the *adhān* standing at different corners. If the mosque is small, they may stand together and call the *adhān* together, provided that they do so in harmony. If they do it differently and their voices create a disturbance, then only one may call the *adhān*. If they disagree, then drawing lots decides the matter.[i]

Who is to call the *iqāmah* when there are several callers of the *adhān*? If they call the *adhān* one after the other, then the first is the most entitled to it provided that he is considered the regular caller of the *adhān* or if there is no regular one. If the first is not the regular caller, then our scholars give two views as to the preferability of the regular caller or the one who is the first, and the more correct view is that the regular one is more entitled to it. If anyone other than what we have mentioned calls the *iqāmah*, this is valid according to the correct view approved by the majority of our scholars. However, some say that it is not valid, just as is the situation of one person giving the *Khuṭbah* on Friday and another leading the prayer. Some scholars say that this is not valid. If they call the *adhān* together and they agree that one of them calls the *iqāmah*, this is fine, but if they disagree, lots are drawn. Our scholars say that only one person should call the *iqāmah* in the same mosque, unless one is not enough. Some of our scholars say that it is acceptable that they may call the *iqāmah* together if this does not create disturbance.

i. All this is no longer applicable in most cases, as the use of loudspeakers makes the *adhān* well heard in the mosque's neighbourhood.

CHAPTER 5

A BLIND MAN MAY CALL THE *ADHĀN*

[678–8]. (Dār al-Salām 0743) Abū Kurayb Muhammad ibn al-ʿAlā' al-Hamdānī narrated to me: Khālid (meaning Ibn Makhlad) narrated; from Muhammad ibn Jaʿfar; Hishām narrated; from his father; from ʿĀ'ishah. She said: **'Ibn Umm Maktum used to call the *adhān* for God's Messenger (peace be upon him) and he was blind'**.

حَدَّثَنِي أَبُو كُرَيْبٍ مُحَمَّدُ بْنُ الْعَلَاءِ الْهَمْدَانِيُّ، حَدَّثَنَا خَالِدٌ يَعْنِي ابْنَ مَخْلَدٍ، عَنْ مُحَمَّدِ بْنِ جَعْفَرٍ، حَدَّثَنَا هِشَامٌ، عَنْ أَبِيهِ، عَنْ عَائِشَةَ قَالَتْ: «كَانَ ابْنُ أُمِّ مَكْتُومٍ يُؤَذِّنُ لِرَسُولِ اللهِ صَلَّى اللهُ عَلَيْهِ وَسَلَّمَ وَهُوَ أَعْمَى»

[000–000]. (Dār al-Salām 0744) Muhammad ibn Salamah al-Murādī narrated:[i] ʿAbdullāh ibn Wahb narrated; from Yaḥyā ibn ʿAbdullāh and Saʿīd ibn ʿAbd al-Raḥmān; from Hishām; with this chain of transmission: **the same text**.

وَحَدَّثَنَا مُحَمَّدُ بْنُ سَلَمَةَ الْمُرَادِيُّ، حَدَّثَنَا عَبْدُ اللهِ بْنُ وَهْبٍ، عَنْ يَحْيَى بْنِ عَبْدِ اللهِ، وَسَعِيدِ بْنِ عَبْدِ الرَّحْمَنِ، عَنْ هِشَامٍ، بِهَذَا الْإِسْنَادِ مِثْلَهُ.

Text Explanation

Most of what may be said about this hadith has already been said in the previous chapter. The purpose of this chapter is just to say

i. Related by Abū Dāwūd, 535.

that calling the *adhān* by a blind man is perfectly appropriate, if there is a person with clear eyesight with him, as was the case with Bilāl and Ibn Umm Maktūm. Our scholars say that if the blind man is alone, then for him to call the *adhān* is discouraged,[i] but God knows best.

i. A blind man may not be able to determine that the time for a prayer is due, unless he has someone with good eyesight alongside him.

CHAPTER 6

NO ATTACK ON UNBELIEVERS IF THE *ADHĀN* IS HEARD FROM THEIR QUARTERS

[679–9]. (Dār al-Salām 0745) Zuhayr ibn Ḥarb narrated to me:[i] Yaḥyā (meaning Ibn Saʿīd) narrated; from Ḥammād ibn Salamah; Thābit narrated; from Anas ibn Mālik. He said: '**The Prophet would time his attack when the dawn had broken. He would first listen for the *adhān*. If he heard the *adhān*, he would not attack; otherwise he would. He once heard someone say: "*Allāh-u akbar; Allāh-u akbar*". The Prophet said: "That is a sound nature". The man then said: "*Ashhadu an lā ilāha illā Allāh; ashhadu an lā ilāha illā Allāh*". The Prophet said: "You have saved yourself from the Fire". People looked for the man and they found him to be a shepherd with his goats**'.

وَحَدَّثَنِي زُهَيْرُ بْنُ حَرْبٍ، حَدَّثَنَا يَحْيَى يَعْنِي ابْنَ سَعِيدٍ، عَنْ حَمَّادِ بْنِ سَلَمَةَ، حَدَّثَنَا ثَابِتٌ، عَنْ أَنَسِ بْنِ مَالِكٍ، قَالَ: كَانَ رَسُولُ اللهِ صَلَّى اللهُ عَلَيْهِ وَسَلَّمَ يُغِيرُ إِذَا طَلَعَ الْفَجْرُ، وَكَانَ يَسْتَمِعُ الْأَذَانَ، فَإِنْ سَمِعَ أَذَانًا أَمْسَكَ وَإِلَّا أَغَارَ فَسَمِعَ رَجُلًا يَقُولُ: اللهُ أَكْبَرُ اللهُ أَكْبَرُ، فَقَالَ رَسُولُ اللهِ صَلَّى اللهُ عَلَيْهِ وَسَلَّمَ: «عَلَى الْفِطْرَةِ» ثُمَّ قَالَ: أَشْهَدُ أَنْ لَا إِلَهَ إِلَّا اللهُ أَشْهَدُ أَنْ لَا إِلَهَ إِلَّا اللهُ، فَقَالَ رَسُولُ اللهِ صَلَّى اللهُ عَلَيْهِ وَسَلَّمَ: «خَرَجْتَ مِنَ النَّارِ» فَنَظَرُوا فَإِذَا هُوَ رَاعِي مِعْزًى.

---

i. Related by Abū Dāwūd, 2634 (in a shorter version); al-Tirmidhī, 1618.

Text Explanation

When the Prophet heard the man saying '*Allāh-u akbar,*' he said: 'That is a sound nature'. What this means is that the man followed Islam, which is the faith of sound, uncorrupted human nature. When the man said the declaration of God's oneness, the Prophet commented that he had saved himself from Hell, by believing in God. The hadith mentions that the one who said this was a shepherd attending his goats. This serves as evidence that a person who happens to be alone in an area may say the *adhān*. This is the correct and well-known view of our Shāfiʿī school and others.

The hadith shows that the *adhān*, announcing the prayer, prevents an attack on the people of the area from where the *adhān* is heard. It is sufficient evidence that the people are Muslims. The hadith also means that stating the two parts of the declaration of God's oneness and the Prophet's message proves belief in Islam, even if this is not in response to a request. This is the correct view, even though there is disagreement among scholars. We discussed this at the beginning of the Book of Faith.

CHAPTER 7

WHAT TO SAY DURING AND AFTER THE *ADHĀN*

[680–10]. (Dār al-Salām 0746) Yaḥyā ibn Yaḥyā narrated to me:[i] I read out to Mālik; from Ibn Shihāb; from 'Aṭā' ibn Yazīd al-Laythī; from Abū Sa'īd al-Khudrī; that God's Messenger (peace be upon him) said: **'When you hear the *adhān*, say the same as the caller says'**.

حَدَّثَنِي يَحْيَى بْنُ يَحْيَى، قَالَ: قَرَأْتُ عَلَى مَالِكٍ، عَنِ ابْنِ شِهَابٍ، عَنْ عَطَاءِ بْنِ يَزِيدَ اللَّيْثِيِّ، عَنْ أَبِي سَعِيدٍ الْخُدْرِيِّ، أَنَّ رَسُولَ اللهِ صَلَّى اللهُ عَلَيْهِ وَسَلَّمَ قَالَ: «إِذَا سَمِعْتُمُ النِّدَاءَ، فَقُولُوا مِثْلَ مَا يَقُولُ الْـمُؤَذِّنُ»

[681–11]. (Dār al-Salām 0747) Muhammad ibn Salamah al-Murādī narrated:[ii] 'Abdullāh ibn Wahb narrated; from Ḥaywah, Sa'īd ibn Abī Ayyūb and others; from Ka'b ibn 'Alqamah; from 'Abd al-Raḥmān ibn Jubayr; from 'Abdullāh ibn 'Amr ibn al-'Āṣ, that he heard the Prophet say: **'When you hear the caller, say as he says. Then solicit peace and blessings for me. Whoever blesses me once, God will bless him ten times. Then appeal to God to grant me the *wasīlah*. It is a status in Heaven that is granted only to one of God's servants, and I hope to be the one. Whoever prays that I be granted the *wasīlah* will qualify for [my] intercession'**.

---

i. Related by al-Bukhārī, 611; Abū Dāwūd, 522; al-Tirmidhī, 208; al-Nasā'ī, 672; Ibn Mājah, 720.

ii. Related by 'Abdullāh, 523; al-Tirmidhī, 3614; al-Nasā'ī, 677.

حَدَّثَنَا مُحَمَّدُ بْنُ سَلَمَةَ الْمُرَادِيُّ، حَدَّثَنَا عَبْدُ اللهِ بْنُ وَهْبٍ، عَنْ حَيْوَةَ، وَسَعِيدِ بْنِ أَبِي أَيُّوبَ، وَغَيْرِهِمَا عَنْ كَعْبِ بْنِ عَلْقَمَةَ، عَنْ عَبْدِ الرَّحْمَنِ بْنِ جُبَيْرٍ، عَنْ عَبْدِ اللهِ بْنِ عَمْرِو بْنِ الْعَاصِ، أَنَّهُ سَمِعَ النَّبِيَّ صَلَّى اللهُ عَلَيْهِ وَسَلَّمَ يَقُولُ: «إِذَا سَمِعْتُمُ الْمُؤَذِّنَ، فَقُولُوا مِثْلَ مَا يَقُولُ ثُمَّ صَلُّوا عَلَيَّ، فَإِنَّهُ مَنْ صَلَّى عَلَيَّ صَلَاةً صَلَّى اللهُ عَلَيْهِ بِهَا عَشْرًا، ثُمَّ سَلُوا اللهَ لِيَ الْوَسِيلَةَ، فَإِنَّهَا مَنْزِلَةٌ فِي الْجَنَّةِ، لَا تَنْبَغِي إِلَّا لِعَبْدٍ مِنْ عِبَادِ اللهِ، وَأَرْجُو أَنْ أَكُونَ أَنَا هُوَ، فَمَنْ سَأَلَ لِي الْوَسِيلَةَ حَلَّتْ لَهُ الشَّفَاعَةُ»

[682–12]. (Dār al-Salām 0748) Isḥāq ibn Manṣūr narrated to me:[i] Abū Jaʿfar Muhammad ibn Jahḍam al-Thaqafī reported; Ismāʿīl ibn Jaʿfar narrated; from ʿUmārah ibn Ghaziyyah; from Khubayb ibn ʿAbd al-Raḥmān ibn Isāf; from Ḥafṣ ibn ʿĀṣim ibn ʿUmar ibn al-Khaṭṭāb; from his father; from his grandfather ʿUmar ibn al-Khaṭṭāb: **'God's Messenger (peace be upon him) said: "If the caller to the prayer says: *Allah-u akbar; Allah-u akbar*; and any of you says: *Allāh-u akbar; Allāh-u akbar*, then when the caller says: *Ashhadu an lā ilāha illā Allāh*, he says: *Ashhadu an lā ilāha illā Allāh*. And when the caller says: *Ashahadu anna Muhammad rasūlu Allāh*, he says: *Ashahadu anna Muhammadan rasūlu Allāh*, then the caller says: *Ḥayya ʿalā al-ṣalāt*, and he says: *Lā ḥawla walā quwwata illā billāh*, then the caller says: *Ḥayya ʿalā al-falāḥ*, and he says: *Lā ḥawla walā quwwata illā billāh*, and when the caller says: *Allāh-u akbar; Allāh-u akbar*; and any of you says: *Allāh-u akbar; Allāh-u akbar*, then when the caller says: *Lā ilāha illā Allāh*, he says: *lā ilāha illā Allāh*, feeling it all at heart, he will enter Heaven".'**

حَدَّثَنِي إِسْحَاقُ بْنُ مَنْصُورٍ، أَخْبَرَنَا أَبُو جَعْفَرٍ مُحَمَّدُ بْنُ جَهْضَمٍ الثَّقَفِيُّ، حَدَّثَنَا إِسْمَاعِيلُ بْنُ جَعْفَرٍ، عَنْ عُمَارَةَ بْنِ غَزِيَّةَ، عَنْ خُبَيْبِ بْنِ عَبْدِ الرَّحْمَنِ بْنِ إِسَافٍ، عَنْ

i. Related by Abū Dāwūd, 527.

حَفْصِ بْنِ عَاصِمِ بْنِ عُمَرَ بْنِ الْخَطَّابِ، عَنْ أَبِيهِ، عَنْ جَدِّهِ عُمَرَ بْنِ الْخَطَّابِ، قَالَ: قَالَ رَسُولُ اللهِ صَلَّى اللهُ عَلَيْهِ وَسَلَّمَ: «إِذَا قَالَ الْمُؤَذِّنُ: اللهُ أَكْبَرُ اللهُ أَكْبَرُ، فَقَالَ أَحَدُكُمْ: اللهُ أَكْبَرُ اللهُ أَكْبَرُ، ثُمَّ قَالَ: أَشْهَدُ أَنْ لَا إِلَهَ إِلَّا اللهُ، قَالَ: أَشْهَدُ أَنْ لَا إِلَهَ إِلَّا اللهُ، ثُمَّ قَالَ: أَشْهَدُ أَنَّ مُحَمَّدًا رَسُولُ اللهِ قَالَ: أَشْهَدُ أَنَّ مُحَمَّدًا رَسُولُ اللهِ، ثُمَّ قَالَ: حَيَّ عَلَى الصَّلَاةِ، قَالَ: لَا حَوْلَ وَلَا قُوَّةَ إِلَّا بِاللهِ، ثُمَّ قَالَ: حَيَّ عَلَى الْفَلَاحِ، قَالَ: لَا حَوْلَ وَلَا قُوَّةَ إِلَّا بِاللهِ، ثُمَّ قَالَ: اللهُ أَكْبَرُ اللهُ أَكْبَرُ، قَالَ: اللهُ أَكْبَرُ اللهُ أَكْبَرُ، ثُمَّ قَالَ: لَا إِلَهَ إِلَّا اللهُ، قَالَ: لَا إِلَهَ إِلَّا اللهُ مِنْ قَلْبِهِ دَخَلَ الْجَنَّةَ».

[683–13]. (Dār al-Salām 0749) Muhammad ibn Rumḥ narrated:[i] al-Layth reported; from al-Ḥukaym ibn ʿAbdullāh ibn Qays al-Qurashī [H]. Also, Qutaybah ibn Saʿīd narrated; Layth narrated; from al-Ḥukaym ibn ʿAbdullāh; from ʿĀmir ibn Saʿd ibn Abī Waqqāṣ; from Saʿd ibn Abī Waqqāṣ; from God's Messenger (peace be upon him) who said: **'Whoever says when he hears the *adhān* being called: I bear witness that there is no deity other than God, and that Muhammad is God's servant and Messenger. I accept God as my Lord, Muhammad as God's Messenger and Islam as my faith, shall have his sins forgiven'**.

In his narration, Ibn Rumḥ said: **'Whoever says when he hears the *adhān* being called, "And I bear witness", but Qutaybah did not mention in his narration the words, "And I"**.'

حَدَّثَنَا مُحَمَّدُ بْنُ رُمْحٍ، أَخْبَرَنَا اللَّيْثُ، عَنِ الْحُكَيْمِ بْنِ عَبْدِ اللهِ بْنِ قَيْسٍ الْقُرَشِيِّ، ح وَحَدَّثَنَا قُتَيْبَةُ بْنُ سَعِيدٍ، حَدَّثَنَا لَيْثٌ، عَنِ الْحُكَيْمِ بْنِ عَبْدِ اللهِ، عَنْ عَامِرِ بْنِ سَعْدِ بْنِ أَبِي وَقَّاصٍ، عَنْ سَعْدِ بْنِ أَبِي وَقَّاصٍ، عَنْ رَسُولِ اللهِ صَلَّى اللهُ عَلَيْهِ وَسَلَّمَ أَنَّهُ قَالَ: «مَنْ قَالَ حِينَ يَسْمَعُ الْمُؤَذِّنَ أَشْهَدُ أَنْ لَا إِلَهَ إِلَّا اللهُ وَحْدَهُ لَا شَرِيكَ لَهُ، وَأَنَّ

---

i. Related by Abū Dāwūd, 525; al-Tirmidhī, 210; al-Nasā'ī, 678; Ibn Mājah, 721.

مُحَمَّدًا عَبْدُهُ وَرَسُولُهُ، رَضِيتُ بِاللهِ رَبًّا وَبِمُحَمَّدٍ رَسُولًا، وَبِالإِسْلَامِ دِينًا، غُفِرَ لَهُ ذَنْبُهُ» قَالَ ابْنُ رُمْحٍ فِي رِوَايَتِهِ «مَنْ قَالَ حِينَ يَسْمَعُ الْمُؤَذِّنَ: وَأَنَا أَشْهَدُ» وَلَمْ يَذْكُرْ قُتَيْبَةُ قَوْلَهُ: وَأَنَا.

Text Explanation

Hadith No. 681 mentions the *wasīlah* and the Prophet explains this as a status in Heaven. Linguists say that the *wasīlah* is a person's status granted by a king. This hadith mentions that a person who prays that the Prophet be given this status 'qualifies' for the Prophet's intercession. This means that it becomes due to him, and what is due from the Prophet will certainly take place.

In hadith No. 682, the Prophet stresses the importance of repeating the phrases of the *adhān* when one hears the caller. However, the caller repeats each phrase twice, but the hadith mentions it once for brevity. Each phrase the caller says should be repeated by the listener, including when it is repeated. However, when the caller says *ḥayya ʿalā al-ṣalāt* and *ḥayya ʿalā al-falāḥ*, we should say: *la ḥawala wa lā quwwata illā billāh*. As mentioned earlier, *ḥayya* means 'come forward' and *falāḥ* means success. These phrases urge those who hear the call to come forward to join the prayer and this ensures their success. Indeed, *falāḥ* means much more than success. Scholars say that no word in Arabic signifies more goodness than *falāḥ*. The response of the listener is made differently, as he says: *lā ḥawala wa lā quwwata illā billāh*, which means that there is no action and no power except what is given by God. It is said that it means that no effort will repel evil and no power will bring goodness except through God. It is further said that no one can avoid disobeying God except through His protection and no one can do what pleases Him except through His help.

The hadiths in this chapter make clear that it is desirable for everyone who hears the *adhān* being called to repeat after the caller every phrase he says, except for the phrases that invite people to come to the prayer so as to ensure their success. When the caller says these four phrases, the listener should say *lā ḥawala wa lā quwwata illā billāh*, which acknowledges his need for God's help. In hadith No. 680, the Prophet is quoted as saying that we should repeat what the caller says. This is a general instruction, to which a restriction is added in hadith No. 682, which gives the variation. The hadith is clear that the listener repeats each phrase when the caller says it. The listener does not wait until the entire *adhān* is called.

Hadith No. 683 also tells us to add: 'And I bear witness that there is no deity other than God, and that Muhammad is God's servant and Messenger. I accept God as my Lord, Muhammad as God's Messenger and Islam as my faith'. From these hadiths we learn that when we encourage others to do something good, it is useful to mention what will motivate people to do it. We note that the Prophet said: 'Whoever blesses me once, God will bless him ten times … . Whoever prays that I be granted the *wasīlah* will qualify for [my] intercession'. These hadiths also make clear that for actions to be well rewarded, they must be clearly intended and sincerely done. This is evident in hadith No. 682, which tells us to repeat the phrases of the *adhān*, feeling them all at heart.

It should be understood that repeating the phrases of the *adhān* after we hear them is recommended for all people, whether one has performed ablution or not, and even for a man in a state of major ritual impurity and a woman having her period. Only when there is a reason to prevent such repetition, such as being at the toilet or having intercourse with one's spouse, should it be omitted. Another reason that prevents repetition is to be offering an obligatory or recommended prayer. The worshipper should wait until he finishes his prayer then he can say the phrases of the *adhān*. The question that arises here is: if a person is offering a prayer and the *adhān* is being called and he repeats the phrases of the *adhān*: is this reprehensible? Al-Shāfiʿī gives two rulings, the stronger of which is that it is reprehensible because it interrupts the prayer but does not invalidate it because these phrases are normal glorifications. However, if he says *ḥayya ʿalā al-ṣalāt* or *al-ṣalāt khayrun mina al-nawm*, his prayer becomes invalid provided that he knows that it is forbidden, because these words are human speech, not glorifications. If a person is reciting the Qur'an or saying some glorifications of God, or something similar and he or she hears the *adhān*, they interrupt what they are doing and repeat the phrases of the *adhān*. Likewise, when the *iqāmah* is called we repeat its phrases, except when the phrase indicating the prayer, *qad qāmat al-ṣalāt* is called out, when we should say *aqāmahā Allāhu wa adāmahā*, meaning: 'may it ever continue'. If the caller adds in the *adhān* for Fajr, or Dawn prayer, the phrase: *al-ṣalāt khayrun mina al-nawm*, which means 'prayer is better than sleeping', we say: *ṣadaqt wa barrart*, which means 'you tell the truth'.

Qāḍī ʿIyāḍ said:

> Our [Mālikī] scholars differ with regard to whether a person who is offering a prayer should repeat the phrases of the *adhān* when he hears them or not, and whether this applies to both obligatory and recommended prayers, or in recommended prayers only. Different scholars give three different answers. Abū Ḥanīfah does not approve of such repetition in both obligatory and recommended prayers. As to the question of whether repeating the phrases of the *adhān* after the caller is obligatory or recommended if a person is not offering prayers, scholars hold different views which are explained by al-Ṭaḥāwī. The correct view, which is shared by the majority of scholars, is that it is recommended, not obligatory. Scholars also differ as to whether the repetition should be made when one hears every caller saying the *adhān*, or after the first one only. Mālik gives two views also regarding repeating all the phrases of the *adhān* or only up to the end of the declaration of God's oneness and Prophet Muhammad's message. These are all glorifications of God, while the rest of the *adhān* includes some phrases that are not so, in addition to glorifications. Moreover, some of it repeats what was said earlier, but God knows best.

Qāḍī ʿIyāḍ also comments on hadith No. 682, which gives the instruction to repeat what the caller says in the *adhān* before stating that whoever does so feeling these phrases at heart will be in Heaven. He said:

> This is the case because all this is an assertion of God's oneness, glorifying Him and submission to His will and command. It adds acknowledgement of His authority and power over all things by saying: *lā ḥawala wa lā quwwata illā billāh.* Whoever accomplishes this gains the truth of faith and the perfection of his belief in Islam. As such he deserves to be in Heaven, by God's grace. This is what is meant by the Prophet's advice in the other hadith that we should say: 'I accept God as my Lord, Muhammad as God's Messenger and Islam as my faith'.
>
> The *adhān* is a comprehensive formula that combines faith in its both rational and verbal parts. It begins with an affirmation of God's existence and His attributes of perfection and freedom of their opposites. This is summed up by our saying *Allāh-u akbar,* which means 'God is supreme'. Brief as this word is, it indicates all that we have mentioned. Then the *adhān* confirms God's oneness and negates the impossible opposite of Him having partners. This represents the essence of faith and belief in God's oneness, which takes precedence over all functions of faith. Then it confirms prophethood and testifies that our Prophet, Muhammad (peace be upon him), is God's Messenger. This is a very important rule that follows the declaration of belief in God's oneness. It comes next to that belief because it is a possible event. All these initial phrases are obligatory rules. With them the rational beliefs concerning what is essential, possible or impossible with regard to our duties towards God are completed. The *adhān* follows this with a call on them to offer their worship, stressing the importance of prayer after having confirmed prophethood, because knowledge of such worship can only be through the Prophet, not through reason and logic. It then calls on them to seek success, which is to win a permanent abode in bliss. It thus refers to matters of the life to come, such as resurrection and recompense. This is the last of Islamic beliefs. All this is

then repeated when the *iqāmah* is called, so as to inform the people that it is about to happen. It incorporates a re-emphasis of belief as one starts to offer worship in which one's mind and tongue take part. The worshipper thus starts his worship, fully aware of his position, realizing what his faith means, feeling the great importance of what he is starting and the great duty he owes to his Lord whom he worships and from whom he seeks reward.

This is the explanation given by *Qāḍī* ʿIyāḍ, which reflects perfect understanding and profound insight. To God we owe all success.

Transmission

Regarding the names of narrators, we note that the last of these four hadiths includes al-Ḥukaym ibn ʿAbdullāh. In Arabic, Ḥukaym is written in the same form as Ḥakīm. It should be noted that all names given this form in both al-Bukhārī's and Muslim's *Ṣaḥīḥ* anthologies are pronounced Ḥakīm, except for two: the present one al-Ḥukaym ibn ʿAbdullāh and Zurayq ibn Ḥukaym.

The chain of transmission of hadith No. 682 includes: 'Isḥāq ibn Manṣūr narrated to me: Abū Jaʿfar Muhammad ibn Jahḍam al-Thaqafī reported; Ismāʿīl ibn Jaʿfar narrated; from ʿUmārah ibn Ghaziyyah, etc.' In his book *al-Istidrāk*, Imam ʿAlī ibn ʿUmar al-Dāraquṭnī said: 'This hadith is narrated by al-Dārawardī and others as *mursal*, with an incomplete chain of transmission'. Al-Dāraquṭnī also said in his book *Kitāb al-ʿIlal*: 'It is related with a complete chain of transmission. It is completed by Ismāʿīl ibn Jaʿfar, a reliable and highly respected Hadith scholar. His addition is accepted and the hadith is related by al-Bukhārī and Muslim in their *Ṣaḥīḥ* anthologies'. What al-Dāraquṭnī said in *al-ʿIlal* is certainly correct. The hadith is authentic, and an addition by a reliable narrator is acceptable. Similar cases were given in this commentary, but God knows best.

CHAPTER 8

THE IMPORTANCE OF THE *ADHĀN*

[684–14]. (Dār al-Salām 0750) Muhammad ibn ʿAbdullāh ibn Numayr narrated:[i] ʿAbdah narrated; from Ṭalḥah ibn Yaḥyā; from his paternal uncle. He said: **'I was at Muʿāwiyah ibn Abī Sufyān's when the caller came over to announce the prayer. Muʿāwiyah said: "I heard God's Messenger (peace be upon him) say: 'The [prayer] announcers are the ones with the longest necks on the Day of Judgement'".'**

حَدَّثَنَا مُحَمَّدُ بْنُ عَبْدِ اللهِ بْنِ نُمَيْرٍ، حَدَّثَنَا عَبْدَةُ، عَنْ طَلْحَةَ بْنِ يَحْيَى، عَنْ عَمِّهِ، قَالَ: كُنْتُ عِنْدَ مُعَاوِيَةَ بْنِ أَبِي سُفْيَانَ، فَجَاءَهُ الْمُؤَذِّنُ يَدْعُوهُ إِلَى الصَّلَاةِ فَقَالَ مُعَاوِيَةُ: سَمِعْتُ رَسُولَ اللهِ صَلَّى اللهُ عَلَيْهِ وَسَلَّمَ يَقُولُ: «الْمُؤَذِّنُونَ أَطْوَلُ النَّاسِ أَعْنَاقًا يَوْمَ الْقِيَامَةِ»

This was also narrated to me by Isḥāq ibn Manṣūr: Abū ʿĀmir reported; Sufyān narrated; from Ṭalḥah ibn Yaḥyā; from ʿĪsā ibn Ṭalḥah. He said: 'I heard Muʿāwiyah say: "God's Messenger said"': **the same text**.

وَحَدَّثَنِيهِ إِسْحَاقُ بْنُ مَنْصُورٍ، أَخْبَرَنَا أَبُو عَامِرٍ، حَدَّثَنَا سُفْيَانُ، عَنْ طَلْحَةَ بْنِ يَحْيَى، عَنْ عِيسَى بْنِ طَلْحَةَ، قَالَ: سَمِعْتُ مُعَاوِيَةَ يَقُولُ: قَالَ رَسُولُ اللهِ صَلَّى اللهُ عَلَيْهِ وَسَلَّمَ بِمِثْلِهِ.

---

i. Related by Ibn Mājah, 725.

[685–15]. (Dār al-Salām 0751) Qutaybah ibn Saʿīd, ʿUthmān ibn Abī Shaybah and Isḥāq ibn Ibrāhīm narrated: Jarīr (Isḥāq said: 'reported', but the other two said: 'narrated'); from al-Aʿmash; from Abū Sufyān; from Jābir. He said: **'I heard God's Messenger (peace be upon him) say: "When Satan hears the prayer announcement [i.e. *adhān*], he goes as far away as al-Rawḥā'".'**

Sulayman said: **'I asked him about al-Rawḥā', and he said that it is thrity-six miles**[i] **from Madinah'**.

حَدَّثَنَا قُتَيْبَةُ بْنُ سَعِيدٍ، وَعُثْمَانُ بْنُ أَبِي شَيْبَةَ، وَإِسْحَاقُ بْنُ إِبْرَاهِيمَ، - قَالَ إِسْحَاقُ، أَخْبَرَنَا، وَقَالَ الآخَرَانِ - حَدَّثَنَا جَرِيرٌ، عَنِ الأَعْمَشِ، عَنْ أَبِي سُفْيَانَ، عَنْ جَابِرٍ، قَالَ: سَمِعْتُ النَّبِيَّ صَلَّى اللهُ عَلَيْهِ وَسَلَّمَ يَقُولُ: «إِنَّ الشَّيْطَانَ إِذَا سَمِعَ النِّدَاءَ بِالصَّلاَةِ ذَهَبَ حَتَّى يَكُونَ مَكَانَ الرَّوْحَاءِ»

قَالَ سُلَيْمَانُ: فَسَأَلْتُهُ عَنِ الرَّوْحَاءِ فَقَالَ: «هِيَ مِنَ الْمَدِينَةِ سِتَّةٌ وَثَلاَثُونَ مِيلاً»

[000–000]. (Dār al-Salām 0752) Abū Bakr ibn Abī Shaybah and Abū Kurayb narrated it: both said: Abū Muʿāwiyah narrated; from al-Aʿmash; with the same chain of transmission.

وَحَدَّثَنَاهُ أَبُو بَكْرِ بْنُ أَبِي شَيْبَةَ، وَأَبُو كُرَيْبٍ، قَالاَ: حَدَّثَنَا أَبُو مُعَاوِيَةَ، عَنِ الأَعْمَشِ بِهَذَا الإِسْنَادِ.

[686–16]. (Dār al-Salām 0753) Qutaybah ibn Saʿīd, Zuhayr ibn Ḥarb and Isḥāq ibn Ibrāhīm narrated (Qutabah's text): Jarīr (Isḥāq said: 'reported'; but the other two said: 'narrated'); from al-Aʿmash; from Abu Ṣāliḥ; from Abū Hurayrah; from the

i. This refers to the Arabian mile, which is a little longer than the well-known British mile used nowadays. The Arabian mile is said to be equal to 1855 metres.

Prophet (peace be upon him): **'When Satan hears the prayer announcement [i.e. *adhān*], he moves away, making a farting noise, so that he does not hear the caller. When he finishes, Satan comes back to whisper. When Satan hears the prayer announcement [i.e. *iqāmah*], he moves away so that he does not hear the announcer. When he finishes, Satan comes back to whisper'**.

حَدَّثَنَا قُتَيْبَةُ بْنُ سَعِيدٍ، وَزُهَيْرُ بْنُ حَرْبٍ، وَإِسْحَاقُ بْنُ إِبْرَاهِيمَ، - وَاللَّفْظُ لِقُتَيْبَةَ، قَالَ إِسْحَاقُ، أَخْبَرَنَا، وَقَالَ الآخَرَانِ - حَدَّثَنَا جَرِيرٌ، عَنِ الأَعْمَشِ، عَنْ أَبِي صَالِحٍ، عَنْ أَبِي هُرَيْرَةَ، عَنِ النَّبِيِّ صَلَّى اللهُ عَلَيْهِ وَسَلَّمَ قَالَ: «إِنَّ الشَّيْطَانَ إِذَا سَمِعَ النِّدَاءَ بِالصَّلاَةِ أَحَالَ لَهُ ضُرَاطٌ حَتَّى لاَ يَسْمَعَ صَوْتَهُ. فَإِذَا سَكَتَ رَجَعَ فَوَسْوَسَ فَإِذَا سَمِعَ الإِقَامَةَ ذَهَبَ حَتَّى لاَ يَسْمَعَ صَوْتَهُ فَإِذَا سَكَتَ رَجَعَ فَوَسْوَسَ»

[687–17]. (Dār al-Salām 0754) ʿAbd al-Ḥamīd ibn Bayān al-Wāsiṭī narrated to me: Khālid (meaning Ibn ʿAbdullāh) narrated; from Suhayl; from his father; from Abū Hurayrah: God's Messenger (peace be upon him) said: **'When the announcer makes the call to prayer [i.e. *adhān*], Satan will move away making a farting noise'**.

حَدَّثَنِي عَبْدُ الْحَمِيدِ بْنُ بَيَانٍ الْوَاسِطِيُّ، حَدَّثَنَا خَالِدٌ يَعْنِي ابْنَ عَبْدِ اللهِ، عَنْ سُهَيْلٍ، عَنْ أَبِيهِ، عَنْ أَبِي هُرَيْرَةَ، قَالَ: قَالَ رَسُولُ اللهِ صَلَّى اللهُ عَلَيْهِ وَسَلَّمَ: «إِذَا أَذَّنَ الْمُؤَذِّنُ أَدْبَرَ الشَّيْطَانُ وَلَهُ حُصَاصٌ»

[688–18]. (Dār al-Salām 0755) Umayyah ibn Bisṭām narrated: Yazīd (meaning Ibn Zurayʿ) narrated; Rawḥ narrated; from Suhayl. He said: **'My father sent me to Banī Ḥārithah and a young lad of ours (or a friend of ours) was with me. Someone called out to him by name from a farm. My companion**

looked over to the farm but could see no one. I mentioned this to my father and he said: "Had I felt that you may experience this, I would not have sent you. However, if you hear such a voice, then make the call to prayer. I heard Abu Hurayrah narrating from God's Messenger (peace be upon him): 'When Satan hears the call to prayer, he runs away making a farting noise'".'

حَدَّثَنِي أُمَيَّةُ بْنُ بِسْطَامَ، حَدَّثَنَا يَزِيدُ يَعْنِي ابْنَ زُرَيْعٍ، حَدَّثَنَا رَوْحٌ، عَنْ سُهَيْلٍ، قَالَ: أَرْسَلَنِي أَبِي إِلَى بَنِي حَارِثَةَ، قَالَ: وَمَعِي غُلَامٌ لَنَا - أَوْ صَاحِبٌ لَنَا - فَنَادَاهُ مُنَادٍ مِنْ حَائِطٍ بِاسْمِهِ قَالَ: وَأَشْرَفَ الَّذِي مَعِي عَلَى الْحَائِطِ فَلَمْ يَرَ شَيْئًا، فَذَكَرْتُ ذَلِكَ لِأَبِي فَقَالَ: لَوْ شَعَرْتُ أَنَّكَ تَلْقَ هَذَا لَمْ أُرْسِلْكَ، وَلَكِنْ إِذَا سَمِعْتَ صَوْتًا فَنَادِ بِالصَّلَاةِ فَإِنِّي سَمِعْتُ أَبَا هُرَيْرَةَ يُحَدِّثُ عَنْ رَسُولِ اللهِ صَلَّى اللهُ عَلَيْهِ وَسَلَّمَ أَنَّهُ قَالَ: «إِنَّ الشَّيْطَانَ إِذَا نُودِيَ بِالصَّلَاةِ وَلَّى وَلَهُ حُصَاصٌ»

[689–19]. (Dār al-Salām 0756) Qutaybah ibn Saʿīd narrated: al-Mughīrah (meaning al-Ḥizāmī) narrated; from Abū al-Zinād; from al-Aʿraj; from Abu Hurayrah; that the Prophet (peace be upon him) said: **'When the call to prayer is made, Satan moves away making a farting noise so that he does not hear the prayer announcement. When the *adhān* is over, he comes back. Then when the *iqāmah* is made, he runs away, and when it finishes he comes back, taking his position even between a person and himself. He tells the worshipper: remember this and remember that, [mentioning] things that he did not remember earlier. [He continues] until the worshipper does not know how much of his prayer he has performed.'**

حَدَّثَنَا قُتَيْبَةُ بْنُ سَعِيدٍ، حَدَّثَنَا الْـمُغِيرَةُ يَعْنِي الْحِزَامِيَّ، عَنْ أَبِي الزِّنَادِ، عَنِ الْأَعْرَجِ، عَنْ أَبِي هُرَيْرَةَ، أَنَّ النَّبِيَّ صَلَّى اللهُ عَلَيْهِ وَسَلَّمَ قَالَ: «إِذَا نُودِيَ لِلصَّلَاةِ أَدْبَرَ الشَّيْطَانُ

لَهُ ضُرَاطٌ، حَتَّى لَا يَسْمَعَ التَّأْذِينَ، فَإِذَا قُضِيَ التَّأْذِينُ أَقْبَلَ حَتَّى إِذَا ثُوِّبَ بِالصَّلَاةِ أَدْبَرَ حَتَّى إِذَا قُضِيَ التَّثْوِيبُ، أَقْبَلَ حَتَّى يَخْطُرَ بَيْنَ الْمَرْءِ وَنَفْسِهِ يَقُولُ لَهُ: اذْكُرْ كَذَا وَاذْكُرْ كَذَا لِمَا لَمْ يَكُنْ يَذْكُرُ مِنْ قَبْلُ حَتَّى يَظَلَّ الرَّجُلُ مَا يَدْرِي كَمْ صَلَّى»

[690–20]. (Dār al-Salām 0757) Muhammad ibn Rāfiʿ narrated: ʿAbd al-Razzāq narrated; Maʿmar narrated; from Hammām ibn Munabbih; from Abū Hurayrah, from the Prophet: the same text, but he said at the end: ‘**until the worshipper is left unaware how he prayed**’.

حَدَّثَنَا مُحَمَّدُ بْنُ رَافِعٍ، حَدَّثَنَا عَبْدُ الرَّزَّاقِ، حَدَّثَنَا مَعْمَرٌ، عَنْ هَمَّامِ بْنِ مُنَبِّهٍ، عَنْ أَبِي هُرَيْرَةَ، عَنِ النَّبِيِّ صَلَّى اللهُ عَلَيْهِ وَسَلَّمَ بِمِثْلِهِ غَيْرَ أَنَّهُ قَالَ: «حَتَّى يَظَلَّ الرَّجُلُ إِنْ يَدْرِي كَيْفَ صَلَّى»

Text Explanation

The first hadith, No. 684, mentions that the Prophet said that the prayer announcers, i.e. the *mu'dhdhins*, are the people with the longest necks on the Day of Judgement. Scholars of earlier and later generations differ as to the meaning of this statement. It is said that they are the ones who most look up to God’s grace, because the one who is eager to get something tries to stretch his neck so as to see it better. Thus, the hadith means that they see great reward and they stretch their necks towards it. Al-Naḍr ibn Shumayl said: ‘When people’s perspiration is made to reach their mouths on the Day of Judgement, they stretch their necks so that they do not feel this great distress’. Others say that those who announce the prayer are the chiefs of people. The Arabs used to describe their chiefs as having long necks, meaning that they have greater following. Ibn al-Aʿrābī said that it means they are the ones with the greatest good works to show. *Qāḍī* ʿIyāḍ and other scholars read the hadith as meaning ‘they are the fastest running on the Day of Judgement’, which means that they move quickly towards Heaven.

The hadiths mention that when Satan hears the call to prayer [i.e. *adhān*], he runs away, and he makes a farting noise. The expression used by the Prophet is also said to mean running fast. Both meanings were stated by Abū ʿUbayd and other leading scholars. Scholars also say that Satan runs away when he hears the *adhān* because he does not want to testify in favour of the announcer on the Day of Judgement. The Prophet said that anyone who hears the *adhān*, whether human or jinn or inanimate object, will testify in favour of the caller on the Day of Judgement. *Qāḍī* ʿIyāḍ said: 'It is suggested that only the believers among humans and jinn will testify, because an unbeliever is unacceptable as a witness'. *Qāḍī* ʿIyāḍ further said: 'This is totally unacceptable, no matter who says it, because the hadiths contradict it. It is further said that this applies to anyone who qualifies as a witness, provided that he has the sense of hearing. On the other hand, it is said that it applies to all animate and inanimate objects, as God creates for them an understanding of the *adhān* and a rational sense and knowledge. Furthermore, it is said that Satan runs away because of the great importance of the *adhān*, as it incorporates principles of the belief in God's oneness and proclaims the essentials of Islam. It is also suggested that Satan despairs of being able to seduce man at the time when the principle of God's oneness is declared'.

The hadiths mention that Satan runs away when he hears the *adhān* and the *iqāmah*, because they are calls inviting people to come to the prayer and to join it. However, he returns when they are over and he approaches people, trying his best to divert them from their prayer by reminding them of their daily affairs, so that they are distracted and do not know how far they have got in their prayers.

The hadiths in this chapter highlight the importance and great merit of the *adhān*. Many hadiths are related in the two *Ṣaḥīḥ* anthologies of al-Bukhārī and Muslim stressing its importance. Our scholars hold different views on whether it is better for a person to dedicate himself to proclaiming the *adhān* or leading the congregational prayer. The more correct view is that the *adhān* is better. This is stated by al-Shāfiʿī himself in his book *al-Umm*, and this is shared by the majority of our scholars. A second view makes leading the prayer better, and it is also stated by al-Shāfiʿī. The third view makes the two of equal merit. The fourth suggests that if a person feels that he meets the requirements of leading the prayer, then it is better for him. Otherwise, the *adhān* is more preferable. This last view is stated by Abū ʿAlī al-Ṭabarī, Abū al-Qāsim ibn Kujj, al-Masʿūdī and *Qāḍī* Ḥusayn, all of whom belong to our Shāfiʿī school.

Should a person combine both roles of calling the *adhān* and leading the prayer? A number of our scholars maintain that it is undesirable, and some go further so as to say that it is discouraged. However, the more scrupulous scholars and the majority say that it is acceptable and even desirable. This is more correct, but God knows best.

Transmission

In the first hadith of this chapter, No. 684, the chain of transmission includes Ṭalḥah ibn Yaḥyā reporting from his paternal uncle, whose name is ʿĪsā ibn Ṭalḥah ibn ʿUbaydullāh, as clearly stated in the other narration in this chapter.

In hadith No. 685, al-Aʿmash narrates from Abū Sufyān. The name of Abū Sufyān is Ṭalḥah ibn Nāfiʿ, as we explained on more than one occasion. The hadith ends with Sulaymān asking about al-Rawḥā'. Sulaymān who is mentioned here is Sulaymān ibn Mahrān, who is better known as al-Aʿmash, and the one who is asked is Abū Sufyān Ṭalḥah ibn Nāfiʿ.

CHAPTER 9

LIFTING ONE'S HANDS PARALLEL WITH ONE'S SHOULDERS

[691–21]. (Dār al-Salām 0758) Yaḥyā ibn Yaḥyā al-Tamīmī, Saʿīd ibn Manṣūr, Abū Bakr ibn Abī Shaybah, ʿAmr al-Nāqid, Zuhayr ibn Ḥarb and Ibn Numayr narrated: all from Sufyān ibn ʿUyaynah (Yaḥyā's text); He said: Sufyān ibn ʿUyaynah reported; from al-Zuhrī; from Sālim; from his father. He said: **'I saw God's Messenger raising his hands when he started the prayer so that they were parallel with his shoulders, and he so did before bowing, and when lifting himself from bowing, but he did not raise his hands in between the two prostrations'**.

حَدَّثَنَا يَحْيَى بْنُ يَحْيَى التَّمِيمِيُّ، وَسَعِيدُ بْنُ مَنْصُورٍ، وَأَبُو بَكْرِ بْنُ أَبِي شَيْبَةَ، وَعَمْرٌو النَّاقِدُ، وَزُهَيْرُ بْنُ حَرْبٍ، وَابْنُ نُمَيْرٍ، كُلُّهُمْ عَنْ سُفْيَانَ بْنِ عُيَيْنَةَ - وَاللَّفْظُ لِيَحْيَى - قَالَ: أَخْبَرَنَا سُفْيَانُ بْنُ عُيَيْنَةَ، عَنِ الزُّهْرِيِّ، عَنْ سَالِمٍ، عَنْ أَبِيهِ، قَالَ: رَأَيْتُ رَسُولَ اللهِ صَلَّى اللهُ عَلَيْهِ وَسَلَّمَ «إِذَا افْتَتَحَ الصَّلَاةَ رَفَعَ يَدَيْهِ حَتَّى يُحَاذِيَ مَنْكِبَيْهِ، وَقَبْلَ أَنْ يَرْكَعَ، وَإِذَا رَفَعَ مِنَ الرُّكُوعِ، وَلَا يَرْفَعُهُمَا بَيْنَ السَّجْدَتَيْنِ»

[692–22]. (Dār al-Salām 0759) Muhammad ibn Rāfiʿ narrated to me: ʿAbd al-Razzāq narrated; Ibn Jurayj reported; Ibn Shihāb narrated to me; from Sālim ibn ʿAbdullāh; that Ibn ʿUmar said: **'When God's Messenger (peace be upon him) stood up for prayer, he raised his hands so as to be parallel with his shoulders, then he would glorify God, saying *Allāh-u akbar*.**

When he wanted to bow, he did the same, and when he lifted himself from the position of bowing, he did the same. But he did not do this when he lifted his head from the prostration position'.

حَدَّثَنِي مُحَمَّدُ بْنُ رَافِعٍ، حَدَّثَنَا عَبْدُ الرَّزَّاقِ، أَخْبَرَنَا ابْنُ جُرَيْجٍ، حَدَّثَنِي ابْنُ شِهَابٍ، عَنْ سَالِمِ بْنِ عَبْدِ اللهِ، أَنَّ ابْنَ عُمَرَ، قَالَ: «كَانَ رَسُولُ اللهِ صَلَّى اللهُ عَلَيْهِ وَسَلَّمَ إِذَا قَامَ لِلصَّلَاةِ رَفَعَ يَدَيْهِ حَتَّى تَكُونَا حَذْوَ مَنْكِبَيْهِ، ثُمَّ كَبَّرَ، فَإِذَا أَرَادَ أَنْ يَرْكَعَ فَعَلَ مِثْلَ ذَلِكَ، وَإِذَا رَفَعَ مِنَ الرُّكُوعِ فَعَلَ مِثْلَ ذَلِكَ، وَلَا يَفْعَلُهُ حِينَ يَرْفَعُ رَأْسَهُ مِنَ السُّجُودِ»

[693–23]. (Dār al-Salām 0760) Muhammad ibn Rāfiʿ narrated to me: Ḥujayn (who is Ibn al-Muthannā) narrated; al-Layth narrated; from ʿUqayl [H]. Also, Muhammad ibn ʿAbdullāh ibn Quhzādh narrated to me; Salamah ibn Sulaymān narrated; ʿAbdullāh reported; Yūnus reported; both from al-Zuhrī, with the same chain of transmission, the same text as stated by Ibn Jurayj: '**When God's Messenger (peace be upon him) stood up for prayer, he raised his hands so as to be parallel with his shoulders, then he would glorify God**'.

حَدَّثَنِي مُحَمَّدُ بْنُ رَافِعٍ، حَدَّثَنَا حُجَيْنٌ وَهُوَ ابْنُ الْمُثَنَّى، حَدَّثَنَا اللَّيْثُ، عَنْ عُقَيْلٍ، ح وَحَدَّثَنِي مُحَمَّدُ بْنُ عَبْدِ اللهِ بْنِ قُهْزَاذَ، حَدَّثَنَا سَلَمَةُ بْنُ سُلَيْمَانَ، أَخْبَرَنَا عَبْدُ اللهِ، أَخْبَرَنَا يُونُسُ، كِلَاهُمَا عَنِ الزُّهْرِيِّ، بِهَذَا الْإِسْنَادِ كَمَا قَالَ ابْنُ جُرَيْجٍ: «كَانَ رَسُولُ اللهِ صَلَّى اللهُ عَلَيْهِ وَسَلَّمَ إِذَا قَامَ لِلصَّلَاةِ رَفَعَ يَدَيْهِ حَتَّى تَكُونَا حَذْوَ مَنْكِبَيْهِ ثُمَّ كَبَّرَ»

[694–24]. (Dār al-Salām 0761) Yaḥyā ibn Yaḥyā narrated: Khālid ibn ʿAbdullāh reported; from Khālid; from Abū Qilābah; that he saw Mālik ibn al-Ḥuwayrith: '**When he prayed, he glorified God then raised his hands, and when he wanted to bow he raised his hands, and when he lifted his head from bowing**

he raised his hands. He narrated that God's Messenger (peace be upon him) used to do this'.

حَدَّثَنَا يَحْيَى بْنُ يَحْيَى، أَخْبَرَنَا خَالِدُ بْنُ عَبْدِ اللهِ، عَنْ خَالِدٍ، عَنْ أَبِي قِلَابَةَ، أَنَّهُ رَأَى مَالِكَ بْنَ الْحُوَيْرِثِ، «إِذَا صَلَّى كَبَّرَ، ثُمَّ رَفَعَ يَدَيْهِ، وَإِذَا أَرَادَ أَنْ يَرْكَعَ رَفَعَ يَدَيْهِ، وَإِذَا رَفَعَ رَأْسَهُ مِنَ الرُّكُوعِ رَفَعَ يَدَيْهِ»، وَحَدَّثَ «أَنَّ رَسُولَ اللهِ صَلَّى اللهُ عَلَيْهِ وَسَلَّمَ كَانَ يَفْعَلُ هَكَذَا»

[695–25]. (Dār al-Salām 0762) Abū Kāmil al-Jaḥdarī narrated to me: Abū ʿAwānah narrated; from Qatādah; from Naṣr ibn ʿĀṣim; from Mālik ibn al-Ḥuwayrith; that **'When God's Messenger glorified God [to begin his prayer], he raised his hands so that they were parallel with his ears; and when he bowed he raised his hands so that they were parallel with his ears; and when he lifted himself from bowing and said *samiʿa Allāhu liman ḥamidah*, he did the same.'**

حَدَّثَنِي أَبُو كَامِلٍ الْجَحْدَرِيُّ، حَدَّثَنَا أَبُو عَوَانَةَ، عَنْ قَتَادَةَ، عَنْ نَصْرِ بْنِ عَاصِمٍ، عَنْ مَالِكِ بْنِ الْحُوَيْرِثِ: «أَنَّ رَسُولَ اللهِ صَلَّى اللهُ عَلَيْهِ وَسَلَّمَ كَانَ إِذَا كَبَّرَ رَفَعَ يَدَيْهِ حَتَّى يُحَاذِيَ بِهِمَا أُذُنَيْهِ، وَإِذَا رَكَعَ رَفَعَ يَدَيْهِ حَتَّى يُحَاذِيَ بِهِمَا أُذُنَيْهِ، وَإِذَا رَفَعَ رَأْسَهُ مِنَ الرُّكُوعِ» فَقَالَ: «سَمِعَ اللهُ لِمَنْ حَمِدَهُ» فَعَلَ مِثْلَ ذَلِكَ.

[696–26]. (Dār al-Salām 0763) Muhammad ibn al-Muthannā narrated it: Ibn Abī ʿAdī narrated; from Saʿīd; from Qatādah; with this transmission; that **'He saw God's Messenger (peace be upon him), and added: until he made them parallel with the top of his ears'.**

وَحَدَّثَنَاهُ مُحَمَّدُ بْنُ الْمُثَنَّى، حَدَّثَنَا ابْنُ أَبِي عَدِيٍّ، عَنْ سَعِيدٍ، عَنْ قَتَادَةَ، بِهَذَا الْإِسْنَادِ أَنَّهُ رَأَى نَبِيَّ اللهِ صَلَّى اللهُ عَلَيْهِ وَسَلَّمَ وَقَالَ: حَتَّى يُحَاذِيَ بِهِمَا فُرُوعَ أُذُنَيْهِ.

Text Explanation

Muslims are unanimous that it is desirable to raise one's hands when saying *Allāh-u akbar* for the first time, starting the prayer. They differ with regard to raising them in other positions. Al-Shāfiʿī, Ahmad and the majority of scholars from among the Prophet's companions and subsequent generations maintain that it is also desirable to raise one's hands before bowing, i.e. *rukūʿ*, and when lifting oneself from bowing. This is also reported from Mālik. Al-Shāfiʿī further adds that it is desirable to raise one's hands in a fourth position, which is when standing up after the first *tashahhud*. This is correct, as evidenced by an authentic hadith related by al-Bukhārī in which Ibn ʿUmar mentions that the Prophet used to do so. Another hadith narrated by Abū Ḥumayd al-Sāʿidī with good chains of transmission also mentions this, and this hadith is related by Abū Dāwūd and al-Tirmidhī. Abū Bakr ibn al-Mundhir and Abū ʿAlī al-Ḥasan ibn al-Qāsim al-Ṭabarī, both of whom belong to the Shāfiʿī school, as well as some Hadith scholars say that it is also desirable to raise one's hands at prostration. Abū Ḥanīfah and his disciples, as well as a number of the scholars of Kufah, said that raising one's hands is desirable only at the first glorification to start the prayer. This is the best-known view of Mālik. They all agree that no raising of hands in prayer is a duty. However, it has been mentioned that Dāwūd makes it a duty at the start of prayer, and this view is shared by Imam Abū al-Ḥasan Ahmad ibn Sayyār al-Sayyārī, who is one of our scholars with independent views. I reported this from him in *Sharḥ al-Muhadhdhab* and in *Tahdhīb al-Lughāt*.

How are the hands raised? The best-known condition approved by our school and the great majority of scholars is that one should make one's hands close to the top of one's shoulders, so that the tips of one's fingers are parallel with the top of one's ears; one's thumbs close to the ends of one's ears and one's palms parallel with one's shoulders. In this way, al-Shāfiʿī fulfilled all reports, and thus he gained people's approval.

At what time does one raise one's hand? The first report mentions that the Prophet raised his hands then glorified God, saying *Allāh-u akbar*, and the second says that he said *Allāh-u akbar* then raised his hands, and the third mentions that when he glorified God he would raise his hands. Our scholars mention various ways: 1) one raises one's hands before the glorification then starts to say *Allah-u akbar* as one begins to lower one's hands finishing the glorification as one's hands settle down; 2) one raises one's hands before the glorification, then one says *Allāh-u akbar* as one's hands are raised stationary, then one lowers them; 3) one starts to raise one's hands as one begins to glorify God and finishes both actions together; 4) one starts both actions together and finishes the glorification as one completes lowering one's hands; 5) and this is the most correct: one begins to raise one's hands as one starts the glorification, and nothing is particularly desirable as to how they are finished. Thus, if one finishes the glorification before completing the raising of one's hands, or had done the reverse, one completes what is left. When both are finished, one puts one's hands in position without continuing to raise them.

If a person has one or both hands cut off at his wrists, he should raise his arms, and if his hands are cut off at the elbows, he raises his upper arms, according to the more accurate view. Some scholars say that he need not raise them if he cannot do so without doing more than what is required. If he can only do it in part, he does what he can. Or, if it is possible, he may do what is more than required.

It is also desirable to turn one's palms towards the *qiblah* when one raises hands, and that they should not be covered, and to slightly separate one's fingers. If one delays raising one's hands until some of the glorification has been said, one raises one's hands during saying the rest. If one has completed the glorification, *Allāh-u akbar*, without beginning to raise one's hands, one does not raise one's hands after that. The glorification should not be mumbled so that it is not understood, and should not be excessively elongated. It should be said clearly and understandably. Should it be elongated a little or not? Two views are expressed, but the more correct is not. When one lowers one's hands, one places them under one's chest, above the navel. This is the view of al-Shāfiʿī and the majority, but Abū Ḥanīfah and some of al-Shāfiʿī's disciples say that the hands should be placed under the navel. The more correct view is that one lowers one's hands gently to a position below the chest, then places one's right hand above the left one. It is also said that one may lower the hands well down then raise them to a position below the chest, but God knows best.

Scholars said different things about the reason for raising one's hands. Al-Shāfiʿī said: it is a gesture to acknowledge that God is great and to confirm following His Messenger. Other scholars have said that it signifies submission and humiliation before God and a willingness to do as we are bid. It used to be the practice in battle that a soldier who was overpowered and wanted to give up the fight would raise his hand as a gesture of surrender. Others say that it is an indication of appreciating the seriousness of what one is embarking upon, or an indication of abandoning worldly affairs and standing in full submission before God to address Him. All this is included in the person saying: *Allāh-u akbar*. Thus, the action of raising one's hands confirms what one says of glorifying God. It is also said that raising one's hands indicates entry into prayer, but this applies only to the first glorification, which is also called *takbīrat al-iḥrām*. Other views are expressed, and they may be subject to discussion, but God knows best.

In hadith Nos 692 and 693, we read: 'When God's Messenger (peace be upon him) stood up for prayer, he raised his hands so as to be parallel with his shoulders, then he would glorify God, saying *Allāh-u akbar*'. This statement confirms the first glorification called *takbīrat al-iḥrām*. The Prophet said: 'Pray as you have seen me pray'. This hadith is related by al-Bukhārī on the authority of Mālik ibn al-Ḥuwayrith. He also told one of his companions, teaching him how to pray: 'When you stand up to pray, say *Allāh-u akbar*'. *Takbīrat al-iḥrām* is obligatory according to Mālik, al-Thawrī, al-Shāfiʿī, Abū Ḥanīfah, Ahmad and all scholars from the generation of the Prophet's companions, the Tābiʿīn and the following generations. The only exception is that reported by *Qāḍī* ʿIyāḍ and others stating that Ibn al-Musayyib, al-Ḥasan, al-Zuhrī, Qatādah, al-Ḥakam and al-Awzāʿī considered it a Sunnah, not obligatory. They considered that the intention is sufficient to start the prayer. I do not think that this could have been the view of such eminent scholars, considering all these authentic hadiths. There is also, in addition, the hadith narrated by ʿAlī, quoting God's Messenger: 'The key to prayer is ablution, and it is consecrated with the *takbīr* and ended with *salām*'. The word of the *takbīr* is *Allāh-u akbar*. These words are appropriate according to the unanimous view of all Muslims. Al-Shāfiʿī says that to say *Allāh-u al-akbar* is also appropriate, and that these two are the only valid ones. Mālik says only *Allah-u akbar* is appropriate. This is the one confirmed to have been used by the Prophet. This view is also reported to have been expressed by al-Shāfiʿī in his old teachings. Abū Yūsuf also approves saying *Allāh-u al-kabīr*, while Abū Ḥanīfah approves any phrase that extols God's greatness, such as *al-Raḥmān akbar* or *Allāh-u ajall* or *Allāh-u aʿẓam*, but the majority of scholars of early and later generations disagree with him. The purpose of starting the prayer with the *takbīr* is to begin it with extolling God's fine attributes and describing him with perfect qualities, but God knows best.

CHAPTER 10

CONFIRMATION OF GLORIFYING GOD AT EVERY MOVE IN PRAYER

[697–27]. (Dār al-Salām 0764) Yaḥyā ibn Yaḥyā narrated:[i] I read out to Mālik; from Ibn Shihāb; from Abū Salamah ibn ʿAbd al-Raḥmān; that Abū Hurayrah '**led the prayer, saying the *takbīr* glorification every time he went down or up. When he finished, he said: "By God, mine is the closest resemblance to the Prophet's prayer".**'

وَحَدَّثَنَا يَحْيَى بْنُ يَحْيَى، قَالَ: قَرَأْتُ عَلَى مَالِكٍ، عَنِ ابْنِ شِهَابٍ، عَنْ أَبِي سَلَمَةَ بْنِ عَبْدِ الرَّحْمَنِ، أَنَّ أَبَا هُرَيْرَةَ، «كَانَ يُصَلِّي لَهُمْ فَيُكَبِّرُ كُلَّمَا خَفَضَ، وَرَفَعَ» فَلَمَّا انْصَرَفَ قَالَ: «وَاللهِ إِنِّي لَأَشْبَهُكُمْ صَلَاةً بِرَسُولِ اللهِ صَلَّى اللهُ عَلَيْهِ وَسَلَّمَ»

[698–28]. (Dār al-Salām 0765) Muhammad ibn Rāfiʿ narrated:[ii] ʿAbd al-Razzāq narrated; Ibn Jurayj reported; Ibn Shihāb reported to me; from Abū Bakr ibn ʿAbd al-Raḥmān; that he heard Abū Hurayrah say: '**When God's Messenger (peace be upon him) stood up to pray, he said the *takbīr* glorification [i.e. *Allāh-u akbar*, meaning God is supreme] when he was standing; then said the glorification when he bowed. When he stood up from the bowing position he said *samiʿa Allāhu***

i. Related by al-Bukhārī, 785; al-Nasāʾī, 1154.
ii. Related by al-Bukhārī, 789; Abū Dāwūd, 738; al-Nasāʾī, 1149.

liman ḥamidah **[i.e. may God answer the one who praises Him]. In his standing position he said: *Rabbanā wa laka al-ḥamd* [i.e. Our Lord, all praise is due to You]. He then said *Allāh-u akbar* as he went down to prostration, then again when he raised his head, and when he prostrated himself the second time, and when he raised his head. He did this throughout the prayer until he finished. He also said *Allāh-u akbar* when he stood up after being seated following the first two *rak'ahs*'. Abū Hurayrah then said: 'By God, mine is the closest resemblance to the Prophet's prayer'.**

حَدَّثَنَا مُحَمَّدُ بْنُ رَافِعٍ، حَدَّثَنَا عَبْدُ الرَّزَّاقِ، أَخْبَرَنَا ابْنُ جُرَيْجٍ، أَخْبَرَنِي ابْنُ شِهَابٍ، عَنْ أَبِي بَكْرِ بْنِ عَبْدِ الرَّحْمَنِ، أَنَّهُ سَمِعَ أَبَا هُرَيْرَةَ، يَقُولُ: «كَانَ رَسُولُ اللهِ صَلَّى اللهُ عَلَيْهِ وَسَلَّمَ إِذَا قَامَ إِلَى الصَّلَاةِ يُكَبِّرُ حِينَ يَقُومُ، ثُمَّ يُكَبِّرُ حِينَ يَرْكَعُ» ثُمَّ يَقُولُ: «سَمِعَ اللهُ لِمَنْ حَمِدَهُ حِينَ يَرْفَعُ صُلْبَهُ مِنَ الرُّكُوعِ» ثُمَّ يَقُولُ: وَهُوَ قَائِمٌ «رَبَّنَا وَلَكَ الْحَمْدُ، ثُمَّ يُكَبِّرُ حِينَ يَهْوِي سَاجِدًا، ثُمَّ يُكَبِّرُ حِينَ يَرْفَعُ رَأْسَهُ، ثُمَّ يُكَبِّرُ حِينَ يَسْجُدُ، ثُمَّ يُكَبِّرُ حِينَ يَرْفَعُ رَأْسَهُ، ثُمَّ يَفْعَلُ مِثْلَ ذَلِكَ فِي الصَّلَاةِ كُلِّهَا حَتَّى يَقْضِيَهَا وَيُكَبِّرُ حِينَ يَقُومُ مِنَ الْمَثْنَى بَعْدَ الْجُلُوسِ» ثُمَّ يَقُولُ: أَبُو هُرَيْرَةَ «إِنِّي لَأَشْبَهُكُمْ صَلَاةً بِرَسُولِ اللهِ صَلَّى اللهُ عَلَيْهِ وَسَلَّمَ»

[699–29]. (Dār al-Salām 0766) Muhammad ibn Rāfi' narrated: Ḥujayn narrated; al-Layth narrated; from 'Uqayl; from Ibn Shihāb; Abū Bakr ibn 'Abd al-Raḥmān ibn al-Ḥārith reported to me; that he heard Abū Hurayrah say: **'When God's Messenger (peace be upon him) stood up to pray, he said the *takbīr* glorification [i.e. *Allāh-u akbar,* meaning God is supreme] when he was standing ... the same as Ibn Jurayj's narration'. He did not mention Abu Hurayrah's words: 'Mine is the closest resemblance to the Prophet's prayer'.**

حَدَّثَنِي مُحَمَّدُ بْنُ رَافِعٍ، حَدَّثَنَا حُجَيْنٌ، حَدَّثَنَا اللَّيْثُ، عَنْ عُقَيْلٍ، عَنِ ابْنِ شِهَابٍ، أَخْبَرَنِي أَبُو بَكْرِ بْنُ عَبْدِ الرَّحْمَنِ بْنِ الْحَارِثِ، أَنَّهُ سَمِعَ أَبَا هُرَيْرَةَ يَقُولُ: كَانَ رَسُولُ اللهِ صَلَّى اللهُ عَلَيْهِ وَسَلَّمَ إِذَا قَامَ إِلَى الصَّلَاةِ يُكَبِّرُ حِينَ يَقُومُ بِمِثْلِ حَدِيثِ ابْنِ جُرَيْجٍ وَلَمْ يَذْكُرْ قَوْلَ أَبِي هُرَيْرَةَ «إِنِّي أَشْبَهُكُمْ صَلَاةً بِرَسُولِ اللهِ صَلَّى اللهُ عَلَيْهِ وَسَلَّمَ»

[700–30]. (Dār al-Salām 0767) Ḥarmalah ibn Yaḥyā narrated to me:[i] Ibn Wahb reported; Yūnus reported to me; from Ibn Shihāb; Abū Salamah ibn ʿAbd al-Raḥmān reported to me; that when Marwān appointed Abū Hurayrah as his deputy as Governor of Madinah, Abū Hurayrah [would lead the prayer]. **'When Abū Hurayrah stood up to offer the obligatory prayer, he said the *takbīr* glorification, *Allāh-u akbar* … .' He added what is similar to Ibn Jurayj's narration. In his narration also: 'When he finished the prayer and said the *salām*, he would turn to the people in the mosque and say: "By Him who holds my soul in His hand, mine is the closest resemblance to the Prophet's prayer".'**

وَحَدَّثَنِي حَرْمَلَةُ بْنُ يَحْيَى، أَخْبَرَنَا ابْنُ وَهْبٍ، أَخْبَرَنِي يُونُسُ، عَنِ ابْنِ شِهَابٍ، أَخْبَرَنِي أَبُو سَلَمَةَ بْنُ عَبْدِ الرَّحْمَنِ، أَنَّ أَبَا هُرَيْرَةَ كَانَ حِينَ يَسْتَخْلِفُهُ مَرْوَانُ عَلَى الْمَدِينَةِ إِذَا قَامَ لِلصَّلَاةِ الْمَكْتُوبَةِ كَبَّرَ فَذَكَرَ نَحْوَ حَدِيثِ ابْنِ جُرَيْجٍ وَفِي حَدِيثِهِ فَإِذَا قَضَاهَا وَسَلَّمَ أَقْبَلَ عَلَى أَهْلِ الْمَسْجِدِ قَالَ: وَالَّذِي نَفْسِي بِيَدِهِ إِنِّي لَأَشْبَهُكُمْ صَلَاةً بِرَسُولِ اللهِ صَلَّى اللهُ عَلَيْهِ وَسَلَّمَ

[701–31]. (Dār al-Salām 0768) Muhammad ibn Mihrān al-Rāzī narrated: al-Walīd ibn Muslim narrated; al-Awzāʿī narrated; from Yaḥyā ibn Abī Kathīr; from Abū Salamah: '**Abū Hurayrah**

i. Related by al-Nasāʾī, 1022.

used to say *Allāh-u akbar* whenever he went down or up in prayer. We asked him: "Abū Hurayrah, what is all this *takbīr* about?" He said: "Such was the way God's Messenger (peace be upon him) prayed".'

حَدَّثَنَا مُحَمَّدُ بْنُ مِهْرَانَ الرَّازِيُّ، حَدَّثَنَا الْوَلِيدُ بْنُ مُسْلِمٍ، حَدَّثَنَا الْأَوْزَاعِيُّ، عَنْ يَحْيَى بْنِ أَبِي كَثِيرٍ، عَنْ أَبِي سَلَمَةَ، أَنَّ أَبَا هُرَيْرَةَ، «كَانَ يُكَبِّرُ فِي الصَّلَاةِ كُلَّمَا رَفَعَ وَوَضَعَ»، فَقُلْنَا يَا أَبَا هُرَيْرَةَ مَا هَذَا التَّكْبِيرُ؟ قَالَ: «إِنَّهَا لَصَلَاةُ رَسُولِ اللهِ صَلَّى اللهُ عَلَيْهِ وَسَلَّمَ»

[702–32]. (Dār al-Salām 0769) Qutaybah ibn Saʿīd narrated: Yaʿqūb (meaning ibn ʿAbd al-Raḥmān) narrated; from Suhayl; from his father; from Abū Hurayrah; that '**He used to say *Allāh-u akbar* every time he went down or raised himself. He would say that the Prophet (peace be upon him) used to do that**'.

حَدَّثَنَا قُتَيْبَةُ بْنُ سَعِيدٍ، حَدَّثَنَا يَعْقُوبُ يَعْنِي ابْنَ عَبْدِ الرَّحْمَنِ، عَنْ سُهَيْلٍ، عَنْ أَبِيهِ، عَنْ أَبِي هُرَيْرَةَ: «أَنَّهُ كَانَ يُكَبِّرُ كُلَّمَا خفض ورفع»، وَيُحَدِّثُ «أَنَّ رَسُولَ اللهِ صَلَّى اللهُ عَلَيْهِ وَسَلَّمَ كَانَ يَفْعَلُ ذَلِكَ»

[703–33]. (Dār al-Salām 0770) Yaḥyā ibn Yaḥyā and Khalaf ibn Hishām narrated:[i] both from Ḥammād. Yaḥya said: Ḥammād ibn Zayd reported from Ghaylān; from Muṭarrif who said: '**ʿImrān ibn Ḥuṣayn and I prayed behind ʿAlī ibn Abī Ṭālib. Whenever he prostrated himself he said *Allāh-u akbar*, and when he raised his head he said *Allāh-u akbar*, and when he stood up after the second *rakʿah* he said *Allāh-u akbar*. When we finished, ʿImrān took me by the hand and said: "This one**

i. Related by al-Bukhārī, 786 and 826; Abū Dāwūd, 835; al-Nasā'ī, 1081 and 1179 (in a shorter version).

has led the prayer in the same way as Muhammad (peace be upon him) did", or "This one has reminded me of the way Muhammad (peace be upon him) prayed".'

حَدَّثَنَا يَحْيَى بْنُ يَحْيَى، وَخَلَفُ بْنُ هِشَامٍ، جَمِيعًا عَنْ حَمَّادٍ، قَالَ يَحْيَى: أَخْبَرَنَا حَمَّادُ بْنُ زَيْدٍ، عَنْ غَيْلَانَ، عَنْ مُطَرِّفٍ، قَالَ: صَلَّيْتُ أَنَا وَعِمْرَانُ بْنُ حُصَيْنٍ، خَلْفَ عَلِيِّ بْنِ أَبِي طَالِبٍ، فَكَانَ «إِذَا سَجَدَ كَبَّرَ، وَإِذَا رَفَعَ رَأْسَهُ كَبَّرَ، وَإِذَا نَهَضَ مِنَ الرَّكْعَتَيْنِ كَبَّرَ»، فَلَمَّا انْصَرَفْنَا مِنَ الصَّلَاةِ، قَالَ: أَخَذَ عِمْرَانُ بِيَدِي. ثُمَّ قَالَ: «لَقَدْ صَلَّى بِنَا هَذَا صَلَاةَ مُحَمَّدٍ صَلَّى اللهُ عَلَيْهِ وَسَلَّمَ» - أَوْ قَالَ: «قَدْ ذَكَّرَنِي هَذَا صَلَاةَ مُحَمَّدٍ صَلَّى اللهُ عَلَيْهِ وَسَلَّمَ»

Text Explanation

The hadiths in this chapter confirm that saying the *takbīr* glorification, in the form *Allāh-u akbar,* which means 'God is supreme', is said in prayer every time the worshipper bows or goes down or raises himself, except when rising from the bowing position when he says *samiʿa Allāhu liman ḥamidah,* which means 'may God answer the one who praises Him'. This is unanimously agreed upon today and in past generations, but some disagreement took place during Abū Hurayrah's own time. Some people considered that this glorification was to be said only at the beginning of the prayer, while others added some of what Abū Hurayrah mentioned in this hadith. Both groups did not learn what the Prophet did. Hence, Abū Hurayrah used to assert that his action was in the manner that the Prophet prayed. Eventually, matters settled and prayer was standardized in the manner Abū Hurayrah explained.

Thus, a prayer that consists of two *rakʿahs* only includes eleven *takbīr* glorifications, or *Allah-u akbar,* which are: the one to start the prayer, i.e. *takbīrat al-iḥrām,* and five in each *rakʿah.* A three-*rakʿah* prayer includes seventeen *Allāh-u akbar*, i.e. *takbīrat al-iḥrām* and the one when the worshipper rises for his third *rakʿah,* and five in each of the three *rakʿahs.* A four-*rakʿah* prayer includes twenty-two *takbīr* glorifications. This means that in the five obligatory prayers alone, a Muslim says *Allāh-u akbar* ninety-four times.

It should be clear that the first glorification, i.e. *takbīrat al-iḥrām*, which starts the prayer is obligatory, while all the rest are Sunnah or recommended. This means that if these are left out, the prayer is valid but one misses out on their reward and on following the Sunnah. This is the view of all scholars, except for one of the two versions reported from Imam Ahmad ibn Ḥanbal, which suggests that all these glorifications are obligatory.

The evidence in support of the majority view is that when the Prophet taught the bedouin how to pray, he taught him all its obligatory parts. He mentioned *takbīrat al-iḥrām*, but did not mention the rest. This was a time when clarification was needed and could not be delayed.

In hadith No. 698, 'He then said *Allāh-u akbar* as he went down to prostrate, then again when he raised his head ... and when he stood up after the first two *rakʿahs*. This is clear evidence that the glorification is coupled with these movements and runs through them. Thus, one starts to say the glorification as one starts to bow and extends the glorification so that it finishes when one is in full bowing. One then says the glorifications recommended for that position. Likewise, when one goes down from the standing to the prostration position, one starts saying *Allāh-u akbar* as one begins the move and extends it so that it finishes when one puts one's forehead on the floor. One then says the glorifications recommended for the prostration position. Similarly, when one rises from the bowing, i.e. *rukūʿ*, position, one begins saying *samiʿa Allāhu liman ḥamidah* and extends it so as to finish as one's body is erect. One then says *Rabbanā wa laka al-ḥamd*, meaning: 'All praise is due to You, our Lord'.

The worshipper should also start to say *Allāh-u akbar* as he begins to rise after the first *tashahhud* in order to perform the third *rakʿah*. He should extend it so as it takes the time of the whole movement. This is the view of our school and all scholars, except what is reported from ʿUmar ibn ʿAbd al-ʿAzīz and endorsed by Mālik, which is to say this when one is in the standing position. The view of the majority is evidenced by the apparent meaning of this hadith.

This hadith also provides evidence in support of the view of the Shāfiʿī school and other scholars that it is desirable that everyone who is offering a prayer, whether an imam or one in the congregation or praying alone, should say both *samiʿa Allāhu liman ḥamidah* and *Rabbanā wa laka al-ḥamd*. One says the first phrase as one rises from the bowing position and says the second when one is in the standing position. It is confirmed that the Prophet said both, and he ordered us: 'Pray as you have seen me pray'. We shall speak about this point in detail, explaining its words and their meanings when Muslim mentions it, God willing.

In the last hadith in this chapter, ʿImrān ibn Ḥuṣayn says: 'This one has reminded me of the way Muhammad (peace be upon him) prayed'. This refers to the fact that at one stage, the use of the *takbīr* glorification was left out when moving from one position to another in prayer, but God knows best.

CHAPTER 11

RECITING THE *FĀTIḤAH* IN EVERY *RAKʿAH*

[704–34]. (Dār al-Salām 0771) Abū Bakr ibn Abī Shaybah, ʿAmr al-Nāqid and Isḥāq ibn Ibrāhīm narrated:[i] all from Sufyān; Abū Bakr said: Sufyān ibn ʿUyaynah narrated; from al-Zuhrī; from Maḥmūd ibn al-Rabīʿ; from ʿUbādah ibn al-Ṣāmit; attributing it to the Prophet (peace be upon him): **'No prayer is valid if one does not recite the Opening Surah of the Book'**.

حَدَّثَنَا أَبُو بَكْرِ بْنُ أَبِي شَيْبَةَ، وَعَمْرٌو النَّاقِدُ، وَإِسْحَاقُ بْنُ إِبْرَاهِيمَ، جَمِيعًا عَنْ سُفْيَانَ، قَالَ أَبُو بَكْرٍ: حَدَّثَنَا سُفْيَانُ بْنُ عُيَيْنَةَ، عَنِ الزُّهْرِيِّ، عَنْ مَحْمُودِ بْنِ الرَّبِيعِ، عَنْ عُبَادَةَ بْنِ الصَّامِتِ، يَبْلُغُ بِهِ النَّبِيَّ صَلَّى اللهُ عَلَيْهِ وَسَلَّمَ «لَا صَلَاةَ لِمَنْ لَمْ يَقْرَأْ بِفَاتِحَةِ الْكِتَابِ»

[705–35]. (Dār al-Salām 0772) Abū al-Ṭāhir narrated to me: Ibn Wahb narrated; from Yūnus [H]. Also, Ḥarmalah ibn Yaḥyā narrated to me; Ibn Wahb reported; Yūnus reported to me; from Ibn Shihāb; Maḥmūd ibn al-Rabīʿ reported to me; from ʿUbādah ibn al-Ṣāmit: **'God's Messenger (peace be upon him) said: "No prayer is valid if one does not recite the Mother of the Qur'an"**.'

i. Related by al-Bukhārī, 756; Abū Dāwūd, 822; al-Tirmidhī, 247; al-Nasāʾī, 910; Ibn Mājah, 837.

حَدَّثَنِي أَبُو الطَّاهِرِ، حَدَّثَنَا ابْنُ وَهْبٍ، عَنْ يُونُسَ، ح وَحَدَّثَنِي حَرْمَلَةُ بْنُ يَحْيَى، أَخْبَرَنَا ابْنُ وَهْبٍ، أَخْبَرَنِي يُونُسُ، عَنِ ابْنِ شِهَابٍ، أَخْبَرَنِي مَحْمُودُ بْنُ الرَّبِيعِ، عَنْ عُبَادَةَ بْنِ الصَّامِتِ، قَالَ: قَالَ رَسُولُ اللهِ صَلَّى اللهُ عَلَيْهِ وَسَلَّمَ: «لَا صَلَاةَ لِمَنْ لَمْ يَقْتَرِئْ بِأُمِّ الْقُرْآنِ»

[706–36]. (Dār al-Salām 0773) Al-Ḥasan ibn ʿAlī al-Ḥulwānī narrated: Yaʿqūb ibn Ibrāhīm ibn Saʿd narrated; my father narrated; from Ṣāliḥ; from Ibn Shihāb; that Maḥmūd ibn al-Rabīʿ, in whose face the Prophet spat some water from their well, reported to him; that ʿUbādah ibn al-Ṣāmit reported to him; that God's Messenger (peace be upon him) said: **'No prayer is valid if one does not recite the Mother of the Qur'an'**.

حَدَّثَنَا الْحَسَنُ بْنُ عَلِيٍّ الْحُلْوَانِيُّ، حَدَّثَنَا يَعْقُوبُ بْنُ إِبْرَاهِيمَ بْنِ سَعْدٍ، حَدَّثَنَا أَبِي، عَنْ صَالِحٍ، عَنِ ابْنِ شِهَابٍ، أَنَّ مَحْمُودَ بْنَ الرَّبِيعِ، الَّذِي مَجَّ رَسُولُ اللهِ صَلَّى اللهُ عَلَيْهِ وَسَلَّمَ فِي وَجْهِهِ مِنْ بِئْرِهِمْ، أَخْبَرَهُ، أَنَّ عُبَادَةَ بْنَ الصَّامِتِ، أَخْبَرَهُ أَنَّ رَسُولَ اللهِ صَلَّى اللهُ عَلَيْهِ وَسَلَّمَ قَالَ: «لَا صَلَاةَ لِمَنْ لَمْ يَقْرَأْ بِأُمِّ الْقُرْآنِ»

[707–37]. (Dār al-Salām 0774) Isḥāq ibn Ibrāhīm and ʿAbd ibn Ḥumayd narrated it to me: they said: ʿAbd al-Razzāq reported; Maʿmar reported; from al-Zuhrī; with this chain of transmission: **the same text, and he added: 'and something more'**.

وَحَدَّثَنَاهُ إِسْحَاقُ بْنُ إِبْرَاهِيمَ، وَعَبْدُ بْنُ حُمَيْدٍ، قَالَا: أَخْبَرَنَا عَبْدُ الرَّزَّاقِ، أَخْبَرَنَا مَعْمَرٌ، عَنِ الزُّهْرِيِّ، بِهَذَا الْإِسْنَادِ مِثْلَهُ وَزَادَ: فَصَاعِدًا.

[708–38]. (Dār al-Salām 0775) Isḥāq ibn Ibrāhīm al-Ḥanẓalī narrated it: Sufyān ibn ʿUyaynah reported; from al-ʿAlā'; from his father; from Abū Hurayrah; from the Prophet (peace be upon him). He said: **'If anyone offers a prayer without reciting the Mother of the Qur'an, it falls short'. He repeated it three times, 'not perfect'. It was said to Abū Hurayrah: 'We are praying behind the imam'. He said: 'Recite it in silence. I heard God's Messenger (peace be upon him) say: "God, the Exalted, said: I have divided prayer in two halves between Myself and My servant. My servant shall have what he requests. When God's servant says: 'All praise be to God, the Lord of all the worlds', God will say: 'My servant has praised Me'. When he says: 'the Lord of Grace, the Ever-Merciful', God will say: 'My servant has extolled Me'. When he says: 'Master of the Day of Judgement', God will say: 'My servant has glorified Me'. (In one narration: My servant has submitted himself to Me.) When he says: 'You alone do we worship and to You alone do we turn for help', God will say: 'This is between Myself and My servant. My servant shall have what he requests'. When he says: 'Guide us on the straight path, the path of those on whom You have bestowed Your favours, not those who have incurred Your wrath, nor those who have gone astray', God will say: 'This is granted to My servant, and My servant shall have what he requests'".'**

Sufyān said: 'Al-ʿAlā' ibn ʿAbd al-Raḥmān ibn Yaʿqūb narrated it to me. I visited him when he was ill at home and I asked him about it'.

وَحَدَّثَنَاهُ إِسْحَاقُ بْنُ إِبْرَاهِيمَ الْحَنْظَلِيُّ، أَخْبَرَنَا سُفْيَانُ بْنُ عُيَيْنَةَ، عَنِ الْعَلَاءِ، عَنْ أَبِيهِ، عَنْ أَبِي هُرَيْرَةَ، عَنِ النَّبِيِّ صَلَّى اللهُ عَلَيْهِ وَسَلَّمَ قَالَ: «مَنْ صَلَّى صَلَاةً لَمْ يَقْرَأْ فِيهَا بِأُمِّ الْقُرْآنِ فَهِيَ خِدَاجٌ» ثَلَاثًا غَيْرُ تَمَامٍ. فَقِيلَ لِأَبِي هُرَيْرَةَ: إِنَّا نَكُونُ وَرَاءَ الْإِمَامِ؟ فَقَالَ: «اقْرَأْ بِهَا فِي نَفْسِكَ»؛ فَإِنِّي سَمِعْتُ رَسُولَ اللهِ صَلَّى اللهُ عَلَيْهِ وَسَلَّمَ يَقُولُ: « قَالَ اللهُ تَعَالَى: قَسَمْتُ الصَّلَاةَ بَيْنِي وَبَيْنَ عَبْدِي نِصْفَيْنِ، وَلِعَبْدِي مَا سَأَلَ، فَإِذَا قَالَ الْعَبْدُ: «الْحَمْدُ للهِ رَبِّ الْعَالَمِينَ»، قَالَ اللهُ تَعَالَى: حَمِدَنِي عَبْدِي، وَإِذَا قَالَ: «الرَّحْمَنِ الرَّحِيمِ»،

قَالَ اللهُ تَعَالَى: أَثْنَى عَلَيَّ عَبْدِي، وَإِذَا قَالَ: «مَالِكِ يَوْمِ الدِّينِ»، قَالَ: مَجَّدَنِي عَبْدِي - وَقَالَ مَرَّةً فَوَّضَ إِلَيَّ عَبْدِي - فَإِذَا قَالَ: «إِيَّاكَ نَعْبُدُ وَإِيَّاكَ نَسْتَعِينُ» قَالَ: هَذَا بَيْنِي وَبَيْنَ عَبْدِي، وَلِعَبْدِي مَا سَأَلَ، فَإِذَا قَالَ: «اهْدِنَا الصِّرَاطَ الْـمُسْتَقِيمَ صِرَاطَ الَّذِينَ أَنْعَمْتَ عَلَيْهِمْ غَيْرِ الْـمَغْضُوبِ عَلَيْهِمْ وَلَا الضَّالِّينَ» قَالَ: هَذَا لِعَبْدِي وَلِعَبْدِي مَا سَأَلَ»

قَالَ: سُفْيَانُ، حَدَّثَنِي بِهِ الْعَلَاءُ بْنُ عَبْدِ الرَّحْمَنِ بْنِ يَعْقُوبَ، دَخَلْتُ عَلَيْهِ وَهُوَ مَرِيضٌ فِي بَيْتِهِ. فَسَأَلْتُهُ أَنَا عَنْهُ.

[000–39]. (Dār al-Salām 0) Qutaybah ibn Sa'īd narrated:[i] from Mālik ibn Anas; from al-'Alā' ibn 'Abd al-Raḥmān; that he heard Abū al-Sā'ib, Hishām ibn Zuhrah's *mawlā*, say: I heard Abū Hurayrah say: God's Messenger (peace be upon him) said: **[the same text]**.

حَدَّثَنَا قُتَيْبَةُ بْنُ سَعِيدٍ، عَنْ مَالِكِ بْنِ أَنَسٍ، عَنِ الْعَلَاءِ بْنِ عَبْدِ الرَّحْمَنِ، أَنَّهُ سَمِعَ أَبَا السَّائِبِ، مَوْلَى هِشَامِ بْنِ زُهْرَةَ، يَقُولُ: سَمِعْتُ أَبَا هُرَيْرَةَ، يَقُولُ: قَالَ رَسُولُ اللهِ صَلَّى اللهُ عَلَيْهِ وَسَلَّمَ.

[709–40]. (Dār al-Salām 0776) Muhammad ibn Rāfi' narrated to me: 'Abd al-Razzāq narrated; Ibn Jurayj reported; al-'Alā' ibn 'Abd al-Raḥmān ibn Ya'qūb reported to me; that Abū al-Sā'ib, Hishām ibn Zuhrah's family's *mawlā* reported to him; that he heard Abū Hurayrah say: God's Messenger (peace be upon him) said: **'Whoever offers a prayer and does not recite in it the Mother of the Qur'an', the same as Sufyān's narration. In their narration: 'God, the Exalted, says: I have divided prayer between Me and My servant in two halves: one half of it is Mine and one half belongs to My servant'**.

i. Related by Abū Dāwūd, 821; al-Tirmidhī, 2953; al-Nasā'ī, 908; Ibn Mājah, 838.

وَحَدَّثَنِي مُحَمَّدُ بْنُ رَافِعٍ، حَدَّثَنَا عَبْدُ الرَّزَّاقِ، أَخْبَرَنَا ابْنُ جُرَيْجٍ، أَخْبَرَنِي العَلَاءُ بْنُ عَبْدِ الرَّحْمَنِ بْنِ يَعْقُوبَ، أَنَّ أَبَا السَّائِبِ، مَوْلَى بَنِي عَبْدِ اللهِ بْنِ هِشَامِ بْنِ زُهْرَةَ، أَخْبَرَهُ أَنَّهُ سَمِعَ أَبَا هُرَيْرَةَ، يَقُولُ: قَالَ رَسُولُ اللهِ صَلَّى اللهُ عَلَيْهِ وَسَلَّمَ: «مَنْ صَلَّى صَلَاةً فَلَمْ يَقْرَأْ فِيهَا بِأُمِّ الْقُرْآنِ» بِمِثْلِ حَدِيثِ سُفْيَانَ وَفِي حَدِيثِهِمَا قَالَ اللهُ تَعَالَى: «قَسَمْتُ الصَّلَاةَ بَيْنِي وَبَيْنَ عَبْدِي نِصْفَيْنِ فَنِصْفُهَا لِي وَنِصْفُهَا لِعَبْدِي»

[710–41]. (Dār al-Salām 0777) Ahmad ibn Jaʿfar al-Maʿqirī narrated to me: al-Naḍr ibn Muhammad narrated; Abū Uways narrated; al-ʿAlā' reported to me: I heard from my father and from Abū al-Sā'ib—and both used to attend Abū Hurayrah. They said: Abū Hurayrah said: God's Messenger (peace be upon him) said: **'Whoever offers a prayer and does not recite the Opening of the Qur'an in it, it falls short'. He repeated it three times. The same as their narration**.

حَدَّثَنِي أَحْمَدُ بْنُ جَعْفَرٍ الْـمَعْقِرِيُّ، حَدَّثَنَا النَّضْرُ بْنُ مُحَمَّدٍ، حَدَّثَنَا أَبُو أُوَيْسٍ، أَخْبَرَنِي الْعَلَاءُ، قَالَ: سَمِعْتُ مِنْ أَبِي، وَمِنْ أَبِي السَّائِبِ - وَكَانَا جَلِيسَيْ أَبِي هُرَيْرَةَ - قَالَا: قَالَ أَبُو هُرَيْرَةَ: قَالَ رَسُولُ اللهِ صَلَّى اللهُ عَلَيْهِ وَسَلَّمَ: «مَنْ صَلَّى صَلَاةً لَمْ يَقْرَأْ فِيهَا بِفَاتِحَةِ الْكِتَابِ، فَهِيَ خِدَاجٌ» يَقُولُهَا ثَلَاثًا بِمِثْلِ حَدِيثِهِمْ.

[711–42]. (Dār al-Salām 0778) Muhammad ibn ʿAbdullāh ibn Numayr narrated: Abū Usāmah narrated; from Ḥabīb ibn al-Shahīd: I heard ʿAṭā' narrating from Abū Hurayrah that God's Messenger (peace be upon him) said: **'No prayer is valid without recitation'. Abū Hurayrah added: 'What God's Messenger (peace be upon him) said aloud, we say aloud to you, and what he did not, we do not'**.

حَدَّثَنَا مُحَمَّدُ بْنُ عَبْدِ اللهِ بْنِ نُمَيْرٍ، حَدَّثَنَا أَبُو أُسَامَةَ، عَنْ حَبِيبِ بْنِ الشَّهِيدِ، قَالَ: سَمِعْتُ عَطَاءً، يُحَدِّثُ عَنْ أَبِي هُرَيْرَةَ، أَنَّ رَسُولَ اللهِ صَلَّى اللهُ عَلَيْهِ وَسَلَّمَ قَالَ: «لَا صَلَاةَ إِلَّا بِقِرَاءَةٍ» قَالَ أَبُو هُرَيْرَةَ: «فَمَا أَعْلَنَ رَسُولُ اللهِ صَلَّى اللهُ عَلَيْهِ وَسَلَّمَ أَعْلَنَّاهُ لَكُمْ، وَمَا أَخْفَاهُ أَخْفَيْنَاهُ لَكُمْ»

[712–43]. (Dār al-Salām 0779) ʿAmr al-Nāqid and Zuhayr ibn Ḥarb narrated (ʿAmr's text);[i] they said: Ismāʿīl ibn Ibrāhīm narrated; Ibn Jurayj reported; from ʿAṭā'; Abū Hurayrah said: **'He recited throughout the prayer. What God's Messenger (peace be upon him) recited aloud, we recite aloud to you, and what he recited silently, we do likewise'. A man said to him: 'If I do not read more than the Mother of the Qur'an?' He said: 'If you add more, it is better; and if you confine yourself to it, it is sufficient for you'.**

حَدَّثَنَا عَمْرٌو النَّاقِدُ، وَزُهَيْرُ بْنُ حَرْبٍ، - وَاللَّفْظُ لِعَمْرٍو -، قَالَا: حَدَّثَنَا إِسْمَاعِيلُ بْنُ إِبْرَاهِيمَ، أَخْبَرَنَا ابْنُ جُرَيْجٍ، عَنْ عَطَاءٍ، قَالَ: قَالَ أَبُو هُرَيْرَةَ: «فِي كُلِّ الصَّلَاةِ يَقْرَأُ، فَمَا أَسْمَعَنَا رَسُولُ اللهِ صَلَّى اللهُ عَلَيْهِ وَسَلَّمَ، أَسْمَعْنَاكُمْ، وَمَا أَخْفَى مِنَّا، أَخْفَيْنَا مِنْكُمْ» فَقَالَ لَهُ رَجُلٌ: إِنْ لَمْ أَزِدْ عَلَى أُمِّ الْقُرْآنِ؟ فَقَالَ: «إِنْ زِدْتَ عَلَيْهَا فَهُوَ خَيْرٌ، وَإِنِ انْتَهَيْتَ إِلَيْهَا أَجْزَأَتْ عَنْكَ»

[713–44]. (Dār al-Salām 0780) Yaḥyā ibn Yaḥyā narrated: Yazīd (meaning Ibn Zurayʿ) reported; from Ḥabīb al-Muʿallim; from ʿAṭā': Abū Hurayrah said: **'A recitation is due in every prayer. What the Prophet (peace be upon him) recited aloud, we recite aloud to you, and what he recited silently, we do the same. He who reads the Mother of the Book only, it is sufficient for him, and whoever adds more does better'.**

---

i. Related by al-Bukhārī, 772 (in a longer version); al-Nasā'ī, 969.

حَدَّثَنَا يَحْيَى بْنُ يَحْيَى، أَخْبَرَنَا يَزِيدُ يَعْنِي ابْنَ زُرَيْعٍ، عَنْ حَبِيبٍ الْمُعَلِّمِ، عَنْ عَطَاءٍ، قَالَ: قَالَ أَبُو هُرَيْرَةَ: «فِي كُلِّ صَلَاةٍ قِرَاءَةٌ فَمَا أَسْمَعَنَا النَّبِيُّ صَلَّى اللهُ عَلَيْهِ وَسَلَّمَ، أَسْمَعْنَاكُمْ، وَمَا أَخْفَى مِنَّا، أَخْفَيْنَاهُ مِنْكُمْ، وَمَنْ قَرَأَ بِأُمِّ الْكِتَابِ فَقَدْ أَجْزَأَتْ عَنْهُ، وَمَنْ زَادَ فَهُوَ أَفْضَلُ»

[714–45]. (Dār al-Salām 0781) Muhammad ibn al-Muthannā narrated to me:[i] Yaḥyā ibn Saʿīd narrated; from ʿUbaydullāh; Saʿīd ibn Abī Saʿīd narrated to me; from his father; from Abū Hurayrah: **'God's Messenger (peace be upon him) entered the mosque. A man came in and offered a prayer, then came forward and greeted God's Messenger (peace be upon him). The Prophet replied with a greeting then said: "Go back and pray, for you have not prayed". The man went back and prayed in the same way as he prayed earlier. He then returned to the Prophet and greeted him. The Prophet said: "And peace be to you". He then said: "Go back and pray, for you have not prayed". He did this three times. The man said: "By Him who sent you with the message of the truth, I know nothing better than this. Teach me". The Prophet said: "When you stand up to pray, say *Allāh-u akbar*, then recite of the Qur'an what comes easy to you. Then bow until you are well positioned in bowing, then raise yourself until you stand up well. Then you prostrate yourself until you are well positioned in prostration, then raise yourself until you are well positioned seated. Do this throughout your prayer".'**

حَدَّثَنِي مُحَمَّدُ بْنُ الْمُثَنَّى، حَدَّثَنَا يَحْيَى بْنُ سَعِيدٍ، عَنْ عُبَيْدِ اللهِ، قَالَ: حَدَّثَنِي سَعِيدُ بْنُ أَبِي سَعِيدٍ، عَنْ أَبِيهِ، عَنْ أَبِي هُرَيْرَةَ: أَنَّ رَسُولَ اللهِ صَلَّى اللهُ عَلَيْهِ وَسَلَّمَ دَخَلَ

i. Related by al-Bukhārī, 757, 793 and 6252; Abū Dāwūd, 856; al-Tirmidhī, 303; al-Nasā'ī, 883.

الْـمَسْجِدَ فَدَخَلَ رَجُلٌ فَصَلَّى، ثُمَّ جَاءَ فَسَلَّمَ عَلَى رَسُولِ اللهِ صَلَّى اللهُ عَلَيْهِ وَسَلَّمَ، فَرَدَّ رَسُولُ اللهِ صَلَّى اللهُ عَلَيْهِ وَسَلَّمَ السَّلَامَ قَالَ: «ارْجِعْ فَصَلِّ فَإِنَّكَ لَمْ تُصَلِّ» فَرَجَعَ الرَّجُلُ فَصَلَّى كَمَا كَانَ صَلَّى، ثُمَّ جَاءَ إِلَى النَّبِيِّ صَلَّى اللهُ عَلَيْهِ وَسَلَّمَ فَسَلَّمَ عَلَيْهِ فَقَالَ رَسُولُ اللهِ صَلَّى اللهُ عَلَيْهِ وَسَلَّمَ: «وَعَلَيْكَ السَّلَامُ» ثُمَّ قَالَ: «ارْجِعْ فَصَلِّ فَإِنَّكَ لَمْ تُصَلِّ» حَتَّى فَعَلَ ذَلِكَ ثَلَاثَ مَرَّاتٍ. فَقَالَ الرَّجُلُ: وَالَّذِي بَعَثَكَ بِالْحَقِّ مَا أُحْسِنُ غَيْرَ هَذَا عَلِّمْنِي، قَالَ: «إِذَا قُمْتَ إِلَى الصَّلَاةِ فَكَبِّرْ، ثُمَّ اقْرَأْ مَا تَيَسَّرَ مَعَكَ مِنَ الْقُرْآنِ، ثُمَّ ارْكَعْ حَتَّى تَطْمَئِنَّ رَاكِعًا، ثُمَّ ارْفَعْ حَتَّى تَعْدِلَ قَائِمًا، ثُمَّ اسْجُدْ حَتَّى تَطْمَئِنَّ سَاجِدًا، ثُمَّ ارْفَعْ حَتَّى تَطْمَئِنَّ جَالِسًا، ثُمَّ افْعَلْ ذَلِكَ فِي صَلَاتِكَ كُلِّهَا»

[715–46]. (Dār al-Salām 0782) Abū Bakr ibn Abī Shaybah narrated:[i] Abū Usāmah and ʿAbdullāh ibn Numayr narrated [H]. Also, Ibn Numayr narrated; my father narrated; both said: ʿUbaydullāh narrated; from Saʿīd ibn Abī Saʿīd; from Abū Hurayrah; that '**A man came into the mosque and offered a prayer. The Prophet was close by. They narrated the hadith with a similar story, but added in it: "When you stand up to pray, do the ablution well, then face the *qiblah* and glorify God".**'

حَدَّثَنَا أَبُو بَكْرِ بْنُ أَبِي شَيْبَةَ، حَدَّثَنَا أَبُو أُسَامَةَ، وَعَبْدُ اللهِ بْنُ نُمَيْرٍ، ح وَحَدَّثَنَا ابْنُ نُمَيْرٍ، حَدَّثَنَا أَبِي، قَالَا: حَدَّثَنَا عُبَيْدُ اللهِ، عَنْ سَعِيدِ بْنِ أَبِي سَعِيدٍ، عَنْ أَبِي هُرَيْرَةَ، أَنَّ رَجُلًا دَخَلَ الْـمَسْجِدَ فَصَلَّى وَرَسُولُ اللهِ صَلَّى اللهُ عَلَيْهِ وَسَلَّمَ فِي نَاحِيَةٍ، وَسَاقَا الْحَدِيثَ بِمِثْلِ هَذِهِ الْقِصَّةِ وَزَادَا فِيهِ «إِذَا قُمْتَ إِلَى الصَّلَاةِ فَأَسْبِغِ الْوُضُوءَ، ثُمَّ اسْتَقْبِلِ الْقِبْلَةَ فَكَبِّرْ»

i. Related by al-Bukhārī, 6251 and 6667 (in a longer version); Abū Dāwūd, 865; al-Tirmidhī, 2692; Ibn Mājah, 1060.

Text Explanation

The Prophet describes a prayer without reciting the opening surah, *al-Fātiḥah,* as falling short. He borrows a word that is used about camels giving birth before they are due, and the newborn is not well developed. The Prophet refers to the first surah of the Qur'an, *al-Fātiḥah,* as Mother of the Qur'an, because it is at its beginning. Indeed, *al-Fātiḥah* means 'the Opening' or 'the starter'. Makkah is called Umm al-Qurā, or Mother of Cities, because it is the leading settlement.

The hadiths in this chapter make clear that reciting the opening surah, *al-Fātiḥah,* in prayer is obligatory, and that it is particularly required and cannot be replaced by any other, except by one who is unable to recite it. This is the view of Mālik, al-Shāfiʿī and the majority of scholars among the Prophet's companions, the Tābiʿīn and subsequent generations. Abū Ḥanīfah and a small number of scholars said that reciting *al-Fātiḥah* is not obligatory, but the obligation is to recite a verse of the Qur'an, because in the hadith No. 714, the Prophet said to the one who requested to be taught how to pray: 'Recite of the Qur'an what comes easy to you'. The majority of scholars cite in evidence the hadith that says that 'no prayer is valid without reciting the Mother of the Qur'an'. If the others argue that this means that 'no prayer is complete', we say that this is contrary to the apparent meaning of the wording of the hadith. This is further confirmed by the hadith in which the Prophet says: 'No prayer is valid if the Opening of the Book [i.e. *al Fātiḥah*] is not recited in it'. This hadith is related by Ibn Khuzaymah in his *Ṣaḥīḥ* anthology and by Ibn Ḥibbān. The Prophet's statement, 'recite what comes easy to you' is taken to mean *al-Fātiḥah,* because it is easy for everyone, or meaning what is more than *al-Fātiḥah,* or a concession to a person who cannot recite *al-Fātiḥah.*

Hadith No. 704 quotes the Prophet (peace be upon him): 'No prayer is valid if one does not recite the Opening Surah of the Book'. This hadith provides evidence supporting the view of al-Shāfiʿī and scholars who agree with him that reciting *al-Fātiḥah* is obligatory for the imam, everyone in the congregation and whoever is praying alone. That it is also obligatory on those in the congregation is further confirmed by Abū Hurayrah, who said to those who told him that they may be in the congregation: 'recite it silently'. This means to recite it inaudibly. The argument of some Mālikī scholars and others that it means merely to reflect on it is unacceptable, because recitation refers only to utterance with tongue movement, when one hears oneself. Indeed, scholars are all agreed that a person who reflects on the meaning of the Qur'an when he is in a state of major ritual impurity does not violate the restriction that makes reciting the Qur'an in this state forbidden. *Qāḍī* 'Iyāḍ reports that 'Alī ibn Abī Ṭālib, Rabī'ah and Muhammad ibn Abī Ṣufrah, a Mālikī scholar, said no recitation is obligatory in the first place. This is an uncorroborated report attributed to Mālik. On the other hand, al-Thawrī, al-Awzā'ī and Abū Ḥanīfah said that recitation of the Qur'an is not obligatory in the last two *rak'ahs*, but the worshipper has the choice to recite, glorify God or remain silent. The correct view subscribed by the majority of scholars of early and later generations is that reciting *al-Fātiḥah* is obligatory in every *rak'ah*, because the Prophet said to the bedouin: 'Then do this in all parts of your prayer'.

In hadith No. 708, God, the Exalted, says: 'I have divided the prayer in two halves between Myself and My servant'. Scholars say that 'prayer' in this instance means *al-Fātiḥah*, and that it is called prayer because it is a condition for the validity of prayer, just like the hadith that says: 'The Pilgrimage is attendance at Arafat'. Hence, this hadith provides further evidence that *al-Fātiḥah* is obligatory to recite in prayer. Scholars add that its division refers to its meaning, because its first half consists of praise and glorification of God and surrendering to Him, while the second half consists of supplication and appeal for help.

Scholars who argue that *bismi-Llāhi al-Raḥmāni al-Raḥīm*, i.e. 'In the name of God, the Lord of Grace, the Ever-Merciful' is not a verse of *al-Fātiḥah* cite this hadith in support. This is one of their clearest arguments. They said that it is unanimously agreed that *al-Fātiḥah* consists of seven verses: the first three of which glorify God, beginning with 'all praise be to God ...' and the last three include supplication, starting with 'guide us on the straight path'. The seventh verse comes in the middle: 'You alone do we worship and to You alone do we turn for help'. They add that God, the Exalted, said: 'I have divided the prayer in two halves between Myself and My servants', then adds, 'When God's servant says: "Praise be to God, the Lord of all the worlds"'. He does not mention, 'In the name ...'. Had it been part of *al-Fātiḥah,* he would have mentioned it.

Our Shāfiʿī scholars and others who maintain that *bismi-Llāhi al-Raḥmāni al-Raḥīm,* i.e. 'In the name of God, the Lord of Grace, the Ever-Merciful' is a verse of *al-Fātiḥah* make several counter arguments. One of these is that the division applies to the prayer as a whole, not to the surah, as this is the proper meaning of the words. A second argument is that the division refers to the complete verses in *al-Fātiḥah,* and a third one is that the hadith means: 'when the worshipper reaches the verse saying "praise be to God".' Scholars add that God says 'My servant has praised, extolled and glorified Me', because praise extols good action while glorification extols majestic attributes. It is also said that he extolled God's praise in all that. Hence, God says this when the worshipper says 'the Lord of Grace, the Ever-Merciful'. These two attributes refer to attributes that are essential to God and describe His action. In one narration of the hadith, God is quoted as saying, 'My servant has surrendered himself to Me'. This fits perfectly with the verse that describes God as 'Master of the Day of Judgement'. It is God who has the absolute dominion of the universe on that day, and it is He who determines people's recompense for their deeds. He alone reckons their deeds and determines their destiny. No one else has any claim, real or figurative. In the present life, some people may have some sort of dominion, and some may make false claims. None of this can be made on the Day of Judgement. This is the meaning of this verse, but the reality is that God is the Master and the King, who has all dominion in both this life and the life to come, and all that they contain. Every other being is subject to His authority. Hence, when the worshipper says: 'Master of the Day of Judgement', he acknowledges God's greatness and surrenders to Him. This is absolutely clear.

Hadith No. 708 concludes with: 'When he says: "Guide us on the straight path, the path of those on whom You have bestowed Your favours, not those who have incurred Your wrath, nor those who have gone astray", God will say: "This is granted to My servant, and My servant shall have what he requests".' This is how the hadith is reported in Muslim's *Ṣaḥīḥ*, 'this is granted to My servant'; but in other anthologies its wording is 'these are granted to My servant'. The fact that it is given in the plural confirms that these are three verses, not two.[i] The point is subject to different opinions by scholars, and their disagreement is based on whether the opening phrase, *bismi-Llāhi al-Raḥmāni al-Raḥīm,* is part of *al-Fātiḥah* or not. Our view, which is also the view of the majority of scholars, is that it is a verse of *al-Fātiḥah,* and that the part of the surah beginning with 'guide us on the straight path' consists of two verses only. Mālik and other scholars who say that it is not part of *al-Fātiḥah* say that this part of the surah consists of three verses. The majority may say that the wording 'these are granted to My servant' refer to the words, not to to verses, supporting their argument by Muslim's version which says: 'this is granted to My servant'. This is a better explanation than to say that the plural form is applicable in this instance to the dual, because this becomes figurative. To give a statement a figurative meaning instead of its real one requires a reason that serves as evidence, but God knows best.

In hadith No. 711, Abū Hurayrah says: 'No prayer is valid without recitation. What God's Messenger (peace be upon him) said aloud, we say aloud to you, and what he did not, we do not'. This means that he followed the Prophet's guidance, and he would recite aloud what the Prophet recited aloud, but what he recited in private should remain so. The Muslim community is unanimous that the Qur'an is recited aloud in the two *rakʿahs* of Fajr and Friday Prayers, as well as the first two *rakʿahs* of Maghrib and ʿIshā Prayers, but the recitation is silent in Ẓuhr and ʿAṣr Prayers as well as the third *rakʿah* of Maghrib and the last two *rakʿahs* of ʿIshā. Scholars hold different views regarding the Eid Prayer and the Prayer for Rain. The view of our Shāfiʿī school is that the recitation in both these two prayers is

i. This argument is based on the fact that Arabic has a special form for dual numbers, which is completely different from the plural which starts at three, not two.

aloud. Recitation of the Qur'an in the recommended prayers offered at night is said to be aloud, but another view says that it should be between aloud and silent. When recommended prayers are offered during the day, the recitation is silent. The recommended prayer at the time of a solar or lunar eclipse should have a silent recitation if it is offered during the day while the recitation is aloud if it is offered at night. Recitation during the Funeral Prayer is silent, whether done at night or during the day, although some scholars favour that it should be aloud if it is offered at night. If a person misses out on an obligatory night prayer, such as 'Ishā, and he prays it on a later night, he recites the Qur'an aloud, but if he makes up for it during the day, there are two views but the more correct one is that he recites the Qur'an silently, while the other is that he recites it aloud. If a person misses out on a day prayer, such as Ẓuhr, and he offers it later during the day, he recites the Qur'an silently. If he offers it at night, scholars give two views, the more correct of which is that he recites aloud, and the second is that he recites silently. Wherever we said that the recitation should be aloud or silent, this is recommended. If not done, the prayer remains valid. No *sahw* prostration, i.e. prostration to correct an error, is due according to our school.

In hadith No. 713: 'He who reads the Mother of the Book only, it is sufficient for him, and whoever adds more does better'. This provides further evidence that reciting *al-Fātiḥah* is obligatory and that it cannot be substituted by reciting anything else. It also makes clear that it is desirable to recite a surah or a passage of the Qur'an after reciting *al-Fātiḥah*. This is unanimously agreed for the Fajr and Friday Prayers as well as the first two *rak'ahs* of all prayers. To add such recitation is a Sunnah according to all scholars. *Qāḍī* 'Iyāḍ reports that some associates of Mālik consider adding a surah after *al-Fātiḥah* to be obligatory, but this is a strange, unacceptable view. Reciting a surah in the third and fourth *rak'ahs* is viewed differently by scholars. Mālik dislikes it, while al-Shāfi'ī considers it desirable, but this is his later view, not the older one. In this case, the older view is the more correct one. Other scholars say that the worshipper has the choice to recite a surah or to say some glorifications, but this view is lacking support. Reciting a surah is desirable in voluntary prayers, but not in the funeral or *janāzah* prayer, because the latter is made simple and light. Nothing is added to *al-Fātiḥah* except to say 'Amen' after it. It is desirable that the surah to be recited in Fajr and the first two *rak'ahs* of Ẓuhr is one of the longer surahs of the part of the Qur'an starting with Surah 50, *Qāf*. In the first two *rak'ahs* of 'Aṣr and 'Ishā prayers, it is desirable to choose one of the middle length from this part, and in Maghrib a shorter surah.

Scholars give different views on whether the recitation in the first *rak'ah* should be longer than in the second. The best-known view of our school is that it is not desirable, but they should be of equal length. The more correct view is that the first *rak'ah* is made longer, as this is stated in an authentic hadith that says: 'He [i.e. the Prophet] used to recite longer in the first *rak'ah* than he did in the second'. Scholars who say that reciting a surah or a passage in the last two *rak'ahs* of a four-*rak'ah* prayer also say that this recitiation should be shorter than in the first two *rak'ahs*. They also differ on whether the recitation in the fourth *rak'ah* should be shorter than the recitation in the third, but God knows best. Wherever a recitation is desirable but the worshipper omits it, he simply misses on what is better, but he does not add a *saḥw* prostration, to compensate for an omission. To recite a short surah is better than reciting an equivalent passage from a longer surah. Choosing the surahs to read in different *rak'ahs* should be according to their order in the Qur'an. To do the opposite, reciting a later surah in the first *rak'ah*, is discouraged, but does not invalidate the prayer. One may read according to any of the seven variant methods of recitation, but it is not permissible to read according to those that are *shādhdh*, or discarded. If one makes a mistake that alters the meaning when reciting *al-Fātiḥah*, such as saying *an'amtu* or *an'amti* instead of *an'amta*, or saying *iyyāki* instead of *iyyāka*, the prayer becomes invalid. If the mistake does not alter the meaning, then this is reprehensible but the prayer remains valid. It is obligatory to recite *al-Fātiḥah* in its correct order and to read it together, without a long gap separating its verses. Moreover, it must be recited in Arabic. It is forbidden to recite it in prayer in a foreign language. The prayer is not valid if *al-Fātiḥah* is recited in a language other than Arabic, whether the person doing so knows Arabic or not. It is a condition when reciting and in all glorifications to utter the words so that one hears oneself. A dumb person, and one similarly considered, should move his tongue and lips as he may be able to. This is sufficient for him, but God knows best.

Hadith No. 714 mentions the situation of a person who offered a prayer but the Prophet told him to repeat because it was not valid. This he did three times, but the man said that he did not know any better and requested the Prophet to teach him. The Prophet gave him the proper instructions. In hadith No. 715, the same story is mentioned with the addition that the Prophet told the man to do the ablution well first and to face the *qiblah* and start the prayer with the *takbīr*. This hadith includes many very useful points. It should be clear at first that it only mentions the duties of prayer, not the recommended parts. If someone suggests that it does not mention all the duties, or that there are other unanimously agreed duties and ones that are considered duties by some scholars, but not by others, this is true. The answer is that the Prophet did not mention these to the man because they were known to him. The duties that are unanimously agreed upon but not mentioned by the Prophet are the intention, the last sitting for *tashahhud* and doing the essential parts of the prayer in the right order. Other parts of the prayer that are not considered obligatory by all scholars include the last *tashahhud*, praying for peace and blessings for the Prophet in this *tashahhud* and finishing the prayer with *salām*. These three are considered duties by al-Shāfiʿī. The *salām* at the end is considered a duty by the majority of scholars, while many scholars consider the last *tashahhud* a duty. The prayer for the Prophet is also considered a duty by al-Shaʿbī and Ahmad ibn Ḥanbal and their disciples. A number of disciples of al-Shāfiʿī add a duty of formulating the intention of finishing the prayer. Ahmad considers the first *tashahhud* a duty, and also the glorifications in the positions of bowing and prostration, as well as the *takbīr* to signify moving from one position to the next. As we said earlier, the Prophet did not mention these because they were known to the person being taught. The hadith also indicates that the *iqāmah* is not obligatory.

The hadith makes clear that to perform the ablution and to face the *qiblah* and say the first *takbīr* are duties of prayer, as also the recitation of the Qur'an.

The hadith also shows that saying *a'ūdhu billāh min al-shayṭāni al-rajīm*, which means 'I seek shelter with God from Satan, the accursed', the opening supplication, lifting one's hands when saying the first *takbīr*, putting one's right hand over one's left hand, the *takbīr* signalling movements, the glorifications during bowing and prostration, how one sits down, and puts one's hands on one's thighs, as other matters not mentined in the hadith are not duties of prayer. The only duties are those we have outlined as unanimously agreed on or over which scholars have differed.

The hadith further mentions that it is obligatory to rise fully when lifting oneself from bowing, and to sit up between the two prostrations. It is a duty to take each of these positions, bowing, rising, prostration and sitting fully and comfortably. This is the view of our Shāfi'ī school and the majority of scholars, but Abū Ḥanīfah and a small number of scholars do not consider this a duty. This hadith provides clear argument in opposition to this view, and they cannot give a satisfactory answer.

When rising from the bowing position, it is a duty to stand up fully. This is the best-known view of our school and other schools, just like it is a duty to be well positioned and comfortable when one sits down between the two prostrations. Some of our scholars stop short of saying that it is a duty, because the hadith mentions rising up without mentioning being well positioned as it is mentioned in the cases of sitting down between the two prostrations, bowing and prostration.

The hadith indicates that recitation is a duty in all *rak'ahs*. This is the view of our school and the majority of scholars, as we have explained earlier.

Another point in the hadith is that if a scholar is asked about something and he realizes that there is something else his questioner needs but has not asked about, then it is desirable for that scholar to give such information. This is considered as sincere advice, not as interference in other people's affairs. The evidence for this is that the Prophet's companion said to him: 'Teach me'. His request was to be taught how to pray, but the Prophet taught him this and added that he should face the *qiblah* and have ablution. Neither is part of the prayer itself, but they are essential for the validity of prayer.

The hadith shows that it is important to take a gentle approach when teaching someone or speaking to one who does not know how to do things properly. Things should be put clearly to such a person, making them short and simple, pointing out what is essential without adding the extras that are not duties, because he may not be able to absorb and fulfil all. Another point in the hadith is that it is desirable to offer the greeting of peace, i.e. *salām*, when meeting others, and such a greeting must be answered. It is desirable to repeat the greeting if they meet again, even after a short while. The greeting must be responded to every time it is offered. The response is in the same wording preceded by *wa*, which means 'and'. Adding it is desirable according to the majority, but some of our scholars claim that it is obligatory, but their claim cannot be substantiated. It is indeed a Sunnah.

It is clear from the hadith that a person who does not fulfil some of the duties of prayer renders his prayer invalid and cannot be deemed to have prayed. Indeed, he is told that he has not prayed. The question, however, may well arise as to why did the Prophet leave the man to offer an invalid prayer more than once? The answer is that the man was not allowed to offer an invalid prayer, and the Prophet did not know that he would offer such an invalid prayer on the second or the third time. In other words, he might have been able to offer a valid prayer. The Prophet did not begin to teach him after the first invalid prayer so that he would be more attentive and learn better when such education was offered. Moreover, others would also be attentive and learn how to pray well. A similar scenario is that in which the Prophet ordered his companions to start their *iḥrām* intending to perform the pilgrimage, but then ordered them to change and offer the *ʿumrah* instead. This was certain to make it clear to them, but God knows best.

Transmission

Abu al-Sā'ib is mentioned in the chains of transmission of several hadiths in this chapter. Yet, his name is unknown, but he is graded as reliable. Ahmad ibn Jaʿfar al-Maʿqirī is mentioned in hadith No. 710, and he belonged to Maʿqir, an area in Yemen.

As mentioned in Muslim, hadith No. 714 features the following chain of transmission: 'Muhammad ibn al-Muthannā narrated to me: Yaḥyā ibn Saʿīd narrated; from ʿUbaydullāh; Saʿīd ibn Abī Saʿīd narrated to me; from his father; from Abū Hurayrah'. In his work *al-Istidrāk*, al-Dāraquṭnī says that 'Yaḥyā ibn Saʿīd differs here with all who learnt from ʿUbaydullāh. They all narrated the hadith from ʿUbaydullāh from Saʿīd from Abū Hurayrah, without mentioning Saʿīd's father.' Al-Dāraquṭnī adds that Yaḥyā was a good memorizer, and therefore his reporting is accepted as correct.

What this means is that the hadith is authentic and without defect. Even if the other report, narrated by the majority, is the correct version, this does not affect the authenticity of the text of the hadith. We have explained this on several occasions earlier in this book. I am only mentioning it here so that people may not give much importance to the comments of al-Dāraquṭnī or others concerning this point, but God knows best.

AUDIBLE RECITATION IS ONLY MADE BY THE IMAM

[716–47]. (Dār al-Salām 0783) Saʿīd ibn Manṣūr and Qutaybah ibn Saʿīd narrated:[i] both from Abū ʿAwānah. Saʿīd said: Abū ʿAwānah narrated; from Qatādah; from Zurārah ibn Awfā; from ʿImrān ibn Ḥuṣayn; who said: **'God's Messenger (peace be upon him) led the Ẓuhr (or the ʿAṣr) Prayer, then said: "Who of you recited behind me [the surah starting with] 'Extol the limitless glory of the name of your Lord, the Most High'?" A man said: "I did, but I meant nothing but good". The Prophet said: "I realized that some of you pulled against me".'**

حَدَّثَنَا سَعِيدُ بْنُ مَنْصُورٍ، وَقُتَيْبَةُ بْنُ سَعِيدٍ، كِلَاهُمَا عَنْ أَبِي عَوَانَةَ، قَالَ سَعِيدٌ: حَدَّثَنَا أَبُو عَوَانَةَ، عَنْ قَتَادَةَ، عَنْ زُرَارَةَ بْنِ أَوْفَى، عَنْ عِمْرَانَ بْنِ حُصَيْنٍ، قَالَ: صَلَّى بِنَا رَسُولُ اللهِ صَلَّى اللهُ عَلَيْهِ وَسَلَّمَ صَلَاةَ الظُّهْرِ - أَوِ الْعَصْرِ - فَقَالَ: «أَيُّكُمْ قَرَأَ خَلْفِي بِسَبِّحِ اسْمَ رَبِّكَ الْأَعْلَى؟» فَقَالَ رَجُلٌ: أَنَا وَلَمْ أُرِدْ بِهَا إِلَّا الْخَيْرَ، قَالَ: «قَدْ عَلِمْتُ أَنَّ بَعْضَكُمْ خَالَجَنِيهَا»

[717–48]. (Dār al-Salām 0784) Muhammad ibn al-Muthannā and Muhammad ibn Bashshār narrated: they said: Muhammad ibn Jaʿfar narrated; Shuʿbah narrated; from Qatādah. He said: I heard Zurārah ibn Awfā narrating from ʿImrān ibn Ḥuṣayn

i. Related by Abū Dāwūd, 828 and 829; al-Nasāʾī, 916 and 917.

that **'God's Messenger (peace be upon him) offered the Ẓuhr Prayer. One man praying behind him also recited "Extol the limitless glory of the name of your Lord, the Most High". When he finished he said: "Who of you so recited?" or "Who of you was the reciter?" A man said: "I did". The Prophet said: "I felt that some of you were pulling against me".'**

حَدَّثَنَا مُحَمَّدُ بْنُ الْـمُثَنَّى، وَمُحَمَّدُ بْنُ بَشَّارٍ، قَالَا: حَدَّثَنَا مُحَمَّدُ بْنُ جَعْفَرٍ، حَدَّثَنَا شُعْبَةُ، عَنْ قَتَادَةَ، قَالَ: سَمِعْتُ زُرَارَةَ بْنَ أَوْفَى، يُحَدِّثُ عَنْ عِمْرَانَ بْنِ حُصَيْنٍ، أَنَّ رَسُولَ اللهِ صَلَّى اللهُ عَلَيْهِ وَسَلَّمَ صَلَّى الظُّهْرَ، فَجَعَلَ رَجُلٌ يَقْرَأُ خَلْفَهُ بِسَبِّحِ اسْمَ رَبِّكَ الْأَعْلَى، فَلَمَّا انْصَرَفَ قَالَ: «أَيُّكُمْ قَرَأَ» - أَوْ أَيُّكُمُ الْقَارِئُ - فَقَالَ رَجُلٌ أَنَا، فَقَالَ: «قَدْ ظَنَنْتُ أَنَّ بَعْضَكُمْ خَالَـجَنِـيهَا»

[718–49]. (Dār al-Salām 0785) Abū Bakr ibn Abī Shaybah narrated: Ismāʿīl ibn ʿUlayyah narrated [H]. Muhammad ibn al-Muthannā narrated; Ibn Abī ʿAdī narrated; both from Ibn Abī ʿArūbah; from Qatādah; with this chain of transmission that **'God's Messenger (peace be upon him) prayed Ẓuhr ... he said: "I knew that some of you were pulling against me".'**

حَدَّثَنَا أَبُو بَكْرِ بْنُ أَبِي شَيْبَةَ، حَدَّثَنَا إِسْمَاعِيلُ ابْنُ عُلَيَّةَ، ح وَحَدَّثَنَا مُحَمَّدُ بْنُ الْـمُثَنَّى، حَدَّثَنَا ابْنُ أَبِي عَدِيٍّ، كِلَاهُمَا عَنِ ابْنِ أَبِي عَرُوبَةَ، عَنْ قَتَادَةَ، بِهَذَا الْإِسْنَادِ أَنَّ رَسُولَ اللهِ صَلَّى اللهُ عَلَيْهِ وَسَلَّمَ صَلَّى الظُّهْرَ. وَقَالَ: «قَدْ عَلِمْتُ أَنَّ بَعْضَكُمْ خَالَـجَنِـيهَا»

Text Explanation

The first hadith mentions that the Prophet was offering either Ẓuhr or ʿAṣr Prayer, but the other two narrations state that it was Ẓuhr, without doubt. The Prophet mentions that someone was 'pulling the surah against him'. This means that the man was reciting the surah like the Prophet did, and hence the Prophet's criticism of him for reciting the surah aloud, so that others could hear. It was not that the mere recitation the Prophet objected to, but the fact that it was heard by others. Indeed, the hadith shows that the Prophet's companions recited a surah, in addition to *al-Fātiḥah*, in prayers offered silently. It also shows that both the imam and those in the congregation recite a surah in Ẓuhr Prayer. This is the ruling according to our Shāfiʿī school, although there is an odd and insupportable view that those in the congregation do not recite a surah in the prayers offered silently, in the same way as in prayers where the recitation by the imam is made aloud. This is wrong. In the latter prayers, the worshipper is commanded to listen to the recitation. In prayers offered silently, he cannot hear anything, and to refrain from reciting is of no benefit. Likewise, a person who is standing far from the imam and cannot hear his recitation should, according to the more correct view, recite a surah even in the prayers where the imam recites aloud. But God knows best.

Transmission

The chains of transmission of the first two hadiths reflect a fine point. The first includes: 'from Qatādah, from Zurārah', while the second mentions: 'from Qatādah. He said: I heard Zurārah'. Qatādah (may God bestow mercy on him) was graded as a 'misleading narrator'. A report by a misleading narrator that is given 'from someone' is not accepted, unless it is proven in some other way that he actually heard the hadith from that narrator. The second narration provides this evidence. We have pointed this out on several occasions, but God knows best.

CHAPTER 13

THE ARGUMENT THAT THE *BASMALAH* SHOULD NOT BE READ ALOUD

[719–50]. (Dār al-Salām 0786) Muhammad ibn al-Muthannā and Ibn Bashshār narrated:[i] both from Ghundar. Ibn al-Muthannā said Muhammad ibn Jaʿfar narrated; Shuʿbah narrated. He said: I heard Qatādah narrating from Anas that he said: **'I offered prayers with God's Messenger (peace be upon him) and with Abū Bakr, ʿUmar and ʿUthmān. I never heard any of them reciting "*Bismillāhi al-Raḥmāni al-Raḥīm,* i.e. in the name of God, the Lord of Grace, the Ever-Merciful".'**

حَدَّثَنَا مُحَمَّدُ بْنُ الْـمُثَنَّى، وَابْنُ بَشَّارٍ، كِلَاهُمَا عَنْ غُنْدَرٍ، قَالَ ابْنُ الْـمُثَنَّى: حَدَّثَنَا مُحَمَّدُ بْنُ جَعْفَرٍ، حَدَّثَنَا شُعْبَةُ، قَالَ: سَمِعْتُ قَتَادَةَ، يُحَدِّثُ عَنْ أَنَسٍ، قَالَ: «صَلَّيْتُ مَعَ رَسُولِ اللهِ صَلَّى اللهُ عَلَيْهِ وَسَلَّمَ وَأَبِي بَكْرٍ، وَعُمَرَ، وَعُثْمَانَ، فَلَمْ أَسْمَعْ أَحَدًا مِنْهُمْ يَقْرَأُ «بِسْمِ اللهِ الرَّحْمَنِ الرَّحِيمِ»

[000–51]. (Dār al-Salām 0787) Muhammad ibn al-Muthannā narrated: Abū Dāwūd narrated; Shuʿbah narrated; with this transmission. He added: Shuʿbah said: I said to Qatādah: Did you hear it from Anas? He said: Yes, we asked him about it.

حَدَّثَنَا مُحَمَّدُ بْنُ الْـمُثَنَّى، حَدَّثَنَا أَبُو دَاوُدَ، حَدَّثَنَا شُعْبَةُ، فِي هَذَا الْإِسْنَادِ، وَزَادَ قَالَ شُعْبَةُ: فَقُلْتُ لِقَتَادَةَ: أَسَمِعْتَهُ مِنْ أَنَسٍ قَالَ: نَعَمْ نَحْنُ سَأَلْنَاهُ عَنْهُ.

i. Related by al-Bukhārī, 473; al-Nasāʾī, 906.

[720–52]. (Dār al-Salām 0788) Muhammad ibn Mihrān al-Rāzī narrated: al-Walīd ibn Muslim narrated; al-Awzāʿī narrated; from ʿAbdah; that ʿUmar ibn al-Khaṭṭāb **used to recite aloud the following phrases:** ***Subhānaka Allahumma wa biḥamdik; tabāraka ismuk; wa taʿālā Jadduk; wa lā ilāha ghayruk*** **[i.e. Limitless are You, God, in Your glory, and all praise is due to You. Blessed is Your name and superior is Your greatness. There is no diety other than You]**.

حَدَّثَنَا مُحَمَّدُ بْنُ مِهْرَانَ الرَّازِيُّ، حَدَّثَنَا الْوَلِيدُ بْنُ مُسْلِمٍ، حَدَّثَنَا الْأَوْزَاعِيُّ، عَنْ عَبْدَةَ، أَنَّ عُمَرَ بْنَ الْخَطَّابِ، كَانَ يَجْهَرُ بِهَؤُلَاءِ الْكَلِمَاتِ يَقُولُ: «سُبْحَانَكَ اللهُمَّ وَبِحَمْدِكَ، تَبَارَكَ اسْمُكَ، وَتَعَالَى جَدُّكَ، وَلَا إِلَهَ غَيْرُكَ»

And from Qatādah that he wrote to him reporting that Anas ibn Mālik narrated to him: **'I prayed behind the Prophet (peace be upon him) and Abū Bakr, ʿUmar and ʿUthmān. They started with "*Alḥamdu lillāh rabbi-l ʿālamīn*, i.e. Praise be to God, the Lord of all the worlds". They did not say "in the name of God, the Lord of Grace, the Ever-Merciful" at the beginning or end of any recitation'**.

وَعَنْ قَتَادَةَ أَنَّهُ كَتَبَ إِلَيْهِ يُخْبِرُهُ عَنْ أَنَسِ بْنِ مَالِكٍ، أَنَّهُ حَدَّثَهُ قَالَ: «صَلَّيْتُ خَلْفَ النَّبِيِّ صَلَّى اللهُ عَلَيْهِ وَسَلَّمَ وَأَبِي بَكْرٍ، وَعُمَرَ، وَعُثْمَانَ، فَكَانُوا يَسْتَفْتِحُونَ بِالْحَمْدُ لِلَّهِ رَبِّ الْعَالَمِينَ، لَا يَذْكُرُونَ [بِسْمِ اللهِ الرَّحْمَنِ الرَّحِيمِ] فِي أَوَّلِ قِرَاءَةٍ وَلَا فِي آخِرِهَا»

[000–000]. (Dār al-Salām 0789) Muhammad ibn Mihrān narrated: al-Walīd ibn Muslim narrated; from al-Awzāʿī; Isḥāq ibn ʿAbdullāh ibn Abī Ṭalḥah reported to me that he heard Anas ibn Mālik mentioning this.

حَدَّثَنَا مُحَمَّدُ بْنُ مِهْرَانَ، حَدَّثَنَا الْوَلِيدُ بْنُ مُسْلِمٍ، عَنِ الْأَوْزَاعِيِّ، أَخْبَرَنِي، إِسْحَاقُ بْنُ عَبْدِ اللهِ بْنِ أَبِي طَلْحَةَ، أَنَّهُ سَمِعَ أَنَسَ بْنَ مَالِكٍ يَذْكُرُ ذَلِكَ.

Text Explanation

Hadith Nos 719 and 720 are cited as evidence in support of the views of those who say that the *basmalah*, i.e. *bismi-Llāhi al-Raḥmāni al-Raḥīm*, which means 'In the name of God, the Lord of Grace, the Ever-Merciful', is not a verse of the opening surah, *al-Fātiḥah*, and also those who say that it is a verse of this surah but should not be recited aloud. The view of al-Shāfiʿī (may God bestow mercy on him), as well as large numbers of scholars of early and later generations is that the *basmalah* is a verse of *al-Fātiḥah*, and it should be recited aloud whenever *al-Fātiḥah* is recited aloud. Our scholars and others who say that it is a verse of *al-Fātiḥah* cite in evidence the fact that it is written in the Qur'an with the same calligraphy as the Qur'an. It was the unanimous agreement of the Prophet's companions that they would not write anything other than the Qur'an with the same calligraphy. Subsequently, all Muslims in all generations up to our present day have been unanimously committed to this. They are also unanimous that it is not mentioned at the beginning of Surah 9, Repentance, and that it must not be written there. This confirms what we have said.

Transmission

The chain of transmission of hadith No. 719 includes: 'Qatādah from Anas', but the second chain of transmission quotes Shuʿbah as asking Qatādah whether he himself heard the hadith from Anas, and Qatādah confirms that he did. This is the same case as mentioned in the previous chapter, where a reporter graded as 'misleading' is not acceptable unless his hearing from the narrator before him is specifically confirmed, as is the case here.

In the chain of transmission of hadith No. 720 we have ʿAbdah mentioning that ʿUmar used to recite aloud the phrases of the opening praise of God. Abū ʿAlī al-Ḥusayn ibn Muhammad al-Ghassānī said that this is how the transmission of this hadith occurs, with ʿAbdah reporting from ʿUmar. As such, it is a *mursal*, i.e. with an incomplete chain of transmission, because ʿAbdah, who is Ibn Abī Lubābah, did not hear directly from ʿUmar. However, in the second route of the transmission we have: 'And from Qatādah that he wrote to him …'. This means that the transmission is al-Awzāʿī, from Qatādah, from Anas. This is what is intended, to show that the chain of transmission is complete. This is what al-Ghassānī explained. What he meant is that 'and from Qatādah' is joined to 'from ʿAbdah', which came earlier in the first route. Muslim did this because this is how he heard the hadith, and he narrated it in the same way. His purpose is to show the second route, which is complete, rather than the first which is incomplete, or *mursal*. There are many instances like this in Muslim's *Ṣaḥīḥ*.

CHAPTER 14

THE ARGUMENT THAT THE *BASMALAH* IS A VERSE OF EVERY SURAH EXCEPT SURAH 9

[721–53]. (Dār al-Salām 0790) ʿAlī ibn Ḥujr al-Saʿdī narrated:[i] ʿAlī ibn Mushīr narrated; al-Mukhtār ibn Fulful reported; from Anas ibn Mālik [H]. Also, Abū Bakr ibn Abī Shaybah narrated (his text); ʿAlī ibn Mushīr narrated; from al-Mukhtār; from Anas. He said: **'One day, God's Messenger (peace be upon him) was with us when he dozed off. He then lifted his head smiling. We asked: "What makes you laugh, Messenger of God?" He said: "A surah has been revealed to me a short while ago. He then recited: *'In the name of God, the Lord of Grace, the Ever Merciful. We have certainly given you al-Kawthar. So pray to your Lord and sacrifice to Him. Surely, he who hates you is the one cut off'*." (108: 1–3) He then asked: "Do you know what al-Kawthar is?" We said: "God and His Messenger know best". He said: "It is a river God, the Mighty and Majestic, has promised me, running with plenty of goodness. It is a pool to which my community will come on the Day of Judgement. The containers around it are as numerous as stars. Yet, a person may be whisked away, and I would say: 'My Lord, he belongs to my community'. He will say: 'You do not know what they invented after you had gone'".'**

i. Related by Abū Dāwūd, 784 (in a shorter version) and 4747; al-Nasāʾī, 903.

In his narration, Ibn Ḥujr added: 'God's Messenger was with us in the mosque'. He also said: 'You do not know what he invented after you had gone'.

حَدَّثَنَا عَلِيُّ بْنُ حُجْرٍ السَّعْدِيُّ، حَدَّثَنَا عَلِيُّ بْنُ مُسْهِرٍ، أَخْبَرَنَا الْـمُخْتَارُ بْنُ فُلْفُلٍ، عَنْ أَنَسِ بْنِ مَالِكٍ، ح وَحَدَّثَنَا أَبُو بَكْرِ بْنُ أَبِي شَيْبَةَ، - وَاللَّفْظُ لَهُ - حَدَّثَنَا عَلِيُّ بْنُ مُسْهِرٍ، عَنِ الْـمُخْتَارِ، عَنْ أَنَسٍ، قَالَ: بَيْنَا رَسُولُ اللهِ صَلَّى اللهُ عَلَيْهِ وَسَلَّمَ ذَاتَ يَوْمٍ بَيْنَ أَظْهُرِنَا إِذْ أَغْفَى إِغْفَاءَةً ثُمَّ رَفَعَ رَأْسَهُ مُتَبَسِّمًا، فَقُلْنَا: مَا أَضْحَكَكَ يَا رَسُولَ اللهِ قَالَ: «أُنْزِلَتْ عَلَيَّ آنِفًا سُورَةٌ» فَقَرَأَ: بِسْمِ اللهِ الرَّحْمَنِ الرَّحِيمِ «إِنَّا أَعْطَيْنَاكَ الْكَوْثَرَ. فَصَلِّ لِرَبِّكَ وَانْحَرْ. إِنَّ شَانِئَكَ هُوَ الْأَبْتَرُ» ثُمَّ قَالَ: «أَتَدْرُونَ مَا الْكَوْثَرُ؟» فَقُلْنَا اللهُ وَرَسُولُهُ أَعْلَمُ، قَالَ: « فَإِنَّهُ نَهْرٌ وَعَدَنِيهِ رَبِّي عَزَّ وَجَلَّ، عَلَيْهِ خَيْرٌ كَثِيرٌ، هُوَ حَوْضٌ تَرِدُ عَلَيْهِ أُمَّتِي يَوْمَ الْقِيَامَةِ، آنِيَتُهُ عَدَدُ النُّجُومِ، فَيُخْتَلَجُ الْعَبْدُ مِنْهُمْ، فَأَقُولُ: رَبِّ، إِنَّهُ مِنْ أُمَّتِي فَيَقُولُ: مَا تَدْرِي مَا أَحْدَثَتْ بَعْدَكَ»

زَادَ ابْنُ حُجْرٍ، فِي حَدِيثِهِ: بَيْنَ أَظْهُرِنَا فِي الْـمَسْجِدِ. وَقَالَ: «مَا أَحْدَثَ بَعْدَكَ»

[722–000]. (Dar al-Salām 0791) Abū Kurayb Muhammad ibn al-'Alā' narrated: Ibn Fuḍayl reported; from Mukhtār ibn Fulful. He said: I heard Anas ibn Mālik say: **'God's Messenger (peace be upon him) dozed off, giving a narration similar to that of Ibn Mushīr, but he said: "It is a river in Heaven my Lord, the Mighty and Majestic has promised me. It has a pool …". He did not mention: "Its containers are as numerous as stars".**'

حَدَّثَنَا أَبُو كُرَيْبٍ مُحَمَّدُ بْنُ الْعَلَاءِ، أَخْبَرَنَا ابْنُ فُضَيْلٍ، عَنْ مُخْتَارِ بْنِ فُلْفُلٍ، قَالَ: سَمِعْتُ أَنَسَ بْنَ مَالِكٍ، يَقُولُ: أَغْفَى رَسُولُ اللهِ صَلَّى اللهُ عَلَيْهِ وَسَلَّمَ إِغْفَاءَةً، بِنَحْوِ حَدِيثِ ابْنِ مُسْهِرٍ غَيْرَ أَنَّهُ قَالَ: «نَهْرٌ وَعَدَنِيهِ رَبِّي عَزَّ وَجَلَّ فِي الْجَنَّةِ عَلَيْهِ حَوْضٌ» وَلَمْ يَذْكُرْ «آنِيَتُهُ عَدَدُ النُّجُومِ»

Text Explanation

It is said that the surah entitled *al-Kawthar* refers to one of the chiefs of the Quraysh called al-ʿĀṣ ibn Wā'il. The Prophet mentions here that al-Kawthar is a river in Heaven, but it is stated elsewhere as meaning 'abundance of goodness'.

This hadith includes several useful points, the first of which is that the *basmalah* which occurs at the beginning of Qur'anic surahs is part of the Qur'an. This is the reason why Muslim includes this hadith at this point. The hadith also points out that it is permissible to sleep in the mosque, and to sleep when one is with friends. It further tells us that if a subordinate person sees his superior smiling, or doing something that suggests that something has occurred, it is desirable to enquire about it.

The hadith further confirms the existence of the Prophet's pool on the Day of Judgement, and to believe in it is obligatory. This will be discussed in more detail, God willing, when Muslim mentions the hadiths confirming it towards the end of his book.

The sentence, 'You do not know what they invented after you had gone', was explained at the beginning of the Book of Cleansing.

CHAPTER 15

WHERE TO PLACE ONE'S HANDS IN PRAYER

[723–54]. (Dār al-Salām 0792) Zuhayr ibn Ḥarb narrated: ʿAffān narrated; Hammām narrated; Muhammad ibn Juḥādah narrated; ʿAbd al-Jabbār ibn Wā'il narrated to me; from ʿAlqamah ibn Wā'il and a *mawlā* of theirs that they both narrated to him; from his father, Wā'il ibn Ḥujr, that **'He saw the Prophet (peace be upon him) raising his hands when he started the prayer. He said *Allāh-u akbar* (Hammām described that his hands were close to his ears), then he covered himself with his robe. He then placed his right [hand] over his left one. When he wanted to bow, he brought his hands out of his robe and raised them. He said *Allāh-u akbar* and bowed. When he said *samiʿa Allāhu liman ḥamidah,* he raised his hands. When he prostrated himself, he did so in between his hands'**.

حَدَّثَنَا زُهَيْرُ بْنُ حَرْبٍ، حَدَّثَنَا عَفَّانُ، حَدَّثَنَا هَمَّامٌ، حَدَّثَنَا مُحَمَّدُ بْنُ جُحَادَةَ، حَدَّثَنِي عَبْدُ الْجَبَّارِ بْنُ وَائِلٍ، عَنْ عَلْقَمَةَ بْنِ وَائِلٍ، وَمَوْلًى لَهُمْ أَنَّهُمَا حَدَّثَاهُ عَنْ أَبِيهِ وَائِلِ بْنِ حُجْرٍ: أَنَّهُ «رَأَى النَّبِيَّ صَلَّى اللهُ عَلَيْهِ وَسَلَّمَ رَفَعَ يَدَيْهِ حِينَ دَخَلَ فِي الصَّلَاةِ كَبَّرَ - وَصَفَ هَمَّامٌ حِيَالَ أُذُنَيْهِ - ثُمَّ الْتَحَفَ بِثَوْبِهِ، ثُمَّ وَضَعَ يَدَهُ الْيُمْنَى عَلَى الْيُسْرَى، فَلَمَّا أَرَادَ أَنْ يَرْكَعَ أَخْرَجَ يَدَيْهِ مِنَ الثَّوْبِ، ثُمَّ رَفَعَهُمَا، ثُمَّ كَبَّرَ فَرَكَعَ، فَلَمَّا قَالَ: سَمِعَ اللهُ لِمَنْ حَمِدَهُ رَفَعَ يَدَيْهِ فَلَمَّا، سَجَدَ سَجَدَ بَيْنَ كَفَّيْهِ»

Text Explanation

The narrator, Hammām, describes that the Prophet placed his hands close to his ears, which means parallel to them. We have explained how the hands should be raised. The hadith includes several useful points, one of which is that a small number of movements does not invalidate the prayer. This is understood from the fact that the hadith mentions that the Prophet said *Allāh-u akbar* then covered himself with his robe. The hadith makes clear that it is desirable to raise one's hands when one starts the prayer and also when bowing and raising oneself after bowing. It is also desirable to uncover one's hands when raising them and to place them on the floor, next to one's shoulders, when prostrating oneself. It is further recommended to place one's right hand over one's left hand after starting the *takbīr*, and to place both hands below one's chest and above one's navel. This is the best known view of our school, and confirmed by the majority of scholars. Abū Ḥanīfah, Sufyān al-Thawrī and Isḥāq ibn Rāhawayh, as well as Abū Isḥāq al-Marwazī, who belonged to our school, said that the worshipper should place his hands below his navel.

Two reports mentioning both ways are attributed to ʿAlī ibn Abī Ṭālib, and also two similar reports are quoted from Ahmad, as well as a third report that the worshipper has the choice to do either, without preference. This is also attributed to al-Awzāʿī and Ibn al-Mundhir. Two reports are mentioned from Mālik: one says that the worshipper places his hands below his chest, and the other that he lets them down without putting one on top of the other. This last way is the one endorsed by most of his disciples and the best known of their school. It is also the view of al-Layth ibn Saʿd. Another report from Mālik is that it is desirable to place one hand on top of the other when praying voluntary prayers and to let one's hands down when offering obligatory prayers. This is the view endorsed by his followers from Basrah.

The evidence supporting the view of the majority of scholars of the desirability of placing one's right hand over the left is this hadith narrated by Wā'il, as well as another hadith narrated by Abū

Ḥāzim from Sahl ibn Saʿd, who said: 'People were ordered to place their right hands over their arms in prayer'. Abū Ḥāzim said: 'To the best of my knowledge, he attributed this to the Prophet'. This hadith is related by al-Bukhārī, and it is authentic and attributed to the Prophet, as we have explained in the Introduction.

Halb al-Ṭā'ī narrated: 'God's Messenger (peace be upon him) used to lead us in prayer and hold his left hand with his right one'. This hadith is related by al-Tirmidhī, who said that it is graded as good. There are many hadiths speaking about this point. The evidence that one's hands are to be placed above the navel is the hadith narrated by Wā'il ibn Ḥujr: 'I prayed with God's Messenger (peace be upon him) and he placed his right hand over his left hand on his chest'. This hadith is related by Ibn Khuzaymah in his *Ṣaḥīḥ* anthology. A different hadith narrated by ʿAlī mentions: 'It is a Sunnah to place hands over hands below the navels in prayer'. This hadith is agreed by scholars to be lacking in authenticity. It is related by al-Dāraquṭnī and al-Bayhaqī as narrated by Abū Shaybah ʿAbd al-Raḥmān ibn Isḥāq al-Wāsiṭī, and he is graded by scholars as unreliable.

Scholars say that the purpose of placing one hand over the other is that it is closer to showing humility in prayer, and it stops one's hands from moving around, but God knows best.

CHAPTER 16

THE *TASHAHHUD* IN PRAYER

[724–55]. (Dār al-Salām 0793) Zuhayr ibn Ḥarb, ʿUthmān ibn Abī Shaybah and Isḥāq ibn Ibrāhīm narrated:[i] Jarīr (Isḥāq said: 'reported' while the other two said: 'narrated'); from Manṣūr; from Abū Wā'il; from ʿAbdullāh. He said: '**When we prayed behind God's Messenger (peace be upon him) we used to say: "Peace be to God; peace be to so-and-so". God's Messenger said to us one day: "God is peace. When any of you sits down in prayer, he should say: 'Greetings be to God, as well as blessings and all good things. Peace be to you, Prophet, together with God's mercy and blessings. Peace be to us and to all good servants of God'. When he says this, it goes to every good servant of God in the heavens and earth. 'I bear witness that there is no deity other than God, and I bear witness that Muhammad is His servant and Messenger'. He may then choose whatever supplication he wishes"**.'

حَدَّثَنَا زُهَيْرُ بْنُ حَرْبٍ، وَعُثْمَانُ بْنُ أَبِي شَيْبَةَ، وَإِسْحَاقُ بْنُ إِبْرَاهِيمَ، - قَالَ إِسْحَاقُ: أَخْبَرَنَا، وَقَالَ الْآخَرَانِ - حَدَّثَنَا جَرِيرٌ، عَنْ مَنْصُورٍ، عَنْ أَبِي وَائِلٍ، عَنْ عَبْدِ اللهِ، قَالَ: كُنَّا نَقُولُ فِي الصَّلَاةِ خَلْفَ رَسُولِ اللهِ صَلَّى اللهُ عَلَيْهِ وَسَلَّمَ: السَّلَامُ عَلَى اللهِ السَّلَامُ عَلَى فُلَانٍ. فَقَالَ لَنَا رَسُولُ اللهِ صَلَّى اللهُ عَلَيْهِ وَسَلَّمَ ذَاتَ يَوْمٍ: «إِنَّ اللهَ هُوَ السَّلَامُ، فَإِذَا قَعَدَ أَحَدُكُمْ فِي الصَّلَاةِ فَلْيَقُلْ: التَّحِيَّاتُ للهِ وَالصَّلَوَاتُ وَالطَّيِّبَاتُ السَّلَامُ عَلَيْكَ أَيُّهَا النَّبِيُّ وَرَحْمَةُ اللهِ وَبَرَكَاتُهُ، السَّلَامُ عَلَيْنَا وَعَلَى عِبَادِ اللهِ الصَّالِحِينَ، فَإِذَا قَالَهَا أَصَابَتْ

i. Related by al-Bukhārī, 6328; al-Nasā'ī, 1168, 1169 and 1276 (in a longer version); Ibn Mājah, 899.

كُلَّ عَبْدٍ لِلّٰهِ صَالِحٍ فِي السَّمَاءِ وَالْأَرْضِ، أَشْهَدُ أَنْ لَا إِلَهَ إِلَّا اللهُ، وَأَشْهَدُ أَنَّ مُحَمَّدًا عَبْدُهُ وَرَسُولُهُ، ثُمَّ يَتَخَيَّرُ مِنَ الْـمَسْأَلَةِ مَا شَاءَ»

[725–56]. (Dār al-Salām 0794) Muhammad ibn al-Muthannā and Ibn Bashshār narrated: both said: Muhammad ibn Jaʿfar narrated; Shuʿbah narrated; from Manṣūr; with this transmission: **the same text, but did not mention: 'He may then choose whatever supplication he wishes'.**

حَدَّثَنَا مُحَمَّدُ بْنُ الْـمُثَنَّى، وَابْنُ بَشَّارٍ، قَالَا: حَدَّثَنَا مُحَمَّدُ بْنُ جَعْفَرٍ، حَدَّثَنَا شُعْبَةُ، عَنْ مَنْصُورٍ بِهَذَا الْإِسْنَادِ مِثْلَهُ وَلَمْ يَذْكُرْ: «ثُمَّ يَتَخَيَّرُ مِنَ الْـمَسْأَلَةِ مَا شَاءَ»

[726–57]. (Dār al-Salām 0795) ʿAbd ibn Ḥumayd narrated: Ḥusayn al-Juʿfī narrated; from Zā'idah; from Manṣūr; with this transmission: **the same as both narrated. He mentioned in the hadith: 'He may then choose whatever supplication he wishes (or he likes)'.**

حَدَّثَنَا عَبْدُ بْنُ حُمَيْدٍ، حَدَّثَنَا حُسَيْنٌ الْجُعْفِيُّ، عَنْ زَائِدَةَ، عَنْ مَنْصُورٍ بِهَذَا الْإِسْنَادِ مِثْلَ حَدِيثِهِمَا وَذَكَرَ فِي الْحَدِيثِ: «ثُمَّ لْيَتَخَيَّرْ بَعْدُ مِنَ الْـمَسْأَلَةِ مَا شَاءَ - أَوْ مَا أَحَبَّ»

[727–58]. (Dār al-Salām 0796) Yaḥyā ibn Yaḥyā narrated:[i] Muʿāwiyah reported; from al-Aʿmash: from Shaqīq; from ʿAbdullāh ibn Masʿūd. He said: **'When we sat with the Prophet (peace be upon him) for prayer … the same as Manṣūr's narration. He added: "He may then select whatever he wishes of supplication".'**

i. Related by al-Bukhārī, 831, 853, 6230, 6328 and 7381 (in longer versions); Abū Dāwūd, 968 (in a longer version); al-Nasā'ī, 1164, 1168 and 1169, and 1276, 1278 and 1297 in longer versions; Ibn Mājah, 899 (in a longer version).

حَدَّثَنَا يَحْيَى بْنُ يَحْيَى، أَخْبَرَنَا أَبُو مُعَاوِيَةَ، عَنِ الْأَعْمَشِ، عَنْ شَقِيقٍ، عَنْ عَبْدِ اللهِ بْنِ مَسْعُودٍ، قَالَ: كُنَّا إِذَا جَلَسْنَا مَعَ النَّبِيِّ صَلَّى اللهُ عَلَيْهِ وَسَلَّمَ فِي الصَّلَاةِ بِمِثْلِ حَدِيثِ مَنْصُورٍ وَقَالَ: «ثُمَّ يَتَخَيَّرُ بَعْدُ مِنَ الدُّعَاءِ»

[728–59]. (Dār al-Salām 0797) Abū Bakr ibn Abī Shaybah narrated:[i] Abū Nuʿaym narrated; Sayf ibn Sulaymān narrated. He said: I heard Mujāhid say: ʿAbdullāh ibn Sakhbarah narrated to me; I heard Ibn Masʿūd say: **'God's Messenger (peace be upon him) taught me the *tashahhud,* holding my hand in his two hands, as he used to teach me a surah of the Qur'an'. He mentioned the *tashahhud* in the same wording they mentioned**.

وَحَدَّثَنَا أَبُو بَكْرِ بْنُ أَبِي شَيْبَةَ، حَدَّثَنَا أَبُو نُعَيْمٍ، حَدَّثَنَا سَيْفُ بْنُ سُلَيْمَانَ، قَالَ: سَمِعْتُ مُجَاهِدًا يَقُولُ: حَدَّثَنِي عَبْدُ اللهِ بْنُ سَخْبَرَةَ، قَالَ: سَمِعْتُ ابْنَ مَسْعُودٍ يَقُولُ: «عَلَّمَنِي رَسُولُ اللهِ صَلَّى اللهُ عَلَيْهِ وَسَلَّمَ التَّشَهُّدَ، كَفِّي بَيْنَ كَفَّيْهِ كَمَا يُعَلِّمُنِي السُّورَةَ مِنَ الْقُرْآنِ، وَاقْتَصَّ التَّشَهُّدَ بِمِثْلِ مَا اقْتَصُّوا»

[729–60]. (Dār al-Salām 0798) Qutaybah ibn Saʿīd narrated:[ii] Layth narrated [H]. Also, Muhammad ibn Rumḥ ibn al-Muhājir narrated; al-Layth reported; from Abū al-Zubayr; from Saʿīd ibn Jubayr and from Ṭāwūs; from Ibn ʿAbbās. He said: **'God's Messenger (peace be upon him) used to teach us the *tashahhud* as he would teach us a surah of the Qur'an. He would say: "Greetings, blessings, prayers and all good things be to God. Peace be to you, Prophet, together with God's mercy and blessings. Peace be to us and to all good servants**

i. Related by al-Bukhārī, 6265 (in a longer version); al-Nasā'ī, 1170.
ii. Related by Abū Dāwūd, 974; al-Tirmidhī, 290; al-Nasā'ī, 1173; Ibn Mājah, 900.

of God. I bear witness that there is no deity other than God, and I bear witness that Muhammad is God's Messenger".'

In Ibn Rumḥ's narration: **'As he would teach us the Qur'an'**.

حَدَّثَنَا قُتَيْبَةُ بْنُ سَعِيدٍ، حَدَّثَنَا لَيْثٌ، ح وَحَدَّثَنَا مُحَمَّدُ بْنُ رُمْحِ بْنِ الْمُهَاجِرِ، أَخْبَرَنَا اللَّيْثُ، عَنْ أَبِي الزُّبَيْرِ، عَنْ سَعِيدِ بْنِ جُبَيْرٍ، وَعَنْ طَاوُسٍ، عَنِ ابْنِ عَبَّاسٍ، أَنَّهُ قَالَ: كَانَ رَسُولُ اللهِ صَلَّى اللهُ عَلَيْهِ وَسَلَّمَ يُعَلِّمُنَا التَّشَهُّدَ كَمَا يُعَلِّمُنَا السُّورَةَ مِنَ الْقُرْآنِ فَكَانَ يَقُولُ: «التَّحِيَّاتُ الْمُبَارَكَاتُ، الصَّلَوَاتُ الطَّيِّبَاتُ لِلهِ، السَّلَامُ عَلَيْكَ أَيُّهَا النَّبِيُّ وَرَحْمَةُ اللهِ وَبَرَكَاتُهُ، السَّلَامُ عَلَيْنَا وَعَلَى عِبَادِ اللهِ الصَّالِحِينَ، أَشْهَدُ أَنْ لَا إِلَهَ إِلَّا اللهُ، وَأَشْهَدُ أَنَّ مُحَمَّدًا رَسُولُ اللهِ»

وَفِي رِوَايَةِ ابْنِ رُمْحٍ «كَمَا يُعَلِّمُنَا الْقُرْآنَ»

[730–61]. (Dār al-Salām 0799) Abū Bakr ibn Abī Shaybah narrated: Yaḥyā ibn Adam narrated; ʿAbd al-Raḥmān ibn Ḥumayd narrated; Abū al-Zubayr narrated to me; from Ṭāwūs; from Ibn ʿAbbās. He said: **'God's Messenger used to teach us the *tashahhud* as he would teach us a surah of the Qur'an'**.

حَدَّثَنَا أَبُو بَكْرِ بْنُ أَبِي شَيْبَةَ، حَدَّثَنَا يَحْيَى بْنُ آدَمَ، حَدَّثَنَا عَبْدُ الرَّحْمَنِ بْنُ حُمَيْدٍ، حَدَّثَنِي أَبُو الزُّبَيْرِ، عَنْ طَاوُسٍ، عَنِ ابْنِ عَبَّاسٍ، قَالَ: «كَانَ رَسُولُ اللهِ صَلَّى اللهُ عَلَيْهِ وَسَلَّمَ يُعَلِّمُنَا التَّشَهُّدَ، كَمَا يُعَلِّمُنَا السُّورَةَ مِنَ الْقُرْآنِ»

[731–62]. (Dār al-Salām 0800) Saʿīd ibn Manṣūr, Qutaybah ibn Saʿīd, Abū Kāmil al-Jaḥdarī and Muhammad ibn ʿAbd al-Malik al-Umawī narrated (Abū Kāmil's text):[i] They said:

---

i. Related by Abū Dāwūd, 972 and 973 (in a longer version); al-Nasāʾī, 1063 (in a longer version), 1172 (in a shorter version), 1279 and 829; Ibn Mājah, 901 (in a shorter version) and 847.

Abū ʿAwānah narrated; from Qatādah; from Yūnus ibn Jubayr; from Ḥiṭṭān ibn ʿAbdullāh al-Riqāshī. He said: '**I offered a prayer with Abū Mūsā al-Ashʿarī. When he was at the *tashahhud*, a man in the congregation said: "Prayer was coupled with righteousness and zakat". When Abū Mūsā finished the prayer and said the *salām*, he turned around and asked: "Who of you said these words?" All people remained silent. He again said: "Who of you said so-and-so?" The people remained silent. He said: "Was it you, Ḥiṭṭān, who said it?" I said: "I did not say it; but I feared that you might accuse me of doing so". A man in the congregation said: "I said it, and I meant nothing but good". Abū Mūsā said: "Do you not know what to say in your prayer? God's Messenger (peace be upon him) addressed us and explained to us our ways and taught us how to pray. He said: 'When you want to pray, stand in rows and let one of you lead the prayer. When he says *Allāh-u akbar*, you also say *Allāh-u akbar*; and when he says: "not those who have incurred Your wrath, nor those who have gone astray", say: "Amen", for then God will answer your prayer. When the imam says *Allāh-u akbar* and bows, you also say *Allāh-u akbar* and bow. The imam bows before you and rises before you'. God's Messenger (peace be upon him) then said: 'This for that. When the imam says *samiʿa Allāhu liman ḥamidah*, you say: *Allahumma rabbanā laka al-ḥamd*, and God will listen to you. For God, the Blessed and Exalted, has said through His Prophet *samiʿa Allāhu liman ḥamidah*. Then when the imam says *Allāh-u akbar* and prostrates himself, you also say *Allāh-u akbar* and prostrate yourselves. The imam prostrates himself before you do and rises before you do'. God's Messenger (peace be upon him) then said: 'This for that. When the imam sits for the *tashahhud*, let it be**

among the first things to say: "Greetings, all good things and peace be to God. Peace be to you, Prophet, together with God's mercy and blessings. Peace be to us and to all good servants of God. I bear witness that there is no deity other than God, and I bear witness that Muhammad is God's servant and Messenger".'"'

حَدَّثَنَا سَعِيدُ بْنُ مَنْصُورٍ، وَقُتَيْبَةُ بْنُ سَعِيدٍ، وَأَبُو كَامِلٍ الْجَحْدَرِيُّ، وَمُحَمَّدُ بْنُ عَبْدِ الْـمَلِكِ الْأُمَوِيُّ - وَاللَّفْظُ لِأَبِي كَامِلٍ - قَالُوا: حَدَّثَنَا أَبُو عَوَانَةَ، عَنْ قَتَادَةَ، عَنْ يُونُسَ بْنِ جُبَيْرٍ، عَنْ حِطَّانَ بْنِ عَبْدِ اللهِ الرَّقَاشِيِّ، قَالَ: صَلَّيْتُ مَعَ أَبِي مُوسَى الْأَشْعَرِيِّ صَلَاةً فَلَمَّا كَانَ عِنْدَ الْقَعْدَةِ قَالَ رَجُلٌ مِنَ الْقَوْمِ: أُقِرَّتِ الصَّلَاةُ بِالْبِرِّ وَالزَّكَاةِ؟ قَالَ فَلَمَّا قَضَى أَبُو مُوسَى الصَّلَاةَ وَسَلَّمَ انْصَرَفَ فَقَالَ: أَيُّكُمُ الْقَائِلُ كَلِمَةَ كَذَا وَكَذَا؟ قَالَ: فَأَرَمَّ الْقَوْمُ، ثُمَّ قَالَ: أَيُّكُمُ الْقَائِلُ كَلِمَةَ كَذَا وَكَذَا؟ فَأَرَمَّ الْقَوْمُ، فَقَالَ: لَعَلَّكَ يَا حِطَّانُ قُلْتَهَا؟ قَالَ: مَا قُلْتُهَا، وَلَقَدْ رَهِبْتُ أَنْ تَبْكَعَنِي بِهَا فَقَالَ رَجُلٌ مِنَ الْقَوْمِ: أَنَا قُلْتُهَا، وَلَمْ أُرِدْ بِهَا إِلَّا الْخَيْرَ فَقَالَ أَبُو مُوسَى: أَمَا تَعْلَمُونَ كَيْفَ تَقُولُونَ فِي صَلَاتِكُمْ؟ إِنَّ رَسُولَ اللهِ صَلَّى اللهُ عَلَيْهِ وَسَلَّمَ خَطَبَنَا فَبَيَّنَ لَنَا سُنَّتَنَا وَعَلَّمَنَا صَلَاتَنَا. فَقَالَ: «إِذَا صَلَّيْتُمْ فَأَقِيمُوا صُفُوفَكُمْ ثُمَّ لْيَؤُمَّكُمْ أَحَدُكُمْ، فَإِذَا كَبَّرَ فَكَبِّرُوا، وَإِذْ قَالَ «غَيْرِ الْـمَغْضُوبِ عَلَيْهِمْ وَلَا الضَّالِّينَ»، فَقُولُوا: آمِينَ، يُجِبْكُمُ اللهُ. فَإِذَا كَبَّرَ وَرَكَعَ فَكَبِّرُوا وَارْكَعُوا، فَإِنَّ الْإِمَامَ يَرْكَعُ قَبْلَكُمْ، وَيَرْفَعُ قَبْلَكُمْ»، فَقَالَ رَسُولُ اللهِ صَلَّى اللهُ عَلَيْهِ وَسَلَّمَ: «فَتِلْكَ بِتِلْكَ وَإِذَا قَالَ: سَمِعَ اللهُ لِمَنْ حَمِدَهُ. فَقُولُوا: اللهُمَّ رَبَّنَا لَكَ الْحَمْدُ يَسْمَعُ اللهُ لَكُمْ، فَإِنَّ اللهَ تَبَارَكَ وَتَعَالَى، قَالَ عَلَى لِسَانِ نَبِيِّهِ صَلَّى اللهُ عَلَيْهِ وَسَلَّمَ: سَمِعَ اللهُ لِمَنْ حَمِدَهُ. وَإِذَا كَبَّرَ وَسَجَدَ فَكَبِّرُوا وَاسْجُدُوا فَإِنَّ الْإِمَامَ يَسْجُدُ قَبْلَكُمْ وَيَرْفَعُ قَبْلَكُمْ» فَقَالَ رَسُولُ اللهِ صَلَّى اللهُ عَلَيْهِ وَسَلَّمَ: «فَتِلْكَ بِتِلْكَ، وَإِذَا كَانَ عِنْدَ الْقَعْدَةِ فَلْيَكُنْ مِنْ أَوَّلِ قَوْلِ أَحَدِكُمْ: التَّحِيَّاتُ الطَّيِّبَاتُ الصَّلَوَاتُ للهِ السَّلَامُ عَلَيْكَ أَيُّهَا النَّبِيُّ وَرَحْمَةُ اللهِ وَبَرَكَاتُهُ، السَّلَامُ عَلَيْنَا وَعَلَى عِبَادِ اللهِ الصَّالِحِينَ، أَشْهَدُ أَنْ لَا إِلَهَ إِلَّا اللهُ وَأَشْهَدُ أَنَّ مُحَمَّدًا عَبْدُهُ وَرَسُولُهُ»

[732–63]. (Dār al-Salām 0801) Abū Bakr ibn Abī Shaybah narrated: Abū Usāmah narrated; Saʿīd ibn Abī ʿArūbah narrated [H]. Also, Abū Ghassān al-Mismaʿī narrated; Muʿādh ibn Hishām narrated; my father narrated [H]. And, Isḥāq ibn Ibrāhīm narrated; Jarīr reported; from Sulaymān al-Taymī. All these from Qatādah, with this transmission: **the same text**.

حَدَّثَنَا أَبُو بَكْرِ بْنُ أَبِي شَيْبَةَ، حَدَّثَنَا أَبُو أُسَامَةَ، حَدَّثَنَا سَعِيدُ بْنُ أَبِي عَرُوبَةَ، ح وَحَدَّثَنَا أَبُو غَسَّانَ الْمِسْمَعِيُّ، حَدَّثَنَا مُعَاذُ بْنُ هِشَامٍ، حَدَّثَنَا أَبِي، ح وَحَدَّثَنَا إِسْحَاقُ بْنُ إِبْرَاهِيمَ أَخْبَرَنَا جَرِيرٌ، عَنْ سُلَيْمَانَ التَّيْمِيِّ، كُلُّ هَؤُلَاءِ عَنْ قَتَادَةَ، فِي هَذَا الْإِسْنَادِ بِمِثْلِهِ.

In Jarīr's narration from Sulaymān, from Qatādah, there is the addition: **'When the imam recites, you listen'. The sentence: 'For God, the Blessed and Exalted, has said through His Prophet *samiʿa Allāhu liman ḥamidah*', does not occur in the narration of anyone of them except in Abū Kāmil's narration from Abū ʿAwānah**.

وَفِي حَدِيثِ جَرِيرٍ، عَنْ سُلَيْمَانَ، عَنْ قَتَادَةَ مِنَ الزِّيَادَةِ وَإِذَا قَرَأَ فَأَنْصِتُوا «وَلَيْسَ فِي حَدِيثِ أَحَدٍ مِنْهُمْ فَإِنَّ اللهَ قَالَ عَلَى لِسَانِ نَبِيِّهِ صَلَّى اللهُ عَلَيْهِ وَسَلَّمَ: «سَمِعَ اللهُ لِمَنْ حَمِدَهُ» إِلَّا فِي رِوَايَةِ أَبِي كَامِلٍ، وَحْدَهُ عَنْ أَبِي عَوَانَةَ.

Abū Isḥāq said: 'Abū Bakr, Abū al-Naḍr's nephew, criticized this hadith'. Muslim said: 'Is anyone better than Sulaymān in memorization?' Abū Bakr said to him: 'How about Abū Hurayrah's hadith then?' He said: 'It is authentic'. He meant: 'When he recites, you listen'. He said: 'As far as I know, it is authentic'. He said: 'Why have you not included it here?' He said: 'I have not included here everything that is authentic. I only included here what they agreed upon'.

قَالَ أَبُو إِسْحَاقَ: قَالَ أَبُو بَكْرٍ: ابْنُ أُخْتِ أَبِي النَّضْرِ فِي هَذَا الْحَدِيثِ. فَقَالَ مُسْلِمٌ: تُرِيدُ أَحْفَظَ مِنْ سُلَيْمَانَ؟ فَقَالَ لَهُ أَبُو بَكْرٍ: فَحَدِيثُ أَبِي هُرَيْرَةَ؟ فَقَالَ: هُوَ صَحِيحٌ يَعْنِي وَإِذَا قَرَأَ فَأَنْصِتُوا فَقَالَ: هُوَ عِنْدِي صَحِيحٌ فَقَالَ: لِمَ تَضَعْهُ هَا هُنَا؟ قَالَ: لَيْسَ كُلُّ شَيْءٍ عِنْدِي صَحِيحٍ وَضَعْتُهُ هَا هُنَا إِنَّمَا وَضَعْتُ هَا هُنَا مَا أَجْمَعُوا عَلَيْهِ.

[733–64]. (Dār al-Salām 0802) Isḥāq ibn Ibrāhīm and Ibn Abī ʿUmar narrated: from ʿAbd al-Razzāq; from Maʿmar; from Qatādah; with this transmission. He said in the narration: **'For God, the Mighty and Exalted, has ordained through His Prophet *samiʿa Allāhu liman ḥamidah*'**.

حَدَّثَنَا إِسْحَاقُ بْنُ إِبْرَاهِيمَ، وَابْنُ أَبِي عُمَرَ، عَنْ عَبْدِ الرَّزَّاقِ، عَنْ مَعْمَرٍ، عَنْ قَتَادَةَ، بِهَذَا الْإِسْنَادِ. وَقَالَ فِي الْحَدِيثِ: «فَإِنَّ اللهَ عَزَّ وَجَلَّ قَضَى عَلَى لِسَانِ نَبِيِّهِ صَلَّى اللهُ عَلَيْهِ وَسَلَّمَ سَمِعَ اللهُ لِمَنْ حَمِدَهُ»

Text Explanation

These hadiths include the *tashahhud* as reported by Ibn Masʿūd, Ibn ʿAbbās and Abū Mūsā al-Ashʿarī. Scholars agree that they are all valid, but they differ as to which is best. The view of al-Shāfiʿī and some of Mālik's associates is that Ibn ʿAbbās's version is best because of the addition of the word 'blessings' in it, and this is a word that is consistent with God's saying: 'But when you enter houses, greet one another with a blessed, goodly greeting, as enjoined by God'. Furthermore, he confirmed it by saying that the Prophet 'used to teach us the *tashahhud* as he taught us a surah of the Qur'an'. Abū Ḥanīfah and Ahmad, as well as the majority of scholars of *fiqh* and Hadith said that Ibn Masʿūd's *tashahhud* is better, because it is considered by Hadith scholars to be more authentic, even though all are authentic. Mālik said that ʿUmar ibn al-Khaṭṭāb's *tashahhud* is best, even though its transmission does not go back to the Prophet but stops at ʿUmar. It is best because he taught it to people as he addressed them standing on the *minbar*, or platform, with no one disputing what he said. This confirms its preference. It runs like this: 'Greetings to God; all pure things belong to God; all good things and peace be to God. Peace be to you, Prophet …'.

Scholars differ as to whether the *tashahhud* is a duty or Sunnah. Al-Shāfiʿī and a number of scholars say that the first *tashahhud* is a Sunnah, while the last one is a duty. The majority of Hadith scholars say that both are duties. Ahmad considers the first a duty, or *wājib*, and the second obligatory, or *farḍ*. Abū Ḥanīfah and Mālik, as well as the majority of *fiqh* scholars, say that both are Sunnah. One report mentions that Mālik also said that the last *tashahhud* is a duty. Scholars who do not consider the *tashahhud* a duty agree that it is a duty to sit down for a while equal to saying it at the end of prayer.

The word *tashahhud* is derived from *shahādah*, which means 'to testify'. The *tashahhud* includes a testimony of belief in God's oneness and in Prophet Muhammad's message.

The Prophet says in hadith No. 724 that 'God is peace'. This means that peace, which is *salām* in Arabic, is one of God's fine names. What this name means is that He is free of all defects, signs of events, partners or equals. It is also said that it means that He keeps His good servants safe, or He greets them. Other meanings are also given.

Al-taḥiyyāt is the plural form of *taḥiyyah*, and it means greetings. Originally, the word is said to have meant dominion, survival, greatness, or life. It is used here in the plural because every Arab king had his own special greeting which was addressed to him by his followers. Therefore, all their greetings are put together and offered to God, who deserves them all.

'All pure things and all good things' mentioned in ʿUmar's hadith mean the same thing, and blessing means goodness in plenty. It is also said to mean growth. Growth is also the meaning attached to the word zakāt. Prayers, which is mentioned in Ibn ʿAbbās's version, refers to the well known prayers, and it is also said that it refers to supplication, or to God's grace which He bestows. The blessed things refer to the good and blessed words.

The *tashahhud* includes 'Peace be to you, Prophet, with God's grace and blessings. Peace be to us and to all God's good servants', and at the end of the prayer we say, 'Peace be to you'. Scholars say that it means seeking refuge with God, because peace, or *salām* in Arabic, is a name of God. Thus, the meaning is 'may God protect you and look after you'. This is the same as when we say 'God be with you', meaning 'may He keep you safe and help you'. It is also said that it means 'may you have safety'.

It should be noted that in both instances of 'peace be to you, Prophet' and 'peace be to us', the definite article, *'al'* is used before the word *'salām'*. In both cases the definite article may be dropped, and this is agreed by all scholars, but using it is preferable, because it is how the *tashahhud* is stated in both al-Bukhārī's and Muslim's *Ṣaḥīḥs*. In the case of 'peace be to you' with which the prayer is concluded, our scholars have different views, with some permitting including or dropping the definite article, while others say that it must be included, because this is how it is always mentioned.

'Peace be to us and to all God's good servants.' Al-Zajjāj, Ibn Qaraqūl the author of *Maṭāliʿ al-Anwār*, as well as other scholars say that a good servant of God is the one who fulfils what is due to God and what is due to other people.

The *tashahhud* also includes 'I bear witness that Muhammad is God's servant and Messenger'. Linguists say that a person is described as *muḥammad* or *maḥmūd* if he has many qualities that are worthy of praise. Ibn Fāris said: This is the reason why our prophet was called Muhammad, because God knew that he would have many good qualities. He inspired his family to call him Muhammad.

The Prophet says: 'He may then choose whatever supplication he wishes'. This makes clear that supplication at the end of prayer, before finishing with *salām* is desirable, and that it may include whatever one wishes of matters related to the present life or the life to come, unless it is sinful. This is the view of our Shāfiʿī school and the majority of scholars. Abu Ḥanīfah said that only supplications mentioned in the Qur'an or the Sunnah are permissible. The majority of scholars are of the view that praying for peace and blessings for the Prophet in the last *tashahhud* is not a duty, but the view of al-Shāfiʿī, Ahmad, Isḥāq and some Mālikī scholars is that it is a duty in the last *tashahhud*, and if one leaves it out one's prayer is rendered invalid. In one narration of this hadith, but not in Muslim's *Ṣaḥīḥ*, an addition is included: 'If you do this, then your prayer is complete'. But this addition is not authentically reported from the Prophet (peace be upon him).

The Prophet instructed his companions to 'stand in rows' and, according to the unanimous view of the Muslim community, this is a general order, but it is an order of preference, not obligation. What it means is that the rows should be straight with people standing next to each other, and completing the rows one by one, leaving no gaps. We will, God willing, be discussing this aspect in more detail where Muslim mentions the relevant hadiths.

The Prophet then says: 'Let one of you lead the prayer'. This is an order to offer the obligatory prayers in congregation, i.e. *jamāʿah.* There is no disagreement about this, but scholars disagree on whether this is an order of preference or obligation. They hold four different views. The more supported view of our school, which is stated by al-Shāfiʿī himself and endorsed by most of our scholars, is that it is a collective duty. This means that if it is done by a number sufficient to publicize this aspect, then the rest are free of responsibility. If all people fail to do it, all of them are at fault and accountable. A number of our scholars say that it is a Sunnah. Ibn Khuzaymah, who is of our school, said that it is a personal duty, but not a condition. This means that a person who does not do it, without a valid reason, but prays alone, commits a sin but his prayer is valid. Some scholars of the Ẓāhirī School say that it is a condition for the validity of prayer. Each one of the first three views is supported by groups of scholars. The question will be fully discussed at the appropriate place, God willing.

'When he says *Allāh-u akbar*, you also say *Allāh-u akbar*'. This is an order to those in congregation to say their *takbīr* after the imam has said it. There are two points here: the first is that worshippers in the congregation may not say their *takbīr* before or with the imam. They must do it after him. Thus, if a person intending to join the imam begins to say his *takbīrat al-iḥrām*, which signals the start of prayer, when the imam has not uttered the last letter of his first *takbīr*, then the prayer of that person is not valid. This is because it means joining someone who is not yet an imam, but will become one after he has completed his *takbīr*. The second point is that it is desirable that the one in the congregation should say his *takbīrat al-iḥrām* without delay. If he delays it, his prayer is valid but he misses out on the preferable situation of joining immediately.

The next instruction given by the Prophet is: 'When he says: "not those who have incurred Your wrath, nor those who have gone astray", say: "Amen".' This provides clear evidence supporting what our scholars and others say that the congregation say 'Amen' together with the imam, not after he has said it. Thus, when the imam says *walāḍḍālīn*, he and the congregation say 'Amen' together. The hadith that says, 'When the imam says, Amen, you say it also', is interpreted as meaning: 'when he is about to say it'. Thus, it is reconciled with this hadith, as it means saying Amen when the imam has read this verse at the end of *al-Fātiḥah*. The word 'Amen' is recited in two versions, with long vowels and short ones. The longer one is preferable. Its meaning is 'Answer our prayer'. We shall discuss it further, God willing, at its appropriate place in Muslim's book.

The Prophet said: 'Say, "Amen", for then God will answer your prayer'. This is a strong encouragement to say 'Amen', so that people pay attention to it. He then said: 'When the imam says *Allāh-u akbar* and bows, you also say *Allāh-u akbar* and bow. The imam bows before you and rises before you'. God's Messenger (peace be upon him) then said: 'This for that'. This means that the people in the congregation should say their *takbīr* to signal their bowing after the imam has said his *takbīr*, and their bowing after he has bowed. The same applies for raising oneself after bowing. 'This for that' means that the imam went into bowing a moment ahead of you, and you regain this moment as you stay in the bowing position a little after him. Thus one moment lost is for one moment gained. The time you spend in the bowing position is the same as that of the imam. The Prophet said the same about the prostration.

The next instruction by the Prophet is: 'When the imam says *samiʿa Allāhu liman ḥamidah*, you say: *Allahumma rabbanā laka al-ḥamd*, and God will listen to you'. This provides evidence supporting the view of our scholars and others that it is desirable that the imam raises his voice when he says, '*samiʿa Allāhu liman ḥamidah*'. The congregation will then hear him and will say their praise. It also gives evidence in support of the view that the people in the congregation only say '*rabbanā laka al-ḥamd*', and does not say before it '*samiʿa Allāhu liman ḥamidah*'. The view of our school is that everyone: the imam, the one in the congregation and the one praying alone, says them both, because it is confirmed that the Prophet said them both and it is also confirmed that he said, 'Pray as you have seen me pray'. More of this will come at the appropriate place, God willing. The meaning of *samiʿa Allāhu liman ḥamidah* is 'may God answer the supplication of whoever praises Him', and the meaning of 'God will listen to you' is that he will answer your supplication.

In hadith No. 731, the Prophet's instruction in response to the imam's saying '*samiʿa Allāhu liman ḥamidah*', is to say '*rabbanā laka al-ḥamd*'. This is how it occurs here, without the particle *wa* before *laka*. In other hadiths the particle *wa* is included. Authentic hadiths are narrated with many adding this particle and many others without it. The view of choice is that both are acceptable and neither is given preference over the other. *Qāḍī* ʿIyāḍ reports some disagreement attributed to Mālik and others on which of the two is preferable.

The Prophet says: 'When the imam sits for *tashahhud*, let it be among the first things to say: Greetings'. Some scholars consider this as evidence that one should not say *Bismillāh* at this point, but must say 'greetings be to God', but this argument is not clear. The instruction is that it should be among the first things to say, not the absolute first, but God knows best.

Transmission

In hadith No. 732 we read: 'In Jarīr's narration from Sulaymān, from Qatādah, there is the addition: "When the imam recites, you listen"'. This is how it occurs, before it continues: 'Abū Isḥāq said:

"Abū Bakr, Abū al-Naḍr's nephew, criticized this hadith". Muslim said: "Is anyone better than Sulaymān in memorization?" Abū Bakr said to him: "How about Abū Hurayrah's hadith then?" He said: "It is authentic". He meant: "When he recites, you listen". He said: "As far as I know, it is authentic". He said: "Why have you not included it here?" He said: "I have not included here everything that is authentic. I only included here what they agreed upon".'

Abū Isḥāq mentioned here is Abū Isḥāq Ibrāhīm ibn Sufyān, Muslim's companion who narrated his book as he learnt it from him. He mentions to Muslim that Abū Bakr criticized the hadith, but Muslim says: 'Is anyone better than Sulaymān in memorization?' He meant that Sulaymān was perfect in his memorization and accurate reporting. As such, disagreement by others does not detract from what he narrates. Abū Bakr then asks Muslim what he thought about the hadith narrated by Abū Hurayrah. Muslim confirms that he considered it authentic. To the next question about the reason for Muslim not including it in his *Ṣaḥīḥ*, Muslim said that not all scholars considered it authentic, adding: 'I have not included here everything that is authentic. I only included here what they agreed upon'.

Some people may question this and say that Muslim has included many hadiths that are not agreed upon. The answer is that according to Muslim, they are considered as though agreed upon. He is not obliged to follow anyone's lead on this point. We have discussed this point and its answer at the beginning of our commentary.

It should be noted that this addition, 'When he recites, you listen', is a subject of disagreement among scholars of Hadith with regard to its authenticity. In his *al-Sunan al-Kubrā*, al-Bayhaqī quotes Abū Dāwūd al-Sijistānī that this phrase is not authentic. The same is attributed to Yaḥyā ibn Maʿīn, Abū Ḥātim al-Rāzī, al-Dāraquṭnī and Abū ʿAlī al-Naysabūrī, the teacher of al-Ḥākim Abū ʿAbdullāh. Al-Bayhaqī quotes Abū ʿAlī that this phrase is not authentic and that Sulaymān al-Taymī is the only one among Qatādah's reporters who mentions it. That all these scholars agree in considering it unauthentic is given greater weight than Muslim's accepting it as authentic, particularly because he has not included it in his *Ṣaḥīḥ* with a proper chain of transmission, but God knows best.

CHAPTER 17

INVOKING BLESSING ON THE PROPHET AFTER THE *TASHAHHUD*

[734–65]. (Dār al-Salām 0803) Yaḥyā ibn Yaḥyā al-Tamīmī narrated:[i] he said: I read out to Mālik; from Nu'aym ibn 'Abdullāh al-Mujmir; that Muhammad ibn 'Abdullāh ibn Zayd al-Anṣārī reported to him (this 'Abdullāh ibn Zayd was the one who saw the *adhān* for prayer in his dream); from Abū Mas'ūd al-Anṣārī; he said: **'God's Messenger (peace be upon him) came to us as we were at Sa'd ibn 'Ubādah's meeting place. Bashīr ibn Sa'd said to him: "God, the Exalted, has commanded us to pray for you, Messenger of God. How do we pray for you?" The Prophet remained silent, until we wished that he did not ask him. The Prophet then said: "Say: *Allahumma ṣalli 'alā Muḥammadin wa 'alā āli Muḥammadin kamā ṣallayta 'alā Ibrāhīma wa 'alā āli Ibrāhīm. Wa bārik 'alā Muhammadin wa 'alā āli Muhammadin kamā bārakta 'alā Ibrāhīma wa 'alā āli Ibrāhīma fī'l 'ālamīn. Innaka ḥamīdun majīd*, and the greeting is as you know".'**

These phrases mean: 'Our Lord, grant peace to Muhammad and to Muhammad's household as you granted peace to Ibrāhīm and to Ibrāhīm's household. And bless Muhammad and Muhammad's household as you blessed Ibrāhīm and Ibrāhīm's household, among all mankind. You are certainly worthy of praise, glorious'.

---

i. Related by Abū Dāwūd, 980 and 981; al-Tirmidhī, 3220; al-Nasā'ī, 1284.

حَدَّثَنَا يَحْيَى بْنُ يَحْيَى التَّمِيمِيُّ، قَالَ: قَرَأْتُ عَلَى مَالِكٍ، عَنْ نُعَيْمِ بْنِ عَبْدِ اللهِ الْمُجْمِرِ، أَنَّ مُحَمَّدَ بْنَ عَبْدِ اللهِ بْنِ زَيْدٍ الْأَنْصَارِيَّ، وَعَبْدُ اللهِ بْنُ زَيْدٍ، هُوَ الَّذِي كَانَ أُرِيَ النِّدَاءَ بِالصَّلَاةِ أَخْبَرَهُ عَنْ أَبِي مَسْعُودٍ الْأَنْصَارِيِّ، قَالَ: أَتَانَا رَسُولُ اللهِ صَلَّى اللهُ عَلَيْهِ وَسَلَّمَ وَنَحْنُ فِي مَجْلِسِ سَعْدِ بْنِ عُبَادَةَ، فَقَالَ لَهُ بَشِيرُ بْنُ سَعْدٍ: أَمَرَنَا اللهُ تَعَالَى أَنْ نُصَلِّيَ عَلَيْكَ يَا رَسُولَ اللهِ، فَكَيْفَ نُصَلِّي عَلَيْكَ؟ قَالَ: فَسَكَتَ رَسُولُ اللهِ صَلَّى اللهُ عَلَيْهِ وَسَلَّمَ، حَتَّى تَمَنَّيْنَا أَنَّهُ لَمْ يَسْأَلْهُ ثُمَّ قَالَ رَسُولُ اللهِ صَلَّى اللهُ عَلَيْهِ وَسَلَّمَ: «قُولُوا اللَّهُمَّ صَلِّ عَلَى مُحَمَّدٍ وَعَلَى آلِ مُحَمَّدٍ، كَمَا صَلَّيْتَ عَلَى آلِ إِبْرَاهِيمَ وَبَارِكْ عَلَى مُحَمَّدٍ وَعَلَى آلِ مُحَمَّدٍ كَمَا بَارَكْتَ عَلَى آلِ إِبْرَاهِيمَ فِي الْعَالَمِينَ، إِنَّكَ حَمِيدٌ مَجِيدٌ، وَالسَّلَامُ كَمَا قَدْ عَلِمْتُمْ»

[735–66]. (Dār al-Salām 0804) Muhammad ibn al-Muthannā and Muhammad ibn Bashshār narrated (Ibn al-Muthannā's text):[i] both said: Muhammad ibn Jaʿfar narrated; Shuʿbah narrated; from al-Ḥakam. He said: I heard Ibn Abī Laylā say: Kaʿb ibn ʿUjrah met me and said: **'Shall I give you a present? God's Messenger (peace be upon him) came to us. We said: "We know how to greet you, but how do we pray for you?" He said: "Say: *Allahumma ṣalli ʿalā Muḥammadin wa ʿalā āli Muḥammadin kamā ṣallayta ʿalā āli Ibrāhīm. Innaka ḥamīdun majīd. Allahumma bārik ʿalā Muḥammadin wa ʿalā āli Muḥammadin kamā bārakta ʿalā āli Ibrāhīm. Innaka ḥamīdun majīd*".'**

حَدَّثَنَا مُحَمَّدُ بْنُ الْمُثَنَّى، وَمُحَمَّدُ بْنُ بَشَّارٍ - وَاللَّفْظُ لِابْنِ الْمُثَنَّى - قَالَا: حَدَّثَنَا مُحَمَّدُ بْنُ جَعْفَرٍ، حَدَّثَنَا شُعْبَةُ، عَنِ الْحَكَمِ، قَالَ: سَمِعْتُ ابْنَ أَبِي لَيْلَى، قَالَ: لَقِيَنِي كَعْبُ بْنُ عُجْرَةَ، فَقَالَ: أَلَا أُهْدِي لَكَ هَدِيَّةً خَرَجَ عَلَيْنَا رَسُولُ اللهِ صَلَّى اللهُ عَلَيْهِ وَسَلَّمَ فَقُلْنَا: قَدْ عَرَفْنَا كَيْفَ نُسَلِّمُ عَلَيْكَ فَكَيْفَ نُصَلِّي عَلَيْكَ؟ قَالَ: «قُولُوا اللَّهُمَّ صَلِّ عَلَى مُحَمَّدٍ،

i. Related by al-Bukhārī, 3370 (in similar wording), 4797 and 6357; Abū Dāwūd, 976, 977 and 978; al-Tirmidhī, 483; al-Nasā'ī, 1286, 1287 and 1288; Ibn Mājah, 904.

وَعَلَى آلِ مُحَمَّدٍ، كَمَا صَلَّيْتَ عَلَى آلِ إِبْرَاهِيمَ، إِنَّكَ حَمِيدٌ مَجِيدٌ، اللهُمَّ بَارِكْ عَلَى مُحَمَّدٍ وَعَلَى آلِ مُحَمَّدٍ، كَمَا بَارَكْتَ عَلَى آلِ إِبْرَاهِيمَ، إِنَّكَ حَمِيدٌ مَجِيدٌ»

[000–67] (Dār al-Salām 0805) Zuhayr ibn Ḥarb and Abū Kurayb narrated: they said: Wakī' narrated; from Shu'bah and Mis'ar; from al-Ḥakam; with this chain of transmission: **the same. Mis'ar's narration does not include: 'Shall I give you a present?'**

حَدَّثَنَا زُهَيْرُ بْنُ حَرْبٍ، وَأَبُو كُرَيْبٍ، قَالَا: حَدَّثَنَا وَكِيعٌ، عَنْ شُعْبَةَ، وَمِسْعَرٍ، عَنِ الْحَكَمِ، بِهَذَا الْإِسْنَادِ مِثْلَهُ وَلَيْسَ فِي حَدِيثِ مِسْعَرٍ: أَلَا أُهْدِي لَكَ هَدِيَّةً؟

[736–68] (Dār al-Salām 0806) Muhammad ibn Bakkār narrated: Ismā'īl ibn Zakariyyā' narrated; from al-A'mash; and from Mis'ar; and from Mālik ibn Mighwal: all of them from al-Ḥakam; with this chain of transmission: **the same text: except that he said, *'wa bārik 'alā Muhammad'*, not *'allāhumma'*.**

حَدَّثَنَا مُحَمَّدُ بْنُ بَكَّارٍ، حَدَّثَنَا إِسْمَاعِيلُ بْنُ زَكَرِيَّا، عَنِ الْأَعْمَشِ، وَعَنْ مِسْعَرٍ، وَعَنْ مَالِكِ بْنِ مِغْوَلٍ، كُلُّهُمْ عَنِ الْحَكَمِ، بِهَذَا الْإِسْنَادِ مِثْلَهُ غَيْرَ، أَنَّهُ قَالَ: «وَبَارِكْ عَلَى مُحَمَّدٍ» وَلَمْ يَقُلْ: اللهُمَّ.

[737–69]. (Dār al-Salām 0807) Muhammad ibn 'Abdullāh ibn Numayr narrated:[i] Rawḥ and 'Abdullāh ibn Nāfi' narrated [H]. Also, Isḥāq ibn Ibrāhīm narrated (his text); Rawḥ reported; from Mālik ibn Anas; from 'Abdullāh ibn Abu Bakr; from his father; from 'Amr ibn Sulaym; Abū Ḥumayd al-Sā'idī reported to me; that '**They said: "Messenger of God, how do we pray for**

i. Related by al-Bukhārī, 3369 and 6360; Abū Dāwūd, 979; Ibn Mājah, 905.

you?" He said: "Say: *Allahumma ṣalli ʿalā Muḥammadin wa ʿalā azwājihi wa dhuriyyatih; kamā ṣallayta ʿalā āli Ibrāhīm. Wa bārik ʿalā Muḥammadin wa ʿalā azwājihi wa dhuriyyatih; kamā bārakta ʿalā āli Ibrāhīm. Innaka ḥamīdun majīd*".'

حَدَّثَنَا مُحَمَّدُ بْنُ عَبْدِ اللهِ بْنِ نُمَيْرٍ، حَدَّثَنَا رَوْحٌ، وَعَبْدُ اللهِ بْنُ نَافِعٍ، ح وَحَدَّثَنَا إِسْحَاقُ بْنُ إِبْرَاهِيمَ، - وَاللَّفْظُ لَهُ - قَالَ: أَخْبَرَنَا رَوْحٌ، عَنْ مَالِكِ بْنِ أَنَسٍ، عَنْ عَبْدِ اللهِ بْنِ أَبِي بَكْرٍ، عَنْ أَبِيهِ، عَنْ عَمْرِو بْنِ سُلَيْمٍ، أَخْبَرَنِي أَبُو حُمَيْدٍ السَّاعِدِيُّ، أَنَّهُمْ قَالُوا: يَا رَسُولَ اللهِ، كَيْفَ نُصَلِّي عَلَيْكَ؟ قَالَ: «قُولُوا اللهُمَّ صَلِّ عَلَى مُحَمَّدٍ، وَعَلَى أَزْوَاجِهِ، وَذُرِّيَّتِهِ كَمَا صَلَّيْتَ عَلَى آلِ إِبْرَاهِيمَ، وَبَارِكْ عَلَى مُحَمَّدٍ وَعَلَى أَزْوَاجِهِ، وَذُرِّيَّتِهِ كَمَا بَارَكْتَ عَلَى آلِ إِبْرَاهِيمَ، إِنَّكَ حَمِيدٌ مَجِيدٌ»

[738–70]. (Dār al-Salām 0808) Yaḥyā ibn Ayyūb, Qutaybah and Ibn Ḥujr narrated:[i] they said: Ismāʿīl (who is Ibn Jaʿfar) narrated; from al-ʿAlā'; from his father; from Abū Hurayrah; that God's Messenger (peace be upon him) said: '**Whoever blesses me once, God will bless him ten times**'.

حَدَّثَنَا يَحْيَى بْنُ أَيُّوبَ، وَقُتَيْبَةُ، وَابْنُ حُجْرٍ، قَالُوا: حَدَّثَنَا إِسْمَاعِيلُ وَهُوَ ابْنُ جَعْفَرٍ، عَنِ الْعَلَاءِ، عَنْ أَبِيهِ، عَنْ أَبِي هُرَيْرَةَ، أَنَّ رَسُولَ اللهِ صَلَّى اللهُ عَلَيْهِ وَسَلَّمَ قَالَ: «مَنْ صَلَّى عَلَيَّ وَاحِدَةً صَلَّى اللهُ عَلَيْهِ عَشْرًا»

Text Explanation

It should be clear to all that scholars hold different views with regard to how the Prophet is to be blessed at the end of the last *tashahhud* in prayer. Abū Ḥanīfah, Mālik and the large majority of scholars maintain that it is recommended, or Sunnah, which means that if it is omitted, the prayer remains valid. Al-Shāfiʿī and Ahmad, on

i. Related by Abū Dāwūd, 1530; al-Tirmidhī, 485; al-Nasā'ī, 1295.

the other hand, say that it is obligatory, and that if it is omitted, the prayer is rendered invalid. This is also reported from ʿUmar ibn al-Khaṭṭāb and his son ʿAbdullāh, and it is al-Shaʿbī's view.

Some scholars accuse al-Shāfiʿī of going against the unanimity of scholars on this point, but they are wrong. As we have just said, it is al-Shaʿbī's view, and it is reported from him by al-Bayhaqī. The argument that it is a duty lacks some clarity. Our scholars cite in evidence the hadith narrated by Abū Masʿūd al-Anṣārī included in this chapter. The hadith mentions that his Companions asked the Prophet: 'How do we pray for you?' He said: 'Say: *Allahumma ṣalli ʿala Muhammad*, etc.' They add that an order is meant as an imperative constituting a duty. This part does not serve as sufficient evidence, unless it is coupled with another narration in which they asked: 'How do we pray for you when we are to pray for you during our prayers?' He said: 'Say: *Allahumma ṣalli ʿalā Muhammadin wa ʿalā āli Muhammad*, etc'. This addition is authentic, related by two leading hadith scholars, Abū Ḥātim ibn Ḥibbān and al-Ḥākim Abū ʿAbdullāh, in their *Ṣaḥīḥ* anthologies, within what they related from Fuḍālah ibn ʿUbaydullāh, a companion of the Prophet: 'God's Messenger (peace be upon him) saw a man praying, but he did not praise or glorify God and did not pray for the Prophet. The Prophet said: "This man has hastened". He then called him and said: "When any of you offers a prayer, he should start by praising his Lord and extol Him, and pray for the Prophet. He may then add any supplication he wishes". Al-Ḥākim said that this hadith is authentic according to the critieria set by Muslim. Although these two hadiths include what is unanimously agreed not to be a duty, such as praying for the Prophet's household and offspring, as well as supplication, they may still be cited in evidence. An order signifies a duty. If a part of what the order includes is not a duty, the rest continues to be a duty, but God knows best. What is a duty according to our scholars is to say: *Allahumma ṣalli ʿalā Muhammad*. Whatever more is merely a Sunnah. We also have an unsupported view that prayer for the Prophet's household is also a duty, but this view is of no value, but God knows best.

Scholars differ as to the meaning of 'the Prophet's household', suggesting different meanings. The most apparent, which is endorsed by al-Azharī and other leading scholars, is that it means the entire Muslim community. Another view suggests that they are the clans of Banū Hāshim and Banū al-Muṭṭalib of the Quraysh tribe. A third view says that they are his immediate family and his offspring, but God knows best.

In hadith No. 734, Bashīr ibn Saʿd says to the Prophet: 'God, the Exalted, has commanded us to pray for you, Messenger of God. How do we pray for you?' This refers to the Qur'anic verse that gives the order: '*Believers! Pray for him and give him greetings of peace*'. (33: 56) The question means: 'how do we say such a prayer?' This makes clear that if a person is given an order and he does not understand its import, he should enquire about it. *Qāḍī* ʿIyāḍ said: 'It is probable that their question means how do they pray for him when they are not offering their prayers, and it is also probable that it refers to when they are in prayer'. He adds that the second is more likely. I think this is the apparent view of Muslim, because he enters this hadith at this point.

The narrator says that 'the Prophet remained silent until we wished that he did not ask him'. This means that his companions disliked the fact that Bashīr put the question to the Prophet, fearing that the Prophet himself disliked and was troubled by it.

The Prophet then said: 'The greeting is as you know'. This means that God has ordered you to pray and greet me. I have explained to you how you should pray for me, and as for the greeting, you know it as it is included in the *tashahhud*, which is, 'Peace be to you, Prophet, together with God's grace and blessings'.

In hadith No. 735, the Prophet gives them the following answer: 'Say: *Allahumma ṣalli ʿalā Muḥammadin wa ʿalā āli Muḥammad; kamā ṣallayta ʿalā āli Ibrāhīm. Innaka ḥamīdun majīd. Allahumma bārik ʿalā Muḥammad wa ʿalā āli Muḥammad; kamā bārakta ʿalā āli Ibrāhīm*'. These phrases mean: 'Our Lord, grant peace to Muhammad and to Muhammad's household as you granted peace to Ibrāhīm's household. You are certainly worthy of praise, glorious. And bless Muhammad and Muhammad's household as you blessed Ibrāhīm's household'. Scholars said that 'blessing' here means an 'increase of goodness and honour'. It is also said that it means 'cleansing and growth'. Scholars also have different opinions about the reason for saying in this supplication: 'Our Lord, grant peace to Muhammad and to Muhammad's household as you granted peace to Ibrāhīm's household'. How is it that he says 'as you granted peace to Ibrāhīm's household', when Muhammad is superior to Ibrāhīm, or Abraham?

Qāḍī ʿIyāḍ said:

> The best opinion is that our Prophet (peace be upon him) asked this for himself and his household so that God would perfect His grace to them as He perfected it to Abraham and his household. It is also said that he asked this for his community. Another suggestion is he wanted this to be his at all times, up to the Day of Judgement, so that he would have the privilege of advocating the truth in later generations, just like Abraham had. It is further said that this supplication was made before Prophet Muhammad knew that he was of a higher status than Abraham. Yet another suggested meaning is that he requested a prayer that would make him a friend of God, just like Abraham was His friend.

The opinion of choice provides three meanings to choose from. The first is reported by some of our scholars as having been expressed by al-Shāfiʿī. It means that these sentences are not joined. Rather, they go like this: 'Our Lord, grant peace to Muhammad'. This is a complete sentence. He then starts a new sentence, saying: 'And to Muhammad's household …'. This means: 'And grant peace to Muhammad's household as you granted peace to Ibrāhīm and Ibrāhīm's household'. Thus, what was granted to Abraham and his household is requested to be granted to Muhammad's household, not to Muhammad himself. The second opinion is that it means: Grant a prayer from You to Muhammad and his household as You did with Abraham and his household. This means that what is being requested is prayer, not its extent. The third opinion is that it is as the words actually mean. Thus, it is a request to give Muhammad and his household a prayer that is the same as was given to Abraham and his household. What is being requested is a similar total. As we said earlier, the preferred meaning of 'household' is all followers. As such Abraham's household include a countless number of prophets, while Muhammad's household does not include any prophet. Therefore, the request is to grant this total that includes no prophet the same as the other total that includes countless prophets, but God knows best.

Qāḍī ʿIyāḍ said:

> These hadiths do not mention prayer for mercy to be granted to the Prophet (peace be upon him), although it occurs in some strange hadiths. However, our teachers hold different opinions on whether it is permissible to pray for mercy to be bestowed on the Prophet. Some of them maintain that it is not permissible, and this is the view endorsed by Abū ʿUmar ibn ʿAbd al-Barr. Other scholars say that it is permitted, and this is the view of Abū Muhammad ibn Abū Zayd. The majority argue that the hadiths outline how the Prophet taught us how to pray for him, and they do not mention mercy. This is the view of choice. The supplication includes: *wa bārik ʿalā Muḥammadin wa ʿalā āli Muḥammad*, which means 'bless Muhammad and his household'. 'Blessing' as used here is said to mean an increase of goodness and honour. It is also said to mean 'steadfastness'. Another suggested meaning is 'purity of all defects'.

The Prophet taught his followers to say: '*Allahumma ṣalli ʿalā Muḥammadin wa ʿalā āli Muḥammad*'. A number of scholars cite this as evidence supporting their view that it is possible to make this prayer in favour of people who are not prophets. This is subject to different views by scholars. Mālik, al-Shāfiʿī and the majority say that it is not permissible to offer such a prayer for ordinary people on their own, but they may be included in a prayer for a prophet. Thus, we may not say: '*Allahumma ṣalli ʿalā* Abū Bakr, ʿUmar, ʿAlī or anyone else', but we may say '*Allahumma ṣalli ʿalā* Muhammad, his household, companions, wives and offspring' as mentioned in different hadiths. Ahmad and a number of scholars maintain that it is permissible to say such a prayer for any believer. Their argument is based on the hadiths mentioned in this chapter and that the Prophet said: '*Allahumma ṣalli 'alā āli Abī Awfā*', which means 'My Lord, grant peace to Abu Awfā's household'. When any people brought him their zakāt, the Prophet used to pray that they be granted peace. It is also consistent with the Qur'anic verse: '*It is He who bestows His blessings upon you, with His angels*'. (33: 43) The majority say that this type is special and that it was not used by the people of the earlier generations in favour of ordinary people, but they used it only for prophets. Likewise, expressions of holiness and glorification are used only for God. We say: 'God, limitless He is in His glory', and 'God, the Mighty and Majestic', or 'superior is His greatness', 'hallowed be His names', 'the Blessed and Exalted', etc. We may not say this about the Prophet, although he is great and exalted. To the argument using the above verse, 'It is He who bestows His blessings upon you', and to the hadiths, they reply that what is from God and His Messenger is a form of prayer and granting mercy. It is not an acknowledgement of greatness and respect which is shown by others.

Prayers to bless the Prophet's household, wives and offspring are used in addition to prayers for the Prophet. They are not addressed by such prayers on their own. We have mentioned that it is perfectly permissible to add them when we pray for the Prophet, because an addition is different from speaking about them separately.

Our scholars differ in their views concerning prayer for ordinary people, other than prophets, and whether it is merely impolite or discouraged. The correct and well-known view is that it is discouraged. Abū Muhammad 'Abdullāh ibn Yūsuf al-Juwaynī, Imam al-Ḥaramayn's father, said: 'Greeting is synonymous with prayer, because God used them together. Therefore, it should not be addressed to anyone who is not present other than prophets. It is wrong to say: 'Abū Bakr, 'Umar and 'Alī, peace be upon them'. However, it may be said as a direct address to people who are alive or dead. Thus, we may say: 'Peace be to you, together with God's mercy', but God knows best.

In the last hadith, No. 738, the Prophet says: 'Whoever blesses me once, God will bless him ten times'. *Qāḍī* ʿIyāḍ said that it means that his reward will be multiplied. This is the same as the Qur'anic verse which says: "*Whoever does a good deed shall be credited with ten times as much*". (6: 160) It may also be as its literal meaning, and this would mean that such a person will be honoured in front of the angels, as in the hadith which quotes God as saying: "If [My servant] remembers Me among a group of people, I will remember him among a better group".'

Transmission

The chain of transmission of hadith No. 734 includes Nuʿaym ibn ʿAbdullāh al-Mujmir. We mentioned him earlier and explained at the beginning of the Book of Cleansing why he was called al-Mujmir and that this is a description of either Nuʿaym or his father. The chain of transmission also mentions Abū Masʿūd al-Anṣārī, whose name is ʿUqbah ibn ʿĀmir. He took part in the Battle of Badr. He was also mentioned earlier.

CHAPTER 18

SUPPLICATION AND PRAISE

[739–71]. (Dār al-Salām 0809) Yaḥyā ibn Yaḥyā narrated: he said:[i] I read out to Mālik; from Sumayy; from Abū Ṣāliḥ; from Abū Hurayrah; that God's Messenger (peace be upon him) said: **'When the imam says *samiʿa Allāhu liman ḥamidah*, you say: *Allahumma; Rabbanā laka al-ḥamd*. Whoever says it as the angels say it shall have all his past sins forgiven'**.

حَدَّثَنَا يَحْيَى بْنُ يَحْيَى، قَالَ: قَرَأْتُ عَلَى مَالِكٍ، عَنْ سُمَيٍّ، عَنْ أَبِي صَالِحٍ، عَنْ أَبِي هُرَيْرَةَ، أَنَّ رَسُولَ اللهِ صَلَّى اللهُ عَلَيْهِ وَسَلَّمَ قَالَ: «إِذَا قَالَ الْإِمَامُ سَمِعَ اللهُ لِمَنْ حَمِدَهُ، فَقُولُوا: اللهُمَّ رَبَّنَا لَكَ الْحَمْدُ، فَإِنَّهُ مَنْ وَافَقَ قَوْلُهُ قَوْلَ الْمَلَائِكَةِ، غُفِرَ لَهُ مَا تَقَدَّمَ مِنْ ذَنْبِهِ»

[000–000]. (Dār al-Salām 0810) Qutaybah ibn Saʿīd narrated: Yaʿqūb (meaning Ibn ʿAbd al-Raḥmān) narrated; from Suhayl; from his father; from Abū Hurayrah; from the Prophet (peace be upon him): **the same meaning as Sumayy's narration**.

حَدَّثَنَا قُتَيْبَةُ بْنُ سَعِيدٍ، حَدَّثَنَا يَعْقُوبُ يَعْنِي ابْنَ عَبْدِ الرَّحْمَنِ، عَنْ سُهَيْلٍ، عَنْ أَبِيهِ، عَنْ أَبِي هُرَيْرَةَ، عَنِ النَّبِيِّ صَلَّى اللهُ عَلَيْهِ وَسَلَّمَ بِمَعْنَى حَدِيثِ سُمَيٍّ.

[740–72]. (Dār al-Salām 0811) Yaḥyā ibn Yaḥyā narrated:[ii] he said: I read out to Mālik; from Ibn Shihāb; from Saʿīd ibn

---

i. Related by al-Bukhārī, 796 and 3228; Abū Dāwūd, 848; al-Tirmidhī, 267; al-Nasāʾī, 1062.

ii. Related by al-Bukhārī, 780; Abū Dāwūd, 936; al-Tirmidhī, 250; al-Nasāʾī, 927.

al-Musayyib and Abū Salamah ibn ʿAbd al-Raḥmān; that they both reported to him from Abū Hurayrah; that God's Messenger (peace be upon him) said: **'When the imam says "Amen", say "Amen". Whoever says it as the angels say it shall have all his past sins forgiven'**.

Ibn Shihāb said: **'God's Messenger (peace be upon him) used to say "Amen".'**

حَدَّثَنَا يَحْيَى بْنُ يَحْيَى، قَالَ: قَرَأْتُ عَلَى مَالِكٍ، عَنِ ابْنِ شِهَابٍ، عَنْ سَعِيدِ بْنِ الْمُسَيِّبِ، وَأَبِي سَلَمَةَ بْنِ عَبْدِ الرَّحْمَنِ، أَنَّهُمَا أَخْبَرَاهُ عَنْ أَبِي هُرَيْرَةَ أَنَّ رَسُولَ اللهِ صَلَّى اللهُ عَلَيْهِ وَسَلَّمَ قَالَ: «إِذَا أَمَّنَ الْإِمَامُ فَأَمِّنُوا، فَإِنَّهُ مَنْ وَافَقَ تَأْمِينُهُ تَأْمِينَ الْمَلَائِكَةِ، غُفِرَ لَهُ مَا تَقَدَّمَ مِنْ ذَنْبِهِ»

قَالَ ابْنُ شِهَابٍ كَانَ رَسُولُ اللهِ صَلَّى اللهُ عَلَيْهِ وَسَلَّمَ يَقُولُ: «آمِينَ»

[741–73]. (Dār al-Salām 0812) Ḥarmalah ibn Yaḥyā narrated to me:[i] Ibn Wahb reported; Yūnus reported to me; from Ibn Shihāb; Ibn al-Musayyib and Abū Salamah ibn ʿAbd al-Raḥmān reported to me; that Abu Hurayrah said: I heard God's Messenger (peace be upon him) say: **the same as Mālik's narration, but did not mention what Ibn Shihāb said**.

حَدَّثَنِي حَرْمَلَةُ بْنُ يَحْيَى، أَخْبَرَنَا ابْنُ وَهْبٍ، أَخْبَرَنِي يُونُسُ، عَنِ ابْنِ شِهَابٍ، أَخْبَرَنِي ابْنُ الْمُسَيِّبِ، وَأَبُو سَلَمَةَ بْنُ عَبْدِ الرَّحْمَنِ، أَنَّ أَبَا هُرَيْرَةَ، قَالَ: سَمِعْتُ رَسُولَ اللهِ صَلَّى اللهُ عَلَيْهِ وَسَلَّمَ بِمِثْلِ حَدِيثِ مَالِكٍ، وَلَمْ يَذْكُرْ قَوْلَ ابْنِ شِهَابٍ.

[742–74]. (Dār al-Salām 0813) Ḥarmalah ibn Yaḥyā narrated to me: Ibn Wahb narrated to me; ʿAmr reported to me; that Abū Yūnus narrated to him; from Abū Hurayrah; that God's

i. Related by Ibn Mājah, 852.

Messenger (peace be upon him) said: **'If any of you says "Amen" in prayer and the angels in Heaven say "Amen" and the one coincides with the other, he will have all his past sins forgiven'**.

حَدَّثَنِي حَرْمَلَةُ بْنُ يَحْيَى، حَدَّثَنِي ابْنُ وَهْبٍ، أَخْبَرَنِي عَمْرٌو، أَنَّ أَبَا يُونُسَ حَدَّثَهُ عَنْ أَبِي هُرَيْرَةَ أَنَّ رَسُولَ اللهِ صَلَّى اللهُ عَلَيْهِ وَسَلَّمَ قَالَ: «إِذَا قَالَ أَحَدُكُمْ فِي الصَّلَاةِ: آمِينَ. وَالْمَلَائِكَةُ فِي السَّمَاءِ: آمِينَ. فَوَافَقَ إِحْدَاهُمَا الْأُخْرَى، غُفِرَ لَهُ مَا تَقَدَّمَ مِنْ ذَنْبِهِ»

[743–75]. (Dār al-Salām 0814) ʿAbdullāh ibn Maslamah al-Qaʿnabī narrated: al-Mughīrah narrated; from Abū al-Zinād; from al-Aʿraj; from Abū Hurayrah: God's Messenger (peace be upon him) said: **'If any of you says "Amen" and the angels in Heaven say "Amen" and the one coincides with the other, he will have all his past sins forgiven'**.

حَدَّثَنَا عَبْدُ اللهِ بْنُ مَسْلَمَةَ الْقَعْنَبِيُّ، حَدَّثَنَا الْمُغِيرَةُ، عَنْ أَبِي الزِّنَادِ، عَنِ الْأَعْرَجِ، عَنْ أَبِي هُرَيْرَةَ قَالَ: قَالَ رَسُولُ اللهِ صَلَّى اللهُ عَلَيْهِ وَسَلَّمَ: «إِذَا قَالَ أَحَدُكُمْ: آمِينَ. وَالْمَلَائِكَةُ فِي السَّمَاءِ: آمِينَ. فَوَافَقَتْ إِحْدَاهُمَا الْأُخْرَى، غُفِرَ لَهُ مَا تَقَدَّمَ مِنْ ذَنْبِهِ».

[000–000]. (Dār al-Salām 0815) Muhammad ibn Rāfiʿ narrated: ʿAbd al-Razzāq narrated; Maʿmar narrated; from Hammām ibn Munabbih; from Abū Hurayrah; from the Prophet (peace be upon him): **the same text**.

حَدَّثَنَا مُحَمَّدُ بْنُ رَافِعٍ، حَدَّثَنَا عَبْدُ الرَّزَّاقِ، حَدَّثَنَا مَعْمَرٌ، عَنْ هَمَّامِ بْنِ مُنَبِّهٍ، عَنْ أَبِي هُرَيْرَةَ، عَنِ النَّبِيِّ صَلَّى اللهُ عَلَيْهِ وَسَلَّمَ بِمِثْلِهِ.

[744–76]. (Dār al-Salām 0816) Qutaybah ibn Saʿīd narrated: Yaʿqūb (meaning Ibn ʿAbd al-Raḥmān) narrated; from Suhayl; from his father; from Abū Hurayrah that God's Messenger (peace be upon him) said: '**When the imam says, "*not those who have incurred Your wrath, nor those who have gone astray*", (1: 7) and a person praying behind him says "Amen", and his word coincides with the word of the people of Heaven, he will have all his past sins forgiven**'.

حَدَّثَنَا قُتَيْبَةُ بْنُ سَعِيدٍ، حَدَّثَنَا يَعْقُوبُ يَعْنِي ابْنَ عَبْدِ الرَّحْمَنِ، عَنْ سُهَيْلٍ، عَنْ أَبِيهِ، عَنْ أَبِي هُرَيْرَةَ أَنَّ رَسُولَ اللهِ صَلَّى اللهُ عَلَيْهِ وَسَلَّمَ قَالَ: «إِذَا قَالَ الْقَارِئُ: «غَيْرِ الْمَغْضُوبِ عَلَيْهِمْ وَلَا الضَّالِّينَ» فَقَالَ: مَنْ خَلْفَهُ: آمِينَ، فَوَافَقَ قَوْلُهُ قَوْلَ أَهْلِ السَّمَاءِ، غُفِرَ لَهُ مَا تَقَدَّمَ مِنْ ذَنْبِهِ»

Text Explanation

A hadith included in the chapter concerning *tashahhud* gives the instruction that when the imam finishes reciting *al-Fātiḥah*, the congregation should say, 'Amen'. The present hadiths make clear that it is desirable that the imam, the congregation and the person praying on his own should say 'Amen' when *al-Fātiḥah* is completed. As noted, the congregation say 'Amen' with the imam, not before or after him. The Prophet said: 'When he says *walāḍḍālīn*, [which is the last word of *al-Fātiḥah*], say: Amen'. Hadith No. 740 says: 'When the imam says "Amen" say "Amen".' This means: when the imam is saying it. We explained this earlier when we talked about the hadith narrated by Abū Mūsā which is included in the chapter on *tashahhud*. It is a Sunnah that the imam and any person praying on his own should say 'Amen' aloud. The same applies to people in the congregation, according to the correct view. This is the detailed view of our Shāfiʿī school.

The Muslim community is unanimous that a person praying alone says 'Amen' in any prayer where the recitation is silent. The same applies to the imam and the people in the congregation. The majority of scholars say that the same applies to prayer when *al-Fātiḥah* is recited aloud. Mālik said that the imam does not say 'Amen' when the recitation is aloud. Abū Ḥanīfah and scholars of Kufah, as well as one report from Mālik, maintain that 'Amen' should not be said aloud, but the majority of scholars say it should.

The Prophet said: 'Whoever says it as the angels say it', and 'when the one coincides with the other'. This means that the worshippers say it at the same time as the angels. This is the correct view. *Qāḍī* ʿIyāḍ mentioned a different view, stating that there is identity of form, humility and sincerity. Scholars differ as to the identity of the angels. Some say these are the guardian angels appointed to people, while other scholars say they are different, because in one narration the Prophet says that the people's word 'coincides with that of the people of Heaven'. The first group respond by saying that when the guardian angels say it, the angels above them will also say it, and then the next ones until it reaches the angels in Heaven.

Ibn Shihāb said: 'God's Messenger (peace be upon him) used to say "Amen".' This means that this was how the Prophet said it in response. It explains his instruction: 'When the imam says "Amen", say "Amen".' It rejects the claim of anyone who says that it means that it is a response to the imam's supplication when reciting *al-Fātiḥah*: 'Guide us along the straight path …' to the end of the surah. This hadith provides further evidence of the requirement of reciting *al-Fātiḥah*, because 'Amen' only occurs after it is recited, but God knows best.

CHAPTER 19

THE REQUIREMENT TO DO LIKE THE IMAM

[745–77]. (Dār al-Salām 0817) Yaḥyā ibn Yaḥyā, Qutaybah ibn Saʿīd; Abū Bakr ibn Abī Shaybah, ʿAmr al-Nāqid, Zuhayr ibn Ḥarb and Abū Kurayb narrated:[i] all from Sufyān. Abū Bakr said: Sufyān ibn ʿUyaynah narrated; from al-Zuhrī. He said: I heard Anas ibn Mālik say: '**The Prophet (peace be upon him) fell off a horse and he injured his right side. We visited him, and it was time for prayer. He led us in prayer, seated. We prayed behind him seated. When he finished the prayer, he said: "The imam is there to be followed: when he glorifies God [i.e. says: *Allāh-u akbar*], say the same; when he prostrates himself, prostrate yourselves; and when he raises himself, raise yourselves. When he says: *samiʿa Allāhu liman ḥamidah*, say: *Rabbanā wa laka al-ḥamd*. If he prays seated, pray seated: all of you"**.'

حَدَّثَنَا يَحْيَى بْنُ يَحْيَى، وَقُتَيْبَةُ بْنُ سَعِيدٍ، وَأَبُو بَكْرِ بْنُ أَبِي شَيْبَةَ، وَعَمْرٌو النَّاقِدُ، وَزُهَيْرُ بْنُ حَرْبٍ، وَأَبُو كُرَيْبٍ، جَمِيعًا عَنْ سُفْيَانَ - قَالَ أَبُو بَكْرٍ: حَدَّثَنَا سُفْيَانُ بْنُ عُيَيْنَةَ - عَنِ الزُّهْرِيِّ، قَالَ: سَمِعْتُ أَنَسَ بْنَ مَالِكٍ، يَقُولُ: سَقَطَ النَّبِيُّ صَلَّى اللهُ عَلَيْهِ وَسَلَّمَ عَنْ فَرَسٍ فَجُحِشَ شِقُّهُ الْأَيْمَنُ، فَدَخَلْنَا عَلَيْهِ نَعُودُهُ، فَحَضَرَتِ الصَّلَاةُ، فَصَلَّى بِنَا قَاعِدًا، فَصَلَّيْنَا وَرَاءَهُ قُعُودًا، فَلَمَّا قَضَى الصَّلَاةَ قَالَ: «إِنَّمَا جُعِلَ الْإِمَامُ لِيُؤْتَمَّ بِهِ، فَإِذَا

i. Related by al-Bukhārī, 805; al-Nasāʾī, 792 and 1060; Ibn Mājah, 1238.

كَبَّرَ فَكَبِّرُوا، وَإِذَا سَجَدَ فَاسْجُدُوا، وَإِذَا رَفَعَ فَارْفَعُوا وَإِذَا قَالَ: سَمِعَ اللهُ لِمَنْ حَمِدَهُ. فَقُولُوا: رَبَّنَا وَلَكَ الْحَمْدُ، وَإِذَا صَلَّى قَاعِدًا، فَصَلُّوا قُعُودًا أَجْمَعُونَ»

[746–78]. (Dār al-Salām 0818) Qutaybah ibn Saʿīd narrated:[i] Layth narrated [H]. Also, Muhammad ibn Rumḥ narrated; al-Layth narrated; from Ibn Shihāb; from Anas ibn Mālik. He said: **'God's Messenger (peace be upon him) fell off a horse and was injured. He prayed seated. He then gave a similar report'**.

حَدَّثَنَا قُتَيْبَةُ بْنُ سَعِيدٍ، حَدَّثَنَا لَيْثٌ، ح وَحَدَّثَنَا مُحَمَّدُ بْنُ رُمْحٍ، أَخْبَرَنَا اللَّيْثُ، عَنِ ابْنِ شِهَابٍ، عَنْ أَنَسِ بْنِ مَالِكٍ، قَالَ: خَرَّ رَسُولُ اللهِ صَلَّى اللهُ عَلَيْهِ وَسَلَّمَ عَنْ فَرَسٍ فَجُحِشَ فَصَلَّى لَنَا قَاعِدًا، ثُمَّ ذَكَرَ نَحْوَهُ.

[747–79]. (Dār al-Salām 0819) Ḥarmalh ibn Yaḥyā narrated to me:[ii] Ibn Wahb reported; Yūnus reported to me; from Ibn Shihāb; Anas ibn Mālik reported to me; that **'God's Messenger (peace be upon him) fell off a horse to the ground and he injured his right side, giving a hadith similar to theirs, adding: "If he prays standing, you pray standing"**.'

حَدَّثَنِي حَرْمَلَةُ بْنُ يَحْيَى، أَخْبَرَنَا ابْنُ وَهْبٍ، أَخْبَرَنِي يُونُسُ، عَنِ ابْنِ شِهَابٍ، أَخْبَرَنِي أَنَسُ بْنُ مَالِكٍ، أَنَّ رَسُولَ اللهِ صَلَّى اللهُ عَلَيْهِ وَسَلَّمَ صُرِعَ عَنْ فَرَسٍ فَجُحِشَ شِقُّهُ الْأَيْمَنُ، بِنَحْوِ حَدِيثِهِمَا وَزَادَ: «فَإِذَا صَلَّى قَائِمًا فَصَلُّوا قِيَامًا»

[748–80]. (Dār al-Salām 0820) Ibn Abī ʿUmar narrated:[iii] Maʿn ibn ʿĪsā narrated; from Mālik ibn Anas; from al-Zuhrī; from

i. Related by al-Bukhārī, 733; al-Tirmidhī, 361.
ii. Related by al-Bukhārī, 1114.
iii. Related by al-Bukhārī, 689; Abū Dāwūd, 601; al-Nasā'ī, 831.

Anas; that '**God's Messenger (peace be upon him) rode a horse, but he fell off it and injured his right side, giving a report similar to theirs, and it includes: "If he prays standing, you pray standing"**.'

حَدَّثَنَا ابْنُ أَبِي عُمَرَ، حَدَّثَنَا مَعْنُ بْنُ عِيسَى، عَنْ مَالِكِ بْنِ أَنَسٍ، عَنِ الزُّهْرِيِّ، عَنْ أَنَسٍ، أَنَّ رَسُولَ اللهِ صَلَّى اللهُ عَلَيْهِ وَسَلَّمَ رَكِبَ فَرَسًا فَصُرِعَ عَنْهُ، فَجُحِشَ شِقُّهُ الْأَيْمَنُ، بِنَحْوِ حَدِيثِهِمْ وَفِيهِ: «إِذَا صَلَّى قَائِمًا فَصَلُّوا قِيَامًا»

[749–81]. (Dār al-Salām 0821) ʿAbd ibn Ḥumayd narrated; ʿAbd al-Razzāq reported; Maʿmar reported; from al-Zuhrī; Anas reported to me; that '**The Prophet (peace be upon him) fell off his horse and he injured his right side. He narrated the hadith, but it does not include the addition given by Yūnus and Mālik**'.

حَدَّثَنَا عَبْدُ بْنُ حُمَيْدٍ، أَخْبَرَنَا عَبْدُ الرَّزَّاقِ، أَخْبَرَنَا مَعْمَرٌ، عَنِ الزُّهْرِيِّ، أَخْبَرَنِي أَنَسٌ، أَنَّ النَّبِيَّ صَلَّى اللهُ عَلَيْهِ وَسَلَّمَ سَقَطَ مِنْ فَرَسِهِ فَجُحِشَ شِقُّهُ الْأَيْمَنُ، وَسَاقَ الْحَدِيثَ وَلَيْسَ فِيهِ زِيَادَةُ يُونُسَ، وَمَالِكٍ.

[750–82]. (Dār al-Salām 0822) Abū Bakr ibn Abī Shaybah narrated:[i] ʿAbdah ibn Sulayman narrated; from Hishām; from his father; from ʿĀ'ishah. She said: '**God's Messenger (peace be upon him) was unwell. A number of his companions came to visit him. God's Messenger prayed seated and they joined him praying in the standing position. He signalled to them to sit down and they sat down. When he finished, he said: "The imam is there to be followed: when he bows, you bow; and when he rises, you rise. If he prays seated, you pray seated"**.'

i. Related by Ibn Mājah, 1237.

حَدَّثَنَا أَبُو بَكْرِ بْنُ أَبِي شَيْبَةَ، حَدَّثَنَا عَبْدَةُ بْنُ سُلَيْمَانَ، عَنْ هِشَامٍ، عَنْ أَبِيهِ، عَنْ عَائِشَةَ، قَالَتْ: «اشْتَكَى رَسُولُ اللهِ صَلَّى اللهُ عَلَيْهِ وَسَلَّمَ فَدَخَلَ عَلَيْهِ نَاسٌ مِنْ أَصْحَابِهِ يَعُودُونَهُ، فَصَلَّى رَسُولُ اللهِ صَلَّى اللهُ عَلَيْهِ وَسَلَّمَ جَالِسًا، فَصَلَّوْا بِصَلَاتِهِ قِيَامًا فَأَشَارَ إِلَيْهِمْ: أَنِ اجْلِسُوا فَجَلَسُوا». فَلَمَّا انْصَرَفَ قَالَ: «إِنَّمَا جُعِلَ الْإِمَامُ لِيُؤْتَمَّ بِهِ فَإِذَا رَكَعَ فَارْكَعُوا وَإِذَا رَفَعَ فَارْفَعُوا وَإِذَا صَلَّى جَالِسًا فَصَلُّوا جُلُوسًا»

[000–83]. (Dār al-Salām 0823) Abū al-Rabīʿ al-Zahrānī narrated: Ḥammād (meaning Ibn Zayd) narrated [H]. Also, Abū Bakr ibn Abī Shaybah and Abū Kurayb narrated; both said: Ibn Numayr narrated [H]. And, Ibn Numayr narrated; my father narrated; all of them from Hishām ibn ʿUrwah; with the same chain of transmission: **giving a similar narration**.

حَدَّثَنَا أَبُو الرَّبِيعِ الزَّهْرَانِيُّ، حَدَّثَنَا حَمَّادٌ يَعْنِي ابْنَ زَيْدٍ، ح وَحَدَّثَنَا أَبُو بَكْرِ بْنُ أَبِي شَيْبَةَ، وَأَبُو كُرَيْبٍ، قَالَا: حَدَّثَنَا ابْنُ نُمَيْرٍ ح وَحَدَّثَنَا ابْنُ نُمَيْرٍ، قَالَ: حَدَّثَنَا أَبِي، جَمِيعًا عَنْ هِشَامِ بْنِ عُرْوَةَ، بِهَذَا الْإِسْنَادِ نَحْوَهُ.

[751–84]. (Dār al-Salām 0824) Qutyabah ibn Saʿīd narrated:[i] Layth narrated [H]. Also, Muhammad ibn Rumḥ narrated; al-Layth reported; from Abū al-Zubayr; from Jābir. He said: **'God's Messenger (peace be upon him) was unwell, and we prayed behind him as he was seated. Abu Bakr was behind him [raising his voice] to make people hear his *takbīr*. He turned to us and saw that we were standing. He signalled to us and we sat down. We prayed with him seated. When he finished saying the *salām*, he said: "You were about to do what the Persians and Byzantines do: they stand up in**

---

i. Related by Abū Dāwūd, 606 (in a shorter version); al-Nasāʾī, 1119; Ibn Mājah, 1240.

the presence of their kings who would be seated. Do not do that; rather, do as your imam. If he prays standing, you pray standing; and if he prays seated, you pray seated".'

حَدَّثَنَا قُتَيْبَةُ بْنُ سَعِيدٍ، حَدَّثَنَا لَيْثٌ، ح وَحَدَّثَنَا مُحَمَّدُ بْنُ رُمْحٍ، أَخْبَرَنَا اللَّيْثُ، عَنْ أَبِي الزُّبَيْرِ، عَنْ جَابِرٍ، قَالَ: اشْتَكَى رَسُولُ اللهِ صَلَّى اللهُ عَلَيْهِ وَسَلَّمَ فَصَلَّيْنَا وَرَاءَهُ وَهُوَ قَاعِدٌ، وَأَبُو بَكْرٍ يُسْمِعُ النَّاسَ تَكْبِيرَهُ، فَالْتَفَتَ إِلَيْنَا فَرَآنَا قِيَامًا، فَأَشَارَ إِلَيْنَا فَقَعَدْنَا فَصَلَّيْنَا بِصَلَاتِهِ قُعُودًا فَلَمَّا سَلَّمَ قَالَ: «إِنْ كِدْتُمْ آنِفًا لَتَفْعَلُونَ فِعْلَ فَارِسَ وَالرُّومِ يَقُومُونَ عَلَى مُلُوكِهِمْ، وَهُمْ قُعُودٌ فَلَا تَفْعَلُوا ائْتَمُّوا بِأَئِمَّتِكُمْ إِنْ صَلَّى قَائِمًا فَصَلُّوا قِيَامًا وَإِنْ صَلَّى قَاعِدًا فَصَلُّوا قُعُودًا»

[752–85]. (Dār al-Salām 0825) Yaḥyā ibn Yaḥyā narrated:[i] Ḥumayd ibn ʿAbd al-Raḥmān al-Ru'āsī reported; from his father; from Abū al-Zubayr; from Jābir. He said: '**God's Messenger (peace be upon him) led us in prayer, and Abu Bakr was behind him. When God's Messenger said *Allāh-u akbar*, Abū Bakr said *Allāh-u akbar*, so that we could hear. He narrated the same as al-Layth's narration**'.

حَدَّثَنَا يَحْيَى بْنُ يَحْيَى، أَخْبَرَنَا حُمَيْدُ بْنُ عَبْدِ الرَّحْمَنِ الرُّؤَاسِيُّ، عَنْ أَبِيهِ، عَنْ أَبِي الزُّبَيْرِ، عَنْ جَابِرٍ، قَالَ: «صَلَّى بِنَا رَسُولُ اللهِ صَلَّى اللهُ عَلَيْهِ وَسَلَّمَ وَأَبُو بَكْرٍ خَلْفَهُ فَإِذَا كَبَّرَ رَسُولُ اللهِ صَلَّى اللهُ عَلَيْهِ وَسَلَّمَ كَبَّرَ أَبُو بَكْرٍ لِيُسْمِعَنَا» ثُمَّ ذَكَرَ نَحْوَ حَدِيثِ اللَّيْثِ.

[753–86]. (Dār al-Salām 0826) Qutaybah ibn Saʿīd narrated: al-Mughīrah (meaning al-Ḥizāmī) narrated; from Abū al-Zinād; from al-Aʿraj; from Abū Hurayrah; that God's Messenger (peace be upon him) said: '**The imam is there to be followed.**

i. Related by al-Bukhārī, 797.

Therefore, do not disagree with him. When he says *Allāh-u akbar,* you say *Allāh-u akbar,* and when he bows, you bow. When he says: *samiʿa Allah liman ḥamidah,* say: *Rabbanā laka al-ḥamd.* When he prostrates himself, you prostrate yourselves. If he prays seated, you pray seated: all of you'.

حَدَّثَنَا قُتَيْبَةُ بْنُ سَعِيدٍ، حَدَّثَنَا الْـمُغِيرَةُ يَعْنِي الْحِزَامِيَّ، عَنْ أَبِي الزِّنَادِ، عَنِ الْأَعْرَجِ، عَنْ أَبِي هُرَيْرَةَ: أَنَّ رَسُولَ اللهِ صَلَّى اللهُ عَلَيْهِ وَسَلَّمَ قَالَ: «إِنَّـمَا الْإِمَامُ لِيُؤْتَمَّ بِهِ، فَلَا تَخْتَلِفُوا عَلَيْهِ فَإِذَا كَبَّرَ فَكَبِّرُوا، وَإِذَا رَكَعَ فَارْكَعُوا وَإِذَا قَالَ: سَمِعَ اللهُ لِمَنْ حَمِدَهُ، فَقُولُوا: اللهُمَّ رَبَّنَا لَكَ الْحَمْدُ، وَإِذَا سَجَدَ فَاسْجُدُوا، وَإِذَا صَلَّى جَالِسًا فَصَلُّوا جُلُوسًا أَجْمَعُونَ»

[000–000]. (Dār al-Salām 0827) Muhammad ibn Rāfiʿ narrated:[i] ʿAbd al-Razzāq narrated; Maʿmar narrated; from Hammām ibn Munabbih; from Abū Hurayrah; from the Prophet: **the same text**.

حَدَّثَنَا مُحَمَّدُ بْنُ رَافِعٍ، حَدَّثَنَا عَبْدُ الرَّزَّاقِ، حَدَّثَنَا مَعْمَرٌ، عَنْ هَمَّامِ بْنِ مُنَبِّهٍ، عَنْ أَبِي هُرَيْرَةَ، عَنِ النَّبِيِّ صَلَّى اللهُ عَلَيْهِ وَسَلَّمَ بِمِثْلِهِ.

Text Explanation

Hadith No. 745 mentions that it was time for prayer. It appears that it was one of the obligatory prayers. The hadith shows that it is permissible to make a signal and do some small action when necessary. It also shows that the congregation must follow the imam and in all his actions when he glorifies God. The hadith includes the instruction to say *Rabbanā wa laka al-ḥamd* when rising from the bowing position. Here it occurs including the particle *wa,* which means 'and' or signifies the start of a new sentence. In other hadiths the phrase is stated without this particle. As explained earlier, both versions are correct and whichever one says is acceptable.

i. Related by al-Bukhārī, 722.

The hadith also instructs us to follow the imam in all his actions, including glorifications, standing sitting, bowing and prostrating. The congregation should do these after the imam.

When the imam has finished saying *takbīrat al-iḥrām*, which is the first glorification signalling the start of the prayer, people in the congregation may say it. If one starts it before the imam has completed saying it, one's prayer is not valid. One must bow after the imam has started to bow and before rising from it. If one does it at the same time as the imam, or before him, one does badly but it does not invalidate one's prayer. The same applies to the prostrations. Everyone in the congregation says *salām* at the end of the prayer after the imam has finished his *salām*. If one says it before the imam, one's prayer becomes invalid unless one intends to part from the imam, thus leaving the congregational prayer. This is a case that is subject to well-known disagreement among scholars. If one says the *salām* at the same time as the imam, i.e. neither before nor after the imam, one does badly but such prayer is not invalid according to the correct view, even though some scholars say that it is invalid.

In this hadith, the Prophet says: 'If he prays seated, pray seated'. Scholars hold different views on this point. A number of them, including Ahmad ibn Ḥanbal and al-Awzāʿī, said that it should be taken at face value. In one report, Mālik says that a person who is able to stand up may not pray, whether seated or standing, behind an imam praying seated. Abū Ḥanīfah, al-Shāfiʿī and the majority of scholars of the earlier generations said that a person who is able to stand up must pray standing if the imam is praying seated. Their evidence is that sometime after this occasion, when he was ill just before he passed away, the Prophet prayed seated, and Abū Bakr and his companions were praying behind him standing. Some scholars claim that Abū Bakr was the imam and the Prophet was praying behind him, but the correct case was that the Prophet was the imam. Muslim mentions this after this chapter in clear, or almost clear terms. Muslim relates from Abu Bakr ibn Abi Shaybah, with a chain of transmission going up to ʿĀ'ishah, who said: 'God's Messenger came up and sat to Abū Bakr's left. Thus, God's Messenger (peace be upon him) was leading the prayer seated and Abū Bakr standing, following the Prophet's prayer, and the congregation following Abu Bakr'.

According to al-Shāfiʿī and other scholars, the Prophet's statement, 'the imam is there to be followed', means that he should be followed in his apparent actions. Otherwise, it is permissible to offer an obligatory prayer behind an imam offering a voluntary prayer, or the reverse. It is also permissible to offer Ẓuhr prayer behind an imam praying ʿAṣr, or the reverse. Mālik, Abu Ḥanīfah and others say that this is not permissible. They consider that 'to be followed' applies to apparent actions and to intentions. The evidence cited by al-Shāfiʿī and those who agree with him is that the Prophet led the special prayer done in a situation of fear twice, once with each group of his companions. This means that his second prayer was voluntary in his case, but obligatory for the congregation joining him. A hadith mentions the case of Muʿādh, who used to offer the ʿIshā Prayer with the Prophet then he would go to his people and lead them in prayer. In this situation he would be offering a voluntary prayer, leading his people who would be offering an obligatory prayer. All this clearly indicates that following the imam is meant in his apparent actions.

In a narration by Jābir, the Prophet is quoted: 'Follow your imams. If the imam prays standing, you pray standing, and if he prays seated, you pray seated'.

The Prophet said: 'The imam is a shield'. This means that he protects his congregation from anything that may affect their prayer, such as an oversight or someone passing across in front of them. Thus, he is like a shield which protects its holder from any harm.

The Prophet told his companions who were standing in prayer while he was seated that they were about to do like the Persians and the Byzantines, who stood up while their kings were seated. This is a clear instruction that young ones and subordinates should not be made to stand up close to their seated leaders for no real need. This does not apply to the case of standing up to welcome an honourable person as he comes in. Indeed, this is perfectly permissible, stated in some hadiths and it is agreed by scholars of earlier and later generations. I have collected the evidence supporting this in a pamphlet devoted to it. To God we pray for success and protection from error.

CHAPTER 20

THE ORDER NOT TO BE AHEAD OF THE IMAM IN ANY ACTION

[754–87]. (Dār al-Salām 0828) Isḥāq ibn Ibrāhīm and Ibn Khashram narrated: they said ʿĪsā ibn Yūnus reported; al-Aʿmash narrated; from Abū Ṣāliḥ; from Abū Hurayrah. He said: **'God's Messenger (peace be upon him) used to teach us. He said: Do not precipitate the imam. When he says *Allāh-u akbar*, say likewise, and when he says *walāḍḍālīn*, [which is the last word of *al-Fātiḥah*] say "Amen". When he bows, you bow; and when he says: *samiʿa Allahu liman ḥamidah*, you say: *Allahumma Rabbunā laka al-ḥamd*'**.

حَدَّثَنَا إِسْحَاقُ بْنُ إِبْرَاهِيمَ، وَابْنُ خَشْرَمٍ قَالَا: أَخْبَرَنَا عِيسَى بْنُ يُونُسَ، حَدَّثَنَا الْأَعْمَشُ، عَنْ أَبِي صَالِحٍ، عَنْ أَبِي هُرَيْرَةَ، قَالَ: كَانَ رَسُولُ اللهِ صَلَّى اللهُ عَلَيْهِ وَسَلَّمَ يُعَلِّمُنَا يَقُولُ: «لَا تُبَادِرُوا الْإِمَامَ إِذَا كَبَّرَ فَكَبِّرُوا وَإِذَا قَالَ: وَلَا الضَّالِّينَ فَقُولُوا: آمِينَ، وَإِذَا رَكَعَ فَارْكَعُوا، وَإِذَا قَالَ: سَمِعَ اللهُ لِمَنْ حَمِدَهُ، فَقُولُوا: اللهُمَّ رَبَّنَا لَكَ الْحَمْدُ»

[755–000]. (Dār al-Salām 0829) Qutaybah narrated: ʿAbd al-ʿAzīz (meaning al-Darāwardī) narrated; from Suhayl ibn Abī Ṣāliḥ; from his father; from Abū Hurayrah; from the Prophet (peace be upon him): **the same text. Except the words '*walāḍḍālīn*, say "Amen".' He added: 'Do not rise before him'**.

حَدَّثَنَا قُتَيْبَةُ، حَدَّثَنَا عَبْدُ الْعَزِيزِ يَعْنِي الدَّرَاوَرْدِيَّ، عَنْ سُهَيْلِ بْنِ أَبِي صَالِحٍ، عَنْ أَبِيهِ عَنْ أَبِي هُرَيْرَةَ، عَنِ النَّبِيِّ صَلَّى اللهُ عَلَيْهِ وَسَلَّمَ بِنَحْوِهِ إِلَّا قَوْلَهُ وَلَا الضَّالِّينَ فَقُولُوا: آمِينَ، وَزَادَ وَلَا تَرْفَعُوا قَبْلَهُ

[756–88]. (Dār al-Salām 0830) Muhammad ibn Bashshār narrated: Muhammad ibn Jaʿfar narrated; Shuʿbah narrated [H]. Also, ʿUbaydullāh ibn Muʿādh narrated (his text); my father narrated; Shuʿbah narrated; from Yaʿlā (who is Ibn ʿAṭā'); he heard Abū ʿAlqamah; who heard Abū Hurayrah say: God's Messenger (peace be upon him) said: **'The imam is a shield. If he prays seated, pray seated; and when he says: *samiʿa Allāhu liman ḥamidah,* you say: *Allahumma Rabbanā laka al-ḥamd.* If what the people on earth say coincides with what the people of Heaven say, they will be forgiven their sins'**.

حَدَّثَنَا مُحَمَّدُ بْنُ بَشَّارٍ، حَدَّثَنَا مُحَمَّدُ بْنُ جَعْفَرٍ، حَدَّثَنَا شُعْبَةُ، ح وَحَدَّثَنَا عُبَيْدُ اللهِ بْنُ مُعَاذٍ، وَاللَّفْظُ لَهُ، حَدَّثَنَا أَبِي، حَدَّثَنَا شُعْبَةُ، عَنْ يَعْلَى وَهُوَ ابْنُ عَطَاءٍ، سَمِعَ أَبَا عَلْقَمَةَ، سَمِعَ أَبَا هُرَيْرَةَ، يَقُولُ: قَالَ رَسُولُ اللهِ صَلَّى اللهُ عَلَيْهِ وَسَلَّمَ: «إِنَّمَا الْإِمَامُ جُنَّةٌ، فَإِذَا صَلَّى قَاعِدًا فَصَلُّوا قُعُودًا، وَإِذَا قَالَ: سَمِعَ اللهُ لِمَنْ حَمِدَهُ. فَقُولُوا: اللهُمَّ رَبَّنَا لَكَ الْحَمْدُ، فَإِذَا وَافَقَ قَوْلُ أَهْلِ الْأَرْضِ قَوْلَ أَهْلِ السَّمَاءِ غُفِرَ لَهُ مَا تَقَدَّمَ مِنْ ذَنْبِهِ»

[757–89]. (Dār al-Salām 0831) Abu al-Ṭāhir narrated to me: Ibn Wahb narrated; from Ḥaywah; that Abū Yūnus, Abū Hurayrah's *mawlā,* narrated to him, saying: I heard Abū Hurayrah say, from God's Messenger (peace be upon him) that he said: **'The imam is there to be followed. When he says *Allāh-u akbar* say the same; and when he bows you bow; and when he says: *samiʿa Allahu liman ḥamidah,* you say: *Allahumma Rabbanā***

***laka al-ḥamd*. If he prays standing, pray standing; and if he prays seated, you pray seated: all of you'.**

حَدَّثَنِي أَبُو الطَّاهِرِ، حَدَّثَنَا ابْنُ وَهْبٍ، عَنْ حَيْوَةَ، أَنَّ أَبَا يُونُسَ، مَوْلَى أَبِي هُرَيْرَةَ، حَدَّثَهُ قَالَ: سَمِعْتُ أَبَا هُرَيْرَةَ، يَقُولُ: عَنْ رَسُولِ اللهِ صَلَّى اللهُ عَلَيْهِ وَسَلَّمَ أَنَّهُ قَالَ: «إِنَّمَا جُعِلَ الْإِمَامُ لِيُؤْتَمَّ بِهِ، فَإِذَا كَبَّرَ فَكَبِّرُوا، وَإِذَا رَكَعَ فَارْكَعُوا، وَإِذَا قَالَ سَمِعَ اللهُ لِمَنْ حَمِدَهُ، فَقُولُوا: اللهُمَّ رَبَّنَا لَكَ الْحَمْدُ، وَإِذَا صَلَّى قَائِمًا، فَصَلُّوا قِيَامًا وَإِذَا صَلَّى قَاعِدًا، فَصَلُّوا قُعُودًا أَجْمَعُونَ»

Note: Al-Nawawī does not include any explanation of these hadiths, as their meaning has been explained in the previous chapter. Indeed, the last paragraph of that chapter relates specifically to these hadiths. However, he has given these hadiths a separate chapter heading, and we follow his lead.

CHAPTER 21

APPOINTMENT OF A DEPUTY IMAM AND PRAYER BEHIND A DISABLED IMAM

[758–90]. (Dār al-Salām 0832) Ahmad ibn ʿAbdullāh ibn Yūnus narrated:[i] Zā'idah narrated; Mūsā ibn Abī ʿĀ'ishah narrated; from ʿUbaydullāh ibn ʿAbdullāh. He said: I visited ʿĀ'ishah and said: Could you tell me about God's Messenger's illness? She said: '**Yes, the Prophet was very ill. He asked: "Have the people prayed?" We said: "No, and they are waiting for you, Messenger of God". He said: "Put some water for me in the tub". We did and he bathed. He then tried to rise, but he fainted. When he came to, he asked: "Have the people prayed?" We said: "No, and they are waiting for you, Messenger of God". He said: "Put some water for me in the tub". We did and he bathed. He then tried to rise, but he fainted. When he came to, he asked: "Have the people prayed?" We said: "No, and they are waiting for you, Messenger of God". He said: "Put some water for me in the tub". We did and he bathed. He then tried to rise, but he fainted. When he came to, he asked: "Have the people prayed?" We said: "No, and they are waiting for you, Messenger of God".' She added: 'The people were still in the mosque awaiting God's Messenger (peace be upon him) to offer the prayer of the last ʿIshā. The Prophet sent a message to Abū Bakr to lead the prayer. The messenger went to him and said: "God's Messenger (peace be upon him) commands**

i. Related by al-Bukhārī, 687; al-Nasā'ī, 833.

you to lead the prayer". Abū Bakr was soft-hearted. He said: "'Umar, you lead the prayer". 'Umar said: "You are more qualified for that". Abū Bakr led the prayer on those days.

'Later, God's Messenger (peace be upon him) felt himself better, and he went out for the Ẓuhr Prayer, supported by two men, one of whom was al-'Abbās. Abū Bakr was leading the prayer, but when he saw the Prophet, he wanted to move back. The Prophet signalled him not to do so. He said to the two men: "Sit me down next to him". They sat him down next to Abū Bakr. Abū Bakr was praying standing and following the prayer of the Prophet (peace be upon him) while the people were following Abū Bakr's prayer. The Prophet (peace be upon him) was praying seated'.

'Ubaydullāh said: **'I visited 'Abdullāh ibn 'Abbās and said: "May I check with you what 'Ā'ishah narrated to me concerning God's Messenger's illness?" He said: "Go ahead". I narrated what she told me and he did not object to anything she said, except that he asked: "Did she name the other man with al-'Abbās?" I said: "No". He said: "He was 'Alī".'**

حَدَّثَنَا أَحْمَدُ بْنُ عَبْدِ اللهِ بْنِ يُونُسَ، حَدَّثَنَا زَائِدَةُ، حَدَّثَنا مُوسَى بْنُ أَبِي عَائِشَةَ، عَنْ عُبَيْدِ اللهِ بْنِ عَبْدِ اللهِ، قَالَ: دَخَلْتُ عَلَى عَائِشَةَ فَقُلْتُ لَهَا أَلَا تُحَدِّثِينِي عَنْ مَرَضِ رَسُولِ اللهِ صَلَّى اللهُ عَلَيْهِ وَسَلَّمَ؟ قَالَتْ: بَلَى ثَقُلَ النَّبِيُّ صَلَّى اللهُ عَلَيْهِ وَسَلَّمَ فَقَالَ: «أَصَلَّى النَّاسُ؟» قُلْنَا: لَا، وَهُمْ يَنْتَظِرُونَكَ يَا رَسُولَ اللهِ قَالَ: «ضَعُوا لِي مَاءً فِي الْمِخْضَبِ» فَفَعَلْنَا فَاغْتَسَلَ ثُمَّ ذَهَبَ لِيَنُوءَ فَأُغْمِيَ عَلَيْهِ ثُمَّ أَفَاقَ فَقَالَ: «أَصَلَّى النَّاسُ؟» قُلْنَا لَا، وَهُمْ يَنْتَظِرُونَكَ يَا رَسُولَ اللهِ فَقَالَ: «ضَعُوا لِي مَاءً فِي الْمِخْضَبِ» فَفَعَلْنَا فَاغْتَسَلَ، ثُمَّ ذَهَبَ لِيَنُوءَ فَأُغْمِيَ عَلَيْهِ ثُمَّ أَفَاقَ، فَقَالَ: «أَصَلَّى النَّاسُ؟» قُلْنَا لَا، وَهُمْ يَنْتَظِرُونَكَ يَا رَسُولَ اللهِ، فَقَالَ: «ضَعُوا لِي مَاءً فِي الْمِخْضَبِ» فَفَعَلْنَا فَاغْتَسَلَ ثُمَّ ذَهَبَ لِيَنُوءَ فَأُغْمِيَ عَلَيْهِ، ثُمَّ أَفَاقَ فَقَالَ: «أَصَلَّى النَّاسُ؟» فَقُلْنَا لَا، وَهُمْ يَنْتَظِرُونَكَ يَا رَسُولَ اللهِ، قَالَتْ: وَالنَّاسُ عُكُوفٌ فِي الْمَسْجِدِ يَنْتَظِرُونَ رَسُولَ اللهِ صَلَّى اللهُ عَلَيْهِ وَسَلَّمَ

لِصَلَاةِ الْعِشَاءِ الْآخِرَةِ، قَالَتْ: فَأَرْسَلَ رَسُولُ اللهِ صَلَّى اللهُ عَلَيْهِ وَسَلَّمَ إِلَى أَبِي بَكْرٍ أَنْ يُصَلِّيَ بِالنَّاسِ، فَأَتَاهُ الرَّسُولُ فَقَالَ: إِنَّ رَسُولَ اللهِ صَلَّى اللهُ عَلَيْهِ وَسَلَّمَ يَأْمُرُكَ أَنْ تُصَلِّيَ بِالنَّاسِ، فَقَالَ أَبُو بَكْرٍ وَكَانَ رَجُلًا رَقِيقًا يَا عُمَرُ صَلِّ بِالنَّاسِ، قَالَ: فَقَالَ عُمَرُ: أَنْتَ أَحَقُّ بِذَلِكَ، قَالَتْ: فَصَلَّى بِهِمْ أَبُو بَكْرٍ تِلْكَ الْأَيَّامَ، ثُمَّ إِنَّ رَسُولَ اللهِ صَلَّى اللهُ عَلَيْهِ وَسَلَّمَ وَجَدَ مِنْ نَفْسِهِ خِفَّةً فَخَرَجَ بَيْنَ رَجُلَيْنِ أَحَدُهُمَا الْعَبَّاسُ، لِصَلَاةِ الظُّهْرِ وَأَبُو بَكْرٍ يُصَلِّي بِالنَّاسِ فَلَمَّا رَآهُ أَبُو بَكْرٍ ذَهَبَ لِيَتَأَخَّرَ فَأَوْمَأَ إِلَيْهِ النَّبِيُّ صَلَّى اللهُ عَلَيْهِ وَسَلَّمَ أَنْ لَا يَتَأَخَّرَ وَقَالَ لَهُمَا: أَجْلِسَانِي إِلَى جَنْبِهِ» فَأَجْلَسَاهُ إِلَى جَنْبِ أَبِي بَكْرٍ، وَكَانَ أَبُو بَكْرٍ يُصَلِّي وَهُوَ قَائِمٌ بِصَلَاةِ النَّبِيِّ صَلَّى اللهُ عَلَيْهِ وَسَلَّمَ وَالنَّاسُ يُصَلُّونَ بِصَلَاةِ أَبِي بَكْرٍ، وَالنَّبِيُّ صَلَّى اللهُ عَلَيْهِ وَسَلَّمَ قَاعِدٌ قَالَ عُبَيْدُ اللهِ: فَدَخَلْتُ عَلَى عَبْدِ اللهِ بْنِ عَبَّاسٍ فَقُلْتُ لَهُ: أَلَا أَعْرِضُ عَلَيْكَ مَا حَدَّثَتْنِي عَائِشَةُ عَنْ مَرَضِ رَسُولِ اللهِ صَلَّى اللهُ عَلَيْهِ وَسَلَّمَ فَقَالَ: هَاتِ فَعَرَضْتُ حَدِيثَهَا عَلَيْهِ فَمَا أَنْكَرَ مِنْهُ شَيْئًا غَيْرَ أَنَّهُ قَالَ: «أَسَمَّتْ لَكَ الرَّجُلَ الَّذِي كَانَ مَعَ الْعَبَّاسِ قُلْتُ: لَا. قَالَ: هُوَ عَلِيٌّ»

[759–91]. (Dār al-Salām 0833) Muhammad ibn Rāfiʿ and ʿAbd ibn Ḥumayd narrated (Ibn Rāfiʿ's text). Both said:[i] ʿAbd al-Razzāq narrated; Maʿmar reported; al-Zuhrī said: and ʿUbaydullāh ibn ʿAbdullāh ibn ʿUtbah reported to me; that ʿĀ'ishah reported to him. She said: **'God's Messenger (peace be upon him) was at Maymūnah's home when his illness first started. He asked his wives' permission to be nursed in her [i.e. ʿĀ'ishah's] home and they agreed. He went out, putting one hand on al-Faḍl ibn ʿAbbās and one hand on another man, dragging his feet on the ground'**.

ʿUbaydullāh said: **'I narrated this to Ibn ʿAbbās, and he said: "Do you know who the man ʿĀ'ishah did not name was? He was ʿAlī"**.'

i. Related by al-Bukhārī, 198, 665, 2588, 3099 (in a shorter version), 4442 and 5714; Ibn Mājah, 1618.

حَدَّثَنَا مُحَمَّدُ بْنُ رَافِعٍ، وَعَبْدُ بْنُ حُمَيْدٍ - وَاللَّفْظُ لِابْنِ رَافِعٍ - قَالَا: حَدَّثَنَا عَبْدُ الرَّزَّاقِ، أَخْبَرَنَا مَعْمَرٌ، قَالَ: قَالَ الزُّهْرِيُّ: وَأَخْبَرَنِي عُبَيْدُ اللهِ بْنُ عَبْدِ اللهِ بْنِ عُتْبَةَ، أَنَّ عَائِشَةَ أَخْبَرَتْهُ قَالَتْ: «أَوَّلُ مَا اشْتَكَى رَسُولُ اللهِ صَلَّى اللهُ عَلَيْهِ وَسَلَّمَ فِي بَيْتِ مَيْمُونَةَ فَاسْتَأْذَنَ أَزْوَاجَهُ أَنْ يُمَرَّضَ فِي بَيْتِهَا وَأَذِنَّ لَهُ قَالَتْ: فَخَرَجَ وَيَدٌ لَهُ عَلَى الْفَضْلِ بْنِ عَبَّاسٍ وَيَدٌ لَهُ عَلَى رَجُلٍ آخَرَ، وَهُوَ يَخُطُّ بِرِجْلَيْهِ فِي الْأَرْضِ». فَقَالَ عُبَيْدُ اللهِ: فَحَدَّثْتُ بِهِ ابْنَ عَبَّاسٍ فَقَالَ: «أَتَدْرِي مَنِ الرَّجُلُ الَّذِي لَمْ تُسَمِّ عَائِشَةُ هُوَ عَلِيٌّ»

[760–92]. (Dār al-Salām 0834) ʿAbd al-Malik ibn Shuʿayb ibn al-Layth narrated to me: my father narrated to me; from my grandfather. He said: ʿUqayl ibn Khālid narrated to me. Ibn Shihāb said: ʿUbaydullāh ibn ʿAbdullāh ibn ʿUtbah ibn Masʿūd reported to me; that ʿĀ'ishah, the Prophet's wife said: '**When God's Messenger was weighed down by his illness and was in severe pain, he requested his wives' permission to be nursed in my home and they agreed. He came out supported by two men, dragging his feet on the ground; supported by ʿAbbās ibn ʿAbd al-Muṭṭalib and another man**'.

ʿUbaydullāh said: '**I told ʿAbdullāh what ʿĀ'ishah had said. ʿAbdullāh ibn ʿAbbās said to me: "Do you know who the other man ʿĀ'ishah did not name?" I said: "No". Ibn ʿAbbās said: "He was ʿAlī"**.'

حَدَّثَنِي عَبْدُ الْمَلِكِ بْنُ شُعَيْبِ بْنِ اللَّيْثِ، حَدَّثَنِي أَبِي، عَنْ جَدِّي، قَالَ: حَدَّثَنِي عُقَيْلُ بْنُ خَالِدٍ، قَالَ: ابْنُ شِهَابٍ، أَخْبَرَنِي عُبَيْدُ اللهِ بْنُ عَبْدِ اللهِ بْنِ عُتْبَةَ بْنِ مَسْعُودٍ، أَنَّ عَائِشَةَ زَوْجَ النَّبِيِّ صَلَّى اللهُ عَلَيْهِ وَسَلَّمَ قَالَتْ: «لَمَّا ثَقُلَ رَسُولُ اللهِ صَلَّى اللهُ عَلَيْهِ وَسَلَّمَ وَاشْتَدَّ بِهِ وَجَعُهُ اسْتَأْذَنَ أَزْوَاجَهُ أَنْ يُمَرَّضَ فِي بَيْتِي، فَأَذِنَّ لَهُ فَخَرَجَ بَيْنَ رَجُلَيْنِ تَخُطُّ رِجْلَاهُ فِي الْأَرْضِ، بَيْنَ عَبَّاسِ بْنِ عَبْدِ الْمُطَّلِبِ وَبَيْنَ رَجُلٍ آخَرَ»

قَالَ عُبَيْدُ اللهِ: فَأَخبَرْتُ عَبْدَ اللهِ بِالَّذِي قَالَتْ عَائِشَةُ: فَقَالَ لِي عَبْدُ اللهِ بْنُ عَبَّاسٍ: «هَلْ تَدْرِي مَنِ الرَّجُلُ الْآخَرُ الَّذِي لَمْ تُسَمِّ عَائِشَةُ؟» قَالَ: قُلْتُ: لَا. قَالَ: ابْنُ عَبَّاسٍ: «هُوَ عَلِيٌّ»

[761–93]. (Dār al-Salām 0835) ʿAbd al-Malik ibn Shuʿayb ibn al-Layth narrated:[i] my father narrated to me; from my grandfather. He said: ʿUqayl ibn Khālid narrated to me. Ibn Shihāb said: ʿUbaydullāh ibn ʿAbdullāh ibn ʿUtbah ibn Masʿūd reported to me; that ʿĀʾishah, the Prophet's wife said: **'I spoke to God's Messenger against that. Nothing prompted me to speak much against this except that I felt that the people will never love a man who would stand in his place; and that I felt that anyone that stands in his place would incur people's ill-feelings. Therefore, I wanted God's Messenger to choose someone other than Abū Bakr'.**

حَدَّثَنَا عَبْدُ الْمَلِكِ بْنُ شُعَيْبِ بْنِ اللَّيْثِ، حَدَّثَنِي أَبِي، عَنْ جَدِّي، حَدَّثَنِي عُقَيْلُ بْنُ خَالِدٍ، قَالَ: قَالَ ابْنُ شِهَابٍ: أَخْبَرَنِي عُبَيْدُ اللهِ بْنُ عَبْدِ اللهِ بْنِ عُتْبَةَ بْنِ مَسْعُودٍ، أَنَّ عَائِشَةَ زَوْجَ النَّبِيِّ صَلَّى اللهُ عَلَيْهِ وَسَلَّمَ قَالَتْ: «لَقَدْ رَاجَعْتُ رَسُولَ اللهِ صَلَّى اللهُ عَلَيْهِ وَسَلَّمَ فِي ذَلِكَ وَمَا حَمَلَنِي عَلَى كَثْرَةِ مُرَاجَعَتِهِ، إِلَّا أَنَّهُ لَمْ يَقَعْ فِي قَلْبِي أَنْ يُحِبَّ النَّاسُ بَعْدَهُ رَجُلًا، قَامَ مَقَامَهُ أَبَدًا، وَإِلَّا أَنِّي كُنْتُ أَرَى أَنَّهُ لَنْ يَقُومَ مَقَامَهُ أَحَدٌ إِلَّا تَشَاءَمَ النَّاسُ بِهِ، فَأَرَدْتُ أَنْ يَعْدِلَ ذَلِكَ رَسُولُ اللهِ صَلَّى اللهُ عَلَيْهِ وَسَلَّمَ عَنْ أَبِي بَكْرٍ»

[762–94]. (Dār al-Salām 0836) Muhammad ibn Rāfiʿ and ʿAbd ibn Ḥumayd narrated (Ibn Rāfiʿ's text): ʿAbd al-Razzāq (ʿAbd said: 'reported' and Ibn Rāfiʿ said: 'narrated'); Maʿmar reported; al-Zuhrī said: Ḥamzah ibn ʿAbdullāh ibn ʿUmar reported to me; from ʿĀʾishah. She said: **'When God's Messenger (peace be upon him) came in my home, he said: "Order Abū Bakr**

---

i. Related by al-Bukhārī, 4445.

to lead the prayer". I said: "Messenger of God, Abū Bakr is soft-hearted. When he recites the Qur'an, he cannot stop weeping. Would you mind ordering someone other than Abū Bakr?" By God, I had no reason other than that I hated that people may have ill-feelings towards the first man to stand in God's Messenger's place. I repeated my suggestion twice or three times. He said: "Order Abū Bakr to lead the prayer. You are like Joseph's women".'

حَدَّثَنَا مُحَمَّدُ بْنُ رَافِعٍ، وَعَبْدُ بْنُ حُمَيْدٍ، - وَاللَّفْظُ لِابْنِ رَافِعٍ قَالَ عَبْدٌ: أَخْبَرَنَا وَقَالَ ابْنُ رَافِعٍ حَدَّثَنَا عَبْدُ الرَّزَّاقِ، أَخْبَرَنَا مَعْمَرٌ، قَالَ الزُّهْرِيُّ: وَأَخْبَرَنِي حَمْزَةُ بْنُ عَبْدِ اللهِ بْنِ عُمَرَ، عَنْ عَائِشَةَ، قَالَتْ: لَمَّا دَخَلَ رَسُولُ اللهِ صَلَّى اللهُ عَلَيْهِ وَسَلَّمَ بَيْتِي قَالَ: «مُرُوا أَبَا بَكْرٍ فَلْيُصَلِّ بِالنَّاسِ» قَالَتْ: فَقُلْتُ يَا رَسُولَ اللهِ، إِنَّ أَبَا بَكْرٍ رَجُلٌ رَقِيقٌ إِذَا قَرَأَ الْقُرْآنَ لَا يَمْلِكُ دَمْعَهُ فَلَوْ أَمَرْتَ غَيْرَ أَبِي بَكْرٍ، قَالَتْ: وَاللهِ، مَا بِي إِلَّا كَرَاهِيَةُ أَنْ يَتَشَاءَمَ النَّاسُ، بِأَوَّلِ مَنْ يَقُومُ فِي مَقَامِ رَسُولِ اللهِ صَلَّى اللهُ عَلَيْهِ وَسَلَّمَ، قَالَتْ: فَرَاجَعْتُهُ مَرَّتَيْنِ أَوْ ثَلَاثًا، فَقَالَ: «لِيُصَلِّ بِالنَّاسِ أَبُو بَكْرٍ فَإِنَّكُنَّ صَوَاحِبُ يُوسُفَ»

[763–95]. (Dār al-Salām 0837) Abū Bakr ibn Abī Shaybah narrated:[i] Abū Muʿāwiyah and Wakīʿ narrated [H]. Also, Yaḥyā ibn Yaḥyā narrated (his text); Abu Muʿāwiyah reported; from al-Aʿmash; from Ibrāhīm; from al-Aswad; from ʿĀ'ishah. She said: **'When God's Messenger was weighed down by his illness, Bilāl came over to say that it was time for prayer. He said: "Order Abū Bakr to lead the prayer". I said: "Messenger of God, Abū Bakr is soft-hearted, and when he stands up in your place, he will not be heard by the people. You may wish to order ʿUmar". He said: "Order Abū Bakr to lead the prayer". I said to Ḥafṣah: Say to him: "Abū Bakr is soft-hearted, and**

i. Related by al-Bukhārī, 664, 712 and 713; Ibn Mājah, 1232.

when he stands up in your place, he will not be heard by the people. You may wish to order 'Umar". God's Messenger (peace be upon him) said: "You, women, are like Joseph's women. Order Abū Bakr to lead the prayer". They told Abū Bakr to lead the prayer. When Abū Bakr started the prayer, God's Messenger (peace be upon him) felt better, and he stood up walking between two men, dragging his feet on the ground. When he entered the mosque, Abū Bakr heard him and he tried to move back, but God's Messenger signalled him to stay in his place. The Prophet came up and sat to Abū Bakr's left. God's Messenger thus was leading the prayer seated and Abū Bakr standing. Abū Bakr was following the Prophet's prayer and the people were following Abū Bakr's prayer'.

حَدَّثَنَا أَبُو بَكْرِ بْنُ أَبِي شَيْبَةَ، حَدَّثَنَا أَبُو مُعَاوِيَةَ، وَوَكِيعٌ، ح وَحَدَّثَنَا يَحْيَى بْنُ يَحْيَى، - وَاللَّفْظُ لَهُ - قَالَ: أَخْبَرَنَا أَبُو مُعَاوِيَةَ، عَنِ الْأَعْمَشِ، عَنْ إِبْرَاهِيمَ، عَنِ الْأَسْوَدِ، عَنْ عَائِشَةَ، قَالَتْ: لَمَّا ثَقُلَ رَسُولُ اللهِ صَلَّى اللهُ عَلَيْهِ وَسَلَّمَ جَاءَ بِلَالٌ يُؤْذِنُهُ بِالصَّلَاةِ. فَقَالَ: «مُرُوا أَبَا بَكْرٍ فَلْيُصَلِّ بِالنَّاسِ» قَالَتْ: فَقُلْتُ يَا رَسُولَ اللهِ، إِنَّ أَبَا بَكْرٍ رَجُلٌ أَسِيفٌ وَإِنَّهُ مَتَى يَقُمْ مَقَامَكَ لَا يُسْمِعِ النَّاسَ فَلَوْ أَمَرْتَ عُمَرَ، فَقَالَ: «مُرُوا أَبَا بَكْرٍ فَلْيُصَلِّ بِالنَّاسِ» قَالَتْ: فَقُلْتُ لِحَفْصَةَ قُولِي لَهُ: إِنَّ أَبَا بَكْرٍ رَجُلٌ أَسِيفٌ وَإِنَّهُ مَتَى يَقُمْ مَقَامَكَ لَا يُسْمِعِ النَّاسَ، فَلَوْ أَمَرْتَ عُمَرَ، فَقَالَتْ لَهُ: فَقَالَ رَسُولُ اللهِ صَلَّى اللهُ عَلَيْهِ وَسَلَّمَ: «إِنَّكُنَّ لَأَنْتُنَّ صَوَاحِبُ يُوسُفَ» مُرُوا أَبَا بَكْرٍ فَلْيُصَلِّ بِالنَّاسِ، قَالَتْ: فَأَمَرُوا أَبَا بَكْرٍ يُصَلِّي بِالنَّاسِ، قَالَتْ: فَلَمَّا دَخَلَ فِي الصَّلَاةِ وَجَدَ رَسُولُ اللهِ صَلَّى اللهُ عَلَيْهِ وَسَلَّمَ مِنْ نَفْسِهِ خِفَّةً فَقَامَ يُهَادَى بَيْنَ رَجُلَيْنِ، وَرِجْلَاهُ تَخُطَّانِ فِي الْأَرْضِ، قَالَتْ: فَلَمَّا دَخَلَ الْمَسْجِدَ سَمِعَ أَبُو بَكْرٍ حِسَّهُ، ذَهَبَ يَتَأَخَّرُ، فَأَوْمَأَ إِلَيْهِ رَسُولُ اللهِ صَلَّى اللهُ عَلَيْهِ وَسَلَّمَ، قُمْ مَكَانَكَ، فَجَاءَ رَسُولُ اللهِ صَلَّى اللهُ عَلَيْهِ وَسَلَّمَ حَتَّى جَلَسَ عَنْ يَسَارِ أَبِي بَكْرٍ قَالَتْ: فَكَانَ رَسُولُ اللهِ صَلَّى اللهُ عَلَيْهِ وَسَلَّمَ يُصَلِّي بِالنَّاسِ جَالِسًا وَأَبُو بَكْرٍ قَائِمًا يَقْتَدِي أَبُو بَكْرٍ بِصَلَاةِ النَّبِيِّ صَلَّى اللهُ عَلَيْهِ وَسَلَّمَ وَيَقْتَدِي النَّاسُ بِصَلَاةِ أَبِي بَكْرٍ.

[764–96] (Dār al-Salām 0838) Minjāb ibn al-Ḥārith al-Tamīmī narrated: Ibn Mushīr reported [H]. Also, Isḥāq ibn Ibrāhīm narrated; ʿĪsā ibn Yūnus reported; both from al-Aʿmash; with this chain of transmission: a similar text. In their narration: **'When God's Messenger (peace be upon him) was in his final illness'**. In Ibn Mushīr's narration: **'God's Messenger was brought forward until he was sat to his left. The Prophet was leading the prayer and Abū Bakr was [raising his voice] to let them hear the *takbīr*'**. In ʿĪsā's narration: **'God's Messenger (peace be upon him) sat praying and Abū Bakr was to his side. Abū Bakr was enabling people to hear'**.

حَدَّثَنَا مِنْجَابُ بْنُ الْحَارِثِ التَّمِيمِيُّ، أَخْبَرَنَا ابْنُ مُسْهِرٍ، ح وَحَدَّثَنَا إِسْحَاقُ بْنُ إِبْرَاهِيمَ، أَخْبَرَنَا عِيسَى بْنُ يُونُسَ، كِلاَهُمَا عَنِ الأَعْمَشِ، بِهَذَا الإِسْنَادِ نَحْوَهُ، وَفِي حَدِيثِهِمَا لَمَّا مَرِضَ رَسُولُ اللهِ صَلَّى اللهُ عَلَيْهِ وَسَلَّمَ مَرَضَهُ الَّذِي تُوُفِّيَ فِيهِ، وَفِي حَدِيثِ ابْنِ مُسْهِرٍ فَأُتِيَ بِرَسُولِ اللهِ صَلَّى اللهُ عَلَيْهِ وَسَلَّمَ حَتَّى أُجْلِسَ إِلَى جَنْبِهِ وَكَانَ النَّبِيُّ صَلَّى اللهُ عَلَيْهِ وَسَلَّمَ يُصَلِّي بِالنَّاسِ وَأَبُو بَكْرٍ يُسْمِعُهُمُ التَّكْبِيرَ، وَفِي حَدِيثِ عِيسَى فَجَلَسَ رَسُولُ اللهِ صَلَّى اللهُ عَلَيْهِ وَسَلَّمَ يُصَلِّي وَأَبُو بَكْرٍ إِلَى جَنْبِهِ وَأَبُو بَكْرٍ يُسْمِعُ النَّاسَ.

[765–97]. (Dār al-Salām 0839) Abū Bakr ibn Abī Shaybah and Abū Kurayb narrated:[i] both said: Ibn Numayr narrated; from Hishām [H]. Ibn Numayr narrated (with similar wording); my father narrated; Hishām narrated; from his father; from ʿĀ'ishah. She said: **'God's Messenger (peace be upon him) ordered Abū Bakr to lead the prayer when he [the Prophet] was ill. And he led the prayer'**.

ʿUrwah said: **'God's Messenger felt better and he came out, and there was Abū Bakr leading the prayer. When Abu Bakr**

i. Related by al-Bukhārī, 683; Ibn Mājah, 1233.

saw him, he moved back, but the Prophet signalled him to stay where he was. God's Messenger sat down parallel with Abū Bakr, to his side. Abu Bakr was following God's Messenger's prayer and the people followed Abu Bakr's prayer'.

حَدَّثَنَا أَبُو بَكْرِ بْنُ أَبِي شَيْبَةَ، وَأَبُو كُرَيْبٍ، قَالَا: حَدَّثَنَا ابْنُ نُمَيْرٍ، عَنْ هِشَامٍ، ح وحَدَّثَنَا ابْنُ نُمَيْرٍ - وَأَلْفَاظُهُمْ مُتَقَارِبَةٌ - قَالَ: حَدَّثَنَا أَبِي، قَالَ: حَدَّثَنَا هِشَامٌ، عَنْ أَبِيهِ، عَنْ عَائِشَةَ، قَالَتْ: «أَمَرَ رَسُولُ اللهِ صَلَّى اللهُ عَلَيْهِ وَسَلَّمَ أَبَا بَكْرٍ أَنْ يُصَلِّيَ بِالنَّاسِ فِي مَرَضِهِ فَكَانَ يُصَلِّي بِهِمْ»

قَالَ عُرْوَةُ: «فَوَجَدَ رَسُولُ اللهِ صَلَّى اللهُ عَلَيْهِ وَسَلَّمَ مِنْ نَفْسِهِ خِفَّةً فَخَرَجَ وَإِذَا أَبُو بَكْرٍ يَؤُمُّ النَّاسَ فَلَمَّا رَآهُ أَبُو بَكْرٍ اسْتَأْخَرَ، فَأَشَارَ إِلَيْهِ رَسُولُ اللهِ صَلَّى اللهُ عَلَيْهِ وَسَلَّمَ أَيْ كَمَا أَنْتَ. فَجَلَسَ رَسُولُ اللهِ صَلَّى اللهُ عَلَيْهِ وَسَلَّمَ حِذَاءَ أَبِي بَكْرٍ إِلَى جَنْبِهِ، فَكَانَ أَبُو بَكْرٍ يُصَلِّي بِصَلَاةِ رَسُولِ اللهِ صَلَّى اللهُ عَلَيْهِ وَسَلَّمَ، وَالنَّاسُ يُصَلُّونَ بِصَلَاةِ أَبِي بَكْرٍ»

[766–98]. (Dār al-Salām 0840) ʿAmr al-Nāqid, Ḥasan al-Ḥulwānī and ʿAbd ibn Ḥumayd narrated to me: Yaʿqūb (who is Ibn Ibrāhīm ibn Saʿd) (ʿAbd said: 'reported to me', while the other two said: 'narrated'); and my father narrated to me; from Ṣāliḥ; from Ibn Shihāb. He said: Anas ibn Mālik reported to me: **'Abū Bakr was leading the prayer during the Prophet's last illness. Then on Monday, when they were standing in rows in prayer, God's Messenger moved the curtain of his home and he was standing as he looked at us. His face was like a sheet of the Qur'an. Then a broad smile was on God's Messenger's face. We were surprised as we were praying, delighted that God's Messenger had come out. Abū Bakr stepped back to join the row, thinking that God's Messenger was coming out for the prayer. God's Messenger (peace be upon him) signalled them with his hand to complete their**

prayer. Then God's Messenger entered [his home] and dropped the curtain. God's Messenger (peace be upon him) passed away on that day'.

حَدَّثَنِي عَمْرٌو النَّاقِدُ، وَحَسَنٌ الْحُلْوَانِيُّ، وَعَبْدُ بْنُ حُمَيْدٍ - قَالَ عَبْدٌ: أَخْبَرَنِي، وَقَالَ الْآخَرَانِ: حَدَّثَنَا يَعْقُوبُ وَهُوَ ابْنُ إِبْرَاهِيمَ بْنِ سَعْدٍ - وَحَدَّثَنِي أَبِي، عَنْ صَالِحٍ، عَنِ ابْنِ شِهَابٍ، قَالَ: أَخْبَرَنِي أَنَسُ بْنُ مَالِكٍ، أَنَّ أَبَا بَكْرٍ كَانَ يُصَلِّي لَهُمْ فِي وَجَعِ رَسُولِ اللهِ صَلَّى اللهُ عَلَيْهِ وَسَلَّمَ، الَّذِي تُوُفِّيَ فِيهِ حَتَّى إِذَا كَانَ يَوْمُ الِاثْنَيْنِ وَهُمْ صُفُوفٌ فِي الصَّلَاةِ «كَشَفَ رَسُولُ اللهِ صَلَّى اللهُ عَلَيْهِ وَسَلَّمَ، سِتْرَ الْحُجْرَةِ، فَنَظَرَ إِلَيْنَا، وَهُوَ قَائِمٌ كَأَنَّ وَجْهَهُ وَرَقَةُ مُصْحَفٍ، ثُمَّ تَبَسَّمَ رَسُولُ اللهِ صَلَّى اللهُ عَلَيْهِ وَسَلَّمَ ضَاحِكًا» قَالَ: «فَبُهِتْنَا وَنَحْنُ فِي الصَّلَاةِ مِنْ فَرَحٍ بِخُرُوجِ رَسُولِ اللهِ صَلَّى اللهُ عَلَيْهِ وَسَلَّمَ، وَنَكَصَ أَبُو بَكْرٍ عَلَى عَقِبَيْهِ لِيَصِلَ الصَّفَّ، وَظَنَّ أَنَّ رَسُولَ اللهِ صَلَّى اللهُ عَلَيْهِ وَسَلَّمَ خَارِجٌ لِلصَّلَاةِ، فَأَشَارَ إِلَيْهِمْ رَسُولُ اللهِ صَلَّى اللهُ عَلَيْهِ وَسَلَّمَ بِيَدِهِ أَنْ أَتِمُّوا صَلَاتَكُمْ»، قَالَ: «ثُمَّ دَخَلَ رَسُولُ اللهِ صَلَّى اللهُ عَلَيْهِ وَسَلَّمَ فَأَرْخَى السِّتْرَ» قَالَ: «فَتُوُفِّيَ رَسُولُ اللهِ صَلَّى اللهُ عَلَيْهِ وَسَلَّمَ مِنْ يَوْمِهِ ذَلِكَ»

[767–99]. (Dār al-Salām 0841) ʿAmr al-Nāqid and Zuhayr ibn Ḥarb narrated it to me. They said:[i] Sufyān ibn ʿUyaynah narrated; from al-Zuhrī; from Anas. He said: **'The last time I saw God's Messenger (peace be upon him) was when he opened the curtain on Monday'. He related the same story, but Ṣāliḥ's narration is fuller and more complete**.

وَحَدَّثَنِيهِ عَمْرٌو النَّاقِدُ، وَزُهَيْرُ بْنُ حَرْبٍ، قَالَا: حَدَّثَنَا سُفْيَانُ بْنُ عُيَيْنَةَ، عَنِ الزُّهْرِيِّ، عَنْ أَنَسٍ، قَالَ آخِرُ نَظْرَةٍ نَظَرْتُهَا إِلَى رَسُولِ اللهِ صَلَّى اللهُ عَلَيْهِ وَسَلَّمَ. كَشْفُ السِّتَارَةِ يَوْمَ الِاثْنَيْنِ بِهَذِهِ الْقِصَّةِ، وَحَدِيثُ صَالِحٍ أَتَمُّ وَأَشْبَعُ.

---

i. Related by al-Nasāʾī, 1830; Ibn Mājah, 1624.

[000–000]. (Dār al-Salām 0842) Muhammad ibn Rāfiʿ and ʿAbd ibn Ḥumayd narrated to me: both from ʿAbd al-Razzāq; Maʿmar reported; from al-Zuhrī. He said: Anas ibn Mālik reported to me. He said: **'When it was Monday …': a similar narration**.

وَحَدَّثَنِي مُحَمَّدُ بْنُ رَافِعٍ، وَعَبْدُ بْنُ حُمَيْدٍ، جَمِيعًا عَنْ عَبْدِ الرَّزَّاقِ، أَخْبَرَنَا مَعْمَرٌ، عَنِ الزُّهْرِيِّ، قَالَ: أَخْبَرَنِي أَنَسُ بْنُ مَالِكٍ، قَالَ: «لَمَّا كَانَ يَوْمُ الِاثْنَيْنِ بِنَحْوِ حَدِيثِهِمَا»

[768–100]. (Dār al-Salām 0843) Muhammad ibn al-Muthannā and Hārūn ibn ʿAbdullāh narrated:[i] both said: ʿAbd al-Ṣamad narrated; I heard my father narrating; ʿAbd al-ʿAzīz narrated; from Anas. He said: **'The Prophet did not come out to join us for three days. Then the prayer was called, and Abū Bakr stepped forward. The Prophet lifted the curtain. When we saw the Prophet's face in its brightness, nothing looked to us more splendid than the Prophet's face when it appeared to us. The Prophet signalled with his hand to Abu Bakr to step forward. Then the Prophet dropped the curtain. We did not see him again until he died'**.

حَدَّثَنَا مُحَمَّدُ بْنُ الْمُثَنَّى، وَهَارُونُ بْنُ عَبْدِ اللهِ، قَالَا: حَدَّثَنَا عَبْدُ الصَّمَدِ، قَالَ: سَمِعْتُ أَبِي يُحَدِّثُ قَالَ: حَدَّثَنَا عَبْدُ الْعَزِيزِ، عَنْ أَنَسٍ، قَالَ: لَمْ يَخْرُجْ إِلَيْنَا نَبِيُّ اللهِ صَلَّى اللهُ عَلَيْهِ وَسَلَّمَ ثَلَاثًا فَأُقِيمَتِ الصَّلَاةُ، فَذَهَبَ أَبُو بَكْرٍ يَتَقَدَّمُ فَقَالَ: «نَبِيُّ اللهِ صَلَّى اللهُ عَلَيْهِ وَسَلَّمَ بِالْحِجَابِ فَرَفَعَهُ، فَلَمَّا وَضَحَ لَنَا وَجْهُ نَبِيِّ اللهِ صَلَّى اللهُ عَلَيْهِ وَسَلَّمَ، مَا نَظَرْنَا مَنْظَرًا قَطُّ، كَانَ أَعْجَبَ إِلَيْنَا مِنْ وَجْهِ النَّبِيِّ صَلَّى اللهُ عَلَيْهِ وَسَلَّمَ حِينَ وَضَحَ لَنَا، قَالَ: «فَأَوْمَأَ نَبِيُّ اللهِ صَلَّى اللهُ عَلَيْهِ وَسَلَّمَ بِيَدِهِ إِلَى أَبِي بَكْرٍ أَنْ يَتَقَدَّمَ، وَأَرْخَى نَبِيُّ اللهِ صَلَّى اللهُ عَلَيْهِ وَسَلَّمَ الْحِجَابَ فَلَمْ نَقْدِرْ عَلَيْهِ حَتَّى مَاتَ»

i. Related by al-Bukhārī, 681.

[769–101]. (Dār al-Salām 0844) Abū Bakr ibn Abī Shaybah narrated:[i] Ḥusayn ibn ʿAlī narrated; from Zā'idah; from ʿAbd al-Malik ibn ʿUmayr; from Abū Burdah; from Abū Mūsā. He said: **'God's Messenger (peace be upon him) was ill and his illness became more severe. He said: "Order Abū Bakr to lead the prayer". ʿĀ'ishah said: "Messenger of God, Abū Bakr is soft-hearted. When he stands in your place he will not be able to lead the prayer". The Prophet said: "Order Abū Bakr to lead the prayer. You, women, are the same as those women of Joseph". Abū Bakr led the prayer for the rest of the Prophet's life.'**

حَدَّثَنَا أَبُو بَكْرِ بْنُ أَبِي شَيْبَةَ، حَدَّثَنَا حُسَيْنُ بْنُ عَلِيٍّ، عَنْ زَائِدَةَ، عَنْ عَبْدِ الْمَلِكِ بْنِ عُمَيْرٍ، عَنْ أَبِي بُرْدَةَ، عَنْ أَبِي مُوسَى، قَالَ: مَرِضَ رَسُولُ اللهِ صَلَّى اللهُ عَلَيْهِ وَسَلَّمَ فَاشْتَدَّ مَرَضُهُ، فَقَالَ: «مُرُوا أَبَا بَكْرٍ فَلْيُصَلِّ بِالنَّاسِ» فَقَالَتْ عَائِشَةُ: يَا رَسُولَ اللهِ إِنَّ أَبَا بَكْرٍ رَجُلٌ رَقِيقٌ مَتَى يَقُمْ مَقَامَكَ لَا يَسْتَطِعْ أَنْ يُصَلِّيَ بِالنَّاسِ، فَقَالَ: «مُرِي أَبَا بَكْرٍ فَلْيُصَلِّ بِالنَّاسِ فَإِنَّكُنَّ صَوَاحِبُ يُوسُفَ» قَالَ: فَصَلَّى بِهِمْ أَبُو بَكْرٍ حَيَاةَ رَسُولِ اللهِ صَلَّى اللهُ عَلَيْهِ وَسَلَّمَ.

Text Explanation

The first hadith, No. 758, mentions that the Prophet fainted. This shows that prophets may faint and become unconsious as this is a case of illness. Needless to say, prophets may become ill but they may not suffer madness, because madness is a deficiency, rather than an illness. The reason that prophets may suffer from illness and other life ordeals is to increase their reward and to provide examples to people in how to tolerate life's reverses. Moreover, it shows their humanity so that people may not come to worship them, particularly when God grants them miracles, but God knows best.

---

i. Related by al-Bukhārī, 3385 and 678.

The Prophet asked: 'Have the people prayed?' and he was told: 'No, and they are waiting for you'. This shows that if the imam has not arrived at the beginning of the prayer's time range, and it is hoped that he will soon arrive, the people should wait for him and no one else should come forward to take his place. We shall discuss this further in the next chapter, God willing.

The Prophet ordered that some water should be placed in the tub, and he washed himself. This proves that it is desirable to take a bath after being unconscious. If one loses consciousness repeatedly, it is desirable to take a bath after each time. If one has not done so but repeatedly fell unconscious, it is sufficient to have one bath. *Qāḍī* ʿIyāḍ suggests that 'washing himself' in this instance means performing minor ablution, i.e. *wuḍū'*, because the loss of consciousness invalidates the ablution. However, the correct meaning is washing all one's body, because it is the apparent meaning of the hadith, and there is nothing to suggest that it is different. Moreover, it is recommended to take a bath after being unconscious. Indeed, some of our scholars say that it is a duty, but this view has no solid basis.

The hadith mentions that the people were 'still in the mosque, awaiting God's Messenger' to come out and offer the ʿIshā Prayer in congregation led by him. The hadith describes this prayer as 'the last ʿIshā', which means that it is correct to describe the ʿIshā Prayer as 'the last'. Al-Aṣmaʿī objects to this description, but it has been authentically reported that the Prophet, ʿĀ'ishah, Anas, al-Barā' and others used it. I have explained this in detail in *Tahdhīb al-Asmā' wal-Lughāt*.

ʿĀ'ishah reports: 'The Prophet sent a message to Abū Bakr to lead the prayer … Abū Bakr was soft-hearted. He said: "ʿUmar, you lead the prayer". ʿUmar said: "You are more qualified for that".' This shows the great merits of Abū Bakr al-Ṣiddīq and that he was the most distinguished among all the Prophet's companions. It also indicates that he was more qualified to succeed the Prophet. The hadith also makes clear that if the imam is prevented by some valid excuse from leading the prayer, he should appoint someone else to lead the prayer, and his choice should be based on the best qualified. The hadith further tells us that the most distinguished of the Prophet's companions next to Abū Bakr was ʿUmar, because Abū Bakr did not think of anyone else. The attitude of the Prophet's companions also tells us that if a person is offered a position by someone who is better than himself, he should not accept it. He should leave it to the one he knows to be better than himself, unless there is a valid reason for not doing so. The hadith tells us that praising someone when he is present is permissible, provided that does not lead to self-adulation. This is clear as ʿUmar says to Abū Bakr: 'You are more qualified for that'. That Abū Bakr had suggested that ʿUmar should lead the prayer was due to what ʿĀ'ishah explained: Abū Bakr was soft-hearted, often weeping when reciting the Qur'an. Some people explain that it was merely a gesture of humility, but the preferred opinion is the one mentioned.

ʿĀ'ishah mentions that when the Prophet went out to the mosque, he was supported by al-ʿAbbās and another man. Ibn ʿAbbās explains that the other man was ʿAlī ibn Abī Ṭālib. In the other version, she says the Prophet had one hand on al-Faḍl ibn ʿAbbās and the other on another person. In other anthologies, it is mentioned that the Prophet was supported by Usāmah ibn Zayd. These reports may be reconciled by saying that they held his hand in turn, one at a time, and they competed for this honour. These honourable men were the closest of his relatives. Al-ʿAbbās was the one who supported the Prophet most, holding his hand, or perhaps he was holding it all the time, and the others took turns in holding the Prophet's other hand, giving al-ʿAbbās the honour of continuing to hold the Prophet's hand as he was their elder and the Prophet's uncle. This is the reason ʿĀ'ishah mentioned al-ʿAbbās in particular and left the other person unidentified as none of the three others helped through the whole distance or most of it, but God knows best.

The hadith mentions that the Prophet said to them, 'Sit me down next to him' and they did so, sitting him next to Abū Bakr. This shows that it is permissible that one man from the congregation may stand next to the imam for some need or purpose, such as raising his voice to let the congregation hear, or because of lack of space, etc.

In hadith No. 759, the Prophet asks his wives' permission to be nursed in ʿĀ'ishah's home. Some scholars take this as evidence that fairness in dividing his time between his wives was a permanent duty of the Prophet, as it is also applicable to anyone of us who is married to more than one wife. Our scholars hold two views, one is this and the other is that it is a Sunnah. They interpret the Prophet's asking his wives' permission in this instance as a gesture of the Prophet's perfect manners and his kind treatment of his wives. They say the same about the hadith in which he said: 'My Lord, this is my division in what I can control. Please do not hold me accountable for what You control and I do not'. The hadith highlights ʿĀ'ishah's merits and higher standing than all the Prophet's nine wives living at the time. There is no disagreement among scholars on this point, but they differ as to who had greater merit: ʿĀ'ishah or Khadījah.

The hadiths mention that when the Prophet was taken to the mosque, he dragged his feet on the ground. This means that he could not lift his feet and place them on the floor, standing on them.

The Prophet says to his wives: 'You are like Joseph's women'. He meant that women gang up together and insist on what they want. The fact that ʿĀ'ishah kept suggesting an alternative to the Prophet shows that it is permissible to point out to a ruler a different course of action, by way of suggestion and advice, provided that it appears to serve an interest. This should be made in a gentle way. A similar example is when ʿUmar suggested to the Prophet not to give too much hope to people so that they would not slacken in their efforts.

In hadith No. 763, Bilāl came to the Prophet to tell him that it was time for the prayer. This supports our scholars' view that it is permissible to call on an imam to come over and lead the prayer. ʿĀ'ishah describes her father, Abū Bakr, as a soft-hearted person, meaning that sadness was one of his characteristics, and he wept easily. She describes that the Prophet went out supported by two men, meaning that he was leaning on them.

In hadith No. 763, the Prophet looks at his companions as they were praying behind Abū Bakr and his face looked like a sheet of the Qur'an. This is a description of perfect beauty, fine skin, a clear and bright face. He then smiles, and the reason for his smiling was that he was delighted to see his companions as a united community behind their imam, attending to their religious duties and showing that they are a community united by faith. Hence his face brightened, as this was part of his nature. Whenever he saw or heard something that delighted him, it showed in the brightness of his face. It also suggests a different meaning, which was to reassure them that his illness was soon to be over. It is said also that he might have wanted to come out and lead them in prayer, but he felt too weak and turned back.

Hadith No. 764 and other hadiths mention that when the Prophet led the prayer in his illness and Abū Bakr was by his side, Abū Bakr raised his voice so that people could hear him saying *Allāh-u akbar* to indicate the moves of prayer. This shows that raising one's voice for this purpose is permissible, and it is also permissible for people in the congregation to follow the raised voice. This is the view of our school and the majority of scholars. Indeed, some say that it is a unanimous view, but I do not think that such a statement of unanimity is correct. *Qāḍī* ʿIyāḍ reports that some scholars of the Mālikī School consider the prayer of the one who follows the raised voice to be invalid. Others do not say it is invalid. Still others say that if the imam permits the person raising his voice to do so, then the prayer of those who follow him is valid; otherwise, it is not valid. Some scholars also say that the prayer of the one who raises his voice is invalid, while others say it is valid. Some make it valid on condition that the imam permits it. Others say that if that person affects to raise his voice louder, his prayer and the prayer of those who follow him are invalid. All these views lack firm support. The correct view is that all these situations are permissible, and the prayers of the one who raises his voice and those who hear him are valid, and the permission of the imam is not a condition of such validity, but God knows best.

Transmission

The chain of transmission of hadith No. 768 runs as follows: 'Muhammad ibn al-Muthannā and Hārūn ibn ʿAbdullāh narrated: ʿAbd al-Ṣamad narrated; I heard my father narrating; ʿAbd al-ʿAzīz narrated; from Anas'. All the narrators in this chain of transmission belonged to Basrah.

Hadith No. 769 has the following chain of transmission: 'Abū Bakr ibn Abī Shaybah narrated: Ḥusayn ibn ʿAlī narrated; from Zā'idah; from ʿAbd al-Malik ibn ʿUmayr; from Abū Burdah; from Abū Mūsā'. This transmission features narrators who were all from Kufah.